The Authors

Christopher Pass, BSc (Econ), M Phil, PhD is a reader, Bryan Lowes, BSc, M Phil, PhD, ACMA is a senior lecturer, and Leslie Chadwick, MBA, FCCA is a lecturer at Bradford University School of Management. Andrew Pendleton is a professor at Manchester Metropolitan University, Malcolm Afferson is a senior lecturer at Sheffield Hallam University and Daragh O'Reilly, BA, MBA, MCIM, Dip. M is a lecturer at Leeds University. Their teaching and research in business studies is complemented by their varied work as consultants to a number of companies and public organizations.

Christopher Pass and Bryan Lowes are authors of the *Collins Dictionary of Economics*.

Collins dictionary *of* Business

William Collins' dream of knowledge for all began with the publication of his first book in 1819. A self-educated mill worker, he not only enriched millions of lives, but also founded a flourishing publishing house. Today, staying true to this spirit, Collins books are packed with inspiration, innovation, and practical expertise. They place you at the centre of a world of possibility and give you exactly what you need to explore it.

Collins. Do more.

Collins dictionary *of*

Business

third edition

Christopher Pass, Bryan Lowes,
Andrew Pendleton, Leslie Chadwick,
Daragh O'Reilly & Malcolm Afferson

Collins

HarperCollins Publishers
Westerhill Road, Bishopbriggs,
Glasgow G64 2QT

www.collins.co.uk

First published 1991
Second edition published 1995
Third edition published 2002
Revised and updated 2005

A catalogue record for this book is available from the British Library

ISBN 0 00 720583-X

Typeset by Davidson Pre-Press Graphics Ltd, Glasgow
Printed and bound in Great Britain by Clays Ltd, St Ives plc.

Preface

This third edition of the dictionary, now updated, contains material especially suitable for students reading specialist business studies courses at schools, universities and polytechnics and for students undertaking a business studies course as part of a broader-based economics and commerce degree or professional qualification. It will also be useful to people working in industry, commerce and public service who may need to familiarize themselves with a particular concept or practice.

Entries have been selected and structured to reflect the following considerations: (1) the various strategies and policies which firms and other organizations can pursue in order to achieve their objectives; (2) the 'nuts and bolts' of business practice, that is, the various concepts, techniques and methods used in the functional areas of business: marketing, finance, production, personnel, etc.; (3) the industrial and economic environment of business, that is, the various factors which impinge *directly* on the operations of business (for example, market structure and competitive influences) and those which have a more general and *indirect* impact (for example, government economic policy and international trade influences).

It is, of course, difficult to draw a precise dividing line between business-orientated material and other subject matter. Accordingly, readers are recommended to consult other volumes in this series (in particular, the *Collins Dictionary of Economics* and *Collins Dictionary of Computing*) should they fail to find a particular entry in this dictionary.

To cater for a wide-ranging readership with varying degrees of knowledge requirements, the entries have been structured, where appropriate, to provide a basic definition followed by an explanation of a particular concept, which leads through cross-references to related terms.

Selected key entries have been highlighted in the main text.

Cross-references are denoted both in the text and at the end of entries by SMALL CAPITAL LETTERS.

Acknowledgements

We should like to thank Edwin Moore and Monica Thorp for their invaluable editorial advice and work in preparing the book for publication; and Sylvia Ashdown, Gill Sharpley, Sylvia Bentley, Chris Barkby and Lorna Pickersgill for their painstaking and efficient typing of the manuscript.

a

ABC analysis *or* **Pareto analysis** a means of classifying items such as sales, stock, etc., in which items are ranked according to their relative importance to the firm. For example, products may be ranked according to their sales value, as in Fig. 1, with sales items plotted cumulatively on the horizontal axis and sales cumulated on the vertical axis to show a Pareto curve. Using this curve it is possible to place items into three classes: A items, often the first 10% of items, which may account for up to 60% of sales value; B items, often the second 30% accounting for perhaps 30% of sales value; and finally C items. Having classified items in this manner it is possible to develop STOCK CONTROL procedures which are appropriate for each class of item.

In retailing, for example, products could be ranked according to their profit margins and the speed at which they sell, for example a high margin, fast-moving product could be ranked A and at the other extreme a low margin, slow-moving product could be ranked C. The rankings can assist management to decide the frequency with which the items will be monitored, for example A items daily, B items weekly and C items monthly. See PARETO DISTRIBUTION.

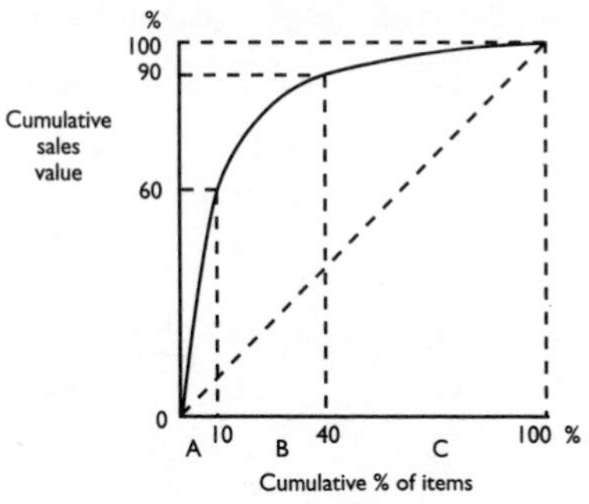

Fig. 1 **ABC Analysis.** The Pareto curve.

'above-the-line' promotion a form of promotion, especially ADVERTISING, where an ADVERTISING AGENCY is paid a commission for buying space or time in the MASS MEDIA such as a newspaper or commercial television company.

'below-the-line' promotions such as POINT OF SALE DISPLAYS and demonstrations, by contrast, do not involve the payment of a commission. See PROMOTIONAL MIX.

absenteeism 1 the level of unsanctioned absences from work in an organization. 2 chronic unsanctioned absence from work by individuals.

Absence from work may be sanctioned by managers in advance for certain reasons (for example for a forthcoming visit to the dentist), or may be sanctioned subsequently (for example for illness – see SICK PAY). The difficulty arises where there are no acceptable reasons for absence or where managers believe the excuses tendered to be untrue. In theory, DISCIPLINARY PROCEDURES can be activated but it can be difficult to prove that employees were absent without due cause. Managers could visit absentees at home to establish the facts but this can be time-consuming and counter-productive since it can indicate to committed employees that they are not trusted. Whilst punishing absence can be difficult, measures can be taken to encourage attendance, such as extra pay (see ATTENDANCE BONUS). A high level of absenteeism is often seen as an indicator of the quality of a workforce but it can equally be an indicator of poor working conditions. Improvement of the latter may also reduce absenteeism.

absorption the sharing of indirect costs or OVERHEADS to units of product by means of COST RATES. Provided that actual overheads do not exceed BUDGET and that actual output is the same as budgeted output, then the overhead cost rate should allow total product cost to be determined, and a selling price set which will recover the overhead costs involved in producing and selling the product. See STANDARD COST, OVERHEAD COST VARIANCE.

absorption costing a system of product COSTING which assigns materials and labour, and OVERHEAD costs to units of product manufactured (as in STANDARD COSTS). Fixed overhead costs are assigned to products by means of an appropriate COST RATE which divides planned overhead costs by planned output. Fig. 2 shows an illustration of absorption costing.

With absorption costing, fixed overhead costs are included in the value of work in progress and finished goods stock. By contrast, with MARGINAL COSTING systems fixed overhead costs are charged as a single block against revenues in the period when they are incurred, and work in progress and finished goods stocks are valued at direct materials and labour cost only.

absorption rate *or* **cost rate** *or* **recovery rate** a means of charging OVERHEADS to products. By relating budgeted overhead costs to budgeted output, it is possible to calculate an overhead absorption rate per unit of product to add to the standard DIRECT COST (direct materials cost and direct labour cost) of a product in order to determine its production cost. Alternatively, production overheads can be charged as a percentage on the direct labour cost of a product; or a percentage on the direct materials cost of the product; or on the basis of the direct labour hours to make the product (at a rate per direct labour hour); or on the basis of the machine hours needed to make the product (at a rate per machine hour).

Once the production cost of a product has been determined by adding production overheads, then a further addition must be made to cover selling, distribution and administration overheads. These can be allowed for by means of other cost rates, such as by adding an appropriate percentage to the production cost of the product. The addition of overhead cost rates to the standard direct cost of products serves to establish their total cost, and facilitates their ABSORPTION through selling prices. See BUDGET, STANDARD COST.

ACAS see ADVISORY CONCILIATION AND ARBITRATION SERVICE.

ACCA see CHARTERED ASSOCIATION OF CERTIFIED ACCOUNTANTS.

accelerated depreciation a DEPRECIATION method which charges a higher proportion

	TOTAL £	*Tables* £	*Chairs* £	*Stools* £
Sales	500	200	200	100
Material cost	250	100	75	75
Wages	100	35	50	15
Overheads (100% wages)	100	35	50	15
TOTAL COST	450	170	175	105
PROFIT (LOSS)	50	30	25	(5)

Fig. 2 **Absorption costing**. Table showing an example.

of the HISTORIC COST of an ASSET against profits during the early years of its life than is charged in the later years of its life, for example the *reducing balance* method of depreciation. It is often argued that an accelerated depreciation method is more appropriate since it levies higher depreciation charges in the early years of an asset's life when maintenance and repair charges are modest, while charging less for depreciation in the later years of the asset's life when maintenance and repair charges are higher.

acceptable quality level (AQL) an agreed standard for error-free products. AQLs are often denoted as a percentage, the lower the percentage agreed for errors then the fewer defects allowed in the final product. AQLs are typically applied also to the supply of raw material and components and penalty clauses are incorporated into supply contracts to minimize defective inputs. See ACCEPTANCE SAMPLING, QUALITY CONTROL.

acceptance see CONTRACT.

acceptance sampling a process in which a sample is taken from a batch of raw materials, work in progress or finished goods to be inspected and tested so as to ensure a predetermined QUALITY standard is consistently achieved. The whole batch will then be accepted or rejected according to whether or not the sample is of an ACCEPTABLE QUALITY LEVEL. This saves the business from having to carry out 100% INSPECTION and testing of the goods involved. For example, a manufacturer taking delivery of 100 identical components from a supplier might inspect and test 10 components (10%) and specify that if more than 2 components (20% of the sample) fail to meet the required specification, then the whole batch will be rejected. In order to specify the performance of a particular sampling plan or evaluate alternative sampling plans, managers can develop OPERATING CHARACTERISTIC CURVES which show the relationship between percentage defects in batches of raw materials or components and the probability of their acceptance.

With JUST-IN-TIME production systems, a company or department may reduce its own acceptance sampling and place the onus of providing fault-free raw materials or components on its supplier. See TOTAL QUALITY MANAGEMENT, QUALITY CONTROL.

accepting house a division of a MERCHANT BANK or similar organization that 'accepts' (guarantees to honour) a BILL OF EXCHANGE, should a borrower default on the loan, in return for an agreed fee. By 'accepting' the bill the accepting house makes the bill more negotiable and so enables the bill to be discounted at more favourable interest rates.

Accepting Houses Committee an organization which represents the interests of UK ACCEPTING HOUSES.

account 1 a LEDGER record in which is entered details of all financial transactions relating to an individual supplier (in the creditors' ledger), or customer (in the debtors' ledger), or particular asset or liability (in the assets ledger), or type of expense or receipt (in the nominal ledgers). See DOUBLE ENTRY ACCOUNTS, ACCOUNTING.

2 a BANK OR BUILDING SOCIETY's record of its dealings with a particular customer which itemizes the customer's business with the bank such as deposits of cash and cheques and withdrawals of funds.

3 a CUSTOMER. A 'key account' is an important customer.

accountability an employee's RESPONSIBILITY for the exercise of certain duties and the requirement to report to his superiors on his performance of them. In recent years, many managers have attempted to strengthen lines of accountability so as to achieve improvements in the job performance of their subordinates.

One approach to this has been th creation of PROFIT CENTRES. The profit performance of these subunits of the organization can be closely monitored by organizational leaders, thereby increasing the accountability of those working in the profit centres. In so far as creation of profit centres involves a measure of decentralization of decision-making, decentralization of responsibility

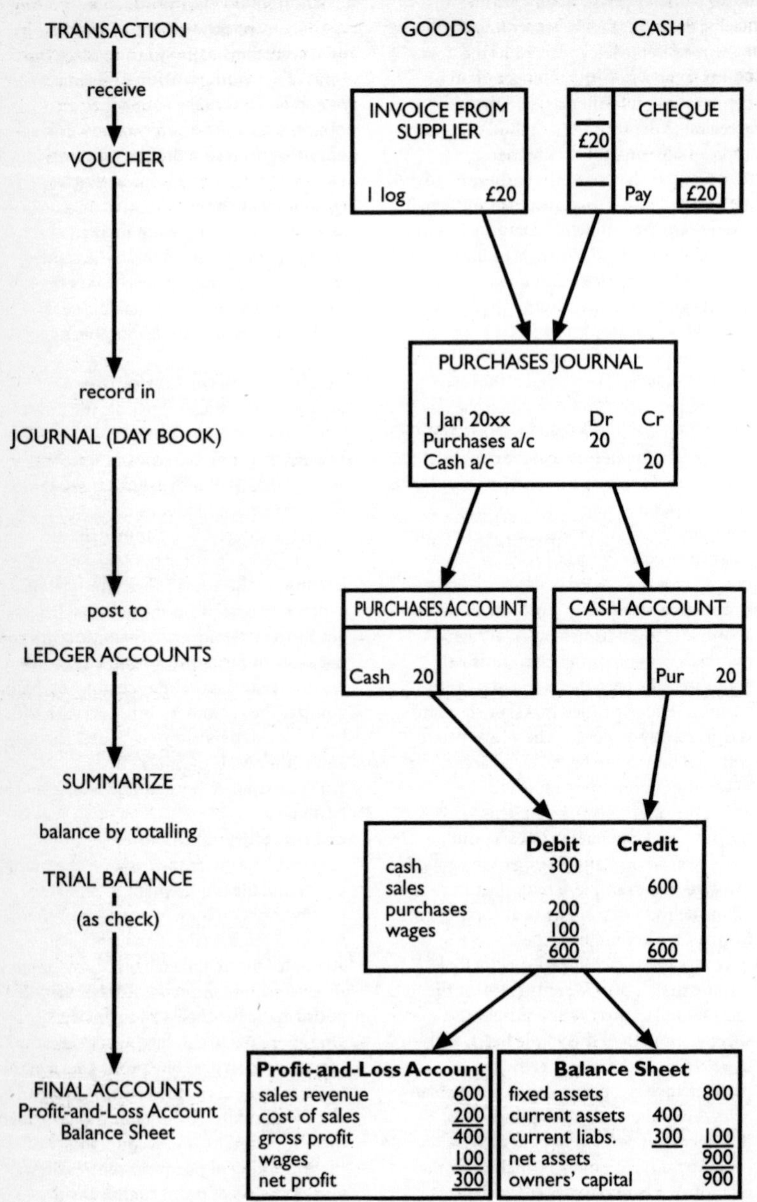

Fig. 3 **Accounting.** A typical data-recording sequence.

and AUTHORITY can be coupled with increased accountability. See MANAGEMENT, ORGANIZATION.

account executive an employee of an ADVERTISING AGENCY who is responsible for looking after the interests of a particular client's ACCOUNT with the agency.

accounting the process of recording a firm's financial transactions in appropriate book-keeping records and of summarizing this information in the form of accounting reports, using acknowledged methods and conventions. FINANCIAL ACCOUNTING is geared to the preparation of summary reports for the shareholders or owners of the business, while MANAGEMENT ACCOUNTING is geared to the preparation of more detailed reports for managers. Fig. 3 shows a typical data-recording sequence.

accounting concepts, principles and policies

The concepts, principles and policies which must be followed in preparing accounting records and summarizing them in financial statements:

(a) the *money measurement* concept suggests that only items which can be measured in money terms will be shown in a company's accounts;

(b) the *going concern* concept suggests that all financial reports be prepared to reflect the business's expected continuation as a going concern which will trade in the future, rather than being a one-off venture or a business which is likely to cease trading imminently and have its assets sold off;

(c) the *accruals* concept suggests that all revenues and expenses should be taken into account when they become due rather than when they are actually received or paid. In this way revenues and profits are *matched* with the associated expenses incurred in earning them;

(d) the *consistency* concept suggests that all accounting information should be consistently based between one year and the next, to aid comparisons of performance over time. This means, for example, that a business should not readily switch from one DEPRECIATION method to another from year to year;

(e) the *prudence* or *conservatism* concept suggests that revenues and profits should never be anticipated in the accounts of a business, but should only be included in the PROFIT-AND-LOSS ACCOUNT when such revenues and profits are reasonably certain. This means, for example, that companies would take account only of sales made, not of orders taken, and even then might make provision for some customers who have bought goods not paying up. Companies would also take a fairly conservative view of the value of assets such as stock in following this principle, adjusting the book value of stocks down to their realizable market value when market values fall. The prudence principle aims to ensure that a business's profits and assets are not overstated nor its liabilities understated;

(f) the *materiality* concept suggests that only data which are significant enough to be relevant need be disclosed, minor items being ignored in accounting reports;

(g) the *objectivity* concept suggests a need to establish rules for recording and summarizing financial transactions which avoid the exercise of personal judgement by the person doing the recording and summarizing. Thus accountants usually account for ASSETS on the basis of their HISTORIC COST, since historic cost provides an objective basis, rather than estimating the changing market value of assets.

In preparing financial accounts for shareholders, joint-stock companies are required to disclose the specific accounting policies (based on the above principles) which they have used in valuing stocks, calculating depreciation and the like.

accounting equation the idea that capital is equal to assets minus liabilities, and thus may be expressed as C = A – L. This may also be described as *'the balance sheet identity'*. See BALANCE SHEET.

accounting exposure see EXCHANGE RATE EXPOSURE.

accounting period the time period over which a firm prepares its PROFIT-AND-LOSS ACCOUNT and at the end of which it draws up its BALANCE SHEET. JOINT-STOCK COMPANIES are required by law to prepare ANNUAL REPORTS AND ACCOUNTS for the shareholders. Many firms now prepare quarterly, monthly or even weekly trading accounts to give managers prompt feedback about performance.

accounting ratio a means of placing a firm's accounting results in context by expressing the figures as ratios or percentages of other figures in order to appraise their 'bigness' or 'smallness'. Examples include RETURN ON CAPITAL EMPLOYED and STOCK TURNOVER RATIO. Fig. 4 shows the main ratios used and the relationship between them.

accounting return a criterion used in INVESTMENT APPRAISAL to evaluate the desirability of an INVESTMENT project. Accounting return involves calculating the anticipated return on an investment in terms of the average yearly accounting profit expected from the project, expressed as a percentage of the capital invested. Fig. 5 shows a typical calculation for a proposed machine purchase, which in this case promises an accounting return of 36% per year. If a firm's target rate of return for new investment projects was, say, 30% plus, then this particular project would be undertaken.

Whether or not the calculated return is realized depends upon how accurate the future estimates of sales volume, selling prices, materials costs, machine life, etc. turn out to be. Since all investments involve assessments of future revenues and costs they are all subject to a degree of uncertainty. This problem, in part, can be handled by undertaking a sensitivity analysis, making not one but three estimates from each item of project cost or revenue ('optimistic', 'most likely', 'pessimistic') to indicate the range of possible outcomes.

accounting standards guidelines relating to the accounting treatment of the figures which are reported in the accounts of companies. They were introduced to reduce the possibility of having large variations in reported profits and to restrict the room available for manoeuvre by those charged with the task of preparing the accounts.

Prior to 1990 Statements of Recommended Practice (SORPs) and Statements of Standard Accounting Practice (SSAPs) were

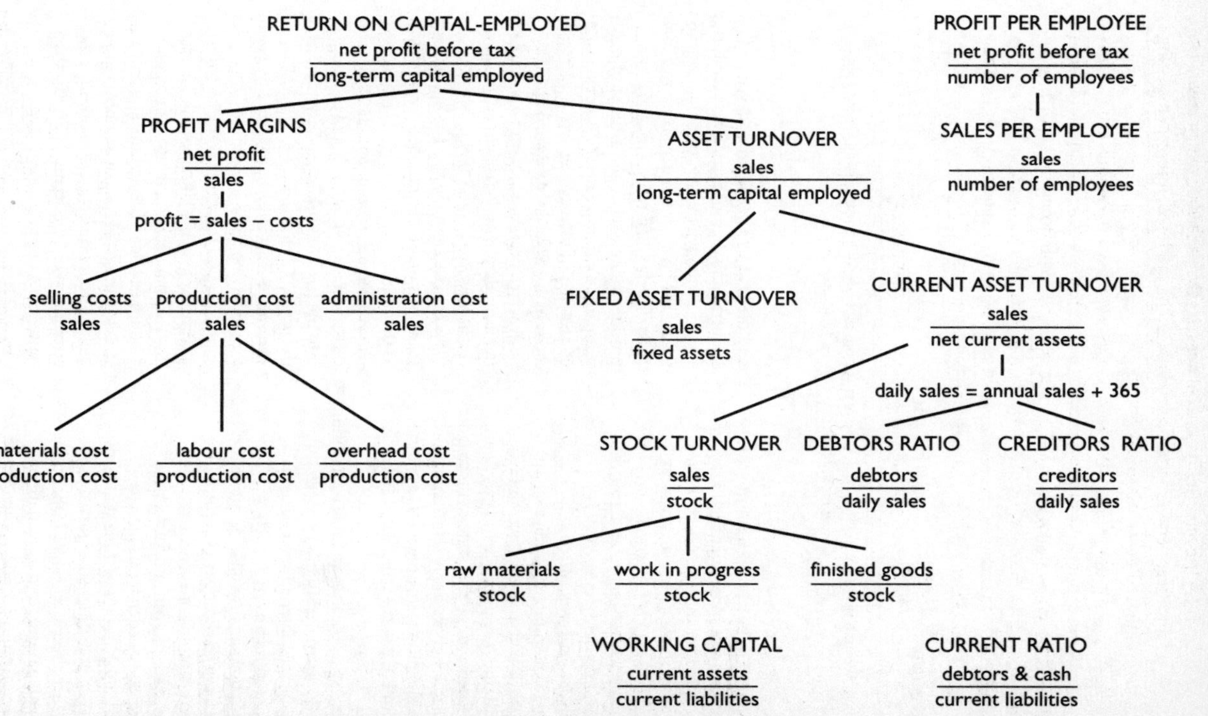

Fig. 4 **Accounting ratio**. The ratio pyramid.

	Year 1 £	Year 2 £	Yearly average £
unit sales	3,000	2,000	2,500
price	x3	x3	x3
revenue	9,000	6,000	7,500
materials, labour and overhead costs	4,000	3,000	3,500
gross profit	5,000	3,000	4,000
depreciation	2,200	2,200	2,200
Profit	2,800	800	1,800

accounting return = $\frac{£1,800}{£5,000} \times 100 = 36\%$ per year

Fig. 5 **Accounting return.** Example: machine: cost £5,000, estimated life 2 years, residual value £600, depreciation $\frac{£5,000 - 600}{2}$ = £2,200 per year.

issued in the UK by a joint committee of the professional accounting organizations. These covered various matters, including:

Accounting policies; post balance sheet events and contingencies; earnings per share; taxation; stocks and long-term contracts; cash flow statements; research and development; and group accounts.

In 1990 the accountancy bodies set up a new organization to oversee accounting standards, the Accounting Standards Board which issued a number of statements that are now called Financial Reporting Standards (FRSs). The FRSs were drawn up to comply with both UK law, the Republic of Ireland law, and EU directives.

In recent years the International Accounting Standards Board (IASB) has overseen the development of International Financial Reporting Standards (IFRS). These standards now apply to all large quoted companies in the European Union, which from the beginning of 2005 are required to report their interim and final annual accounts expressed in terms of these standards. Application of these standards initially generate different reported profits and balance sheet asset values from those which would result from using national generally-agreed accounting principles or national financial reporting standards.

To date IFRS apply only to EU companies, and the USA, Japan and other developed countries use their own national accounting standards, though the US Financial Accounting Standards Board and the IASB are working to harmonize their rules. The goal is to produce a single set of global accounting standards to improve the transparency and consistency of financial reports.

Accounting Standards Board the UK body which prior to 1990 was responsible for the formulation of *Statements of Standard Accounting Practice (SSAPs).*

It was replaced in 1990 by The Accounting Standards Board Limited. See ACCOUNTING STANDARDS.

account payee a means of indicating on a CHEQUE that the money should only be paid into the bank or building society account of the payee.

account period a designated trading period for the buying and selling of FINANCIAL SECURITIES on the STOCK MARKET. Until 1994 trading on the UK Stock Market took place within a series of end-on fortnightly account periods with all purchases and sales struck during a particular account period being paid for or settled six working days after the end of the account period – the 'settlement' day or 'account' day.

In 1994 this system was replaced by a 'rolling settlement' system in which settlement takes place ten working days after a deal has been struck. Thus, *every* working day is a settlement day.

Settlement was cut to five days in 1995. See TALISMAN, CREST.

accounts the financial statements of a business prepared from a system of recorded financial transactions. Public limited JOINT-STOCK COMPANIES are required to publish their year-end financial statements, which must comprise at least a PROFIT-AND-LOSS ACCOUNT and BALANCE SHEET, to enable SHAREHOLDERS to assess their company's financial performance during the period. AUDITORS also require a set of year-end accounts to enable them to undertake appropriate tests of the LEDGER records and submit their opinion on the accuracy of the company's reported results to shareholders. Nonincorporated bodies such as sole proprietors and partnerships are not subject to such rigorous legislation but most prepare appropriate financial statements to submit to the INLAND REVENUE as a basis for tax assessments.

accounts payable see CREDITORS.

accounts receivable see DEBTORS.

accreditation of experiential learning the award of credit for a period of relevant work experience or similar to gain admission to or exemption from some part of an educational or TRAINING course. The principle underlying it is that the technical skills ('competences') and conceptual understanding likely to have been gained during this time is broadly equivalent to that which would have been obtained from a specified programme of education or training. Some method of assessment might be used as part of the accreditation process. This type of accreditation is linked to the attempt to establish national standards of competence found in the NATIONAL VOCATIONAL QUALIFICATION initiative.

accreditation of prior learning the award of credit for a course of study or TRAINING previously undertaken to give exemption from some part of an educational or training course currently being taken. It facilitates greater flexibility in the provision of training and education, and is therefore thought likely to encourage take-up of vocational training and education. Accreditation of prior learning is likely to be facilitated by the attempts to set national standards of training and education in the NATIONAL VOCATIONAL QUALIFICATION initiative.

accrual an expense which is outstanding at the end of a trading period and which needs to be included in the accounting results for the period. For example, an unpaid INVOICE for car repairs would be included in the expenses of the trading period in calculating profits, since the repair costs relate to that period; the unpaid bill is counted as a liability of the firm at the period end, and afterwards until it is paid, and is added to CURRENT LIABILITIES in the firm's BALANCE SHEET. See PREPAYMENT.

accruals concept of accounting the principle that all a firm's costs and revenues should be counted in the company's accounts from the date when the expenses are legally incurred and when the revenues are receivable, not when the expenses are actually paid or the cash received. Organizations such as local drama groups which require less formal accounts may settle for RECEIPTS AND PAYMENTS ACCOUNTS which deviate from the accruals principle in the interests of simplicity; though even here *income and expenditure accounts* which follow the accruals principle are more common.

accumulated fund a non-profit-making organization's balance sheet description for the capital and retained earnings figure.

accumulated profit see RETAINED PROFIT.

achievement test see PSYCHOLOGICAL TEST.

acid test ratio see CURRENT RATIO.

Acquired Rights Directive see TRANSFER OF UNDERTAKINGS (PROTECTION OF EMPLOYMENT) REGULATIONS.

acquisition see TAKEOVER.

ACT see advance CORPORATION TAX.

action learning see MANAGEMENT DEVELOPMENT.

action programme a STRATEGY for achieving prompt results, which sets deadlines for meeting targets. For instance, a company targeting a new MARKET SEGMENT will draw up an action plan specifying which market segment is being aimed at and how the company is going to market the product (in terms of price, special offers, methods of selling, etc.), thus establishing sales and market share targets.

activity chart *or* **process chart** *or* **flowchart** a means of recording all the work tasks performed by a person and/or machine at a 'work station'. Activity charts break down work tasks into five main categories: operation (altering materials, assembly, etc.); transportation (moving materials, components or products); inspection (checking for defects); delay (hold-ups in production caused by lack of materials, machine breakdowns, etc.); storage (items placed in stock).

Fig. 6 shows the symbols which are conventionally used to depict these activities:

Activity charts are used in METHOD STUDY to record the methods used to perform work tasks as a basis for improving these methods by reducing delays, minimizing materials handling and combining operations. They are also used to assist in the planning of FACTORY LAYOUTS and in PRODUCTION SCHEDULING by depicting the sequence of work tasks involved.

Where several machines or operatives are deployed alongside each other in a work station, *multiple activity charts* may be used to depict their interactions.

activity-based costing a system of product costing which seeks to break down the divide between FIXED COSTS and VARIABLE COSTS by looking at the total cost to the business of making a product. All costs are related to *cost drivers* – the factors which influence the cost of a product.

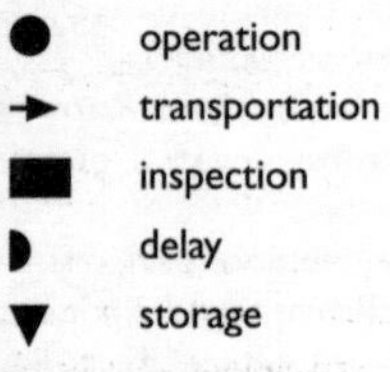

● operation
➔ transportation
■ inspection
◗ delay
▼ storage

Fig. 6 **Activity chart symbols**

Activity costing is suggested as an alternative to STANDARD COSTING, which analyses labour costs in detail and tends to share out overheads between products by reference to the *direct* labour hours involved in making different products. However, in automated factories, where labour is a relatively unimportant part of the total product cost, such detailed analysis of labour may not be justified and direct labour costs may be an inappropriate basis for analysing overheads. For such automated plants activity costing may be preferable, focusing as it does on the forces driving the costs of being in business.

activity level a measure of output which can be expressed in units of production, direct labour hours, machine hours or some other basis.

activity sampling *or* **work sampling** a means of studying the work of managers, staff and indirect factory workers (see INDIRECT LABOUR). Activity sampling involves noting at predetermined time intervals, say every five minutes, what activity or work a particular individual or group of employees is engaged in. From these observations it is then possible to calculate the percentage of their time which the individual or group of workers is spending upon various tasks. Activity sampling information can be used to assess the proportions of productive and non-productive time and to help managers and workers to use their time more efficiently. See METHOD STUDY.

actuary a statistician employed by an INSURANCE COMPANY to calculate insurance risks and premiums.

added value see VALUE ADDED.

Additional Voluntary Contribution (AVC) an additional payment to a PENSION scheme, to supplement contributions to an occupational pension scheme.

ad-hocracy those ORGANIZATIONS in which work roles and routines tend not to be specialized or standardized. Job content is not closely or formally defined. Thus individuals' tasks can be adapted as required to meet current exigencies. An important feature of this type of organization is that employees determine among themselves who does what when new tasks arise. Hence organizations of this sort can normally respond flexibly to new situations. However, a negative feature of organizations of this sort is the lack of strategy, to guide the organization; this results in the absence of clearly-defined or consistent policies to ensure achievement of organizational goals. See MECHANISTIC AND ORGANISMIC.

administered price a PRICE for a product which is set and controlled by an individual supplier, a group of suppliers or the government, as opposed to being determined by the free interplay of market forces. See MONOPOLY, CARTEL, PRICE CONTROL, FIXED EXCHANGE RATE.

administration see MANAGEMENT.

administrator see INSOLVENCY.

ADR see AMERICAN DEPOSITORY RECEIPT.

ad valorem tax a TAX which is levied as a percentage of the price or value of a unit of OUTPUT. See VALUE ADDED TAX. Compare SPECIFIC TAX.

advance corporation tax (ACT) see CORPORATION TAX.

advertisement a written or visual presentation in the MEDIA of a BRAND of good or service supplied by a firm or some other organization, which is aimed at encouraging either prospective buyers to purchase the product, or greater usage of a facility, or to provide information. See ADVERTISING, ADVERTISING CAMPAIGN, ADVERTISING COPY, ADVERTISING EFFECTIVENESS TEST, REINFORCEMENT ADVERTISING, ADVERTISING STANDARDS AUTHORITY, CONTROL OF MISLEADING ADVERTISEMENTS REGULATION 1988.

advertising

A means by which a seller of a BRAND of good or service attempts to increase its sales by communicating with BUYERS, informing them of the nature and attributes of the brand and persuading them to buy it in preference to competitors' brands. Advertising comprises part of a firm's PROMOTIONAL MIX and is undertaken in a variety of ways, including the use of mass MEDIA channels such as television, national newspapers and magazines, posters, websites etc., and more targeted approaches through 'special interest' magazines and trade journals, and regional and local newspapers.

Although some advertising is largely concerned with providing buyers with information about the product, the majority of advertising is 'persuasive' in intent. Persuasive advertising aims to encourage consumers to purchase products, and the skill of advertising copywriters lies in designing ADVERTISEMENTS which are visually attractive and which appeal to deep-seated consumer motivations, both physical and psychological. If advertisements appeal sufficiently to consumer motives they will encourage repeat buying of the product, thereby establishing BRAND LOYALTY and increasing or maintaining the firm's MARKET SHARE.

The selection of the advertising medium will depend upon the MARKET or market segment which is being targeted (see MARKET SEGMENTATION) and the relative costs and effectiveness of using different media. For example, in respect of specialized INDUSTRIAL BUYERS advertisements may be placed in appropriate trade/professional journals. On the other hand, if large numbers of final consumers are being targeted, it may be more cost-effective to use the mass media which, although more expensive in absolute terms, actually costs less per potential customer reached.

Advertising is an important part of a firm's MARKETING MIX which seeks to differentiate its brand of product from competitors' offerings. See ADVERTISING COPY, ADVERTISING COVERAGE, ADVERTISING EFFECTIVENESS TEST, ADVERTISING FREQUENCY, DIRECT MARKETING, PRODUCT DIFFERENTIATION, COMPETITIVE ADVANTAGE, ADVERTISING CAMPAIGN, ADVERTISING OBJECTIVE, BUYER BEHAVIOUR, PRODUCT IMAGE, ADVERTISING STANDARDS AUTHORITY, CONTROL OF MISLEADING ADVERTISEMENTS REGULATIONS 1988.

advertising agency a business which specializes in providing various MARKETING services for firms and other organizations, particularly ADVERTISING services. Advertising agents devise, programme and manage specific ADVERTISING CAMPAIGNS on behalf of clients as well as undertaking more general MARKET RESEARCH, product and market analyses, SALES PROMOTION planning and public relations activities. See ADVERTISING COPY.

advertising campaign a planned series of ADVERTISEMENTS aimed at increasing the sales of a particular BRAND of good or service. Such campaigns may include a set of linked advertisements stressing a common promotional theme and this same theme will be deployed across several advertising MEDIA. A campaign might run over a short period of time, or over a number of years if it proves successful. See ADVERTISING EFFECTIVENESS TEST.

advertising copy the specific wording of an ADVERTISEMENT of a BRAND of good or service, which highlights the 'theme' or 'message' the advertisement is intended to convey to prospective BUYERS or users of that product. Advertising copy may be pitched to appeal to consumers in general or targeted to attract the attention of a particular type of buyer (see MARKET SEGMENTATION).

Advertising copy can take a variety of forms, but ADVERTISING AGENCIES and other writers and producers of advertising material must be mindful that an advertisement should not be misleading, untruthful or in bad taste. See ADVERTISING STANDARDS AUTHORITY, ADVERTISING EFFECTIVENESS TEST, MOTIVATIONAL RESEARCH.

advertising coverage the number of prospective buyers of a BRAND of good or service reached by an ADVERTISEMENT of that product. This will depend largely on the choice of MEDIA (commercial television, newspapers, etc.) selected for the advertisement and the frequency with which the advertisement appears. See ADVERTISING, ADVERTISING FREQUENCY, ADVERTISING CAMPAIGN.

advertising effectiveness test a means of measuring the impact or likely impact of an ADVERTISEMENT or an ADVERTISING CAMPAIGN on the sales of a product. Such tests fall into two basic categories:

(a) *pre-testing* in which particular advertisements are tried out on a representative sample of buyers or potential buyers (see TEST MARKETING) to decide, in advance, which one of them is likely to make the biggest impact on prospective buyers. Methods used for this purpose include the *sales conviction test* and the *blind product test.* In the former case established buyers of the product are asked which of a number of advertisements would induce them to buy the product, while in the latter case respondents are given ADVERTISING COPY and asked to select from a number of unidentified products the one which best 'fits' the advertisement;

(b) *post-testing* which aims to measure the impact of the advertisements currently used by the firm. Various *recognition tests* can be used for this purpose, including asking readers of a newspaper or viewers of commercial television where the advertisement has been placed whether they have read or seen the advertisement in question. Deeper probing of the impression an advertisement may have made can be done by the *unaided recall test* where respondents are asked to comment from memory on particular details of the advertisement.

advertising frequency the number of times an ADVERTISEMENT appears in the MEDIA (commercial television, newspapers, etc.). Advertising frequency can be extended by increasing over a specific time period the number of times the advertisement appears in the firm's existing choice of media, or by placing the advertisement in a wider range of media. A high advertising frequency is often required to launch a NEW PRODUCT onto the market and is also important in supporting existing BRANDS over time, encouraging repeat purchasing and maintaining BRAND LOYALTY.

advertising message a communication designed to influence BUYER BEHAVIOUR. See ADVERTISING COPY.

advertising objective the goal of ADVERTISING which can be stated in qualitative terms such as increasing consumers' awareness of a particular BRAND of good or service or the company itself. Alternatively, the objective may be operationalized as a specific target such as increasing the SALES/MARKET SHARE of a product by x% over a one-year period.

advertising platform the aspect of the seller's product that is most persuasive and relevant to the target consumer.

Advertising Standards Authority (ASA) a body which regulates (on a 'voluntary' basis) the UK ADVERTISING industry. The ASA administers the British Code of Advertising Practice which aims to ensure that ADVERTISEMENTS provide a fair, honest and unambiguous representation of the products they promote, including the wording of, and impressions conveyed by, ADVERTISING COPY. The ASA gives guidance to advertisers on whether a proposed advertisement would be regarded as acceptable, and deals with complaints from the general public about cases of allegedly untruthful, misleading or offensive advertisements.

Advisory, Conciliation and Arbitration Service (ACAS) an independent service set up in 1975, financed by the government and used to resolve collective and individual INDUSTRIAL DISPUTES in the UK. It is able to provide CONCILIATION to bring the parties together and to provide ARBITRATION and MEDIATION where it is deemed desirable. ACAS also provides advisory services to employers, employees and trade unions on work and employment issues. See CENTRAL ARBITRATION COMMITTEE, EMPLOYMENT TRIBUNAL.

AEEU see AMALGAMATED ENGINEERING AND ELECTRICAL UNION.

AESOP see SHARE INCENTIVE PLAN.

AESP see SHARE INCENTIVE PLAN.

after-sales service back-up services and facilities provided by the suppliers of goods and services to their customers. After-sales service can include free maintenance and repairs, a telephone service for dealing with customers' queries, and an express PARTS delivery service. An after-sales service is an important part of the MARKETING MIX, serving to enhance customer loyalty and provide valuable feedback about its goods and services. See CUSTOMER SERVICES, GUARANTEE, REPLACEMENT PARTS.

agency costs the failure of employees (as 'agents'), hired by the owners (the 'principals') of a business, to fully comply with the terms and responsibilities stipulated in their CONTRACT OF EMPLOYMENT. For example, operatives may 'shirk', indulging in time wasting (long tea breaks etc) thus leading to a loss of potential output. The companies executive directors may fail to put shareholder interests first and pursue other BUSINESS OBJECTIVES of more 'value' to themselves. See PRINCIPAL-AGENT THEORY.

Strategists are concerned not only with agency costs (*internal* to the firm) but also with the TRANSACTION COSTS of using *external* markets. Together these can be important considerations in influencing the extent of VERTICAL INTEGRATION/DISINTEGRATION.

age analysis profile for debtors a summary analysis of outstanding DEBTOR balances in the debtors LEDGER classified according to how long these debts have been outstanding. For example, the age analysis profile might distinguish between debts which are less than one month old; those which are two months old; those which are three months old (stale debts); those which are four months old (doubtful as to repayment); and five months or older (mostly bad debts to be written off as irrecoverable). Preparation of periodic age analysis profiles which monitor the proportions of total outstanding debt falling into each age category can provide useful data for CREDIT CONTROL purposes. See CREDIT PERIOD, DEBTORS RATIO.

Agency status a UK civil service function which operates at arm's length from the civil service. Agencies developed in the wake of the 'Next Steps' report in the late 1980s which argued that the service provision function of the civil service (e.g. payment of unemployment benefit) should be separated from the policy-formulation part and become the responsibility of executive agencies. See NEW PUBLIC MANAGEMENT.

agenda a list of items of business scheduled for discussion at a meeting.

agent a person or company employed by another person or company (called the PRINCIPAL) for the purpose of arranging CONTRACTS between the principal and third parties. An agent generally has authority to act within broad limits in conducting business on behalf of his or her principal and has a basic duty to carry out the tasks involved with due skill and diligence.

An agent or broker acts as an intermediary in bringing together buyers and sellers of a good or service, receiving a flat or sliding scale commission or fee related to the nature and comprehensiveness of the work undertaken and/or value of the transaction involved. Agents and agencies are encountered in one way or another in most economic activities and play an important role in the smooth functioning of the market mechanism. A *stockbroker*, for example, acts on behalf of clients wishing to buy and sell financial securities; an *estate agent* acts as an intermediary between buyers and sellers of houses, offices, etc.; while an *insurance broker* negotiates insurance cover on behalf of clients with an insurance company. A *recruitment agency* performs the services of advertising for, interviewing and selecting employees on behalf of a company. In addition to the role of agents as market intermediaries, organizational theorists have paid particular attention to the *internal* relationship between the employees ('agents') and owners ('principals') of a company. See PRINCIPAL-AGENT THEORY.

aggregate demand the total demand for a firm's product/s. The term is also used to describe the total demand placed on a production unit in order to calculate MANUFACTURING RESOURCE PLANNING (MRP II) requirements.

aggregated rebate *or* **overriding discount** a business practice whereby a supplier offers distributors/retailers a discount on their *total* purchases over a specified time period (usually one year) rather than on individual orders. The operation of aggregated rebates, by encouraging dealers/retailers to place the whole or a substantial part of their regular orders with one supplier, may help the supplier increase his sales and protect market share. However, if undertaken by a DOMINANT FIRM, the practice may serve to limit competition in a market by depriving rival suppliers of distribution outlets. See COMPETITION ACT, 1980, QUANTITY DISCOUNT, BULK BUYING.

aggregate inventory the total INVENTORY (stocks) held by a firm.

aggregate plan the overall plan for the deployment of people, inventory, machines and other resources necessary to meet the demands for the product on the firm. See MATERIALS REQUIREMENT PLANNING (MRP), MANUFACTURING RESOURCE PLANNING (MRP II).

AGM see ANNUAL GENERAL MEETING.

AIDA awareness, interest, desire, action – the stages through which a consumer is intended to be taken by ADVERTISING messages before purchasing a product.

AIM see ALTERNATIVE INVESTMENT MARKET.

aims see BUSINESS OBJECTIVES.

AITC see ASSOCIATION OF INVESTMENT TRUST COMPANIES.

alienation the separation of people from their essential qualities as human beings in capitalist societies. Karl Marx (1818–83), who first developed the concept, believed that 'free conscious activity' was the hallmark of human activity. Work in modern capitalist society, which involves the worker producing goods and services for the profit of an employer and in a manner dictated by the employer, separates (i.e. alienates) people from their essence. In effect an individual's labour power is reduced to a commodity to be bought and sold. Job dissatisfaction may well result, but the possibility arises that alienation from 'true' human desires is so deep that individuals have no standard against which to compare their lot and hence may nevertheless experience job satisfaction. Since alienation, as defined here, has no clear discernible relationship with SATISFACTION, many critics have argued that its use in the analysis of work attitudes and behaviour is decidedly limited.

A closer link between alienation and job satisfaction has been provided by American sociologist Robert Blauner (1929–). He defined alienation as a 'fragmentation in man's consciousness', experienced as dissatisfaction. The dimensions of this are a sense of powerlessness (i.e. inability to control what happens at work), a feeling of meaninglessness (i.e. the job tasks seem pointless), a sense of isolation from others, and a feeling of self-estrangement (i.e. that one's creativity is stifled). In Blauner's view, technology is the most important determinant of alienation.

In assembly-line work (see FORDISM) alienation reaches its peak. By contrast, more recent process technology, in which the worker oversees a range of operations rather than being subjugated to the machine, is associated with lower levels of alienation. The logic of Blauner's account, in contrast to that of Marx, is that alienation can be reduced by managerial policies to modify the nature of workers' tasks (see JOB DESIGN AND REDESIGN) and to integrate workers into a work community (see HUMAN RELATIONS). See ANOMIE.

all-current method see FOREIGN CURRENCY TRANSLATION.

All Employee Share Ownership Plan see SHARE INCENTIVE PLAN.

All Employee Share Plan see SHARE INCENTIVE PLAN.

allocation 1 the breakdown of COSTS (and REVENUES) between different products, functions or company departments where it is possible to attribute costs (and revenues) directly to the departments where the cost (revenue) arises. For example, in analysing costs, the depreciation OVERHEADS of factory departments can be allocated precisely between the production departments where the specific fixed assets are located. Such allocations help in tracing responsibility for costs to the managers responsible, as well as assessing the profitability of different departments or products. Fig. 7 shows a typical departmental revenue/cost breakdown where some costs are precisely allocated while others are apportioned on an equitable basis. See BUDGETING, STANDARD COST.
2 the process of assigning or 'earmarking' materials which are in STOCK in order to fulfil specified product orders. The stock of materials that has not been currently allocated is referred to as the 'free balance', which is available for allocation to future orders.

allotment the allocation of shares by directors of a company to intending shareholders who have made applications for new shares. In the event of a new SHARE ISSUE being oversubscribed (i.e. more applications for shares than the number being issued), then the company must use some formula to allocate shares among applicants. Often this involves granting applicants for small blocks of shares the

Expense	Total £	Basis used	Frame shop £	Upholstery section £
DIRECT COSTS				
Direct Materials	350,000	Actual	200,000	150,000
Direct Labour	174,000	Actual	74,000	100,000
Prime cost	524,000		274,000	250,000
PRODUCTION OVERHEADS				
Factory Rent and Rates	10,800	Floor area	5,000	5,800
Power and Light	10,750	Metered Consumption	5,750	5,000
General Labour	21,850	Actual	10,000	11,850
Depreciation	23,300	Plant Installed	12,300	11,000
Works Management	5,000	Time Occupied Estimate	2,000	3,000
	71,700		35,050	36,650

Fig. 7 **Allocation and Apportionment.** Budgeted production costs: departmental analysis.

full number of shares applied for, while applicants for large blocks of shares may be granted only a proportion of the numbers they applied for, or, in the event of a ballot, receive none at all if unsuccessful.

allowances 1 the additional time which is added to the 'basic time' allowed for the completion of a particular work task in order to calculate a 'standard time' for that task. These include:

(a) Relaxation allowances, which are made to take account of the mental and physical needs of workers, who require rest periods;

(b) contingency allowances which are made to cover the unforeseen circumstances such as the extra work caused by defective machines or substandard materials;

(c) interference allowances which are made to take account of nonproductive or IDLE TIME caused by delays in materials, machine breakdowns and machine SET-UP TIMES. See WORK MEASUREMENT.

2 the additional raw materials or components which are added to the basic materials allowed for the completion of a particular product or subassembly in a PRODUCT SPECIFICATION, to allow for cutting losses and anticipated wastage of materials.

3 tax allowances. See INCOME TAX ALLOWANCE, CAPITAL ALLOWANCE, CORPORATION TAX.

allowed time the maximum amount of time which an employee should take to perform a specific production task. Allowed times tend to be used in INCENTIVE BONUS SCHEMES as the basis for computing bonus payments. If the allowed time is exceeded no bonus is payable. However, if the actual time taken to perform the particular task is less than the allowed time, a bonus would be payable based upon the amount of time saved. See WORK MEASUREMENT.

alpha stock the STOCKS and SHARES (generally of large well-established companies) listed on the STOCK MARKET which are highly regarded by investors.

Alternative Investment Market (AIM) a market for corporate STOCKS and SHARES that have not obtained a full STOCK MARKET listing. An *unlisted securities market* (USM) was established in the UK in 1980 in order to provide smaller companies with a means of raising new capital (see SHARE ISSUE) without the expense and the same formalities required by the main stock market. For example, such companies need only have a brief trading record to qualify and the proportion of their shares sold in the open market need only be 10% of their ISSUED CAPITAL instead of the usual 25%. The USM was phased out in 1996 and superseded by the Alternative Investment Market (AIM). AIM imposes no minimum on the percentage of a company's shares in public hands and no minimum trading record.

Amalgamated Engineering and Electrical Union (AEEU) see AMICUS.

amalgamation see MERGER.

ambush marketing originally referred to activities of companies who try to associate themselves with an event (e.g. the Olympics) without paying any fee to the event owner; now meaning the sponsoring of the television coverage of a major event, national teams and the support of individual sportspeople.

American Depository Receipt (ADR) a certificate of ownership issued to an individual or company investor by a US bank which holds (on deposit) the investor's or company's STOCKS and SHARES. The ADR serves as proof of the ownership of the securities held by the bank and can be used as a negotiable instrument.

American Depository Receipts have been used extensively by UK companies wishing to encourage investment by US institutional investors. Such companies lodge a proportion of their shares with a US bank, which then issues depository shares which can be traded on the US stock market.

AMICUS a TRADE UNION representing technical and blue collar workers, especially in manufacturing. It was formed in 2002 from a merger of the Amalgamated Engineering and Electrical Union (AEEU) and the Manufacturing, Science and Finance union (MSF). It has around 1,125,000 members and is the UK's second largest trade union.

amortization see DEPRECIATION, definition 1.

Amsterdam Treaty, 1997 a EUROPEAN UNION (EU) statute which extended various provisions of the MAASTRICHT TREATY in the areas of social policy (particularly discriminations against persons and the integration of the SOCIAL CHAPTER), internal procedures for the administration of EU institutions and the EU's Common Foreign and Security Policy (including defence).

analytical estimating see WORK MEASUREMENT.

ancillary operation an operation in which material or plant is being cleaned, prepared or put away, where the work performed does not result in added value to the material or plant. For example, the time spent setting up or cleaning a machine contributes to the smooth running of the production presses even though it does not contribute directly to the manufacture of the product. See MAINTENANCE, SET-UP TIME.

Andean Pact a regional alliance originally formed in 1969 with the general objective of establishing a 'common market' (see TRADE INTEGRATION entry for details). The original members of the Andean Pact were Peru, Chile, Ecuador, Columbia and Bolivia. However, by the mid 1980s it had all but collapsed due to various economic and political instabilities. The Pact was re-launched in 1990 minus Chile but with a new member Venezuela.

andon a Japanese term referring to call lights installed at workstations to notify management and other workers of a quality and/or process problem in production. Andons act as part of the team working and quality circles structure within the JUST-IN-TIME (JIT) SYSTEM/TOYOTA PRODUCTION SYSTEM (TPS). The light is activated by the worker at the workstation when he or she has found a problem with the work being carried out. Invariably work is stopped until a solution has been found. Andons are also considered to be a tool of the continual improvement cycle (see KAIZAN and JIDOKA) promoted by the JIT/TPS.

annual general meeting (AGM) the yearly meeting of SHAREHOLDERS which JOINT-STOCK COMPANIES are required by law to convene, in order to allow shareholders to discuss their company's ANNUAL REPORT AND ACCOUNTS, elect directors and agree the DIVIDEND payouts suggested by directors. In practice, annual general meetings are usually poorly attended by shareholders and only rarely do directors fail to be re-elected on the strength of PROXY votes cast in favour of the directors.

Extraordinary or *special* general meetings may also be called by directors or shareholders to deal with major changes in, say, the firm's capital structure. See BOARD OF DIRECTORS.

annual hours the contractual requirement that employees work a number of hours over the year rather than a standard number of hours each week. This means that the length of the working day can be varied day by day to fit in with production requirements ('flexible rostering'). Alternatively, at certain times of the year employees work very short days whilst at other times they work long days. This can be advantageous to employers when product demand is seasonal in nature and storage of the product is either difficult or impossible (for example where a service is provided). Thus annual hours facilitate the synchronization of labour utilization with production requirements, thereby potentially improving labour productivity. A common feature of annual hours contracts is that the right to determine daily working hours is largely reserved to the employer (compare with FLEXITIME system).

annual report and accounts a yearly report by the directors of a JOINT-STOCK COMPANY to the SHAREHOLDERS. It includes a copy of the company's BALANCE SHEET and a summary PROFIT-AND-LOSS ACCOUNT for the current and immediately-prior year, along with other information which directors are required by law to disclose to shareholders. Large quoted joint-stock companies must also include a SOURCES AND USES OF FUNDS STATEMENT and an Operating and Financial Review. A copy of the annual report and accounts is sent to every shareholder prior to the company's ANNUAL GENERAL MEETING.

annual return a document which must be completed by the COMPANY SECRETARY and DIRECTORS of a JOINT-STOCK COMPANY after its ANNUAL GENERAL MEETING and forwarded to the COMPANY REGISTRAR. The annual return includes details about company directors, MORTGAGES and charges, the updated SHARE REGISTER and the ANNUAL REPORT AND ACCOUNTS. Annual returns can be inspected by members of the public on payment of a fee.

annuity a series of equal payments at fixed intervals deriving from an original lump-sum INVESTMENT.

annuity table a table that shows the effect of compound interest on an annually invested sum. Specifically, the table shows what the investment of the same amount of money on an annual basis at a fixed rate of interest for a certain number of years will accumulate to. For example, if £250 is invested at 10% at the end of each of the next 6 years, using the annuity table (which shows a figure of 7.716), it would accumulate to £250 x 7.716 = £1,929.

anomie a state of normlessness (i.e. a sense of confusion and loss about values and personal objectives) which French sociologist Emile Durkheim (1858–1917) believed could arise from the disruption of community caused by growing specialization in the division of labour. It could be expressed in job dissatisfaction and 'deviant' behaviour at work. The solution was to create a sense of community appropriate to the new division of labour. See ALIENATION, HUMAN RELATIONS, JOB SATISFACTION.

answering machine see VOICE MESSAGING.

anti-competitive agreement a form of COLLUSION between suppliers aimed at restricting or removing competition between them. For the most part such agreements concentrate on fixing common selling prices and discounts but may also contain provisions relating to market-sharing, production quotas and coordinated capacity adjustments. The main objection to such agreements is that they raise prices above competitive levels, impose unfair terms and conditions on buyers and serve to protect inefficient suppliers from the rigours of competition. In the UK, anti-competitive agreements are *prohibited* by the COMPETITION ACT, 1998.

anti-competitive practice a practice employed by a firm which has the effect of restricting or eliminating competition in a market. Practices which may potentially adversely affect the position of a firm's rivals, suppliers or distributors include EXCLUSIVE DEALING, REFUSAL TO SUPPLY, FULL LINE FORCING, TIE-IN SALES and AGGREGATED REBATES. These practices are likely to be particularly restrictive if employed by a DOMINANT FIRM as a means of buttressing its market position against competitive encroachment. The COMPETITION ACT, 1980, gives the OFFICE OF FAIR TRADING and the COMPETITION COMMISSION powers to investigate and, where appropriate, prohibit offending practices. See COMPETITION POLICY.

anti-trust policy the US version of COMPETITION POLICY.

AOQL see AVERAGE OUTGOING QUALITY LEVEL.

APEC see ASIA PACIFIC ECONOMIC COOPERATION.

application money the amount payable per share on application for a new SHARE ISSUE.

apportionment the breakdown of COSTS (and REVENUES) between different products, functions or company departments, where it is not possible to attribute costs (and revenues) directly to the departments where the cost or revenue concerned arises. For example, it is generally impossible to allocate rent and rates OVERHEADS exactly between departments in a factory and they can only be apportioned on some equitable basis such as the respective floor areas of departments. Such apportionments can help in assessing the profitability of different departments or products. See ALLOCATION, BUDGETING, STANDARD COST.

appraisal see PERFORMANCE APPRAISAL.

appraisal costs see QUALITY COSTS.

appreciation *or* **capital appreciation**
1 an increase in the price of an ASSET. Assets held for long periods, such as factory buildings, offices or houses, are most likely to appreciate in value because of the effects of INFLATION and increasing site values, though the value of short-term assets like STOCKS can also appreciate. Where assets appreciate their REPLACEMENT COST will exceed their HISTORIC COST and such assets may need to be revalued periodically to keep their book values in line with their market values. See DEPRECIATION, definition 1, INFLATION ACCOUNTING, REVALUATION PROVISION.
2 an increase in the EXCHANGE RATE of a currency against other currencies under a FLOATING EXCHANGE RATE SYSTEM, reflecting an increase in market demand for that currency combined with a decrease in market demand for other countries' currencies. The effect of an appreciation is to make imports (in the local currency) cheaper, thereby increasing import demand, and EXPORTS (in the local currency) more expensive, thereby reducing export demand, ultimately working towards keeping a country's BALANCE OF PAYMENTS in equilibrium on a more or less continuous basis.

Appreciations, like REVALUATIONS, can adversely affect the profitability and market position of domestic firms by making imports more price competitive in the home market and, similarly, reducing their price competitiveness in export markets. See REVALUATION, definition 2, for further discussion. Contrast with DEPRECIATION, definition 2, EXCHANGE RATE EXPOSURE.

apprenticeship a form of TRAINING which involves workers committing themselves to one employer for a period of time during which they are to acquire the skills of the trade, mainly through informal instruction by those already skilled (supplemented by some college-provided tuition). Once trained in this way such workers have a set of recognized skills which can, in theory, lead to employment in any organization in the industry. The apprenticeship system has been much censured because it can transmit outdated skills, because competence is defined in terms of time served rather than skills acquired, and because it serves to limit the supply of skilled labour. The employer may not recoup the costs of an apprenticeship in the long run because the apprentice, once trained, may leave for alternative employment. The long-term decline in the apprenticeship system in the UK accelerated towards the end of the 1980s as government removed many of its statutory supports, e.g. by abolishing the

Industry Training Boards (established in 1964) and removing the right of those remaining to levy 'taxes' on employers to support training. However, mounting alarm about skill shortages led to the apprenticeship system being revitalized in the mid-1990s as the *modern apprenticeship*. This new form of apprenticeship leads to a NATIONAL VOCATIONAL QUALIFICATION, whilst progress during the apprenticeship is monitored more systematically (with reference to clear industry standards) than under the traditional system.

appropriation account see PROFIT-AND-LOSS APPROPRIATION ACCOUNT.

approved supplier a raw material or component supplier which is selected as the 'preferred' source of inputs as part of a firm's PURCHASING requirements. In recent years many firms have sought to reduce the number of their suppliers and this has led to greater emphasis being placed on the means of approving suppliers. The trend has been to move away from item price as the single determinant of who supplies, to a list of attributes the supplier must constantly keep to. For example, accuracy of delivery times, or agreed quality standards and specifications, as well as total item cost. Approved suppliers benefit from this arrangement because it usually involves longer-term agreements to supply. See SOURCING.

APR the 'annualized percentage rate of INTEREST' charged on a LOAN. The APR rate will depend on the total 'charge for credit' applied by the lender and will be influenced by such factors as the general level of INTEREST RATES, and the nature and duration of the loan.

Where lenders relate total interest charges on INSTALMENT CREDIT loans to the *original* amount borrowed, this can give a misleading impression of the interest rate being charged, for as borrowers make monthly or weekly repayments on the loan they are reducing the amount borrowed, and interest charges should be related to the lower *average* amount owed. For example, if someone borrows £1,000 for one year with a total credit charge of £200 the 'simple interest' charge on the original loan is 20%. However, if the loan terms provide for monthly repayments of £100, then at the end of the *first* month the borrower would have repaid a proportion of the original £1,000 borrowed and by the end of the *second* month would have repaid a further proportion of the original loan, etc. In effect, therefore, the borrower does *not* borrow £1,000 for one whole year but much less than this over the year *on average* as he or she repays parts of the outstanding loan. If the total credit charge of £200 were related to this much smaller *average* amount borrowed to show the 'annualized' percentage rate' then this credit charge would be nearer 40% than the 20% quoted.

To make clear to the borrower the *actual* charge for credit and the 'true' rate of interest the CONSUMER CREDIT ACT 1974 requires lenders to publish both rates to potential borrowers.

aptitude test see PSYCHOLOGICAL TEST.

AQL see ACCEPTABLE QUALITY LEVEL.

arbitrage the buying and selling of PRODUCTS, FINANCIAL SECURITIES or FOREIGN CURRENCIES between two or more markets in order to take profitable advantage of any differences in the prices quoted in those markets.

If the price of the *same* product is different, as between two markets, a dealer, by simultaneously buying in the lower-priced market and reselling in the higher-priced market, stands to make a profit on the transaction (allowing for dealing expenses). Arbitrage thus serves to narrow or eliminate price differentials between markets, with buying in the lower-priced market causing prices to rise there, and selling in the higher-priced market causing prices to fall. See SPOT MARKET, ARBITRAGEUR, SPECULATION, COVERED INTEREST ARBITRAGE.

arbitrageur a person or firm which purchases SHARES in a company and other FINANCIAL SECURITIES in the hope of making a windfall profit. Arbitrageurs deliberately put a company into 'play'; that is, by making strategic share purchases in the company the arbitrageur fuels SPECULATION that a

TAKEOVER BID is in the offing, causing the company's share price to rise. The arbitrageur then sells off his stake at a suitable profit. See ARBITRAGE.

arbitration a procedure for settling INDUSTRIAL DISPUTES in which a neutral third party (arbitrator) makes an award which is usually binding on all parties to the dispute. Arbitration is usually used as a last resort when it has been impossible to reach agreement under normal procedures. Some PROCEDURAL AGREEMENTS, especially those forming part of a NO STRIKE AGREEMENT, include an automatic reference to arbitration if agreement cannot be reached during COLLECTIVE BARGAINING. The benefit of arbitration is that it facilitates a compromise solution to a dispute in a way which allows both parties to save face. The arbitrator in effect finds a middle way.

A relatively novel form of arbitration in Britain is *pendulum* arbitration (also known as 'flip-flop' or 'last-offer' arbitration), in which the arbitrator has to decide for one case in its entirety rather than 'splitting the difference'. The benefits of this are said to be that it encourages more reasonable bargaining behaviour and that it precludes potentially unworkable compromises. Some of the Japanese companies which have recently opened factories in the UK have included this form of arbitration in their NO STRIKE AGREEMENTS/SINGLE UNION DEALS. See also JAPANIZATION, ADVISORY, CONCILIATION AND ARBITRATION SERVICE, CENTRAL ARBITRATION COMMITTEE.

arms-length price the PRICE at which unrelated sellers and buyers agree to transact a product or asset.

articles of association the legal constitution of a JOINT-STOCK COMPANY which governs the internal relationship between the company and its members or SHAREHOLDERS. The articles govern the rights and duties of the membership and aspects of administration of the company. They will contain, for instance, the powers of the directors, the conduct of meetings, the dividend and voting rights assigned to separate classes of shareholders, and other miscellaneous rules and regulations. See MEMORANDUM OF ASSOCIATION.

ASA see ADVERTISING STANDARDS AUTHORITY.

ASEAN see ASSOCIATION OF SOUTHEAST ASIAN NATIONS.

ASCII (American Standard Code for Information Interchange) a system for coding individual numbers, letters and punctuation marks which is widely used in COMPUTERS.

'A' shares see NONVOTING SHARES.

Asia Pacific Economic Cooperation (APEC) a regional alliance formed in 1990 with the general objective of establishing a 'free trade area' (see TRADE INTEGRATION entry for details). There are currently 18 members of APEC: USA, Canada, Japan, China, Mexico, Chile, Australia, New Zealand, Papua New Guinea, South Korea, Taiwan, Hong Kong, Thailand, Philippines, Brunei, Malaysia, Singapore and Indonesia. The USA, Canada and Mexico are also members of the NORTH AMERICAN FREE TRADE AGREEMENT (NAFTA), and Brunei, Indonesia, Malaysia, Philippines, Singapore and Thailand are also members of the ASSOCIATION OF SOUTHEAST ASIAN NATIONS (ASEAN).

ask price see BID PRICE.

assembly chart see MATERIALS FLOW MANAGEMENT.

assembly drawings see MATERIALS FLOW MANAGEMENT.

assembly line see PRODUCTION LINE, PRODUCT-FOCUSED LAYOUT.

assembly-line balancing see PRODUCTION-LINE BALANCING.

assembly time the time taken to assemble a group of sub-components so as to create a further sub-component – or final product. Knowledge of the time taken to assemble an item allows for a better indication of the cost of the item as well as being a determinant in capacity management.

assented shares SHARES in a company which a shareholder has agreed to sell to a takeover bidder for the company. If in the interim the shareholder sells his shares in the market, any purchaser is automatically committed to accept the bid.

assessment centre see RECRUITMENT AND SELECTION, PSYCHOLOGICAL TEST.

asset an item or property which is owned by a business or individual and which has a money value. Assets are of three main types:

(a) physical assets such as plant and equipment, land, consumer durables (cars, etc.);

(b) financial assets such as currency, bank deposits, stocks and shares;

(c) intangible assets, such as BRANDS.

Alternatively, assets can be classified into FIXED ASSETS (those intended for long-term use by a business); and CURRENT ASSETS (those intended to be turned over, in trading, as raw materials are converted into finished goods, then sold to generate cash). See INVESTMENT, LIQUIDITY, BALANCE SHEET, LIABILITY.

asset register a LEDGER record which notes the HISTORIC COST of each physical asset owned by a business, any DEPRECIATION charged on that asset to date and its NET BOOK VALUE. Such information is summarized periodically in the FIXED ASSETS section of the BALANCE SHEET.

asset-stripper a predator firm which takes control of another firm (see TAKEOVER) with a view to selling off that firm's ASSETS, wholly or in part, for financial gain rather than continuing the firm as an ongoing business.

The classical recipe for asset-stripping arises when the realizable MARKET VALUE of the firm's assets is much greater than what it would cost the predator to buy the firm; i.e., where there is a marked discrepancy between the asset-backing per share of the target firm and the price per share required to take the firm over. This discrepancy usually results from a combination of two factors:

(a) gross under-valuation of the firm's assets in the BALANCE SHEET;

(b) mismanagement or bad luck resulting in low profits or losses, both of which serve to depress the firm's share price.

asset structure the proportions of various types of ASSET held by a firm as shown in the BALANCE SHEET. For example, a large manufacturing company or public utility is likely to have proportionately large FIXED ASSETS, while retail companies are likely to have proportionately large CURRENT ASSETS, such as DEBTORS and STOCK. A firm's asset structure helps to determine the way in which finance is raised, in particular the balance of long-term LOANS and short-term DEBT. See CAPITAL GEARING.

asset turnover, asset utilization *or* **sales-to-capital-employed ratio** a measure of a firm's ASSET turnover, which expresses the firm's sales revenue as a ratio of its size to measure the amount of sales revenue generated by each pound's worth of assets employed in the business. Often total assets are taken as the basis for comparison with sales, though sometimes long-term capital employed is used instead, taking a narrower definition of assets. The asset turnover ratio is often regarded as an important test of business efficiency. Asset turnover has a significant impact upon a firm's RETURN ON CAPITAL EMPLOYED.

asset utilization see ASSET TURNOVER.

asset value per share *or* **break-up value** the total value of a firm's tangible book ASSETS less all short- and long-term LIABILITIES as shown in the BALANCE SHEET. The net assets figure is divided by the number of ORDINARY SHARES the company has, to show approximately how much asset value supports each share. In the case of a LIQUIDATION it would be of some use to the SHAREHOLDERS in estimating how much they may reasonably expect to receive from the sale of the firm or of its assets. Book values of assets may be a reasonable estimate of their value to the firm as a going concern, but upon break-up they tend to be worth considerably less depending upon the alternative uses to which they can be put. See also ASSET-STRIPPER, SHARE CAPITAL.

assisted area a region of economic decline designated under European Union and UK REGIONAL POLICY as in need of industrial regeneration. Financial assistance in the form of REGIONAL SELECTIVE ASSISTANCE is available to manufacturing and service businesses prepared to undertake new investment in designated areas.

associated company *or* **related company** a JOINT-STOCK COMPANY in which another company, the HOLDING COMPANY, has a significant but not controlling shareholding (specifically 20% or more of the voting shares but not more than 50%). In such a situation the investing company can exert influence on the commercial and financial policy decisions of the associated company, though in principle the associated company remains independent under its own management, producing its own annual accounts, and is not a SUBSIDIARY COMPANY of the holding company.

If the second company held 50% or more of the first company's shares then the first company's assets and profits would be *consolidated* with those of the second, and the two companies would be regarded as part of the same group of firms. Where the second company holds 20% or more of the first company's shares then it must note in its own accounts information about the profits, capital and reserves of the first company in which it is heavily invested. If the second company holds less than 20% of the first company's shares it may still exercise influence over that company, though it is not obliged to disclose details of its shareholding. See CONSOLIDATED ACCOUNTS.

Association of British Insurers a TRADE ASSOCIATION which represents the collective interests of INSURANCE COMPANIES and INSURANCE BROKERS in the UK.

Association of Futures Brokers and Dealers (AFBD) see FINANCIAL SERVICES ACT, 1986.

Association of Investment Trust Companies (AITC) the TRADE ASSOCIATION which represents the collective interests of INVESTMENT TRUST COMPANIES in the UK.

Association of Southeast Asian Nations (ASEAN) a regional alliance formed in 1967 with the general objective of creating a 'free trade area' (see TRADE INTEGRATION entry for details) The current member countries of ASEAN are Brunei, Indonesia, Malaysia, Philippines, Singapore and Thailand. See ASIA PACIFIC ECONOMIC COOPERATION.

assurance a contractual saving arrangement whereby a person pays premiums at regular intervals to an INSURANCE COMPANY in return for a sum of money to be received at a later date. With *life* assurance a lump sum payment and/or annuity becomes due to the dependants of the person assured. With *endowment* assurance a lump sum payment and/or annuity is payable to the person assured at an agreed future date.

Aston School see CONTINGENCY THEORY.

asymmetrical information a situation where the parties to a CONTRACT have differing degrees of information, including 'hidden' information, concerning the terms, conditions and operational details of the contract. Thus, it may be possible for one party to 'exploit' this knowledge to their advantage and to the detriment of the other party. See PRINCIPAL-AGENT THEORY.

attack strategy the specific manoeuvres a business adopts to establish COMPETITIVE ADVANTAGE over rival suppliers. Such an attack may be designed to eliminate a competitor or reduce his MARKET SHARE. In order to formulate an attack strategy a MARKET CHALLENGER must define clearly his own marketing objective and identify those businesses or MARKET SEGMENTS where his rivals are vulnerable.

attainment test see PSYCHOLOGICAL TEST.

attendance bonus a payment made to employees by their employer as part of their wage to reward satisfactory attendance at work. Although many would argue that such payments should not be necessary because satisfactory attendance is usually a condition of the CONTRACT OF EMPLOYMENT, it can be a useful means of discouraging ABSENTEEISM.

attitude survey see SURVEY.

auction a means of selling goods and services to the highest bidder among a number of potential customers. Auctions can take several forms. One form is an open auction – increasing bid – competition in which the bids of all parties are observable and bidders drop out as the price increases until only the highest bidder remains. Another form is an open auction – decreasing price – auction in which the auctioneer starts off from a very high price that is then slowly decreased until one bidder agrees to buy at the last announced price. This form of auction is often called 'Dutch auction'. Yet another form is a sealed-bid, closed auction in which all bidders have to submit their bids in sealed envelopes at the same time. In open auctions, bidders can gain some information about the private valuations that other bidders place upon the goods to be sold, while in sealed-bid auctions the private valuations of bidders remain unobservable.

The principles of auctions apply to situations where firms seek TENDER to supply products.

audit 1 the legal requirement for a JOINT-STOCK COMPANY to have its BALANCE SHEET and PROFIT-AND-LOSS ACCOUNT (the financial statements) and underlying accounting system and records examined by a qualified AUDITOR, so as to enable an opinion to be formed as to whether such financial statements show a TRUE AND FAIR VIEW of the company's state of affairs and that they comply with the relevant statutes. Auditing involves inspecting documentary evidence of transactions such as INVOICES, STATEMENTS and DELIVERY NOTES to ensure that the DOUBLE-ENTRY accounting entries are complete and authentic.

Where the auditor is satisfied that the financial statements show a 'true and fair view' he will report this to the SHAREHOLDERS in the ANNUAL REPORT AND ACCOUNTS. However, if he is not satisfied that the financial statements show a 'true and fair view' or he is unhappy about any explanations given by the managers, then he may make a 'qualified report' to the shareholders expressing his precise misgivings.

2 internal audits of accounting procedures, marketing activities, production operations, quality control systems, and safety may be undertaken to monitor and review the efficiency and effectiveness with which these various activities are undertaken. In addition, a company may undertake a *value-for-money* audit, to evaluate whether the organization is operating effectively. See also MARKETING AUDIT.

Auditing Practices Board the UK body which is responsible for the work of AUDITORS and which issues guidelines on auditing practice.

auditor a professional accountant appointed to check the accuracy of a JOINT-STOCK COMPANY'S LEDGER accounts and ANNUAL REPORT AND ACCOUNTS, and to present an independent report to SHAREHOLDERS on whether the accounts present a *true and fair view* of the company's affairs.

audit trail a trail of primary documents such as INVOICES, and LEDGER entries, for example sales ledger records, which are used to identify how ACCOUNTING records have been kept. By selecting a sample of primary documents and ledger entries an AUDITOR can check the completeness and accuracy of a firm's accounting system.

authority the capacity to give commands which are accepted as legitimate by others. In the modern ORGANIZATION the manager's authority to give instructions to subordinates is drawn primarily from his formal position as a manager, and the set of rights and obligations formally associated with the post, rather than from the manager's individual leadership qualities. However, both sources of authority can be important. Managers whose personal standing with their subordinates is low may find that their authority is not fully accepted. Equally, some managers claim that they are given insufficient powers to exercise their authority fully.

Modern analysis of authority relationships owes much to German sociologist Max Weber (1864–1920). He discerned three forms of authority:

(a) *traditional authority*, where people obey those who occupy religious or monarchical positions;

(b) *charismatic authority*, where people obey those who have special inspirational personal qualities;

(c) rational–legal authority, where individuals obey laws or rules which have been devised as a result of the application of reason to achieve certain objectives.

In Weber's view the last is the distinctive

form of authority in modern industrial societies, and is exemplified in the workings of the modern ORGANIZATION or BUREAUCRACY.

authorization the granting of permission by a senior manager to a subordinate to undertake a particular task. For example, the chief executive could empower his purchasing officer to buy raw materials and authorize his production manager to buy machinery. The authorization process attempts to make sure that subordinates know the extent of their DELEGATED AUTHORITY.

authorized depository a UK agent such as a stockbroker or commercial bank, which holds foreign STOCKS and SHARES on behalf of its owners, and which is authorized to conduct such business by the Bank of England.

authorized share capital *or* **registered share capital** the maximum amount of SHARE CAPITAL which a JOINT-STOCK COMPANY can issue at any time. This amount is authorized by the company's ARTICLES OF ASSOCIATION, is disclosed in the BALANCE SHEET and may be altered by SHAREHOLDERS at the company ANNUAL GENERAL MEETING. The ISSUED SHARE CAPITAL cannot exceed the authorized amount, though not all the authorized capital need be issued.

automated guided vehicle (AGV) computer controlled vehicles that are used to convey goods between one part of a production unit and another. AGVs are used in manufacturing organizations to convey part finished and finished items between WORKSTATIONS. They can also be used as part of AUTOMATED STORAGE AND RETRIEVAL SYSTEMS in WAREHOUSING. See STORE, MATERIALS MANAGEMENT.

automated storage and retrieval system computer managed systems that control the movement of goods in and out of WAREHOUSING. All PICK LISTS, forklift movement, bin movement, conveying and inventory records are managed by the system. See STORE, MATERIALS MANAGEMENT, MATERIALS FLOW MANAGEMENT.

automatic till machine (ATM) a cash point ('hole in the wall') facility in which a bankers card can be used by a customer of a COMMERCIAL BANK or BUILDING SOCIETY to withdraw cash both inside and *outside* banking hours. The 'Link' network enables customers to use their cards in the ATMs of other banks as well as their own.

automatic vending a means of retailing products to consumers via vending machines. Vending machines augment conventional point-of-sale retailing (shops and stores) and provide a comparatively inexpensive and convenient way of making products available. Automatic vending has been employed extensively in selling, for instance, food and beverages, stamps and latterly money. See RETAIL OUTLET.

automation the use of mechanical or electrical machines such as robots to undertake frequently-repeated PRODUCTION processes to make them self-regulating, thus avoiding human intervention in these processes. Automation often involves high initial capital investment but, by reducing labour costs, cuts VARIABLE COST per unit.

Automation can be applied to mass production, PRODUCTION-LINE operations which are performed in a fixed sequence with high volumes but in a relatively inflexible way, where changes in the process to accommodate product changes are difficult and costly to implement (fixed automation). Automation can also be applied to lower volume BATCH PRODUCTION type operations, allowing in this case for greater flexibility in accommodating product changes by reprogramming the numerically-controlled machine's/robot's instructions to facilitate rapid changeovers (flexible or programmable automation). See FLEXIBLE MANUFACTURING SYSTEM.

autonomous production *or* **assembly** a situation where all work on a product is produced at one WORKSTATION by an individual or group of individuals. Sometimes also known as ONE WORKER-MULTIPLE MACHINES production. See CELL, CELLULAR MANUFACTURING. Contrast PRODUCTION-LINE.

autonomous work teams a development in JOB DESIGN closely linked to the concept of team based work organizations. Requires employees with overlapping work skills, collectively performing a defined task, with a degree of autonomy over how the task is performed. See CELL, CELLULAR MANUFACTURING.

AVC see ADDITIONAL VOLUNTARY CONTRIBUTION.

average collection period see DEBTORS RATIO.

average cost the unit cost of a product (total cost divided by number of units produced). Average total cost (ATC) can be split up into average FIXED COST (AFC) and average VARIABLE COST (AVC). AFC declines continuously as output rises, as a given total amount of fixed cost is 'spread' over a greater number of units. For example, with fixed costs of £1,000 per year and annual output of 1000 units, fixed costs per unit would be £1, but if annual output rose to 2000 units the fixed cost per unit would fall to 50p. Unit variable cost (AVC) tends to remain constant over the output range.

average outgoing quality level (AOQL) the lowest quality which will be accepted by INSPECTION when inspection/testing a sample from a batch of raw materials, work in progress or finished goods. See ACCEPTABLE QUALITY LEVEL, ACCEPTANCE SAMPLING, QUALITY CONTROL.

avoidance (tax) see TAX AVOIDANCE.

b

backlog a build-up of customer orders which a firm has agreed to deliver at specified future dates. Backlogging is one means by which a firm can 'even out' demand in relation to its production capacity, allowing delivery lead times to increase during peaks in demand and shorten during slack periods. Backlogs of orders can provide an alternative to STOCK-HOLDING or OVERTIME working, and varying the backlog may be the only way of dealing with demand fluctuations in some service industries. See PRODUCTION SCHEDULING.

back order see BACKLOG.

back-to-back loan *or* **parallel loan** an arrangement under which two companies in different countries borrow each other's currency and agree to repay the loans at a specified future date. At the expiry date of the loans each company receives the full amount of its loan in its domestic currency without risk of losses from exchange-rate changes. In this way back-to-back loans serve to minimize EXCHANGE RATE EXPOSURE.

backward integration see VERTICAL INTEGRATION.

backward scheduling the calculation of the time to manufacture or provide a service deducted from the agreed time for delivery. This provides the start date for manufacture or service design. It requires a detailed knowledge of the time for each process of activity required. See PRODUCTION SCHEDULING.

BACS (Bank Automated Credit System) a money transmission system whereby a payer instructs their commercial bank to debit a specified sum of money from their account and transfer it to a named payee's bank account. This obviates the need for the payer to issue and post a cheque to the payee and for the payee then to bank it, thus saving on time and expense. Many employers now use BACs to pay their employees' monthly salaries, and many companies use the system to transfer dividend payments to shareholders.

bad debt an accounting term for money owed to a company by customers or borrowers which is highly unlikely to be paid because, for example, a customer has become insolvent (see INSOLVENCY). Such bad debts are written off against the PROFITS of the trading period as a business cost. See CREDIT CONTROL, DEBTORS RATIO, DOUBTFUL DEBTS.

balanced scorecard a tool for setting and communicating corporate goals and for measuring corporate performance. The balanced scorecard incorporates four groups of goals and derived performance indicators: *External Indicators* (financial goals and measures); (customer goals and measures); *Internal Indicators* (internal business process goals and measures); (learning and growth goals and measures).

The balanced scorecard approach balances traditional financial measures such as net profit and return on capital with customer measures such as market share and customer satisfaction; business process measures such as productivity and stock turnover; and learning and growth goals such as employee turnover and training. Balanced scorecards provide a broader set of performance measures and related management systems for judging overall performance, than financial targets alone. See BUSINESS STRATEGY.

balance of payments

A record of a country's trade and financial transactions with the rest of the world over a particular period of time, usually one year. Fig. 8 shows the UK's balance of payments account for 2003. The account is divided into two main sections, the current account and the investment and other capital transactions account. The current account shows the country's day-to-day dealings in goods and services, together with various short-run income flows such as profit, dividend, and interest payments and receipts. The current account is split into two main components:

(a) the balance of trade in goods, i.e. sterling receipts from the EXPORTS of UK goods, and foreign currency payments for IMPORTS of overseas goods (referred to as 'visible' trade, as flows of goods are measured by the CUSTOMS AND EXCISE authorities as they physically enter or leave the country);

(b) sterling receipts from the provision (export) of UK services and from the repatriation of profits, dividends and interest on UK-owned foreign assets, and foreign currency payments for the provision (import) of services by foreign businesses and from the repatriation abroad of profits, dividends and interest on foreign-owned UK assets (referred to as 'invisible' trade since such transactions can only be measured indirectly).

The investment and other capital transactions account embraces a number of capital items including:

(a) the purchase of overseas physical assets (the establishment of a new factory or acquisition of a company);

(b) the purchase of financial assets (stocks and shares, government bonds, etc.) by UK individuals, companies, financial institutions and the government;

(c) the purchase of UK physical and financial assets by foreigners;

(d) banking and money market transactions in financial instruments and lending and borrowing in sterling and foreign currencies;

(e) various intergovernment transfers, for example UK payments to, and receipts from the European Union, and

(f) the provision of economic aid to less developed countries. Included also in the capital transactions account are movements in the UK's stock of INTERNATIONAL RESERVES of gold and FOREIGN EXCHANGE, an overall balance of payments deficit being financed by a fall in the reserves (and/or increased borrowing), and a surplus leading to an addition to the reserve position (and/or increased lending).

Broadly speaking, governments aim to maintain a balance of payments equilibrium over a run of years, avoiding in particular a build-up of deficits. The external payments position of the country often acts as a major constraint on the government's ECONOMIC POLICIES and in consequence the general economic climate in which businesses operate. For example, balance of payments deficits are usually rectified by a combination of domestic DEFLATION and DEVALUATION/DEPRECIATION of the country's EXCHANGE RATE, which can pose difficulties for domestic firms as well as providing opportunities for the more enterprising of them. Deflationary measures which reduce domestic demand may limit sales potential in the home market, but by damping down INFLATION can make a firm's exports more competitive and thus increase its overseas sales. A devaluation can be even more helpful since it works to increase the prices of foreign products in the home market, and by lowering export prices serves, like deflation, to make exports more price competitive. See FIXED EXCHANGE RATE SYSTEM, FLOATING EXCHANGE RATE SYSTEM, INTERNATIONAL TRADE, FOREIGN EXCHANGE MARKET, FOREIGN EXCHANGE CONTROLS.

Current Account		
	£ million	
Visible balance[1] (Balance of Trade)		
Food, beverages and tobacco	−10,259	
Basic materials	−2,806	
Oil, lubricants	5,050	
Manufactures	−38,533	
Other items	−742	
		−47,290
Invisible balance[2]		
Services	14,617	
Interest, profits and dividends	22,097	
Transfers, including European Union commitments	−9,854	
		26,860
Current balance		−20,430
Capital and financial account		
Direct investment	−22,287	
Portfolio investment	56,509	
Other items	−15,524	
		18,698
Overall balance		−1,732

Notes

(1) *Visible trade – flows of goods which are recorded by the customs and excise authorities as they enter or leave the country.*

(2) *Invisible trade – transactions that are recorded by the Bank of England from company and bank foreign currency receipts and payments data.*

Fig. 8 **Balance of payments.** UK balance of payments, 2003. (Source: UK balance of payments, ONS, 2004.)

balance sheet

An accounting statement of a firm's ASSETS and LIABILITIES on the last day of a trading period. The balance sheet lists the assets which the firm owns and sets against these the balancing obligations or claims of those groups of people who provided the funds to acquire the assets. Assets take the form of FIXED ASSETS and CURRENT ASSETS, while obligations take the form of SHAREHOLDERS' CAPITAL EMPLOYED, long-term loans and CURRENT LIABILITIES. The balance sheet is compiled by summarizing information derived from the LEDGER accounts and provides a condensed financial snapshot of a company's state of affairs.

A simple balance sheet is illustrated in Fig. 9 overleaf. Assets include fixed assets (such as equipment and buildings) and current assets (stocks, debtors and cash); liabilities include money owed to the bank and suppliers of raw materials and components. The difference between current assets and current liabilities is referred to as the net current assets or WORKING CAPITAL. Working capital plus fixed assets equals NET ASSETS employed or NET WORTH. This is equal to LONG-TERM CAPITAL of the company and represents monies subscribed by SHARE HOLDERS (the owners of the company), together with any profits retained in the business. Thus, fixed assets + (current assets – current liabilities) = long-term capital ('net worth').

ASSETS EMPLOYED	£	£	£
Fixed assets			
Equipment	500,000		
Factory	300,000		
		800,000	
Current assets			
Stock	600,000		
Debtors	175,000		
Cash	25,000		
		800,000	
Current liabilities			
Trade creditors	300,000		
Bank overdraft	200,000		
		500,000	
Net current assets			300,000
Net assets employed			1,100,000
FINANCED BY:			
Ordinary shareholders capital			900,000
Retained profits			200,000
			1,100,000

Fig. 9 **Balance sheet.** Balance sheet of Y Co as at 31 December 20xx.

balance of trade see BALANCE OF PAYMENTS.

balance sheet identity see ACCOUNTING EQUATION.

Baldridge Award an internationally recognised QUALITY award originated in the United States and named after a US Secretary of Commerce. The award program focuses on QUALITY as a strategic and integral part of management within the organization. The awards criteria are widely accepted as a standard for excellence in quality.

balk the term used in queuing analysis where a customer decides that a QUEUE is too long and decides to leave.

Baltic Mercantile and Shipping Exchange a London-based MARKET which is concerned with arranging FREIGHT facilities for cargo consignments moved by sea and air, and which also acts as a retail commodity exchange for dealings in cereals. See CORN EXCHANGE, COMMODITY MARKET.

banded pack offer a free sample of one BRAND banded to another.

bank a deposit-taking institution which is licensed by the monetary authorities of a country (the BANK OF ENGLAND in the UK) to act as a repository for money deposited by persons, companies and institutions, and which undertakes to repay such deposits either immediately on demand or subject to due notice being given. Banks perform various services for their customers (money transmission, investment advice, etc.) and lend out money deposited with them in the form of loans and overdrafts or use their funds to purchase financial securities, in order to operate at a profit. There are many types of banks, including COMMERCIAL BANKS, MERCHANT BANKS, SAVINGS BANKS and INVESTMENT BANKS. See BANKING SYSTEM, BANK OF ENGLAND, CENTRAL BANK.

bank advance see BANK LOAN.

banking system a network of COMMERCIAL BANKS and other more specialized BANKS (INVESTMENT BANKS, SAVINGS BANKS, MERCHANT BANKS) which accept deposits and savings from the general public, firms and other institutions, and which provide money transmission and other financial services for customers, operate loan and credit facilities for borrowers and invest in corporate and government securities. The banking system is part of a wider FINANCIAL SYSTEM and exerts a major influence on the functioning of the 'money economy' of a country. Bank deposits occupy a central position in the country's MONEY SUPPLY and hence the banking system is closely regulated by the monetary authorities. See CENTRAL BANK, BANK OF ENGLAND, CLEARING HOUSE SYSTEM.

bank loan *or* **bank advance** the advance of a specified sum of money to an individual or business (the borrower) by a COMMERCIAL BANK, SAVINGS BANK. etc. (the lender). A bank loan is a form of CREDIT which is extended for a specified period of time, usually on fixed-interest terms related to the base rate of interest, with the principal being repaid either on a regular instalment basis or in full on the appointed redemption date. Depending upon the nature of the loan and the degree of risk involved, a bank loan may be unsecured or secured, the latter requiring the borrower to deposit with the bank an approved form of COLLATERAL SECURITY (for example the property deeds to his house). In the case of businesses, bank loans are usually renegotiated shortly before expiring, thus providing the borrower with a 'revolving' line of credit used mainly to finance WORKING CAPITAL requirements. See OVERDRAFT, INTEREST RATE.

Bank of England the CENTRAL BANK of the UK which acts as banker to the government and the BANKING SYSTEM and acts as the authority responsible for implementing MONETARY POLICY. The Bank of England handles the government's financial accounts in conjunction with the TREASURY, taking in receipts from taxation and the sale of government assets, and making disbursements to the various government departments to fund their activities. The Bank acts as the government's broker in its borrowing and lending operations, issuing and dealing in government BONDS and TREASURY BILLS to underpin its year-to-year budgetary position and management of the country's NATIONAL DEBT.

COMMERCIAL BANKS hold accounts with the Bank of England and, in its role as banker to the banking system, the Bank makes it possible for banks to settle their indebtedness with one another by adjusting their accounts as appropriate (see CLEARING HOUSE SYSTEM).

The Bank of England and its satellite, the Royal Mint, are responsible for issuing the country's basic stock of money – LEGAL TENDER consisting of bank notes and coins (see MONEY SUPPLY). The bank occupies a key role in the implementation of monetary policy through controls on the money supply, influencing the level of bank deposits and credit creation by the financial institutions, particularly commercial banks. (See BANK DEPOSIT CREATION), while the MONETARY POLICY COMMITTEE has the responsibility for setting 'official' INTEREST RATES in the UK which in turn determines all other short-term interest rates (BASE RATE, BILL DISCOUNTING INTEREST RATE, INTERBANK CLEARING INTEREST RATE).

The Bank is also responsible for managing the country's EXCHANGE RATE and holding the country's stock of INTERNATIONAL RESERVES to be used in the financing of balance of payments deficits. The Bank of England operates a 'Foreign Exchange Equalization Account' which it uses to intervene in the FOREIGN EXCHANGE MARKET, buying and selling currencies to support the exchange rate at a particular level or to ensure that it falls (depreciates) or rises (appreciates) in an 'orderly' manner. See LENDER OF LAST RESORT.

bank rate see INTEREST RATE.

bank reconciliation the process of reconciling an individual's or business's CASH ACCOUNT records of receipts and payments with the BANK STATEMENT record of receipts and payments. These two need not coincide exactly since cheques drawn and received but not yet banked do not appear on the bank statement until a later date.

bankruptcy see INSOLVENCY.

bank statement a periodic record of an individual's or business's transactions with a BANK (or BUILDING SOCIETY) which itemizes on the one hand cash deposits and cheques paid in, and on the other hand cash withdrawals and cheques drawn and presented against the account.

A company's bank statement needs to be reconciled periodically against the firm's own CASH ACCOUNT to verify the accuracy of its cash account. See BANK RECONCILIATION.

bar code an alpha or alpha-numeric code, converted into a series of lines and spaces which are marked on products. Bar coding and the use of bar code scanners enables a firm to obtain accurate data quickly on its STOCK position to help with planning its reordering of goods; and can be used to adjust the prices of goods more easily than by replacing price tags. See EPOS.

bar-code reader a device which reads bar codes using a light scanner, widely used in supermarket checkouts.

bargain 1 the sale of a product at a cut price as a means of promoting sales of the product. See SALES PROMOTION.

2 the sale or purchase of a FINANCIAL SECURITY on the STOCK MARKET.

bargaining depth see COLLECTIVE BARGAINING.

bargaining level see COLLECTIVE BARGAINING.

bargaining scope see COLLECTIVE BARGAINING.

bargaining structure see COLLECTIVE BARGAINING.

bargaining unit see COLLECTIVE BARGAINING.

barriers to entry obstacles in the way of firms attempting to enter a MARKET, which operate to give established firms particular advantages over newcomers. There are a number of potential barriers to entry, including:

(a) ECONOMIES OF SCALE – where unit costs of production (marketing, distribution and research and development) decline with the volume produced, the minimum efficient scale of operation may require entry on a large scale; otherwise entrants would be put at a relative cost disadvantage;

(b) PRODUCT DIFFERENTIATION – entrants with 'unknown' and 'untried' products may be unable to win a viable share of the market because of customer loyalty to existing brands built up by established firms through cumulative investment in advertising and sales promotion;

(c) capital requirements – the cost of financing investment in plant and product differentiation, and meeting initial operating losses, may be prohibitively high;

(d) vertical restrictions – key raw materials, component sources and distribution channels – may be controlled by established firms, thereby limiting access to inputs and market outlets. See VERTICAL INTEGRATION;

(e) absolute cost disadvantages – entrants, for example, may be denied access to 'best state-of-the-art technology' because of PATENT rights accruing to established firms, and thus be forced to adopt inferior, higher cost methods of production, etc.

One, or some combination, of the above factors may pose particular problems for a small scale, GREENFIELD type of entrant. However, they may be of little consequence to a large conglomerate firm possessing ample financial resources, and which chooses to effect entry by MERGER with, or TAKEOVER of, an established producer. Moreover, the basic assumption of much entry theory that established firms invariably possess advantages over potential entrants must also be challenged. In a dynamic market situation entrants may be in a position to introduce new technology ahead of existing firms, or develop innovative new products, thereby giving them COMPETITIVE ADVANTAGES over established firms. See MARKET ENTRY, MARKET STRUCTURE, DIVERSIFICATION, BRAND PROLIFERATION, MARKET SYSTEM, MOBILITY BARRIER.

barriers to exit obstacles in the way of a firm contemplating leaving a market which serve to keep the firm in the market despite falling sales and profitability. There are a number of potential exit barriers including:

(a) whether the firm owns the assets used to make the product, or leases them;

(b) the age of the firm's assets used to serve the particular market and the extent to which they have been depreciated. Where DEPRECIATION charges on old assets are low then operating costs will be lower, and this may encourage the firm to remain in the market despite low prices. On the other hand, with fully-depreciated assets the firm would suffer little capital loss in writing off these assets and exiting the market;

(c) the nature of the firm's assets. Specifically, if the assets are special purpose and so difficult to redeploy to other uses;

(d) the extent to which the firm's plant and equipment is re-saleable in second-hand markets;

(e) whether the firm needs to make any additional investment in order to remain competitive;

(f) the extent of market excess capacity, and thus related price and profit levels;

(g) the extent of shared production and distribution facilities. For example, where a multiproduct firm's plant produces a number of different products rather than just one, then a decision to drop one product could affect the cost and availability of other products;

(h) the extent of VERTICAL INTEGRATION. A vertically-integrated petrochemical firm, for example, may find it difficult to drop one product without affecting downstream operations which use that product as a raw material, or upstream operations which rely upon the product as a use for their intermediate material;

(i) the spread of a firm's product range. A single product firm would be reluctant to cease making its product, for then the firm would cease trading, whilst a diversified firm would find it easier to exit from one particular market since it has many others available. See DIVERSIFICATION.

Barriers to exit determine the ease with which firms can leave declining markets, and thus affect both the profitability of firms and the smooth functioning of markets. See BUSINESS STRATEGY, ENDGAME STRATEGY, PRODUCT LIFE CYCLE, MARKET SYSTEM.

barriers to imitation see MOBILITY BARRIER.

BARS see BEHAVIOURALLY-ANCHORED RATING SCALE.

barter an exchange mechanism for buying and selling goods and services which involves the physical 'swapping' of one product for another. Generally, barter is a cumbersome and inefficient means of organizing exchanges in an economy, since a large amount of time is wasted in seeking out and finding compatible 'swap' partners (i.e. each selling what the other wants to buy), and then haggling over an appropriate exchange rate (for example how many tomatoes equal a sewing machine?). All these difficulties can be overcome by the use of MONEY as a common denominator to conclude transactions and 'price' individual products.

For all its disadvantages, barter (or COUNTERTRADE as it is often referred to) is still widely used in the context of INTERNATIONAL TRADE. Firms which are unable to obtain the necessary foreign currencies they require to finance a trade deal (because the government operates FOREIGN EXCHANGE CONTROLS or because the country has simply run out of currencies due to a balance of payment deficit), often enter into a bilateral 'swap' deal with firms in other countries arranging a suitable product exchange.

base rate see INTEREST RATE.

base stock system see STOCK CONTROL.

BASIC (Beginners All-Purpose Symbolic Instruction Code) a simple COMPUTER programming language widely used by nonspecialists for programming computers.

basic time the time that it should take an operative with the appropriate level of skill to complete a task. However, it should be noted that this ignores any ALLOWANCES designed to compensate for contingencies, interferences and relaxation. See WORK MEASUREMENT, STANDARD TIME.

basing point price system see GEOGRAPHICAL PRICING.

batch production a method of organizing PRODUCTION whereby a number of identical components or products are passed through one or more production operations or processes as a 'batch'. Batch-production systems are used to make components or products in comparatively small quantities using 'general purpose' machines on an intermittent basis. See BATCH SIZE, PROCESS-FOCUSED LAYOUT, PRODUCTION SCHEDULING, SET-UP TIME, SET-UP COSTS.

batch size the number of items which constitute a 'batch' in BATCH PRODUCTION. The use of very large batch sizes, whilst having the advantage of minimizing the total costs associated with setting up the production facilities, has the disadvantage of incurring high stock-holding costs. On the other hand, the manufacture of many small batches of items, whilst keeping average stock levels down and thus reducing stock-holding costs, increases total SET-UP COSTS since more set ups are required for the production of a given total quantity of items in a given time. Some compromise must therefore be reached which has the effect of minimizing total stock-holding and setting-up costs.

The economic batch quantity which minimizes total costs can be calculated in similar fashion to the economic order quantity in the STOCKHOLDING MODEL. See LEAN MANUFACTURING.

bath tub curve see FAILURE RATE CURVE.

bear a person who sells a financial security (stock, share, foreign currency, etc.) in expectation that its market price is likely to fall. See SPECULATION. Compare BULL.

bearer bonds FINANCIAL SECURITIES which are not registered under the name of a particular holder but whose possession serves as proof of ownership. Such securities are popular in the US financial system but fairly rare in the UK, where the names of holders of STOCKS and SHARES are recorded in a company's SHARE REGISTER.

bear market a situation in which the prices of FINANCIAL SECURITIES (stocks, shares, etc.) or COMMODITIES (tin, wheat, etc.) tend to fall as a result of persistent selling and only limited buying. See SPECULATION. Compare BULL MARKET.

beauty contest a competition between TRADE UNIONS to gain recognition by an employer for COLLECTIVE BARGAINING and/or representational purposes. See BRIDLINGTON RULES.

bed and breakfast the process of selling SHARES at the end of a trading day on the STOCK MARKET and buying them back at the beginning of the following day's trading. This is done primarily to establish on a formal basis the amount of profit or loss made on these shares over the period when they are held, in order to calculate CAPITAL GAINS TAX.

behaviourally-anchored rating scale (BARS) a scale of behaviour patterns against which observed behaviour can be compared as a tool for analysing an individual's behaviour at work or elsewhere. To construct a BARS, various patterns of behaviour associated with a particular activity or aspect of work performance are compiled on a scale. These patterns are derived from earlier observation of behaviour or from behaviour patterns identified by analysis of CRITICAL INCIDENTS. The scale can thus be said to be 'anchored' in real behaviour. The behaviour of particular individuals can then be rated on this scale. The advantage of BARS is that they facilitate a fairly objective rating of behaviour since individual behaviour can be compared systematically against real behaviour patterns of other people. However, construction of these scales can be time-consuming and expensive because to be reliable they need to be based on a large population. An important use of rating scales of this type is in PERFORMANCE APPRAISAL. See OCCUPATIONAL PSYCHOLOGY.

behavioural observation scale (BOS) a scale upon which observed behaviour can be graded. For example, the degree to which an individual consults with his colleagues can be graded from 'never' through to 'always'. This method of rating behaviour can be used where behaviour is observed as part of RECRUITMENT AND SELECTION and where behaviour is a subject of PERFORMANCE APPRAISAL. Such scales are easy to compile but observation of behaviour may be difficult (it may not be possible to scrutinize all relevant behaviour), and it can be difficult to exclude the observer's subjective opinion of the nature of the behaviour observed.

behaviour reinforcement see OCCUPATIONAL PSYCHOLOGY.

below-the-line an accounting term describing items (other than dividends and retained profit) which appear below the net profit figure in the PROFIT-AND-LOSS ACCOUNT. These would normally include items relating to previous trading periods or extraordinary nonrecurring items, for example losses associated with the reorganization of a company division involving significant sales of assets. Below-the-line items are deducted directly from the company's RESERVES rather than being charged against the profits of the trading period, to avoid affecting the trading profit with one-off, non-trading revenues or costs.

'below-the-line' promotion see 'ABOVE-THE-LINE' PROMOTION.

benchmarking the practice whereby a firm studies the 'best' PRODUCTION and MARKETING processes used by immediate competitors and firms from other similar industries so as to identify possible ways for the firm to improve its own methods. Benchmarking usually involves a number of steps: selection of critical processes that may need improvement; in depth study of other firms who perform these processes particularly well; adaptations of the processes identified so as to facilitate their implementation by the firm.

beneficial owner the ultimate owner of a FINANCIAL SECURITY rather than any NOMINEE who may have been appointed to hold legally the financial security on behalf of the beneficial owner.

benefit see CONSUMER SURPLUS, VALUE CREATED MODEL.

benefit advantage strategy the establishment of a COMPETITIVE ADVANTAGE over rival suppliers which seeks to offer higher product benefits (better quality, better performance etc) than rivals while maintaining cost levels that are comparable to competitors. See VALUE CREATED MODEL, BENEFIT DRIVERS, COMPETITIVE STRATEGY. Compare COST ADVANTAGE STRATEGY.

benefit drivers elements of a firm's operations which individually and collectively create BENEFIT ADVANTAGES for consumers who buy the firm's product. The ability to offer a product which is 'perceived' by customers to offer superior value to them is an important consideration where PRODUCT DIFFERENTIATION is the key basis of the firm's COMPETITIVE ADVANTAGE over rival suppliers.

There are four main categories of benefit drivers:

(a) the physical attributes of the product, including QUALITY, DESIGN, features, performance in use etc;

(b) the provision of back-up services and products by the firm or its dealers, including product pre-sale advice and demonstrations and various AFTER-SALES SERVICES (GUARANTEES/WARRANTIES, repair and maintenance, replacement parts) etc;

(c) sale/delivery characteristics, including the availability of the product, the provision of credit facilities, the speed and promptness of delivery, etc.

(d) consumers' perceptions and expectations of the product's performance, including the reputation of the supplying firm, BRAND awareness, the 'image' of the brand and the psychological satisfaction gained from the brand built by ADVERTISING and other promotional means. See VALUE CREATED MODEL, RESOURCE BASED THEORY OF THE FIRM. Compare COST DRIVERS.

best before date see SHELF LIFE.

best practice see BENCHMARKING.

best value the duty of local authorities to provide services with regard to economy, efficiency and effectiveness. Local authorities are required to seek continuous improvement in these services. In awarding contracts for services, local authorities are required to consult with users. The performance of these services is to be regularly compared with service provision by other local authorities (BENCHMARKING). See COMPETITIVE TENDERING.

beta coefficient a measure of the responsiveness of the expected return on a particular FINANCIAL SECURITY relative to movements in the average expected return on all other securities in the market. The Financial Times all-share index or the Dow-Jones index are usually taken as proxy measurements for general market movements. In the CAPITAL-ASSET PRICING MODEL, the beta coefficient (β) is taken as a measure of the market (or non-diversifiable) RISK of a particular security. The beta coefficient links the return on the security and the average market return. The average market risk of all securities is where $\beta = 1$, that is, a 10% increase in market return is reflected as a 10% increase in the return of, say, security A. If the return on, say, security B, is 20%, but there is only a 10% increase in market return, this security has a $\beta = 2$ which indicates a risk greater than the market. If security C has a $\beta = 0.5$, this indicates a security less risky than the market in general. See EFFICIENT-MARKETS HYPOTHESIS.

bid 1 an offer by one company to purchase all or the majority of the SHARES of another company as a means of effecting a TAKEOVER. The bid price offered by the predator for the voting shares in the victim company must generally exceed the current market price of those shares, the difference being a premium which the predator must pay for control of the company. However, on occasions, the market price of the shares may subsequently rise to exceed the initial bid price where investors either feel that the bid price undervalues the company, or where investors anticipate, for example, the possibility of a second party making a higher bid. The offer price could be paid solely in cash, or in a mix of cash and shares in the acquirer's own company, or solely in terms of the acquirer's shares (called a paper bid). In order to finance a takeover bid, a predator company may raise loans. See TAKEOVER BID (leveraged bid).

2 an offer to purchase an item (for example, a house or antique vase) which has been put up for sale at a specified price or is to be sold subject to receipt of 'other prices'. The latter may occur at an AUCTION where a number of would-be buyers each put in a bid for an item, the final sale going to the highest bidder unless a predetermined 'reserve' has been set but not reached.

bid price the price at which a dealer in a FINANCIAL SECURITY (such as a STOCK or SHARE), FOREIGN CURRENCY or COMMODITY (tin, wheat, etc.) is prepared to buy a security, currency or commodity. Such dealers usually cite two prices to potential customers, the smaller bid price, and a higher *offer price* or 'ask price' at which they are prepared to sell a security, etc. The difference between the bid and offer price (referred to as the 'spread') represents the dealer's profit margin on the transaction. See MARKET MAKER, MIDDLE PRICE.

bilateral netting see MULTILATERAL NETTING.

bill-discounting rate see INTEREST RATE.

bill of exchange a FINANCIAL SECURITY which is used to extend business CREDIT for a limited time period. The lender draws up a bill of exchange for a specified sum of money payable at a given future date, usually three months hence, and the borrower signifies his agreement to pay the amount involved by signing (i.e. accepting) the bill. In addition, a borrower will often arrange for a bill to be guaranteed by an ACCEPTING HOUSE, which in return for a fee will agree to repay the debt should the borrower be unable to do so. Most bills are in fact 'discounted' (i.e. bought from the drawer) by a DISCOUNT HOUSE for an amount less than the face value of the bill (the difference between the two sums being the interest charged). The bill may then be held until maturity or sold at a lower price ('rediscounted') to another discount house, or, more commonly, on-sold to the COMMERCIAL BANKS. See DISCOUNT, DISCOUNT MARKET, REDISCOUNTING, INTEREST RATE.

bill of lading a document used to ship internationally traded goods that gives the holder (the consignee) the right to take possession of the goods. The bill of lading gives details of the goods shipped, the identification marks and numbers on crates, etc., the name of the ship, ports of embarkation and destination, rate of freight, etc. Bills of lading are drawn up by shipowners, the original being sent to the consignee with copies being retained by the captain of the ship and the FREIGHT FORWARDER. See EXPORTING.

bill of materials see PRODUCT SPECIFICATION.

bin card a STORES record card of quantities of a particular material or component received, quantities issued and the balance of the material in store. These balances can be checked against the actual quantities in stock by STOCKTAKING.

birth rate see POPULATION.

bit a digit which takes the value zero or one and which can therefore be represented electronically by an off/on switch in a COMPUTER. Computers use groups of bits to represent numbers or letters for storage, transmission and processing of numerical or alphabetical data. Specifically, computers use various off/on permutations of eight bits to represent all numbers, letters and punctuation characters. Most computers use multiples of eight bits to handle data in this way and various eight-bit, sixteen-bit and thirty-two bit machines are available, the larger ones generally being able to process data faster.

black-coated worker see WORKER.

blacking a form of INDUSTRIAL ACTION in which workers in one organization refuse to handle goods or services either bought from or intended for sale to another organization which is engaged in an INDUSTRIAL DISPUTE with its workforce; this is a way of providing support to the workforce in dispute. See SECONDARY ACTION.

black knight see TAKEOVER BID.

blackleg a worker who reports for work normally whilst the majority of his or her colleagues are on STRIKE.

black market an unofficial or 'under-the-counter' MARKET trading in a product which the government has declared to be illegal (for example narcotic drugs), or on the sale of which the government has imposed controls thus limiting its availability.

blind product test see ADVERTISING EFFECTIVENESS TESTS.

block model a scaled model, using blocks of plastic or card outlines to assist in the layout of a factory or office complex etc. See FACTORY LAYOUT.

'blue-chip' company a large well-established JOINT-STOCK COMPANY, with considerable assets whose SHARES investors regard as a low-risk investment.

blue-collar worker see WORKER.

board of directors the group responsible to the SHAREHOLDERS for running a JOINT-STOCK COMPANY. Often boards of directors are composed of full-time, salaried company executives (the executive directors) and part-time, nonexecutive directors. The board of directors meets periodically under the company chairman to decide on major policy matters within the company and the appointment of key managers. DIRECTORS are elected annually at the company ANNUAL GENERAL MEETING.

In recent years the responsibilities of British directors have been increased under the terms of the Insolvency Act and they may be held personally liable for company debts incurred if they knowingly and recklessly trade after the company is insolvent (see INSOLVENCY).

In certain European countries, like Germany, there are two-tier boards of directors with a supervisory board composed of representatives of shareholders, employees, etc., which appoints a management board to deal with the detailed management of the company. See FIFTH DIRECTIVE, CORPORATE GOVERNANCE.

bond a FINANCIAL SECURITY issued by a company or by the government as a means of borrowing long-term funds. Bonds are, typically issued for a set number of years (often 10 years plus), being repayable on maturity. They are issued in units of a fixed (nominal) face value and bear a fixed (nominal) rate of interest. Purchasers of bonds include private individuals, commercial banks and institutional investors (pension funds, etc.) who hold them as a form of portfolio investment.

Once issued, bonds can be bought and sold on the STOCK MARKET. Bond prices tend to fluctuate at prices below their face value, reflecting buying and selling strengths, but are closely linked to prevailing market interest rates so as to remain attractive to potential buyers. For example, a £100 bond with a nominal 5% interest rate returning £5 per year would have to be priced at £50 if current market interest rates were 10% so that a buyer could earn an effective return of £5/£50 = 10% on his investment.

In addition to their role as a means of borrowing money, the sale and purchase of bonds is used by the monetary authorities to control the MONEY SUPPLY. See MONETARY POLICY. See also EUROCURRENCY MARKET, GILT-EDGED SECURITY.

bonus payment a form of incentive payment made to individual employees of a firm or groups of employees who exceed specified output or sales targets. Bonus payments are usually paid in cash (monthly or annually) but could also take the form of an allocation of shares in the company (see GOLDEN HANDCUFF). See PERFORMANCE-RELATED PAY, INCENTIVE BONUS SCHEME, GROUP INCENTIVE BONUS SCHEME.

bonus shares additional SHARES issued to existing SHAREHOLDERS in a JOINT-STOCK COMPANY without further payment on their part. See CAPITALIZATION ISSUE.

book-keeping see ACCOUNTING.

books of prime entry the JOURNALS or DAY BOOKS in which information about business transactions are first recorded. The books of prime entry include the purchases and sales day books, and the cash book. See LEDGER, ACCOUNTING.

book value the money amount of an ASSET as stated in a company's LEDGER accounts and BALANCE SHEET. FIXED ASSETS are often stated at NET BOOK VALUE (original cost less cumulative DEPRECIATION), while CURRENT ASSETS are stated at original cost or market value, whichever is the lower.

boom see BUSINESS CYCLE.

borrower a person, company or institution who obtains MONEY or some other asset (for example machinery, property) in the form of a LOAN, MORTGAGE or LEASING arrangement from a LENDER in order to finance consumption and investment. See DEBT, FINANCIAL SYSTEM, COLLATERAL SECURITY.

BOS see BEHAVIOURAL OBSERVATION SCALE.

Boston matrix a framework for highlighting and analysing PRODUCT DEVELOPMENT policy and associated CASH FLOW implications in a firm, used by corporate planners in formulating BUSINESS STRATEGY.

		MARKET SHARE	
		High	*Low*
MARKET	*High*	Star	Problem Child
GROWTH RATE	*Low*	Cash Cow	Dog

Fig. 10 **Boston Matrix.** The matrix identifies cash generators and cash users.

Fig. 10 shows the matrix which depicts market growth rate on one axis and the product's market share on the other; the matrix indicates that the higher the product's growth rate, the greater will be the capital investment required and hence cash used, while the greater the product's market share, the greater will be the profit earned and hence cash generated. The four market growth/share segments relate to four product types:

(a) cash cows – products, usually in the mature phase of the PRODUCT LIFE CYCLE, which have a low growth rate, so that they require little new investment to support them, and a high market share yielding a high profit return. Cash cows are the firm's primary source of internal funds for financing the introduction and development of new products;

(b) stars – products which have a high growth rate and need a considerable amount of new investment to keep up with market demand, and a high market share often yielding sufficient cash to make their operations self-financing. Star products are usually relatively new products in the growth phase of the product life cycle that it is hoped, with proper handling, will become the firm's cash cows of the future;

(c) problem children – products which have a high growth rate and so require heavy injections of capital to support them, and a low market share providing only a modest profit return if at all. Such products are a cash drain but they have 'star' potential if their market shares can be improved;

(d) dogs – products which have both a low growth rate and a low market share and which seemingly lack potential for future development. Such products are prime candidates for DIVESTMENT if a suitable buyer can be found.

The Boston matrix can be used in conjunction with the PRODUCT-MARKET MATRIX to assist the firm in planning for a suitable 'balanced' portfolio of mature, growth and newly-launched products so as to sustain the growth of the firm's profits over time. See COMPETITIVE ADVANTAGE.

BOT see BUILD, OPERATE, TRANSFER PROJECT.

bottleneck a hold-up in some part of a PRODUCTION LINE which disrupts the smooth flow of work. See PRODUCTION-LINE BALANCING, OPTIMISED PRODUCTION TECHNOLOGY.

bottom line an accounting term denoting the NET PROFIT from a business operation after all costs have been paid. In financial accounting terms, profit would be sales revenue less all the costs of production, marketing, finance, etc., and frequently after taxation charges for the period. However, profit would generally be stated before the payment of dividends or appropriation to RESERVES.

bought day book see JOURNAL OR DAY BOOK, ACCOUNTING.

bought journal see JOURNAL OR DAY BOOK, ACCOUNTING.

bought ledger see LEDGER, ACCOUNTING.

boycott 1 the withholding of supplies of products to a trader by a producer because the trader is, for example, in breach of CONTRACT or the trader is selling the products as LOSS LEADERS. See REFUSAL TO SUPPLY.
2 the cessation of INTERNATIONAL TRADE, wholly or in part, with a particular country by other countries. See EMBARGO.

brainstorming a technique for generating ideas in which members of a group express ideas as they think of them. The object is to compile a list of ideas which can subsequently be considered and evaluated in greater depth. It is often recommended as a means of stimulating creativity when a group is experiencing difficulties in generating new ideas or solutions to apparently intractable problems. However, it is uncertain whether the ideas so generated are of any greater value than those arising in more conventional discussions. See DELPHI TECHNIQUE, NOMINAL GROUP TECHNIQUE.

brand a distinctive name, term, sign, symbol or design used to identify a firm's product and to distinguish it from similar products offered by competitors. A brand may be given legal protection through the use of TRADEMARKS and COPYRIGHT. See BRANDING.

brand equity the goodwill associated with a BRAND NAME which adds tangible value to a company through the resulting higher profits and sales.

brand extension *or* **brand transference** the use of an existing BRAND for new or modified products. Where the new product is in a significantly different category this is called 'brand stretching'. Brand extension seeks to capitalize on consumer awareness of and loyalty towards a firm's established brands in order to gain rapid consumer approval and acceptance of the new or modified product.

Where a modified product simply serves another segment of the same market the term brand extension is generally used (see MARKET SEGMENTATION). The term brand transference is used where an established brand name is associated with a new product serving a different market. For instance, the manufacturer of a well-known vacuum cleaner might use that brand name to launch a new product in some other market, for example washing machines. See PRODUCT POSITIONING.

brand identity the meaning of a BRAND, seen from the firm's point of view, as encoded in the promotional messages and business actions of the brand owners.

brand image the perceptions and beliefs held by consumers about a particular BRAND of GOOD or SERVICE which reinforce BRAND LOYALTY and encourage repeat purchases. The image may have been cultivated by media ADVERTISING, SALES PROMOTION and word-of-mouth recommendation by existing consumers.

branding a means of helping consumers to identify a particular firm's BRAND of product, and to create and maintain consumer confidence in the performance of the brand. This is achieved by ensuring consistent brand quality and reinforcing this by appropriate ADVERTISING and SALES PROMOTION in order to foster consumer goodwill. Once the supplier has created significant BRAND LOYALTY this enables him to exert greater control over the advertising, sales promotion and distribution of the brand, and may well enable him to command a premium price over competitors' offerings. A well established brand has considerable value in giving a supplier COMPETITIVE ADVANTAGE over rival suppliers and such brands can have a significant impact upon the valuation of a business. See BRAND VALUATION.

brand loyalty the extent to which consumers buy a particular BRAND of a product in preference to similar brands. Consumers may be totally loyal to a single brand but more usually will switch irregularly between two or more brands. Brand loyalty will depend largely upon consumer satisfaction with the intrinsic qualities and attributes of the brand but may also be swayed by persuasive ADVERTISING and SALES PROMOTION.

Strong brand loyalty serves to protect and increase the firm's MARKET SHARE vis-à-vis competitors, and may afford opportunities to charge a premium price for the brand. See BRANDING, BRAND SWITCHING, COMPETITIVE ADVANTAGE.

brand manager see PRODUCT MANAGER.

brand mark the symbol, design or distinctive colouring or lettering used to identify a particular BRAND, for example the jaguar symbol used by Jaguar cars or the lion used by Peugeot cars.

brand name the name used to identify a particular BRAND. This can consist of a newly created word or phrase, or a conventional word or phrase adapted to have a particular meaning. The skill of advertising copywriters lies in creating or finding words which have a broad-ranging and powerful appeal, and which are meaningful and pronounceable in several languages. Once created, brand names can be given legal protection against unauthorized use by registering them as TRADEMARKS. See BRAND EXTENSION, GLOBAL BRAND.

brand positioning and repositioning the matching of a particular BRAND with a selected MARKET SEGMENT(S) which offers good sales potential. This will involve developing a new brand with characteristics which match the identified needs of the segment. Alternatively, an existing brand whose market segment is declining or which is experiencing intense competition may be adapted to target alternative market segments. For example, a company which manufactures shampoo or talcum powder for babies may attempt to market those products to adults. See SEGMENTATION, PRODUCT POSITIONING.

brand preference the selection of a particular BRAND over other brands by a consumer. See BRAND LOYALTY.

brand proliferation the availability in a market of an extensive number of similar brands reflecting the MARKET SEGMENTATION policies of suppliers and the need to offer a comprehensive range of brands to compete against rivals. By offering a number of brands, suppliers may be able to expand their sales. However, they have to be mindful of the extra production and marketing costs this involves and the particular danger of 'cannibalizing' their own sales (i.e. an increase in the sales of one particular brand may be largely at the expense of their other brands rather than taking away sales from rivals' brands). From a wider public interest perspective, brand proliferation is sometimes considered objectionable by the COMPETITION POLICY authorities, because, while ostensibly serving to increase consumer choice, the 'saturation' of a market by established firms' brands may result in 'excessive' advertising and act as a BARRIER TO ENTRY to new firms. See PRODUCT DIFFERENTIATION, PRODUCT RANGE, PRODUCT VARIETY.

brand repositioning see BRAND POSITIONING.

brand stretching see BRAND EXTENSION.

brand switching the decision by consumers to substitute alternative BRANDS for the ones they currently consume. This may be a response to dissatisfaction with their existing brand, the attractions of newly-available brands or consumers' search for variety. Brand switching may be induced by ADVERTISING and SALES PROMOTION designed to overcome BRAND LOYALTY to existing brands.

brand transference see BRAND EXTENSION.

brand value the money value attached to an established BRAND name by consumer goods companies. The valuation attached to a brand name reflects past advertising by the company to create public awareness of the brand and gives the brand a value to the company and to a potential takeover bidder. Valuation of brands and their incorporation in a company's accounts serves to create an INTANGIBLE FIXED ASSET. See GOODWILL.

breakaway union a TRADE UNION formed by disaffected members of another union who feel that their particular interests are given insufficient weight in union decision-making. Such unions rarely have much impact because managements are often reluctant to recognize an additional union for COLLECTIVE BARGAINING purposes (the Union of Democratic Mine-workers in the UK coal industry is an important exception).

break-even the short-run rate of output and sales at which a supplier generates just enough revenue to cover his fixed and variable costs, earning neither a PROFIT nor a LOSS. If the selling price of a product exceeds its unit VARIABLE COST then each unit of product sold will earn a CONTRIBUTION towards FIXED COSTS and profits. Once sufficient units are being sold so that their total contributions cover the supplier's fixed costs then the company breaks even. If less than the break-even sales volume is achieved then total contributions will not meet fixed costs and the supplier will make a loss. If the sales volume achieved exceeds the break-even volume, total contributions will cover the fixed costs and leave a surplus which constitutes profit. See Fig. 11.

Differences in cost structures can have a significant effect upon companies' break-even points. For example, a company with low levels of automation and so little capital equipment (for example Rolls Royce cars) would have low fixed depreciation costs but

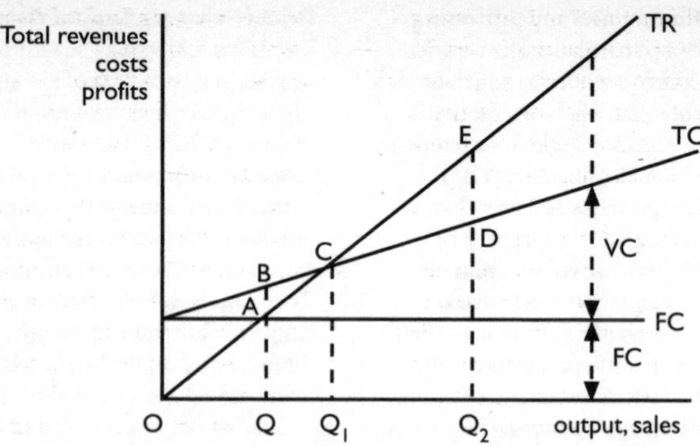

Fig. 11 **Break-even.** A supplier's typical short-run costs and revenues. Fixed costs do not vary with output and so are shown as the horizontal line FC. Total cost comprises both fixed costs and total variable costs and is shown by line TC. Total revenue rises as output and sales are expanded and is depicted by line TR. At low levels of output such as Q total costs exceed total revenues and the supplier makes a loss equal to AB. At high levels of output such as Q_2 revenues exceed costs and the supplier makes a profit equal to DE. At output Q_1 total revenues exactly match total costs (at C) and the supplier breaks even.

high direct labour costs. With high unit direct costs relative to selling prices such a firm would have a low unit contribution but low fixed costs, so would break even at a low sales volume, though profits would climb only slowly beyond the break-even point because of low unit contribution. By contrast, a highly automated plant would have high fixed depreciation costs, but with low unit direct labour costs, would have a higher unit contribution. Firms with such plants (for example Ford) would not break even until a much higher sales volume was achieved, but thereafter profits would increase rapidly with larger unit contributions. See MARGINAL COSTING, PROFIT-VOLUME CHART.

break-even pricing see COST-BASED PRICING.

breaking bulk an activity performed by intermediaries in a DISTRIBUTION CHANNEL which involves the buying-in of products in large quantities and on-selling them in much smaller quantities. See WHOLESALER.

break-up value the value of a business's ASSETS when sold off separately, as opposed to selling the business as a going concern.

bridging loan a form of short-term LOAN that is used by a borrower as a continuing source of funds to 'bridge' the period until the borrower obtains a medium or long-term loan to replace it. Bridging loans are used in particular in the housing market to finance the purchase of a new house while arranging long-term MORTGAGE finance and awaiting the proceeds from the sale of any existing property.

Bridlington Rules a code of practice operated by the TRADES UNION CONGRESS (TUC) to regulate inter-union competition for members in the UK, so called because they were agreed by the TUC at its Congress in Bridlington (in 1939). Where a TRADE UNION believes that its 'sphere of influence' has been encroached upon by another it may take the issue to a disputes committee of the TUC for resolution.

Brisch system a coding/classification system used to identify the characteristics of a part or component which is to be used in the manufacture of a product. See PARTS FAMILY CODING AND CLASSIFICATION SYSTEM.

British Institute of Management see INSTITUTE OF MANAGEMENT.

British Standard see BS5750.

British Standards Institution (BSI) an organization which produces national standards for products and processes at the request of particular industries. The BSI generally seeks to produce national standards which are consistent with the international standards established by the International Standardization Organization (ISO).

In designing products and processes firms must generally meet the QUALITY, performance and safety standards laid down by the BSI if their products are to be acceptable to consumers. Products which meet these specifications are entitled to bear the BSI's 'kite' mark. See BS5750.

British Technology Group (BTG) a UK government-owned organization which assists in the development of inventions made both in the private and public sectors (government and university/polytechnic research laboratories). The BTG (formed by the merger in 1981 of the National Research and Development Council and the National Enterprise Board) works in tandem with private sector VENTURE CAPITAL specialists in providing start-up finance for projects unable, because of the high risks involved, to attract conventional finance. See RESEARCH AND DEVELOPMENT.

British Venture Capital Association see VENTURE CAPITAL.

broker a business such as a stockbroker, insurance broker, commodity broker, which acts as a market intermediary in bringing together buyers and sellers of a financial asset, financial service or commodity. See AGENT, TRADER/DEALER, STOCK MARKET, COMMODITY MARKET, INSURANCE.

brownfield location a derelict industrial site or housing estate which has been demolished and redeveloped to accommodate new industrial premises, often as part of a regional industrial regeneration programme. See INDUSTRIAL LOCATION, REGIONAL DEVELOPMENT AGENCY. Contrast GREENFIELD LOCATION.

BS5750 a QUALITY standard drawn up by the BRITISH STANDARDS INSTITUTION. To obtain BS5750 certification a supplier is required to establish, document and maintain an effective and economical quality system to ensure and demonstrate that materials, products or services conform to the specified requirements.

BSI see BRITISH STANDARDS INSTITUTION.

BTG see BRITISH TECHNOLOGY GROUP.

budget

1 a firm's predetermined plan (expressed in quantitative or financial terms) for a given future period. The *sales budget* is generally compiled with the aid of sales forecasts and shows quantities and values of planned sales broken down by product group, area and type of customer. The linked *selling costs budget* shows planned salesforce and advertising costs; while the *distribution costs budget* shows planned distribution activity measured in packages handled, tonnage, etc. and associated warehousing and transport costs. Once the sales budget is complete then the consequences of planned sales can be spelled out in the production budget, after making allowance for any planned changes in finished goods stock. The *production budget* specifies the quantities of various goods to be produced and the planned DIRECT MATERIALS, DIRECT LABOUR and factory OVERHEADS associated with these production plans, with a *purchases budget* showing planned purchases of raw materials. The *administration costs budget* shows the planned cost of personnel, accounts and similar administrative departments.

The *capital expenditure budget* is concerned with planned expenditure on FIXED ASSETS, itemizing what new or replacement assets are to be acquired during the forthcoming period and making the necessary finance available. The *cash budget* shows the overall cash position, with cash inflows resulting from planned sales and cash outflows resulting from planned expenditure on raw materials, wages, capital expenditure, etc. (so that any anticipated cash surpluses or deficits show up in good time to deal with them). Finally the *master budget* aggregates all the former budgets to produce a budgeted PROFIT-AND-LOSS ACCOUNT and a budgeted BALANCE SHEET, showing what profit will be earned and what the year-end position will be, provided that actual operations go according to plan. Fig. 12 shows the steps involved in developing a budget while Fig. 13 overleaf shows a simple company budget. See BUDGETING, BUDGETARY CONTROL.

2 a statement of the government's financial position which is used for the government's economic and social welfare programmes and as part of FISCAL POLICY in managing the level and distribution of spending in the economy. Government revenue comes primarily from receipts from various taxes such as income tax and value added tax (see DIRECT TAX, INDIRECT TAX), NATIONAL INSURANCE CONTRIBUTIONS, and miscellaneous sales, including the proceeds from selling off State industries. Government expenditure is directed towards a variety of current and capital commitments. A large proportion of current spending is taken up by social welfare payments (social security and unemployment benefits (JOBSEEKERS ALLOWANCE), old age pensions etc.) and the payment of wages and salaries to central and local authority employees in the Health Service, schools etc. National defence payments also take up a sizeable part of current spending. Capital spending is undertaken on various projects, including investment in infrastructure (roads, schools, hospitals and other public works) and the nationalized industries.

Taxation and government expenditure changes are used by the government to redistribute income and WEALTH (see DISTRIBUTION OF INCOME) and to influence the total amount of spending in the economy. For example, if the authorities consider it necessary to reduce total spending, they can aim for a budget surplus, increasing taxes and cutting government expenditure. Alternatively, if a stimulus to the economy is needed, the government can run a budget deficit, cutting taxes and increasing government spending.

Recently (post 1997) the government has accepted that fiscal stability is an important element in the fight against INFLATION and UNEMPLOYMENT. To this end, fiscal 'prudence', specifically a current budget deficit within the European Union's MAASTRICHT TREATY limits of no more that 3% of GDP (and an outstanding total debt limit of 60% of GDP) was endorsed as being a necessary adjunct to avoid excessive monetary creation of the kind which fuelled previous runaway inflation.

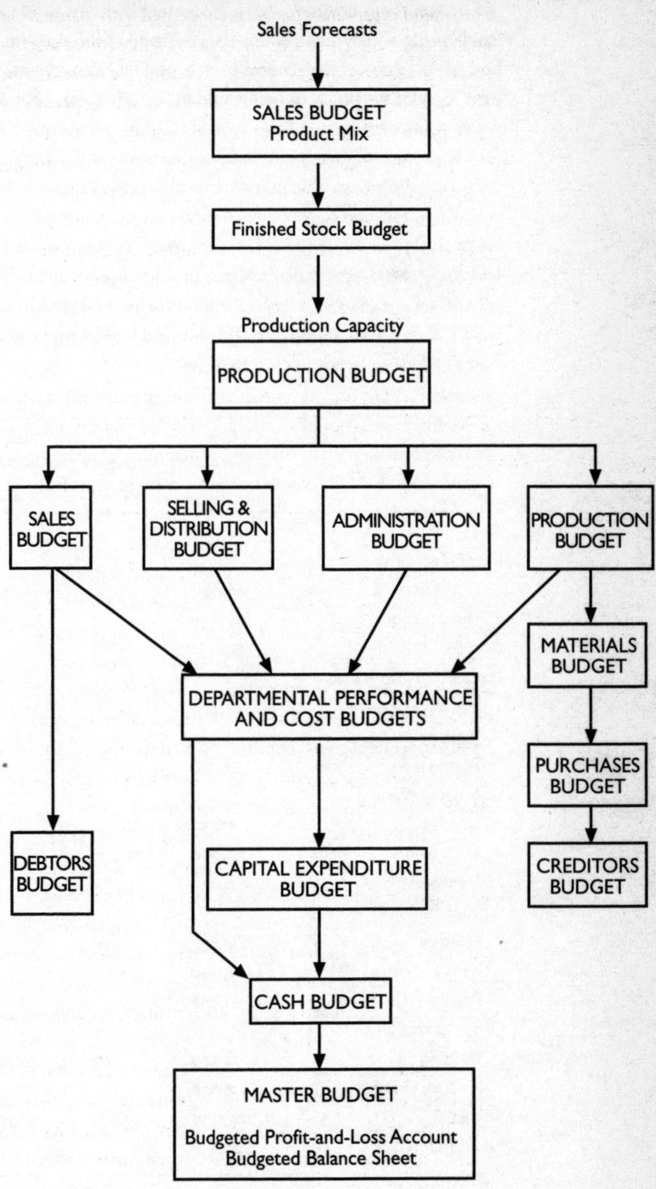

Fig. 12 **Budget.** Development of budgets.

In fact the government has gone further than this in adopting the so-called 'golden rule' which requires that the government should "aim for an overall budget surplus over the economic cycle (defined as 1998/99 to 2003/04)" with some of the proceeds being used to pay off government debt to reduce outstanding debt eventually to 40% of GDP. Along the way it has introduced more rigorous standards for approving increases in public spending, in particular the 'sustainable investment rule' which stipulates that the government should only borrow to finance capital investment and not to pay for general spending. In addition, the government has announced it will 'ring fence' increases in particular tax receipts to be used only for funding specific activities. For example, receipts from future increases in fuel taxes and tobacco taxes will be spent, respectively, only on road building programmes and the National Health Service. See PUBLIC SECTOR BORROWING REQUIREMENT.

	TOTAL	Sales Manager	Production Manager	Secretary/ Accountant
	£	£	£	£
Sales Net	826,000	826,000		
Less Direct Costs:				
Direct Materials	366,000		366,000	
Direct Labour	147,550		147,550	
GROSS MARGIN	312,450			
Production Overheads:				
Indirect Wages	44,400		44,400	
Maintenance	2,000		2,000	
Depreciation	9,350		9,350	
Selling Overheads:				
Salaries	47,150	47,150		
Advertising	31,000	31,000		
Transport	21,250	21,250		
Administration Overheads:				
Salaries	15,850			15,850
Rent and rates	21,000			21,000
Postage/telephone	7,500			7,500
Other Costs:				
Training	1,500	300	1,000	200
Finance charges	2,000			2,000
Sub Total	203,000	99,700	56,750	46,550
NET PROFIT	109,450			

Fig. 13 **Budget.** Operational budget for year beginning 1 January 20xx.

budgetary control a system for controlling COSTS and REVENUES by comparing actual results with BUDGET estimates and then taking corrective action where necessary. See COMPARISON STATEMENT.

Budgetary control involves two main stages:

(a) *preparation of the budget* prior to the start of the budget period, forecasting and planning activities for that future period;

(b) *control* by taking action based upon an evaluation of actual performance during the budget period in the light of the plans and standards developed in the budget.

budgeting the process of preparing BUDGETS and exercising BUDGETARY CONTROL. Budgeting encourages forward thinking by managers; serves to help coordinate different functions and departments in the firm; defines the responsibilities of individual managers; provides a framework for delegating responsibility; and provides incentives by setting standards of achievement. Budgeting also provides an instrument for control by pointing out where corrective action is required and a basis for modifying plans where necessary. Finally budgeting enables managers to practise MANAGEMENT BY EXCEPTION concentrating only on important deviations from plans.

buffer stock 1 a reserve of a particular COMMODITY or product held by some appointed body (often a government agency) which is used as part of a support mechanism to stabilize its price at some agreed level. If current production exceeds current demand, surplus output is bought up and held in reserve (otherwise excess supply would force the price down). Similarly, if current production cannot meet current demand then stock is released onto the market (otherwise excess demand would force prices up). Buffer stocks are used, for example, in connection with the operation of an INTERNATIONAL COMMODITY AGREEMENT.
2 see STOCK CONTROL.

building society a financial institution which offers a variety of savings accounts to attract deposits, mainly from the general public, and which specializes in the provision of long-term MORTGAGE loans used to purchase property. In recent years, many of the larger UK building societies have moved into the estate agency business. Additionally, they have entered into arrangements with other financial institutions whereby they are enabled to provide their depositors with limited banking facilities (the use of cheque books and credit cards, for instance) and other financial services, a development which has been given added impetus by the BUILDING SOCIETIES ACT 1986. Most notably, major building societies such as the Abbey National and Halifax have taken advantage of changes introduced by the BUILDING SOCIETIES ACT, 1986 and the FINANCIAL SERVICES ACT, 1986 and have converted themselves into public JOINT STOCK COMPANIES setting themselves up as 'financial supermarkets' offering customers a banking service and a wide range of personal financial products, including insurance, personal pensions, unit trusts, individual savings accounts (ISAs) etc. This development has introduced a powerful new competitive impetus into the financial services industry, breaking down traditional 'demarcation' boundaries in respect of 'who does what', allowing former building societies to 'cross sell' these services and products in competition with traditional providers such as the COMMERCIAL BANKS, INSURANCE COMPANIES, UNIT TRUSTS, etc. See ESTATE AGENT.

Building Societies Act 1986 a UK Act which consolidated earlier legislation in respect of the legal framework governing the activities of BUILDING SOCIETIES and, importantly, extended their powers to provide a range of financial services beyond that of providing principally MORTGAGE loans. In effect, the Act has opened the door to societies to engage in the provision of an extensive package of financial services for their clients in competition with the COMMERCIAL BANKS and other financial institutions, including money transmission facilities (via cheque books and cheque cards), foreign exchange (via travellers cheques and foreign currencies), and buying and selling of shares and other securities, the management of UNIT TRUST schemes for pensions and PERSONAL EQUITY PLANS, arranging all kinds of INSURANCE, and the provision of estate agency facilities, surveying and valuation services.

The Act established an authority, the Building Societies Commission, to regulate the sector, replacing the Registrar of Friendly Societies in this capacity. In the past the larger building societies have expanded their mortgage business by merger with, and takeover of, other building societies while retaining their 'friendly society' status (i.e. being owned by their subscribing members). In addition to widening the scope of their business, the 1986 Act also permitted building societies to increase their capital resources and growth potential by incorporating themselves as JOINT-STOCK COMPANIES, (as have the Abbey National and the Halifax) issuing shares to the investing public and securing a listing on the stock exchange.

build, operate, transfer project (BOT) a 'one-off' major construction project such as the building of a petrochemical complex in a country, in which the government is involved in contracting a foreign firm (or firms) not only to design and construct the facility, but also to finance it and run it on completion for a number of years. During this time the firm will expect to recoup its investment on the project before eventually transferring it to the government. See TURNKEY PROJECT.

bulk buying the purchase of raw materials, components and finished products in large quantities, which enables a BUYER to take advantage of DISCOUNTS off suppliers' LIST PRICES. A supplier may offer a price discount to encourage the placement of large orders as a means of obtaining extra sales. In many cases, however, the initiative lies with buyers, with powerful retailing and wholesaling groups exacting favourable price concessions from suppliers by playing one supplier off against another. See RETAILER, WHOLESALER, CHAIN STORE.

bulk discount see QUANTITY DISCOUNT, BULK BUYING.

bulletin board a COMPUTER accessory which enables users to post, read and reply to electronic messages transmitted through a computer network.

bull a person who buys a financial security (stock, share, foreign currency, etc.) in expectation that its market price is likely to rise. See SPECULATION. Compare BEAR.

bullion precious metals such as GOLD, silver, platinum, etc., which are traded commercially in the form of bars and coins for investment purposes, and which are used to produce jewellery and as industrial base metals.

bullion market a MARKET established for the buying and selling of precious metals such as GOLD and silver, and of gold and silver coins such as 'Krugerrands' and 'Sovereigns'. The London Bullion Market is a leading centre for such transactions.

bull market a situation in which the prices of FINANCIAL SECURITIES (stocks, shares, etc.) or COMMODITIES (tin, wheat, etc.) tend to rise as a result of persistent buying and only limited selling. See SPECULATION. Compare BEAR MARKET.

Bullock Report the report of the Committee of Inquiry on Industrial Democracy, chaired by Sir Alan Bullock and published in 1977. The Committee was created in response to growing interest in the UK in the 1970s in INDUSTRIAL DEMOCRACY, among both TRADE UNIONS and the population at large. The report recommended that company BOARDS OF DIRECTORS be restructured to include equal numbers of representatives of the workforce and of shareholder representatives, plus a third group of independent members (known as the 2x + y formula). The Report was never implemented, though an experiment in board representation took place in the Post Office.

bundled prices the PRICING of a number of separable products as one package, usually effectively lowering the price.

bureaucracy a structured ORGANIZATION formed to achieve specified goals. The term is commonly used in a pejorative sense to refer to those organizations which appear to have an excessive number of levels in the HIERARCHY, where job roles are narrow and sharply defined and where rules are rigidly adhered to, whatever the circumstances.

As developed by German sociologist Max Weber (1864–1920), however, the term is used to apply to all organizations which include the following features: clearly defined jobs; a hierarchy; a set of rules to govern operations; employees who are appointed (not elected) to posts which constitute their main occupation; and a system of promotion. In Weber's view personal emotions should not enter into the running of the bureaucracy. Weber viewed the bureaucratic organization as a distinctive feature of the modern world. In contrast to traditional societies, the bureaucracy involved a clear separation of home and work life.

In his writing on bureaucracy Weber pioneered the analytical device of the 'ideal type' as a means of identifying the essential features of a phenomenon. The features outlined above constitute the essential features that are present to a greater or lesser extent in bureaucracies. The notion of ideal type has no evaluation or prescriptive connotations.

Subsequent research has questioned Weber's contention that the bureaucracy is a highly efficient form of organization. The emphasis on following the rules can deflect employees' attention from the efficient or effective production of goods and services (see GOAL DISPLACEMENT).

American sociologist Alvin Gouldner (1920–80) identified three types of bureaucracy in terms of the function and observance of rules:

(a) *mock bureaucracy*, where rules are imposed from outside the organization, e.g. by legislation, and where all or most employees, including managers, evade or ignore them;

(b) *representative bureaucracy*, where rules are supported by all organization members, and hence are willingly obeyed;

(c) *punishment-centred bureaucracy*, where rules are enforced by one group upon another in the organization, using punishments to achieve compliance.

This approach can lead to CONFLICT.

burn-in period see FAILURE RATE CURVE.

business *or* **firm** *or* **enterprise** a producer or distributor of GOODS OR SERVICES. The economic form of a business consists of:

(a) a *horizontal business*, a business which specializes in a single activity, for example the production of bread. See HORIZONTAL INTEGRATION;

(b) a *vertical business*, a business which combines two or more successively-related vertical activities, for example flour milling and bread production. See VERTICAL INTEGRATION;

(c) a *conglomerate* or *diversified business*, a business that is engaged in a number of unrelated production activities, for example bread production and the supply of financial services.

See DIVERSIFICATION.

A business can take a number of 'legal' forms:

(a) a *sole proprietorship*, a business owned and controlled by a single person;

(b) a *partnership*, a business owned and controlled by two or more persons who are parties to a partnership agreement;

(c) a JOINT-STOCK COMPANY, a business owned by a group of SHAREHOLDERS and whose capital is divided up into a number of shares;

(d) a *cooperative*, a business owned and controlled by a group of workers. See WORKERS' COOPERATIVE.

For purposes of COMPANY LAW and the application of many company taxes and allowances (for example, CORPORATION TAX and CAPITAL ALLOWANCES) a distinction is made between 'small and medium-sized' companies and 'large' companies. Small and medium-sized companies (SMEs) are defined as follows (Companies Act, 1995):

(i) annual turnover of less than £11.2 million;

(ii) gross assets of under £5.6 million;

(iii) not more than 250 employees

In 2000 there were some 3,662,000 firms in the UK, of which 80% were run by the self-employed. Most businesses are small with around 3,630,000 firms employing under 50 people; 24,600 firms employed between 50 and 249 people, while only 6,700 firms employed over 250 people. However, in terms of their contribution to gross domestic product (GDP) firms employing over 50 people contributed in excess of 75% of total output.

The total stock of firms fluctuates from year to year depending on the *net* balance of new start-up businesses and those businesses ceasing trading (see INSOLVENCY). Generally, the total stock of firms increases when the economy is expanding (or as a result of some 'special' factor, e.g. the surge in newly established INTERNET businesses) and falls in a recession.

A final point to note is that with the increasing globalization of the world economy MULTINATIONAL ENTERPRISES are becoming more prevalent in economies such as the UK.

business clusters a system of market and non-market links between geographically concentrated companies and institutions. The links enable cooperation among suppliers and competitors on business processes, purchasing, investments and technical research.

business cycle fluctuations in the level of business activity in an economy brought about by changes in demand conditions, particularly increases and decreases in investment spending. The business cycle is characterized by four phases, with the economy moving upwards from 'depression' through 'recovery' to 'boom' and back through 'recession' to depression once again. The *depression* stage of the cycle is characterized by a very low level of demand relative to supply capacity, accompanied by low levels of output, unsold stock and high unemployment. As demand picks up in the *recovery* stage, stock levels fall and output and employment increases. *Boom* conditions are characterized by full-capacity levels of output and employment, but with a tendency for the economy to 'overheat', producing inflationary pressures. The ending of a boom is followed by a period of *recession,* with falling demand leading to modest falls in output and employment at first but then accelerating into *depression* as demand continues to fall. In practice, however, governments attempt to use anticyclical FISCAL POLICY and MONETARY POLICY to stabilize the economy, aiming in general to keep total demand in balance with the supply capabilities of the economy, thus avoiding undesirable output- and employment-losses as well as containing inflation. See ECONOMIC POLICY.

business establishment see BUSINESS PREMISES.

business ethics moral guidelines for the conduct of business based on notions of what is right, wrong and fair. Most business people rely upon their own consciences in making business decisions, falling back upon their own moral and religious backgrounds for guidance. However, business people are also affected by their superiors and immediate colleagues when making business decisions and may feel pressurized to behave unethically when seeking to make profits. Over recent years many firms and industries have attempted to develop codes of conduct which can be used to guide managers when making decisions.

Business Expansion Scheme see ENTERPRISE INVESTMENT SCHEME.

business format franchising a FRANCHISING method whereby marketing approaches, quality control and operating procedures are offered to the franchisee.

business *or* **firm growth** the expansion of the size of a business or firm over time. Typical measures of firm growth are the growth of assets or capital employed, turnover, profits and number of employees. Some firms remain small either by choice or circumstances (e.g. the 'corner shop'); other firms expand to become large, either in a national or international context (see MULTINATIONAL ENTERPRISE) through either/or INTERNAL GROWTH and EXTERNAL GROWTH (MERGERS, TAKEOVERS and STRATEGIC ALLIANCES). Firms may expand in their original lines of business (HORIZONTAL INTEGRATION), become VERTICALLY INTEGRATED or they may expand into new business activities (DIVERSIFICATION). See PRODUCT MARKET MATRIX.

The process of growth is initiated and facilitated by a combination of managerial, economic, financial and 'chance' factors:

(a) *Managerial.* A typical catalyst underpinning firm growth is an ambitious

ENTREPRENEUR, he or she establishing a new firm and setting out to create a 'big business'. Over time, as a firm expands, the original founder is usually unable to manage all facets of the business and will need the assistance of other directors and professional managers. While firms may develop a growth philosophy and impetus, however, serious management 'mistakes' may occur in the form of a failure to identify changing customer needs (see, for example, the recent setbacks at the retailing group Marks & Spencer and the car producer BMW/Rover), or ill-judged diversifications may reverse growth potential and put the very survival of the firm under threat;

(b) *Economic.* Some firms thrive and grow whilst others decline or go bankrupt (or are taken over) because the former firms are superior in creating and sustaining COMPETITIVE ADVANTAGES, which enables them to 'meet and beat' rival firms (see RESOURCE-BASED THEORY OF THE FIRM). Firms that are able to take full advantage of ECONOMIES OF SCALE and the EXPERIENCE CURVE are able to expand their sales and market shares by producing their products at lower cost and selling them at lower prices than rivals; similarly, firms that are able to exploit PRODUCT DIFFERENTIATION advantages, particularly through developing new products are able to expand at the expense of less innovative rivals. For example, Microsoft has gained a worldwide dominance of software systems through its 'Windows' technology. ECONOMIES OF SCOPE are often important in underpinning growth through concentric diversification, where firms 'transfer' resources and skills from their core activities into related areas of business;

(c) *Financial.* As they grow, firms will need to obtain additional financial resources. This may involve the firm in steadily ploughing back profits over the years. A quicker way to fund expansion, however, often involves the firm converting from a 'sole proprietor' status to one of public JOINT-STOCK COMPANY (Plc) by floating the business on the STOCK MARKET (see FLOTATION). Plcs typically continue to finance their expansion by issuing new shares to their existing shareholders (see RIGHTS ISSUE), by increased borrowing from the COMMERCIAL BANKS and investors (see CORPORATE BOND) and financing mergers and takeovers by exchanging new shares in the enlarged company for those of target companies;

(d) *Chance or luck factors.* Being in the 'right place at the right time' often affects the fortunes of firms. A growth opportunity may occur, for example, through the discovery of a hitherto unknown North Sea oilfield by an oil company such as BP; or from the UK government's decision to deregulate the telecommunications and bus markets, which have provided growth opportunities for new suppliers to enter these markets such as Vodaphone and Stagecoach, respectively.

The comparative rates of growth achieved by firms determines the eventual number and size distribution of the firms supplying a particular market and thus affects MARKET STRUCTURE.

business incubators an organization of services designed to nurture young businesses. They aim to reduce the failure rate of early stage companies and speed the growth of companies which have the potential to create employment and wealth. The incubator could take the form of property offering small workshops units with secretarial and management services.

Business Link a nationwide network of agencies which brings together the business support activities of many Chambers of Commerce, enterprise agencies, training and skills councils and local authorities to provide a single local point of access for business information and advisory services to small- and medium-sized business (SMEs see BUSINESS entry). A particular responsibility of the Business Link is to assist small business take full advantage of the SMART scheme (aimed at promoting new innovative techniques and products). The Business link operates under the auspices of the SMALL BUSINESSES SERVICE (SBS), an arm of the DEPARTMENT OF TRADE AND INDUSTRY (DTI).

business location see INDUSTRIAL LOCATION.

business objectives

The goals which a firm sets for itself in respect of profit returns, sales and assets growth, etc., which in turn determine the strategic and operational policies it adopts.

The firm may pursue a single objective or multiple objectives; objectives may be operationalized in 'maximization' or 'satisfactory' target level terms; the time frame in which objectives are pursued may be short term or long term. Thus, it can be seen that objective-setting can be a complex matter, Critical factors affecting the setting of objectives include *who* controls decision-making in the firm, and the various constraints – institutional, financial and environmental, etc. – impinging upon this process.

Economic theories of the firm emphasize that firms which are *owner*-controlled will tend to pursue single period or multi-period profit maximization; likewise, theories of finance suggest that the operational goal of the firm will be to maximize the value of the firm (shareholders' wealth) over the long term. Firms which are *management*-controlled will tend to pursue objectives such as multi-period sales revenue maximization and asset growth maximization. In this latter case, although shareholders are the owners of the firm, there is a de facto 'divorce of ownership from control' enabling the appointed representatives of the shareholders, namely members of the Board of Directors, to make the key decisions affecting the firm's business. In general, shareholdings are too fragmented and shareholders, as 'outsiders', are too remote from the seat of power to be able to exercise control over the business, thus leaving the incumbent managers relatively free to run the company as they see fit. Obviously shareholders' interests cannot be ignored (i.e. directors can be removed at the ANNUAL GENERAL MEETING (AGM) if the firm is badly managed and dividends are not paid). However, within this constraint managers will be able to set objectives which enhance their own interests; sales revenue maximization and asset growth maximization objectives, it is argued, result in 'bigger' firms – big firms pay higher salaries to managers and accord them power and status.

An alternative framework to the largely normative maximization view of objective setting is provided by the 'organizational' or 'behavioural' schools, which argue that the decision-making process at work in most firms tends to produce objectives couched in 'satisfactory' terms – objectives tend to reflect organizational bargaining between the various divisions of the firm (marketing, production, finance, etc.), resulting in the specification of objectives generally 'acceptable' (i.e. satisfactory) to all participants rather than optimal for one group alone. Other economists have drawn attention to the fact that the presence of uncertainty and incomplete information in most market situations means that profit maximization in the way depicted in the theoretical models is unattainable and that in practice 'real world' firms use more pragmatic performance targets to guide their actions. For example,

Philips, the electrical products company, aims to achieve a 24% return on capital employed, while other companies are concerned to enhance shareholder value:

Our aim is to "substantially outperform the support services sector as measured by shareholder return over a five year period" (Rentokil Initial, Annual Report and Accounts 2000).

In the case of food and drinks group Cadbury Schweppes: "Our primary objective is to grow the value of the business for our shareholders. 'Managing for Value' is the business philosophy which unites all our activities in pursuit of this objective. The objective is quantified. We have set three financial targets to measure our progress:

1 to increase our earnings per share by at least 10% every year;

2 to generate £150 million of free cash flow every year; and

3 to double the value of our shareholder's investment within four years".

(Annual Report and Accounts, 2000). Also instructive are the objectives which are set to trigger awards to company executive directors (i.e. those persons responsible for determining company objectives and policies) under EXECUTIVE STOCK OPTION SCHEMES. For example, Wolseley, a leading distributor of heating, plumbing and building materials, requires that the company's earnings per share growth is greater than the increase in the RETAIL PRICE INDEX by at least 9% over three years and the achievement also of a rate of return on capital of at least 17.5% over three years. (Annual Report and Accounts 2000). See BUSINESS STRATEGY, STRATEGY, MISSION STATEMENT, PRINCIPAL-AGENT THEORY, CORPORATE GOVERNANCE.

business park see SCIENCE PARK.

business plan a detailed statement of the objectives, proposed operations, resource requirements, financial forecasts etc. of a completely new business or an established business which is being developed further. It is particularly important to draw up such a plan not only to ensure that the owners/managers of the business themselves understand clearly what is required to make a success of the venture but also that external parties, in particular providers of capital and loan facilities, can evaluate the viability of what is being attempted.

There is no set formula for a business plan but typical elements would include:

* name, address, products and objectives of the business; what product is to be supplied
* market analysis – customer needs, competitors, size of market etc. and proposed marketing/competitive strategy
* operations analysis – production, purchasing, selling etc.
* financial analysis – profit and loss forecasts, cash flow forecasts, capital expenditure requirements
* management information/business controls – recording procedures, monitoring progress. See BUSINESS STRATEGY.

business policy see BUSINESS STRATEGY.

business premises *or* **establishment** a building which is used to produce a good or provide a service. The main types of business premises are: FACTORY, OFFICE, retail or work SHOP OR STORE, WAREHOUSE. See UNIFORM BUSINESS RATE.

business process re-engineering (BPR) an approach to management which emphasizes the need to organize business operations in a multi-functional way rather than the conventional 'compartmentalized' way built round separate functions such as production and marketing.

Under the traditional functional-focused approach, employees tend to identify with 'their' own function rather than with the firm as a whole. Given, however, the growing complexity of modern business and the need to adapt to change quickly to remain competitive, BPR requires firms to take a holistic view of their operations stressing that everything which affects outcomes – processes, people, technology, etc. – must be effectively coordinated *across* departmental boundaries. Thus the 'focus' of the business is clearly based on satisfying external customer needs as competitively as possible and internal processes are 're-engineered' as appropriate to meet this objective. See DE-LAYERING, DOWNSIZING.

business rate see UNIFORM BUSINESS RATE.

business strategy, business policy, corporate strategy *or* strategic management

The formulation of a unified body of strategic plans by a firm in order to achieve its BUSINESS OBJECTIVES. Business STRATEGY interlocks all aspects of a firm's activities including:

(a) objective setting: determining the general goals of the firm (for example increasing the rate of return on capital employed, or increasing earnings per share, etc);

(b) ENVIRONMENTAL SCANNING: determining the opportunities and threats presented by the firm's business environment (see SWOT ANALYSIS, PEST, COMPETITIVE STRATEGY);

(c) POSITION AUDIT: determining the strengths and weaknesses in the firm's available resources (see RESOURCE BASED THEORY OF THE FIRM);

(d) strategic direction: deciding what business activities the firm should operate in, and where: for example continue its existing activities, DIVEST some of them and/or DIVERSIFY into new product markets (see PRODUCT MARKET MATRIX, BOSTON MATRIX); remain a national supplier or globalize its operations (see MULTINATIONAL ENTERPRISE);

(e) choice of growth mode: deciding for each particular area of activity the most appropriate means of expanding its business interests; for example ORGANIC GROWTH or EXTERNAL GROWTH via MERGERS, TAKEOVERS, JOINT VENTURES and other forms of STRATEGIC ALLIANCES.

(f) COMPETITIVE STRATEGY: deciding on the basis of an evaluation of the firm's own competitive strengths and weaknesses vis-à-vis those of its rivals and the requirements of customers, the best means of establishing a position of COMPETITIVE ADVANTAGE (lower price, innovative products, etc.) over rival suppliers.

(g) establishment of appropriate ORGANIZATIONAL STRUCTURES to facilitate the firm's goals. This involves ensuring an efficient and co-ordinated effort from the various operational divisions of the firm: MARKETING, PRODUCTION, etc. through appropriate management and organizational structures.

(h) strategy implementation: designing appropriate management CONTROL and reward systems (see PAY) which will motivate employees and encourage them to achieve the firm's strategies;

(i) review and control: to identify problems which are preventing the firm from achieving its goals and devise means of overcoming these problems or amend goals and strategies where problems cannot be overcome.

Fig. 14 shows the various steps in the business strategy process.

Strategists have attempted to 'model' the business strategy formulation process noted above so as to provide company executives with a practical 'action plan'. Typically, business strategy formulation is depicted as consisting of three key elements:

(i) *strategic analysis*, which involves an examination of the firm's objectives, its relationship with its environment and its resources

(ii) *strategy development*, which involves the development and selection of strategy options and consideration of which competitive strategies to adopt in the firm's chosen markets

(iii) *strategy implementation*, which involves implementation of the selected strategies.

One model of business strategy formulation suggests that the three steps above follow sequentially with top management determining objectives and developing strategies which are then communicated to middle and junior managers and arrangements made for strategy implementation. This model is often characterised as the *rational* or *prescriptive approach* to strategy which is based upon formal, top-down strategy processes, using designated strategy teams, planning units and formal collection of information.

Some authorities on strategy such as Mintzberg argue that strategic processes are less rational than those implied in figure 14. They argue that the three steps involved in strategy formulation are not linear and rational and that all three steps happen at the same time in different parts of the organization. They argue that objectives change and can conflict; that senior managers share responsibility for setting and implementing strategy with middle managers, that strategy cannot be decided in advance by top management; that formal processes are too slow to allow business to be dynamic; and that formal strategic processes are impossible to pursue in uncertain business environments characterised by complexity and dynamism.

The critics of the rational strategy model suggest instead that the strategies which emerge in businesses are a combination of planned strategies and unanticipated "emergent" strategies. This *emergent strategy* approach suggests that strategies may be realised because of, despite, or in the absence of, objectives – they simply happen along the way. Such an approach sees the essential role of managers as moving their organizations along in small incremental steps rather than relying on visions or strategic plans. The emergent strategy approach sees no clear distinction between the steps of strategy

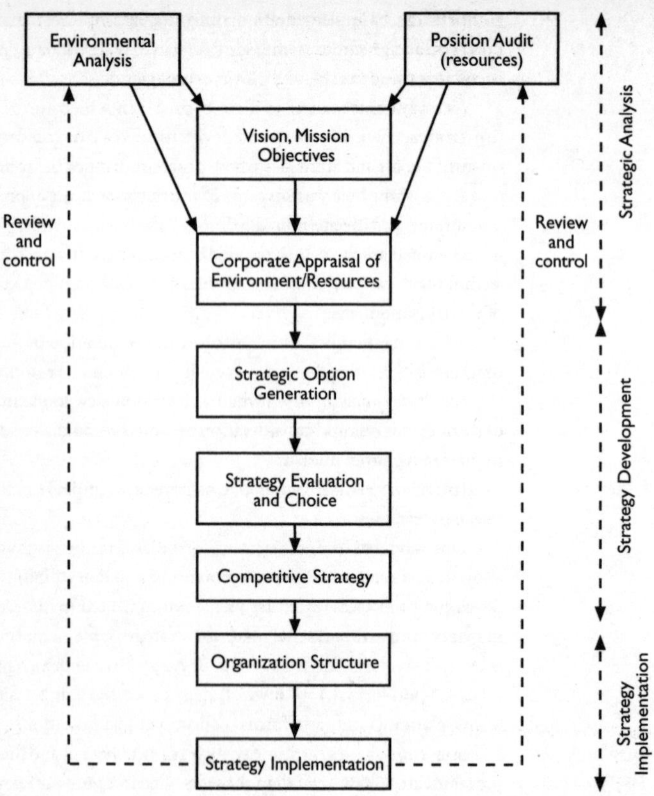

Fig. 14 **The Business Strategy process.**

development and strategy implementation: instead it views the business as learning by experimentation and discussion as strategies are developed, implemented, revised and adapted.

A further distinction is often made between *market based* and *resource based* business strategies. The market based view suggests that strategy should start with strategic objectives which seek to define what markets the business is in and which markets it seeks to serve. By contrast the resource based view starts with an audit of the business's resources which seeks to identify which of the business's activities cannot easily be copied or improved upon by competitors. These activities represent the core competences of the business and management should seek to develop products and markets which utilize these competences. Such a resource based approach focuses on developing core competences, bases strategy on present resource endowments and avoids the business losing sight of what it is good at. Resource based strategy tends to be incremental and fits well with the emergent strategy approach.

Strategy exists at three main levels in a business:

(i) Corporate Strategy which is determined at the corporate centre or head office of the organization. Corporate Strategy deals with the overall purpose and scope of the business dealing with such issues as acquisitions and mergers; divestment; and diversification.

(ii) Business Strategy which is determined by strategic business units within the organization, each unit being responsible for developing, producing and marketing a related group of products. Such business units deal with COMPETITIVE STRATEGIES for beating competitors in the relevant markets.

(iii) Functional Strategy which is determined by operational units within each strategic business unit which are responsible for business functions such as marketing, production and human resources. See BUSINESS PLAN, HORIZONTAL INTEGRATION, VERTICAL INTEGRATION, DIVERSIFICATION, INVESTMENT, ENDGAME STRATEGY, TURN-ROUND, MANAGEMENT BUY-OUT, MANAGEMENT BUY-IN, MARKET ENTRY, MARKET STRUCTURE, MARKET CONDUCT, MARKET PERFORMANCE, STRATEGIC GROUP, FRANCHISE, BARRIERS TO EXIT, BARRIERS TO ENTRY, CORE SKILL, CORPORATE RESTRUCTURING, BUSINESS PROCESS RE-ENGINEERING, CRITICAL or KEY SUCCESS FACTORS.

business unionism see TRADE UNION.

buyback see COUNTERTRADE.

buyer a purchaser of a GOOD, SERVICE or FINANCIAL SECURITY. A broad distinction can be made between purchasers of goods and services such as raw materials, components, plant and equipment which are used to produce other products (referred to as 'industrial buyers') and purchasers of products for personal consumption (referred to as 'consumers').

The distinction between the two groups is important in terms of the application of appropriate MARKETING STRATEGIES. In general, industrial buyers, mainly purchasing/procurement officers, are involved in the purchase of 'functional' inputs to the production process, usually in large quantities and often involving the outlay of thousands of pounds. Their particular concern is to obtain input supplies which are of an appropriate quality and possess the technical attributes necessary to ensure that the production process goes ahead smoothly and efficiently. In selling to industrial buyers, personal contacts, the provision of technical advice and back-up services are important. Buyers of consumer goods, by contrast, typically buy a much wider range of products, mainly in small quantities. Purchases are made to satisfy some physical or psychological need of the consumer. Thus, it is important for marketers to understand the basis of these needs and to produce and promote BRANDS which satisfy identifiable consumer demands. In this context, ADVERTISING and SALES PROMOTION are important tools for shaping consumers' perceptions of a brand and establishing BRAND LOYALTY. See BUYER BEHAVIOUR, BUYING CENTRE, BUYING PROCESS, PURCHASING.

buyer behaviour the purchasing decisions of BUYERS as shaped by their functional and psychological motivations and needs. A broad distinction can be made between industrial buyers and consumers in general. Industrial buyers purchase products purely on the basis of functional or technical requirements: the producer of a motor car, for instance may seek to buy suitable components such as tyres, batteries, etc. for incorporation into a particular car model. Consumers too buy many products on the basis of some functional or physical requirement, for example a consumer may decide to purchase a motor car as a means of personal transport. However, a consumer's decision to buy a product such as a car is also influenced by his or her personality and the image he or she desires to project to others ('extrovert', 'sporty', 'affluent', etc.).

It is thus important for producers of consumer goods to understand the psychological impulses of prospective buyers of their products as well as their practical needs. This requires careful MARKET RESEARCH into the motivation and perception of buyers aimed at matching products with identified customer needs, and the deployment of appropriate MARKETING MIX strategies (product quality, pricing, advertising, etc.) designed to maximize sales potential. See PRE-PURCHASE BEHAVIOUR, POST-PURCHASE BEHAVIOUR, PRODUCT IMAGE, PSYCHOLOGICAL PRICING, ADVERTISING, LIFE STYLE, MOTIVATIONAL RESEARCH, BUY-RESPONSE METHOD, BUY.

buyer concentration see MARKET CONCENTRATION.

buyer's market a MARKET situation characterized by the temporary excess supply of a GOOD OR SERVICE often leading to cut-throat price competition. In such markets BUYERS are advantageously placed to obtain price concessions. Compare SELLER'S MARKET.

buy-in see MANAGEMENT BUY-IN.

buying centre a group of persons usually within a firm which is responsible for the buying decision. The roles within the buying centre, or decision-making unit, include the initiator, who sets the process in motion; the buyer who negotiates the terms of any purchase deal; the specifier, or influencer, who specifies the precise product requirements; the decider who has the ultimate authority to approve the award of the supply contract; a gatekeeper, who controls the flow of information and contacts in the BUYING PROCESS; and finally the user(s), namely the individual(s) who will make use of the bought inputs in their working operations. See PURCHASING.

buying criteria the requirements on which a prospective buyer bases his or her decision on whether or not to buy a product or service. See BUYER BEHAVIOUR.

buying intentions survey an investigation designed to discover BUYERS' future plans in respect of purchasing a particular GOOD or SERVICE. Such a survey is undertaken to enable a firm to produce more realistic forecasts of the anticipated future demand for their product. Surveys are generally carried out by interviewers or direct mail questionnaires. See SALES FORECASTING.

buying process the various stages involved in a buying (PURCHASING) decision. In the case of *industrial* buying this requires the identification of the need to purchase a good or service, the development of a strategy for the handling of the purchase, the specification of the requirement, the search for suppliers, the evaluation of supplier's offerings, final negotiations, the award of the contract, operationalization of the supply relationship and subsequent feedback and control of the arrangements. For example, if an organization is purchasing an IT system, this buying process may have been initiated by the operations director. The IT department will then be asked to specify a system, usually in consultation with potential users. Once this is done, a buyer or contracts manager on the purchasing department may be asked, with support from technical staff, to identify suppliers, solicit proposals, and negotiate best value for this contract. Once the purchase is made, the operational staff will work with supplier staff to secure the inputs. The purchasing staff will usually check that the value which they negotiated is actually delivered.

In *consumer* buying, the process may be very quick, such as in an impulse buy, or may take longer depending on the importance of the purchase. For bigger purchases, a consumer will go through the stages of need awareness, information search, evaluation of alternatives, purchase and post-purchase evaluation.

buying signal a statement by a BUYER which indicates that he or she is interested in buying.

buy-out see MANAGEMENT BUY-OUT.

buy-response method a study of the value customers place on a product by asking them if they would be willing to buy it at varying price levels. See BUYER BEHAVIOUR.

by-product a product which results from a common production process but which is secondary to the main product being produced from that process. The refining of crude oil to produce petrol, for example, also produces by-products such as tar and creosote. See BY-PRODUCT PRICING, PROCESS PRODUCTION.

by-product pricing the PRICING of the various BY-PRODUCTS emerging from a common production process. The PRICE of each by-product should, if possible, cover its cost. However, the precise individual cost of each by-product is very difficult to determine given the *common* process costs involved. As a consequence by-products are often priced according to what the market will bear. See PROCESS COSTING.

byte a group of eight bits (zeros/ones) used to represent a single number or letter in a COMPUTER. The capacity of a computer is often measured in terms of thousands of bytes (K), for example 640K; or millions of bytes, for example 20 megabytes.

C

CAD see COMPUTER-AIDED DESIGN.

Cadbury Committee Report see CORPORATE GOVERNANCE.

CAE (computer-aided engineering) see COMPUTER-AIDED DESIGN.

c&f see COST AND FREIGHT.

cafeteria benefits a PAY system where employees are able to design their own remuneration package selecting from a menu of pay and FRINGE BENEFIT items up to a value stipulated by the employer.

call centre a location where CUSTOMER SERVICE employees handle customer queries by phone and e-mail.

called-up capital the amount of issued share capital which shareholders have been called upon to subscribe to date, where a JOINT-STOCK COMPANY issues shares with phased payment terms. For example, a company may issue £1 shares with 50p payable immediately upon application by intending share-holders, a further 25p upon ALLOTMENT of the shares to shareholders and the final 25p three months later. Here the called-up capital at the time of allotment of shares would be 75p times the number of shares allotted. Called-up capital is usually equal to PAID-UP CAPITAL unless there are any calls in arrears – shares on which subsequent instalments are owing. See SHARE ISSUE.

call option see OPTION.

call reports reports completed by sales representatives after visiting customers and potential customers as a basis for compiling MARKETING INTELLIGENCE and monitoring representatives' performance. The reports may include information about new customers, reasons why particular customers have been lost and creditworthiness of buyers. See CALLS.

calls visits by SALES REPRESENTATIVES to customers and potential customers as a means of securing SALES and maintaining customer contact. Calls provide a useful opportunity for sales persons to inform customers about the firm's product offerings and promotions. Additionally, calls may be used to obtain data about customer needs for SALES FORECASTING and NEW PRODUCT DEVELOPMENT purposes. See CALL REPORTS, COLD CALL.

CAM see COMPUTER-AIDED MANUFACTURING.

campaign a planned marketing or advertising activity designed to increase a firm's sales. See ADVERTISING CAMPAIGN, PROMOTION, PROMOTIONAL MIX.

campaigning a technique for manufacture where product set up costs are high or considered to be difficult. Items are manufactured to stock possibly to meet a 12 month period of demand.

campaign objectives goals set by an organization for a promotional campaign in terms of e.g. sales, profits, customers won or retained or awareness creation. See PROMOTION.

cannibalization a situation where a new brand gains sales at the expense of another of the company's brands.

capacity the maximum amount of output that a firm is physically capable of producing, at a point in time, given the fullest and most efficient use of its existing plant or plants.

Over time, a firm may adjust its capacity to meet changes in demand and the competitive situation facing it, investing in new plant or extending existing plant to meet an increase in demand, or closing down plant, permanently or temporarily ('MOTHBALLING'), to meet a situation of OVERCAPACITY.

When preparing a PRODUCTION BUDGET, it is necessary to ensure that the firm has sufficient production capacity to meet planned output levels. A firm's capacity or the capacity of industry in general may be limited by the availability of capital equipment and labour.

The maximum rate of output which the firm can produce will depend upon the capacity of its individual factories which in turn depends upon the capacity of various departments and work stations within each factory. See INPUT-OUTPUT CONTROL, PRODUCTION SCHEDULING, PRODUCTION-LINE BALANCING. See CAPACITY UTILIZATION, LIMITING FACTOR, RATIONALIZATION, INDIVISIBILITIES, CAPACITY CONSTRAINED RESOURCE, CAPACITY CONTROL, CAPACITY CUSHION, CAPACITY PLANNING, CAPACITY REQUIREMENTS PLANNING.

capacity constrained resource the identification of a resource within manufacture or service provision which limits the total output, the constraining resource acting as a bottleneck.

capacity control the management of resource, so that utilization approaches the maximum possible without straining the whole system. See CAPACITY UTILIZATION.

capacity cushion the amount of capacity commonly available within a working period. See CAPACITY UTILIZATION.

capacity planning the management of available resource over a planned time period. See CAPACITY UTILIZATION.

capacity requirements planning the management of resource over a planned time period when related to manufacturing planning. See MATERIALS REQUIREMENT PLANNING, MANUFACTURING RESOURCE PLANNING. (See MRP and MRP II).

capacity utilization the proportion of a firm's available CAPACITY which is currently being employed in producing output. This depends to a great extent on the state of demand and a firm's competitive abilities. A fall in demand, or a failure to win orders against competition, may force a firm to operate at below BREAK-EVEN levels of capacity utilization. See INDIVISIBILITIES, BUSINESS CYCLE, MACHINE UTILIZATION.

capacity utilization rate the ratio of designed CAPACITY to used capacity.

capital 1 the funds invested in a BUSINESS in order to acquire the ASSETS which the business needs to trade. Capital can consist of SHARE CAPITAL subscribed by SHAREHOLDERS or LOAN CAPITAL provided by lenders.
2 GOODS such as plant, machinery and equipment which are used to produce other goods and services. See CAPITAL STOCK, INVESTMENT.

capital accumulation see CAPITAL FORMATION.

capital allowances standard allowances, for TAXATION purposes, against expenditure on FIXED ASSETS by a firm in lieu of DEPRECIATION. In the UK currently (as at 2004/05) a 25% 'writing-down allowance' against tax is available for firms which invest in new plant and equipment. Additionally in the case of small and medium-sized firms a 40% 'first year allowance' is available for INVESTMENT in new plant and equipment and a 100% tax write-off (for the three year period 2000/03) for investment in computers and e-commerce. A business may choose its own rates of depreciation for fixed assets which may differ from the statutory capital allowances. Capital allowances may also be varied by the government to encourage or discourage capital INVESTMENT. See DEPRECIATION, CORPORATION TAX.

capital appreciation see APPRECIATION.

capital-asset pricing model a share-price valuation model in which the major factors of short-term share-price determination are explained. The capital-asset pricing model provides a method of computing the return on a FINANCIAL SECURITY which specifically identifies and measures the risk factor within a PORTFOLIO holding. The expected rate of return on a particular investment has two components:

(a) the risk-free percentage return which could be obtained from, say, a gilt-edged, government financial security;

(b) the risk return associated with the investment.

(Risk itself can be split into market or nondiversifiable risk and specific or diversifiable risk.) This relationship between risk and return is shown in Fig. 15.

The total expected return on an investment is or$_m$, but risk only attaches to non gilt-edged securities which is why the capital market line intercepts the vertical axis at r_f. The capital market line shows how, in a competitive market, the additional risk premium varies in direct proportion to β. known as the BETA COEFFICIENT. At point M in the figure there is perfect correlation between movements in the market generally, as detailed by an all-share index, and a particular investment. Therefore β = 1 at point M. Where there is no risk, as in Treasury bills, β = 0. β is a measure of market risk because investors have it within their power to diversify away specific risk to almost zero by holding a broad portfolio of shares. It is possible to estimate the beta coefficient of a security from published information.

See also EFFICIENT MARKETS HYPOTHESIS, PORTFOLIO THEORY.

capital budgeting the process of planning and controlling CAPITAL expenditure within a firm. Capital budgeting involves the search for suitable investment opportunities; evaluating particular investment projects; raising LONG-TERM CAPITAL to finance investments; assessing the COST OF CAPITAL; applying suitable expenditure controls to ensure that investment outlays conform with the expenditures authorized; and ensuring that adequate cash is available when required for investments. See INVESTMENT APPRAISAL, BUDGETING.

capital employed the total funds invested in a business made up of SHAREHOLDERS' funds and long-term LOAN CAPITAL. It is equivalent in value to the company's NET ASSETS in its BALANCE SHEET. See SHAREHOLDER'S CAPITAL EMPLOYED, LONG-TERM CAPITAL EMPLOYED.

capital expenditure expenditure on the acquisition or improvement of FIXED ASSETS that is subsequently written off against profits over several ACCOUNTING PERIODS. Contrast with REVENUE EXPENDITURE. See INVESTMENT, CAPITAL BUDGETING.

capital export see EXPORT, BALANCE OF PAYMENTS.

capital formation *or* **capital accumulation** 1 the process of increasing the internally available CAPITAL of a business by retaining earnings to add to RESERVES.

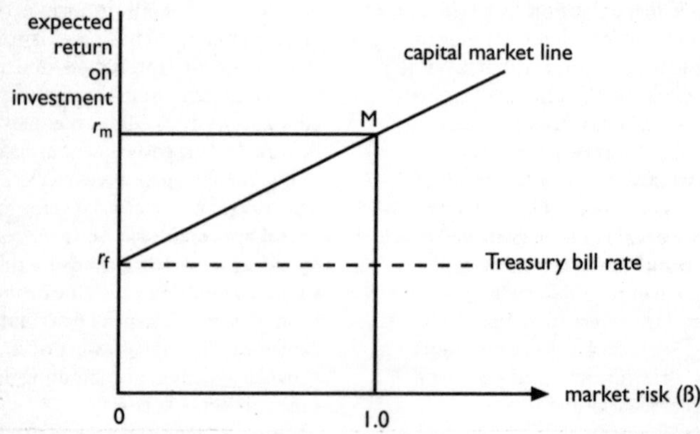

Fig. 15 **Capital-asset pricing model.** This identifies the market risk factor for the expected rate of investment.

2 the process of adding to the net physical CAPITAL STOCK of an economy as a means of increasing the economy's capacity to produce goods and services. INVESTMENT by businesses in new plant and equipment is one important source of capital formation, as is investment by the government in INFRASTRUCTURE (roads, railways, etc.).

capital gain the surplus realized when an ASSET (house, SHARE, etc.) is sold at a higher price than was originally paid for it. However, because of INFLATION it is important to distinguish between NOMINAL VALUES and REAL VALUES. Thus what appears to be a large nominal gain may, after allowing for the effects of inflation, turn out to be a very small real gain. Furthermore, in an ongoing business, provision has to be made for the REPLACEMENT COST of assets, which can be much higher than the HISTORIC COST of these assets being sold. See CAPITAL GAINS TAX, CAPITAL LOSS, REVALUATION PROVISION, APPRECIATION, definition 1.

capital gains tax a TAX on the surplus obtained from the sale of an ASSET for more than was originally paid for it.

In the UK, CAPITAL GAINS tax for business assets is based (as at 2005/06) on a sliding scale, from 40% on gains from assets held for under one year to 10% on gains realised after 4 years. For persons, capital gains on 'chargeable' assets (e.g. shares) up to £8,500 per year are exempt from tax; above this they are taxed at 40%.

capital gearing *or* **leverage** the proportion of fixed-interest LOAN CAPITAL to share capital employed in financing a company. Where a company raises most of the funds required by issuing shares and uses very few fixed-interest loans it has a low capital gearing; where a company raises most of the funds needed from fixed-interest loans and few funds from SHAREHOLDERS it is highly geared.

Capital gearing is important to company shareholders because fixed-interest charges on loans have the effect of gearing up or down the eventual residual return to

	Firm A: ungeared £		*Firm B: highgeared* £	
Ordinary Shares	1,000		500	
Fixed-interest loans	–		500	
Total capital employed	1,000		1,000	
Year 1 trading profit = 30% on total capital employed				
Trading profit	300		300	
Less loan interest (at 10%)	–		50	
Net profit	300		250	
Return to shareholders	300/1,000	= 30%	250/500	= 50%
Year 2 trading profit = 7% on total capital employed				
Trading profit	70		70	
Less loan interest (at 10%)	–		50	
Net profit	70		20	
Return to shareholders	70/1,000	= 7%	20/500	= 4%

Fig. 16 **Capital gearing.** Table comparing the effects of ungeared and highgeared capital on returns to shareholders.

shareholders from trading profits. When the trading return on total funds invested exceeds the interest rate on loans, any residual surplus accrues to shareholders, enhancing their return. On the other hand, when the average return on total funds invested is less than interest rates, then interest still has to be paid and this has the effect of reducing the residual return to shareholders. For example, compare two companies, one financed solely from share capital (*ungeared*) and another which raises half of its capital from fixed-interest loans on which it must pay 10% interest (*highgeared*). Fig. 16 (above) shows how returns to shareholders vary more widely when highgeared.

The extent to which a company can employ fixed-interest capital as a source of long-term funds depends to a large extent upon the stability of its profits over time. For example, large retailing companies whose profits tend to vary little from year to year tend to be more highly geared than, say, mining companies whose profit record is more volatile.

capital good see GOOD.

capital import see IMPORT, BALANCE OF PAYMENTS, CAPITAL INFLOW.

capital inflow a movement of funds into a particular country, the HOST COUNTRY, from one or more foreign countries, the source countries. The host country may attract capital inflows for a variety of reasons, including:

(a) FOREIGN DIRECT INVESTMENT by MULTINATIONAL ENTERPRISES in physical assets such as the establishment of a local manufacturing plant or the acquisition of a local firm;

(b) Portfolio investment in financial securities (equities and bonds etc. issued in the host country by overseas residents and financial institutions, pension funds, insurance companies etc.);

(c) Host government borrowing from international banks or from other governments to finance a BALANCE OF PAYMENTS deficit, borrowing by individuals and companies from international banks and inter-company transfers to finance current consumption and investment;

(d) Short-term deposits with money market and banking institutions in the host country relating to interest rate differentials between countries and/or speculation in the hope that a country's EXCHANGE RATE may appreciate, thereby producing a CAPITAL GAIN.

By contrast, a CAPITAL OUTFLOW is the outward movement of funds from one country to other countries for the kinds of reasons listed above. See FOREIGN INVESTMENT.

capitalist economy see ECONOMY.

capital intensiveness the extent to which capital (plant, equipment, etc.) is used in the PRODUCTION of goods and services. Where capital is relatively cheap and labour is comparatively expensive, then firms will be inclined to use large amounts of capital in their production processes and automate (see AUTOMATION) their production.

See CAPITAL LABOUR RATIO.

Compare LABOUR INTENSIVENESS.

capitalization issue *or* **scrip issue**, the issue by a JOINT-STOCK COMPANY of additional SHARES to existing SHAREHOLDERS without any further payment being required. Capitalization issues are usually made when a company has ploughed back profits over several years and so has accumulated substantial RESERVES, or has revalued its fixed assets and accumulated capital reserves. If the company wishes to capitalize the reserves it can do so by creating extra shares to match the reserves, and issue them as BONUS SHARES to existing shareholders in proportion to their existing shareholdings. In the USA the term *stock dividend* is used to describe this same process. See also RETAINED PROFIT.

capitalization rate the rate at which the STOCK MARKET capitalizes the current earnings of a company. It is calculated by dividing a company's earnings per ordinary share by the current market price per ordinary share in order to arrive at the EARNINGS YIELD.

capitalizing the process of converting an expense into an equivalent capital sum, carrying forward that expense as a FIXED ASSET in the BALANCE SHEET of a firm rather than writing off that expense as a current cost. Capitalization is applied to expenditure on assets that have been acquired for use in the business for periods in excess of a year and which are not for resale, for example motor vehicles, plant, machinery, equipment, land and buildings, patents, goodwill, trademarks, brands etc.

capital labour ratio the proportion of CAPITAL to LABOUR inputs in a company. This can be measured by means of a number of accounting ratios. One measure is total assets per pound of employee remuneration: the higher the ratio (the more capital per pound of labour cost), the greater the degree of capital intensity. Alternatively, we could take FIXED ASSETS per employee, or more narrowly plant and machinery per employee, as an index of the degree of mechanization in a firm. Where a company employs a high proportion of part-time workers, numbers employed may need to be adjusted to full-time equivalent numbers to assist comparability. Alternatively, assets may be expressed as a proportion of total employee remuneration.

capital loss the deficit realized when an ASSET (house, SHARE, etc.) is sold at a lower price than was originally paid for it. Compare CAPITAL GAIN.

capital market see STOCK MARKET.

capital outflow a movement of funds out of a particular country into one or more foreign countries, representing, on the one hand, investments by individuals, companies and institutions and by government in foreign physical assets and financial securities, and on the other hand, the provision of borrowing facilities and loans to foreigners. See CAPITAL INFLOW, FOREIGN INVESTMENT, FOREIGN DIRECT INVESTMENT, BALANCE OF PAYMENTS.

capital rationing a situation where a firm selects an annual capital budget which is less than the amount required to undertake all INVESTMENTS promising a rate of return in excess of the cost of capital. For example, if a firm requires a minimum 20% return on any investment then *all* of the appropriate investment opportunities available to the firm which promise a return of 20% or more may involve a total expenditure of, say, £10 million. However, if the firm decides that it is willing to spend only £6 million, then it must rank investment opportunities in descending order of rate of return, undertaking those with the highest promised return and rejecting others even though the latter opportunities promise a re- turn greater than the 20% cost of capital. The firm is said to be in a situation of capital rationing because it is investing less than the amount dictated by usual profit maximizing criteria. See CAPITAL BUDGETING, INVESTMENT APPRAISAL.

capital reserves see RESERVES.

capital servicing cost interest paid on long-term and medium-term loan capital, and on overdrafts.

capital stock the total amount of capital GOODS (plant, offices, machinery and equipment) currently available to a firm or an economy with which to produce goods and services. The firm's/economy's capital stock requires maintaining by INVESTMENT to replace worn out or obsolete capital items (see DEPRECIATION) but more importantly, the size of the capital stock can be increased over time by new investment. Capital formation or accumulation plays a crucial role in expanding the firm's/economy's productive capacity and hence its ability to sustain a high rate of business growth and ECONOMIC GROWTH.

capital structure the composition of a JOINT-STOCK COMPANY's long-term capital which reflects the source of that capital, for example SHARE CAPITAL and long-term LOAN CAPITAL. See CAPITAL GEARING.

capital transfer tax see INHERITANCE TAX.

CAPP (computer-aided process planning) see COMPUTER-AIDED DESIGN.

captive product a product which needs to be bought on a continuing basis once a main product has been bought in order to operate the main product; for example films for a camera. See CAPTIVE PRODUCT PRICING.

captive product pricing the PRICING of a CAPTIVE PRODUCT. When a supplier's main product and captive product are unique (i.e. there is no interchangeability with competing products), the supplier may choose to charge a low price for the main product to encourage people to buy it, with the objective of thereafter making the bulk of his profits from continuing sales of captive products.

career break an interruption to an individual's career for the purpose of childcare or achievement of personal goals outside work. Some organizations now allow staff to take career breaks of several years' duration without loss of seniority or occupational position. It can be a way of reducing LABOUR TURNOVER and tackling DISCRIMINATION against female employees.

cargo see FREIGHT.

carousel a closed loop conveying system frequently used between final store and loading bay. Used in some airports for the final distribution of passenger luggage after discharge from the aircraft.

cartel a form of COLLUSION between a group of suppliers aimed at suppressing competition between themselves, wholly or in part. Cartels can take a number of forms. For example, suppliers may set up a sole selling agency which buys up their individual output at an agreed price and arranges for the marketing of these products on a coordinated basis. Another form is where suppliers operate an agreement (see RESTRICTIVE TRADE AGREEMENT) which sets uniform selling prices for their products, thereby suppressing price competition, but with suppliers then competing for market share through PRODUCT DIFFERENTIATION strategies. A more comprehensive version of a cartel is the application not only of common selling prices and joint marketing, but also of restrictions on production involving the assignment of specific output quotas to individual suppliers, and the making of coordinated capacity adjustments, thereby either removing over-capacity or extending capacity on a coordinated basis.

Cartels are usually established either to exploit the joint marketing power of suppliers to extract MONOPOLY profits, or as a means of preventing cutthroat competition from forcing firms to operate at a loss, often resorted to in times of depressed demand (a so-called 'crisis cartel').

A number of factors are crucial to the successful operation of a cartel, in particular the participation of all significant suppliers of the product and their full compliance with the policies of the cartel. Nonparticipation of some key suppliers and 'cheating' by cartel

	January £	*February* £	*March* £	*etc.*
Opening Balance	3,000	(2,000)	4,000	
Add Inflows				
cash sales	5,000	6,000	5,500	
collections on credit sales	15,000	17,000	16,000	
sale of short-term investments	–	4,000	–	
Total inflows	20,000	27,000	21,500	
Less Outflows				
payments to materials suppliers	6,000	5,000	7,000	
payments of wages	8,000	8,500	9,500	
interest and dividend payments	4,500	500	500	
expenditure on plant and equipment	6,500	7,000	2,000	
Total outflows	25,000	21,000	19,000	
Excess of Inflows over Overflows				
(Outflows over Inflows)	(5,000)	6,000	2,500	
Closing Balance	(2,000)	4,000	6,500	

Fig. 17 **Cash budget** *or* **cash flow forecast.** A typical example.

members, together with the ability of buyers to switch to substitute products, may well serve to undermine a cartel's ability to control prices. In many countries, most notably the US, UK and EUROPEAN UNION, cartels concerned with price fixing, market sharing and restrictions on production and capacity are prohibited by law. See COMPETITION POLICY, ORGANIZATION OF PETROLEUM EXPORTING COUNTRIES (OPEC).

case law see COMMON LAW.

cash see CURRENCY.

cash account *or* **cash book** a LEDGER account which records all of a company's cash incomings and outgoings. See ACCOUNTING.

cash and carry a form of wholesaling which requires customers (predominantly RETAILERS) to pay cash for products bought and to collect these products themselves from a warehouse. By eliminating the costs involved in offering credit terms and a delivery service, such WHOLESALERS are able to offer products at highly-competitive prices. See DISTRIBUTION CHANNEL.

cash book see CASH ACCOUNT.

cash budget *or* **cash flow forecast** an accounting statement which analyses expected cash receipts and payments over forthcoming trading periods with a view to anticipating any potential cash shortages or surpluses before they arise and thus allow appropriate remedial action to be taken. This action could take the form of tightened CREDIT CONTROL to get cash in from customers more quickly, or arranging short-term loans in advance to cover an expected cash shortage, or plans to invest profitably any expected cash surplus. Fig. 17 shows a typical cash budget. See BUDGET, BUDGETING, BUDGETARY CONTROL.

cash card see COMMERCIAL BANK.

cash cow see BOSTON MATRIX.

cash discount a reduction in the total amount of money owed by a customer to a supplier in return for prompt payment. Cash discounts are offered by suppliers as a means of persuading customers to pay for their CREDIT purchases more quickly and thereby improve the supplier's CASH FLOW.

cash equivalents short-term investments and advances which can be quickly converted into cash.

cash flow the money coming into a business from sales and other receipts and going out of the businesses in the form of cash payments to suppliers, workers, etc. Cash

	Buy	*Sell*	*Profit* £	*Cash flow* £	*Difference*
Cash purchase Cash sale	10 units (cash) –£50	10 units (cash) +£100	50	50 (–50+100)	
Cash purchase Credit sale	10 units (cash) –£50	10 units (credit) +£0	50	–50 (–50+0)	*Debtors £100*
Credit purchase Cash sale	10 units (credit) –£0	10 units (cash) +£100	50	100 (–0+100)	*Creditors £50*
Purchases exceed Sales	12 units (cash) –£60	10 units (cash) +£100	50	40 (–60+100)	*Stock £10*

Fig. 18 **Cash flow.** A trader sells 10 units at £10 each will cost £5 each.
Sales: 10 x £10 = £100
Cost: 10 x £5 = £50
Profit: 10 x £5 = £50

receipts and cash payments in a trading period are not necessarily the same as the accounting revenues and cost applicable to that same period, because customers need not pay cash for goods sold until some time afterwards while the firm may not pay for materials and services used until afterwards. Fig. 18 overleaf shows the main causes of disparities between cash flow and profit. See SOURCES AND USES OF FUNDS STATEMENT.

cash flow exposure see EXCHANGE RATE EXPOSURE.

cash flow forecast see CASH BUDGET.

cash flow statement a statement which is included as part of a UK company's published annual report and accounts. The one used in the UK in 2002 is prepared in accordance with the provisions of FRS 1 (*Financial Reporting Standard 1*). This shows where the finance came from and where it went out to during the period under review and helps to explain the movements in the cash and bank balances, as illustrated in Fig. 19. See also, FUNDS FLOW ANALYSIS, SOURCES AND USES OF FUNDS STATEMENTS.

cash on delivery (COD) an arrangement whereby goods previously ordered are paid for when delivered.

cash settlement purchases of FINANCIAL SECURITIES which have to be paid for immediately rather than being settled after the end of the stock exchange ACCOUNT PERIOD.

catalogue shopping see MAIL ORDER.

catalogue showroom a means of retailing products from premises displaying catalogues from which consumers purchase products for immediate collection and payment. See RETAILER, RETAIL OUTLET. Contrast with MAIL ORDER.

category discounter *or* **killer** a RETAILER or WHOLESALER which sells an extensive range of a *particular* product category at low, 'discounted' prices on a SELF SERVICE basis. Toys–R–Us is a prominent discounter of toy products. See DISTRIBUTION CHANNEL, DISCOUNT STORE.

Cash flow statement for year ended 31 December 20xx

	£m	£m
Net cash flow from operating activities		60
Returns on investments, and the servicing of finance:		
Dividends received	4	
Dividends paid	(8)	
Interest paid	(6)	(10)
		50
Taxation		
Tax paid		(18)
		32
Investing activities:		
Purchase of tangible fixed assets	(22)	
Sale of tangible fixed assets	5	
Proceeds from sale of trade investments	nil	(17)
		15
Financing:		
Proceeds from new share capital	56	
Repayment of borrowings	(36)	20
Increase (or decrease) in cash and cash equivalents		**35**

Fig. 19 **FRS 1 cash flow statement.**

category management the management of BRANDS in a group, portfolio or category with specific emphasis on the retail trade's requirements.

cause and effect analysis a technique used in the control of QUALITY in which all possible causes of defective production are investigated. Its purpose is to detect causes of defects and to take any necessary corrective action to prevent a recurrence of the problem. See FISHBONE CHART.

caveat emptor 'let the buyer beware': a situation where a supplier of a good or service is under no legal obligation to inform buyers of any defects or deficiencies in the products supplied. It is thus the responsibility of buyers to determine for themselves whether or not the product is satisfactory. Compare CAVEAT VENDOR.

caveat vendor 'let the seller beware': a situation where a supplier of a good or service is legally obliged to inform buyers of any defects in the product. Compare CAVEAT EMPTOR.

CBI see CONFEDERATION OF BRITISH INDUSTRY.

CCT see COMPETITIVE TENDERING.

celebrity endorsement a form of ADVERTISING in which a well-known sports or media person is used to endorse a product.

cell an independent team of operatives who work together in a CELLULAR MANUFACTURING production environment.

cellular layout a defined work space (work centre) where multiple operations may be carried out by one or a group of individual(s). See CELLULAR MANUFACTURING, AUTONOMOUS WORK TEAMS, AUTONOMOUS PRODUCTION.

cellular manufacturing *or* **group technology** a means of obtaining the benefits of PROCESS-FOCUSED LAYOUT and PRODUCT-FOCUSED LAYOUT by seeking similarities within tasks, jobs, products and processes. These are identified and formed into families and the resources required are formed into 'groups' or 'cells'. The net effect is to reduce work in progress, set up times and throughput times as well as creating better social relationships amongst employees using the system. The technique relies on a coding system (see PARTS FAMILY CODING AND CLASSIFICATION SYSTEMS). The components need not be for the same product but will all be worked on in the same cell.

Cellular manufacturing applications have the following characteristics:

groups are team oriented, groups produce or carry out a specific 'family' or set of tasks or products, groups are equipped with a specific set of equipment solely for the use of the group, equipment is located in one area – the cell, the workers within the group share a specific target and the group operates as independently as possible self assigning workloads within the cell. See LEAN MANUFACTURING.

census a survey carried out by a government department to obtain economic and social data which can be used in the formulation of social and industrial policies. In the UK a *production census* is conducted yearly to provide information on industrial production, employment, exports, capital investment etc.; a *population census* is carried out every ten years to obtain data on demographic trends.

Central Arbitration Committee a UK body with power to arbitrate in cases where employers contest the legal right of TRADE UNIONS to receive information relevant to COLLECTIVE BARGAINING and where unions claim that pay structures are discriminatory. Since 2000 it has overseen the STATUTORY UNION RECOGNITION PROCEDURE. See ARBITRATION, DISCLOSURE OF INFORMATION, DISCRIMINATION.

central bank a country's leading BANK generally responsible for overseeing the BANKING SYSTEM, acting as a 'clearing' banker for the COMMERCIAL BANKS (SEE CLEARING HOUSE SYSTEM) and for implementing MONETARY POLICY. In addition, many central banks are responsible for handling the government's budgetary accounts and for managing the country's external monetary affairs, in particular the EXCHANGE RATE.

Examples of central banks include the USA's Federal Reserve, Germany's Deutsche

Bundesbank, France's Banque de France and the European Union's EUROPEAN CENTRAL BANK. (For a more detailed discussion of a central bank's activities see the BANK OF ENGLAND entry).

centralization the vertical dimension of ORGANIZATION structure. Organizations are centralized when important decisions are largely taken by managers at the top of the organization. There is a persistent tension between DECENTRALIZATION and centralization organizations. Centralization of decisions is useful to provide central direction to the organization. However, it can mean that the organization cannot respond quickly to PRODUCT MARKET developments. Also, if lower level managers are precluded from making important decisions it can have negative effects on their job satisfaction. See ORGANIZATIONAL ANALYSIS.

centrally-planned economy see ECONOMY.

Central Processing Unit see CPU.

Central Statistical Office see Office for National Statistics.

centre for inter-firm comparisons a non-profit-making organization which collects and processes data from subscribing firms and provides them with a useful range of ACCOUNTING RATIOS for assessing their comparative financial performance, and in so doing, maintains a high level of confidentiality.

certainty equivalent see DECISION TREE.

certificate a document signifying ownership of a FINANCIAL SECURITY (STOCK, SHARE etc.). In the UK such certificates are issued in the name of the person or company recorded in the company's register of SHAREHOLDERS as the owner of these shares, new certificates being issued to buyers when shares are sold. In countries like the USA where BEARER BONDS are used, stock certificates merely note the number of stocks or shares represented and do not include the name of the owner, the holder of the certificate being presumed to be the owner.

certificate of deposit a FINANCIAL SECURITY issued by BANKS, BUILDING SOCIETIES and other financial institutions as a means of borrowing money for periods ranging from one month to five years. Once issued, certificates of deposit may be bought and sold on the MONEY MARKET and are redeemable on their maturity for their face value plus accrued interest.

certificate of incorporation a certificate issued by the REGISTRAR OF COMPANIES to a new JOINT-STOCK COMPANY whose MEMORANDUM OF ASSOCIATION and ARTICLES OF ASSOCIATION are acceptable to the Registrar. A company starts its legal existence from the date of its incorporation and thereafter is able to enter into CONTRACTS in its own name.

certificate of origin a document used to authenticate the country of origin of internationally traded goods. Most trading countries are prepared to accept certificates of origin issued by government departments of their trade partners or their appointees (CHAMBERS OF COMMERCE in the UK). However, complications as to their precise country of origin often arise in the case of goods which are assembled in one country using components which are in the main imported from other countries. See LOCAL CONTENT RULE, EXPORTING.

certification 1 a means of recording the details of a transaction in SHARES involving noting on the TRANSFER DEED that the SHARE CERTIFICATE has been placed with the company or its representative. Certification is necessary where a seller is not selling all of his shareholding or where a block of shares are bought by more than one person to enable new share certificates to be issued which reflect the new ownership of the shares.

2 a status granted by a manufacturer to a supplier which is able to demonstrate that it is able to achieve consistent QUALITY in the materials or components it supplies. The materials or components supplied by a certified supplier can be used directly by the manufacturer without the need for INSPECTION of these items. See QUALITY CONTROL.

Certification Officer the UK officer responsible for overseeing the accounts of TRADE UNIONS and EMPLOYERS'

ASSOCIATIONS, and ensuring that unions observe the statutory procedures relating to POLITICAL FUNDS, mergers between unions, and ballots to elect union executive members.

chain of command the line of command flowing down from the top of an ORGANIZATION to the bottom. In theory, the chief executive issues commands to his or her subordinates which are then relayed down to those they have AUTHORITY over. In practice, those in the chain of command often do not follow such commands, either because they do not have the resources to meet them or because they believe them to be incorrect or otherwise inappropriate. See UNITY OF COMMAND, LINE AND STAFF, HIERARCHY.

chain store a multibranch retail business. All types of RETAILER, ranging from SPECIALIST SHOPS to SUPERMARKETS can be organized to take advantage of the growth and competitive opportunities deriving from large-scale operations. Unlike single-shop concerns, chain stores, by operating a network of stores each located strategically in catchment areas serving large populations, are in a position to expand their sales potential. Moreover, by selling the same general range of products in all of their stores and utilizing a central buying system, chain stores are able to secure BULK BUYING price discounts from manufacturers. In addition, the larger chain stores have found it advantageous to establish their 'OWN LABEL' BRANDS as a means of maximizing the group's sales potential. See DISTRIBUTION CHANNEL.

chairperson 1 a person who organizes and runs a committee, drawing up the agenda for each committee meeting, ensuring the orderly conduct of the meeting and approving the minutes or records of the meeting.

2 a person who organizes and runs the BOARD OF DIRECTORS of a JOINT STOCK COMPANY. See DIRECTOR.

Chamber of Commerce an organization which operates primarily to serve the needs of the business community in an industrial city or area. Chambers of Commerce provide a forum for local businessmen and traders to discuss matters of mutual interest and provide a range of services to their members, especially small businesses, including, for example in the UK, information on business opportunities locally and nationally and, in conjunction with the DEPARTMENT OF TRADE AND INDUSTRY, export advisory services, export market intelligence, participation in overseas visits and trade fairs, and the issue of CERTIFICATES OF ORIGIN. In recent years, a particular concern of many chambers has been the provision of training facilities and centres, run either independently or in conjunction with the government's LEARNING AND SKILLS COUNCILS. At the national level the movement is represented by the Association of British Chambers of Commerce. See EXPORTING, TRAINING.

changeover cost see SET-UP COST.

channel the means of physically distributing a product from the producer to the ultimate customer. See DISTRIBUTION CHANNEL.

channel integration the way in which the businesses in a CHANNEL are linked together. See DISTRIBUTION CHANNEL.

channel intermediaries businesses (WHOLESALERS, RETAILERS) which facilitate the distribution of products to customers. See DISTRIBUTION CHANNEL.

channel of distribution see DISTRIBUTION CHANNEL.

channel strategy the selection of the most effective DISTRIBUTION CHANNEL, the most appropriate level of distribution intensity and the degree of channel integration.

chargeable gain see CAPITAL GAINS TAX.

charismatic authority see AUTHORITY.

Charities (Accounts and Reports) Regulations UK legislation requiring all charities that are not companies to state in their accounts whether or not they have been prepared in accordance with accounting standards.

Chartered Association of Certified Accountants (ACCA) a large UK body of accountants, some of whose members operate in professional practice (auditing, taxation, etc.), whilst others work in industry.

Chartered Institute of Management Accountants (CIMA) a large UK body of professional accountants whose members work primarily in industry undertaking MANAGEMENT ACCOUNTING work.

Chartered Institute of Marketing (CIM) the representative UK body for marketing professionals.

Chartered Institute of Personnel and Development (CIPD) the main UK body representing personnel managers and publicizing the benefits of effective PERSONNEL MANAGEMENT. It operates a system of training and examination of personnel managers so as to promote professional standards of personnel work. Currently it has over 100,000 members. See PROFESSIONAL, HUMAN RESOURCE MANAGEMENT.

Chartermark see CITIZENS' CHARTER.

chartism the monitoring of price movements of financial securities such as STOCKS and SHARES and FOREIGN CURRENCIES as a means of indicating appropriate buying and selling positions. See SHARE PRICE INDEX, STOCK MARKET, FOREIGN EXCHANGE MARKET.

check-off agreement an agreement between EMPLOYER and TRADE UNION, enabling the employer to deduct the union membership subscription ('union dues') from employees' pay (with their consent) and pass them to the union as a lump sum. This is a more efficient method of collecting membership fees than the traditional method whereby shop stewards or officials collected union dues in cash from each member each week. After legislative restrictions in the 1990s, many union members now pay their union dues directly to the union by direct debit. See CLOSED SHOP.

cheque a means of transferring or withdrawing money from a BANK or BUILDING SOCIETY current account. In the former case, the drawer of a cheque creates a written instruction to his bank or building society to transfer funds to some other person's or company's bank or building society account (the 'payee'). In the latter case, money may be withdrawn in cash by a person or company writing out a cheque payable to themselves. See COMMERCIAL BANK.

cheque card see COMMERCIAL BANK.

chief executive the person who has overall responsibility for the MANAGEMENT of a firm. In a JOINT-STOCK COMPANY the chief executive is usually the full-time managing director, or the full-time executive chairman appointed by the BOARD OF DIRECTORS.

chinese wall the segregation of the related activities of a financial institution in order to protect the interests of its clients. For example, a stock market firm could be responsible for 'making a market' in a particular share (see MARKET MAKER),' while at the same time offering investment advice to clients to purchase this share, bringing with it the danger that the advice given will not be impartial.

cif see COST, INSURANCE AND FREIGHT.

CIM see COMPUTER-INTEGRATED MANUFACTURING, CHARTERED INSTITUTE OF MARKETING.

CIMA see CHARTERED INSTITUTE OF MANAGEMENT ACCOUNTANTS.

CIPD see CHARTERED INSTITUTE OF PERSONNEL AND DEVELOPMENT.

circles see QUALITY CIRCLES.

circulating capital another way of describing WORKING CAPITAL which stresses how stock, debtors and cash circulate continuously through the business, as raw materials stocks are converted into finished goods stocks, sold to customers who become debtors, then are converted back to cash as the debtors pay, making funds available to buy yet more raw materials stock and so on.

Citizens' Charter an initiative launched by the UK government in 1991 to promote high-quality service delivery in the public services. The Charter sets out the government's view on what citizens should expect to get from public services. Public sector organizations are now encouraged to set public targets for service delivery e.g. that 90% of trains should arrive on time, and to communicate to the public the extent to which these targets are achieved. Those organizations judged by a government committee to have set and achieved targets which bring about significant improvements to services may be awarded a *Chartermark*. The philosophy behind the Charter is that public services do not experience the market pressures faced by commercial organizations and hence some mechanism like the Citizens' Charter is necessary to ensure responsiveness to consumers. See NEW PUBLIC MANAGEMENT.

City code on takeovers and mergers a regulatory system operated voluntarily by interested parties to the UK STOCK MARKET that lays down rules of good conduct governing the tactics and procedures used in TAKEOVERS and MERGERS. The general purpose of the code is to ensure that all SHAREHOLDERS (both the shareholders of the firm planning the takeover and those of the target firm) are treated equitably. For example, a potential bidder who has been acquiring shares in the open market is required to make a formal bid for all outstanding shares at a price not less than the highest price paid in the market over the previous 12 months, once his holding exceeds 30%. There are various other rules covering such areas as the accumulation of shares by several buyers acting together (see TAKEOVER BID). The City code is administered by the City panel on Takeovers and Mergers, which is responsible for formulating rules of practice and for investigating suspected cases of malpractice.

civil law legal arrangements whereby the State acts as an impartial judge of a dispute between two parties, the *plaintiff*, who sues and the *defendant*; the plaintiff usually requires *damages* which are a form of monetary compensation paid to him by the defendant. Civil law can be invoked for breach of CONTRACT or behaviour which constitutes a TORT and if the plaintiff wins his case he will receive damages to compensate him financially for the harm done to him by the defendant. As an alternative to damages the court may instead grant an injunction ordering the defendant to stop doing the act which is harming the plaintiff. Civil law judgements are enforced by the threat of imprisonment for contempt of court.

CKD (completely knocked down) a kit supplied either for self-assembly by a final customer (for example, a do-it-yourself kitchen flat pack) or for assembly by a firm as part of a manufacturing operation.

claimant count unemployment measure see UNEMPLOYMENT.

classical management theory the body of theory mainly associated with French mining engineer and manager Henri Fayol (1841–1925) but also with English army Colonel Lyndall Urwick (1891–1983). Common to all members of this school was an attempt to extrapolate from their practical experiences in management roles in large organizations a set of rules about how to manage effectively and efficiently. Fayol defined MANAGEMENT in terms of forecasting, planning, organizing, commanding, coordinating and controlling. To this end, management should function according to a set of principles which were valid whatever the ORGANIZATION's environment and goals. These included the principle of UNITY OF COMMAND, a clear HIERARCHY and JOB SPECIALIZATION. Fayol's analysis could be viewed as the first attempt to generate a theory of management and can be seen as a prescriptive version of Weber's ideal type of BUREAUCRACY. Compare CONTINGENCY THEORY.

clearing bank see COMMERCIAL BANK.

clearing house system a centralized mechanism for settling indebtedness between financial institutions involved in money transmission and dealers in commodities and financial securities. In the case of UK commercial banking, for example, the London Clearing House collates all of the many thousands of cheques drawn, transfers bank deposits from one bank to another, cross-cancels them, and calculates the net balances owing or receivable for each bank. The COMMERCIAL BANKS' balances at the Bank of England are then debited or credited as appropriate. A similar 'clearing' function is performed in the commodities and financial securities market by, for example, the International Commodities Clearing House and the London Financial Futures Exchange and TAURUS. See FINANCIAL SERVICES ACT 1986, FINANCIAL SYSTEM, BANKING SYSTEM, COMMODITY MARKET, STOCK MARKET, FORWARD MARKET.

clerical work measurement a technique for measuring and controlling clerical work. It involves setting targets or standards for clerical activities such as filing and typing against which actual clerical outputs can be assessed. See STANDARD TIME, WORK MEASUREMENT.

client a BUYER of a professional SERVICE.

clock card a document on which an employee records the precise time at which he or she arrives to start work and departs at the end of the work period. Such time records are used to check on employees' punctuality and to calculate wages due where employees are paid on a time basis. See FLEXITIME.

close company a JOINT-STOCK COMPANY which is under the control of five or fewer larger SHAREHOLDERS or directors.

closed shop a requirement that all employees in a given workplace or organization be members of a specified TRADE UNION. There are two types of closed shop:

(a) *pre-entry closed shop*, where union membership is necessary to gain employment;

(b) *post-entry closed shop*, where union membership is necessary once employment has commenced.

The pre-entry closed shop, traditionally found in parts of the printing and food wholesaling industries, was often unilaterally imposed by unions, whereas the post-entry closed shop has often been formally recognized in Union Membership Agreements with managements. Many managers found the post-entry closed shop advantageous since it helped to ensure that union representatives speak for all employees. However, it can be viewed as an infringement of individual rights. See CONTRACT OF EMPLOYMENT.

closed union see TRADE UNION.

closing off the process of listing all the balances in the LEDGERS and CASH ACCOUNT of a firm after the TRIAL BALANCE. PROFIT AND LOSS ACCOUNT and BALANCE SHEET have been completed. It ensures that all the balances have been carried forward to the next accounting period before any more transactions are recorded or posted. See ACCOUNTING.

closing price the price of a STOCK or SHARE ruling at the close of the day's trading on the STOCK MARKET.

closing rate method see FOREIGN CURRENCY TRANSLATION.

COBOL (Common Business Orientated Language) a COMPUTER programming language used for business applications.

COD see CASH ON DELIVERY.

code of practice a set of guidelines used to encourage desirable patterns of behaviour but which generally lack any formal sanctions to punish inappropriate behaviour. Often codes of practice are developed as an alternative to legal regulation. For instance, companies engaged in food production might develop a code of practice between them to define hygiene standards, possibly to forestall government action in this area. Critics of this voluntaristic approach to regulation argue that they provide insufficient deterrents to wrong-doing. However, codes of practice are sometimes developed by official agencies and whilst not legally binding they are taken into account by courts in any legal action in the area covered by the code. For instance, employer adherence to the guidelines in the ADVISORY, CONCILIATION AND ARBITRATION SERVICE's code of practice on DISCIPLINARY PROCEDURES is often an issue in UNFAIR DISMISSAL cases. Where the employer fails to follow the code the tribunal may award against the employer.

co-determination the German form of INDUSTRIAL DEMOCRACY in which all companies with more than 2000 employees are required to have an equal number of employee and shareholder representatives n the upper tier of a two-tier board of directors. However, full parity representation is not achieved (except in the coal and steel industries) because the chairperson, nominated by the shareholders, has a casting vote. In enterprises of 500-2000 employees one-third of the seats on the supervisory board are reserved for employee representatives. Employee representatives are nominated by the Works Council, elected by all employees in the company. These Councils have the legal right to co-determine with management methods and changes in WORK organization, hours of work, payments by results, HEALTH AND SAFETY regulations and discipline. To support them in this activity Works Councils have the right to DISCLOSURE OF INFORMATION from management. The Works Council system is formally separate from TRADE UNION representation but in practice union representatives are often deeply involved in the Works Council system. See BULLOCK REPORT, FIFTH DIRECTIVE, WORKER DIRECTOR, EUROPEAN WORKS COUNCIL.

coding system a numerical or alpha-numerical referencing system which is used to identify specific factor inputs and costs within a business. Code numbers (reference numbers) can be used for many purposes, for instance to identify STOCK items and for the allocation of costs to COST CENTRES.

coinage metal coins made of brass, nickels etc., issued by a country's CENTRAL BANK which constitute the 'low value' or 'small change' component of the MONEY SUPPLY. See CURRENCY.

cold calling a method of selling products which involves a business making unsolicited approaches to potential customers by door-to-door visits by SALES REPRESENTATIVES, TELEPHONE SELLING or DIRECT MAIL.

collateral security an ASSET which a BORROWER is required to deposit with, or pledge to, a LENDER as a condition of obtaining a LOAN, which can be sold off if the loan is not repaid. For example, a bank may require a borrower to hand over the title deeds to his house as collateral for a BANK LOAN, or a company may issue DEBENTURE stock as a means of obtaining loan capital, which is secured by a charge on the company's business assets.

collective agreement see COLLECTIVE BARGAINING, MULTI EMPLOYER AGREEMENT.

collective bargaining NEGOTIATION between employers or managers and representatives of the workforce to determine rates of pay (see WAGE), conditions of employment, etc. The desired outcome of collective bargaining is a collective agreement between the parties. In the UK these agreements have no legal force (see VOLUNTARISM) and, except where they incorporate statutory requirements, there are no legal sanctions that can be used if one party chooses to break the agreement. It is now customary in the UK for collective bargaining over pay rates to take place annually, though some employers have recently sought collective agreements of a longer duration. Collective bargaining usually takes place in accordance with procedures which are themselves generally established through bargaining (see PROCEDURAL AGREEMENT). Although there are no conclusive figures, it is reliably estimated that currently around a third of the employed labour force in the UK have their pay and conditions determined by collective bargaining.

Contrasts can be drawn between two fundamentally different approaches to collective bargaining. *Distributive bargaining* is where one side's gain is seen as the other's loss. The money to be distributed as a result of this bargaining process is essentially seen as a 'cake' of a fixed size. This sort of bargaining is inevitably adversarial as each side seeks to minimize the concessions it makes to the other. In *integrative bargaining*, by contrast, the parties seek ways of increasing the size of cake. For instance, the money available for wage increases could be enlarged by agreeing changes to working practices. This approach therefore tends to be more cooperative in character.

In the UK, integrative bargaining is more widely known as productivity bargaining. This involves employers offering to improve pay or conditions of employment in return for the relaxation by the workforce and trade union of DEMARCATION LINES, 'RESTRICTIVE

LABOUR PRACTICES' and other restraints on the efficient utilization of labour (see LABOUR FLEXIBILITY). SOCIAL PARTNERSHIP, whereby employers and unions agree to flexibility in return for job security, is a form of integrative bargaining. Productivity bargaining enjoyed renewed popularity in the 1980s because of the imperative for many firms to secure improvements in productivity. An alternative approach known as *concession bargaining* also occurred in the 1980s. Whereas productivity bargaining trades extra payments for changes in working practices, this form involves no offer of payment, management arguing instead that unemployment will result if changes are not agreed. It can, therefore, involve a more confrontational approach and can be viewed as a form of distributive bargaining.

To compare patterns of collective bargaining between firms, various dimensions of collective bargaining are used in INDUSTRIAL RELATIONS analysis:

(a) *extent of bargaining:* the proportion of employees who are covered by collective agreements;

(b) *bargaining depth:* the extent to which workforce representatives are involved in the administration of agreements achieved through collective bargaining;

(c) *bargaining scope:* the range of issues which are subject to bargaining;

(d) *bargaining level:* the level of an industry at which bargaining takes place (see below);

(e) *bargaining unit:* the occupations which are covered by an agreement. There may be one bargaining unit – covering an entire workforce in a plant or industry – or separate units for different categories of employee.

These dimensions taken together are said to form the *bargaining structure.*

Industrial relations research in the UK has been especially concerned with the level of bargaining over pay. Three levels are most important:

(a) *industry-wide or multi-employer bargaining:* where representatives of all or most employers in a particular industry and TRADE UNION negotiate pay rates for employees in that industry. See EMPLOYERS' ASSOCIATION, MULTI-EMPLOYER AGREEMENT;

(b) *company or single employer bargaining:* where head office managers in a firm and either SHOP STEWARDS or trade union officials negotiate pay rates for employees at all locations of the company;

(c) *plant, decentralized or workplace bargaining:* where shop stewards bargain on behalf of employees at a particular plant or workplace with managers at that plant.

Broadly speaking, there has been a trend in UK industry away from industry-wide bargaining to company and plant bargaining.

In practice the structure of bargaining in the UK is highly complex. Collective bargaining on behalf of a given set of employees may occur at more than one level. Some issues may be determined in industry-wide bargaining, others by plant bargaining, whilst particular issues may be subject to negotiations at more than one level. Where collective bargaining breaks down, the parties may refer the issue to a third party for ARBITRATION. If this is not done it is possible that a STRIKE or some other form of INDUSTRIAL ACTION could occur. See SINGLE TABLE BARGAINING.

collective labour law see LABOUR LAW.

Collective Redundancies Directive see REDUNDANCY.

collectivism the philosophy that society is composed of groups or classes of people, each with its own interests, and that social CONFLICT stems largely from conflicts of interest between them. To achieve general wellbeing, policy makers should seek to balance group interests. Political action to advance the claims of disadvantaged groups and to regulate the actions of individuals is generally viewed as desirable by those subscribing to this philosophy. TRADE UNIONS are often viewed as vehicles of collectivism in that they represent and advance group interests. Critics of this philosophy argue that it subsumes the unique interests of each individual. See INDIVIDUALISM.

collusion the deliberate suppression of competition between themselves by a group of rival suppliers. Collusion may be confined to a single area of business activity, for example prices, or cover a wider range of limitations including coordinated marketing, production and capacity adjustments. Collusion may be practised through formalized arrangements specifying obligations (either in writing or orally) and institutional mechanisms for coordinating behaviour, as in a CARTEL or ANTI-COMPETITIVE AGREEMENT/ RESTRICTIVE TRADE AGREEMENT, or operated by more informal means through, for example, an INFORMATION AGREEMENT or CONCERTED PRACTICE.

The purpose of collusion may be to monopolize jointly the supply of a product in order to extract MONOPOLY profits, or it may be a defensive response to poor trading conditions, seeking to prevent prices from dropping to uneconomic levels. Because, however, of its generally adverse effects on market efficiency (cushioning inefficient, high-cost suppliers), and because it deprives buyers of the benefits of competition (particularly lower prices), collusion is usually prohibited outright, by COMPETITION POLICY, as in the UK, under the COMPETITION ACT 1998.

combine committee a committee of TRADE UNION representatives, usually SHOP STEWARDS, drawn from a number of plants in a company with the objective of coordinating pressure (for example to improve pay) on the management of the company. Combine committees are rarely effective in the long term because it is often difficult to identify all the plants in a company and because the interests of workers between plants are often divergent (especially where there is plant-level COLLECTIVE BARGAINING).

combined code see CORPORATE GOVERNANCE.

commercial bank *or* clearing bank

A BANK which accepts deposits of money from persons and businesses and provides them with a payments transmission service and various saving and loan facilities.

Commercial banking in the UK is conducted on the basis of an interlocking branch network system, which caters for local and regional needs as well as allowing the major banks such as Barclays, Lloyds, NatWest and the HSBC to cover the national market. Increasingly, the leading banks have globalized their operations to provide traditional banking services to international companies as well as diversifying (see DIVERSIFICATION) into a range of related financial services such as the provision of MORTGAGES, INSURANCE and UNIT TRUST investment.

Bank deposits are of two types:

(a) *sight deposits*, or *current account* deposits, which are withdrawable on demand and which are used by depositors to finance day-to-day personal and business transactions as well as to pay regular commitments such as instalment credit repayments. Most banks now pay interest on outstanding current account balances;

(b) *time deposits*, or *deposit accounts*, which are usually withdrawable subject to some notice being given to the bank and which are held as a form of personal and corporate saving and to finance irregular, 'one-off' payments.

Interest is payable on deposit accounts, normally at rates above those paid on current accounts, in order to encourage clients to deposit money for longer periods of time, thereby providing the bank with a more stable financial base.

Customers requiring to draw on their bank deposits may do so in a number of ways; direct cash withdrawals are still popular and have been augmented by the use of *cheque/cash cards* for greater convenience (i.e. cheque/cash cards can be used to draw cash from a dispensing machine outside normal business hours). However, the greater proportion of banking transactions are undertaken by *cheque* and CREDIT CARD payments and by such facilities as *standing orders* and *direct debits*. Some of these services, like cheque payments for customers in current account surplus, are provided free, while for others a small charge is made. Payment by cheque is the commonest form of non-cash payment involving the drawer detailing the person or business to receive payment and authorizing his bank to make payment by signing the cheque, with the recipient then depositing the cheque with his own bank. Cheques are 'cleared' through an inter-bank CLEARING HOUSE SYSTEM with customers' accounts being debited and credited as appropriate. Credit cards enable a client of the bank to make a number of individual purchases of goods and services on CREDIT over a particular period of time which are then settled by a single debit to the person's current account, or, alternatively, paid off on a loan basis (see below).

Under a standing order arrangement, a depositor instructs his bank to pay from his account a regular fixed sum of money into the account of a person or firm he is indebted to, again involving the respective debiting and crediting of the two accounts concerned. In the case of a direct debit, the customer authorizes the person or firm to whom he is indebted to arrange with his bank for the required regular payment to be transferred from the account.

Commercial banks have the dual objective of being able to meet money withdrawals on demand and of putting their resources to profitable use (i.e. they are in business to make profits for their shareholders). This influences the structure of their asset holdings. A proportion of the banks' funds are held in a highly liquid form (till money, 'call money' with the DISCOUNT MARKET, BILLS OF EXCHANGE and TREASURY BILLS) to cover short-term needs. The remaining funds are deployed in areas yielding a higher return, specifically portfolio investment, in particular government BONDS and corporate fixed interest securities such as DEBENTURES and, to a much greater extent, in the provision of *bank loans* (*bank advances*) to personal and corporate borrowers. Loans are used by personal borrowers to finance the purchase of a variety of products, while they are a major source of WORKING CAPITAL finance for businesses, covering the purchase of short-term assets such as the materials and components and the financing of work in progress and the stockholding of final products. Loans may be for a specified amount and made available for fixed periods of time at agreed rates of interest, or take the form of an *overdraft* facility where the person or firm can borrow as much as they require up to a prearranged total amount and is charged interest on outstanding balances. In recent years, the banks have introduced more flexible and varied loan arrangements for clients of suitable creditworthiness, which enables them to borrow money on a more or less continuous basis without the formality of having to make separate loan applications.

In recent times the commercial banks have been markedly affected by changes introduced by the FINANCIAL SERVICES ACT, 1986 which has allowed other financial institutions to set themselves up as 'financial supermarkets' offering customers a banking service and a wide range of personal financial products, including insurance, mortgages, personal pensions, unit trusts and individual savings accounts (ISAs) etc. This development has introduced a powerful new competitive impetus into the financial services industry breaking down traditional 'demarcation' boundaries in respect of 'who does what', allowing banks to 'cross sell' these services and products in competition with traditional providers such as the BUILDING SOCIETIES, INSURANCE COMPANIES, UNIT TRUSTS etc.

This and other developments (in particular, the globalization of investment banking) have in turn caused a number of structural changes. Intra and inter takeovers-mergers have occurred (e.g. The Lloyds-TSB Banks' tie-up and their takeover of Cheltenham and Gloucester building society); foreign banks have increasingly moved into the UK through either takeover (e.g. Hong Kong and Shanghai Banking Corp's takeover of the Midland Bank and Deutsche Bank's acquisition of Morgan Grenfell investment house) or setting up local offices; building societies such as the Abbey National, Woolwich and Halifax have converted themselves into banks. Direct banking services (via the telephone and the internet) have increasingly taken market share away from traditional branch networks. This has led to pressure on banks to cut costs by reducing the number of their branches. Another notable development has been the rapid rise in ATMs (automatic till machines, referred to popularly as 'hole in the wall' machines). See MONEY SUPPLY, BANKING SYSTEM, BANK OF ENGLAND, MONETARY POLICY, LOAN GUARANTEE SCHEME, VENTURE CAPITAL, SHARE PURCHASE/SALE.

commission 1 a payment to an AGENT or employee for performing particular services on behalf of a buyer or seller of a product, for example the sale of a financial security by a stockbroker (paid by the client); the sale of a car by a salesperson (paid by the garage owners). Commissions may be paid on a fixed or sliding scale basis related to the value of the transaction involved.

2 a body which acts as an official regulatory or administrative authority with respect to a specified activity. For example, the COMPETITION COMMISSION hears cases of monopolies, mergers and anticompetitive practices referred to it by the Office of Fair Trading under UK competition policy. The European Commission is the main body responsible for the day-to-day administration of the affairs of the EUROPEAN UNION.

Commission for Racial Equality see DISCRIMINATION.

commodity any economic GOOD but in commercial circles more specifically agricultural produce and minerals such as wheat, tea, copper, iron ore, etc. See COMMODITY MARKET, INTERNATIONAL COMMODITY AGREEMENT.

commodity broker see COMMODITY MARKET.

commodity market a MARKET for the buying and selling of agricultural produce and minerals such as coffee and tin. Commodity business is conducted through various inter-national commodity exchanges, some of the more prominent ones being based in London, for example the London Metal Exchange and the London International Financial Futures Exchange. Commodity markets provide an organizational framework for the establishment of market prices and 'clearing' deals between buyers and sellers (see CLEARING HOUSE SYSTEM). Commodity dealers and brokers act as intermediaries between buyers and sellers wishing to conclude immediate spot transactions (see SPOT MARKET) or to buy or sell forward (see FORWARD MARKET). See BALTIC MERCANTILE AND SHIPPING EXCHANGE, CORN EXCHANGE, EQUILIBRIUM MARKET PRICE.

commodity-type product a good or service which is highly standardized so that the offerings of competing suppliers are perceived by buyers as being virtually identical. Such products offer little scope for PRODUCT DIFFERENTIATION and are mainly sold on price. See PRODUCT LIFE-CYCLE.

Common Agricultural Policy the EUROPEAN UNION's programme for the subsidization and protection of the farm sector.

Common Business Orientated Language see COBOL.

common law *or* **case law** laws based upon the outcome of previous court cases which serve as a precedent in guiding the judgement of present court cases. Where important legal principles are involved in a particular court case, the plaintiff or defendant may appeal against the judgement of a court to a higher court such as the High Court and then the House of Lords in the UK and finally the European Court of Justice. Compare STATUTE LAW.

common market see TRADE INTEGRATION.

common stock a North American term for ORDINARY SHARES.

communication the exchange of information in an ORGANIZATION. For organizations to work effectively, it is vital that information be communicated to those who need it. For example, the pay department would not be able to function properly if it were not notified of employees' hours of work. In this sense organizations can be conceived of as systems for exchanging information. Withholding information, i.e. failure to communicate, can be an effective means of exerting power over others in the organization. If a manager is not fully aware of what is going on in the organization he or she may be unable to influence decisions or events.

Often the effective transmission of information is impeded. As a piece of information is passed from top to bottom of an organization it may be modified by the misinterpretation or bias of each individual involved, so that by the time the information reaches its final destination it has a very different content. Effective communication can also be time-consuming, and hence arduous to perform. However, the effort can be worthwhile since those employees who feel they are not fully informed about matters relevant to their job may become demotivated and dissatisfied. As a result performance suffers. There is also evidence that individuals are more likely to respect bosses who they feel keep them informed.

In addition to these 'behavioural' aspects of communication the *process* or 'technology' of internal and external communication has changed dramatically in the last decade. For example, conventional telephone systems (based on fixed-wired handsets) have been increasingly augmented by the cordless (mobile) telephone and accessories such as VOICE MESSAGING. Moreover, many businesses have integrated their

PC (personal computer) networks and telecommunications to take advantage of value-added network services such as ELECTRONIC MAIL, VIDEO CONFERENCING and ELECTRONIC DATA INTERCHANGE. These developments, while enhancing the immediacy and effectiveness of communications, have also facilitated flexibility and mobility, allowing staff to reduce their dependency on being physically present at an office in order to conduct business. See CONSULTATION, EMPLOYEE INVOLVEMENT, EMPLOYEE PARTICIPATION, INDUSTRIAL DEMOCRACY, COMMUNITY CHARTER OF FUNDAMENTAL SOCIAL RIGHTS, DISCLOSURE OF INFORMATION, INFORMATION MANAGEMENT, INFORMATION HIGHWAY, BUSINESS PROCESS RE-ENGINEERING.

communications mix see PROMOTIONAL MIX.

community charge see LOCAL TAX.

Companies Acts see COMPANY LAW.

Companies House see REGISTRAR OF COMPANIES.

company see JOINT-STOCK COMPANY.

company bargaining see COLLECTIVE BARGAINING.

company council an institution composed of top managers and employee representatives which discusses company strategy and policies. Usually these organs perform an advisory and consultative rather than decision-making function, but in some of the Japanese companies in the UK they provide the forum for COLLECTIVE BARGAINING over pay. See CONSULTATION, INDUSTRIAL DEMOCRACY, PARTICIPATION.

Company Directors Disqualification Act 1986 see INSOLVENCY.

company formation the process of forming a JOINT-STOCK COMPANY, which involves a number of steps:

(a) drawing up a MEMORANDUM OF ASSOCIATION;

(b) preparation of ARTICLES OF ASSOCIATION;

(c) application to the REGISTRAR OF COMPANIES for a CERTIFICATE OF INCORPORATION;

(d) issuing SHARE CAPITAL;

(e) commencing trading.

company image commonly held beliefs and impressions about a firm as a supplier of products, an employer and member of the community. Companies seek to promote positive public perceptions of themselves as progressive and enlightened organizations, caring for their employees and the environment and looking after the interests of consumers, because of the beneficial impact of good image upon, for example, company recruitment and sales. See PUBLIC RELATIONS, CORPORATE IDENTITY.

company law a body of legislation providing for the regulation of JOINT-STOCK COMPANIES. British company law encouraged. the development of joint-stock companies by establishing the principle of LIMITED LIABILITY and provides for the protection of SHAREHOLDERS' interests by controlling the formation and financing of companies. The major provisions of UK company law are contained in the 1948, 1967, 1976, 1981, 1985 and 1989 Companies Acts. See ARTICLES OF ASSOCIATION, MEMORANDUM OF ASSOCIATION.

company registrar the officer of a JOINT-STOCK COMPANY who is responsible for maintaining an up-to-date SHARE REGISTER and for issuing new SHARE CERTIFICATES and cancelling old share certificates as shares are bought and sold on the STOCK MARKET.

Many companies, however, have chosen to sub-contract these tasks to specialist institutions, often departments of commercial banks.

The role of the company registrar identified above should not be confused with that of the role of the government's REGISTRAR OF COMPANIES, who is responsible for supervising *all* joint-stock companies.

company secretary an officer of a JOINT-STOCK COMPANY with responsibility for maintaining the company's SHARE REGISTER, for notifying shareholders of ANNUAL GENERAL MEETINGS and for preparing the company's ANNUAL RETURN.

Company Securities (Insider Dealing) Act 1985 see INSIDER DEALING.

company share option plan see EMPLOYEE SHARE OWNERSHIP PLAN.

company union a TRADE UNION which is in effect run by the management of a company and which is intended to defuse employee grievances or wage demands. As such it cannot be considered to be a genuine union, and would therefore find it difficult to secure a certificate of independence from the CERTIFICATION OFFICER, and hence would be denied the benefits unions usually obtain as FRIENDLY SOCIETIES. See STAFF ASSOCIATION.

comparability an approach to PAY determination in which levels or increases in pay are sought or offered which maintain a relationship to those for other industries or occupations. The notion of the *going rate* is a form of comparability in that workers seek pay increases which are similar to those being achieved or sought by others. See JOB EVALUATION, PAY DIFFERENTIAL.

comparative advantage see INTERNATIONAL TRADE.

comparison statement a management accounting statement which sets out budgeted revenues and costs alongside actual revenues and costs in order to facilitate comparisons between the two. Fig. 20 shows a typical comparison statement. See BUDGET, BUDGETARY CONTROL, STANDARD COST.

compatibility the extent to which COMPUTER HARDWARE OR SOFTWARE is compatible with the user's existing hardware or software, that is, capable of running existing programs on new machines or alongside existing programs.

compensation deal see COUNTERTRADE.

competence-based pay a PAYMENT SYSTEM where bonuses or increments are based on the acquisition of recognised levels of competence in key skills required by the job.

competency see CORE SKILL, NATIONAL VOCATIONAL QUALIFICATION.

competition the process of active rivalry between the sellers of a particular product as they seek to win and retain buyer demand for their offerings. Competition can take a number of forms including price cutting, ADVERTISING and SALES PROMOTION, quality variations, packaging and design, and market segmentation (see MARKETING MIX).
The nature and intensity of competitive relationships in a market, in turn, depends on various factors such as product and buyer characteristics, the extent of market concentration, and cost and demand considerations (see MARKET STRUCTURE, MARKET CONDUCT). For example, where

	Month ended 30 April 20xx					
PRODUCTION	This month			4 months to date		
MANAGER	Budget	Actual	Variance	Budget	Actual	Variance
	£	£	£	£	£	£
Value of production	65,750	68,725	+2,975	270,000	291,000	+21,000
Expenditure:						
Direct Wages	11,550	11,975	– 425	45,700	47,500	– 1,800
Direct Materials	22,450	23,147	– 697	81,350	92,177	–10,827
PRIME COST	34,000	35,122	–1,122	127,050	139,677	– 12,627
Production Overheads:						
Indirect Wages	2,711	2,588	+ 123	10,794	10,774	+ 20
Maintenance	200	176	+ 24	800	680	+ 120
Depreciation	650	650		2,600	2,600	
Training	100	125	– 25	400	125	+ 275
TOTAL PRODUCTION OVERHEADS:	3,661	3,539	+ 122	14,594	14,179	+ 415

Fig. 20 **Comparison statement.** A typical example.

products are standardized, competition is usually focused on price, whereas in markets where buyers demand a wide range of product variety and quality mixes, PRODUCT DIFFERENTIATION competition tends to be emphasized. In markets characterized by high levels of seller concentration, suppliers tend wherever possible to substitute product differentiation competition for price competition because of the mutually ruinous consequences of price wars. Moreover, in some instances, mutual interest considerations may well lead suppliers to control competition so as to promote orderly and profitable trading conditions by, for example, establishing price-fixing CARTELS.

Business strategy and marketing analysts are especially concerned with identifying and exploiting product and buyer characteristics as a means of establishing COMPETITIVE ADVANTAGES over rival suppliers. From a wider public interest angle, the nature and strength of competition has an important effect on MARKET PERFORMANCE and hence is of particular relevance to the application of COMPETITION POLICIES.

Competition Act 1980 an Act which extended UK COMPETITION LAW by providing for the investigation of potentially ANTI-COMPETITIVE PRACTICES such as EXCLUSIVE DEALING, REFUSAL TO SUPPLY, etc. on an individual 'one-off' basis rather than as part of a wider-ranging monopoly investigation. Under the Act, anti-competitive practices are examined in the first instance by the OFFICE OF FAIR TRADING which may itself order the discontinuance of an offending practice, or may refer it to the COMPETITION COMMISSION for further investigation and report.

Competition Act 1998 a UK Act which consolidated existing COMPETITION LAWS but which also contained new prohibitions, powers of investigation and penalties for infringements of the Act. The Act is designed to bring UK competition law into line with European Union competition law as currently enshrined in Articles 85 and 86 of the Treaty of Rome.

The Act covers two key areas of competition policy: anti-competitive agreements and market dominance.

(1) The *Act prohibits outright* agreements between firms (ie. COLLUSION) and CONCERTED PRACTICES which prevent, restrict or distort competition within the UK (the Chapter 1 prohibition). This prohibition applies to both formal and informal agreements, whether oral or in writing, and covers agreements which contain provisions to jointly fix prices and terms and conditions of sale; to limit or control production, markets, technical development or investment; and to share markets or supply sources.

(2) The Act *prohibits* the 'abuse' of a 'dominant position' within the UK. (The Chapter 2 prohibition). The Act specifies dominance as a situation where a supplier "can act independently of its competitors and customers". As a general rule, a dominant position is defined as one where a supplier possesses a market share of 40% or above.

Examples of 'abuse' of a dominant position specified in the Act include charging 'excessive' prices, imposing restrictive terms and conditions of sale to the prejudice of consumers and limiting production, markets and technical development to the prejudice of consumers.

The Act established a new regulatory authority, the COMPETITION COMMISSION which took over the responsibilities previously undertaken by the Monopolies and Mergers Commission and the Restrictive Practices Court. Under the Act, the OFFICE OF FAIR TRADING (OFT) has the power to refer dominant firm cases and cases of suspected illegal collusion to the Competition Commission for investigation and report.

The Act gives the OFT wide-ranging powers to uncover malpractices. For example, if there are reasonable grounds for suspecting that firms are operating an illegal agreement OFT officials can mount a 'dawn raid' – "entering business premises, using reasonable force where necessary, and search for incriminating documents". The Act also introduces stiff new financial penalties. Firms found to have infringed either prohibition may be liable to a financial penalty of up to 10% of their annual turnover in the UK (up to a maximum of 3 years).

See COMPETITION POLICY, COMPETITION POLICY (UK), COMPETITION POLICY (EU), ANTICOMPETITIVE AGREEMENT, RESTRICTIVE TRADE AGREEMENT.

competition-based pricing pricing methods which determine the PRICE of a product primarily on the basis of the prices charged by competitors.

In markets where products are highly standardized (i.e. COMMODITY-TYPE PRODUCTS), customers are likely to see competing brands as close substitutes for one another, so that any price differences would cause switching to the lower-priced brand. In such markets a seller has little pricing latitude and must set the price at the going rate as determined by supply and demand. With few manufacturers supplying the product (i.e. OLIGOPOLY), any one firm will be acutely aware of the harmful effects on its market share and sales volume of a price which is even slightly higher than those of its competitors and will therefore tend to charge an identical price to competitors.

Where suppliers are required to put in a *sealed price bid* or *tender* to supply, for example, components to a manufacturer, or build a complete factory or ship, competitive conditions may be paramount. A firm must guess the likely sealed bid prices of its competitors for the work and in the light of its own cost conditions make an appropriate price bid. See COST-BASED PRICING, DEMAND-BASED PRICING.

Competition Commission (CC) a regulatory body established by the COMPETITION ACT 1998 which was originally set up in 1948 as the *Monopolies Commission* (1948-65), then *the Monopolies and Mergers Commission* (1965-98), which is responsible for the implementation of UK COMPETITION POLICY. The basic task of the Commission is to investigate and report on cases of MONOPOLY/market dominance, MERGER/TAKEOVER, and ANTI-COMPETITIVE PRACTICES referred to it by the OFFICE OF FAIR TRADING (OFT) to determine whether or not they unduly remove or restrict competition, thus producing harmful economic effects (ie. economic results which operate against the 'public interest'). The Commission is also required by the OFT to investigate cases of 'illegal' collusion between suppliers ie. cases where the OFT has good reason to suspect that an ANTI-COMPETITIVE AGREEMENT/RESTRICTIVE TRADE AGREEMENT prohibited by the Competition Act, 1998 is continuing to be operated 'in secret'. (This task was formerly undertaken by the RESTRICTIVE PRACTICES COURT).

Under UK COMPETITION LAW, monopoly/market dominance is defined as a situation where at least 40% of a reference good or service is supplied by one firm or a number of suppliers who restrict competition between themselves (CONCERTED PRACTICE OR COMPLEX MONOPOLY situation). Mergers and takeovers fall within the scope of the legislation where the market share of the combined business exceeds 25% of the reference good or service or where the value of assets being merged or taken over exceeds £70 million. Anti-competitive practices are those which distort, restrict or eliminate competition in a market.

Cases referred to the Competition Commission are evaluated nowadays primarily in terms of whether or not the actions of suppliers' (MARKET CONDUCT) or changes in the structure of the market (MARKET STRUCTURE) are detrimental to the potency of competition in the market and hence prejudicial to the interests of consumers and other suppliers, (the so-called 'public interest' criterion found in earlier legislation). In cases of monopoly/market dominance the Commission scrutinizes the actions of dominant firms for evidence of the 'abuse' of market power, and invariably condemns predatory pricing policies which result in excessive profits. Practices such as EXCLUSIVE DEALING, AGGREGATED REBATES, TIE-IN SALES and FULL-LINE FORCING whose main effect is to restrict competition have been invariably condemned by the Commission, especially when used by a dominant firm to erect barriers to entry and undermine the market positions of smaller rivals. In merger and takeover cases, again the emphasis is on competitive impact. A merger or takeover involving the leading firms who already possess large market shares is likely to be considered detrimental. (See MARKET CONCENTRATION).

In all cases the Commission has powers only of *recommendation.* It can recommend, for example, price cuts to remove monopoly profits, the discontinuance of offending practices and the prohibition of anti-competitive mergers, but it is up to the Office of Fair Trading to implement the recommendations, or not, as it sees fit.

competition law a body of legislation providing for the control of monopolies/market dominance, mergers and takeovers, anti-competitive agreements/restrictive trade agreements and anti-competitive practices. UK legislation aimed at controlling 'abusive' MARKET CONDUCT by monopolistic firms and firms acting in COLLUSION was first introduced in 1948 (The Monopolies and Restrictive Practices (Inquiry and Control) Act), while powers to control undesirable changes in MARKET STRUCTURE were added in 1965 (The Monopolies and Mergers Act). Other notable legislation concerning the control of collusion were the Restrictive Trade Practice Acts of 1956, 1968 and 1976.

Current competition law in the UK is contained in a number of Acts:

FAIR TRADING ACT, 1973, ENTERPRISE ACT, 2002, (applying to mergers and takeovers)

COMPETITION ACT, 1980 (applying to anti-competitive practices)

COMPETITION ACT 1998 (applying to monopolies/market dominance and anti-competitive agreements/restrictive trade agreements)

RESALE PRICES ACTS, 1964, 1976 (applying to resale price maintenance)

These laws are currently administered by the OFFICE OF FAIR TRADING and the COMPETITION COMMISSION (formerly the MONOPOLIES AND MERGERS COMMISSION). See also RESTRICTIVE PRACTICES COURT.

In the EUROPEAN UNION, competition law is enshrined in Articles 85 and 86 of the Treaty of Rome (1958) and the 1980 Merger Regulation. These laws are administered by the European Commission's Competition-Directorate. See COMPETITION POLICY, COMPETITION POLICY (UK), COMPETITION POLICY (EU) COMPLEX MONOPOLY.

competition policy

A policy concerned with the regulation of MONOPOLIES, MERGERS and TAKEOVERS, RESTRICTIVE TRADE AGREEMENTS, RESALE PRICES and ANTI-COMPETITIVE PRACTICES. Competition policy, by promoting greater competition in markets, aims to secure an efficient use of economic resources and the enhancement of consumer welfare; specifically, least-cost supply, 'fair' prices and profit levels, technological advance and product improvement.

Competition policy is implemented mainly through the control of MARKET STRUCTURE and MARKET CONDUCT but also, on occasions, through the direct control of MARKET PERFORMANCE itself (by, for example, the use of PRICE CONTROLS to limit industry profit levels).

There are two basic approaches to the control of market structure and conduct: the nondiscretionary approach and the discretionary approach. The nondiscretionary approach lays down 'acceptable' standards of structure and conduct and prohibits outright any transgression of these standards. Typical ingredients of this approach include:

(a) the stipulation of maximum permitted market share limits (say, no more than 20% of the market) in order to limit the degree of MARKET CONCENTRATION and thus prevent the emergence of a monopoly supplier. Under this stipulation any proposed mergers or takeover which would take the combined group's market share above the permitted limit would be automatically prohibited;

(b) the outright prohibition of all forms of 'shared monopoly' (CARTELS, ANTI-COMPETITIVE AGREEMENTS/RESTRICTIVE TRADE AGREEMENTS) involving price-fixing, market sharing, etc.;

(c) the outright prohibition of specific practices designed to limit competition, for example EXCLUSIVE DEALING, RESALE PRICE MAINTENANCE, etc.

Thus the nondiscretionary approach attempts to promote competitive conditions by a direct attack on the possession and exercise of monopoly power as such.

By contrast, the discretionary approach takes a more pragmatic line, recognizing that often high levels of market concentration and certain agreements between firms may serve to improve economic efficiency rather than impair it. It is the essence of the discretionary approach that each situation be judged on its own merits rather than be automatically condemned. Thus, under the discretionary approach, mergers, restrictive agreements and practices of the kind noted above are evaluated in terms of their possible benefits and detriments, and only prohibited if they are found to be, on balance, detrimental. See COMPETITION POLICY (UK), COMPETITION POLICY (EU), INDUSTRIAL POLICY.

competition policy (European Union) covers three main areas of application:

(a) CARTELS: Articles 85(1) and (2) of the Treaty of Rome prohibit cartel agreements and CONCERTED PRACTICES (i.e. formal and informal collusion) between firms involving price fixing, limitations on production, technical developments and investment, and market sharing whose effect is to restrict competition and trade within the European Union (EU). Certain other agreements (for example, those providing for joint technical research and specialization of production) may be exempted from the general prohibition contained in Articles 85(1) and (2) provided they do not restrict inter-state competition and trade;

(b) MONOPOLIES/DOMINANT FIRMS: Article 86 of the Treaty of Rome prohibits the abuse of a dominant position in the supply of a particular product if this serves to restrict competition and trade within the EU. What constitutes abusive behaviour is similar to that applied in the UK, namely actions which are unfair or unreasonable towards customers (for example PRICE DISCRIMINATION between EU markets), retailers (for example REFUSAL TO SUPPLY) and other suppliers (for example selective price cuts to eliminate competitors). Firms found guilty by the European Commission of illegal cartelization and the abuse of a dominant position can be fined up to 10% of their annual sales turnover;

(c) MERGERS: the Commission can investigate mergers involving companies with a combined worldwide turnover of over €5 billion (£3.7 bn) if the aggregate EU-wide turnover of the companies concerned is greater than €250 million. Again, the main aim is to prevent mergers likely to affect competition and trade adversely within the EU.

These thresholds still apply generally, but in 1998 they were reduced to €3.5 billion and €100 million, respectively, for mergers affecting the competitive situation in three (or more) EU countries in cases where the *combined* turnover of the companies exceed

€25 million in *each* of the three countries.

Generally, where EU competition laws apply they take precedence over the national competition laws of member countries. However, a *subsidiarity* provision can be invoked which permits the competition authority of a member country to request permission from the EU Competition-Directorate to investigate a particular dominant firm or merger case if it appears that the 'European dimension' is relatively minor compared to its purely local impact.

competition policy (UK) covers five main areas of application:

(a) MONOPOLIES/market dominance. The COMPETITION ACT, 1998 *prohibits* actions which constitute the 'abuse' of a dominant position in a UK market. The OFFICE OF FAIR TRADING (OFT) is responsible for the referral of selected goods and services monopolies (both private and public sectors) to the COMPETITION COMMISSION for investigation and report and the implementation (where it sees fit) of the Commission's recommendations.

A dominant position is defined as a situation where one firm controls 40% or more of the 'reference' good or service. (Under previous legislation market dominance was defined in terms of a 25% market share). Abuse consists of acts which are harmful to the interests of consumers and other suppliers; e.g. charging excessive prices to secure monopoly profits and imposing restrictive terms and conditions on the supply of goods (see EXCLUSIVE DEALING, TIE-IN SALES etc). The term 'abuse' can be broadly equated with that of conduct contrary to the 'public interest' – the benchmark used in previous legislation.

Defining the 'reference' market to establish evidence of market dominance can be problematic since it raises the issue of how widely or narrowly the boundaries of 'the market' are to be delineated. (See MARKET, MARKET CONCENTRATION). Thus, the drinks market could be divided as between alcoholic and non-alcoholic drinks, and further divided into sub-markets as between, for example, the various types of alcoholic drink – the beer/lager market, spirits market, wine market etc. Establishing abuse can also be a 'grey area'. For example, high prices and profits may be condoned because they reflect exceptional innovativeness; on the other hand low profits may not be a sign of effective competition but reflect the fact that the firm is grossly inefficient.

(b) ANTI-COMPETITIVE AGREEMENTS/RESTRICTIVE TRADE AGREEMENTS. The Competition Act, 1998 *prohibits outright* agreements between firms (i.e. COLLUSION) and CONCERTED PRACTICES which prevent, restrict or distort competition within the UK. The Office of Fair Trading is responsible for monitoring 'suspected' cases of firms operating agreements illegally and can refer them for further investigation by the Competition Commission. The prohibition applies to both formal and informal agreements, whether oral or in writing, and covers agreements which involve joint price-fixing and common terms and conditions of sale, market-sharing and coordination of capacity adjustments etc. (Under previous legislation it was possible to obtain exemption from prohibition if it could be demonstrated that an agreement conferred 'net economic benefit' – see RESTRICTIVE TRADE PRACTICES ACTS, RESTRICTIVE PRACTICES COURT).

Although anti-competitive agreements are technically illegal, nonetheless there is much evidence that many such agreements have been driven 'underground' and continue to be operated in secret. This problem has been addressed by the authorities in encouraging 'whistleblowers' to come forward and supply them with information about illegal activities and also provisions in the Competition Act, 1998 which allows officials to enter business premises without warning and to seize incriminating documentation.

(c) MERGERS AND TAKEOVERS. Under the ENTERPRISE ACT, 2002 the Office of Fair Trading (OFT) can refer mergers and takeovers to the Competition Commission for investigation and report where (1) the combined firms already have or would have a market share of 25% or over in a 'reference' good or service or (2) the value of assets being combined exceeds £70 million. Clause

(1) effectively covers horizontal mergers and takeovers (see HORIZONTAL INTEGRATION) and clause (2) vertical and conglomerate mergers and takeovers (See VERTICAL INTERGRATION, DIVERSIFICATION/ CONGLOMERATE INTEGRATION). Mergers and takeovers nowadays are mainly evaluated in terms of their likely competitive effects. Unlike in dealing with established monopolies where *past* conduct can be scrutinized to establish harmful effects, mergers and takeovers are about the *future* and predicting the likely future effects of a merger/takeover is problematic. Faced with this difficulty the Commission tends to 'play safe' and recommend the blocking of most mergers/takeovers which reduces competition by *significantly* increasing the level of MARKET CONCENTRATION.

(d) RESALE PRICE MAINTENANCE (RPM): manufacturers' stipulation of the resale prices of their products is generally prohibited in the UK, although under the RESALE PRICES ACTS it is possible for a manufacturer to obtain exemption by satisfying the Competition Commission that, on balance RPM confers net economic benefit. The OFT is responsible for monitoring manufacturers' policies towards retail prices and can take action against suspected cases of manufacturers attempting (illegally) to enforce RPM. Manufacturers can, however, take action against retailers who use their products as LOSS LEADERS;

(e) ANTI-COMPETITIVE PRACTICES: various trade practices such as EXCLUSIVE DEALING, REFUSAL TO SUPPLY, FULL-LINE FORCING, etc. may be investigated both by the OFT itself and (if necessary) by the Competition Commission, and prohibited if they are found to be unduly restrictive of competition.

Where a particular dominant firm or merger case falls within the competition rules of *both* the UK and the European Union (see COMPETITION POLICY (EU)), EU law takes precedence. However, a *subsidiarity* provision can be invoked which permits the Office of Fair Trading to request permission from the EU competition authorities to investigate a particular dominant firm or merger case if it appears that the 'European dimension' is relatively minor compared to its purely local impact. See also CONSUMER PROTECTION.

competitive advantage

The possession by a firm of various ASSETS and attributes (low cost plants, innovative brands, ownership of raw material supplies, etc.) which give it a competitive edge over rival suppliers. To succeed against competitors in winning customers on a viable (profitable) and sustainable (long-run) basis, a firm must, depending on the nature of the market, be cost-effective and/ or able to offer products which customers regard as preferable to the products offered by rival suppliers. The former enables a firm to meet and beat competitors on price, while the latter reflects the firm's ability to establish PRODUCT DIFFERENTIATION advantages over competitors. See VALUE ADDED MODEL.

Cost advantages over competitors are of two major types:

(a) absolute cost advantages, that is, lower costs than competitors at *all* levels of output deriving from, for example, the use of superior production technology (e.g. COMPUTER-AIDED MANUFACTURING, LEAN MANUFACTURING) or from VERTICAL INTEGRATION of input supply and assembly operations;

(b) relative cost advantages, that is, cost advantages related to the scale of output accruing through the exploitation of ECONOMIES OF SCALE in production and marketing and through cumulative EXPERIENCE CURVE effects. Over time, investment in plant renewal, modernization and process innovation (either through in-house research and development or the early adoption of new technology developed elsewhere) is essential to maintain cost advantages.

Product differentiation advantages derive from:

(a) a variety of physical product properties and attributes (notably the ability to offer products which are regarded by customers as having unique qualities or as being functionally better than competitors' products);

(b) the particular nuances and psychological images built into the firm's product by associated advertising and sales promotion. Again, given the dynamic nature of markets, particularly PRODUCT LIFE CYCLE considerations, competitive advantage in this area needs to be sustained by an active programme of new product innovation and upgrading of existing lines. See COST DRIVERS, BENEFIT DRIVERS, VALUE CHAIN ANALYSIS, CRITICAL OR KEY SUCCESS FACTORS, CORE SKILL OR COMPETENCIES, SWOT ANALYSIS, COMPETITIVE STRATEGY, BUSINESS STRATEGY, RESOURCE BASED THEORY OF THE FIRM, CONSUMER SURPLUS, DISTINCTIVE CAPABILITIES.

competitive strategy

The formulation of strategic plans by a firm aimed at ensuring that the firm is able to meet and beat its competitors in supplying a particular product. Competitive strategy constitutes an integral part of overall BUSINESS STRATEGY formulation (deciding *which* markets to operate in etc.), since no matter how few or many product markets the firm chooses to be in, its corporate prosperity depends fundamentally on how well it succeeds in the individual product markets making up its business. A main concern of competitive strategy is to identify:

(a) the competitive strengths and weaknesses of one's own firm and of rival firms (see SWOT ANALYSIS);

(b) the nature and strength of the various forces driving competition in a market (see Fig. 21). The key to a successful competitive strategy is then

(c) to understand fully what product attributes are demanded by buyers (whether it be low prices or product sophistication) with a view to

(d) establishing, operationally, a position of COMPETITIVE ADVANTAGE which makes the firm less vulnerable to attack from established competitors and potential new entrants, and to erosion from the direction of buyers, suppliers and substitute products.

There are three generic strategies for competitive success (Fig. 22): cost leadership, product differentiation and 'focus'. Low costs, particularly in commodity-type markets, help the firm not only to survive price competition should it break out, but, importantly, enable it to assume the role of market leader in establishing price levels which ensure high and stable levels of market

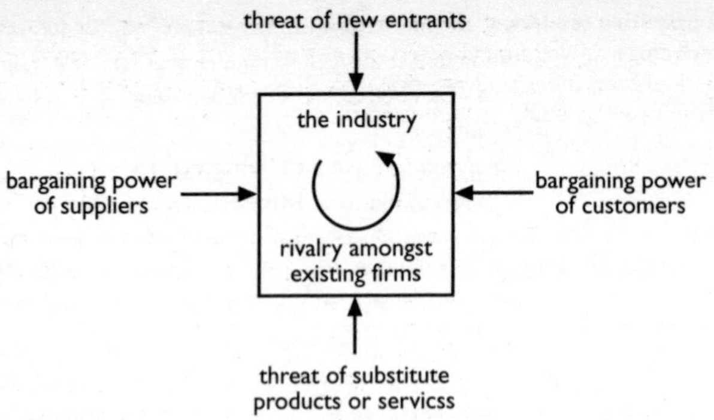

Fig. 21 **Competitive strategy.** Forces driving competition in a market. (Source: Michael Porter).

profitability. The sources of cost-effectiveness are varied, including the exploitation of ECONOMIES OF SCALE, investment in best state-of-the-art technology (e.g. COMPUTER-AIDED MANUFACTURING, LEAN MANUFACTURING) and preferential access to raw materials or distribution channels. By adopting a PRODUCT DIFFERENTIATION strategy a firm seeks to be unique in its market in a way that is valued by its potential customers. Product differentiation possibilities vary from market to market but are associated with the potential for distinguishing products by their physical properties and attributes and the experience of satisfaction – real and psychological – imparted by the product to consumers. General cost leadership and differentiation strategies seek to establish a COMPETITIVE ADVANTAGE over rival suppliers across the whole market. By contrast, 'focus' strategies aim to build competitive advantages in narrower segments of a market, but again either in terms of cost or, more usually, differentiation characteristics, with 'niche' suppliers primarily catering for speciality product demands. See VALUE ADDED MODEL, MARKET STRUCTURE, MARKET CONDUCT, MARKET PERFORMANCE, STRATEGIC GROUP.

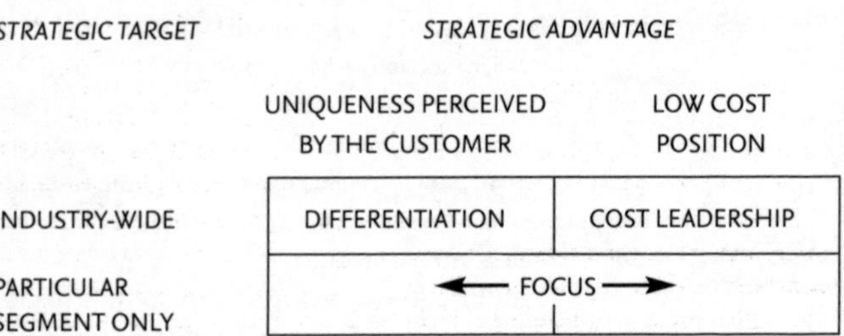

Fig. 22 **Competitive strategy.** Three generic strategies. (Source: Michael Porter).

competitive tendering the system of awarding contracts for public services on the basis of competitive tenders. Private sector firms as well as public sector organizations are invited to submit tenders to provide services previously run directly by public sector organizations e.g. local authority refuse-collection. The assumption underlying this is that competition for contracts will drive down costs and encourage efficiency. Competitive tendering was encouraged from the 1980s onwards and eventually became compulsory (compulsory competitive tendering or CCT) for a range of local authority services. However, CCT was abolished in 2000 and replaced by BEST VALUE, whereby local authorities are under a duty to operate services with regard to economy, efficiency and effectiveness. In most cases contracts have been awarded to the 'in-house' organization. Where they are awarded to an external organization it is common for most of the public sector workforce to be transferred to the contractor. See ENABLING AUTHORITY, NEW PUBLIC MANAGEMENT, PURCHASER-PROVIDER SPLIT.

competitor a business rival of a firm supplying a particular GOOD OR SERVICE which offers buyers an identical or similar product. Where customers regard a rival's products as being close substitutes then the rival's marketing strategies are likely to have a significant effect on the firm's own market position. See COMPETITION, COMPETITIVE ADVANTAGE, COMPETITIVE STRATEGY, PRODUCT DIFFERENTIATION.

competitor analysis the process whereby a firm studies the production and marketing practices used by its immediate competitors so that the firm can gauge its own strengths and weaknesses in relation to its main competitors.

See SWOT ANALYSIS.

completely knocked down see CKD.

completion date the date by which a particular project is scheduled to be finished. In civil engineering projects completion dates are often formally written into the contract terms between the supplier and customer, with financial penalties for late completion and bonuses for early completion. See NETWORK ANALYSIS.

complex monopoly a situation defined by UK COMPETITION POLICY as one in which two or more suppliers of a particular product restrict competition between themselves. Complex monopoly is in essence an OLIGOPOLY situation where the firms concerned, although pursuing individual (i.e. noncollusive) policies, nonetheless behave in a uniform manner and produce a result which is noncompetitive (i.e. similar to COLLUSION). The problem is that it is often difficult to distinguish between competitive and noncompetitive situations. For example, if firms charge identical prices, is this reflective of competition (i.e. prices which are brought together *because* of competition) or a deliberate suppression of competition?

component *or* **part** an item such as a gearbox, steering wheel, etc. which is used in the assembly of another component or final product (such as a motorcar). See PARTS FAMILY CODING AND CLASSIFICATION SYSTEMS, REPLACEMENT PARTS, ORIGINAL EQUIPMENT, AFTER-SALES SERVICE.

compound interest see INTEREST.

comprehensive agreement see MULTI-EMPLOYER AGREEMENT.

compressed hours a method used to reduce the number of days worked each week or month by extending the number of hours worked each day. For instance, employees on a 40 hour week might work four days each week of 10 hours duration. See also ANNUAL HOURS, FLEXITIME, SHIFT WORK.

compulsory competitive tendering see COMPETITIVE TENDERING.

computer an electronic/electromechanical device which accepts alphabetical and numerical data in a predefined form, stores and processes this data according to the instructions contained in a COMPUTER PROGRAM, and presents the analysed data in an organized form. Fig. 23 shows the main items of computer HARDWARE, with input devices like KEYBOARDS, and magnetic tape readers; the CPU (central processing unit) which manipulates data; DISK DRIVES which provide additional data storage capacity;

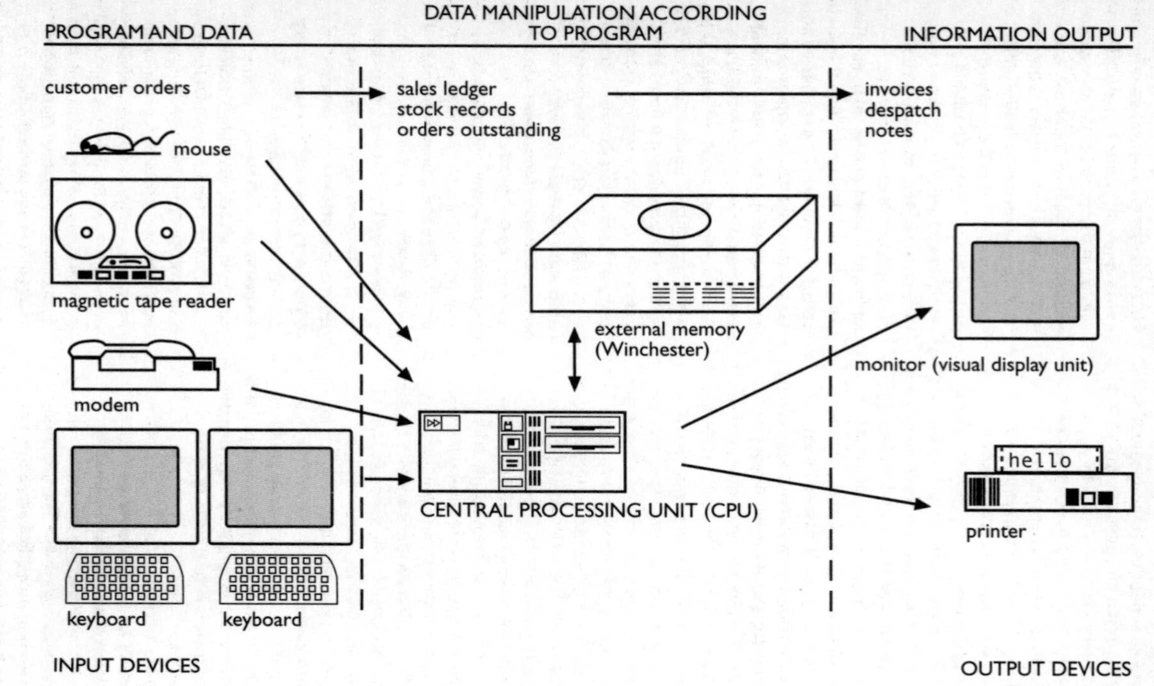

Fig. 23 **Computer**. The main items of hardware.

and output devices like PRINTERS and VISUAL DISPLAY UNITS. The figure shows how a number of computers may be linked in a LOCAL AREA NETWORK, in this case to process customer orders, maintain the sales LEDGER and issue INVOICES.

Big 'mainframe' computers are used to handle large databases. For example, the Driver and Vehicle Licensing Agency in Swansea holds over 60 million records on its mainframe computer. Increasingly, however, with the development of faster, more powerful and more cost-effective microprocessors the mainframe computer has been replaced by the desktop 'personal computer' (PC) in routine office data-processing operations (DOWNSIZING), with PCs being linked together in LOCAL AREA NETWORKS, enabling them to share data. A further development has been the introduction of small portable computers typified by the 'notebook' personal computer which can be carried in a briefcase.

Computers have dramatically improved the productivity of DATA PROCESSING in business, facilitating the keeping of ACCOUNTING ledger records like sales ledger, purchases ledger and payroll and personal records by small numbers of clerical staff. In addition, software packages like SPREADSHEETS and WORD PROCESSORS have improved the presentation and analysis of management information, helping to improve decision-making. See FLEXIBLE MANUFACTURING SYSTEM, PRODUCTION LINE, ELECTRONIC MAIL SYSTEM, COMPUTER-AIDED DESIGN, COMPUTER-AIDED MANUFACTURING, INFORMATION MANAGEMENT, BULLETIN BOARD, MODEM, INTERNET.

computer-aided design (CAD) the use of COMPUTERS in the DESIGN of new components or products and in the re-design of existing products. Unlike hand drawings, CAD design specifications can be shown on a visual display unit and redrawn to produce different versions of the components or product. CAD can also be linked to computer-aided process planning (CAPP) to determine the best methods by which to manufacture a product. Moreover, a component or product can be subjected to various tests of strength, performance, etc. using computer-aided engineering (CAE) software without having to build prototypes; thus changes in product design can be made quickly and cheaply (see NEW PRODUCT DEVELOPMENT). CAD is particularly useful in designing and classifying components and products used in GROUP TECHNOLOGY production and in FLEXIBLE MANUFACTURING SYSTEMS. See COMPUTER-AIDED MANUFACTURING.

computer-aided engineering see COMPUTER-AIDED DESIGN.

computer-aided manufacturing (CAM) the use of COMPUTERS to impart operating instructions to NUMERICALLY-CONTROLLED MACHINES and ROBOTS employed in PRODUCTION systems (mass production, batch production, group technology and flexible manufacturing systems). CAM enables PRODUCTION SCHEDULING to be completed more efficiently and quickly, particularly in rescheduling production to accommodate new or redesigned components or products. CAM systems are especially effective when linked to COMPUTER-AIDED DESIGN (CAD), for with CAD/CAM computer software packages it is possible to provide design specifications and parts lists for components or products *directly* to the machines that will produce these items.

computer-aided process planning see COMPUTER-AIDED DESIGN.

computer-integrated manufacturing (CIM) the use of COMPUTERS to integrate all facets of PRODUCTION planning and control, including product design, factory layout planning, production scheduling and stock control. See COMPUTER-AIDED DESIGN, COMPUTER-AIDED MANUFACTURING.

computer program a set of instructions set out in a clear and logical sequence which tells a processor within a COMPUTER how to perform a particular task. Computer programs are often written in 'high-level' program languages like BASIC (beginners all-purpose symbolic instruction code) or COBOL (common business-orientated language), but must then be converted into MACHINE CODE for use in a computer.

concentrated marketing *or* **targeting strategy** a MARKETING STRATEGY for a product which is based on the use of a MARKETING MIX format (pricing, advertising messages, sales promotion) aimed at *one* particular group of customers in the market. This approach thus focuses exclusively on one MARKET SEGMENT, rather than several market segments (DIFFERENTIATED MARKETING OR TARGETING STRATEGY) or the whole market (UNDIFFERENTIATED MARKETING STRATEGY). Also known as a 'focus' or 'niche' strategy.

A concentrated marketing approach is particularly suited to a smaller firm with limited financial and marketing resources or a specialist producer, and could be used by a new entrant to the market as a means of establishing a toe-hold in the market before undertaking further expansion (see MARKET PENETRATION). By concentrating its resources narrowly, a firm may well be in a better position to boost its sales but, on the debit side, may fail to capitalize on the sales potential of other segments. Worse still, dependency on one segment leaves the firm unduly exposed to a fall in demand in that segment.

concept testing testing a new product concept with a sample of target consumers to assess the product's likely customer acceptability. Concept testing is used at a very early stage of NEW PRODUCT DEVELOPMENT in order to eliminate products which are unlikely to succeed and to pinpoint products whose potential warrants further research and development work.

concerted practice a situation defined by European Union and UK competition law as one where rival firms, without engaging in *formal* COLLUSION (See ANTI-COMPETITIVE AGREEMENT), nonetheless *informally* coordinate their behaviour in respect of selling prices and discounts, and engage in market-sharing and joint capacity adjustments.

Under the EU's Article 85 of the Treaty of Rome and the UK's COMPETITION ACT, 1998 concerted practices are prohibited outright. See COMPETITION POLICY (EU), COMPETITION POLICY (UK).

concert party see TAKEOVER BID.

concession bargaining see COLLECTIVE BARGAINING.

conciliation a form of intervention in collective and individual INDUSTRIAL DISPUTES in which a third party assists the disputants in resolving their differences. The primary role of the conciliator is to encourage the parties to settle the dispute themselves through continued NEGOTIATION, rather than to cast judgement on the disputants' claims (ARBITRATION) or to bring forward the conciliator's own proposals for a settlement (MEDIATION). In the UK, conciliation services are provided officially by the ADVISORY, CONCILIATION AND ARBITRATION SERVICE (ACAS). Conciliation in collective disputes is typically resorted to when agreed procedures for resolving differences have been exhausted and a STRIKE could well occur. Individual conciliation may take place where an employee claims that his or her employer has treated him or her unlawfully. In the UK all such claims that are lodged with EMPLOYMENT TRIBUNALS are automatically referred to ACAS to determine whether conciliation may render a formal hearing unnecessary. See INDUSTRIAL DISPUTE, UNFAIR DISMISSAL, DISCRIMINATION, COLLECTIVE BARGAINING.

concurrent engineering the term used to describe a group who are drawn from different disciplines to work on a problem within the firm. For example, a new product analysis concurrent engineering team may consist of a production engineer, cost accountant, marketing specialist etc. Thus, concurrent engineering can reduce product development time allowing the product to be brought to market more quickly and at a reduced cost. Typically also used as the basis for a team in VALUE ANALYSIS. See NEW PRODUCT DEVELOPMENT. See also MATRIX.

condition-based maintenance a PREVENTIVE MAINTENANCE system in which a firm's plant, machinery or equipment is inspected at frequent intervals to assess maintenance needs. With this type of system the condition of components is monitored and they are replaced when they reach a certain state in order to avoid breakdowns. See INSPECTION.

condition of employment see CONTRACT OF EMPLOYMENT.

Confederation of British Industry (CBI) a UK organization which represents the collective interests of employers. The CBI is run by a centrally-elected committee, a secretariat, and a network of regional and local branches which provide a forum for company executives to meet and discuss affairs of mutual concern, and act as a means of disseminating information on the government's industrial policy, European Union directives on employers' obligations, etc.

A major objective of the CBI is to promote industrial enterprise and efficiency, thereby helping the country to increase its wealth and create employment.

conflict a disagreement or divergence of interests which may result in one party taking action against another. Conflict can occur at the inter-personal, group or societal level and may involve collective or individual action. It may arise out of simple dislike of another person or out of opposed collective interests. Marxists argue that conflict is endemic to capitalist society. In their view capitalism has created two classes of people, the proletariat (i.e. paid employees) and the bourgeoisie (i.e. entrepreneurs and their supporters), whose interests are diametrically opposed. This opposition of interests in the employment sphere leads to various forms of conflict including sabotage and STRIKES. In Marx's view this conflict would lead to the overthrow of capitalism. That this has not happened in most advanced industrial societies has been attributed to various factors, including rising living standards and the institutionalization of conflict. This is the development of DISPUTES PROCEDURES and mechanisms for COLLECTIVE BARGAINING which have provided TRADE UNIONS and managers with the means to resolve many manifestations of conflict. Putting a grievance into procedure (i.e. passing it to a joint management–union committee for discussion and resolution) tends to take the heat out of an issue, thereby lowering overt conflict. Although industrial conflict has not led to revolution in countries such as the UK, radical observers argue that there is nevertheless still a fundamental conflict of interests at work and that this is manifested in less overt or more indirect forms of conflict, such as ABSENTEEISM and LABOUR TURNOVER, which do not necessarily appear to be explicitly directed against the other party.

As against the Marxist view of two diametrically opposed interests in society, PLURALISM suggests that there is a plurality of interests, possibly organized in interest groups, in any society or organization. Although on occasions these interests may conflict, pluralists would dispute that such conflicts are an expression of a fundamental cleavage. Instead conflict tends to arise over specific distributional issues, such as the size of an annual pay increase, and the composition of interest groups varies according to the issue at stake. Indeed some pluralists would go further and assert that there is a basic identity of interests underneath these specific differences. Pluralists argue that conflict can be beneficial in so far as its expression ('giving voice') can both reduce the intensity of conflict and provide the impetus to design procedures for resolving differences.

Pluralism has been an influential approach in political science, in the study of INDUSTRIAL RELATIONS, and in ORGANIZATIONAL ANALYSIS. In industrial relations pluralists argue that TRADE UNIONS are the expression of distinct employee interests and that recognition of them by managers enables the creation of mechanisms for conflict resolution and hence for managers to regain or maintain control of work. Pluralism has been a less explicit approach in the study of organizations but has nevertheless informed much of the recent work in this area.

For instance, writers have showed that whilst all in the organization may subscribe to the organization's broad goals, various departments may acquire specific and divergent interests relating to their contribution to these goals. These interests are expressed in the decision-making process, making it as much a political as a rational or technical process. Although an influential approach, pluralism has been criticized for its assumption that the power of interest groups is more or less equal and that there are no fundamental structural bases to power differences in organizations and society. See INDUSTRIAL DISPUTE, INDUSTRIAL ACTION, MANAGEMENT STYLE.

conformance the extent to which a product meets the standard of QUALITY which was designed into the product. See QUALITY CONTROL.

conglomerate integration see DIVERSIFICATION.

conjoint analysis a MARKETING RESEARCH technique which involves potential buyers in assigning ordinal rankings to attributes possessed by varieties of a particular product.

In assessing television sets, for instance, conjoint analysis would rate particular BRANDS on the characteristics of sound quality, picture quality and layout of controls (see Fig. 24). A 'conjunctive buyer' would distinguish between the alternative brands by requiring minimum performance standards for every attribute, rejecting brands which fail to meet these standards. For example, a consumer might set minimum standards of 5 for picture and sound quality and 3 for layout of controls, in which case brands A and C would be rejected in favour of brand B.

By contrast, a 'disjunctive buyer' would select a brand by setting minimum attribute levels for only certain highly-regarded characteristics and would be indifferent about other attributes.

Conjoint analysis is used to develop product brands which contain combinations of attributes in proportions which appeal to the mass of consumers or to particular MARKET SEGMENTS.

conjunctive buyer see CONJOINT ANALYSIS.

conservatism *or* **prudence** see ACCOUNTING CONCEPTS.

consideration 1 something of value which is offered by a party to a CONTRACT in exchange for something of value received. Consideration usually takes the form of a monetary payment in exchange for GOODS or SERVICES received, but could involve, for example, the direct exchange of one product for another (as in BARTER).

2 the sum of money paid by an investor to purchase SHARES, STOCKS, etc., or the proceeds from selling such securities before allowing for stockbroker's commission and other transfer expenses.

consignment an arrangement between an exporter and an importer of a product under which the exporter only receives payment for the product after it has been transported to, and sold by, the importer. Where exporters sell GOODS on consignment they may experience significant delays in being paid and must make appropriate funding arrangements to maintain their cash flow. See EXPORTING, EXPORT CREDIT GUARANTEE DEPARTMENT.

consignment inventory the practice of supplying components to a customer, where these components are held in STOCK at the user's premises. The user is only invoiced for items actually used in production.

consistency see ACCOUNTING PRINCIPLES.

Brand	*Sound quality*	*Picture quality*	*Layout of controls*
A	4	4	3
B	5	5	3
C	3	4	4

Fig. 24 **Conjoint analysis.** Rating scores for television sets.

consol a FINANCIAL SECURITY issued by the government as a means of raising money. Consols are issued at a fixed price and bear a nominal fixed INTEREST RATE. Unlike other securities issued by the government such as TREASURY BILLS and BONDS, consols are irredeemable, i.e. they do not carry a specified redemption date. However, consols can be bought and sold on the STOCK MARKET at variable prices reflecting the forces of supply and demand for them.

consolidated accounts the aggregate accounts of a group of companies. A consolidated BALANCE SHEET is compiled by adding the assets and LIABILITIES of all companies in the group, after making allowance for any amounts that companiesin the group owe to one another. A consolidated PROFIT-AND-LOSS ACCOUNT is prepared by adding the SALES REVENUES and COSTS of all companies in the group, after deducting the effects of any sales between companies within the group. The claims of any MINORITY INTERESTS in group assets and profits must also be allowed for.

Preparation of consolidated accounts for a MULTINATIONAL ENTERPRISE with subsidiary companies in several countries is complicated by the need to translate the accounts of these subsidiaries, expressed in terms of their local currencies, into the domestic currency of the parent company (see FOREIGN CURRENCY TRANSLATION, EXCHANGE RATE EXPOSURE). See HOLDING COMPANY.

consortium a group of independent companies or financial institutions which agree to work together jointly on some undertaking, for example the construction of an electricity power plant or the provision of a range of financial services, each contributing some particular resource input or expertise. In recent years, many TAKEOVERS of companies have been arranged on a consortium basis, with a view to breaking up the target company and sharing out its assets between the individual participants in the consortium. See CONTRACTOR.

constant failure rate see FAILURE RATE CURVE.

constructive dismissal see UNFAIR DISMISSAL.

consultation the process in which managers inform and seek the views of others before finally deciding what course of action to take. It may take place with interested parties outside the organization, for example local authorities, or with those inside. In INDUSTRIAL RELATIONS, joint consultation is where managers consult with employee representatives. It differs from COLLECTIVE BARGAINING in that managers do not usually seek formal agreement and in theory NEGOTIATION does not occur. Instead, representatives are there to listen to management plans and to express their views on them. However, since these views may be forcefully expressed and may be backed up by substantial power resources, managers may have to modify or even abandon their plans as a result. Thus the difference between consultation and collective bargaining may therefore be more apparent than real, and may hinge on the procedural distinction that disagreements during consultation cannot normally be carried forward to the next stage of a GRIEVANCE PROCEDURE.

Consultation may occur in a variety of bodies – joint consultative committee, works committee, etc. – and may involve workplace trade union representatives (SHOP STEWARDS) or representatives elected by all employees separately from union channels of representation. In the latter case, the consultative body is often known as the Works Council, after the German name for such institutions (see CO-DETERMINATION).

Traditionally, consultation has been viewed as dealing with minor welfare issues ('tea 'n' toilets') though major rationalizations can be the subject of consultation. However, it is a common complaint that employees are either not consulted at all over such important issues or else consultation is left to such a late stage that it is impossible to modify managerial plans. In recent years some companies, e.g. some of the Japanese firms in the UK, have extended consultation to cover issues relating to company strategy, whilst legislation has stipulated that information should be disclosed to unions and their representatives relating to

REDUNDANCY. Equally, there has been a shift in some organizations from formal joint consultation with employee representatives to direct COMMUNICATION with individual employees. Currently the EUROPEAN WORKS COUNCIL directive of the European Union is requiring that large European firms with plants in more than one member state establish works councils composed of employee representatives from all parts of the company for the purpose of consultation on key issues of company strategy. See DISCLOSURE OF INFORMATION, EMPLOYEE INVOLVEMENT, EMPLOYEE PARTICIPATION.

consumer the end user of a final GOOD or SERVICE which is purchased to satisfy a personal consumption need. See BUYER BEHAVIOUR.

consumer adoption the acceptance and purchasing of NEW PRODUCTS or BRANDS by CONSUMERS. The rate at which consumers adopt a new product will determine whether or not it is withdrawn from the market or continues to be sold. A very high proportion of new products launched are rejected by consumers and only a minority gain rapid consumer acceptance. Consumer acceptance of a particular brand of a good determines the extent to which the consumer will continue to purchase that brand in preference to competitors' brands. See BRAND LOYALTY, TEST MARKETING.

consumer behaviour see BUYER BEHAVIOUR.

Consumer Credit Act 1974 a UK Act which provides for the licensing of persons and businesses engaged in the provision of consumer CREDIT (specifically moneylenders, pawnbrokers and INSTALMENT CREDIT traders – but not banks which are covered by separate legislation), and the regulation of debtor-creditor contracts. The former requirement is designed to ensure that only 'fit and proper' persons are allowed to provide consumer finance, and the latter gives borrowers certain rights in respect of withdrawal from an agreement, to complete payments ahead of time and to terminate the agreement. The Act contains important provisions protecting creditors from extortionate rates of interest. The Act is administered by the OFFICE OF FAIR TRADING in conjunction with the DEPARTMENT OF TRADE AND INDUSTRY. See CONSUMER PROTECTION, APR.

consumer decision-making process the stages a consumer goes through when buying something, namely, product awareness, information search, evaluation of alternatives, purchase and post-purchase evaluation. See BUYER BEHAVIOUR.

consumer durables CONSUMER GOODS such as television sets, motorcars and microwave ovens which yield satisfaction to consumers over relatively long periods of time rather than immediately. Consumer durables tend to be purchased infrequently by a consumer, and are generally expensive items which are often purchased on CREDIT terms. Compare CONSUMER NONDURABLES. See GOOD.

consumer goods products such as television sets, bread and clothing, which are purchased by CONSUMERS for their own personal consumption. See GOOD, CONSUMER DURABLES, CONSUMER NONDURABLES.

consumerism an organized movement to protect the interests of CONSUMERS by forcing companies to behave in a more socially responsible manner. The movement developed in response to the increasing technical complexity of products, the growing power of big businesses and environmental pollution. In many countries there are now consumer bodies, such as the Consumer Association in the UK, which provide product-testing facilities and publish comparative information on products through magazines such as *Which*. See GREEN CONSUMER.

consumer loyalty see BRAND LOYALTY.

consumer nondurables CONSUMER GOODS such as coffee, beefburgers and hair shampoos which yield satisfaction to consumers at the time of immediate use. Such GOODS are purchased frequently and are generally low-priced items. Compare CONSUMER DURABLES.

consumer orientation a business philosophy of a company which emphasizes the provision of GOODS and SERVICES that have been specially designed to satisfy the needs of its customers. A CONSUMER or customer orientation involves the identification of customer needs with a view to developing products which satisfy these needs (see NEW PRODUCT DEVELOPMENT).

Once a firm has chosen to operate in a particular MARKET it needs to identify the needs of customers including, where appropriate, the needs of specific subgroups of customers (see MARKET SEGMENTATION).

A consumer orientation strategy thus requires a firm to understand the attitudes, wants and behaviour of a target group of consumers (see MARKETING RESEARCH. BUYER BEHAVIOUR). Having defined consumer wants, a firm can then develop products with characteristics which satisfy these wants and develop an appropriate MARKETING MIX to market them.

Contrast with PRODUCTION ORIENTATION. See MARKETING CONCEPT.

consumer panel see MARKETING INTELLIGENCE.

consumer preference product attributes which CONSUMERS seek and which will lead them to choose one BRAND of a product in preference to other similar brands. Information about consumer preferences may be obtained from MARKETING RESEARCH techniques like interviews or postal questionnaires. PRODUCT DEVELOPMENT can then be geared to designing products which match consumer preferences, offering the appropriate blend of product characteristics to suit the demands of the market as a whole or of particular market segments (see MARKET SEGMENTATION).

consumer price index see RETAIL PRICE INDEX.

consumer products see SELLER.

consumer protection a generic term used to describe various pieces of legislation whose objective is to protect CONSUMERS from unscrupulous, unfair and intrusive trade practices and unsafe products. In the UK the main Acts concerning consumer protection in force at the present time are: the WEIGHTS AND MEASURES ACT 1963; the TRADE DESCRIPTIONS ACTS 1968 and 1972; the UNSOLICITED GOODS AND SERVICES ACT 1971 and 1975; the FAIR TRADING ACT 1973; the CONSUMER CREDIT ACT 1974; the CONSUMER SAFETY ACT 1978; the PRICE MARKING (BARGAIN OFFERS) ORDER 1979, SALE OF GOODS ACT 1979; SALE OF GOODS AND SERVICES ACT 1982; ESTATE AGENCY ACT 1979; CONTROL OF MISLEADING ADVERTISEMENTS REGULATIONS 1988; CONSUMER PROTECTION ACT 1987. See FINANCIAL SERVICES AUTHORITY, OMBUDSMAN, OFFICE OF FAIR TRADING, DEPARTMENT OF TRADE AND INDUSTRY. See also CONSUMERISM, COMPETITION POLICY (UK) (EU).

Consumer Protection Act 1987 a UK Act which extends existing powers to protect consumers in the areas of consumer safety (the Act makes it a criminal offence to supply unsafe goods) and misleading price indications (the Act makes deceptive price advertising an offence and requires price promises to be kept). In addition, the Act introduces new powers for consumers to obtain damages against suppliers whose products prove defective. See CONSUMER SAFETY ACT 1978; TRADE DESCRIPTIONS ACT 1968; CONSUMER PROTECTION.

Consumer Safety Act 1978 a UK Act which empowers the Secretary of State for Trade and Industry to make regulations in respect of a product so as to prevent or reduce the risk of personal injury or death. This Act subsumes the Consumer Protection Acts 1961 and 1971 and the regulations previously made under these Acts covering, for example, gas and electric fires, electric blankets, cooking utensils and perambulators. See CONSUMER PROTECTION ACT 1987.

Consumers' Association see CONSUMERISM.

consumer segmentation an approach to marketing which involves grouping together potential BUYERS of a product on the basis of similarities in their buying characteristics. This enables a firm to match the attributes of its products' requirements or behaviour with that of identified buyer characteristics when selecting MARKET SEGMENTS to target. See MARKET SEGMENTATION.

consumer surplus a difference between the price the consumer is *actually* required to pay for a product compared to the price the consumer *would be prepared* to pay. In Fig 25, which shows a downward-sloping demand curve for a product, the price charged is indicated by P. The shaded area above P represents the consumer surplus. To illustrate: you are a Manchester United Football fan; tickets for a home game are currently priced at £50 but you would be willing to pay £75. Hence you have 'received' as a consumer a 'perceived benefit' or 'surplus' of £25 over and above the price actually charged.

Business strategists can use the concept of the consumer surplus to increase the firm's profits and COMPETITIVE ADVANTAGES over rival suppliers (see VALUE CREATED MODEL). For example, in the case of Manchester United instead of charging a single price of £50 it could segment its market, charging different prices for admission to different parts of the ground. (See PRICE DISCRIMINATION, MARKET SEGMENTATION) in order to 'capture' more of the consumer surplus for itself. Thus, it could continue to charge the 'basic' price of £50 for admission to certain parts of the ground; £75 for seating in the main stand and £120 for an 'executive box' seat. Similarly, BSkyB the television broadcaster offers subscribers not only a basic 'variety' package of some 75 channels but other extra pay channels such as Sky Sports 1, 2 and 3 and the movie channel.

consumer survey see MARKETING RESEARCH.

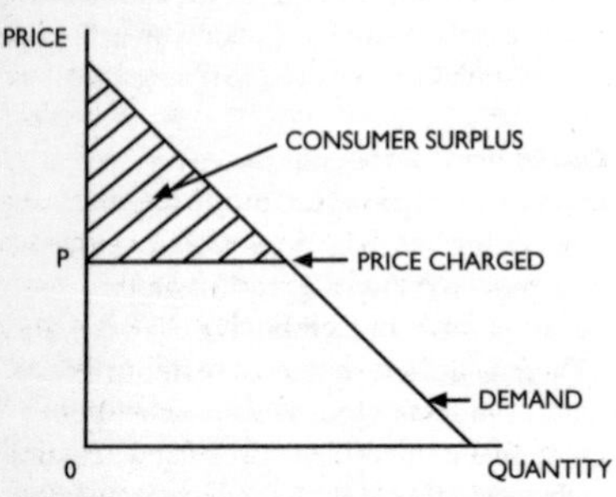

Fig. 25 **Consumer surplus.**

consumer wants the desire of CONSUMERS to have particular NEEDS satisfied by the consumption of GOODS and SERVICES. See BUYER BEHAVIOUR.

contango 1 an additional payment made by an investor or speculator who has purchased or sold a SHARE, STOCK etc. on the UK STOCK MARKET in return for being permitted to carry over the settlement of the share transaction from one ACCOUNT PERIOD to the next.

2 a condition in a FORWARD MARKET where the most distant delivery months trade at a premium to the near term delivery months.

continental shift see SHIFT WORK.

contingency allowance see ALLOWANCES.

contingency plan tactics which would be adopted in the event of a firm's original plans being thwarted. It is important for a BUSINESS to establish contingency plans so that they have a fall-back position. If, for example, a key component supplier is unable to deliver on time, the firm should have alternative suppliers lined up to avoid excessive disruption to its own production process.

contingency theory an approach to ORGANIZATIONAL ANALYSIS which emphasizes that the character and structure of ORGANIZATIONS can take a number of forms, and may be related to the technology in use or the organization's environment. Organizational features can be said to be contingent on such factors.

The idea of contingency is now so widely accepted in the study of organizations, and views premised on it so diverse that it is more accurate to speak of a contingency approach rather than one theory as such. The contingency approach is notable for rejecting the notion that there is one best way of structuring organizations (see CLASSICAL MANAGEMENT THEORY, SCIENTIFIC MANAGEMENT).

The contingency approach initially became popular in the 1960s. British industrial sociologist Joan Woodward (1916–71) found that technology (in itself determined by what product the firm was making) was associated with certain structural characteristics. For instance, the more advanced the technology, the longer the CHAIN OF COMMAND. Woodward argued that there was a particular form of organizational structure appropriate to each technical situation. Other writers emphasized the importance of environment. American writers Paul Lawrence (1922–) and Jay Lorsch (1932–) suggested that the greater the degree of environmental uncertainty and complexity, the greater the need for differentiation of management functions within the organization, but also the need for integrative devices to pull the organization together. Like Woodward they argued that there was an appropriate organizational form for each type of environment. A number of British writers also traced the relationship between environment and organizational form (see MECHANISTIC AND ORGANISMIC).

The most important investigation of these issues in the UK was conducted by the 'Aston School' (members of the Industrial Administration Research Unit at Aston University, including Derek Pugh (1930–) and David Hickson (1931–)) in the 1960s. This project found that the structuring of organizational activities (e.g. specialization of job roles and departments) was correlated not with technology but with the size of the organization, whilst the degree of centralization of decision-making was correlated with the degree of dependence upon other organizations, such as suppliers.

Whilst most writers on organizations now adopt a contingency approach, views differ on how far certain factors, such as environment, determine organizational form and how far top managers can make a strategic choice to model their organizations in certain ways by taking account of such factors.

contingent liability a liability which may or may not occur depending upon an uncertain event, for example, the outcome of a court case in which damages are being claimed against a firm.

continuation day the first day of the UK STOCK MARKET ACCOUNT PERIOD.

continuing professional development (CPD) the regular updating by PROFESSIONALS of their skills and knowledge. Professional institutes encourage their members to undertake CPD, and in some cases progression within the professional body is dependent on a minimum level of regular CPD.

continuous flow manufacturing 1 Used to describe JUST-IN-TIME manufacturing systems.

2 Manufacturing or service provision which because of very high levels of demand have to be made constantly available, for example, the provision of gas, electricity or water. Some pure manufacturing is described as continuous, for example the manufacture of float glass at the Pilkington factory in St Helens or the cracking of petroleum products at an oil refinery.

continuous improvement see KAIZAN, LEAN MANUFACTURING.

continuous production see MASS PRODUCTION, CONTINUOUS FLOW MANUFACTURING.

continuous review system of stock control see FIXED QUANTITY REORDER SYSTEM.

continuous stock-taking see STOCK CONTROL.

contract a legally enforceable agreement between two or more parties generally relating to a TRANSACTION for the purchase or sale of inputs, goods and services. A contract involves obligations on the part of the contractors which may be expressed verbally or in writing. Formation of a contract involves one party making an offer to the other party which must then be *accepted* by the latter party. For example, one firm may offer to supply a product to another company at a given future date and on specified terms. In return, the latter company would agree to pay a specified sum of money as *consideration* for the product to be supplied. Both parties would then be legally bound to honour their agreement to sell and to buy the product. In the event of either party failing to comply with the terms of the contract the other party could seek damages for breach of contract through the courts.

A *complete contract* stipulates each party's responsibilities and rights for every contingency that could conceivably arise during the transaction. Such a complete contract would bind the parties to particular courses of action as the transaction unfolds, with neither party having any freedom to exploit weaknesses in the other's position. It is difficult to develop complete contracts since parties to the contract must be able to specify every possible contingency and the required responsibilities by the contracting parties; stipulate what constitutes satisfactory performance; make the contract enforceable; and have access to complete information about circumstances surrounding the contract.

In practice, most contracts are *incomplete contracts* in which precise terms of the contract cannot be fully specified. In such situations, one or other parties to the agreement may be tempted to take advantage of the open-endedness or ambiguity of the contract at the expense of the other party. See ASYMMETRICAL INFORMATION, MORAL HAZARD.

In addition to contractual relationships between a firm and its *external* suppliers/customers, organizational theorists have paid particular attention to the role of contracts in the *internal* relationship between the employees ('agents') and owners ('principals') of a company in running the business. See PRINCIPAL-AGENT THEORY entry for details. See also CONTRACT OF EMPLOYMENT.

contract costing see COSTING.

contracting-out 1 the nonparticipation in some specific scheme operated by a company or government in favour of an alternative arrangement; for example, in the UK, an employee may opt out of his employer's company PENSION scheme, choosing instead to invest in a personal pension plan.
2 the placement of some or all of a firm's input requirements (raw materials, components, services) with independent suppliers. Whether or not a firm provides these resources itself through backward vertical integration or relies on outside suppliers will depend on a number of financial, technical and strategic considerations. See MAKE OR BUY DECISION, OUTSOURCING.
3 the putting-out to private firms of contracts for the provision of services to a public institution. The term 'contracting-out' has assumed a particular significance in the government's current privatization programme, referring specifically to a situation in which a publicly owned service such as the National Health Service employs private sector firms to supply, for example, laundry, cleaning and catering services. The logic for this is that it is more cost effective for these services to be bought in under conditions of competitive tendering by specialist firms enjoying economies of scale than for them to be provided by hospital staff. See TRANSFER OF UNDERTAKINGS, NATIONALIZATION VERSUS PRIVATIZATION).

contract note a document issued by a STOCKBROKER to a client, which confirms details of a purchase or sale of STOCKS and SHARES on behalf of the client.

contract of employment an agreement whereby a worker undertakes to work for an employer in return for a wage or salary. In the UK most workers are entitled to a written statement of the main elements of the contract, such as rates of pay, hours of work, and notice requirements. These are referred to as the terms and conditions of employment. It is usual for a brief JOB DESCRIPTION to be included in this statement. However, this document is not necessarily the full contract: the requirements stipulated in a separate company rule book and any agreements reached through COLLECTIVE BARGAINING also form part of the contract. Legally, this is encapsulated in a distinction between 'express terms' and 'implied terms': the former are explicitly part of the contract document signed by the employee whilst the latter are the other elements of the contract that are not explicitly agreed between employer and employee but which are nevertheless held to form part of the agreement in law.

The contract provides rights and imposes obligations on each party to it. The employer has the broad right to direct the work of the employee: what to do and how to do it. If the employee fails to carry out their allotted duties satisfactorily the employer can terminate the contract. However, the employer must have a valid reason for sacking the employee and must have carried out the termination in accordance with an acceptable DISCIPLINARY PROCEDURE. If the employee feels that they have been dismissed unfairly or that proper procedures have not been observed, they may take an UNFAIR DISMISSAL case (for reinstatement or compensation) to an EMPLOYMENT TRIBUNAL. See PRINCIPAL-AGENT THEORY.

contract of sale a CONTRACT under which the SELLER of a product transfers or agrees to transfer the product to the BUYER of the product for a money consideration. Contracts of sale contain various terms or conditions on which the product is to be supplied including, typically, product descriptions, qualities, quantities, delivery dates and prices. Remedies for breach of contract can be sought through the Courts. See SALE OF GOODS ACTS 1979, 1962.

contractor a person or firm which enters into a legal CONTRACT with another person or firm to supply goods or services. For example, in the building industry a housebuilder may employ contractors to undertake the plumbing and electrical work involved in the construction of houses, rather than do this work himself. The plumbing and electrical contractors would provide, for the contract price, all piping, wire, etc. needed, plus the specialist workers to install them. In turn, the plumber may enter into an agreement with a *subcontractor* to install the timeclocks and electrical controls for the central heating system. Complex projects requiring a large number of specialist inputs are frequently undertaken on a CONSORTIUM basis.

contribution the difference between SALES REVENUE and VARIABLE COSTS. If total contributions are just large enough to cover FIXED COSTS then the producer BREAKS EVEN; if contributions are less than fixed costs the producer makes a LOSS; while if contributions exceed fixed costs then the producer makes a PROFIT. Fig. 26 shows how contributions provide a fund out of which total fixed costs must be paid before any profit is made. See MARGINAL COSTING.

contribution per £ of sales see PROFIT-VOLUME RATIO.

control the process of ensuring that activities are carried out as intended. Control involves monitoring aspects of performance and taking corrective action where necessary. For instance, control of expenditure involves regular monitoring of expenditure figures, comparison of these with budget targets, and decisions to cut or increase expenditure where any discrepancy is believed to be harmful. Without control an ORGANIZATION cannot function: employees would go their own way (possibly with the best of intentions) and the organization would fragment, making COORDINATION impossible. Control can, therefore, be viewed as a central component of MANAGEMENT.

Outputs (units per annum)	700	800	900	1,000	1,100
	£	£	£	£	£
Sales revenue (at price £20)	14,000	16,000	18,000	20,000	22,000
less Variable cost (£10 per unit)	7,000	8,000	9,000	10,000	11,000
Contribution (£10 per unit)	7,000	8,000	9,000	10,000	11,000
less Fixed costs	9,000	9,000	9,000	9,000	9,000
Profit (Loss)	(2,000)	(1,000)	NIL	1,000	2,000
Note Total cost	16,000	17,000	18,000	19,000	20,000
Unit Total cost	22.86	21.25	20.00	19.00	18.18

Fig. 26 **Contribution.** Output and sales of chairs.

Some writers in the SOCIOLOGY OF WORK have argued that, since (in their view) employers' and employees' interests are opposed, control of labour is the main task of management. Without it, workers would behave in a way which is detrimental to managerial goals. Research has shown, however, that many managers attach more importance to other managerial functions (such as budgeting), whilst it is questionable whether employees would necessarily act in the way suggested. See ORGANIZATIONAL ANALYSIS.

control chart, quality control chart, process chart *or* **P (percent defective control) chart** a diagram used to plot variations in the size or other characteristic of a component or PRODUCT made by a machine and/or operative. Such charts are compiled by taking samples of items produced and measuring their sizes or characteristics. Where variations are small and fall within predefined normal or acceptable limits marked on the control chart, no action is necessary. However, where machine faults, worn tools or defective materials cause larger variations than the control limits then the cause of this variation must be investigated and immediate corrective action taken to avoid any further production of defective items. See QUALITY CONTROL.

Fig. 27 shows a typical control chart which depicts variations in the size of a machine component, and the upper and lower control limits at which the process would require correction.

control costs the costs to a firm of avoiding making defective products. Control costs fall into two main categories. First *prevention costs,* which are the costs of pre-production activities aimed at preventing defects. Prevention costs include costs of preparing quality manuals and procedures, training, process planning and collecting data about product quality.

Second, *appraisal costs,* which are the costs of eliminating defects after they occur but before products reach the customer. These costs include final goods inspection, inspection during the production process, and laboratory testing. See QUALITY COSTS, QUALITY CONTROL, NORMAL CURVE.

control limits see CONTROL CHART.

Control of Misleading Advertisements Regulations 1988 a UK regulatory framework which gives the OFFICE OF FAIR TRADING powers to protect the general buying public from deceptive ADVERTISEMENTS. An advertisement is misleading if it deceives people by, for example, making a false statement of fact or concealing or omitting important facts about the product. See CONSUMER PROTECTION.

convenience goods PRODUCTS such as newspapers which CONSUMERS buy at frequent intervals with little comparison or buying effort. Contrast with SHOPPING, GOODS.

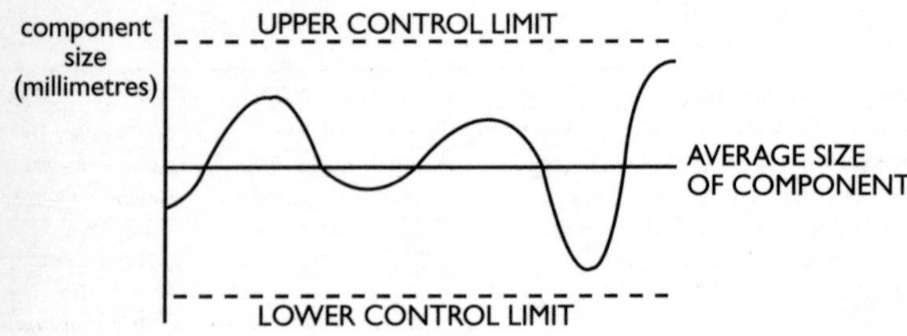

Fig. 27 **Control chart.**

convenience store a retail outlet offering customers the convenience of close location and long opening hours every day of the week.

convenor a senior SHOP STEWARD responsible, in negotiations and discussions with management, for representing the views and policies of the shop stewards' committee in a workplace.

convertibility the extent to which a financial security such as a FOREIGN CURRENCY or CONVERTIBLE LOAN can be exchanged for some other currency or financial ASSET.

convertible currency a currency which can be converted into another currency without special permission from the FOREIGN EXCHANGE CONTROL authorities.

convertible loan stock as convertible debentures long-term LOANS to a JOINT-STOCK COMPANY which may be converted at the option of the lender into ORDINARY SHARES at a predetermined share price.

conveyance a document which transfers the legal ownership of land and buildings from one person/business to another person/ business.

conveyor equipment which is used to transport raw materials, work in progress and finished goods around a factory. Conveyors assist the smooth flow of materials/PRODUCTS and are used extensively in PRODUCTION-LINE/ASSEMBLY-LINE operations.

cooperation 1 the process whereby businesses seek to coordinate their pricing and output policies rather than compete with one another in order to secure higher profits. See OLIGOPOLY, COLLUSION, CARTEL.
2 the process whereby individuals coordinate their work in GROUPS.

cooperative see WORKERS' COOPERATIVE, RETAIL COOPERATIVE.

coordinated marketing see MARKETING STRATEGY.

coordination the process of combining together the work of ORGANIZATION members and departments to achieve the desired end-product or goals of the organization. Coordination is necessary at two levels:

(a) the bringing together of production tasks to achieve production goals with the minimum of waste, buffer stocks, etc.;

(b) the coordination of all organizational functions to achieve effective and efficient operations and the maintenance of the organization as a viable entity.

Coordination of a complex range of activities is fraught with problems, and it is a central issue in the design and running of organizations. Some organizations seek to achieve coordination by formulating a range of rules and procedures to guide and govern the work of employees and departments. Others prefer to rely on the skills, knowledge and commitment of their employees to interpret what forms of coordination are necessary (see MECHANISTIC AND ORGANISMIC, CULTURE). Most organizations adopt a combination of the two. In all organizations, however, the need for coordination is embodied in the formal structure. Some adopt a FUNCTIONAL STRUCTURE, some a PRODUCT-BASED STRUCTURE, whilst others adopt a MATRIX STRUCTURE explicitly to tackle problems of coordination.

co-ownership see WORKERS' COOPERATIVE.

copycat product see MARKET POSITIONING.

copyright the legal ownership by persons or businesses of certain kinds of material, in particular original literary, dramatic, musical and artistic work; sound recordings, films, broadcasts and cable programmes; the typographical arrangement or layout of a published edition; and computer programs. In the UK, the COPYRIGHT, DESIGNS AND PATENTS ACT 1988 gives legal rights to the creators of copyright material so that they can control the various ways in which their work may be exploited. Copyright protection is automatic and there is no registration or other formality. The 1988 Act gives copyright owners protection against unauthorized copying of such material in most cases for a period of 50 years. If copyright is infringed, the copyright owner (or assignee or licensee) may seek an injunction through the courts preventing further abuses, with offenders liable to pay unlimited damages/ fines and prison sentences in extreme cases. See BRAND.

Copyright, Designs and Patents Act 1988 a UK Act which provides for the establishment and protection of the legal ownership rights of persons and businesses in respect of various classes of 'intellectual property', in particular COPYRIGHTS, PERFORMERS RIGHTS, DESIGN RIGHTS (including registered designs) and PATENTS. The Act amends and restates various earlier statutes, including the Copyright Act 1956, the Registered Designs Act 1949, the Performers' Protection Acts 1958–72 and the Patents Act 1977.

The Act is administered in part by the PATENTS OFFICE, with cases of unauthorized copying, patent infringements, etc. being handled by the courts.

core business a division of a conglomerate firm which is considered to be central to the firm's corporate success insofar as it embodies the firm's CORE SKILLS and competencies and generates the bulk of its sales revenue and profits. See DIVERSIFICATION, DIVESTMENT.

By contrast, a non-core business is one which makes only a relatively small contribution to the firm's overall activities. However, the dividing-line between core and non-core businesses can be elastic when viewed over time. For example, BAT Industries' main core business was and continues to be tobacco products but from 1983 it developed through acquisitions a large insurance division which it also regarded as a core business, until it was demerged in 1997.

core competency see CORE SKILLS.

core product-benefit the most important attribute of a product in the judgement of a *particular* buyer when considering the purchase of a PRODUCT. Thus one buyer of a motor-car might look specifically for style, another for comfort, and yet another for speed, so that each is seeking a different version of it. By identifying groups of consumers who are seeking the same core product-benefit, it is possible to undertake appropriate PRODUCT DIFFERENTIATION strategies. See CONJOINT ANALYSIS.

core skill *or* **competency** the particular, often unique, abilities possessed by a firm in supplying a product which provides the basis for the firm's on-going COMPETITIVE ADVANTAGES over rival suppliers. At an individual level, core competencies are the key skills and knowledge required in a job (see RECRUITMENT AND SELECTION). Such skills may reside, for example, in the firm's research and development or marketing capabilities. Essentially they embody the expertise of the firm's incumbent staff, accumulated know-how and intellectual property rights (PATENTS).

From a strategic perspective, the possession of core skills suggests that firms should concentrate on what they do best (that is, 'stick to the knitting') rather than be tempted to diversify (see DIVERSIFICATION) into areas they know little about or dissipate their energies by trying to do too many things. See CORE BUSINESS, RESOURCE BASED THEORY OF THE FIRM, DISTINCTIVE CAPABILITIES, VALUE CHAIN ANALYSIS.

core workforce see LABOUR FLEXIBILITY.

cornering the market an attempt to buy up all the supplies of a particular commodity in order to exploit the market by charging high prices.

Corn Exchange a London-based wholesale commodity exchange which undertakes dealings in cereals, seeds, fertilizers and animal feedstuffs. See BALTIC MERCANTILE AND SHIPPING EXCHANGE, COMMODITY MARKET.

corporate goals see BUSINESS OBJECTIVES.

corporate governance the duties and responsibilities of a company's BOARD OF DIRECTORS in managing the company and their relationship with the SHAREHOLDERS of the company. Typically salaried professional managers have acquired substantial powers in respect of the affairs of the company they are paid to run on behalf of their shareholders. However, directors have not always had the best interests of shareholders in mind when performing their managerial functions (see PRINCIPAL-AGENT THEORY) and this has led to attempts to make directors more accountable for their policies and actions.

A number of reports have been published in the UK in the 1990s prompted by the public's concern at cases of gross mismanagement (for example, the collapse of the BCCI bank and Polly Peck and the misappropriation of employees' pension monies at the Mirror Group) and 'fat cat' pay increases secured by executive directors. The Cadbury Committee Report (1992), recommended a 'Code of Best Practice' relating to the appointment and responsibilities of executive directors, the independence of non-executive directors and tighter internal financial controls and reporting procedures. The Greenbury Committee Report (1995) specifically addressed the issue of directors' pay recommending that executive directors' pay packages should be determined by the company's Remuneration Committee consisting solely of non-executive directors and that share awards under EXECUTIVE SHARE OPTION SCHEMES and LONG-TERM INCENTIVE PLANS (LTIPS) should be linked to the company's financial performance. The Hempel Committee Report (1998) covered many of the same issues raised by these two earlier reports recommending ('Principles of Good Governance') checks on the power of any one individual executive director (by, for example, separating the roles of Chairman and Chief Executive), a more independent and stronger voice for non-executives (including the appointment of a 'senior' non-executive to offer guidance to, and check 'empire building' tendencies on the part of, executive directors, and in liaising with shareholder interests), and more accountability to shareholders at the AGM (including the approval of options and LTIP schemes).

In 1998 the 'Code of Best Practice' and 'Principles of Good Governance' were combined and 'the combined code' was formally incorporated into the listing rules of the London STOCK EXCHANGE.

Increased concern with financial irregularities and malpractice resulted in two reports (Turnbull, 1999 and Smith 2003) proposing guidelines to tighten internal financial control and auditing practices. A similar stricter regime of financial monitoring has been implemented in the USA (the Sarbanes-Oxley Act, 2002) in the wake of 'scandals' such as Enron.

More recently, the Higgs Report (2003) on the role of non-executive directors recommended that they be given a more prominent position including: the company's Chairman should be a non-executive and that at least half of the Board's directors should be non-executive. See BUSINESS OBJECTIVES, SOCIAL RESPONSIBILITY, STAKEHOLDER.

corporate identity 1 the ethos, aims and values of an organization, presenting a sense of its individuality which helps to differentiate it from its competitors
2 a specially designed symbol or printed heading used by a company to make it more easily recognized by the general public. Such symbols or headings are used on company letterheads, business cards, invoices, advertisements and signs. See COMPANY IMAGE.

corporate raider see ARBITRAGEUR.

corporate restructuring 1 a change in a firm's STRATEGIC DIRECTION involving, for example, its expansion into new business activities (see DIVERSIFICATION) and its withdrawal from some existing activities (see DIVESTMENT).
2 a change in a firm's internal ORGANIZATION involving, for example, the replacement of a highly centralized decision-making structure by one based on individual STRATEGIC BUSINESS UNITS. See ORGANIZATIONAL STRUCTURE, BUSINESS PROCESS RE-ENGINEERING.

corporate social responsibility a business philosophy which stresses the need for firms to behave as good corporate citizens, not merely obeying the law but conducting their production and marketing activities in a manner which avoids causing environmental pollution or exhausting finite world resources. Some businesses have begun to behave in a more socially responsible manner, partly because their managers want to do so, and partly because of fear of environmentalist and consumer pressure groups and the media, and concern for their public image. It is argued that socially responsible behaviour can pay off in the long run, even where it involves some short-term sacrifice of profit. See CONSUMERISM, COMPANY IMAGE, CORPORATE GOVERNANCE.

corporate strategy see BUSINESS STRATEGY.

corporate venturing a situation where a major company takes a minority stake in a new or relatively new company and injects cash into that company. However, corporate venturing may go much further than the provision of finance, and may involve a cross-fertilization of skills, talents, know-how and expertise which may be of benefit to both parties involved. See VENTURE CAPITAL.

corporation a North American term for a JOINT-STOCK COMPANY.

corporation tax a DIRECT TAX levied by the government on the PROFITS accruing to businesses. A company's corporation tax is loosely based upon its profit for the accounting period as determined in the COMPANY'S PROFIT-AND-LOSS ACCOUNT. However, since firms use different methods for calculating DEPRECIATION of FIXED ASSETS to charge against revenues and so arrive at different PROFIT figures, the UK government establishes a standard scale of CAPITAL ALLOWANCES which all firms must apply to their fixed assets when computing taxable *profit.*

When a company pays dividends or makes other distributions of profit to shareholders, then it must also make a payment of *advance corporation tax* to the government, currently equal to one third of the dividend paid. This is an advance payment of corporation tax and can be offset by the company against its liability to *mainstream corporation tax* when this liability is assessed at the year end.

Shareholders receiving a dividend are also treated as receiving a *tax credit* equal, at current rates, to one third of the dividend received. This tax credit is added to the dividend received to establish the shareholders' total taxable income. This *imputation system,* whereby the tax paid on distributed profits by the company is credited to the shareholders, avoids double-taxing the shareholders both on their company's profits and on their dividend distributions.

In the UK (as at 2005/06) the general corporation tax rate is 30% of taxable profits per annum, but there is also a 'smaller companies' corporation tax rate. No tax is payable on taxable profits up to £10,000 per annum and 19% on taxable profits over £10,000 up to a maximum of £300,000 per annum.

The level of corporation tax is important to a firm insofar as it determines the amount of after-tax profit which is available to it to pay out DIVIDENDS to shareholders or to reinvest in the business (see RETAINED PROFITS). See INLAND REVENUE.

corporatism see TRIPARTISM.

cost the expenditure upon resources incurred by a firm in producing and selling its output. Each cost is a charge against revenues and profits for the use or consumption of resources during a trading period. (see PROFIT AND LOSS ACCOUNT). Costs can be classified along functional lines, distinguishing between production, selling, distribution, administration and financing costs. Alternatively costs can be classified as either direct costs (usually raw materials and direct labour) or indirect costs (overheads) (see PROFIT AND LOSS ACCOUNT). Costs may also be classified as variable costs and fixed costs, depending on whether they vary with the level of output or activity. In addition, costs may be analysed by product. Finally costs may be classified by location (division, subsidiary, company, department, etc.).

Classification and analysis of costs is necessary for three main business purposes:

(a) for *product costing;*
(b) for *management control;*
(c) for *decision-making.*

Identification and classification of these costs is the core of MANAGEMENT ACCOUNTING. Fig. 28 shows the build up of major cost elements. See PRODUCTION COST, SELLING COST.

cost accounting see MANAGEMENT ACCOUNTING.

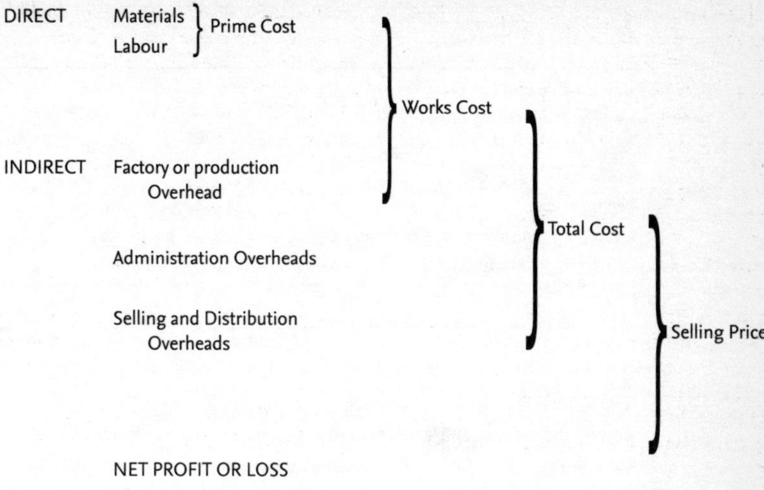

Fig. 28 **Cost.** Major elements of cost.

cost advantage strategy the establishment of a COMPETITIVE ADVANTAGE over rival suppliers which seeks to attain a *lower* supply cost/price than rivals while maintaining product benefits (quality, performance etc) that are comparable to competitors. See VALUE CREATED MODEL, COST DRIVERS, COMPETITIVE STRATEGY. Compare BENEFIT ADVANTAGE STRATEGY.

cost and freight (c&f) a term used to denote the respective contractual obligations of sellers and buyers of a GOOD which is exported. Under a c&f contract, the seller pays the cost of transporting the good to the port of shipment, the loading charges and the freight charges to the port of destination. From then on the buyer bears the cost of unloading and transporting the good to its final destination. The buyer pays *all* the insurance costs incurred.

See COST, INSURANCE AND FREIGHT, FREE ON BOARD, EXPORTING.

cost-based pricing

Pricing methods which determine the PRICE of a product on the basis of its production, distribution and marketing COSTS. Three cost-based pricing methods may be distinguished:

(a) *full-cost* or *mark-up* or *average cost pricing* of a product is determined by adding a percentage profit mark-up to average or unit total cost, unit total cost being composed of average or unit variable cost and average or unit fixed cost (both of which can be determined from MANAGEMENT ACCOUNTING records). Fig. 29 shows an example of full-cost pricing based on an estimated sales/production volume of 1000 units per month. Unit variable costs (costs which vary with the level of output, such as raw materials and direct labour)

Sales/production volume	1,000 units per month £
unit variable cost	2.00
unit fixed cost (FC÷volume)	1.00
total unit cost	3.00
profit mark-up (50%)	1.50
selling price	4.50
resulting total revenue £4.50 x 1,000 = £4,500 per month	
resulting total profit £1.50 x 1,000 = £1,500 per month	

Fig. 29 **Cost-based pricing.** Full cost or mark-up pricing example.

are £2. Total fixed costs (costs which do not vary with output, such as depreciation and factory rent) are £1000 per month so that average fixed cost at a volume of 1000 units is £1. Unit total cost is the sum of average variable cost and average fixed cost, and managers decide on the percentage profit mark-up (here 50%) to add to total cost to arrive at a selling price (here £4.50). At this price, revenue would be £4.50 x 1000 units or £4,500 per month and profits £1.50 x 1000 units or £1,500 per month, provided that 1000 units per month can be sold at this price;

(b) *cost-plus pricing* is very similar to full-cost or mark-up pricing, in so far as the price of a product is determined by adding a percentage profit mark-up to the product's unit total cost. Indeed the terms are often used interchangeably. However, cost-plus pricing is used more specifically to refer to an agreed price between a purchaser and the seller, where the price is based on actual costs incurred plus a fixed percentage of actual cost or a fixed amount of profit per unit. Such pricing methods are often used for large capital projects or high technology contracts where the length of time of construction or changing technical specifications lead to a high degree of uncertainty about the final price;

(c) *break-even* or *target-profit* or *marginal cost* pricing of a product is based upon the CONTRIBUTION needed for the product to BREAK EVEN or provide a predetermined target profit. Fig. 30 shows an example of break-even pricing based on an estimated sales/production volume of 1,000 units per month and total fixed costs (depreciation, rent, etc.) of £1,000 per month. Unit contribution is simply the difference between selling price and unit variable cost or marginal cost. Unit contribution, when multiplied by sales/production volume gives total contribution, and this total contribution should provide sufficient money to cover fixed costs (to break even) or fixed costs and target profit. Fig. 30 shows the unit contribution required in each case. To calculate selling price it is necessary to add unit contribution to unit variable cost or marginal cost as shown in Fig. 30.

Sales/production volume			1,000 units per month
			£
fixed cost			1,000 per month
target profit			1,500 per month

unit contribution to break-even = $\frac{£1{,}000}{1{,}000 \text{ units}} = £1.00$

Selling price to break-even

	£
unit variable cost	2.00
unit contribution	1.00
selling price	3.00

unit contribution to achieve target profit = $\frac{£1{,}000+1{,}500}{1{,}000 \text{ units}} = £2.50$

Selling price to achieve target profit

	£
unit variable cost	2.00
unit contribution	2.50
selling price	4.50

Fig. 30 **Cost-based pricing.** Break-even or marginal cost pricing example.

All three pricing methods are cost-based and to this extent appear to ignore demand. However, demand and competition cannot be ignored in setting prices. For instance, in full-cost and break-even pricing, estimates of sales volume are necessary to calculate average fixed cost and required unit contribution respectively. Yet in both cases the price charged will affect sales volume. In practice, managers take account of demand or competition, so that in using full-cost pricing they tend to vary the percentage mark-up over time to reflect fluctuations in demand, and to use different percentage mark-ups for different products to reflect differences in the intensity of competition. See DEMAND-BASED PRICING, COMPETITION-BASED PRICING.

cost-benefit analysis a technique for enumerating and evaluating the total social costs and social benefits associated with an economic project. Cost-benefit analysis is generally used by public agencies when evaluating large-scale public INVESTMENT projects such as major new motorways or rail lines, in order to assess the welfare or net social benefits which will accrue to the nation from these projects. This generally involves the sponsoring bodies taking a broader and longer-term view of a project than would a commercial organization concentrating on project profitability alone.

cost centre a group of machines, a factory department or some other organizational sub-unit of a firm under the control of a manager, for which costs can be ascertained and used for purposes of COST CONTROL. See STANDARD COST, PROFIT CENTRE, REVENUE CENTRE.

cost code a series of alphabetical or numerical symbols each of which represents a particular labour, material or overhead cost item. Cost codes facilitate the classification and recording of costs for cost control purposes.

cost control the task of controlling all items of expenditure by regular and frequent comparison of actual costs with predetermined budgeted or standard costs, identifying the causes of deviations of actual cost from standard, and taking corrective action to minimize such deviations. With regard to materials cost, deviations from planned materials usage can occur through excessive usage of raw materials for the output achieved or defective production leading to high scrap rates. With regard to labour cost, deviations from planned labour hours can occur, for example, through idle time caused by production bottlenecks. With regard to overheads, deviations from planned production-overheads per unit of product can occur because expenditure on overhead items exceeds budget or because actual output was less than planned. See MATERIALS COST VARIANCE, LABOUR COST VARIANCE, STANDARD COST, PRODUCTION MANAGEMENT, PRODUCTION CONTROL, BUDGETARY CONTROL, VARIANCE ANALYSIS.

cost drivers elements of a firm's operations which individually and collectively determines the level of the firm's (average or unit) COSTS. The ability to 'drive' or 'manage' costs down (or contain cost increases) is an important strategic consideration where cost leadership is the key basis of the firm's COMPETITIVE ADVANTAGE over rival suppliers.

There are four main categories of cost drivers

(a) those related to firm size and scope: ECONOMIES OF SCALE (the reduction in average costs as the scale of operation increases) and ECONOMIES OF SCOPE (the reduction in average costs as the firm produces a greater variety of product);

(b) those related to cumulative experience: the EXPERIENCE CURVE (cost reductions which arise over time as the firm 'learns' to operate technologies and processes more efficiently);

(c) cost drivers not related to the above, industry input prices (e.g. differences in hourly wage rates payable for 'unionised' as opposed to non-unionised workers); location (e.g. differences in transportation costs of local versus long-haul for input procurement and product distribution); process efficiencies (cost differences due to the fact that some firms are able to achieve higher levels of PRODUCTIVITY than others) etc;

(d) those related to the organization of transactions: VERTICAL INTEGRATION AND DISINTEGRATION (cost reductions which arise when buying and selling transactions are conducted within the firm rather than through the market) and the internal organization of the firm (AGENCY COSTS are higher for some firms than others). See VALUE CREATED MODEL, RESOURCE BASED THEORY OF THE FIRM; see also ACTIVITY-BASED COSTING. Compare BENEFIT DRIVERS.

cost focus strategy see COMPETITIVE STRATEGY.

costing the process of ascertaining the cost of a PRODUCT, COMPONENT or SERVICE. With historical costing, costs are ascertained after they have been incurred, though most businesses seek to gauge future costs through STANDARD COSTING.

Product costing seeks to determine the cost of each job or batch of products in order to assess the cost per unit. *Contract* costing is used to determine the construction costs of a large-scale building or civil engineering contract. *Process* costing is used where liquid or gaseous materials such as oil pass through several refining/heating processes to produce products such as petrol and by-products such as tar, and seeks to determine the costs of products by dividing output volume by materials and processing costs.

cost, insurance and freight (c.i.f) a term used to denote the respective contractual obligations of sellers and buyers of a good which is exported. Under a c.i.f. contract, the seller pays the cost of transporting the good to the port of shipment, the loading charges, and the freight charges to the port of destination, plus all insurance cover up to this point. From then on the buyer bears the cost of unloading, transporting, and insuring the good to its final destination. See COST AND FREIGHT, FREE ON BOARD, EXPORTING.

cost leadership strategy see COMPETITIVE STRATEGY.

cost of capital the cost to a firm of the LONG-TERM CAPITAL used to finance its business activities. The average cost of capital to a firm which uses several sources of long-term funds (for example LOANS, SHARE CAPITAL (EQUITY)) to finance its investments will depend upon the individual cost of each separate source of capital (for example INTEREST on loans), weighted in accordance with the proportions of each source used. See CAPITAL GEARING.

cost of goods sold see COST OF SALES.

cost of sales *or* **cost of goods sold** the relevant cost that is compared with SALES REVENUE in order to determine GROSS PROFIT in the PROFIT-AND-LOSS ACCOUNT. Where a trading company has STOCKS of finished goods, the cost of goods sold is not the same as purchases of finished goods. Rather, purchases of goods must be added to stock at the start of the trading period to determine the goods available for sale, then the stocks left at the end of the trading period must be deducted from this to determine the cost of the goods which have been sold during the period. See STOCK VALUATION.

cost of sales adjustment the difference between the COST OF SALES calculated on an HISTORIC COST and on a current cost or replacement cost basis. See INFLATION ACCOUNTING.

cost-plus pricing see COST-BASED PRICING.

cost price a PRICE for a product which just covers its production and distribution COSTS with no PROFIT MARGIN added.

cost-push inflation see INFLATION.

cost rate see ABSORPTION RATE.

cost-volume-profit see MARGINAL COSTING, BREAK-EVEN.

Council of the European Union the organization which arranges periodic meetings of ministers from the national governments of member states of the EUROPEAN UNION. Its role is to set political objectives for the European Union, coordinate national policies and resolve any differences between member states.

counselling see OCCUPATIONAL PSYCHOLOGY.

counterpurchase see COUNTERTRADE.

countertrade the direct or indirect exchange of goods for other goods in INTERNATIONAL TRADE. Countertrade is generally resorted to when particular FOREIGN CURRENCIES are in short supply, or when countries apply FOREIGN EXCHANGE CONTROLS.

There are various forms of countertrade, including:

(a) BARTER – the direct exchange of product for product;

(b) *compensation deal* – where the seller from the exporting country receives part payment in his own currency and the remainder in goods supplied by the buyer;

(c) *buyback* – where the seller of plant and equipment from the exporting country agrees to accept some of the goods produced by that plant and equipment in the importing country as part payment;

(d) *counterpurchase* – where the seller from the exporting country receives part payment for the goods in his own currency and the remainder in the local currency of the buyer, the latter then being used to purchase other products in the buyer's country. See EXPORTING.

country of origin the country in which a product is substantially manufactured. See LOCAL CONTENT RULE.

coupon 1 a voucher used as a means of promoting the sale of a product which is offered to buyers of the product to be redeemed for cash, gifts or other goods. Coupons can be mailed direct to households, printed in newspapers and magazines, incorporated into the packaging of the product, or distributed in a shop. See SALES PROMOTION.

2 a detachable slip which forms part of a SHARE CERTIFICATE or BOND and which is presented in order to claim the owner's entitlement to dividends or interest paid out on the security.

covenant a written agreement by a person to pay a given sum of money to some other person or organization for a specified period of time. Where a covenant arrangement allows a donor relief from income tax on any sums paid over, the covenant provides a tax-efficient means of making financial provision for a relative or charity.

cover see DIVIDEND COVER, INTEREST COVER.

covered interest arbitrage the borrowing and investing of foreign currencies to take advantage of differences in INTEREST RATES between countries. For example, a company could borrow an amount of one currency (say, the UK pound (£)), convert this into another currency (say, the US dollar ($)) and invest the proceeds in the USA. Concurrently, the company would sell $s for £s in the FORWARD MARKET for delivery at a future specified date. The company would earn a profit on such a transaction if the rate of return on its investment in the USA was greater than the combined expenses of interest payments on the amount of £s borrowed and the costs of concluding the forward exchange contract. Covered interest ARBITRAGE takes advantage of (and in the process eliminates) any temporary discrepancies between relative interest rates in two countries and the forward exchange rate of the two countries' currencies. See INTERNATIONAL FISHER EFFECT.

covering a means of protecting the domestic currency value of the future proceeds of an international trade transaction, usually by buying or selling the proceeds of the transaction in the FORWARD MARKET for foreign currencies.

cover note a document issued by an INSURANCE COMPANY to cover temporarily the period between the acceptance of an insurance risk and the issue of a detailed insurance policy to the client.

CPD see CONTINUING PROFESSIONAL DEVELOPMENT.

CPU (Central Processing Unit) the 'brain' of a COMPUTER which stores and processes data.

craft union see TRADE UNION.

crash any breakdown or malfunction of a COMPUTER.

creative accounting the use of discretion in the application of ACCOUNTING CONCEPTS so as to report profit and asset figures which are flattering to the company. By subtle use of different DEPRECIATION methods for fixed assets, or different STOCK VALUATION methods, or techniques like OFF-BALANCE SHEET FINANCING, a company's senior managers can 'massage' or 'window-dress' the profits for any trading period to impress shareholders. Such interpretations are legal, if somewhat dubious. Although the professional accounting bodies have issued Statements of Standard Accounting Practice and Financial Reporting Standards to try to curtail the scope for arbitrariness in the application of accounting concepts when measuring business income, considerable latitude still exists in the interpretation of accounting data and the reporting of accounting results. See ACCOUNTING STANDARDS.

credit 1 a financial facility which enables a person or business to borrow MONEY to purchase (i.e. take immediate possession of) products, raw materials and components, etc. and to pay for them over an extended time period. Credit facilities come in a variety of forms including BANK LOANS and OVERDRAFTS, INSTALMENT CREDIT, CREDIT CARDS and TRADE CREDIT. Interest charges on credit may be fixed or variable according to the type of facilities offered or, in some cases, loans may be interest-free as a means of stimulating business. See CREDIT CONTROL, MONETARY POLICY, EXPORTING, LETTER OF CREDIT, BILL OF EXCHANGE, CONSUMER CREDIT ACT 1974, INTEREST RATE.
2 to acknowledge (in DOUBLE-ENTRY ACCOUNTS) the receipt of services rendered to a firm. This is done by making an accounting entry which records the value of goods or services received by the company in the company's account of the supplier of the goods or services. A credit entry in a company's double entry accounts represents either a decrease in the company's assets or an increase in its liabilities. See DEBIT.

credit card a card issued by a financial institution (mainly COMMERCIAL BANKS and BUILDING SOCIETIES), which can be used generally to purchase goods and services on CREDIT up to an agreed limit, or, for example, by a retail group for in-house purchases only. Credit cards are a convenient way of making purchases and many issuers provide the facility interest-free, provided clients pay off the outstanding balance in full when due. In the UK, retailers pay the credit card companies, on average, around 2% commission to participate in the credit card schemes and may pass on this charge to customers who pay for products by credit card rather than cash.

credit control 1 the control exercised by a firm over its TRADE DEBTORS to ensure that customers pay their debts on time and to minimize the risk of BAD DEBTS. Credit control involves: assessing the creditworthiness of new and established customers to determine borrowing limits and terms; encouraging prompt payment by offering cash discounts and monitoring and recording payments due; the recovering of bad debts. Effective credit control minimizes the funds which a firm has tied up in debtors, so improving profitability and LIQUIDITY. See FACTORING, DEBTORS RATIO, WORKING CAPITAL RATIO.

2 the regulation of borrowing from the COMMERCIAL BANKS, FINANCE HOUSES, etc. by the monetary authorities in order to exercise control over the level of spending in the economy. See MONETARY POLICY.

credit note a document issued by a supplier to a customer giving the customer CREDIT for any products returned by the customer for which payment has already been received.

creditors (accounts payable) the money owed to individuals or firms because they have supplied goods, services or raw materials for which they have not yet been paid (trade creditors), or because they have made LOANS. Amounts falling due for payment within one year are counted as part of a company's CURRENT LIABILITIES in its BALANCE SHEET, while amounts falling due after more than one year appear as part of long-term liabilities.

Some creditors, called secured creditors, are offered collateral or security for their loans by means of a fixed charge on a specific asset owned by a debtor, which they could legally claim in the event of default on the loan. Other secured creditors are offered security by means of a 'floating charge' on the debtors' assets, which would offer them priority in claiming the proceeds from the sale of these assets in the event of default. Unsecured creditors such as trade creditors have less security in the event of default. See DEBTORS (ACCOUNTS RECEIVABLE), CREDIT. CREDITORS RATIO.

creditors ledger see LEDGER. ACCOUNTING.

creditors ratio an accounting measure of a firm's average period of CREDIT taken from suppliers, which expresses the amount owed by the firm to period-end CREDITORS as a ratio of its average daily purchases (or sales). The resulting figure shows how many days on average the firm took to pay its creditors. Compare DEBTORS RATIO.

credit period the average number of days' (or weeks') CREDIT granted to customers by a company, or the average time it takes for the company to collect its debts. See CREDIT CONTROL, AGE ANALYSIS PROFILE FOR DEBTORS.

credit rating an assessment of the creditworthiness of a firm or an individual, which indicates the amount of CREDIT they can reasonably be allowed by a supplier.

The creditworthiness of a company can often be assessed on the basis of information derived from the company's past annual report and accounts, and from confidential details provided by the company's bank. Additionally, there are a number of specialized credit rating companies, such as Dunn and Bradstreet in the UK, who provide information about the creditworthiness of companies in return for a fee.

The creditworthiness of individual customers is more difficult to assess and is often based on some hard information such as court bankruptcy proceedings and default information on hire purchase agreements, together with circumstantial information such as the postal areas in which a potential debtor lives (indicating a suburb or inner city estate, for example). Firms specialize in collecting and processing such data and provide credit ratings in return for a fee. Under the terms of the UK CONSUMER

CREDIT ACT, an individual has a right to inspect any credit record kept about them by such a firm.

Suppliers use credit ratings as a means of determining the maximum amount of credit to allow a customer as part of their CREDIT CONTROL procedures.

credit scoring see CREDIT RATING.

credit squeeze an attempt by the monetary authorities to reduce the amount of CREDIT granted by financial institutions to consumers and businesses, in order to reduce the level of spending in the economy. A credit squeeze forces up INTEREST RATES, affecting businesses by reducing consumer demand and raising the cost of financing stockholding and investment. See MONETARY POLICY.

credit terms the basis (usually the number of days delay in payment) on which goods are released to the customer before payment is received.

creditworthiness see CREDIT CONTROL.

Crest a paperless settlement system which was introduced in 1996 to cut the costs and speed up the completion of dealings on the UK STOCK MARKET. Under Crest, STOCK and SHARE transactions are recorded electronically, in contrast to the existing parallel system (TALISMAN) which involves the issue of settlement papers and share certificates. However, as with Talisman, investors will still receive a contract note from their broker to confirm their purchase or sale.

criminal law a body of rules which the State imposes upon individuals for the protection of other individuals and to restrain antisocial behaviour. Criminal law covers such crimes as theft and fraud. Prosecution of the accused is at the instance of the State and could result in imprisonment or fines as a punishment if the accused is found guilty.

critical function structure an ORGANIZATION structure in which one management function is considered so important that it is organized separately to some extent from the rest of the organization. For example, in retailing the overall structure is often the geographical variant of the PRODUCT-BASED STRUCTURE, with DECENTRALIZATION of AUTHORITY to an area or regional manager; however, standardized merchandising is considered so critical to the organization's success that this function is centralized on a functional basis (see Fig. 31).

critical incident technique an examination of a series of important incidents in an employee's work performance so as to isolate the factors which determine effectiveness. Usually the employees will be asked to suggest these critical incidents themselves and to indicate what influenced their effectiveness, or lack of it, in each case. This method can be used in PERFORMANCE APPRAISAL, especially when a key objective is improving work performance. Its benefits are that it encourages individuals to consider their own performance, and in so far as

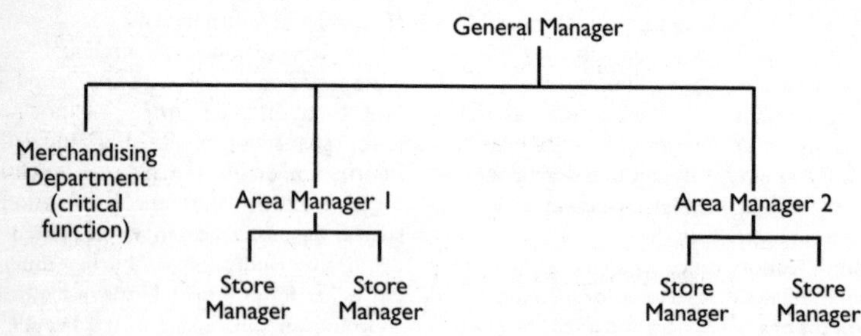

Fig. 31 **Critical function structure.** A typical example.

they propose the issues to be considered it can make appraisal a fairly open and nonthreatening process.

critical path analysis see NETWORK ANALYSIS.

critical *or* **key success factors** the resources and capabilities/competencies/skills a firm *must* possess to achieve some competitive 'success' and profitability in a market. For example, a pharmaceutical firm such as Glaxo Smith Kline must possess financial resources and skilled research staff to fund and develop expensive and innovative new drugs. However, this is not enough in itself to achieve a COMPETITIVE ADVANTAGE over rival suppliers and deliver above-average profits; that is the firm must achieve *greater* differential competitive advantage by having *superior* resources and capabilities (technical, but crucially also managerial expertise) such as to create *more* value than its competitors. See VALUE CREATED MODEL, VALUE ADDED ANALYSIS, RESOURCE BASED THEORY OF THE FIRM, DISTINCTIVE COMPETENCIES.

cross chart see RELATIONSHIP CHART.

cross-elasticity of demand see ELASTICITY OF DEMAND.

cross-licence see LICENCE.

cross rate the EXCHANGE RATE between two foreign currencies derived from the exchange rate of each of these currencies in terms of a common third currency. For example, the exchange rate between the UK pound and the Japanese Yen would be calculated by reference to the exchange rate of each of these currencies against, say, the US dollar.

cross-selling persuading an existing customer to buy another product from the same business.

cross-subsidization see SUBSIDY.

cultural distance the degree to which norms and values or working methods between companies and consumer preferences differ between countries because of differences in their national characteristics.

cultural values the perceptions, beliefs and standards which people acquire from the society in which they grew up. Differences in cultural values both *between* countries and between ethnic groups *within* a country (subcultures) are often important in designing a company's MARKET SEGMENTATION strategies.

culture

The norms and shared attitudes that pervade an ORGANIZATION. It may be expressed in symbols, rituals and the language used by organization members. It thus constitutes the distinctive characteristics of an organization. In recent years managerial interest in organizational culture has grown enormously. It is believed that the culture will influence how individuals behave at work and hence will affect both individual and organizational performances.

A number of types of culture have been identified in this respect:

(a) *power culture,* characterized by an emphasis on personal charisma, risk-taking and a low level of respect for procedures. This might be found in a small entrepreneurial organization, where power tends to be concentrated in the entrepreneur;

(b) *rôle culture,* characterized by well-defined procedures and job roles, and an emphasis on conformity. This might be found in an established BUREAUCRACY for example government administration;

(c) *task culture,* characterized by an emphasis on problem-solving by expert teams. Groups are formed to deal with particular problems. Once the task is completed the group may be disbanded. Here the culture is one which attaches importance to expertise, though in fact expertise may be less developed in organizations of this sort than in role culture organizations, where job roles are more specialized. Task culture places a much greater emphasis on flexibility and creativity than does role culture;

(d) *person-oriented culture*, characterized by an emphasis on meeting the needs of individuals in the organization. This is often found in small, 'alternative' organizations. It may also characterize small organizations composed mainly of PROFESSIONALS, such as small consultancy companies, where it is deemed important that individuals be given some freedom to shape their jobs so that they can pursue particular professional or other 'acceptable' outside interests (for example, being a local councillor).

A concern of many managers in recent years has been that the prevailing culture of their organization is inappropriate, or even obstructive, to a desired change in objectives. For instance, a role culture, where jobs are specialized and well-defined, could obstruct creativity and hence prevent an organization from becoming more entrepreneurial. As a result much attention recently has been devoted to changing cultures. It is doubtful, however, whether managers can actually achieve dramatic cultural change in the short term. Culture is influenced by a complex of factors, such as the character and background of the workforce, many of which are to some extent independent of managerial action. See MANAGEMENT STYLE. MECHANISTIC AND ORGANISMIC, EXCELLENCE CULTURE.

cum-dividend 1 (of a particular SHARE) including the right to receive the DIVIDEND which attaches to a SHARE.
2 with dividend. If shares are purchased on the STOCK MARKET, 'cum-div', the purchaser would be entitled to the dividend accruing to those shares when the dividend is next paid. Compare EX-DIVIDEND.

cumulative preference share see PREFERENCE SHARE.

currency *or* **cash** the coins and bank notes which constitute the physical component of a country's MONEY SUPPLY, i.e. coins and notes have a physical identity, whereas the other assets comprising the money supply, such as bank deposits, are book-keeping entries and have no tangible life of their own. See LEGAL TENDER, FOREIGN CURRENCY.

currency matching the financial management practice within multinational companies of matching their foreign currency holdings with equal foreign currency borrowings in order to minimize their exposure to losses from exchange rate changes. See EXCHANGE RATE EXPOSURE.

currency swap see SWAP.

currency translation the translation of the financial accounts of foreign subsidiaries, which are expressed in terms of local currencies, into the currency of the parent company so that they can be included in the CONSOLIDATED ACCOUNTS. Thus a UK MULTINATIONAL ENTERPRISE with a US subsidiary would need to translate the accounts of the subsidiary expressed in dollars into sterling in order to consolidate them with its UK accounts. The most common method of translation is the *closing rate method* which translates all ASSETS, LIABILITIES, REVENUES and costs at the currency exchange rate ruling at the end-date of the ACCOUNTING PERIOD.

current account 1 an individual's or company's account kept at a COMMERCIAL

BANK OR BUILDING SOCIETY into which the customer can deposit cash or cheques and from which he or she can draw cheques or make withdrawals on a day-to-day basis.
2 a financial record of a country's trade in GOODS and SERVICES with the rest of the world (see BALANCE OF PAYMENTS).
3 an account which keeps a record of individual partner's share of profits or losses, and amounts withdrawn, in a PARTNERSHIP.

current assets ASSETS such as STOCKS, money owed by DEBTORS, and cash, which are held for short-term conversion within a firm as raw materials are bought, made up, sold as finished goods and eventually paid for. See FIXED ASSETS, WORKING CAPITAL, WORKING CAPITAL RATIO.

current cost accounting see INFLATION ACCOUNTING.

current liabilities all obligations to pay out cash at some date in the near future, including amounts which a firm owes to trade CREDITORS and BANK LOANS/OVERDRAFTS. See WORKING CAPITAL, WORKING CAPITAL RATIO.

current/noncurrent method see FOREIGN CURRENCY TRANSLATION.

current purchasing power accounting see INFLATION ACCOUNTING.

current ratio *or* **acid-test ratio** an accounting measure of a firm's ability to pay its short-term liabilities out of its quickly-realizable CURRENT ASSETS, which expresses the firm's liquid current assets (DEBTORS plus cash) as a ratio of CURRENT LIABILITIES. Sometimes called the 'quick ratio', this is a more stringent test of liquidity than the WORKING CAPITAL RATIO, because it excludes STOCK from CURRENT ASSETS on the grounds that STOCKS cannot be as readily convertible into cash to meet short-term debts as can DEBTORS where the goods or services have already been sold and only collecting the money remains.

current yield see YIELD.

custom and practice a way of doing things that receives its justification from the claim that 'things have always been done like this' rather than from any specific rule. In INDUSTRIAL RELATIONS it generally refers to working practices which are operated by workforces and TRADE UNIONS and which are implicitly condoned by management, but have not been explicitly sanctioned in a formal agreement. The buying-out of such practices is often the subject of productivity initiatives tabled by managements during COLLECTIVE BARGAINING. See RESTRICTIVE LABOUR PRACTICE.

customer a BUYER of a good or service from a BUSINESS. See also INTERNAL CUSTOMER.

customer analysis a survey of who the firm's customers are, what choice criteria they use, how they rate competitive offerings and on what variables they can be segmented. See BUYER BEHAVIOUR.

customer centred see CONSUMER ORIENTATION.

customer database a system which records details about the firm's customers.

customer relationship management (CRM) a strategic concept which focuses on business competencies, processes and technologies required to effectively service the needs and requirements of a firm's customers. As such CRM embraces key MARKETING activities and related INFORMATION MANAGEMENT in order to keep existing customers and attract new ones. The issue of customer retention has taken on a new imperative in the digital age, with the INTERNET and E-COMMERCE providing customers with greater opportunities to compare prices, switch suppliers etc. CRM recognises that businesses need to use these new technologies more proactively to their own advantage, either by developing IT capabilities in-house or relying on outside IT specialists, to provide call centres, sales force automation, marketing and data analysis and website management.

customer resistance consumers' unwillingness to buy a product or BRAND because of their misgivings about it. Their objections could be based on some dislike of the product's functional attributes, their view about its price and value to them, or antipathy towards the product's image. See SELLING.

customer satisfaction the fulfilment of customers' requirements or needs.

customer satisfaction measurement a process through which customer satisfaction criteria are set, customers are surveyed and the results interpreted in order to establish the level of customer satisfaction with the firm's product.

customer service the marketing and technical functions within a firm, which deal direct with customers. Customer services can involve offering pre-sales services, such as providing advice to customers on their product needs; and AFTER-SALES SERVICES, such as repair and maintenance back-up and the replacement of faulty products or parts. Customer services are an important part of the MARKETING MIX, serving to attract new customers and reinforcing BRAND LOYALTY among existing customers. See GUARANTEE, CUSTOMER SERVICE LEVEL, CALL CENTRE.

customer service level a measure of the ability of an organization to provide a product with no waiting on the customer's part.

customer-supplier relationship the proposition within TOTAL QUALITY MANAGEMENT (TQM) that the customer-supplier chain is continuous within and exterior to the organization. In effect this means that an individual managing a machine on the factory floor has as a supplier the individual at the preceding operation and is therefore a customer, as he (or she) is also the supplier to the individual at the following process.

customer target the MARKET SEGMENT or segments identified by the firm as offering considerable sales potential and on which the firm focuses its marketing efforts. See MARKET SEGMENTATION.

customization the adaption of a good or service to meet the particular requirements of a specific customer or group of customers. Extreme customization involves the design, and production of a different product for each customer, which tends to be expensive. In order to achieve cost savings associated with ECONOMIES OF SCALE firms may prefer to produce a limited range of standardized products (see STANDARDIZATION). As a compromise firms often seek to produce a single standardized product which can then be varied slightly through customization to meet broadly the requirements of different groups of buyers. See MARKET SEGMENTATION, PRODUCT RANGE.

Customs and Excise a UK government department responsible for the administration and collection of REVENUES from VALUE ADDED TAX, EXCISE DUTIES and CUSTOMS DUTIES. The department is responsible for policing and enforcing the revenue laws and restrictions and prohibitions on the IMPORT and EXPORT of certain goods, as well as for the control of smuggling. Customs and Excise also provides statistical details of taxes raised and the volume and value of UK overseas trade; these are used by the Treasury or the Office for National Statistics in compiling budget and balance of payments returns. See IMPORTING, EXPORTING.

customs duty a form of EXPENDITURE TAX which is levied by the government on foreign products imported into the country. Customs duties are used mainly to raise revenue for the government, although they can serve, like TARIFFS, to reduce domestic spending on imports. See IMPORT, CUSTOMS AND EXCISE.

customs union see TRADE INTEGRATION.

cut-off date the date, coinciding with the end of an accounting period, after which goods received from suppliers or sold to customers will not enter the accounting records for that accounting period but will be recorded at the start of the next accounting period. This date is of particular importance to the stocktaking at the period end and to the measurement of sales, purchases and profit.

cut-off rate the minimum rate of return used in INVESTMENT APPRAISAL for the purpose of deciding if an investment project is to go ahead. A predetermined arbitrary cut-off rate may be used in place of the COST OF CAPITAL as the DISCOUNT RATE. Different cut-off rates may be employed for projects with different degrees of riskiness. See DISCOUNTED CASH FLOW.

cut-throat competition see PRICE WAR.

cycle time the time which is required at each work station (machine or operative) to complete the workload allocated to it. Cycle times are important in PRODUCTION LINE OF ASSEMBLY LINE balancing to ensure the smooth flow of raw materials, components and work in progress from workstation to workstation, thereby avoiding bottlenecks and idle periods.

cyclical fluctuation see BUSINESS CYCLE.

cyclical ordering system see FIXED INTERVAL REORDER SYSTEM.

cyclical unemployment see UNEMPLOYMENT, BUSINESS CYCLE.

cyclical variation see SALES FORECASTING.

d

damages money awarded by a court to a plaintiff who has suffered loss at the hands of the defendant as a result of breach of CONTRACT or a TORT committed by the defendant.

databank a collection of information on a specific topic, such as consumer purchases, which is added to over time.

database a COMPUTER software package which enables data to be created and stored, to be retrieved and analysed later. Databases can, for example, store names and addresses of potential or past customers which can be used to produce mailing lists for SALES PROMOTIONS.

database marketing an interactive approach to MARKETING which uses individually addressable marketing media and channels to provide information to, stimulate demand from, and stay close to, customers.

data processing the organization and processing of information in a business. The use of COMPUTERS to store data (see DATA STORAGE) and to undertake routine data processing activities such as recording purchases, sales, payroll etc. can save time, improve recording accuracy and reduce staffing costs. See INFORMATION MANAGEMENT, LOCAL AREA NETWORK.

Data Protection Act, 1998 a UK Act which contains provisions relating to accuracy, access and confidentiality of information kept by businesses on their employees, suppliers, customers etc in the form of both computerized and paper-based files. To process personal data requires the explicit consent of the individual concerned, with individuals having rights of compensation if it can be shown their interests have been harmed by unauthorised recording and disclosure of personal details.

data storage the storing of business documentation. This can involve the accumulation of physical 'paper mountains' with attendant problems of space availability, extra staff and retrieval. However, many firms now use COMPUTER-based electronic systems such as *document image processing* (DIP). DIP compresses a document into a series of digits which is indexed and stored on a disk file; scanners search and retrieve information held on disk, reproducing items by laser printout.

See INFORMATION MANAGEMENT.

dawn raid a situation in which a potential TAKEOVER bidder for a company buys a substantial shareholding in the target company at current market prices, often through intermediaries (to disguise the identity of the bidder). This shareholding can then be used as a platform for a full takeover bid for all the shares at a stated offer price. In the UK, company law provisions on DISCLOSURE OF SHAREHOLDINGS, requiring shareholders with more than 3% of the shares in a public company to declare such shareholdings to the directors of that company, have made it more difficult to mount a dawn raid. See TAKEOVER BID, CITY CODE ON TAKEOVERS AND MERGERS.

day book see JOURNAL.

dead stock raw materials, work in progress or finished goods which have not been used for a considerable time. Businesses need to employ careful STOCK CONTROLS, monitoring the usage rate of STOCK items in order to avoid tying up WORKING CAPITAL in high levels of redundant stock.

dealer see TRADER.

death duty see INHERITANCE TAX.

death rate see POPULATION.

debentures a means of financing companies through fixed-interest LOANS secured against company ASSETS. In some cases the company may offer a specific asset such as a particular machine as security for the loan (fixed charge); in other cases lenders are offered security by means of a general claim against all company assets in the event of default (floating charge). Most debentures are redeemable by the borrower at a future specified date, say 10 or 15 years from the date of issue. Some debentures, however, are irredeemable and never have to be repaid, the lender continuing to be rewarded through interest payments forever. See LOAN CAPITAL, CONVERTIBLE LOAN STOCK.

debit 1 *n.* a means of charging (in DOUBLE-ENTRY ACCOUNTS) for services rendered by a firm. This is done by making an accounting entry which records the value of GOODS or SERVICES supplied by the company in the company's account of the customer for these goods and services. A debit entry in a company's DOUBLE-ENTRY ACCOUNTS represents either an increase in the company's assets or a decrease in its LIABILITIES.
2 *v.* to enter the value of goods or services supplied to a customer in the supplying company's account of that customer. See CREDIT, definition 2.

debit note a document issued by a supplier to a customer charging the customer for any additional products supplied to the customer for which payment has not been received.

debt an amount of money owed by one person, company, etc. to another. Debts result from borrowing money to purchase a product, service or financial asset (e.g. INSTALMENT CREDIT). Debt contracts provide for the eventual repayment of the sum borrowed and include INTEREST charges for the duration of the LOAN. See DEBTORS. BORROWER.

debt collection see CREDIT CONTROL.

debt control see LOAN CAPITAL.

debt finance see LOAN CAPITAL.

debtors (accounts receivable) the money owed by individuals or firms because they have bought goods, services or raw materials for which they have not yet paid (trade DEBTORS), or because they have borrowed money. See CREDITORS (ACCOUNTS PAYABLE), DEBT, DEBTORS RATIO, CREDIT CONTROL, WORKING CAPITAL, BAD DEBT.

debtors ledger see LEDGER, ACCOUNTING.

debtors ratio, average collection period *or* **debtor days ratio** an accounting measure of a firm's average collection period for DEBTS, which expresses the amount owed by firm's period-end DEBTORS as a ratio of its average daily sales. The resulting figure shows the average period that customers took to pay their debts, expressed in days. See CREDITORS RATIO, CREDIT CONTROL, BAD DEBT, FACTORING.

debt servicing the cost of meeting INTEREST payments and regular contractual repayments of principal on a LOAN, along with any administration charges borne by the BORROWER.

debug to identify and remove errors from a COMPUTER program.

'decency threshold' see LOW PAY.

decentralization the relocation of managerial AUTHORITY and RESPONSIBILITY to a lower level in the ORGANIZATION. A restructuring of a FUNCTIONAL STRUCTURE to a PRODUCT-BASED STRUCTURE will generally involve some degree of decentralization, especially regarding operational (but not strategic) matters. DELAYERING often involves decentralization from middle management to LINE MANAGERS. See CENTRALIZATION, ORGANIZATIONAL ANALYSIS.

decentralized bargaining see COLLECTIVE BARGAINING.

decentralized purchasing a situation where a multi-site firm has a PURCHASING policy that allows individual sites to choose and manage their own supplier base.

decision-making see ORGANIZATIONAL ANALYSIS, 'GARBAGE-CAN' MODEL OF DECISION-MAKING, DISJOINTED INCREMENTALISM.

decision support system a procedure which is concerned with getting appropriate information to managers as and when they need it and which aids the manager in making decisions. Decision support systems are generally based upon interactive COMPUTER networks which can help the manager to solve problems and to gauge the effects of alternative outcomes of a decision. See INFORMATION MANAGEMENT.

decision tree an aid to decision-making in uncertain conditions, that sets out alternative courses of action and the financial consequences of each alternative, and assigns subjective probabilities to the likelihood of future events occurring. For, example, a firm thinking of opening a new factory the success of which will depend upon consumer spending (and thus the state of the economy) would have a decision tree like Fig. 32.

In order to make a decision, the manager needs a decision criterion to enable him to choose which he regards as the best of the alternatives and, since these choices involve an element of risk, we therefore need to know something about his attitudes to risk. If the manager were neutral in his attitude to risk then we could calculate the *certainty equivalent* of the 'open factory' alternative using the expected money value criterion, which takes the financial consequence of each outcome and weights it by the probability of its occurrence, thus:

$$
\begin{aligned}
0.5 \times + £80{,}000 &= + £40{,}000 \\
0.5 \times - £30{,}000 &= - \underline{£15{,}000} \\
& + \underline{£25{,}000}
\end{aligned}
$$

which being greater than the £0 for certain of not opening the factory would justify going ahead with the factory project.

However, if the manager were averse to risk then he might not regard the expected money value criterion as being appropriate, for he might require a risk premium to induce him to take the risk. Application of a more cautious certainty equivalent criterion would reduce the certainty equivalent of the 'open factory' branch and might even tip the decision against going ahead on the grounds of the 'downside risk' of losing £30,000. See UNCERTAINTY AND RISK.

decline phase see PRODUCT LIFE CYCLE.

declining industry strategy see ENDGAME STRATEGY.

defective work work in progress or finished goods which fail to pass INSPECTION because they do not conform to the standards laid down. Defective work may arise because of poor workmanship, poor supervision, poor materials or poor machine maintenance. See QUALITY CONTROL, FISHBONE CHART.

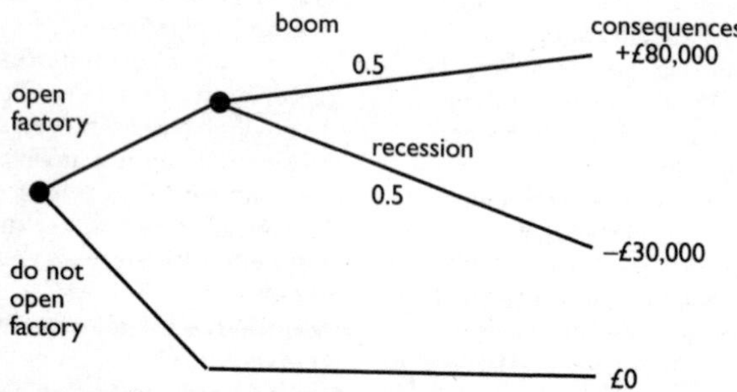

Fig.32 **Decision tree.** The businessman has two options: to open a new factory to boost production capacity or not to open a new factory; and he has to consider two states of nature or events which can occur: economic boom or recession. The businessman must assess the likelihood of each of these events occurring and, in this case, based on his knowledge and experience, he estimates that there is a one-in-two chance of a boom and a 0.5 probability of a recession. Finally, the businessman estimates the financial consequences as an £80,000 profit for the new factory if there is a boom, and a £30,000 loss if there is a recession.

deferred performance liability costs that may have to be paid out in the future, eg, the estimated costs associated with after-sales service agreements.

deferred tax a PROVISION which a company may make to reflect the difference between CORPORATION TAX actually payable (based on CAPITAL ALLOWANCES), and the tax which would have been payable if the charge had been based solely on accounting profits (reflecting DEPRECIATION rates applied).

defined benefit pension see PENSION.

defined contribution pension see PENSION.

deflation a fall in the rate of growth of the general level of prices in an economy, or an absolute reduction in the general level of prices (see PRICE INDEX). The authorities may seek to deflate the economy in order to combat INFLATION and eliminate a BALANCE OF PAYMENTS deficit by using restrictive monetary and fiscal measures, i.e. increasing interest rates and taxes to cut spending. See ECONOMIC POLICY, MONETARY POLICY, FISCAL POLICY, PRICES AND INCOMES POLICY.

DEFRA see DEPARTMENT FOR ENVIRONMENT, FOOD AND LOCAL AFFAIRS.

de-industrialization a sustained fall in the proportion of national output accounted for by the industrial (manufacturing, construction, etc.) sector of the economy. See STRUCTURE OF INDUSTRY.

de-layering the removal of tiers in an ORGANIZATION'S HIERARCHY. This is often implemented to shorten lines of communication and to increase the speed of decision-making. It often forms part of an attempt at DECENTRALIZATION and has been associated with moves to shift authority away from hierarchically organized functional departments to multi-function process teams, as in BUSINESS PROCESS RE-ENGINEERING. Currently a fashionable term, many view it as a euphemism for measures aimed at contraction and labour-shedding. Middle managers are particularly susceptible to REDUNDANCY as a result of de-layering. See DOWNSIZING, SCALAR CONCEPT.

delegation the passing of certain duties or decisions by a manager or SUPERVISOR to a subordinate whilst still retaining overall AUTHORITY for them, Delegation can increase a subordinate's JOB SATISFACTION whilst reducing the workload of a manager. See MANAGEMENT.

delivered price system see GEOGRAPHICAL PRICING.

delivery cost see STOCKHOLDING MODEL.

delivery date the agreed date by which a supplier will deliver GOODS OR SERVICES ordered by a customer. This date is often specified as part of the terms of a CONTRACT OF SALE and the CONTRACT may specify financial penalties for late delivery.

Meeting delivery dates is an important element in the MARKETING MIX for winning and retaining customers. See JUST-IN-TIME (JIT) SYSTEM.

delivery note a document sent by a supplier to a customer at the time when products are supplied, itemizing the physical quantities of product supplied. Thereafter an INVOICE is usually sent to the customer showing the money value of products supplied. Compare STATEMENT OF ACCOUNT.

Delphi technique an approach to generating new ideas or problem-solving amongst a GROUP or team. Each member or interested party submits his or her recommendations or views on the issue under review to a central contact point. All ideas generated in this way are then circulated to all those participating in the process, who then have the opportunity to submit comments on them. This process is repeated until a consensus emerges. Although time consuming, it can be an effective approach to the management of change since it enables all interested parties to express their views, generates consensus and, by incorporating all in the decision-making process, tends to generate commitment to the final outcome. See TECHNOLOGICAL FORECASTING, BRAINSTORMING, NOMINAL GROUP TECHNOLOGY.

demand the amount of a product which is purchased at a particular price at a particular point in time. A *demand curve* is a line showing the relationship between the price of a product and the quantity demanded per time period over a range of possible prices. Demand curves are usually downward sloping, indicating that as the price of the product falls, more is demanded. The extent to which the demand for a product will increase as price falls (and the extent to which demand will drop if the price rises) depends on the product's price-ELASTICITY OF DEMAND. The demand for a product, however, is determined also by a variety of non-price factors. A *demand function* attempts to incorporate *all* the factors that have a statistically. significant influence on demand for example, consumers' incomes, the prices of substitute products, advertising, etc. Demand curves will shift if any of these factors change over time.

In practice, firms are unable to derive definitive demand curves because of incomplete information. For this reason many firms use a COST-BASED PRICING formula for determining prices, but allow for the influence of demand by varying the profit mark-up (see DEMAND-BASED PRICING, COMPETITION-BASED PRICING).

There are various methods a firm can use to 'forecast' demand, including time series analysis, barometric indicators and econometric models. See SALES FORECASTING.

demand-based pricing pricing methods which determine the PRICE of a product primarily on the basis of intensity of demand rather than on costs of production and distribution. There are several facets of demand which are relevant to pricing:

(a) Firms may vary their prices over time as demand for their products changes as a result of BUSINESS CYCLES, charging higher prices when demand is strong and shading down prices in conditions of weak demand. More specifically, particular products will be subject to variations in demand over their PRODUCT LIFE CYCLE with implications for pricing. High skimming prices may be charged for a novel product in the early launch phase of its life cycle when demand is price-inelastic, with lower prices and larger promotion expenditures in the later, growth phase of its life cycle;

(b) Firms may also practise price discrimination, varying prices between types of customers, the location of customers, the time of purchase and versions of a product. Customer-based pricing recognizes the different bargaining power of potential buyers and seeks to capitalize on this by charging whatever price particular customers are prepared to pay. For example, in pricing theatre tickets special low prices may be charged to low income, price-sensitive consumers (for example, students and pensioners), and price discounts may be offered on block bookings. In addition, prices may be scaled for theatre seats in different parts of the theatre, with higher prices for the stalls and lower prices for the upper circle. Furthermore, different prices may be charged on different days or at different times of the day, with higher prices for weekend evening performances and lower prices for mid-week afternoon matinée performances. Finally, prices can be varied according to the version of a product, with different prices for a particular model of car, for example, according to whether the customer specifies fabric or leather seats. See ELASTICITY OF DEMAND, COST-BASED PRICING, COMPETITION-BASED PRICING.

demand curve see EQUILIBRIUM MARKET PRICE.

demand during lead time the demand made on a product required during the delivery or manufacturing lead-time period for that product. An unexpected increase during this period can lead to an out-of-stock situation.

demand forecasting see SALES FORECASTING.

demand management see BUSINESS CYCLE.

demand-pull inflation see INFLATION.

demarcation line the boundary between those tasks workers are permitted to do and those which they are not, as established by their TRADE UNION or by themselves collectively. Characteristically, demarcation lines develop in workplaces where there are several unions representing different occupational groups: their function is to establish which unions' members can work on which job, and hence to ensure that the unions do not damage each others' interests. They are usually policed by SHOP STEWARDS. Demarcation lines have been criticized for their potentially damaging impact on efficiency and LABOUR FLEXIBILITY, especially where tasks either side of the line are very similar. See RESTRICTIVE LABOUR PRACTICE.

de-merger the break-up of a company, often originally formed through a MERGER, into two (or more) separate companies. This is most easily achieved when the original businesses comprising the merger have continued to be run as separate divisions of the enlarged group. In this case, for example, the A-B company could be split into separate quoted companies, A and B, with the company's existing shareholders being given shares in *both* companies. Thus, unlike a DIVESTMENT (the sale of a division to outside interests) or a MANAGEMENT BUY-OUT (the sale of a division to its existing management), initially at least the companies continue to be owned by their existing shareholders.

A de-merger may occur because the merged company has failed to perform up to expectations because of internal conflicts of management, or result from a rethink of the company's BUSINESS STRATEGY favouring a concentration on 'core' businesses.

demographic segmentation the division of a market into SOCIOECONOMIC GROUPS according to demographic variables like age, sex, occupation, education and family size. See MARKET SEGMENTATION.

demography the analysis of human POPULATIONS according to their total size, birth rates, death rates and migration; the age and sex distribution of populations and their geographical and occupational distributions; racial and religious profiles, etc.

Firms need to monitor changes in the demographic environment because these changes can have a significant impact on the demand for particular CONSUMER GOODS and SERVICES. For instance, the increase in the proportions of elderly citizens in the total population in most industrialized countries over recent decades has created new market opportunities for companies in such areas as health care and leisure products; while declining birth rates have reduced the demand for children's clothing and toys. See SOCIOECONOMIC GROUP.

denationalization see NATIONALIZATION VERSUS PRIVATIZATION.

department a grouping of similar or closely related JOB roles into a discrete section within an ORGANIZATION, for example, the finance department. Departments may be confined to one level of the HIERARCHY or, as in FUNCTIONAL STRUCTURED organizations, extend over several levels and contain their own hierarchy. Grouping of tasks in this way is generally necessary to facilitate the integration and CO-ORDINATION of activities, but there is the danger that departments will prioritize internal objectives over those of the organization as a whole. See BUREAUCRACY.

departmental load the amount of work which is allocated to a production department during a specified period of time. The loading will take into account delivery promises and the availability of plant and personnel. In scheduling production it is important to avoid any department becoming over-loaded. See PRODUCTION SCHEDULING.

Department for Education and Skills (DfES) the UK government department responsible for administering the government's general educational programmes, including schools, colleges and universities and vocational training schemes aimed at improving work-related skills.

The emphasis in education is one of providing young people with a basic general education through schools, followed by further education opportunities at colleges and universities with a commitment thereafter to 'lifetime learning' so as to equip people with the necessary basic and vocational skills to adapt to the changing needs of the workplace. This is augmented by more specialised vocational schemes to match up peoples' educational capabilities with the practical requirements of specific work tasks through 'on-the-job-training' (See TRAINING) and the provision of courses designed to teach people new skills (e.g. computer programming courses).

Department for Environment, Food and Rural Affairs (DEFRA) the UK government department responsible for administering government policies in the areas of environmental protection and 'green issues' (see POLLUTION), the countryside, and agriculture, food and fisheries.

Department for Transport the UK government department responsible for administering government policies relating to the roads, railways, aviation and shipping. Local Government and the Regions are now handled by the Office of the Deputy Prime Minister.

Department for Work and Pensions (DWP) the UK government department and its offices (the Benefit Agency, Employment Service and Jobcentre Plus) responsible for administering the government's social welfare and employment programmes. The former includes making payments in respect of old-age PENSIONS, disabilities pensions, child allowance and the JOBSEEKERS ALLOWANCE (formerly, unemployment benefit). Regarding the latter a particular concern has been to instill in people a culture of 'employment' being the norm, playing down the negative aspects of 'unemployment'. This more positive approach is reflected in the work of the DWP's agency, the Employment Service and its nationwide network of 'JOB CENTRES', the introduction of the jobseekers allowance as a replacement for unemployment benefit and the NEW DEAL programme aimed at reducing youth unemployment and long-term unemployment amongst older workers.

The DWP is also responsible for conducting the fact-finding LABOUR FORCE SURVEY which provides data on conditions in the labour market; for overseeing the application of the UK's EMPLOYMENT LAWS; and for implementing employee rights' regulations issued by the European Union (see, for example, the WORKING TIME REGULATION).

Department of Health the UK government department responsible for administering the National Health Service.

Department of Trade and Industry (DTI) the UK Government office which is primarily responsible for implementing and administering the Government's industrial and trade policies. A particular concern at the DTI is the promotion of greater efficiency through an INDUSTRIAL POLICY programme, which includes support for new business start ups, consultancy services for small firms, research and development, and technology transfer. In the past, the DTI has been required by governments to involve itself in the rationalization of declining industries and support for 'failing' firms, but now the emphasis is very much on fostering greater enterprise by business itself, with a minimum of direct State intervention. See SMALL BUSINESS SERVICE.

The DTI is responsible for the operation of REGIONAL POLICY (including the REGIONAL DEVELOPMENT AGENCIES), vetting applications for regional selective assistance by firms investing in the 'assisted areas'. The DTI works closely with the OFFICE OF FAIR TRADING in matters affecting COMPETITION POLICY in general, and MERGER and TAKEOVER investigations in particular; the DTI regulates the formation of companies and their conduct through the REGISTRAR OF COMPANIES, and is responsible for issuing licences to deposit-taking institutions and authorizing dealers in stocks and shares, etc. (see FINANCIAL SERVICES ACT 1986). Finally, the DTI plays a prominent part in the running of the UK's overseas trade affairs, representing the country's interests at international (WORLD TRADE ORGANIZATION) and regional (EUROPEAN UNION) levels. The DTI in conjunction with the foreign office through the *Trade Partner* organization is important in the promotion of exports through the Export Market Information Centre, British Overseas Trade Board and related back-up facilities and services, including the EXPORT CREDIT GUARANTEE DEPARTMENT (see EXPORTING).

In 2002 the DTI's disparate range of support programmes (over 150) was streamlined and re-grouped under three main divisions: Business Support and Regional Policy (including the Small Business Service and the Regional Development Agencies); Competitiveness and Regulation (including trade policy, competition policy and consumer and employee protection); Science Technology and Innovation (including the SMART scheme). See CONSUMER CREDIT ACT 1974, LOAN GUARANTEE SCHEME, PRICES ACT 1974, PRICE MARKING (BARGAIN OFFERS) ORDER 1979, TRADE DESCRIPTIONS ACT 1965, TECHNOLOGY TRANSFER.

department store a RETAILER which sells a great variety of products, the term 'department' denoting the fact that a typical store will be divided up into a large number of sections each offering a particular kind of merchandise: the food department, the footwear department, the toys and games department, etc. Department stores may be under single-shop ownership or run as a multiple CHAIN STORE business.

Department stores compete mainly by offering customers convenience ('everything under one roof'), personal service and good quality products rather than on the basis of SELF SERVICE and cut prices. The larger department stores are able to boost their profitability by obtaining BULK-BUYING discounts from manufacturers as well as by promoting their OWN LABEL BRANDS. See DISTRIBUTION CHANNEL.

dependent inventory an inventory item is said to be dependent (on the final product) when it is a component of that final product. A car's steering wheel is therefore a dependent item. The idea of dependency is important for the ordering of sub-component materials and for the design of Bills of Materials. See STOCK, PRODUCT SPECIFICATION. Contrast INDEPENDENT INVENTORY.

deposit account see COMMERCIAL BANK.

depot 1 a business premise which is used to warehouse (i.e. store) goods in transit as part of a physical DISTRIBUTION CHANNEL engaged in the movement of goods from their place of manufacture to WHOLESALERS and RETAILERS of the product.

2 a business premise which is used to provide a central parking facility for fleet operators of lorries, vans, coaches and buses who are engaged in the distribution of goods and the provision of travel services.

depreciation *or* **amortization** 1 the fall in the value of an ASSET during the course of its working life. The condition of plant and equipment used in production deteriorates over time and these items will eventually have to be replaced. Accordingly, a firm needs to make financial provision for the depreciation of its assets.

Depreciation is an accounting means of dividing up the HISTORIC COST of a FIXED ASSET over a number of accounting periods which correspond with the asset's estimated life. The depreciation charged against the revenue of successive time periods in the PROFIT-AND-LOSS ACCOUNT serves to spread the original cost of a fixed asset yielding benefit to the firm over several trading periods. In the period-end BALANCE SHEET such an asset would be included at its net book value (cost less cumulative depreciation deducted to date). This depreciation charge does not attempt to calculate the reducing market value of fixed assets, so that balance sheets do not show realization values.

Different formulas used to calculate depreciation can lead to variations in the balance sheet value of a fixed asset and in the charge against GROSS PROFIT for depreciation. The second formula in Fig. 33 gives a large depreciation charge in the early periods of the fixed asset's life and a small charge in the later years (accelerated depreciation). In the interests of consistency, firms generally do not change the depreciation formula used for their fixed assets but stick to the same formula indefinitely.

All these depreciation formulas base the depreciation charge on the historic cost of fixed assets. However, during a period of INFLATION it is likely that the REPLACEMENT COST of an asset is likely to be higher than its original cost. Therefore, prudent companies need to make PROVISION for higher replacement costs in the form of a REVALUATION RESERVE. See INFLATION ACCOUNTING, CAPITAL CONSUMPTION, APPRECIATION, CREATIVE ACCOUNTING.

Straight-line methods

	Operating book value	Depreciation (£24,000÷3)	Closing book value
	£	£	£
Year 1	24,000	8,000	16,000
Year 2	16,000	8,000	8,000
Year 3	8,000	8,000	–

The *straight-line method* divides the original cost of a fixed asset (£24,000) by its estimated life (three years), giving equal depreciation charges each trading period.

Reducing-balance or diminishing-balance method

	Operating book value	Depreciation (50%)	Closing book value
	£	£	£
Year 1	24,000	12,000	12,000
Year 2	12,000	6,000	6,000
Year 3	6,000	3,000	3,000

The *reducing-balance method* writes off, each trading period, a fixed percentage of the net book value of the fixed asset at the beginning of the period.

Fig. 33 **Depreciation.** Two methods of calculating depreciation.

2 a decrease in the EXCHANGE RATE of a currency against other currencies under a FLOATING EXCHANGE RATE SYSTEM, reflecting a fall in market demand for that currency combined with a rise in market demand for other countries' currencies. The effect of a depreciation is to make imports (in the local currency) more expensive and exports (in the local currency) cheaper, thereby assisting in the removal of a BALANCE OF PAYMENTS deficit by acting to reduce import demand for goods and services and increasing export demand.

Depreciations, like DEVALUATION, provide firms with an opportunity to expand sales and boost profitability by improving their price competitiveness in both home and export markets. See DEVALUATION for further discussion. Contrast with APPRECIATION, definition 2. See EXCHANGE RATE EXPOSURE.

depreciation adjustment see INFLATION ACCOUNTING.

depression see BUSINESS CYCLE.

deregulation the removal of controls over a particular economic activity which have been imposed by the government or some other regulatory body, for example an industry trade association. Deregulation may be initiated either because the controls are no longer seen as necessary (for example the ending of PRICE CONTROLS to combat inflation); or because they are over-restrictive, preventing companies from taking advantage of business opportunities (for example the ending of most FOREIGN EXCHANGE CONTROLS by the UK in 1979 designed to liberalize overseas physical and portfolio investment).

Deregulation has assumed particular significance in the context of recent initiatives by the UK government to stimulate greater competition by, for example, allowing private companies to compete for business in areas (such as local bus services) hitherto confined to central government or local authority operators. The Government has also initiated programmes of deregulation in the employment protection field, because it believes that extensive regulation imposes an unwelcome burden on business, stifling flexibility and inhibiting the action of market forces.

Conversely, government initiatives can be seen to have promoted regulation in so far as they have imposed rules on how trade unions should conduct their affairs (see TRADE UNION ACT 1984). Also, paradoxically, the privatization of nationalized industries has in some cases led to greater regulation of their activities, because public pressure has necessitated the creation of regulatory agencies to ensure that private monopoly status is not abused at consumers' expense. For example, Ofgas regulates the gas industry, and Oftel the telecommunications industry. See REGULATION, NATIONALIZATION VERSUS PRIVATIZATION, EMPLOYMENT ACT 1989.

derivative a financial instrument such as an OPTION OR SWAP whose value is derived from some other financial asset (for example, a STOCK OR SHARE) or indices (for example, a price index for a commodity such as cocoa). Derivatives are traded on the FORWARD MARKETS and are used by businesses and dealers to 'hedge' against future movements in share, commodity etc. prices and by speculators seeking to secure windfall profits. See LONDON INTERNATIONAL FINANCIAL FUTURES EXCHANGE (LIFFE), EUREX.

derived demand DEMAND for a particular product which is driven by demand for a different product, e.g. the demand for joinery is at least partly derived from the demand for new housing.

de-seasonalize see SALES FORECASTING.

design the process of translating a product idea into a product which can be produced and marketed on a commercial basis. Though design is a creative process it has economic consequences insofar as a product's shape, configuration and performance affect its marketability and its cost of production. In order to achieve high product variety without involving an excessive variety of components, designers often use common, interchangeable parts and design products on a modular basis.

In order to remain competitive, firms need continuously to review the design of their products in the light of new developments in materials and processes. The technique of VALUE ANALYSIS is used to identify possible sources of cost savings without impairing a product's performance. See COMPUTER-AIDED DESIGN, NEW PRODUCT DEVELOPMENT.

design rights the legal ownership by persons or businesses of original designs of the shape or configuration of industrial products. In the UK, the COPYRIGHT, DESIGNS AND PATENTS ACT 1988 gives protection to the creators of industrial designs against unauthorized copying for a period of 10 years after the first marketing of the product. Design right protection is automatic and there are no registration requirements. Design right is an exclusive right for five years after first marketing and then becomes subject to licences of right for the remaining five years. If a design right is infringed, the design right owner (or licensee) may seek an injunction from the courts preventing further abuses, with offenders liable to pay damages/fines.

Under the Registered Design Act 1949, designs judged to be original *solely* by their outward appearance (i.e. by 'eye appeal' and not by their functioning) can be registered with the Designs Registry, a branch of the PATENT OFFICE. This facility has been continued by the 1988 Act which increased the term of protection for registered designs from a maximum of 15 years to 25 years.

desk research see MARKETING INTELLIGENCE.

de-unionization the termination by management of COLLECTIVE BARGAINING and representational rights of TRADE UNIONS in an organization. If managers decide to de-unionize, they will need to withdraw unions' rights to represent aggrieved employees in disputes with management and to cease to negotiate pay and conditions with them. Instead, management will unilaterally determine rates of pay and the relevant terms of the CONTRACT OF EMPLOYMENT. To achieve de-unionization, managers may also need to engineer the dismissal of key union activists.

The rationale for de-unionization is that union action leads to wages being artificially high (i.e. higher than the 'true' market rate) and inhibits LABOUR FLEXIBILITY (by generating RESTRICTIVE LABOUR PRACTICES). However, some labour economists claim that unions bring efficiency benefits. By 'giving voice' to employee grievances they defuse them and, by forcing wages up they provide an incentive to firms to invest in labour-saving technology. Firms also often find it easier to negotiate with employee representatives rather than directly with each individual employee.

Even where organizations de-recognize unions it does not necessarily end union activity. Trade unions may continue to recruit employees into union membership. If a sizeable proportion of the organization's employees remain or become union members, managers may find it difficult to sustain the non-union recognition policy because of the STATUTORY UNION RECOGNITION PROCEDURE. See MANAGEMENT STYLE.

devaluation an administered reduction in the EXCHANGE RATE of a currency against other currencies under a FIXED EXCHANGE RATE SYSTEM; for example, the lowering of the UK pound (£) against the US dollar ($) from one fixed or 'pegged' level to a lower level, say from £1 = $3 to £1 = $2. Devaluations are resorted to by governments to assist in the removal of a BALANCE OF PAYMENTS deficit. The effect of a devaluation is to make imports (in the local currency) more expensive, thereby reducing import demand, and exports cheaper (in the local currency), thereby acting as a stimulus to export demand. Whether or not a devaluation 'works' in achieving balance of payments equilibrium, however, depends on a number of factors, including the sensitivity of import and export demand to price changes (see ELASTICITY OF DEMAND); the availability of resources to expand export volumes and replace imports; and, critically over the longer term, the control of inflation to ensure that domestic price rises are kept in line with or below other countries' inflation rates.

Devaluations can affect the business climate in a number of ways, but in particular provide firms with an opportunity to expand sales and boost profitability. A devaluation increases import prices, which makes imports less competitive against domestic products and encourages domestic buyers to switch to locally-produced substitutes. Likewise, a fall in export prices is likely to cause overseas customers to increase their demand for the country's exported products in preference to locally produced items and to the exports of other overseas producers. If the pound, as in our example above, is devalued by one-third, then this would allow UK exporters to reduce their prices by a similar amount, thus increasing their price competitiveness in the US market Alternatively, they may choose not to reduce their prices by the full amount of the devaluation in order to increase unit profit margins and provide additional funds for advertising and sales promotion, etc. Contrast with REVALUATION, definition 2.

development see NEW PRODUCT DEVELOPMENT. RESEARCH AND DEVELOPMENT. MANAGEMENT DEVELOPMENT.

development area see REGIONAL POLICY.

DfES see DEPARTMENT FOR EDUCATION AND SKILLS.

differential advantage a clear performance differential over competition on factors that are important to target customers. See PRODUCT DIFFERENTIATION, COMPETITIVE ADVANTAGE.

differential costs relevant (or incremental) costs. See RELEVANT CASH FLOWS.

differentiated marketing *or* **targeting strategy** a MARKETING STRATEGY for a product which is based on the use of a *variety* of MARKETING MIX formats (different prices, advertising messages, retail outlets, etc.) each aimed at a particular group of customers in the market, i.e. MARKET SEGMENT. Contrasted with an UNDIFFERENTIATED MARKETING STRATEGY, which applies the same marketing mix formula right across the market, the differentiated approach attempts to customize its marketing mix for each particular segment in order to maximize its appeal to the buyers constituting those segments.

This approach is best suited to a market in which the product being sold is capable of being differentiated either by physical variations of the product itself or by its psychological appeal (see PRODUCT DIFFERENTIATION), and where buyers demand a substantial amount of product variety. In these cases, differentiated marketing is usually much more successful than an across the board approach in boosting sales. However, the targeted approach may prove to be unduly costly in terms of both higher production Costs (for example, with smaller production runs a firm may be unable to lower costs through exploiting economies of scale) and marketing costs (for example, the need to finance a number of separate ADVERTISING and SALES PROMOTION budgets). See CONCENTRATED MARKETING or TARGETING STRATEGY, INTERNATIONAL MARKETING, MARKET SEGMENTATION.

differentiation see DIFFERENTIATED MARKETING or TARGETING STRATEGY, PRODUCT DIFFERENTIATION.

differentiation focus strategy see COMPETITIVE STRATEGY.

differentiation strategy see COMPETITIVE STRATEGY.

diffusion process the spread of a NEW PRODUCT (or process) through society. Initially, new products tend to be purchased by a small number of *pioneering* or *innovator customers* (see PRODUCT LIFE CYCLE) and then by *early adopters* who begin to purchase the product soon after it has been introduced. In due course the product may become a mass market item with a widespread demand.

dilution 1 the decrease in control and EARNINGS PER SHARE experienced by existing shareholders in a JOINT-STOCK COMPANY when SHARE ISSUES are made which attract new shareholders. Dilution is a particular problem in fast-growing, family-controlled companies where the need to raise new capital may dilute the founding family's shareholdings to below 50%, causing them to lose potential control of the company.

In the past, companies have sought to avoid dilution whilst continuing to raise capital by issuing NON-VOTING SHARES; but these are nowadays disapproved of by most STOCK MARKETS.

2 the weakening of the monopoly of skills of a particular occupational group by the recruitment of less-skilled workers to perform the same work. See SKILL.

diminishing balance depreciation see DEPRECIATION.

direct cost *or* **prime cost** the sum of the DIRECT MATERIALS cost and the DIRECT LABOUR cost of a product. Direct costs tend to vary proportionately with the level of output. See COST.

direct debit see COMMERCIAL BANK.

direct exporting see EXPORTING.

direct investment see INVESTMENT.

directive 1 EUROPEAN UNION *Directives* which EU member states are required to incorporate into their own legislation. For example, *The Fourth Directive* introduced standardized formats for presenting company accounts; *the Seventh Directive* tightened up the requirements relating to group accounts; *the Eighth Directive* dealt with the qualifications of auditors.

2 a request' by the monetary authorities that the COMMERCIAL BANKS and other financial institutions should limit the amount of LOANS and OVERDRAFTS they make available, in order to control spending in the economy. See MONETARY POLICY for further details.

direct labour 1 that part of the labour force in a firm which is directly concerned with the manufacture of a good or the provision of a service. Direct labour cost depends on the hours of labour worked by factory operatives engaged directly in making a product. Provided that wage rates remain constant then direct labour cost will tend to vary exactly with output. See VARIABLE COST, STANDARD COST.

2 workers employed directly by local or central government to perform tasks rather than such tasks being contracted out to private-sector companies. See CONTRACTING-OUT, INDIRECT LABOUR.

direct-mail a form of DIRECT MARKETING which involves posting information about a firm's GOODS and SERVICES direct to prospective/existing customers. This type of marketing offers a more targeted approach than conventional forms of advertising which employ mass MEDIA (commercial television, etc.). Potential customers can be identified in terms of various socioeconomic criteria and added to a mailing list which becomes the basis for a targeted mailing shot. See SOCIOECONOMIC GROUP, MARKET SEGMENTATION.

direct marketing a form of MARKETING aimed at obtaining and retaining customers where the supplier contacts customers directly without the use of a coventional DISTRIBUTION CHANNEL intermediary such as a SHOP. Forms of direct marketing include: MAIL ORDER, DIRECT MAIL, TELEPHONE SELLING, ELECTRONIC SHOPPING, INTERNET, FACTORY OUTLET.

direct materials raw materials which are incorporated in a product. Provided that materials prices remain constant, then direct materials cost will tend to vary exactly with output. See INDIRECT MATERIALS, VARIABLE COST.

director an official of A JOINT-STOCK COMPANY elected by the SHAREHOLDERS at the company's ANNUAL GENERAL MEETING and charged with certain powers and responsibilities to run the company on behalf of the shareholders. Each company will have a number of directors who constitute the BOARD OF DIRECTORS and the directors will meet regularly to determine company policy. The board generally elects one of their number to act as *chairman* of the BOARD OF DIRECTORS and may also elect one of their number to serve as *managing director* with responsibility for the day to day management of the company. Some directors will be *executive* directors and will hold senior salaried management posts in the company; others may be *non-executive* directors who are not primarily employed by the company but may be bankers or executives employed by other companies, contributing their expertise at board meetings in return for directors' fees. See CORPORATE GOVERNANCE.

directors' report a report by the directors of a JOINT-STOCK COMPANY to the SHAREHOLDERS which appears alongside the published annual accounts of the company to form the ANNUAL REPORT AND ACCOUNTS. Company law requires the directors to produce an annual report and specifies the information which it should contain; it also requires the AUDIT of any financial information given in the report.

direct quotation see EXCHANGE RATE.

direct response advertising ADVERTISING which solicits a direct response from the consumer by phone or coupon.

direct tax a TAX imposed by the government on the income and wealth of persons and businesses in order to raise revenue, redistribute income and wealth, and as an instrument of FISCAL POLICY in managing the economy. The main forms of direct tax in the UK are INCOME TAX, CORPORATION TAX, NATIONAL INSURANCE CONTRIBUTIONS and INHERITANCE TAX. See BUDGET (GOVERNMENT).

dirty float see FLOATING EXCHANGE RATE SYSTEM.

Disability Rights Commission see DISCRIMINATION.

disciplinary procedure a set of rules governing the way managers should conduct investigations into infringements of company rules or unsatisfactory performance by employees. Generally, disciplinary procedures require that employees be formally notified of the charge against them, have an opportunity to defend themselves (accompanied by a friend or TRADE UNION representative), be formally notified of any punishments, and have a right of appeal. If an employee is dismissed, failure to abide by such a procedure can lay a company open to a charge of UNFAIR DISMISSAL. See GRIEVANCE PROCEDURE.

disclosure of information any release of information from one party to another. Usually it refers to release of management information relevant to COLLECTIVE BARGAINING and potentially useful to trade union negotiators. In the UK, managers are statutorily required to release information, if requested, to union representatives; otherwise, collective bargaining would be impeded. However, managers are allowed to withhold certain categories of information, for example that which would be commercially damaging if released, and are entitled to withhold original documentation from scrutiny. The mechanisms for unions to challenge withholding of information on these grounds are cumbersome and in fact rarely used.

Employers are statutorily required to consult trade unions or other elected employee representatives when it has been decided to make a number of employees redundant. 30 days' notice is required if 10–100 employees in any establishment are to be made redundant, 90 days if over 100. Management is required to state formally the reason for redundancy, how many employees will be made redundant and what methods will be used to select employees for redundancy. See REDUNDANCY, CONSULTATION, COMMUNICATION, VREDELING DIRECTIVE.

disclosure of shareholdings the requirement in the UK under current COMPANY LAW for an investor owning more than 3% of the SHARES of a public JOINT-STOCK COMPANY to declare ownership of these shares to the directors of that company. Where several blocks of shares held by NOMINEE shareholders on behalf of a BENEFICIAL OWNER *collectively* amount to more than 3%, then the identity of the beneficial owner must be declared to the directors of the company. Disclosure provisions make it more difficult for someone to mount a DAWN RAID on a public company.

discount 1 a deduction from the published LIST PRICE of a product by a supplier to a customer. The discount could be offered in respect of bulk purchases (*trade discount*) or for prompt payment in cash (*cash discount*). Discounts may be given when stores offer goods at special low prices as, for example, during a sale period, or on a more permanent basis by DISCOUNT STORES.

2 the purchase of a BOND, TREASURY BILL or BILL OF EXCHANGE for less than its nominal value. Bills and bonds are redeemable at a specific future date at their face values. The original buyer will purchase the bill or bond for less than its nominal value (at a discount). The discount between the price which he pays and the nominal value of the bill or bond represents interest received on the loan made against the security of the bill or bond, which will depend largely on the length of time before maturity. For example, if a bond with a nominal value of £1,000 redeemable in one year's time was bought for £900, then the £100 discount on redemption value represents an interest rate of (£100/900) 11.1% on the loan.

3 the sale of new STOCKS and SHARES at a reduced price. In the UK this involves the issue of a new share at a price below its nominal value. Where shares have no nominal value it involves the sale of new shares at below their current market price.

4 the rating of a particular company's shares at a price below the average market price of the shares of other companies operating in the same sector, the discount reflecting investors' general view that this company is likely to perform less well than the others.

5 the amount by which a foreign currency's spot exchange rate stands below its official par value in a FIXED EXCHANGE RATE SYSTEM which allows some degree of short-term fluctuation either side of the par value.

discount house 1 a financial institution (unique to the UK financial system) which specializes in the buying and selling of commercial BILLS OF EXCHANGE and government TREASURY BILLS. See DISCOUNT MARKET.

2 RETAILERS who sell products at low prices by bulk buying, accepting low margins and selling high volumes.

discounted cash flow

A method used in INVESTMENT APPRAISAL to evaluate the desirability of an INVESTMENT project. Discounted cash flow is the CASH FLOW associated with an investment project that is adjusted to allow for the timing of the cash flow and the potential interest on the funds involved. Such an allowance for timing is important because most investment projects have their main costs or cash outflows in the first year or so, while their revenues or cash inflows are spread over future years.

For example, if the INTEREST RATE was 10% a company could invest £100 now and have it accumulate at compound interest to £110 at the end of one year and £121 at the end of two years. So £100 in the hands of the company now is worth the same as £110 in one year's time, or £121 receivable in two years' time, that is, it has a *present value* of £100.

The *net present value* investment criterion uses this principle to calculate the present value of the estimated stream of future cash outflows associated with an investment project, and the present value of the estimated stream of future cash inflows from the project, and to compare the two. If the present value of the cash inflows from the project exceeds the present value of outflows when both are discounted at, say, 10%, then the net present value is positive (see Fig. 34 A). If the firm's cost of capital (based on market interest rate) was 10% then it would be worthwhile for the company to undertake this project, because it will earn a return in excess of its financing costs.

The *internal rate of return* investment criterion seeks to calculate the percentage internal rate of return which will equate the present value of the stream of cash outflows associated with an investment project, with the present value of the stream of cash inflows from the project, so as to give a zero net present value. For example, in Fig. 34 B, the calculated internal rate of return is just over 42%, this being the rate at which net present value is zero.

This calculated internal rate of return can then be compared with the firm's cost of capital which is usually based on market rates. If the calculated internal rate of return (here 42%) exceeds the cost of capital (say 10%) then the project is worthwhile; otherwise not.

Whether or not the machine has a positive net present value, or an internal rate of return which exceeds the cost of capital, depends upon how accurate the future estimates of sales volumes, selling prices, materials costs, etc. turn out to be. Since all investments involve assessments of future revenues and costs they are all subject to a degree of uncertainty. This problem can to some extent be handled by undertaking sensitivity analysis, and by making not one but three estimates for each item of project cost or revenue ('optimistic', 'most likely', 'pessimistic') to indicate the range of possible outcomes.

A *Net Present Value at discount rate 10%*

Year	Cash Flows	Present Value Index at 10%	Present Value of Cash Flows (at 10%)
	£		£
now	–5,000	1.000	–5,000
end year 1	+5,000	0.909	+4,545
end year 2	+3,000	0.826	+2,478
	+3,400		NPV = +2,023

B *Internal Rate of Return*

Year	Cash Flows	Present Value Index at 42%	Present Value of Cash Flows (at 42%)	Present Value Index at 43%	Present Value of Cash Flows (at 43%)
	£		£		
now	–5,000	1.0000	–5,000	1.0000	–5,000
end year 1	+5,000	0.7042	+3,521	0.6993	+3,496
end year 2	+3,000	0.4959	+1,488	0.4890	+1,467
			NPV = +9		NPV = –37

Fig. 34 **Discounted cash flow.** Examples of two investment criteria for a machine: cost £5,000, estimated life 2 years, cash receipts/inflows £5,000 (year 1), £3,000 (year 2).

discount market a market engaged in the buying and selling of short-dated BILLS OF EXCHANGE and TREASURY BILLS. Such transactions are conducted through a number of DISCOUNT HOUSES which use money borrowed primarily from the COMMERCIAL BANKS (usually on a revolving day-to-day basis) to purchase bills (i.e. to 'discount' them) which they then hold until maturity or sell to each other ('re-discount') or more commonly on-sell to the commercial banks. When the discount houses find themselves temporarily unable to cover their purchase commitments by borrowing from the commercial banks, it is possible for them to obtain additional funds from the BANK OF ENGLAND in its capacity as the 'lender of last resort'. See ACCEPTING HOUSE.

discount rate the INTEREST RATE at which future cash inflows and cash outflows associated with an INVESTMENT project are discounted in order to allow for the timing of these cash flows. The discount rate used by firms in evaluating the desirability of investments is frequently based upon the average COST OF CAPITAL to the firm. See DISCOUNTED CASH FLOW.

discount store a RETAILER which sells a relatively limited range of products at low, 'discounted' prices (that is, prices substantially below manufacturers' RECOMMENDED RETAIL PRICES and the prices charged by other types of retailer) on a SELF SERVICE basis.

Discount stores may be under single-shop ownership or run as a multiple CHAIN STORE business. In the latter case the bigger chains are usually able to obtain substantial price concessions by BULK BUYING direct from manufacturers. See DISTRIBUTION CHANNEL, CATEGORY DISCOUNTER, WAREHOUSE CLUB.

discount tables see PRESENT VALUE TABLES.

discretionary costs managed costs of a non-manufacturing nature; e.g. administrative costs; research and development costs; marketing costs; training costs.

discrimination inequitable treatment of employees of which the main forms are:

(a) *sex discrimination,* where men and women are treated differently by their employer;

(b) *race discrimination,* where people are treated differently according to their colour, nationality, race or ethnic origins.

(c) *disability discrimination*, where disabled people are treated less favourably than others.

Discrimination can be said to be morally unacceptable in that it infringes people's rights and is also counterproductive in that it can result in people's talents being under-utilized. Since the late 1960s legislation has been aimed at tackling the more overt forms of discrimination at work in the UK. The *Equal Pay Act 1970* established the right for men and women to be paid the same rate of pay for performing the *same* job or a job rated as *equivalent.* It was widely believed, however, that employees could circumvent the intentions of this legislation by segregating men's and women's jobs. That the average female wage is only 75% of the average male wage tends to support this contention. In 1983, however, UK law was amended to establish the right to *equal pay* for work of *equal value* (in line with the European Union's directive on equal pay). Thus, a woman doing a job which is shown to be of equal value to a different job done by a man has a right to the rate of pay of the latter. Aggrieved individuals may pursue their claim to an INDUSTRIAL TRIBUNAL, whereupon the techniques of JOB EVALUATION will be used to assess the claim.

The *Sex Discrimination Act 1975* made discrimination on grounds of sex or marital status in RECRUITMENT AND SELECTION, TRAINING and employment benefits unlawful. The 1975 Act also established the Equal Opportunities Commission with a remit to:

(a) work towards the elimination of sex discrimination in employment, education and consumer services;

(b) promote equality of opportunity;

(c) monitor the effectiveness of the Sex Discrimination and Equal Pay Acts.

As well as direct discrimination, indirect discrimination, for example framing a job advertisement in a way which intentionally excludes women, is unlawful. Initially small firms and private household employers were exempt, but the *Sex Discrimination Act 1986* (passed in response to a European Court ruling) removed this exemption.

The *Race Relations Act 1976* is similar to the Sex Discrimination Act 1975 in making both direct and indirect discrimination in employment on grounds of colour, race, nationality or ethnic origins unlawful. As with claims of sex discrimination, aggrieved individuals can pursue a claim to an industrial tribunal. This legislation also created the Commission for Racial Equality to:

(a) work towards the elimination of racial discrimination in employment, education and consumer service;

(b) promote equality of opportunity;

(c) monitor the effectiveness of the 1976 Act.

The approach to combating discrimination against disabled people at work traditionally relied on the imposition of quotas. This changed with the Disability Discrimination Act in the mid-1990s. This legislation required that organizations take positive steps to meet the needs of disabled people in RECRUITMENT AND SELECTION and in EMPLOYMENT. A Disability Rights Commission was established to promote the rights of disabled people. The approach to tackling discrimination differs from measures to promote gender and racial equality. The latter aims at equality of treatment with a reference group (e.g. men) whereas the recent disability legislation aims at promoting measures that respond to the particular needs of disabled people.

Whilst legislation has largely curbed the more blatant forms of sex and race discrimination, it cannot be said to have achieved equality of opportunity. Only a minority of top managerial positions are held by women or black people. To encourage the recruitment and advancement of these people, many organizations have recently styled themselves as 'equal opportunities employers'. What this means in practice varies and many are sceptical of employers' claims in this respect. It is generally believed that to be meaningful such claims need to be supported by explicit equal opportunities policies in the area of recruitment, selection, training, etc., coupled with monitoring procedures to permit assessment of their impact. As part of this, data will need to be collected on the proportion of recruits, trainees, and those promoted, who are drawn from disadvantaged groups (for example ethnic monitoring). In addition DISCIPLINARY PROCEDURES and GRIEVANCE PROCEDURES will probably require amendment so as to discourage discriminatory behaviour and to provide channels of redress for those who feel they have been discriminated against. See GLASS CEILING.

discriminatory pricing see DEMAND-BASED PRICING, PRICE DISCRIMINATION.

diseconomies of scale see ECONOMIES OF SCALE.

disjointed incrementalism a pattern of decision-making in organizations, identified by American political scientist Charles Lindblom, in which decisions are taken step by step as a problem unfolds. The various incremental stages of decision-making are not closely integrated with the preceding stages. Although this differs sharply from the rational-deductive ideal of decision-making (where a problem is fully identified at the outset, all relevant information is collected and finally a set of rational procedures is used to choose the appropriate course of action), Lindblom believed it was a sensible strategy for decision-makers. This is because the human capacity to absorb information is limited, perfect information is unavailable anyway, and it is difficult to determine at the outset what information is relevant. See ORGANIZATIONAL ANALYSIS, 'GARBAGE-CAN' MODEL OF DECISION-MAKING.

disjunctive buyer see CONJOINT ANALYSIS.

disk drive a mechanical device in a COMPUTER which records and retrieves data from a rotating magnetic or vinyl disk.

Disk Operating System see DOS.

dismissal the termination of an employee's employment with an organization due to unsatisfactory work performance or breach of CONTRACT OF EMPLOYMENT. The term *firing* is sometimes used to refer to dismissal. See UNFAIR DISMISSAL.

dispatch 1 the sending out of finished goods for distribution and sale. Such finished goods can be dispatched from STOCK or as particular customers' orders are manufactured.

2 the selection of JOBS or batches of a product to be completed in a PRODUCTION schedule. Various *dispatch rules* can be used to select which particular job should be completed next from a queue of jobs awaiting completion, such as 'first come first served', 'random selection', 'minimum processing time' (starting with the job which has the shortest machine processing time) etc.

displays information presented visually to assist operatives in the control and operation of machinery and equipment. For example, the displays may consist of different coloured lights or data on a VISUAL DISPLAY UNIT (VDU).

disposable income the amount of INCOME which a person has available after paying INCOME TAX, NATIONAL INSURANCE CONTRIBUTIONS and PENSION contributions. The amount of a person's disposable income has an important effect on the ability to buy products.

disputes procedure a set of rules stipulating the procedures to be followed where two (or more) parties are in dispute with each other, with the aim of resolving the difference without recourse to open conflict. Such a procedure may be used to deal with disputes between employers and TRADE UNIONS concerning pay and conditions of employment. Where these matters are the subject of COLLECTIVE BARGAINING within the firm, the procedure will normally form part of the PROCEDURAL AGREEMENT governing relations between management and unions. Where, however, they are dealt with externally (by industry-wide bargaining), the disputes procedure will probably be operated by the EMPLOYERS' ASSOCIATION of which the company is a member. When a dispute arises the company hands it over to the association for resolution. See GRIEVANCE PROCEDURE.

distinctive capabilities the particular skills and attributes possessed by a firm which form the basis of *sustainable* COMPETITIVE ADVANTAGES over rival suppliers. Strategists emphasize three key competencies: *innovative ability* – the capability to bring out a succession of 'leading edge' new technologies and products; *reputation/image* – the accumulated qualities that make a firm 'stand out from the crowd'; *architecture* – the 'networking' of input suppliers and customers through the cultivation of close and mutually beneficial dealings See CORE SKILL OR COMPETENCY, RESOURCE BASED THEORY OF THE FIRM, VALUE CHAIN ANALYSIS.

distributed requirements planning (DRP) *or* **distributed resource planning** is based on a similar structure to MATERIALS REQUIREMENT PLANNING (MRP) and is used to manage the movement of materials *between* organizations within the same SUPPLY CHAIN. See SUPPLY CHAIN MANAGEMENT.

distributed resource planning see DISTRIBUTED REQUIREMENTS PLANNING.

distribution the process of storing and moving products to customers, often through intermediaries such as WHOLESALERS and RETAILERS. The task of *physical distribution management* involves moving specified quantities of products to places where customers can conveniently buy them, in time to replenish stocks, and in good condition. The objective is to maximize the availability of the product whilst minimizing the cost of distribution. Distribution is often described as one of the FOUR P'S of marketing as it is concerned with getting products to the correct *place* where they can be bought. Thus, distribution will include the selection of appropriate DISTRIBUTION CHANNELS in order to bring a firm's products to its selected markets. However where a business employs an *integrated distribution system*, distribution will include inventory, warehousing, materials handling, transport and order processing. SEE MARKETING; LOGISTICS, JUST-IN-TIME (JIT) SYSTEM, DISTRIBUTION RESOURCE PLANNING; FOUR P'S OF MARKETING, FREIGHT, PIGGY BACKING.

distribution channel

The route used in the physical distribution of a PRODUCT from the MANUFACTURER to the ultimate buyer of that product.

Functionally, a typical distribution channel consists of three basic interrelated operations:

(a) manufacturing (making the product);

(b) wholesaling (the holding of large STOCKS and 'breaking-bulk' into retail packs);

(c) retailing (the sale of the product to the final buyer) (see WHOLESALER, RETAILER).

Organizationally, these functions may be undertaken by firms which specialize at a particular stage in the chain or they may be combined wholly or partially, and undertaken by the one firm as an integrated operation (see VERTICAL INTEGRATION). The attractions of 'INTERNALIZING' the distribution function include the avoidance of TRANSACTION COSTS involved in dealing through the market, better control and coordination of the movement of products, various advantages over competitors (see FORECLOSURE, PRICE SQUEEZE) and the more effective MARKETING of products.

1. Manufacturing (M) → wholesaling (W) → retailing (R) → buyers
2. M → [WR] → buyers
3. [MW] → R → buyers
4. [MWR] → buyers

→ = independent function

[ ] = integrated function

Fig. 35 **Distribution channel.** Examples of typical channels of distribution.

Thus, depending upon the traditions of the trade, the nature of the product and the characteristics of the market being served, and the relative costs and marketing effectiveness of using different channel intermediaries, a number of distributive channel configurations may be identified, as Fig. 35 illustrates. Line 1 shows a conventional channel structure with the products being moved on an arms-length basis, that is, through independent intermediaries at each separate stage. Alternatively (line 2), a retailer such as a SUPERMARKET chain may buy in bulk direct from manufacturers and undertake the wholesaling function itself as an integrated wholesaling-retailing operation; a manufacturer may combine the production and wholesaling functions (line 3), on-selling to independent retailers or, alternatively, combine all three operations (line 4), selling direct to final buyers.

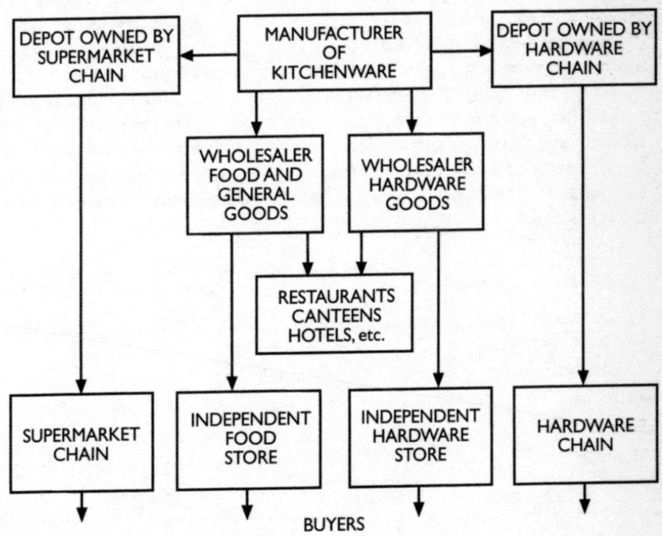

Fig. 36 **Distribution channel.** Some distribution channels for kitchenware.

Additionally, at some stage in a channel. SALES AGENTS, whose primary function is to generate new business contacts, may be employed. Typically, agents do not take title to the goods but are employed by, for example, a manufacturer to obtain new wholesale customers or a wholesaler seeking new retail accounts. For many products, distributive arrangements are multi-dimensional with a variety of modes employed depending upon which MARKET or MARKET SEGMENTS are being targeted (see Fig. 36). See VERTICAL MARKETING SYSTEM, SELECTIVE DISTRIBUTION, EXCLUSIVE DISTRIBUTION.

distribution centre a WAREHOUSE or DEPOT which carries sufficient stock to serve the needs of a particular area.

distribution of income the division of a country's GROSS NATIONAL PRODUCT among the multitude of people making up its POPULATION. In most countries, income (wages and salaries, rent, dividends, profit) is unequally divided; this reflects differences in people's natural abilities, educational attainments, special skills, but most importantly differences in the ownership of WEALTH assets such as businesses, houses, stocks and shares, etc. In many countries, however, governments operate progressive TAXATION systems and SOCIAL SECURITY programmes designed to redistribute income and so assist the poorer members of society. Thus, as Fig. 37 shows for the UK in 2002, the poorest 20% of the population received only 3% of total original income, but after taxation and state benefits they received 10% of total final income. See PER CAPITA INCOME.

distribution ratio a measure of the proportion of NET PROFIT which a company distributes to SHAREHOLDERS instead of ploughing it back into the business. Specifically, the distribution ratio expresses DIVIDENDS as a percentage of net profit after tax and interest. Thus, for example, if a company pays out one-quarter of its profits as dividends, then the distribution ratio is 25%. The distribution ratio is the opposite of the RETENTIONS RATIO and the mirror image of the DIVIDEND COVER ratio. See RESERVES, RETAINED PROFIT.

distribution resource planning (DRP) a computer-based PRODUCTION planning system which integrates a firm's PRODUCTION SCHEDULES, product DISTRIBUTION system and customers' orders, in order both to minimize stockholding costs and to improve customer service by reducing delivery times. See STOCKHOLDING MODEL, DELIVERY DATE, PRODUCTION MANAGEMENT.

distributive bargaining see COLLECTIVE BARGAINING.

Quintile groups of households	*Original income* %	*Final income* %
Bottom fifth	3	10
Second fifth	7	13
Third fifth	16	17
Fourth fifth	25	21
Top fifth	49	39
	100	100

Fig. 37 **Distribution of Income.** The personal distribution of original and final income in the UK, 2002. Final Income = original income less taxes paid, plus state spending on education, health, security benefits. (Source: Social Trends 2004).

distributor a business such as a RETAILER or WHOLESALER which acts as an intermediary in a DISTRIBUTION CHANNEL. Distributors take title to goods (that is, purchase goods) which they then on-sell to customers. See also DISTRIBUTOR BRANDS.

distributor brands brands created and owned by distributors. See OWN-LABEL BRAND.

diversifiable risk see CAPITAL-ASSET PRICING MODEL.

diversification *or* **conglomerate integration** the expansion of a firm into a range of different product areas which leads to its operating in a number of markets rather than a single market. Diversification may be 'concentric' or 'pure', the former involving some carry over of production or marketing functions (for example, two firms which utilize a common technological base – razor blades and garden spades both produced from stainless steel and sold through the same outlets – supermarkets), while in the latter case the products are entirely unrelated (for example cars and cement). Diversification may take the form of ORGANIC (INTERNAL) GROWTH, or firms may choose to expand by EXTERNAL GROWTH, merging with or taking over established firms. Concentric diversification via internal growth often arises as a result of new discoveries and applications made by the firm's RESEARCH AND DEVELOPMENT activities as an extension of its existing technological expertise. For example, many producers of basic chemicals have extended their businesses into areas of chemical derivatives, such as paint and pharmaceuticals. In the case of pure diversification, mergers and takeovers often offer the best prospects of a successful entry into a new area.

The main attraction of diversification as a growth strategy compared with HORIZONTAL INTEGRATION (expansion in the firm's existing markets) and VERTICAL INTEGRATION (expansion into different supply levels, but again within an existing market), is the ability to spread risks and broaden the firm's profit-earning potential. Specifically, a one-market firm is vulnerable not only to erratic, cyclical profit returns resulting from the business cycle, but worse still, its very survival may be threatened by a declining customer base as the firm's product moves into the final stages of the PRODUCT LIFE-CYCLE. Diversification is thus the main way the firm can reduce its exposure to business risk and fluctuating profitability, while reorientating its activities away from mature and declining markets into new areas offering sustained growth and profit opportunities.

Diversification may produce *synergy* (ie, the 2 + 2 = more than 4 effect). Synergy results from complementary activities or from the carry-over of management capabilities. For example, in the case of a diversified merger, one firm may have a strong production organization, while the other excels in marketing – joining the two renders both firms more effective. Similarly, a high degree of carry-over of management expertise may make it possible to reduce production costs and improve product quality of the combined group.

On the other hand a number of problems can arise with diversification, especially if it is of the pure rather than the concentric variety. Diversification may bring with it a loss of 'focus' and 'identity' with top management trying to do too much and failing to fully comprehend the operational and strategic needs of the company's individual business divisions. This may well be exacerbated by spreading financial resouces for development too thinly so that some divisions remain underfunded and unable to attain their true potential. Together these factors may produce 'reverse synergy' (2 + 2 = 3 rather than 5) resulting in under – performance and a depressed share price. Hence the current vogue for 'unlocking shareholder value' through hiving-off or demerging divisions as separate quoted companies. For example, BAT Industries the tobacco company spun-off its financial services division setting up a joint venture company with Zurich the Swiss financial services group, while Hanson the leading UK conglomerate of the 1960s, 1970s and 1980s recently split itself up into four separate companies.

Diversification can produce both pro- and anti-competitive effects and for this reason may attract the attentions of the competition policy authorities. Diversifying firms can redeploy profits earned in other areas of their businesses in order to finance entry into new markets, thereby increasing competition in the entered market; on the other hand, 'cross subsidization' may be used in a predatory manner to undercut competitors' prices and drive them out of business. In the UK, conglomerate mergers and takeovers involving assets in excess of £70 million may be referred by the OFFICE OF FAIR TRADING to the COMPETITION COMMISSION for investigation, to determine whether or not they should be allowed to proceed. See BUSINESS STRATEGY, PRODUCT-MARKET MATRIX, STRATEGIC BUSINESS UNIT, INTERNALIZATION, SYNERGY, CORE SKILL, CORE BUSINESS.

divestment the closure or sale by a firm of one or more of its operating units (for example a production plant) or a whole business division. In the former case, divestment usually occurs in order to rationalize production and/or to concentrate the firm's output in a more modern plant. In contrast, the divestment of a whole business division represents a more fundamental strategic decision on the part of the firm. Divestment in this case may reflect a number of considerations, including a desire to pull out of an unprofitable, loss-making activity deemed to be incapable of TURNROUND; the wish to shed peripheral businesses in order to release cash and managerial resources which, in opportunity cost terms, could be more effectively, redeployed in the firm's other activities; a major rethink of a firm's strategic position involving a retrenchment back to 'core' businesses; and finally, a wish to avoid the opposition of the COMPETITION POLICY authorities, particularly in cases of MERGERS and TAKEOVER.

Divestment by one firm often presents an opportunity for some other firm to diversify (see DIVERSIFICATION), in turn, into new business areas, or for former competitors to increase their market shares. See ENDGAME STRATEGY, BUSINESS STRATEGY, BOSTON MATRIX, DE-MERGER, MANAGEMENT BUY-OUT, JOINT VENTURE, PRODUCT MARKET MATRIX, PRODUCT RATIONALIZATION, CORE BUSINESS.

dividend a payment made by a JOINT-STOCK COMPANY to its SHAREHOLDERS for providing SHARE CAPITAL. Dividends are a distribution of the after-tax PROFITS of the company, and are paid in proportion to the number of shares held. Generally the directors of a company will decide to pay out only a proportion of after-tax profit as dividends, reinvesting the remaining profits in the business (see RETAINED PROFIT).

The DIRECTORS may pay an *interim dividend* during the accounting period then recommend a final rate of dividend per share for approval by shareholders at the ANNUAL GENERAL MEETING, this *final dividend* being paid after the AGM. In the UK dividends are paid net of income tax, though shareholders receive a tax credit for the amount of tax deducted by the company from their dividends, which must be added to the net dividends received to establish the shareholder's gross taxable dividend income (see CORPORATION TAX).

dividend cover *or* **times covered** a measure of the extent to which a firm's earnings (profit after tax and interest) cover DIVIDEND paid, which expresses PROFITS as a multiple of dividends paid. Thus, for example, if a company pays out one quarter of its profit as dividends, then the dividend cover ratio is four. The dividend ratio is the mirror image of the DISTRIBUTION RATIO.

dividend yield the DIVIDEND paid by a JOINT-STOCK COMPANY for a given ACCOUNTING PERIOD expressed as a percentage of the current market price per share. For example, if Company X declared a dividend of £1 per ORDINARY SHARE for the 12 month accounting period ending 31 December, and the current market price of one ordinary share in Company X was £5, the dividend yield would be:

$$\frac{\text{Dividend per share}}{\text{Price per share}} \times 100 = \frac{£1}{£5} \times 100 = 20\%$$

division see PRODUCT-BASED STRUCTURE.

divisionalization see PRODUCT-BASED STRUCTURE.

division of labour see SPECIALIZATION.

document image processing (DIP) see DATA STORAGE.

dogs see BOSTON BOX.

Do-It-Yourself store a RETAILER which sells mainly home improvement and repair equipment and materials (paint, wallpaper, patio doors, etc.) and garden accessories. DIY stores may be under single-shop ownership or run as a multiple CHAIN STORE business.

They compete principally by offering customers both convenience, by stocking an extensive range of products under the one roof, and competitive prices. The bigger DIY chains are able to obtain significant price discounts by BULK BUYING manufacturers' brands and have found it advantageous also to establish their OWN-LABEL BRANDS. See DISTRIBUTION CHANNEL, SELF-SERVICE.

dollar ($) the domestic currency of the USA. In addition the dollar is used extensively as an INTERNATIONAL RESERVE asset, a key currency in the EUROCURRENCY MARKET and is used to finance the international oil business.

domestic labour work performed by household members for the benefit of the household (for example child rearing). It has been argued that since domestic labour ultimately benefits employers by preparing and sustaining a LABOUR FORCE, those performing it should be paid a WAGE.

dominant firm a firm that accounts for a substantial proportion of the total supply of a particular product. Such a firm not only has a high absolute market share, but also often a (relative) market share which is considerably greater than its nearest rival. In consequence, a dominant firm may be in a position to exercise market (monopoly) power to the detriment of both consumers and rival suppliers.

Under UK COMPETITION POLICY, a dominant firm is defined as a firm which supplies 40% or more of a specified GOOD OR SERVICE. See COMPETITION POLICY (UK).

Donovan Commission the Royal Commission on Trades Unions and Employers' Associations which reported in 1968 into the state of INDUSTRIAL RELATIONS in the UK. This landmark report found that informal, uncontrolled bargaining had developed at shop-floor level alongside the existing formal system of industry-wide bargaining, leading to spiralling pay claims, unofficial STRIKES, etc. The solution proposed was the rationalization and formalization of workplace industrial relations. Employee representatives were to be given a formal role in new procedures governing discipline, grievance and pay determination. See COLLECTIVE BARGAINING, EMPLOYERS' ASSOCIATION, MULTI-EMPLOYER AGREEMENTS, TRADE UNION.

DOS (Disk Operating System) a COMPUTER program which enables a computer to record and retrieve data from a rotating magnetic or vinyl disk. The most widely-used disk operating system is MSDOS, which is used on computers that are compatible with the IBM personal computer.

dot.com a term used to refer to a company which makes extensive use of the INTERNET to market its products and whose internet address ends in .com.

'dotted-line relationship' see ORGANIZATION CHART.

double-day shifts see SHIFT WORK.

double-entry accounts the ACCOUNTING records of a firm's day-to-day financial transactions with outside parties which record both aspects of each transaction, namely, what is 'given' and what is received in return. By making a double entry in the accounts the firm can record both aspects of the exchange, for example the exchange of cash for raw materials purchased, or the exchange for cash of GOODS OR SERVICES sold. See LEDGER, DEBIT, CREDIT.

double taxation the TAXATION of INCOMES and PROFITS in both the country where they arise, and again where these incomes and profits are remitted to the income earner's home country. Such double taxation can be a significant deterrent to international labour and capital movements. For this reason many countries have negotiated double taxation agreements which limit taxation liability to the country in which the income is earned. Compare UNITARY TAXATION, WITHHOLDING TAX.

doubtful debts amounts owed to a company by customers or borrowers which may possibly not be paid because the customers or borrowers are in financial difficulties. In anticipation that many doubtful debts will eventually become BAD DEBTS, a company may make a PROVISION against profits for some doubtful debts. See CREDIT CONTROL.

Dow-Jones Index see SHARE PRICE INDEX.

downgrading the re-classification of a product as sub-standard or second quality. See QUALITY CONTROL, TOTAL QUALITY MANAGEMENT.

downside risk the risk of experiencing losses associated with an investment project and the magnitude of these losses. Managers' attitudes towards UNCERTAINTY will influence their assessment of the desirability of a project which has substantial downside risk.

downsizing 1 the use of PERSONAL COMPUTERS in a business in place of large mainframe computers. The introduction of smaller, faster and more cost-effective microprocessors has made it possible for tasks which formerly could only be performed by mainframe computers to be carried out at the personal workstation level, allowing a greater devolution of DATA PROCESSING down to the 'desk top'.
2 a term for policies aimed at organizational contraction, usually leading to REDUNDANCY for some employees. The oft-stated rationale for downsizing is that a smaller, more flexible ORGANIZATION will be able to respond better to market forces. Cost reduction, however, is probably an equally important motive. See DELAYERING, RIGHTSIZING.

downstream integration see VERTICAL INTEGRATION.

downtime time when a machine or COMPUTER is not operating correctly owing to machine failure or because the machine is being set up for the next work task (SET-UP TIME). Downtime in a factory can cause considerable loss of output and disruption to production schedules, and the aim of PREVENTIVE MAINTENANCE is to minimize such downtime. See IDLE TIME.

drawing office the department of a manufacturer's business responsible for producing the technical drawings of products, components and plant lay-out. See COMPUTER-AIDED DESIGN, COMPUTER-AIDED MANUFACTURING.

driver see COST DRIVER, ACTIVITY-BASED COSTING.

drum buffer rope see OPTIMIZED PRODUCTION TECHNOLOGY.

DTI see DEPARTMENT OF TRADE AND INDUSTRY.

DTLR the former Department for Transport, Local Government and the Regions. See DEPARTMENT FOR TRANSPORT

duality the dual aspect of each business transaction, in which something is given by a firm and something is received in return, for example, goods for cash in a cash sale. Both aspects of a transaction are recorded in DOUBLE ENTRY ACCOUNTS. See ACCOUNTING.

dumping the sale of a product by a firm in an EXPORT MARKET at a price *below* that charged in its own domestic market. Firms may choose to lower their overseas sales prices in order, for example, to dispose of surplus output, or as part of a MARKET PENETRATION PRICING strategy aimed at building the firm's market share in export markets over the longer term. Whatever the firm's motivation, such a pricing practice constitutes 'unfair' INTERNATIONAL TRADE under WORLD TRADE ORGANIZATION conventions, and member countries are entitled to protect their domestic producers against dumping by applying anti-dumping duties, or countervailing duties on offending products. See LOCAL CONTENT RULE. PROTECTIONISM.

durability the ability of a product or component to perform its required function under its stated conditions of use until its performance falls below an acceptable level.

durable goods see CONSUMER DURABLES.

DWP see DEPARTMENT OF WORK AND PENSIONS.

dysfunction any consequence of an activity which inhibits the achievement of the desired objective. In the study of ORGANIZATIONS, dysfunctions refer to those aspects of organizations which are essential to the organization's proper functioning but at the same time detract from organizational performance. For instance, a justifiable emphasis on following the correct procedures can also stifle the flexibility that is often needed in work situations. See GOAL DISPLACEMENT.

e

early adopter see DIFFUSION PROCESS.

early failure rate see FAILURE RATE CURVE.

early mover advantage see MOBILITY BARRIER.

earned income that part of a person's income earned from employment or self-employment (WAGES, SALARIES, FEES. COMMISSIONS and PROFITS). By contrast unearned income derives from the ownership of assets (interest and dividends from investment, rents from property, etc.) or can take the form of unemployment benefits, old age pensions, etc. See INCOME.

earnings see EARNED INCOME.

earnings per share NET PROFIT after tax accruing to the ordinary shareholders in a JOINT-STOCK COMPANY, divided by the number of ORDINARY SHARES. Comparison of earnings per share with DIVIDEND per share indicates the proportion of earnings paid out as dividends and the proportion retained in the business.

earnings yield NET PROFIT after tax per ordinary share (EARNINGS PER SHARE) of a JOINT-STOCK COMPANY for a given ACCOUNTING PERIOD, expressed as a percentage of the current market price per share. For example, if profit after tax was £2 per share and the market price per share was £5 then the earnings yield would be 40%. Earnings yield is the mirror image of the PRICE-EARNINGS RATIO.

Earnings yield depends upon DIVIDEND YIELD and DIVIDEND COVER. For example, if dividend yield was 20% and the dividend was covered twice over then the earnings yield would be 20% x 2 or 40%.

EBCDIC (Extended Binary Coded Decimal Interchange Code) a system for coding individual numbers, letters and punctuation marks.

e-business the use of computers and the INTERNET to link both the *internal* operations of a business (that is, transactions and communications between the various departments/divisions of the business) and its *external* dealings and relationships with its suppliers and customers. See E-COMMERCE.

EC see EUROPEAN UNION.

ECB see EUROPEAN CENTRAL BANK.

ECGD see EXPORT CREDIT GUARANTEE DEPARTMENT.

e-commerce a method of buying and selling goods and services over the INTERNET. E-commerce is a form of DIRECT SELLING/MARKETING which enables a supplier to sell direct to the final customer without the need for traditional 'middlemen' – wholesalers and store retailers. E-commerce provides sellers with a means of tapping into a mass market; it reduces BARRIERS TO ENTRY so that even small firms can offer their products alongside big name companies; and by eliminating the 'middleman' selling costs and prices can be lowered conferring COMPETITIVE ADVANTAGE. Apart from lower prices another attraction for customers is the convenience of being able to 'shop' from home rather than have to visit a retail outlet.

The volume and value of transactions conducted via computer and associated networks has grown rapidly from the late 1990s and it is predicted that a large proportion of economic transactions will in future be conducted through electronic commerce. See also E-BUSINESS, CUSTOMER RELATIONSHIP MANAGEMENT.

econometrics the application of statistical techniques in the analysis of economic data. Econometrics is used extensively in establishing statistical relationships between, for example, levels of national income and consumption in the economy, as a basis for formulating government ECONOMIC POLICY, and is used by firms to forecast demand for their products. See SALES FORECASTING, REGRESSION ANALYSIS.

Economic and Monetary Union (EMU) the unification of the economies of member countries of the EUROPEAN UNION (EU) through the introduction of a common ('single') currency and the harmonization (and eventual centralization) of fiscal policy. EMU represents the final stage in a long process towards integration which had its roots initially in the establishment of a 'common market' by the Treaty of Rome (1958) and which was then propelled further by the establishment of the EUROPEAN MONETARY SYSTEM (EMS) to coordinate the exchange rates of member countries' currencies and the attempt to create a 'single market' through the harmonization of business practices (See SINGLE EUROPEAN ACT, 1986). See TRADE INTEGRATION entry.

At present movement towards 'monetary union' is far more advanced than that of fiscal harmonization. The 'building blocks' of monetary union were put in place by the MAASTRICHT TREATY (1991) which envisaged the introduction of a single currency for the EU with EU-wide monetary policy being controlled by a EUROPEAN CENTRAL BANK (ECB). The ECB was duly established in 1998 to oversee EU member countries' 'readiness' for the introduction of EMU in January 1999. This was focused on conformity to various 'convergence' criteria, including low inflation (under 3%) and government debt limits (current budget deficits not to exceed 3% of GDP, and total outstanding debt not to exceed 60% of GDP). Member countries meeting the convergence criteria were required to decide whether to join EMU at the outset or delay their entry to a later date. Eleven of the 15 EU members opted for immediate membership, while the UK, Norway, Greece and Sweden adopted a 'wait-and-see' stance. In 2001 Greece joined the EMU.

The inception of EMU involved a number of stages. On 1 January 1999 the 11 founding members of EMU established irrevocably fixed exchange rates between their currencies; in 2002 individual national currencies were replaced by a new single currency – the EURO (see EURO entry for further details). The Euro itself was introduced in January 1999 as a book-keeping 'unit of account', but took on a physical identity (i.e. as notes and coins) in 2002 and serves as a 'medium of exchange' used to finance personal and business transactions within the EU. At present the exchange rate of the Euro 'floats' against other currencies such as the Japanese yen, US dollar and the UK pound.

Advocates of EMU argue that a common currency will create a more stable economic environment as distortions such as the exchange rate cost and risks associated with the conversion of national currencies will be removed. This will be reinforced by the ECB's primary objective of maintaining a regime of low inflation. Also a common currency will have the advantage of enhancing price transparency so that price differentials for the *same* product as between EU countries will tend to disappear and prices will tend to be driven down to the level of the most efficient supply source. However, other commentators point out that an EU-wide 'one fit' monetary policy has its limitations given continuing business cycle and structural disparities between EU members. Also, by definition, the adoption of a common currency removes the *external* exchange rate option of improving a country's economic position by devaluing/depreciating its currency, placing the whole burden of 'adjustment' on *internal* measures. Furthermore, at present members are relatively free to pursue their own independent budgetary policies (although they are expected to observe Maastricht 'Stability Pact' restraints as noted above, (current budget deficits below 3% of GDP and an overall debt limit of 60% GDP)) increasing the danger that fiscal stimulation may conflict with a 'tight' monetary policy. A particular problem facing the EU is that chronic unemployment which can only be effectively tackled, as some economists argue, by supply-side policies aimed at improving labour market flexibility rather than monetary measures alone.

Regarding the issue of the UK's future entry into the EMU, the present Labour government is 'in principle' in favour of joining the EMU but only if a high degree of 'convergence' with the EMU-zone economies has been attained, and then only after a National Referendum of the electorate secures a majority vote in favour. The government has proposed five 'tests' for joining the EMU relating to 'convergence', 'flexibility', 'inward investment', 'financial services' and 'employment'. These include 'convergence' with the EMU-zone with regard to inflation rates (the UK's current (as at January 2005) inflation rate is under 2%, and the EMU-zone rate is under 2%) and government debt-GDP ratios (the UK's current rate is below 40% which conforms to the EMU-zone maximum permitted rate of 60%). The other criteria are more 'open-ended' and can be interpreted in a number of ways; for example, the UK's leading position as a recipient of inward investment and a major provider of financial services could be put under threat as a number of major MULTINATIONAL ENTERPRISES have declared that they intend to reduce their investments in the UK or even pull out if the UK continues to remain outside the EMU-zone. A big question mark if the UK were to join the EMU hangs over the initial exchange rate of the pound to the EURO. If the rate is too high the results could be disastrous, as was the case when the UK joined the 'exchange rate mechanism' of the old European Monetary System in the early 1990s.

economic exposure see EXCHANGE RATE EXPOSURE.

economic growth an increase in the total real' output of goods and services in an economy over time. Economic growth is usually measured in terms of an increase in GROSS DOMESTIC PRODUCT (GDP) over time, or an increase in GDP per head of population to reflect its impact on living standards over time. Because of the contribution of economic growth to wealth creation, and the fact that it provides the government with extra resources to provide social amenities (without having to raise taxation), most governments accord a high priority to the promotion of economic growth in formulating their ECONOMIC POLICIES.

The ability of an economy to produce m ore goods and services on a sustained basis depends on many factors including an increase in the quantity and quality of the labour force. capital stock and natural resources (the basic factor inputs available to it); the efficient use of these resources so as to attain a high level of PRODUCTIVITY; the introduction of new innovative techniques and methods of production and new products. The latter two factors are especially important in the context of a world economy where a country's economic growth rate is materially affected by INTERNATIONAL TRADE influences. Finally, a country's own level of demand needs to be sufficiently buoyant both to ensure the full utilization of its existing resources and to encourage producers to invest in new plant and research and development to enlarge the supply capabilities of the economy over the longer term.

Governments can stimulate the growth process by increasing current spending in the economy through taxation cuts (see FISCAL POLICY) and by increasing the money supply and reducing interest rates (see MONETARY POLICY). Additionally, it can operate on the supply-side of the economy by promoting enterprise initiatives and providing resources for improving productivity and research (see INDUSTRIAL POLICIES).

economic order quantity model see STOCKHOLDING MODEL.

economic policy the strategies and measures adopted by the government to manage the economy as a means of achieving its economic objectives. In general terms governments are concerned with (at the macro-level) securing full employment (see UNEMPLOYMENT), price stability (see INFLATION), ECONOMIC GROWTH and BALANCE OF PAYMENTS equilibrium, and (at the micro-level) an efficient use of resources. In practice, given the complexities of the economy and its exposure to international influences, the simultaneous achievement of all these objectives is virtually impossible, so that a degree of prioritizing is required. Inevitably, political as well as economic considerations will influence this process.

Various general measures can be employed by governments to achieve their objectives, including FISCAL POLICY (the manipulation of tax rates and government expenditure), MONETARY POLICY (the control of the money supply and interest rates), PRICES AND INCOMES POLICIES (controls on costs and prices) and the management of the EXCHANGE RATE to influence the country's external trade and payments position. These policies are augmented at a more specific level by measures designed to encourage industrial investment, research and development and enterprise, and to protect consumers' interests; see INDUSTRIAL POLICY, REGIONAL POLICY, COMPETITION POLICY.

Fiscal and monetary policies, the main measures used by successive governments in the UK since 1945, operate on the level and distribution of spending in the economy. They are thus essentially demand-side measures. In recent years greater emphasis has been given to the need to improve the supply-side of the economy, reflected, in particular, by attempts to inject greater flexibility into the workings of the labour market by breaking down the power of trade union monopolies.

The government's economic policy is formulated and coordinated through the office of the CHANCELLOR OF THE EXCHEQUER, the TREASURY and the BANK OF ENGLAND and implemented through more specialized agencies such as the OFFICE OF FAIR TRADING, DEPARTMENT OF TRADE AND INDUSTRY, DEPARTMENT FOR WORK AND PENSIONS etc. See BUSINESS CYCLE, MONETARISM.

economics the study of the way in which countries endowed with only a *limited* availability of economic resources (natural resources, labour and capital) can best use these resources so as to gain the maximum fulfilment of society's *unlimited* demands for goods and services. Economics has a macroeconomic and a microeconomic dimension. Macroeconomics is concerned with the *overall* efficiency of resource use in the economy, in particular the achievement of full employment, and with the growth of resources over time (see ECONOMIC POLICY). Micro-economics is concerned with the efficient supply of *particular* goods and services (see MARKET SYSTEM).

economic union see TRADE INTEGRATION, ECONOMIC AND MONETARY UNION (EMU).

economic value added (EVA) a measure of a firm's overall profit (loss) position when allowance is made for the OPPORTUNITY/ECONOMIC COSTS of the firm's capital (that is, the revenues the firm's assets could have earned in some alternative use). Whereas accounting PROFIT = SALES REVENUE less accounting COSTS (see PROFIT AND LOSS ACCOUNT), EVA = sales revenue less accounting cost less opportunity economic costs.

To illustrate: assume sales revenue is £1,000,000 and accounting cost is £900,000; on conventional criteria the firm thus makes an accounting profit of £100,000. However, when allowance is made for the *opportunity* cost of the firm's assets *if liquidated and redeployed in an alternative use* the picture changes. If the firm's assets could have earned, say, £200,000 in some alternative activity (e.g. even putting the money on interest-bearing deposit with a bank) then the positive accounting profit is turned into an economic loss of £100,000. Thus, shareholders' wealth has been 'destroyed' rather than 'created'.

However, whilst producing accurate accounting cost and profit data can be difficult, obtaining reliable economic cost and profit data can be even more problematic. For example, a high proportion of the investment in the firm's *current* activity may represent a 'sunk' cost with little prospect of recovery if liquidated, while there is a difficulty in identifying which are likely to be viable *alternative* activities where the firm's new investment might yield higher profit returns than currently being achieved.

economies of scale the reduction in the unit (average) costs of producing and distributing a product as the size of the firm's operations is increased. The ability to supply a product at a low cost (and hence a low price) represents an important source of COMPETITIVE ADVANTAGE over rival suppliers in markets where price competition is the main form of inter-firm rivalry.

Economies of scale are to be found at the level both of the individual plant and of the firm (operating a number of plants). Important plant level economies include the possibility of using superior techniques or organization of production as scale is increased, for example switching from labour intensive BATCH PRODUCTION to continuous capital-intensive MASS PRODUCTION methods of manufacture; and the economies of increased dimensions, where for many types of capital equipment (boilers, tankers, etc.) both set-up and operating costs rise less than proportionately to increases in capacity. Firm-level economies include the ability of large firms to bulk buy raw materials and components on advantageous terms and, likewise, borrow money at preferential rates.

Unit costs, however, do not fall continuously as the scale of the firm's operations is increased; they tend to level off at some point (the *minimum efficient scale* of operation) and remain relatively constant thereafter, or they may rise because of the growing complexities of managing a larger organization (*diseconomies of scale*). Moreover, the potential for exploiting available economies of scale may be limited by the fact that the overall size of the market is too small or that *firms'* individual market shares are too low. In the latter case, increasing firm size by HORIZONTAL INTEGRATION, particularly through mergers or takeovers, may be one important means of making firms more cost-effective. Where economies of scale are significant, a high level of MARKET CONCENTRATION may also be required to ensure that industry output is produced as efficiently as possible. See SPECIALIZATION.

economies of scope the cost savings which arise by carrying out a number of different activities within the same firm through sharing common inputs or jointly promoting or distributing products. For example, a building society could use its existing branches and staff not only to sell mortgages but also to offer customers other financial services such as insurance, pensions etc. Likewise, Nestlé has used the strategy of UMBRELLA BRANDING to extend its range of instant coffee products all under the 'Nescafé' BRAND NAME thereby reducing promotional costs. See DIVERSIFICATION.

economy a country defined in terms of the total composition of its economic activities and the ultimate location of economic decision-making.

The total value of goods and services produced in any one year is called the *gross domestic product*. The contribution made to total output by the various subdivisions of the economy can be split down in various ways: for example, by broad sectors such as the *primary* sector (agriculture), the *industrial* sector (including manufacturing) and the *tertiary* sector (services); or by individual activities (brewing, coal-mining, etc.).

Economic decision-making in the economy may be either highly centralized or decentralized. In a *centrally planned economy*, the State owns the means of production (except labour) and decides what goods and services are to be produced in accordance with a national plan. Resources are allocated between producing units, and final outputs between consumers by the use of physical quotas. At the other extreme, in a *private enterprise economy* (*free market* or *capitalist economy*) the means of production are held by individuals and firms. Economic decision-making is highly decentralized with resources being allocated through a large number of individual goods and services markets. It is the MARKET which synchronizes the decisions of buyers and sellers by establishing market prices which determine how much of a product will be produced and sold. In practice, a large number of countries, including the UK, are *mixed economies* with some goods and services being provided by private enterprise and others, typically public-utility type products such as postal services and railways, being supplied by the State. The precise mix of private enterprise and State activities to be found in particular countries, however, does vary substantially between the two extremes and is very much influenced by prevailing political ideologies. See INDUSTRY, STRUCTURE OF INDUSTRY, NATIONALIZATION VERSUS PRIVATIZATION.

ECR see EFFICIENT CUSTOMER RESPONSE.

EEA see EUROPEAN ECONOMIC AREA.

EEF see ENGINEERING EMPLOYERS FEDERATION.

effective exchange rate see EXCHANGE RATE.

efficiency the relationship between the quantities of factor inputs (labour, materials, etc.) used by a firm and the quantity of output which it is able to produce using these inputs. Where a firm is able to produce the same output using fewer inputs or produce more output using the same quantity of inputs then it has improved its efficiency. See PRODUCTIVITY.

efficiency wage a WAGE in excess of the market rate, and which contributes to a high level of EFFICIENCY. It does this by establishing a high OPPORTUNITY COST to employees for dismissal for sacking. It may also attract higher quality recruits to employment with the firm.

efficient customer response (ECR) a system used by RETAILERS for planning product ranges, continuous replenishment of inventory, new product introduction and product promotion.

efficient-market hypothesis the proposition that all available information which may influence the price of a FINANCIAL SECURITY is reflected in its *current* market price because financial markets are 'efficient' in adjusting prices to information. If markets are indeed efficient it is impossible for an investor to consistently predict how the price of any particular financial security is likely to change and thus outguess the market.

effort bargain a term in the SOCIOLOGY OF WORK referring to the implicit trade-offs made by workers between the effort expended on work and the payment received from it.

EFTA see EUROPEAN FREE TRADE ASSOCIATION.

EFTPOS (electronic funds transfer at the point of sale) a system for paying for the purchase of goods and services involving the use of at CREDIT CARD (e.g. Visa) or bank debit card (e.g. Switch). The customer's card is 'swiped' across a machine at the till with details of the purchase being transmitted down an electronically connected line to the EFTPOS processing centre for authorization. The advantage of EFTPOS is that like a cheque it removes the need to pay in ready cash, but more particularly computerization of transactions cuts down on the amount of physical paperwork undertaken and related costs. See EPOS.

EIS see ENTERPRISE INVESTMENT SCHEME.

elasticity of demand a measure of the degree of responsiveness of DEMAND for a product to a given change in some economic variable, particularly its own price, the prices of competing products and consumers' income. In general terms, if there is a more than proportionate change in quantity demanded as a result of a change in a variable, then demand is said to be *elastic*, while if there is a less than proportionate change, then demand is *inelastic*. Price elasticity of demand is calculated using the formula:

$$\frac{\text{\% change in quantity demanded}}{\text{\% change in product's own price}}$$

which measures the effect on demand of an increase or decrease in the product's own price. Since the price-quantity demanded relationship determines the firm's total revenue from selling the product, the price elasticity of demand figure thus provides an indication of the way in which a change in price will affect the firm's revenues. For example, if, as in the case of cigarettes as a generic group in the UK, demand is highly inelastic (econometric studies put it at 0.32), then an increase in cigarette prices will increase total industry revenues more than proportionately. However, it is important to note that the demand for each of the many individual brands making up the market is likely to be much more elastic because they face competitive substitutes within the market (i.e. putting up the price of a particular brand is likely to result in buyers switching to other brands, and hence reduce the firm's revenues). The extent to which the demand for a brand is affected by a change in the price of a close substitute brand can be measured by the cross-elasticity of demand formula:

$$\frac{\text{\% change in quantity demanded of brand A}}{\text{\% change in price of brand B}}$$

There are various practical difficulties, however, in the way of measuring elasticity values. For example, there is usually insufficient data available to construct a comprehensive 'demand curve' covering a wide range of price-quantity demanded combinations, and to isolate individual brand cross-elasticity effects in a multi-brand setting. See DEMAND-BASED PRICING.

Income elasticity of demand measures the degree of responsiveness of demand for a product to changes in consumers' income over time, namely:

$$\frac{\text{\% change in quantity demanded}}{\text{\% change in income}}$$

The concept of income elasticity of demand is useful to corporate planners in indicating which industries are likely to decline or expand over time as income levels rise, and hence can make an important contribution to the formulation of a firm's DIVERSIFICATION and DIVESTMENT strategies. See PRICE DISCRIMINATION.

electronic data interchange (EDI) an interactive COMMUNICATION system which enables two firms to exchange business documents using standard electronic forms and COMPUTERS linked through a service provider e.g. electronic links between suppliers and retailers allowing purchase orders, packing lists, delivery notices, invoices and remittance advices, as well as self-billing by retailers. EDI is often a faster, cheaper and more reliable means of exchanging information than traditional paper-based exchanges. See INFORMATION MANAGEMENT, MASS CUSTOMIZATION.

electronic mail (e-mail) a form of COMMUNICATION which involves sending COMPUTER-originated messages and information across a telecommunications network. E-mail usage is expanding rapidly, partly reflected in the introduction of new facilities which provide an integrated approach to sending messages to any combination of fax, telex and electronic mail addresses. See INFORMATION MANAGEMENT, NETWORKING.

electronic point of sale see EPOS.

electronic shopping a form of DIRECT MARKETING in which consumers make purchases from products displayed on their domestic television by means of a telephone or keyboard link to the seller.

e-mail see ELECTRONIC MAIL.

emergent (approach to strategy) see BUSINESS POLICY.

emigration see POPULATION.

emission permit see POLLUTION.

emoluments wages, salaries, bonuses and payments in kind paid to employees or self-employed workers and managers. See PAY.

employee a person who is employed by an EMPLOYER (firm, government, etc.) on a paid basis to perform a JOB or work task specified in his or her CONTRACT OF EMPLOYMENT. See PAY, WORKER.

employee attitude survey see SURVEY.

employee communications see COMMUNICATION, CONSULTATION.

employee involvement the attempt to increase employees' interest and commitment to their work and to the organization without, however, giving them any role in decision-making. SUGGESTION SCHEMES, which encourage employees to think about ways in which work methods could be improved but which generally give them no role in the assessment of their recommendations, are a good example. The term is often used interchangeably with EMPLOYEE PARTICIPATION, but there is a difference in nuance in that the latter usually provides for some, albeit limited, participation in decision-making. See TEAM BRIEFINGS

employee participation the participation of employees in the affairs of the organization through (limited) participation in decision-making or acquisition of a stake in the company through EMPLOYEE SHARE OWNERSHIP schemes (financial participation). Participation in decision-making is usually at the immediate job level, i.e. employees may be given the opportunity to consider, recommend and implement changes to the way tasks are performed (see JOB DESIGN AND REDESIGN, JAPANIZATION). The philosophy behind participation is that employees have talents and knowledge about their jobs which can be utilized to improve performance, and that involvement in decision-making encourages commitment.

It can be contrasted with INDUSTRIAL DEMOCRACY in which employees or their representatives have the *right* to be involved in determining company *policy.* See CONSULTATION, COMMUNITY CHARTER OF FUNDAMENTAL SOCIAL RIGHTS, FIFTH DIRECTIVE, VREDELING DIRECTIVE, EMPLOYEE SHARE OWNERSHIP PLAN, EUROPEAN WORKS COUNCIL.

employee ratios accounting ratios which attempt to assess the productivity and efficiency of a firm's labour force; for example, net profit per employee or sales per employee. See ACCOUNTING RATIO.

employee relations see INDUSTRIAL RELATIONS.

employee share ownership plan (ESOP) a scheme whereby employees acquire shares in the company in which they are employed. Although employees can of course purchase shares in their company on the open market, or companies can simply choose to donate shares to them, employee share ownership in the UK usually refers to three schemes, established by various Finance Acts, which confer tax advantages if formally approved by the Inland Revenue. Currently the main approved schemes are SAVE-AS-YOU-EARN SHARE OPTIONS, SHARE INCENTIVE PLAN, ENTERPRISE MANAGEMENT INCENTIVE PLAN, EXECUTIVE SHARE OPTION SCHEME, LONG-TERM INCENTIVE PLAN.

Employee share ownership schemes of these types are generally seen by companies as a tax-efficient way of rewarding employees rather than as an extension of INDUSTRIAL DEMOCRACY. They are essentially a FRINGE BENEFIT. Employees may of course gain voting rights at the ANNUAL GENERAL MEETING as a result of acquiring shares but the volume and dispersal of shares is usually such that these shareholders cannot by themselves make a significant impact on company policy. Companies often justify these schemes on the basis that they will promote an identity of interest between employees and their employer, which in turn will lead to improvements in job performance. There is some evidence that some share ownership schemes are associated with attitudes of this sort but it is questionable whether this leads to better individual performance. The link between share benefits (dependent to some extent on growing profitability) and individual effort is at best weak and indirect, and it is therefore doubtful whether they provide a strong incentive effect. Also to be noted is the downside of owning shares: through 'bad luck', 'bad management' or adverse trading conditions, a company's share price can go down as well as up!

Some observers see employee share ownership schemes as a way of weakening employee commitment to TRADE UNIONS and strengthening INDIVIDUALISM and entrepreneurial enthusiasm. But given that employees seem to judge these schemes primarily on their capacity to increase incomes, it is questionable whether any major reorientation of employees' attitudes can be achieved in this way. See FINANCIAL PARTICIPATION, PRINCIPAL-AGENT THEORY, PROFIT SHARING, UNAPPROVED EMPLOYEE SHARE OWNERSHIP PLAN, MANAGEMENT BUY-OUT.

employer an organization (firm, government, etc.) which engages EMPLOYEES to perform JOB tasks related to the types of goods and services produced by the organization. See CONTRACT OF EMPLOYMENT.

employers' association an organization of employers in an industry with the function of representing their mutual interests in the promotion of trade (for example, representation at trade fairs) and/or dealing with labour and INDUSTRIAL RELATIONS issues. Regarding the latter, four functions are usually identified:

(a) negotiation of MULTI-EMPLOYER AGREEMENTS regulating rates of pay and conditions of employment in member companies;

(b) operation of a DISPUTES PROCEDURE. Where an INDUSTRIAL DISPUTE arises in a member company the association can step in (if requested) to apply a procedure for resolving the dispute;

(c) provision of advice to member companies on industrial relations and employment questions;

(d) representation of member companies' views to third parties, for example government.

With the growth of COLLECTIVE BARGAINING within companies, employers' associations are not as important in many industries as they once were. Nevertheless, they continue to provide important services for those small companies which do not have the resources to develop these functions in-house.

employers' liability insurance INSURANCE which employers are required by law to take out in order to cover their employees against injury or death at work.

employment the use of LABOUR and CAPITAL to produce goods and services. See LABOUR FORCE, CAPITAL STOCK.

employment agency a business which acts as an AGENT on behalf of firms seeking employees and of persons seeking work. Employment agencies maintain lists of job vacancies notified by prospective employers and details of persons seeking work, and match up the two. In addition, they may advertise jobs on behalf of employers and, where instructed, act as recruitment agents by interviewing and shortlisting job applicants.

Employment Appeals Tribunal a body which hears appeals against the decisions of INDUSTRIAL TRIBUNALS and the CERTIFICATION OFFICER.

employment contract see CONTRACT OF EMPLOYMENT.

employment legislation see LABOUR LAW.

EMS see EUROPEAN MONETARY SYSTEM.

EMU see ECONOMIC AND MONETARY UNION.

enabling authority a local authority or some other public service organization which coordinates service provision by other, possibly private sector, organizations. In this model of public service provision the public authority no longer provides services itself. Instead it contracts with other organizations to deliver them. The philosophy underlying this model is that private sector organizations can provide public services more effectively and efficiently than public sector organizations. COMPETITIVE TENDERING embodies the 'enabling authority' approach. See NEW PUBLIC MANAGEMENT.

endgame strategy *or* **declining industry strategy** a framework for analysing the nature and causes of decline in an industry and for identifying strategies most appropriate to the firm operating in such an environment. Although an industry which has moved into the decline phase of the PRODUCT LIFE CYCLE is characterized overall by falling demand and problems of excess capacity, it nonetheless may still offer attractive returns to firms possessing COMPETITIVE ADVANTAGES over rival suppliers. For others, immediate exit from the industry rather than hanging on may be appropriate to the situation. Each industry differs in its makeup, so that an appraisal needs to be made of:

(a) the *particular* reasons for decline, the rate at which demand is declining and whether there are growth segments in the market;

(b) the structure of the market (see MARKET STRUCTURE) in terms of levels of MARKET CONCENTRATION, buyer characteristics and factors influencing the volatility of competition;

(c) the firm's own perceived strengths and weaknesses vis-à-vis other competitors in the industry (see SWOT ANALYSIS).

A number of strategic possibilities will emerge from this evaluation including:

(a) to hold or increase the firm's investment in the market by, for example, MERGER/TAKEOVER to expand its market share and, simultaneously, remove excess capacity from the market. This is a high-risk strategy but acceptable if the firm possesses competitive advantages (for example, low costs or superior products) and the industry itself exhibits certain favourable endgame characteristics, for example a slow rate of decline in overall demand coupled with the existence of profitable market segments;

(b) to shrink selectively – this strategy involves refocusing the firm by exiting from unprofitable sectors and remaining in profitable ones;

(c) to milk the investment – the firm would continue its operations with a minimum of expenditure and make no effort to maintain its market position;

(d) to divest now – sell the business to competitors wholly or in part, or liquidate. See DIVESTMENT. See BUSINESS STRATEGY, BARRIERS TO EXIT.

Engineering Employers' Federation (EEF) the UK federation of EMPLOYERS' ASSOCIATIONS representing employers in the engineering industry. Over 4,000 engineering firms are members of their regional Engineering Employers' Associations which in turn are affiliated to the EEF. Member firms are known as federated; nonmembers are nonfederated. In the past, the EEF negotiated WAGE RATES and HOURS OF WORK nationally with the industry's TRADE UNIONS. Now, wages and conditions are determined at individual companies or workplaces. See MULTI-EMPLOYER AGREEMENT.

Enterprise Act, 2002 see COMPETITION POLICY (UK).

Enterprise Grant Scheme an instrument of UK INDUSTRIAL/REGIONAL policy introduced in 2000 to facilitate the growth of small and medium sized firms (SMEs), i.e. firms with under 250 employees. Cash grants (up to £75,000) are available to SMEs which meet various criteria, including the introduction of e-commerce, the development of innovatory processes and products and workforce training. The Scheme incorporates a 'regional' element in that it is available only to SMEs located in the ASSISTED AREAS.

Enterprise Investment Scheme (EIS) a facility introduced in 1994 which offers income tax relief on equity investments in unquoted companies. The EIS (which replaced the *Business Expansion Scheme (BES)*) is aimed at assisting smaller businesses in the manufacturing and services industries to raise new capital without having to obtain a STOCK MARKET listing. The scheme specifically excludes investments in private rented housing which had been widely used under the previous BES as a means of avoiding tax.

Under the EIS individuals can invest up to £200,000 in a company writing off the price paid for their shares against their income tax assessment, and can also become paid directors of the companies they invest in without losing entitlement to tax relief. See INVESTMENT INCENTIVE.

Enterprise Management Incentive Scheme a UK arrangement introduced in 2000 which enables small companies (assets under £30 million) to grant SHARE OPTIONS to their employees. Originally the maximum grant which could be made available was £1.5 million and limited to no more than 15 people. In 2001, the threshold for grants was raised to £3 million and the scheme was opened up to cover *all* employees. See EMPLOYER SHARE OWNERSHIP PLAN.

enterprise union see TRADE UNION.

entrepôt trade a form of INTERNATIONAL TRADE, mainly confined to COMMODITIES such as tin and tea, where goods are temporarily imported into a country and then subsequently re-exported to other countries as part of a complex chain of physical distribution and financing deals. See FREEPORT.

entrepreneur a person who undertakes the risks of establishing and running a new business. Entrepreneurs are characterized by their initiative and enterprise in seeking out new business opportunities; inventing and commercializing new goods and services and methods of production. See VENTURE CAPITAL, INDUSTRIAL POLICY, INTRAPRENEURIAL GROUP, MANAGEMENT BUY-OUT.

entry see MARKET ENTRY, BARRIERS TO ENTRY.

environment see CONTINGENCY THEORY, POLLUTION.

Environmental Protection Act 1990 see POLLUTION.

environmental audit see GREEN AUDIT.

environmental scanning the monitoring by a firm of the general (macro) environment and its more immediate market environments in order to identify those factors likely to have a significant impact on its business position and viability. See PEST, SWOT ANALYSIS, COMPETITIVE STRATEGY, BUSINESS POLICY.

environmental standard see POLLUTION.

environmental tax see POLLUTION.

environment monitoring the practice of keeping a watchful eye on what is happening in the external environment in which a business or organization operates. The objective is to identify threats and opportunities in that environment posed by changing technology, competition, etc. and to help the business or organization be flexible and respond quickly to change. See SWOT ANALYSIS.

EPOS (electronic point of sale) a system for recording sales using sophisticated cash tills which record the total amount to be paid by a customer, provide them with itemized bills and simultaneously adjust the firm's STOCK records to assist the firm to plan its reordering of goods. EPOS is increasingly being used in supermarket checkouts, often linked to BAR-CODE scanners and providing for the direct debiting of customers' bank accounts for the total amount owing.

Equal Opportunities Commission see DISCRIMINATION.

equal opportunities employer see DISCRIMINATION.

equal pay the right for men and women to be paid the same rate of PAY for performing the same job, established in the UK by the Equal Pay Act 1970. Until 1984 it was widely believed that employers could circumvent the spirit of this legislation by segregating men's and women's jobs. Since then employees have been entitled to equal pay for work of equal *value*. Aggrieved employees may pursue their claim to an INDUSTRIAL TRIBUNAL. To determine whether different jobs are of equal value the techniques of JOB EVALUATION are used. See DISCRIMINATION.

Equal Pay Act 1970 see DISCRIMINATION.

equal pay for equal value see EQUAL PAY, DISCRIMINATION.

equilibrium market price the market-clearing price at which the demand for a PRODUCT, FINANCIAL SECURITY, FOREIGN CURRENCY or COMMODITY is just equal to the supply of it. The *demand curve* in Fig. 38 is downward sloping, indicating that as price falls buyers will be prepared to purchase more of the product; the *supply curve* is upward sloping, indicating that as the price of the product increases suppliers will be prepared to offer more of it. Price OP is the equilibrium market price and OQ the amount of the product transacted. At prices initially higher than OP there is *excess supply* over demand which in a free market situation will cause the price to fall, while at prices initially lower than OP there is *excess demand* over supply which will cause the price to rise. In many markets, however, price levels are likely to be distorted both

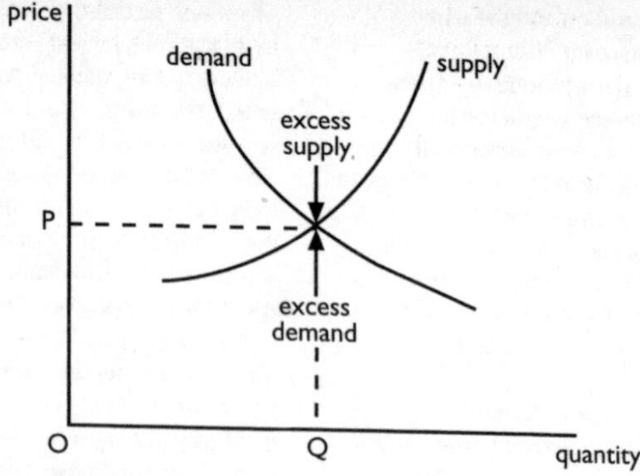

Fig. 38 **Equilibrium market price.** Graph showing demand and supply curves.

by the presence of powerful suppliers (see MONOPOLY, CARTEL, COLLUSION) and by governmental PRICE CONTROLS. See MARKET, MARKET SYSTEM, FLUCTUATING EXCHANGE RATE SYSTEM, STOCK MARKET, SPOT MARKET, FORWARD MARKET, COMMODITY MARKET.

equipment small items of capital such as a hand drill or screwdriver which are used to produce goods. See PLANT, MACHINERY, CAPITAL STOCK, FIXED ASSET.

equity ordinary shareholders' funds, that is, their ORDINARY SHARE capital subscribed plus any RESERVES or ploughed-back profit. Alternatively, equity can be regarded as what would be left to the ordinary shareholders of a company after all the company's debts and liabilities have been met.

ergonomics *or* **human engineering** the study of the interface between people and technology with the objective of achieving a better 'fit' between the two. The twin objectives of ergonomics are the interrelated ones of improvements in efficiency and the provision of better working conditions. For instance, an ergonomist would be concerned to ensure that a typist's chair is of the right height to avoid back and arm strains. As well as minimizing employee dissatisfaction this would prevent productivity from being impaired by physical injury. In more complex technological environments the ergonomist is also concerned with the distribution of functions between human operators and the technology itself.

Ergonomics grew out of SCIENTIFIC MANAGEMENT, one strand of which was concerned with the development of technology that could be matched to the task in hand and to the human physique, and human factor psychology (see OCCUPATIONAL PSYCHOLOGY), which was concerned with the impact of environmental factors on work performance.

ERG Theory see MOTIVATION.

escrow account a special financial account for the temporary deposit of funds before they are paid out (or returned) at the conclusion of, for example, an insurance or will settlement or a merger deal. For example, as part of the terms of the sale of Diageo's (UK) USA food division to General Mills (USA) in 2000, Diageo transferred $642 million into an escrow account. This money will be paid out in full to GM if that company's share price ($38 at the time of the sale) is at or above $42.55c on the first anniversary of the deal. In the event, however, of GM's share price falling below $38 the money will be returned to Diageo.

estate agent a business which acts as an AGENT on behalf of personal and industrial clients in the buying and selling of land and buildings. Estate agents provide various services for their clients including the valuation and pricing of land and buildings, advice on the attributes of the land or building itself and the locality in which it is situated, and conveyancing, surveying, inspection and MORTGAGE contacts. The provision of estate agency services in the UK is regulated by the Estate Agency Act 1979 which lays down general rules of good conduct and can ban persons who are deemed unfit for this purpose. See CONVEYANCE, BUILDING SOCIETY.

estate duty see INHERITANCE TAX.

estimating the process of judging the probable expenditure to be incurred in making a product, as a basis for setting a product price. Estimating is generally less detailed and accurate than COSTING where actual costs of jobs are ascertained, but it may suffice in quoting a price for a job.

ethnic monitoring see DISCRIMINATION.

ETUC (European Trade Union Confederation) the main European TRADE UNION organization and one of the main SOCIAL PARTNERS. It represents the combined interests of national trade unions confederations, such as the TRADES UNION CONGRESS, in European SOCIAL DIALOGUE and the development of European policy and legislation.

EU see EUROPEAN UNION.

Eurex a FORWARD MARKET which is engaged in the buying and selling of FINANCIAL SECURITIES, COMMODITIES, FOREIGN CURRENCIES, DERIVATIVES and SWAPS. Eurex is owned by German STOCK MARKET/EXCHANGE (the Deutsche Börse). See OPTION, LONDON INTERNATIONAL FINANCIAL FUTURES EXCHANGE.

euro (€) the common ('single') currency of the EUROPEAN UNION (EU), introduced in January 1999 as an integral element in the move towards ECONOMIC AND MONETARY UNION (EMU). Initially, the euro served as a book-keeping 'unit of account'; in 2002, however, euro banknotes and coins were put into circulation, to replace the individual domestic currencies of EMU members, so the euro is now used as a 'medium of exchange' to finance day-to-day transactions in goods, services and financial assets (see MONEY).

Eleven of the 15 countries of EU were founding members of the EMU zone in January 1999: Germany, France, Italy, Spain, Netherlands, Belgium, Austria, Finland, Portugal, Ireland and Luxembourg, with the UK, Sweden, Greece and Denmark adopting a 'wait and see' stance. Greece joined the euro-zone in 2001. The UK's position is still to be resolved on the basis of 5 'tests of fitness' (see ECONOMIC AND MONETARY UNION entry for details).

The value of the euro against the currencies of nonmembers of the EMU zone 'floats' on a day-to-day basis according to supply and demand conditions. For example, the value of the euro against the UK pound was around 71 pence when it was launched in January 1999. After falling to a low of 57 pence in May 2000, the Euro has since recovered and is currently (at March 2005) around 69 pence.

The euro is administered by the EUROPEAN CENTRAL BANK, which is responsible for setting EMU-wide interest rates and determining monetary policy.

Eurobond market see EUROCURRENCY MARKET.

Eurocurrency market *or* **Eurobond market** a MARKET based in Europe, comprising a web of international banks and money brokers, which is engaged in the borrowing and lending of FOREIGN CURRENCIES such as US dollars *outside* their countries of origin, as a means of financing trade and investment transactions.

The main instrument used in the Eurocurrency market to finance long-term investment is the Eurobond, a form of fixed interest security which is denominated either in a single currency or is syndicated with a 'lead' bank arranging with other banks a multi-currency loan package. Depositors of funds in the Eurocurrency market include commercial banks, companies and central banks, while borrowers for the most part are industrial and financial companies, particularly MULTINATIONAL ENTERPRISES, who use Eurofinance during times of domestic credit restrictions and/or when domestic interest rates are high in comparison with Eurocurrency rates. See LIBOR.

Euronext see STOCK MARKET/EXCHANGE.

European Central Bank (ECB) the CENTRAL BANK set up in July 1998 by the EUROPEAN UNION (EU) in the run-up to the establishment of ECONOMIC AND MONETARY UNION (EMU) in January 1999. Under EMU, the European Central Bank was given centralized powers to set INTEREST RATES and responsibility for determining monetary policy in the EMU-zone (currently comprising 12 of 15 member countries of the EU). The ECB oversees the operation of the EURO, EMU's single currency, and is the sole issuing authority of Euro banknotes and coins.

The ECB's primary objective is to maintain a low INFLATION rate in the EMU-zone (a target inflation rate of 2% is the current goal). Interest rates are set and managed with the inflation target in mind. Inflation has remained low in recent years (see INFLATION entry) and with an economic downturn affecting many of the EU countries the ECB has been under pressure to reduce interest rates. Between 2001 and 2004 interest rates were reduced – from 4.75% to (as at March 2005) 2%.

The ECB, which is based in Frankfurt, Germany, is managed by an executive board of six members drawn from EMU countries, including the Bank's President. Overall policy is set by a Supervisory Board that consists of these six plus the 12 central bankers of the 12 EMU members.

European Commission the organization which deals with the day to day administration of the EUROPEAN UNION (EU). The Commission ensures that the provisions of European Union treaties are carried out in the legislation of member states and undertakes the detailed implementation of EU policies, including control of budgeted expenditures. The President of the Commission is appointed by the COUNCIL OF THE EUROPEAN UNION and is assisted by 19 commissioners and 26 Director-Generals each responsible for particular areas of the Commission's work such as Agriculture or Transport.

European Community (EC) see EUROPEAN UNION.

European Court of Justice the EUROPEAN UNION court which is responsible for interpreting the laws passed by the EUROPEAN PARLIAMENT which are binding upon the citizens of member states of the European Union. The European Court often interecedes to overrule judgements made by the courts of member states or modify national laws.

European Currency Unit see EUROPEAN MONETARY SYSTEM.

European Economic Area (EEA) an alliance established in 1991 between. the member countries of the EUROPEAN UNION – and the EUROPEAN FREE TRADE ASSOCIATION (EFTA). The EEA's aim is to extend the EU's 'single market freedoms' in the flow of goods, services, capital and labour to include EFTA. EFTA countries will adopt the harmonization directives currently being implemented under the SINGLE EUROPEAN ACT 1986.

European Foundation for Quality Management (EFQM) a body established in 1988 which awards the European Quality Award (EQA) to the most successful exponent of TOTAL QUALITY MANAGEMENT (TQM) in Western Europe each year.

European Free Trade Association (EFTA) a regional 'free trade area' established in 1959 with the general objective of securing the benefits to be derived from greater INTERNATIONAL TRADE (see TRADE INTEGRATION entry for details). There were originally seven members of EFTA: the UK, Sweden, Switzerland, Austria, Denmark, Norway and Portugal; these countries opted for a less comprehensive integration of their economies than that required by membership of the EUROPEAN UNION (EU) formed the year previously. In 1973, however, the UK and Denmark left and joined the EU, and Portugal joined the EU in 1986. Three countries have joined EFTA: Finland in 1961, Iceland in 1970 and Liechtenstein in 1991.

However, the whole future of EFTA has been put in the melting pot as a further three members (Finland, Austria and Sweden) joined the European Union in 1995 and it is possible that others may follow. See EUROPEAN ECONOMIC AREA.

European Investment Bank see REGIONAL POLICY.

European Monetary System (EMS) the former institutional arrangement, established in 1979, for coordinating and stabilizing the EXCHANGE RATES of member countries of the EUROPEAN UNION.

The EMS was replaced in January 1999 by the exchange rate arrangements of the ECONOMIC AND MONETARY UNION (EMU).

The EMS was based on a FIXED EXCHANGE RATE system and the European Currency Unit (ECU), which was used to value, on a common basis, exchange rates and which also acted as a reserve asset to be used by members, alongside their other INTERNATIONAL RESERVE holdings, to settle payments imbalances between themselves.

European Ombudsman the person responsible for monitoring the efficient and fair operation of the EUROPEAN UNION. The ombudsman and his/her secretariat investigate complaints by citizens of the European Union who feel that they have been unfairly affected by any European Union institutions such as the EUROPEAN COMMISSION.

European Parliament the permanent legislative assembly of Members of the European Parliament (MEPs) directly elected by the electors of the member countries of the EUROPEAN UNION.

European Regional Development Fund see REGIONAL POLICY.

European Trade Union Confederation see ETUC.

European Union (EU) a regional alliance established by the Treaty of Rome in 1958 with the general objective of integrating the economies of member countries. The EU was originally called the 'European Economic Community' (EEC) before changing its name to simply the 'European Community' (EC). In 1993, following ratification of the MAASTRICHT TREATY, the current name was adopted to reflect the wider move towards social and political union as well as economic union.

In January 1999 the EU put into place a further major step towards integrating the economies of member countries. Under the ECONOMIC and MONETARY UNION (EMU) programme a new single currency, the EURO, was introduced to replace the individual domestic currencies of EMU participants by the end of 2002. The introduction of EMU has meant the end of the EUROPEAN MONETARY SYSTEM and the European Currency Unit. (For further details of this landmark development see ECONOMIC AND MONETARY UNION, EURO, and EUROPEAN CENTRAL BANK entries).

The deeper integration of member countries implied by EMU has already accentuated a number of underlying difficulties, particularly that of applying 'one fit' policies throughout the EMU-zone despite substantial differences in the industrial structures and extent of economic maturity of members (contrast relatively economically 'advanced' Germany with that of less-developed Greece). Many economists fear that harmonization will become untenable as more and more countries, most of them possessing weak industrial sectors and thus in need of massive structural funding, join the EU.

	Contributions %	*Receipts* %
Germany	25	14
France	18	15
UK	15	10
Italy	14	11
Spain	6	17
Netherlands	6	3
Belgium	3	4
Sweden	3	2
Austria	2	2
Denmark	2	2
Greece	2	8
Finland	1	1
Portugal	1	6
Ireland	1	4
Luxembourg	0.5	1

Fig. 39 **EU Budget 2004.**

The EU has a total population of some 450 million and accounts for around 44% of the world production and world exports.

There were six founding countries of the EU: (West) Germany, France, Italy, Netherlands, Belgium and Luxembourg. Nineteen more countries have since joined the EU bringing its current membership up to 25. The UK, Ireland and Denmark joined in 1973, Greece in 1981, Spain and Portugal in 1986, and Austria, Sweden and Finland in 1995. In 2004 a further 10 countries joined the EU under an 'Accession' arrangement which required them to have undertaken major reforms of their economies to make them market-orientated: Poland, Hungary, Czech Republic, Estonia, Slovenia, Slovakia, Latvia, Lithuania, Cyprus and Malta.

The strategic and operational policies of the EU are formulated by member country governments acting through the Council of Ministers (one appointed member per country) and the European Parliament (democratically elected). The European Commission is responsible for overseeing the day-to-day administration of the EU and in controlling its general budget finances while various other bodies are responsible for running specific programmes such as the Common Agricultural Policy. Agricultural price support and structural operations (the EU's regional and social, programmes) currently account for around four-fifths of the total EU Budget.

In 2004 the EU Budget totalled some 103 billion Euros. Contributions and receipts for the 15 member countries of the EU are listed in Fig 39. The budget is financed from four sources – a charge on each country proportional to their share of the EU's Gross National Product (GNP); a proportional charge on each countries value added tax (VAT) receipts; levies on agricultural imports and customs duties on other imports from non-EU countries.

The main economic developments within the EU down to EMU include:

(a) the creation of a ('single') *common market* providing for free trade in goods and services and the free movement of labour and capital across national boundaries. (See TRADE INTEGRATION entry for details). Member countries are committed to removing TARIFFS, QUOTAS and other obstacles to trade within the EU and to maintaining the EU's 'common external tariff' against nonmember countries' imports. Import restrictions by the six original members against each other were dismantled and their external tariffs harmonized in stages between 1958 and 1968. The creation of an internal market was give further impetus by the SINGLE EUROPEAN ACT, 1986 which embodied some 400 'directives' providing for the implementation of common technical standards, product specification, descriptions and labelling, road haulage regulations etc. In addition, the EU has concluded a number of trade preference agreements with non-member countries, including the multilateral LOME AGREEMENT with over 40 less-developed countries, most of them former colonies of EU members, and bilateral pacts with members of the EUROPEAN FREE TRADE ASSOCIATION. See also EUROPEAN ECONOMIC AREA.

(b) a *competition policy* providing for the prohibition of price-fixing and market-sharing agreements between firms and the abuse of a dominant market position which have the effect of reducing or eliminating intra-EU trade (see COMPETITION POLICY EU)

(c) Common Agricultural Policy providing for the subsidization and protection of the farm sector

(d) a REGIONAL POLICY providing financial assistance for the removal of regional imbalances both within and between member countries.

(e) the establishment of the EUROPEAN MONETARY SYSTEM to provide a close coordination of member countries' currency exchange rates and settlement of payment imbalances.

EU laws generally take precedence over the national laws of member countries but in some areas the principle of *subsidiarity* can be invoked which involves the devolvement of responsibility for decision-making from the European Commission to national administrations. See, for example, COMPETITION POLICY (EU).

In 2000 the Treaty of Nice introduced several changes to the administration of the EU in order to facilitate the enlargement of the EU, and enable the integration of members' economies to proceed more rapidly. Member countries vote allocations were re-weighted in favour of the larger states; qualified majority voting replaced the national veto on a range of issues; limits were introduced on the size of the European Commission (big nations lose their second Commissioner in 2005); groups of eight or more countries can push ahead with integration in agreed policy areas. However, tax and social security matters will remain subject to unanimity in voting.

European Union Directive see DIRECTIVE (1).

European Works Council a pan-European council of employee representatives with transitional firms established to facilitate CONSULTATION between management and employees. Firms with at least 1000 employees in the member states of the EUROPEAN UNION and at least 150 employees in the two or more member states are required to establish a European Works Council.

The UK initially opted out of the *Social Protocol* provision of the MAASTRICHT TREATY and hence UK firms were only partially covered by the European Works Council Directive. However, the UK has now fully implemented the Directive so UK firms are fully covered. Currently, there are around 650 EWC agreements in companies operating in Europe.

evasion see TAX EVASION

everyday low prices a RETAILERS' policy of keeping prices low 'every day' rather than through periodic sales promotions.

excellence culture the elements of a firm's CULTURE which are likely to make it successful. Peter's and Waterman's study of successful American companies led them to identify eight key attributes of excellence: a bias for action; customer orientation; emphasis on staff participation; autonomy and entrepreneurship through staff creativity; management aligned with staff; staying close to the firm's core activities ("sticking to the knitting"); simple organizational structure with few levels of management; local management autonomy, combined with working together towards corporate goals ("loose-tight").

excess capacity see OVERCAPACITY.

excess demand see EQUILIBRIUM MARKET PRICE.

excess supply see EQUILIBRIUM MARKET PRICE.

exchange see MARKET, BARTER.

exchange controls see FOREIGN EXCHANGE CONTROLS.

exchange rate

The price of one country's currency expressed in terms of another country's currency; for example, one UK pound (£) = two US dollars ($). Because there are a large number of countries participating in the international economy, multi-exchange rate systems are required in order to synchronize and, in some cases, coordinate and harmonize exchange rates.

Under a FIXED EXCHANGE RATE SYSTEM, exchange rates, once established, will remain unchanged for longish periods. If a particular country's exchange rate gets too far out of line with underlying market conditions, however, and becomes overvalued for example, resulting in that country being persistently in BALANCE OF PAYMENTS deficit, the exchange rate can be devalued (see DEVALUATION), i.e. refixed at a lower level which makes its imports more expensive and its exports cheaper. Similarly, if the exchange rate becomes undervalued, resulting in a country being persistently in balance of payments surplus, the exchange rate can be revalued, i.e. refixed at a higher value, which makes its imports cheaper and its exports more expensive (see REVALUATION).

Over time, exchange rates, if left unregulated by the authorities, will fluctuate according to changes in underlying market conditions, reflecting such things as differences in INFLATION rates and INTEREST RATES between countries. For example, if the prices of UK goods rise faster than the prices of equivalent US goods, people will tend to buy more US goods, causing the dollar to appreciate and the £ to depreciate. On the other hand, if UK interest rates are higher than US interest rates, this will encourage US investors to deposit money in the UK money markets, causing the £ to appreciate against the dollar.

Under a FLOATING EXCHANGE RATE SYSTEM, the exchange rate is free to fluctuate day by day and will fall (see DEPRECIATION) or rise (see APPRECIATION) in line with changing market conditions, serving (in theory) to keep a country's balance of payments more or less in equilibrium on a continuous basis. In practice, however, the uncertainties and SPECULATION associated with free floats tend to produce erratic and random exchange rate movements which act to inhibit trade as well as producing destabilizing domestic effects. For these reasons countries often prefer to 'manage' their exchange rates, both to moderate the degree of short-run fluctuation and to smooth out the long-run trend line.

The term *effective exchange rate* is used to describe a given currency's value in terms of a weighted average of a 'basket' of other currencies, expressed as an index number. The *sterling exchange rate index* (1990=100) has fluctuated, averaging 104 (in 1999), 107 (2000), 106 (2001), 106 (2002), 100 (2003) and 104 (2004). Recently, the £ has been strong against the USA $ and weak against the EURO. A rise (appreciation) in the effective exchange rate indicates a general deterioration in the price competitiveness of a country's products vis-à-vis trade partners.

In FOREIGN EXCHANGE MARKETS the exchange rate may be quoted either in terms of how many units of a foreign currency may be bought or sold per unit of the domestic currency (an *indirect quotation*), or in terms of how many units of domestic currency may be bought or sold per unit of a particular foreign currency (a *direct quotation*). For example, in the UK an indirect quotation of the exchange rate between the Pound and the US dollar might be £1 = $2, whereas a direct quotation would be $1 = 50 pence.

Exchange rates are usually quoted by dealers as a pair of rates, the offer or sell rate and the bid or buy rate, the difference between the two (the *spread*) representing the dealers' profit margin. Currencies which are traded in large volumes, such as the US dollar and Japanese yen, usually have a narrower spread than currencies which are little used in international dealings. Similarly, the spread on current exchange rates quoted in the SPOT MARKET for currencies is usually narrower than the spread on forward prices quoted in the FORWARD MARKET. See CROSS RATE, EXCHANGE RATE EXPOSURE.

exchange rate exposure the extent of a firm's potential losses/gains on its overseas operations (measured in domestic currency terms) as a result of EXCHANGE RATE changes. The firm can be exposed to variations in exchange rates in a number of ways:

(a) *translation* or *accounting exposure* arises when consolidating (see CONSOLIDATED ACCOUNTS) the assets, liabilities, revenues and expenses of overseas subsidiaries (expressed in foreign currencies) into the parent company's group accounts (expressed in the parent's domestic currency);

(b) *transactions exposure* arises when a firm exports and imports products and borrows funds from abroad or invests overseas. For example, when a firm exports a product, invoicing the customer in terms of the customer's own local currency, and granting the customer 60 days' credit, then the firm is exposed to the effects of exchange rate variations during the 60-day credit period, which may decrease or increase the domestic currency value of the money due. Were the exchange rate of the foreign currency to fall dramatically vis-à-vis the domestic currency, then the exchange rate loss may completely eliminate any expected profit on the transaction;

(c) *economic* or *cash flow exposure* is concerned with the impact of exchange rate variations on the future cash flows generated by a company's production and marketing operations. Long-term or dramatic changes in exchange rates may well force a firm to rethink its FOREIGN MARKET SERVICING STRATEGY and raw material SOURCING strategy. For instance, a firm which serviced its overseas markets by direct exporting from domestic plants might decide to establish local production units to supply these markets instead, if an exchange rate appreciation were to render its export prices uncompetitive.

There are a number of mechanisms whereby a firm can reduce its exposure to potential losses resulting from exchange rate changes. First, a firm can seek to prevent an exposed position from arising by using such internal exposure management techniques as *currency matching* (matching foreign currency holdings with equal foreign currency borrowings); *leading and lagging* (accelerating or delaying foreign currency payments and receipts where the exchange rate of the currency is expected to change); and MULTILATERAL NETTING of currency receipts and payments between subsidiaries of a MULTINATIONAL ENTERPRISE. Second, the firm can use external contractual arrangements to reduce or eliminate whatever exposure remains, hedging risks by: entering into forward exchange contracts to buy or sell currencies as appropriate (see FORWARD MARKET); FACTORING (selling the *firm's* trade debts); buying and selling foreign exchange OPTIONS; foreign currency borrowing; the use of export credit guarantees (see EXPORT CREDIT GUARANTEE DEPARTMENT) and currency SWAPS.

excise duty an INDIRECT TAX imposed by the government on a product, principally those such as tobacco, petrol and alcoholic drinks, the demand for which is highly price-inelastic (see ELASTICITY OF DEMAND). Governments use excise duties both as a means of raising revenue (see BUDGET) and as an instrument of FISCAL POLICY. See CUSTOMS AND EXCISE.

exclusive dealing a business practice whereby a supplier contracts distributors/retailers to sell his products on an exclusive basis (i.e. to refrain from handling the products of rival suppliers). Retailers are rewarded for sole representation in a variety of ways including preferential discounts, back-up services and loans. The practice of exclusive dealing may help the supplier boost his sales and protect market share because distributors have an undivided commitment to the product. However, if undertaken by a DOMINANT FIRM, the practice may serve to limit competition in a market by depriving rival suppliers of distribution outlets. See ANTI-COMPETITIVE PRACTICE, COMPETITION ACT, 1980, OFFICE OF FAIR TRADING.

exclusive distribution a DISTRIBUTION strategy employed by a supplier of a product in which only one RETAILER or WHOLESALER is permitted to sell that supplier's product in a particular area or territory. Designated exclusive sales territories may be defined narrowly (city by city) or more broadly (region by region). Exclusive distribution systems can enable physical distribution costs to be lowered and achieve a greater retailer commitment in boosting sales (especially if this is backed by an EXCLUSIVE DEALING arrangement). On the other hand, if the retailer has an insufficient number of shops then, compared with a multiple-retailer approach, sales potential could be limited.

ex-dividend in a manner which excludes entitlement to the DIVIDEND which attaches to a share. If shares are purchased on the STOCK MARKET 'ex div', the purchasers would not be entitled to the dividend accruing to that share when the dividend is next paid. Compare CUM-DIVIDEND.

executive committee the ruling body of an organization, such as a TRADE UNION, whose function is to decide and implement courses of action consistent with the policy and philosophy established by the organization's membership.

executive director see DIRECTOR, BOARD OF DIRECTORS.

executive share option scheme an arrangement which involves the periodic grant of SHARES in a company to the company's executive directors as an incentive for them to improve the financial performance of the company and align their interests more closely with those of the company's SHAREHOLDERS. Options to buy shares are granted at a specified 'exercise' price which is normally the market price of the company's shares at the date of grant. The exercise of options typically can only occur between three and ten years after the date of grant. Most options can be exercised (that is 'cashed-in') only provided that certain pre-determined financial performance 'targets' are achieved over a specified time period, usually three years. Typically, option schemes require the company's earnings per share (profit after tax divided by the number of shares) to grow at a rate greater than the increase in the RETAIL PRICE INDEX over the same period or growth in total shareholder return (increase in share price with dividends reinvested) to exceed that of companies comprising some SHARE PRICE INDEX, such as the FTSE-100 share index. Compare LONG-TERM INCENTIVE PLAN. See PRINCIPAL-AGENT THEORY, BUSINESS OBJECTIVES, CORPORATE GOVERNANCE, EMPLOYEE SHARE OWNERSHIP PLAN.

exempt products see VALUE ADDED TAX.

exhibition an event which brings buyers and sellers together in a commercial setting. See SALES PROMOTION.

Existence, Relatedness and Growth (ERG) see MOTIVATION.

expectancy theory see MOTIVATION.

expectations the view taken of likely *future* events and changes by persons and firms which serves to influence their *current* economic behaviour. For example, a holder of a FINANCIAL SECURITY may anticipate that its price is likely to fall in the near future, and this may encourage him to sell the security now rather than incur (an expected) reduction in profits or even losses in the future (see SPECULATION, HEDGING); a TRADE UNION may anticipate that INFLATION is likely to rise, which causes it to put in a demand for a wage increase for its members which in part reflects (an expected) higher rate of future inflation.

expected money value see DECISION TREE.

expected number defective the average number of defective products which a firm expects to obtain from taking a number of samples. If the actual number of defectives from a sample is higher than expected, the production process involved will be investigated to determine the cause of the problem. See QUALITY CONTROL.

expected service-perceived service gap see GAP ANALYSIS.

expenditure tax a form of INDIRECT TAX which is added to the selling price of a good or service and which is borne by consumers of these products. VALUE ADDED TAX, EXCISE DUTIES and CUSTOMS DUTIES are the main types of expenditure tax levied in the UK. Expenditure taxes, along with various taxes on income (see DIRECT TAX), are used by the government to raise revenue (see BUDGET) and as a means of regulating the level of spending in the economy (see FISCAL POLICY).

expense any expenditure which is chargeable to the trading activities of an accounting period. This includes cash expenditures on materials and labour, and non-cash items of expenditure such as credit purchases and depreciation.

experience curve *or* **learning curve** the cumulative process whereby, as the managers and labour force of a firm gain greater experience of a new technology by repetitive contact, they become more efficient at operating it, which enables unit costs of production to be reduced. Additionally, familiarity with a technology and the development of associated skills and expertise can provide a platform for further technological advances. Thus, a firm's unique embodied experience can enable it to establish COMPETITIVE ADVANTAGES over rival suppliers.

Experience curve theory states that every time the same task is carried out, then the time taken to complete the task falls by some fixed amount. Thus if a task takes an hour to complete the first time, it will take some proportion less to complete the second time and a similar reduction will take place the fourth time, eighth time and so on, until a stable task time is achieved. Tasks are evaluated on their complexity, the more complex, the lower will be the rate of time reduction. See SPECIALIZATION, PRODUCTIVITY.

expert system a COMPUTER programme which simulates the problem-solving and decision-making behaviour of a technical expert in a particular field such as engineering and medicine. Like human technical experts, expert systems are able to learn from experience and restructure their knowledge in order to improve their future problem-solving.

expired costs costs, the benefits of which have been consumed and used up within the current accounting period and which do not therefore get carried forward into the next account period in the form of closing stock or a prepayment.

exponential smoothing see SALES FORECASTING.

export 1 a good which is produced in the home country and which is then physically transported to, and sold in, an overseas market earning foreign exchange for the home country (*visible export*).
2 a service which is provided for foreigners either in the home country (for example visits by tourists) or overseas (for example banking, insurance) which likewise generates foreign exchange for the home country (*invisible export*).
3 capital which is placed abroad in the form of portfolio investment, foreign direct investment in physical assets, and banking deposits (*capital export*). See FOREIGN INVESTMENT.

Together these items comprise, along with IMPORTS, a country's BALANCE OF PAYMENTS. See INTERNATIONAL TRADE, EXPORTING, EXPORT CREDIT GUARANTEE DEPARTMENT, EXPORT RESTRAINT AGREEMENT, EXPORT SUBSIDY.

Export Credit Guarantee Department (ECGD) the former UK government department which UNDERWRITES (insures) UK EXPORTS sold on CREDIT against nonpayment by foreign customers whether this is due to insolvency of the customer or, for example, the imposition of exchange controls by foreign governments, etc.

Until 1991 the ECGD provided both short-term and long-term export credits. Guarantees covering 90–95% of the loss of sales revenue were available for most exports sold on up to 6 months' credit, while extended cover is provided for certain exports (for example production engineering products) sold on up to 5 years' credit terms. In addition, the ECGD provides long-term cover (normally up to 15 years) for certain FOREIGN INVESTMENT projects against political risk.

In 1991 the provision of short-term export credits was taken over by a private sector concern, NCM. The ECGD itself is was transformed (2001) into a commercial concern outside immediate government control. See FACTORING.

exporting the sale in an overseas market of a product which is produced in the firm's home market.

Exports may be viewed by the firm as merely an extension of home sales, serving to provide extra business as a means of allowing the firm to operate its productive capacity to the full. More fundamentally, exports may be regarded as an important profit centre in their own right, providing the firm with opportunities for worldwide sales expansion and long-term profit growth.

Exporting may be undertaken indirectly or directly. *Indirect* exporting involves the contracting of independent agents to establish wholesale and retail sales contacts, and importers/distributors to handle the physical distribution of the product. Often, however, independent agents/distributors lack the commitment or resources required to maximize the firm's overseas sales potential. For this reason *direct* exporting may be preferred, requiring the appointment of the company's own overseas sales personnel and the establishment of overseas sales offices, depots and sales subsidiaries to handle local distribution and marketing. Exporting may be conducted on a 'standalone' basis or, as in the case of MULTINATIONAL ENTERPRISES as part of a more complex FOREIGN MARKET SERVICING STRATEGY involving also licensing and overseas production.

The physical act of transporting goods to export markets may be done by the supplier's own distribution division or by using the services of independent hauliers, fleet operators and FREIGHT FORWARDERS. Documentation required in connection with export consignments includes a BILL OF LADING, CERTIFICATE OF ORIGIN, WEIGHT NOTE, INSURANCE and (where appropriate) an export licence. Exporting may be undertaken according to a FREE ON BOARD (f.o.b.) contract, a COST, INSURANCE AND FREIGHT (c.i.f.) contract, or a COST AND FREIGHT (c&f) contract.

Export finance is provided by the commercial banks in the form of short-term credits (often underpinned by LETTERS OF CREDIT) and backed in the UK by the government's EXPORT CREDITS GUARANTEE DEPARTMENT (ECGD), FACTORS and FORFAITING HOUSES.

In addition to the ECGD, the *Trade Partners* organization (which incorporates the trade and overseas divisions of the DEPARTMENT OF TRADE AND INDUSTRY (DTI, and the Foreign Office) provides various facilities to support UK exports including:

(a) the *Export Market Information Centre* which provides, amongst other things, access to the British Overseas Trade Information Services worldwide statistical database, market research reports, directories, etc. and an Export Intelligence Service (for subscribers only) providing detailed, up-to-date market and product databases;

(b) the *Export Marketing Research Scheme* which provides professional advice and research on overseas markets, and financial grants to cover exploratory missions;

(c) *Technical Help to Exporters* which provides information and advice in respect of overseas technical standards, national laws covering safety and environmental protection, etc.;

(d) the *Fairs and Promotions* branch which organizes and financially assists exhibitors at overseas trade fairs, sets up contacts with agents and distributors, etc.;

(e) the *Supplier Trade Procedures Board* which provides advice and assistance in preparation of export documentation and provides a system for sending documents by electronic data interchange instead of using paper documents;

(f) the *Projects and Export Policy Division* which provides contacts with overseas governments and companies, and ongoing support for large overseas projects such as power station, railway networks, pipelines, etc.;

(g) finally, the *Trade Partners* provides information and advice on tariffs, local duties and exchange controls, and in the case of certain specific exports is responsible for issuing export licences. See CUSTOMS AND EXCISE, INTERNATIONAL TRADE, INTERNATIONAL MARKETING, CHAMBER OF COMMERCE, SUBSIDY, CONSIGNMENT.

export market an overseas country to which a firm based in one particular country EXPORTS its products. INTERNATIONAL

TRADE provides an opportunity for a firm to increase its sales potential by marketing its products in a number of foreign markets rather than relying solely on sales in its own domestic market. See MARKET DEVELOPMENT, FOREIGN MARKET SERVICING STRATEGY.

Export Market Information Centre see EXPORTING.

Export Market Research Scheme see EXPORTING.

export ratio a measure of the proportion of a firm's sales that are exported, which expresses export sales revenues as a fraction of total sales revenue. To the extent that overseas debts often take longer to collect than money owed by domestic customers, a high export ratio can influence the DEBTORS RATIO.

export subsidy a direct payment, or tax concession, made by the government to firms to encourage them to increase their EXPORTS. This is done in order to generate greater foreign exchange earnings, thereby assisting the balance of payments and helping to create additional domestic jobs.

exposure see EXCHANGE RATE EXPOSURE.

express terms see CONTRACT OF EMPLOYMENT.

extended internal labour market see INTERNAL LABOUR MARKET.

external appraisal see SWOT.

external growth a mode of business growth which involves a firm in expanding its activities by MERGER, TAKEOVER, STRATEGIC ALLIANCES, or JOINT VENTURES, rather than through ORGANIC GROWTH (i.e. internal expansion). External growth may take the form of horizontal, vertical or diversified expansion (see HORIZONTAL INTEGRATION, VERTICAL INTEGRATION, DIVERSIFICATION).

In general terms, external growth allows a firm to expand more rapidly and in a more cost-effective way than internal expansion, while augmenting and widening the firm's resource base. Additionally, external growth has some specific attractions. For example, in the case of *horizontal* growth, a merger with, or takeover of, a competitor can enable a firm significantly to increase its market share while providing scope for exploiting economies of scale through rationalization of the two firms' operations. The alternative of attempting to improve market share through price and product differentiation competition may be prohibitively expensive by comparison. Likewise, in the case of conglomerate expansion, the firm may simply not have the expertise to develop products in non-related areas, whereas external growth allows a firm to move into new activities by acquiring a customized operation and related resource capabilities.

External growth, however, is not without its complications. For example, the merged or acquired firms have to be integrated into the one controlling organization which may require a major streamlining of operations and the creation of new management structures. If this is not done effectively, efficiency may be impaired and financial resources strained. See BUSINESS STRATEGY, ORGANIC GROWTH, PRODUCT-MARKET MATRIX, FRANCHISE.

externalities factors which may result in a benefit or cost to a firm or society which originate, in part, from outside the firm or as an adjunct to productive activity. A firm which does not itself invest in training its labour force, for example, may nonetheless benefit from being able to attract employees who have been trained by other firms or by the government. POLLUTION is an example of an external cost imposed on society: a chemical company which pollutes the air or contaminates river water incurs only the immediate costs of producing its products, while society suffers the extra costs of cleaning up the atmosphere and river.

extraordinary items non-recurring items of expense or revenue which do not arise in the normal course of trading; for example, losses associated with a major reorganization of a company division which involves significant sales of assets. Such losses would be deducted directly from the company's RESERVES below the line rather than being charges against the profits of the trading period, to avoid affecting the results of routine trading operations with one-off non-trading losses.

extrapolation see SALES FORECASTING.

f

face value see PAR VALUE 1.

factor 1 a firm that purchases TRADE DEBTS from client firms. See FACTORING.
2 a firm that buys in bulk and performs a WHOLESALING function.
3 an input (for example raw material, labour, capital) which is used to produce a good or provide a service.

factoring the provision of finance (and other related services) by one firm (the factor) to another firm (the client) by discounting its unpaid INVOICES issued to customers, i.e. purchasing the client's TRADE DEBTS.

Factors typically provide immediate cash up to the value of 85% of the client's invoices, thus releasing ready money for the client to use for WORKING CAPITAL purposes. The remaining balance, less the fee for providing the facility, is paid over when the factor has received payment from the customer.

In addition, factors are usually prepared to undertake the administration of their clients' sales ledgers, assess credit risks and insure clients against bad debts, thus saving the client the trouble and expense of maintaining his own sales accounts and credit control departments.

Factoring extends to both domestic and export sales. It can be especially useful in the latter context where credit periods on exports are, on average, two to three times longer than on domestic sales and where there are additional complications arising from dealings with relatively unknown foreign customers and an unfamiliarity with local customs and laws. See EXPORTING, DEBTORS, CREDIT CONTROL.

factory a BUSINESS PREMISE used by a firm in the PRODUCTION of goods. See CAPITAL STOCK, FIXED ASSET.

Factory Inspectorate see HEALTH AND SAFETY.

factory layout the arrangement of machines and equipment within a factory which includes the layout of departments within the factory site, the layout of machines within the departments and the layout of individual work places. The two principal types of factory layout are PRODUCT-FOCUSED LAYOUTS where a product is routed through the factory on a single path, and PROCESS-FOCUSED LAYOUTS where products may follow a variety of routes through job shops in the factory.

In the two above-mentioned layout systems the product moves past stationary production equipment, but in the case of layout by *fixed position* the reverse applies. In the extreme case, for example civil engineering, neither the partly completed nor the finished product moves. Alternatively, as in shipbuilding, the product remains stationary only until it is completed.

Changes in the level of demand, or the need to produce a new product or a redesigned product, may result in a need to reorganize existing plant or to provide additional plant. Obsolescence or failure of existing equipment may result in the decision to install equipment whose characteristics provoke some rearrangements. The need for cost reductions may promote a reappraisal of layouts, as may factory legislation, accidents, etc. See PRODUCTION, RELATIONSHIP CHART, ACTIVITY CHART, BLOCK MODEL.

factory outlet a FACTORY which not only manufactures products but also sells them directly to visiting customers from the *same* premise rather than through independent retail outlets. See RETAILER.

failure costs the cost to a firm of manufacturing defective products. *Internal* failure costs result from defects which arise during the production process, and include the cost of defective items which have to be scrapped (yield loss); the cost of reworking faulty items which have to be corrected (rework costs); and the loss of revenue from having to downgrade a product which has been identified as second quality and has to be sold as substandard at a lower than normal price.

External failure costs result from defects which arise after the product has reached the customer and include the cost of replacing or repairing defective products (GUARANTEE OR WARRANTY costs); and legal costs or damages to customers who have suffered physical or financial injury from defective products. An additional external failure cost is the loss of consumer goodwill and cancelled orders which, although difficult to quantify, can have a significant potential impact on sales and profits. See QUALITY COSTS, QUALITY CONTROL.

failure mode effect and criticality analysis (FMECA *or* **FMEA)** the detailed study of a product design, manufacturing operation or distribution network to determine how it may fail and to offer options for the reduction in failure rate.

failure rate curve *or* **'bath tub curve'** *or* **Weibull analysis** a curve which reflects the RELIABILITY of a component of a product or machine, measured in terms of the proportion of a sample of that component which fails at different phases of its operational life. Fig. 40 shows a typical failure rate curve for a sample of the component which is divided into three phases:

(a) the 'infant' or *burn-in* period of the component is characterized by an initial high rate of failure. The early failure rate then decreases rapidly as surviving components prove themselves to be reliable;

(b) the *adult* or *normal useful life* period of the component is typified by a low and relatively constant rate of component failure;

(c) the *ageing* or *wear-out* period of the component is characterized by a rise in the failure rate as the component reaches the end of its designed life.

Each of these phases will reflect the adequacy of the design of the component, the quality of the materials used to make it, and the consistency with which it is manufactured.

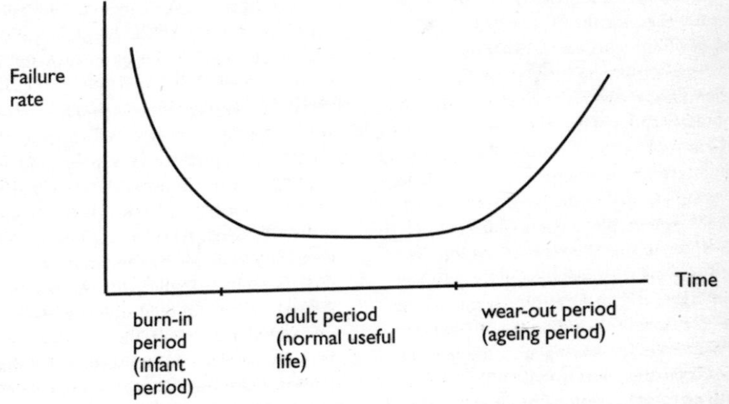

Fig. 40 **Failure rate curve.** Graph showing a typical curve.

In designing finished products, firms may seek to reduce the extent of early failure of components by laboratory testing of new product designs, and by using feedback from consumer panels and test marketing to perfect the design of the product. In determining GUARANTEE or WARRANTY periods for products, firms need to be aware of when the components of the product are likely to reach the end of their normal useful life and begin to experience rising failure rates. Failure rate profiles for components of factory machines can likewise be employed to plan the firm's MAINTENANCE and machine replacement programmes. See QUALITY CONTROL.

Fairs and Promotions see EXPORTING.

Fair Trading Act 1973 an Act which consolidated and extended UK competition law by controlling MONOPOLIES, MERGERS AND TAKEOVERS, RESTRICTIVE TRADE AGREEMENTS and RESALE PRICES. The Act established a new regulatory authority, the OFFICE OF FAIR TRADING (headed by the Director-General of Fair Trading) with powers to supervise all aspects of COMPETITION POLICY, including the monitoring of changes in market structure, companies' commercial policies, the registration of restrictive trade agreements, and the referral, where appropriate, of cases for investigation and report by the Monopolies and Mergers Commission and Restrictive Practices Court. The Act also gave the OFT specific responsibilities to oversee other matters affecting consumers' interests, including weights and measures, trade descriptions and voluntary codes of good practice. The Act's provisions relating to monopolies, restrictive trade agreements and resale prices have now been superceded by the COMPETITION ACT, 1998. However, the Office of Fair Trading continues to supervise these situations as well as being responsible for the regulation of mergers and takeovers under the 1973 Act and the referral of cases to the COMPETITION COMMISSION for investigation and report. See CONSUMER PROTECTION.

family brand a group of products marketed by a company using a common BRAND NAME. See BRAND EXTENSION (BRAND TRANSFERENCE).

fashion see FASHION PRODUCT, TREND 2.

fashion product a product for which demand changes frequently because of changes in consumer tastes or product attributes. Where consumer tastes are fickle and consumers seek to be fashionable, suppliers can take advantage of this by frequent restyling of products. See OBSOLESCENCE.

fast-moving consumer goods (FMCG) i.e. goods which consumers need to buy frequently, such as food and drink.

FAX (Facsimile) machine a machine capable of transmitting a copy of a document over a telephone link.

FDI see FOREIGN DIRECT INVESTMENT.

feasible region see LINEAR PROGRAMMING.

features see PRODUCT ATTRIBUTES.

'federated-firm' see ENGINEERING EMPLOYERS' FEDERATION (EEF).

federation an association of organizations formed to represent and advance their joint interests. In INDUSTRIAL RELATIONS there are both TRADE UNION federations, for example the Confederation of Shipbuilding and Engineering Unions, and federations of EMPLOYERS' ASSOCIATIONS, for example ENGINEERING EMPLOYERS' FEDERATION.

fee a payment to an AGENT or professional person/firm such as an accountant or lawyer for performing particular services for clients. Fees may be paid on a *fixed* or *sliding scale* basis related to the value of the transaction or work undertaken.

fidelity bonus a business practice whereby a supplier rewards distributors/ retailers with preferential supply conditions (prompt delivery times, access to supplies in times of shortage, back-up services) in return for their loyal custom. The operation of fidelity bonuses, by encouraging dealers/retailers to place the whole or a substantial part of their orders with the one supplier, may help the supplier increase his sales and protect market share. However, if undertaken by a DOMINANT FIRM, the practice may serve to limit competition in a market by depriving rival suppliers of distribution outlets. See OFFICE OF FAIR TRADING.

field studies see MARKETING INTELLIGENCE.

FIFO see STOCK VALUATION.

fighter brands low-cost manufacturer's brands introduced to combat OWN-LABEL BRANDS.

FIMBRA see FINANCIAL SERVICES ACT, 1986.

final accounts financial accounts prepared at the end of an accounting period. Final accounts consist of the PROFIT AND LOSS ACCOUNT and the BALANCE SHEET, and may also include a SOURCES AND USES OF FUNDS STATEMENT for the accounting period.

final dividend see DIVIDEND.

final good see GOOD.

final salary pension scheme see PENSION.

finance house a financial institution which accepts deposits of money from savers and which specializes in the provision OF INSTALMENT CREDIT to borrowers and LEASING facilities. See MONETARY SYSTEM, MONETARY POLICY.

financial accounting ACCOUNTING activities directed towards the preparation of annual PROFIT-AND-LOSS ACCOUNTS and BALANCE SHEETS in order to report to shareholders on their company's overall (profit) performance. See MANAGEMENT ACCOUNTING.

financial analysis see RATIO ANALYSIS, ACCOUNTING RATIOS.

financial flexibility see LABOUR FLEXIBILITY.

financial institution an institution that acts primarily as a FINANCIAL INTERMEDIARY in channelling funds from LENDERS to BORROWERS (e.g. COMMERCIAL BANKS, BUILDING SOCIETIES), or from SAVERS to INVESTORS (e.g. PENSION FUNDS, INSURANCE COMPANIES). See FINANCIAL SYSTEM.

Financial Intermediaries, Managers and Brokers Regulatory Association (FIMBRA) see FINANCIAL SERVICES ACT, 1986.

financial intermediary an organization that operates in financial markets linking LENDERS and BORROWERS or SAVERS and INVESTORS. See FINANCIAL SYSTEM, COMMERCIAL BANK, SAVINGS BANK, BUILDING SOCIETY, PENSION FUND, INSURANCE COMPANY, UNIT TRUST, INVESTMENT TRUST COMPANY, INTERMEDIATION.

financial investment see INVESTMENT, PORTFOLIO.

financial management the process of obtaining funds to finance a firm and advising on the use of these funds, which involves analysing the flow of funds through the firm. Financial management seeks to improve the market valuation of a firm by improving its future prospective earnings stream, taking due account of the riskiness of earnings. See CAPITAL GEARING, INVESTMENT APPRAISAL, WORKING CAPITAL.

financial participation the participation of employees in the profits (PROFIT SHARING) or the equity capital (EMPLOYEE SHARE OWNERSHIP PLAN) of their employing organizations. In some countries employees may participate in the financial returns of their company by being granted convertible bonds (CONVERTIBLE LOANS). GAINSHARING may also be seen as a form of financial participation. The objectives of financial participation include the provision of incentives to employees, the encouragement of ORGANIZATIONAL COMMITMENT, and redistribution of income and wealth. See ENTERPRISE MANAGEMENT INCENTIVE SCHEME, SAVE-AS-YOU-EARN SHARE OPTIONS, SHARE INCENTIVE PLAN.

financial ratio see ACCOUNTING RATIO.

Financial Reporting Standards (FRS) see ACCOUNTING STANDARDS.

financial security a financial instrument issued by companies, financial institutions and the government as a means of borrowing money and raising new capital. The most commonly used financial securities are SHARES, STOCKS, DEBENTURES, BILLS OF EXCHANGE, TREASURY BILLS and BONDS. Once issued these securities can be bought and sold either on the MONEY MARKETS or on the STOCK MARKET. See WARRANT, CERTIFICATE OF DEPOSIT, CONSOL.

Financial Services Act 1986 (as amended by the Financial Services and Markets Act, 2000) a UK act which provides a regulatory system for the FINANCIAL SECURITIES and INVESTMENT industry. The Act covers the businesses of securities dealing and investment, commodities and financial futures, unit trusts and some insurance (excluding the Lloyds insurance market). Also excluded from its remit is commercial banking, which is supervised by the Bank of England, and mortgage and other business of the building societies, which is regulated separately by the BUILDING SOCIETIES ACT 1986.

The main areas covered by the Act are the authorization of securities and investment businesses, and the establishment and enforcement of rules of good and fair business practice. The DEPARTMENT OF TRADE AND INDUSTRY, together with its appointed agency, the Financial Services Authority (formerly the Securities and Investment Board), is responsible for the overall administration of the Act, in conjunction with Recognized Investment Exchanges (RIEs) and Recognized Professional Bodies (RPBs).

Originally the Act set up five Self-Regulatory Organizations (SROs) to regulate firms providing financial securities and investment services: The Securities Association (TSA), Association of Futures Brokers and Dealers (AFBD), Investment Management Regulatory Organization (IMRO), Life Assurance and Unit Trust Regulatory Organization (LAUTRO) and Financial Intermediaries, Managers and Brokers Regulatory Association (FIMBRA). The TSA and ABRD merged in 1991 to form the Securities and Futures Authority (SFA) and in 1994 LAUTRO and FIMBRA merged to form the Personal Investment Authority (PIA). In 2000 the newly established Financial Services Authority took over the responsibilities for the three remaining Self-Regulatory Organizations thus bringing all aspects of the regulation of the securities and investment industry under the 'one-roof'.

The general objective of the legislation is to ensure a high level of investor protection by ensuring that only persons deemed to be 'fit and proper' are authorized to undertake securities and investment business, and that they conduct their business according to standards laid down by the SROs, RIEs and RPBs; leading, for example, in the former case, to the clarification of the relationship between the firm and its clients, especially as regards disclosure of fees, charges and the capacities in which the firm may act, and, in the latter case, to open and fair pricing.

The Financial Services Act also paved the way for important changes in the structure of the personal financial services industry. The Act together with the BUILDING SOCIETIES ACT, 1986 has enabled financial services providers such as insurance companies and building societies to broaden their portfolio of product offerings to include, for example, personal pensions, unit trusts and individual savings accounts (ISAs) thus increasing competition in the industry by breaking down traditional 'demarcation' boundaries in respect of 'who does what'.

A Recognized Investment Exchange is a body such as the STOCK MARKET, LONDON DERIVATIVES EXCHANGE which provides an organized framework within which transactions can be effected, including facilities for making a market in a financial asset or commodity (see MARKET MAKER), monitoring and reporting completed transactions and providing for settlement and delivery through an appropriate clearing mechanism.

A Recognized Professional Body is an organization such as the Chartered Accountants in England and Wales, which is responsible for regulating its members in relation to their work in advising clients on their investments.

Financial Services Authority (FSA) a body which is responsible for regulating all aspects of the provision of financial securities and investment under the FINANCIAL SERVICES ACT, 1986 (as amended by the Financial Services and Markets Act, 2000). Previously this task was split between various other organizations, including the Securities and Futures Authority, Personal Investment Authority and the Investment Management Regulatory Organization.

financial structure see CAPITAL STRUCTURE, CAPITAL GEARING.

financial system a network of financial institutions (COMMERCIAL BANKS, BUILDING SOCIETIES, etc.) and markets (MONEY MARKET, STOCK MARKET), dealing in a variety of financial instruments (BANK DEPOSITS, STOCKS and SHARES, etc.), which are engaged in money transmission activities and the provision of LOAN and CREDIT facilities.

The financial institutions and markets occupy a key position in the economy as intermediaries in channelling savings and other funds to borrowers and investors. In doing this one of their main roles is to reconcile the different requirements of savers and borrowers, thereby facilitating a higher level of saving and investment in the economy than would otherwise be the case. Depositors with financial institutions are seeking a relatively risk-free repository for their monies, combining ready access to their money with a longer term investment return, which provides for current income and/or capital appreciation. Borrowers, in general, require access to funds of varying amounts to finance short-, medium- and long-term debt and capital investment, often, as is particularly the case with business investments, under conditions of substantial risk. The financial institutions help to reconcile these different requirements in three main ways:

(a) by combining together the deposits and savings of many individuals, thus making it possible to make single large-scale loans;

(b) by pooling the resources of many depositors and savers to provide both for an individual to withdraw his funds at short notice while maintaining, in the round, a substantially large and stable financial base to underpin long-term lending;

(c) by holding a diversified portfolio of assets and lending for a variety of purposes so as to provide for various risk-return combinations.

In the UK the financial system is regulated by the BANK OF ENGLAND in combination with the FINANCIAL SERVICES AUTHORITY. See FINANCIAL SERVICES ACT 1986, BANKING SYSTEM, CLEARING HOUSE SYSTEM, BUILDING SOCIETIES ACT, 1986.

Financial Times All-Share Index see SHARE PRICE INDEX.

financial year the period from 1 April to 31 March of the following year used for CORPORATION TAX purposes. Compare FISCAL YEAR.

firing see DISMISSAL.

firm see BUSINESS.

firm location see INDUSTRIAL LOCATION.

first in, first out (FIFO) see STOCK VALUATION.

fiscal policy

The regulation of government expenditure and taxation in order to control the level of spending in the economy (see ECONOMIC POLICY).

The fiscal authorities (principally the TREASURY in the UK), can employ a number of taxation measures to control spending: DIRECT TAXES on individuals (INCOME TAX) and companies (CORPORATION TAX) can be increased if spending needs to be reduced, for example, to control inflation, i.e. an increase in income tax reduces people's disposable income, and similarly an increase in corporation tax leaves companies with less profit available to pay dividends and reinvest. Alternatively, spending can be reduced by increasing indirect taxes: an increase in VALUE ADDED TAXES on products in general, or an increase in EXCISE DUTIES on particular products such as petrol and cigarettes will, by increasing their prices, lead to a reduction in purchasing power.

The government can use changes in its own expenditure to affect spending levels; for example, a cut in current purchases of products or capital investment by the government again serves to reduce total spending in the economy.

Taxation and government expenditure are linked together in terms of the government's overall fiscal or BUDGET position: total spending in the economy is reduced by the twin effects of increased taxation and expenditure cuts with the government running a budget surplus. If the objective is to increase spending then the government operates a budget deficit, reducing taxation and increasing its expenditure.

In practice the application of fiscal policy as a *short-term* stabilization technique encounters a number of problems which reduces its effectiveness. Taxation rate changes, particularly alterations to income tax, are administratively cumbersome to initiate and take time to implement: likewise, a substantial proportion of government expenditure on, for example schools, roads, hospitals and defence, reflect *longer-term* economic and social commitments and cannot easily be reversed without lengthy political lobbying. From a technical point of view, changes in taxes or expenditure produce 'multiplier' effects (i.e. some initial change in spending is magnified and transmitted around the economy) but to an indeterminate extent.

Practical experience has indicated that the short-termism approach to economic management has not in fact been especially successful in stabilizing the economy. As a result, *medium-term* management of the economy favoured by the monetarist school has, in recent years, assumed a greater degree of significance.

In the past the authorities have occasionally set 'targets' for fiscal policy, most notably 'caps' on the size of the PUBLIC SECTOR BORROWING REQUIREMENT (PSBR). Recently, the government has accepted that fiscal stability is an important element in the fight against inflation. In 1997, the government set an inflation 'target' of an increase in the RETAIL PRICE INDEX (RPIX) of no more than 2½% per annum and ceded powers to a newly-established MONETARY POLICY COMMITTEE to set official interest rates. In doing this the government explicitly recognised that a low inflation economy was essential in order to achieve another of its priorities – low UNEMPLOYMENT. To this end, fiscal 'prudence', specifically a current budget deficit (PSBR) within the European Union's MAASTRICHT TREATY limits of no more than 3% of GDP (and an outstanding total debt limit of 60% of GDP) was endorsed as a necessary adjunct to avoid excessive monetary creation of the kind which had fuelled previous runaway inflations. See BUDGET (GOVERNMENT) entry for further discussion. See MONETARISM, MONETARY POLICY, BUSINESS CYCLE.

fiscal year the government's accounting year which, in the UK, runs from 6 April to 5 April of the following year, and in the USA from 1 July to 30 June. The fiscal year is the basic period used by the government in assessing personal INCOME TAX and any income earned during the fiscal year is assessable to taxation at the income tax rates applicable for that fiscal year. Compare FINANCIAL YEAR.

fishbone chart *or* **cause and effect chart** *or* **Ishikawa chart** a chart that breaks down the PRODUCTION of a product into its constituent operations as a means of identifying the source of a product defect. Fig. 41 shows a simplified fishbone chart for draught beer. Should a poor QUALITY batch of beer be produced this could be due to a malfunction in any one or more of the operations listed, including faulty or unclean equipment (mash mixers and filters, fermentation vessels), incorrect material mixes or poor strains of malt, hop or yeast, or incorrect boiling and cooling temperatures and periods. Fishbone charts can also be used more proactively to detect and *prevent* quality problems on a continuous basis as part of a commitment to TOTAL QUALITY MANAGEMENT. See QUALITY CONTROL, FIVE M.

five M a checklist designed to ensure that all five Ms, men (people), machine, material, measurement and method are considered in any structured attempt at a problem's solution. Frequently used with a FISHBONE CHART.

five S a framework (Japanese in origin) for imparting PRODUCTION efficiency: *Seiketsu* Standardize. The intent being to standardize work so that consistent work will lead to consistent performance. *Seiri* Removal. The intent being to remove unwanted items from the workplace, for example tools or materials or plans that are not needed for the present task. *Seiso* Keeping clean. Keeping the work place clean and tidy. *Seiton* Organizing. That is, organising materials, tools etc so that the user will know where they are and time will not be wasted looking for them. *Shitsuke* Keeping to the rules. Underpinning the idea that organizations (and society) operate better through cooperation and teamwork. See LEAN MANUFACTURING.

fixed assets ASSETS such as buildings and machinery that are bought for long-term use in a firm rather than for resale. Fixed assets are retained in the business for long periods, and generally each year a proportion of their original cost will be written off against PROFITS for DEPRECIATION to reflect the

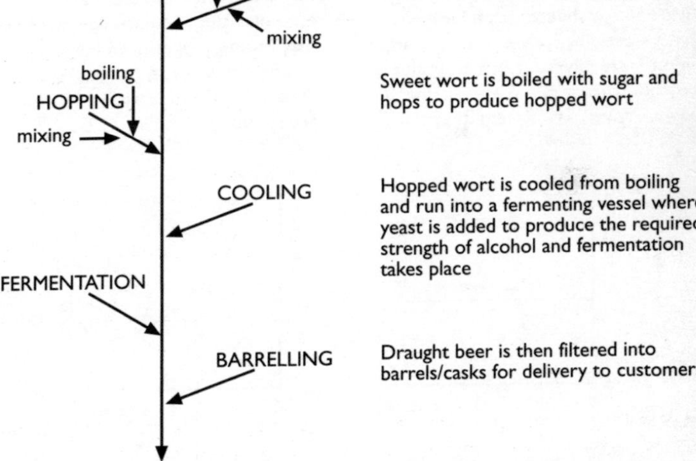
OPERATION
filtering
MASHING
mixing
Malt is mixed with boiled water and filtered to produce sweet wort
boiling
HOPPING
mixing
Sweet wort is boiled with sugar and hops to produce hopped wort
COOLING
Hopped wort is cooled from boiling and run into a fermenting vessel where yeast is added to produce the required strength of alcohol and fermentation takes place
FERMENTATION
BARRELLING
Draught beer is then filtered into barrels/casks for delivery to customers

Fig. 41 **Fishbone chart**. Simplified fishbone chart for draught beer. (Note: Fishbone charts are usually drawn horizontally).

diminishing value of the asset. In a BALANCE SHEET fixed assets are usually shown at cost less depreciation charged to date. Certain fixed assets such as property tend to appreciate in value (see APPRECIATION, definition 1) and need to be revalued periodically to keep their BALANCE SHEET values in line with market values. Other fixed assets such as patents, trademarks and GOODWILL are termed *intangible assets* to distinguish them from tangible assets such as buildings and machinery. All fixed assets are held for the purpose of earning income. See CURRENT ASSETS, REVALUATION, definition 1.

fixed charge see CREDITORS.

fixed costs any COSTS that do not vary with the level of output because they are linked to a time base rather than to a level of activity (see Fig. 42). Sometimes called period costs, they include rent and rates and depreciation.

fixed exchange rate system a mechanism for synchronizing and coordinating the EXCHANGE RATES of participating countries which involves each country setting a fixed par value for its currency against other countries' currencies; for example, 1 US dollar = 260 Japanese yen. Once an exchange rate value is fixed, countries are expected to maintain this rate for fairly lengthy periods of time, but may choose to devalue their currency (repeg the exchange rate at a new lower rate – see DEVALUATION) or revalue it (repeg the exchange rate at a new higher value – see REVALUATION, definition 2) if their BALANCE OF PAYMENTS is, respectively, in chronic deficit or surplus. Fixed exchange rates are maintained by the country's CENTRAL BANK intervening in the FOREIGN EXCHANGE MARKETS on a day-to-day basis, using its foreign exchange equalization account to buy and sell currencies as appropriate to stabilize the rate around its central par value.

The INTERNATIONAL MONETARY FUND formerly operated a system of fixed exchange rates, as did most members of the European Union under the fixed exchange rate requirements of the EUROPEAN MONETARY SYSTEM. Generally speaking, the business and financial community prefer a relatively fixed exchange rate to FLOATING EXCHANGE RATES, since it enables them to conclude trade and financial transactions at known foreign exchange prices so that the profit and loss implications of these deals can be calculated in advance. The disadvantage with such a system is that governments often tend to delay altering the exchange rate, either because of political factors or because they may choose to deal with balance of payments difficulties by using other measures, so that the pegged rate gets seriously out of line with underlying market tendencies. In consequence, for example, a firm's exports may become progressively less price-competitive in foreign markets because the country's currency is 'overvalued'. See ECONOMIC POLICY.

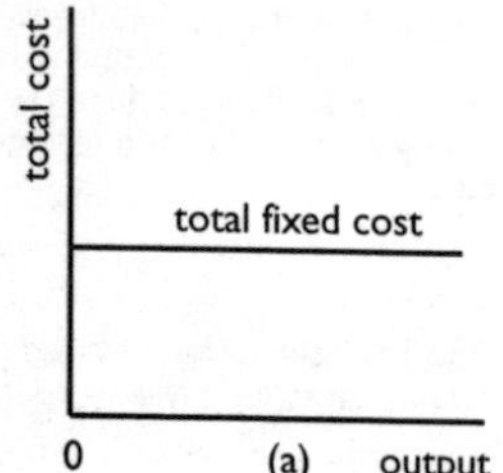

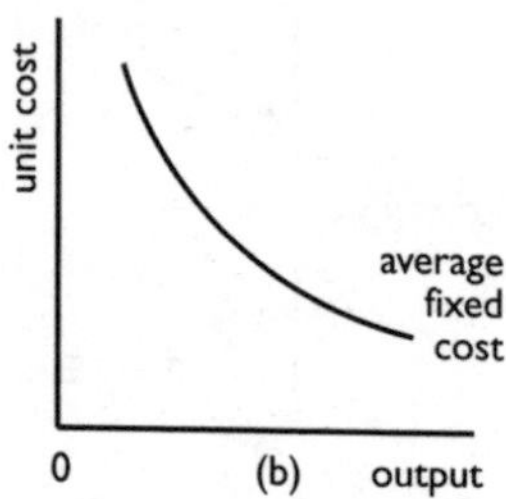

Fig. 42 **Fixed costs.** (a) The graph represents total payments made for the use of buildings, plant and equipment, etc., which must be met irrespective of whether output is high or low.
(b) The graph represents the continuous decline in average fixed cost as output rises, because a given amount of fixed cost is spread over a greater number of units.

fixed interest financial security see DEBENTURE.

fixed interval reorder system *or* **reorder point system** an arrangement whereby STOCK is reordered at regular intervals in variable quantities. In determining the amount to be reordered, account must be taken of usage rate of stock during the interval between placing the order and delivery of the ordered material. Usage during the reorder period should serve to reduce stock to a minimum safety stock level, before then being restored to the planned maximum stock level. With such a periodic review system the stock position is monitored at pre-determined intervals and orders placed to bring the stock position up to a target level. See STOCK CONTROL, STOCKHOLDING COSTS.

fixed overheads any indirect COSTS that do not vary with the level of output of a product. They include such items as rents and depreciation of fixed assets, whose total cost remains unchanged regardless of changes in the level of activity. Consequently, fixed overhead cost per unit of product will tend to fall as output increases (as OVERHEADS are spread over a larger output). See VARIABLE OVERHEADS, SEMI-VARIABLE OVERHEADS, STANDARD COST.

fixed quantity reorder system, reorder level system *or* **continuous review system** an arrangement whereby a specified quantity of materials is reordered at variable intervals. In determining the interval between orders, account must be taken of the usage rate of STOCK during the interval between placing the order and delivery of the ordered material. With such a continuous review system the stock position is monitored after every withdrawal and when the stock level drops to a predetermined reorder point a fixed quantity is ordered. See STOCK CONTROL, STOCK HOLDING COST.

flat organization an ORGANIZATION which has only a few managerial layers. This avoids excessive bureaucracy (see TALL ORGANIZATION); decision-making is more closely in touch with customer needs and the organization is able to adapt quickly to changes in its external environment. Small firms are usually flat organizations, but increasingly larger firms have attempted to improve their competitiveness by cutting down on their management structures and by establishing more focused business divisions. See STRATEGIC BUSINESS UNIT, RIGHTSIZING, HIERARCHY, DELAYERING.

flat yield see YIELD.

flexible budget a BUDGET that is designed to change in accordance with the level of activity actually attained, so that it allows for the variation in COSTS associated with changes in output volume. The costs associated with running a manufacturing plant, for instance, at 50% of capacity are different from running it at 70% or 100% capacity. The budget must allow for variation in plant utilization by distinguishing between FIXED COSTS, VARIABLE COSTS and SEMI-VARIABLE COSTS and their relationship to output. Flexible budgets facilitate more appropriate comparisons between the actual costs associated with the output attained and the budgeted costs for that output level. See BUDGETING, BUDGETARY CONTROL.

flexible firm see LABOUR FLEXIBILITY, FLEXIBLE SPECIALIZATION.

flexible manufacturing system (FMS) a means of PRODUCTION which makes extensive use of programmed AUTOMATION and COMPUTERS to achieve rapid production of small batches of components or products, whilst maintaining flexibility in manufacturing a wide range of these items. In FMS systems computer-controlled machines can be quickly switched from the production of one component or product to another by reprogramming the machines. Such reprogramming also facilitates the smooth running of the production system by allowing a component or product to be processed on several different machines, thus avoiding production bottlenecks or delays caused by machine breakdowns.

flexible specialization a form of industrial organization in which firms specialize in certain products but are able to change at short notice to producing different ones. A notable feature is that such flexibility can make it viable to produce small batches of each product. A prerequisite is the use of advanced flexible technology operated by employees with a broad range of skills who are able to surmount traditional job boundaries. Research by sociologists, however, suggests that, in the UK at least, flexible technology is not being fully exploited and that managers are often reluctant to create multi-skilled workforces. See LABOUR FLEXIBILITY.

flexitime a method of organizing hours of work which permits some flexibility in the times of starting and finishing each working day. Usually the employee will be required to commence work within certain times (for example between 7.00 and 9.30 a.m.) and to remain at work until a specified time (for example 3.30 p.m.). Within these limits employees can choose day by day their hours of work. However, they will usually be required to work a specified total number of hours over a period of, say, one month. Any shortfalls at the end of the period may be carried forward or result in pay deductions whilst excess hours could be dealt with by additional pay or time off in lieu. Flexitime enables employees to adapt their working day to other commitments. However, it also confers advantages to employers: in so far as it requires precise timings to be kept it can tighten control of hours of work; and because potential absences from work (for example, visit to a doctor) can be pushed outside the flexi-day it can improve utilization of staff and productivity. See ANNUAL HOURS.

flip flop arbitration see ARBITRATION.

floating charge see DEBENTURES, CREDITORS.

floating exchange rate system a mechanism for coordinating EXCHANGE RATES between countries' currencies which involves the value of each country's currency in terms of other currencies being determined by the forces of supply and demand in the FOREIGN EXCHANGE MARKET (see EQUILIBRIUM MARKET PRICE). Over time the exchange rate of a particular currency may rise (appreciate) or fall (depreciate) depending, respectively, on the strength or weakness of its underlying BALANCE OF PAYMENTS position and exposure to SPECULATIVE activity. See APPRECIATION, definition 2, DEPRECIATION, definition 2.

Generally speaking, the business and financial community dislikes unregulated floating exchange rates since the market tends to produce erratic and destabilizing exchange rate movements, often prompted by currency speculation, which makes it difficult to conclude meaningful trade and investment transactions, because of the uncertainties surrounding the profit-and-loss implications of such deals when exchange rates are fluctuating widely. Governments too dislike disorderly currency markets and prefer where possible to 'manage' their exchange rates both to moderate the excessive short-term fluctuations and to smooth out the underlying longer-term trend line by buying and selling currencies as appropriate out of their foreign exchange equalization account. While this creates a more settled and controlled environment in which to operate, nonetheless firms are usually forced to cover their currency deals in the forward exchange market.

Government intervention in currency markets sometimes goes beyond merely smoothing its exchange rate and may involve a deliberate attempt to manipulate the exchange rate so as to gain a trading advantage over other countries (a so-called *dirty float*). See FORWARD MARKET, INTERNATIONAL MONETARY FUND, ECONOMIC POLICY, CENTRAL BANK, GROUP OF 7 (G7), PURCHASING POWER PARITY, EXCHANGE RATE EXPOSURE.

floppy disk a data storage device in which data is stored on a vinyl disk which is inserted in a COMPUTER's disk drive to enable the computer to 'read' the information contained on it or to 'write' information onto it.

flotation the process by which a new company or an established PRIVATE LIMITED COMPANY becomes a PUBLIC LIMITED

COMPANY and issues SHARES to the general public. By going public a company is able to raise large amounts of capital by issuing a PROSPECTUS inviting shareholders to subscribe for shares. See SHARE ISSUE.

flowchart 1 a graphic representation of a sequence of COMPUTER operations which is used in presenting computer programs.
2 a graphic representation of a sequence of production operations. See ACTIVITY CHART.

flow of funds statement see CASH FLOW STATEMENT.

flow production see MASS PRODUCTION.

FMCG see FAST-MOVING CONSUMER GOODS.

FMS see FLEXIBLE MANUFACTURING SYSTEM.

fob see FREE ON BOARD.

focus 1 a term used to describe a firm's concentration on a single or limited range of business activities. By focusing on a 'core activity' the firm is better able to reap the benefits of SPECIALIZATION and access ECONOMIES OF SCALE, increase its MARKET SHARE and concentrate management's attention and capabilities on 'what they know best'. On the debit side, however, over-specialization may make the firm vulnerable to cyclical and secular downturns in demand while limiting opportunities for achieving long-run growth. See HORIZONTAL INTEGRATION, COMPETITIVE STRATEGY. Contrast DIVERSIFICATION.
2 a means of organizing production. See PRODUCT-FOCUSED LAYOUT.
3 a means of conducting market research by the use of 'focus groups'. See MARKETING INTELLIGENCE.
4 competing in ('targeting') one MARKET SEGMENT only (also known as niche targeting or marketing.) See CONCENTRATED MARKETING or TARGETING STRATEGY, DIFFERENTIATED MARKETING or TARGETING STRATEGY.

focused factory a term used to describe the division of a manufacturing unit into specialized areas for each complete product. See PRODUCT-FOCUSED LAYOUT.

Fordism a form of MASS PRODUCTION characterized by a high degree of job specialization, so called after the pattern of WORK ORGANIZATION and JOB DESIGN extolled by American car entrepreneur Henry Ford (1863–1947). Large numbers of a product could be produced for a mass market using assembly line technology where each worker performs a single task over and over again. Although high specialization can have efficiency advantages this form of work organization is often associated with low levels of JOB SATISFACTION, high LABOUR TURNOVER and ABSENTEEISM and high levels of CONFLICT and INDUSTRIAL DISPUTES.

forecasting see SALES FORECASTING, TECHNOLOGICAL FORECASTING.

foreclosure the refusal by a VERTICALLY INTEGRATED firm to supply inputs to non-integrated rivals, or distribute their products, as a means of putting them at a competitive disadvantage. Under UK COMPETITION POLICY, cases of vertical integration may be referred to the COMPETITION COMMISSION for investigation. See REFUSAL TO SUPPLY.

foreign currency *or* **foreign exchange** the CURRENCY of an overseas country, which is purchased by a particular country in exchange for its own currency, which is then used to finance trade and capital transactions between the two countries. See INTERNATIONAL TRADE, FOREIGN EXCHANGE CONTROLS, FOREIGN EXCHANGE MARKET, FORWARD MARKET.

foreign currency translation the process of denoting the assets and liabilities of a MULTINATIONAL ENTERPRISE's foreign subsidiary's BALANCE SHEET and the revenues and expenses of the subsidiary's PROFIT-AND-LOSS ACCOUNT, which are expressed in terms of the subsidiary's local currency by translating them into the parent company's domestic currency. This is done in order to prepare CONSOLIDATED ACCOUNTS for the group.

There are two main currency translation methods:

(a) the *closing rate*, or *net investment* method, or *all-current* method, in which all foreign currency items are translated at the EXCHANGE RATE ruling at the date of the balance sheet. With the closing rate method any gains or losses on exchange arising from translation are taken direct to the group balance sheet an dealt with as changes in RESERVES so as not to affect reported PROFIT.

(b) *temporal* method or *current/non-current* method, in which fixed assets and long-term liabilities are translated at the exchange rate ruling at the date of their acquisition, and revenues and expenses at an average exchange rate for the year. With the temporal method any differences arising on translation are taken to the profit-and-loss account where they serve to affect recorded profit.

foreign direct investment (FDI) investment by a MULTINATIONAL ENTERPRISE in establishing production, distribution or marketing facilities abroad. Sometimes foreign direct investment takes the form of GREENFIELD INVESTMENT with new factories, warehouses or offices being constructed overseas and new staff recruited. Alternatively, foreign direct investment can take the form of TAKEOVERS and MERGERS with other companies located abroad. Foreign direct investment differs from overseas portfolio investment by financial institutions which generally involves the purchase of small shareholdings in a large number of foreign companies.

FDI is used alongside STRATEGIC ALLIANCES and EXPORTING as an integral part of a multinational enterprise's FOREIGN MARKET SERVICING STRATEGY.

In 2003/2004, the USA was the world's leading *outward* (overseas) investor accounting for 15.5% of world outward FDI flows, followed by Belgium 13.3%, France 12.8%, the UK 12.7% and the Netherlands 5.8%. The USA was the leading recipient of *inward* FDI accounting for 17.3% of inward investment in 2003/2004, followed by Belgium 14.4%, Germany 9.7%, China 7.8% and the UK 7.1%.

foreign exchange see FOREIGN CURRENCY.

foreign exchange controls the application of restrictions on the availability of FOREIGN CURRENCIES by a country's central bank, to assist in the removal of a BALANCE OF PAYMENTS deficit and to control disruptive short-run capital inflows and outflows which tend to destabilize the country's EXCHANGE RATE. Because importers need to purchase foreign currencies from the country's central bank (via their commercial banks) in order to buy products from overseas suppliers, by cutting off the supply of foreign currencies the authorities can reduce the amount of IMPORTS to a level compatible with the foreign currency earned by the country's EXPORTS. Exchange controls may be applied not only to limit the total amount of currency available but can also be used to discriminate against particular types of imports, thus serving as a form of PROTECTIONISM. See FOREIGN EXCHANGE MARKET.

Foreign Exchange Equalization Account the section of a country's CENTRAL BANK (for example the Bank of England) which uses the country's foreign currency holdings to operate in the FOREIGN EXCHANGE MARKET in order to stabilize the country's currency EXCHANGE RATE.

foreign exchange market a MARKET engaged in the buying and selling of FOREIGN CURRENCIES. Such a market is required because each country involved in INTERNATIONAL TRADE and investment has its own domestic currency and this needs *to be* exchanged for other currencies in order to finance trade and capital transactions. This function is undertaken by a network of private foreign exchange dealers and a country's monetary authorities acting through its central banks.

The foreign exchange market by its very nature is multinational in scope. The leading centres for foreign exchange dealings are London, New York and Tokyo.

Foreign currencies can be transacted on a 'spot' basis for immediate delivery (see SPOT MARKET), or can be bought and sold for future delivery (see FORWARD MARKET). Some two-thirds of London's foreign exchange dealings in 2000 were spot transactions.

The foreign exchange market may be left unregulated by governments, with EXCHANGE RATES between currencies being determined by the free interplay of the forces of demand and supply (see FLOATING EXCHANGE RATE SYSTEM), or they may be subjected to support buying and selling by countries' central banks in order to fix them at particular rates (see FIXED EXCHANGE RATE SYSTEM).

foreign investment the purchase of overseas physical and financial assets. Overseas investment in financial assets, in particular by institutional investors, is undertaken primarily to diversify portfolio risk and to obtain higher returns than would be achievable on comparable domestic investments; while physical investment abroad is one main way for a firm to internationalize its operations. FOREIGN DIRECT INVESTMENT (FDI) in new manufacturing plants and sales subsidiaries, or the acquisition of established businesses, provide the firm with a more flexible approach to supplying foreign markets. See CAPITAL INFLOW, CAPITAL OUTFLOW, FOREIGN MARKET SERVICING STRATEGY, MULTINATIONAL ENTERPRISE.

foreign market servicing strategy the choice of EXPORTING, STRATEGIC ALLIANCES (including JOINT VENTURES), LICENSING and FOREIGN DIRECT INVESTMENT (FDI), or some combination of each, by a MULTINATIONAL ENTERPRISE (MNE) as a means of selling its products in overseas markets. Exporting involves production in one or more locations for sale overseas in target markets; licensing involves the assignment of production and selling rights by a MNE to producers in the target market; strategic alliances involve the combining together on a contractual or equity basis the resources and skills of two firms; foreign direct investment involves the establishment of the firm's own production (and selling) facilities in the target market. In resource terms, exporting from established production plants is a relatively inexpensive way of servicing a foreign market, but the firm could be put at a competitive disadvantage either because of local producers' lower cost structures and control of local distribution channels or because of governmental TARIFFS, QUOTAS, etc. and other restrictions on IMPORTS. Licensing enables a firm to gain a rapid penetration of world markets and can be advantageous to a firm lacking the financial resources to set up overseas operations, or where again local firms control distribution channels, but the royalties obtained may represent a poor return for the technology transferred. Strategic alliances can enable complementary resources and skills to be combined, enabling firms to supply products in a more cost-effective way and to increase market penetration. Foreign direct investment can be expensive and risky (although HOST COUNTRIES often offer subsidies, etc. to attract such inward investment), but in many cases the 'presence' effects of operating locally (familiarity with local market conditions and the cultivation of contacts with local suppliers, distributors and retailers) are important factors in building market share over the long run.

MNEs in practice tend to use various combinations of these modes to service global markets because of the added flexibility it gives to their operations. For example, if governments choose to act on imports by raising tariffs, etc. a MNE may substitute in-market FDI for direct exporting. See FOREIGN INVESTMENT, INTERNATIONAL MARKETING, EXCHANGE RATE EXPOSURE.

foreman an alternative term for SUPERVISOR used mainly in manufacturing organizations.

forex *abbrev. for* foreign exchange. See FOREIGN CURRENCY, FOREIGN EXCHANGE MARKET.

forfaiting the provision of finance by one firm (the forfaiter) to another firm (the client) by purchasing goods the client has pre-sold to a customer but for which he has not yet been paid. The forfaiter (which often is a subsidiary of a commercial bank or a specialist firm) buys the client's goods at a discounted cash price, thus releasing ready money for the client to use to finance his WORKING CAPITAL requirements. The forfaiter then arranges to collect the payment when due from the customer to whom the goods have been sold, thus also saving the client the paperwork involved.

Forfaiting extends to both domestic and export sales. It can be especially useful in the latter context in the case of expensive capital equipment involving long delivery dates, and where there are possible complications arising from dealing with relatively unknown customers, exchange rate fluctuations, etc. See EXPORTING.

formal organization see ORGANIZATION.

forward exchange contract a contract to exchange a given amount of one foreign currency for another at a specified future date (usually one or three months ahead). For example, if a UK importer is due to pay $100,000 for materials in three months' time, then in order to guarantee the pound cost of these materials it might cover the transaction by entering into a forward exchange contract to buy $100,000 for delivery in three months' time in return for a given amount of pounds, the amount of pounds being determined by the forward exchange rate. See FORWARD MARKET.

forward exchange market see FORWARD MARKET.

forward integration see VERTICAL INTEGRATION.

forward market, futures market *or* **forward exchange market** a market which provides for the buying and selling of FINANCIAL SECURITIES (shares, stocks), COMMODITIES (rubber, tin, etc.) FOREIGN CURRENCIES, DERIVATIVES and SWAPS for delivery at some future point in time, as opposed to a SPOT MARKET which provides for immediate delivery. Forward positions are taken by traders in a particular financial asset or commodity whose price can fluctuate greatly over time, in order to minimize the risk and uncertainty surrounding their business dealings in the immediate future (i.e. hedge against adverse price movements), and by dealers and speculators (see SPECULATION) hoping to earn windfall profits from correctly anticipating price movements.

Traders seek to minimize uncertainty about future prices by buying or selling *futures,* particularly OPTIONS, i.e. contracts that promise to buy or sell a commodity or financial asset at a price agreed upon now for delivery at some later point in time, usually within a three-month period. For example, a producer of chocolate could contract to buy a given amount of cocoa at today's price plus a percentage risk premium for delivery in two months' time. Even if the price of cocoa were to go up markedly, the manufacturer knows that he is still able to buy at the (lower) contract price, and is thus able to plan his raw material outlays accordingly. Similarly, the producers of cocoa can contract to sell the commodity at an agreed price now for delivery in the near future in order to cover themselves against adverse price changes.

In between the original buyers and producers, using futures as a hedge to minimize risk, stand the various dealers and speculators who do not themselves actually *physically* hold commodities and financial assets but buy or sell the paper contracts to such items according to their view of probable price movements.

Forward prices reflect anticipated future demand and supply conditions for a financial security, foreign currency or commodity being traded. Specifically, the forward prices will be based partially on current spot prices but will also take into account interest rate and inflation rate trends. The difference between the current spot rate of a foreign currency and the forward exchange rate constitutes the 'forward margin'. The forward margin can be at either a discount or a premium to the spot rate.

The EUREX and the LONDON INTERNATIONAL FINANCIAL FUTURES MARKET (LIFFE), are the largest European Union centres for forward dealings in securities and commodities. The forward markets in the UK are regulated by the FINANCIAL SERVICES AUTHORITY in accordance with various standards of good practice laid down under the FINANCIAL SERVICES ACT 1986. Globally, the Chicago Board of Trade and the Chicago Mercantile Exchange are the world's largest forward markets. See COMMODITY MARKET, FOREIGN EXCHANGE MARKET, STOCK MARKET, CONTANGO, COVERED INTEREST ARBITRAGE, EXCHANGE RATE EXPOSURE, EQUILIBRIUM MARKET PRICE.

Four O's of purchasing the objects and objectives of a purchase, and the organization and operation of buying.

The Four O's help to answer important marketing questions about:

(a) *Objects* – what general uses will the product have?

(b) *Objectives* – what specific functions do buyers expect the product to perform?

(c) *Organization* – who within an organization has power to authorize a purchase?

(d) *Operations* – what procurement procedures do they employ in purchasing it, for example, by inviting tenders?

The answers to these questions will assist a company in formulating its MARKETING MIX. See PURCHASING.

Four P's of marketing product, price, promotion and place, the key variables of the MARKETING MIX.

(a) *Product:* a good or service offered to consumers which satisfies a want or need. Product management involves decisions about PRODUCT LINES, the PRODUCT MIX, BRANDS and PACKAGING;

(b) *Price:* the amount of money which consumers are required to pay for a product or service. Decisions have to be made about the basic price, trade discounts, allowances and special deals, credit terms and carriage terms. Various PRICING METHODS may be employed;

(c) *Promotion:* the means of stimulating demand for the firm's products. Promotion decisions involve consideration of the MEDIA to be used for ADVERTISING the firm's products, SALES PROMOTION and other aspects of the PROMOTIONAL MIX;

(d) *Place:* the physical DISTRIBUTION of the firm's products into the hands of customers. This involves the selection of appropriate DISTRIBUTION CHANNELS which maximize marketing effectiveness.

four-shift working see SHIFT WORK.

franchise the granting by one company to another company (exclusive franchise) or a number of companies (non-exclusive franchise) of the right/s to supply its products. A franchise is a contractual arrangement which is entered into for a specified period of time, with the franchisee paying a royalty to the franchisor for the rights assigned. Examples of franchises include the McDonald Burger and Kentucky Fried Chicken diner chains, Tie Rack and Dyno-Rod.

Franchises are a form of co-partnership, offering mutual benefits. They allow the franchisor to expand sales rapidly and widely, sometimes on a global basis, without having to raise large amounts of capital, by building on the efforts of a highly motivated team of entrepreneurs. Individual franchisees are usually required to contribute the bulk of the investment in physical assets and hence have a personal interest in the success of the venture. For his part, the franchisee obtains access to an innovative product or novel selling method, with the franchisor providing back-up, technical assistance, specialized equipment and advertising and promotion. See VERTICAL MARKETING SYSTEM, BUSINESS STRATEGY, EXTERNAL GROWTH, BUSINESS FORMAT FRANCHISING.

franked investment income interest or dividends received from FINANCIAL SECURITIES net after CORPORATION TAX has been deducted. To avoid taxing such investment income twice, any such income received by a company which has bought financial securities is granted a TAX CREDIT for the tax already paid so that it is not subject to further corporation tax.

Fraser's five-fold grading system see RECRUITMENT AND SELECTION.

fraud the gaining of financial advantage by a person who deliberately deceives another person or business, by mispresenting himself.

'free balance' see ALLOCATION, definition 2.

free enterprise economy see ECONOMY.

freehold property property which is legally owned outright by a person or business. Contrast LEASEHOLD PROPERTY.

free issue raw materials or components which a factory operative can collect from the materials stores without having to obtain a duly authorized MATERIALS REQUISITION.

free on board (f.o.b.) a term used to denote the respective contractual obligations of sellers and buyers of a good which is exported. Under a f.o.b. contract the seller pays the cost of transporting the goods to the port of shipment and loading charges, plus all insurance cover up to this point. From then on it is the buyer who bears the cost of transporting, and insuring, the good to its final destination. See COST, INSURANCE AND FREIGHT, COST AND FREIGHT, EXPORTING.

freeport *or* **free trade zone** an area usually forming part of an airport or shipping port into which goods can be imported without incurring import or customs duties, provided the goods are to be subsequently exported either in their original form or as intermediate products within a final good. See ENTREPÔT TRADE.

free shares see SHARE INCENTIVE SCHEME.

free trade the EXPORT and IMPORT of goods and services between countries totally unhindered by restrictions such as TARIFFS and QUOTAS. In general, free trade leads to a higher level of economic welfare in so far as it favours the location of economic activities in those countries best suited to their production, resulting, through the trade mechanism, in worldwide consumption gains in the form of lower prices and greater product availability. See INTERNATIONAL TRADE, TRADE INTEGRATION, WORLD TRADE ORGANIZATION.

free trade area see TRADE INTEGRATION.

free trade zone see FREEPORT.

freight *or* **cargo** goods that are in the process of being physically transported from a factory or depot to a customer by road, rail, sea or air, involving both domestically and internationally traded goods. The movement of goods may be done by the supplier's own distribution division or by independent fleet operators and FREIGHT FORWARDERS. See DISTRIBUTION, PIGGY BACKING, COST AND FREIGHT, COST, INSURANCE AND FREIGHT, BALTIC MERCANTILE AND SHIPPING EXCHANGE.

freight forwarder *or* **forwarding agent** a firm which specializes in the physical movement of goods in transit, arranging the collection of goods from factory, depot, etc., and delivering them direct to the customer in the case of domestic consignments, and to seaports, airports, etc. in the case of exported goods. In the latter case the forwarder also handles the documentation required by the customs authorities and the booking arrangements. See EXPORTING.

frictional unemployment see UNEMPLOYMENT.

friendly society a business organization which is owned by its members. Friendly societies were the forerunners of many modern Insurance Companies and BUILDING SOCIETIES. See REGISTRAR OF FRIENDLY SOCIETIES, BUILDING SOCIETIES ACT, 1986.

fringe benefit *or* **perk** any benefit offered to employees in addition to their WAGE or SALARY, for example luncheon vouchers, company car or mileage allowance, EMPLOYEE SHARE OWNERSHIP PLAN and private health insurance and employer contributions to a PENSION scheme.

FRS see ACCOUNTING STANDARDS.

FSA see FINANCIAL SERVICES AUTHORITY.

full-cost pricing see COST-BASED PRICING.

full employment see ECONOMIC POLICY.

full-line forcing a business practice whereby a supplier encourages distributors/retailers to stock or provide not only his principal products or services but additionally other products or services from his range. For example, an oil company might require a filling station contracted to sell its petrol also to sell its brands of lubricants, anti-freeze and other motoring accessories. The practice of full-line forcing may help the supplier increase his total sales and reinforce brand loyalty. However, if undertaken by a DOMINANT FIRM, the practice may serve to limit competition in a market by depriving rival suppliers of distribution outlets. See OFFICE OF FAIR TRADING, COMPETITION ACT, 1980.

full-line strategy a product line strategy which involves offering an extensive number of variations of a product.

See PRODUCT RANGE, contrast LIMITED-LINE STRATEGY.

full-time official an official employed by a TRADE UNION to undertake COLLECTIVE BARGAINING with managements, recruitment of new members and administration of union affairs. See SHOP STEWARD.

functional budget a BUDGET which relates to a specific function of a business organization e.g., marketing, production, research and development, purchasing etc.

functional flexibility see LABOUR FLEXIBILITY.

functional foremen see SCIENTIFIC MANAGEMENT.

functional layout a means of organizing production which involves grouping together equipment, machinery and personnel according to the function which they perform in the production process, for example drilling, grinding and assembly. See BATCH PRODUCTION, PROCESS-FOCUSED LAYOUT.

functional structure an ORGANIZATION structure where activities are grouped into DEPARTMENTS by function, and formal COORDINATION occurs at the apex. (See Fig. 43).

Such structures provide a generally effective means of coordination both within departments and across the organization as a whole, when there is a *single* product or service. They also provide clear career paths for functional specialists, though there is a possibility that loyalty to departments will displace loyalty to the organization. Functional structures become less appropriate when an organization *diversifies* – it can be difficult to adapt functions to possibly varying product or service requirements since the centralization of authority in this model tends to encourage uniformity.

This type of structure is often referred to as 'U-form' since authority within the organization can be traced up the CHAIN OF COMMAND to a unitary source. See PRODUCT-BASED STRUCTURE, MATRIX STRUCTURE, CRITICAL FUNCTION STRUCTURE.

funded pension a PENSION scheme where savings contributions are invested to finance future pension payments. This type of scheme can be contrasted with PAY AS YOU GO schemes. See PENSION FUND.

funding the process of replacing maturing short-term LOANS by long-term loans in order to reduce the ratio of short-term borrowing to long-term borrowing. Funding is undertaken by the government in its management of the NATIONAL DEBT, and by companies who use the proceeds of DEBENTURE and LOAN STOCK issues to pay off short-term borrowings and overdrafts.

funds the WORKING CAPITAL of a business, consisting of money tied up in stocks and debtors plus cash, less money owed to creditors. Any change in net working capital has an effect in increasing or decreasing funds.

funds flow analysis a means of analysing the movement of funds within a company by comparing successive BALANCE SHEETS to note where additional funds have come from and where they have been deployed in the business. See also CASH FLOW STATEMENT.

funds flow statement see CASH FLOW STATEMENT.

futures market see FORWARD MARKET.

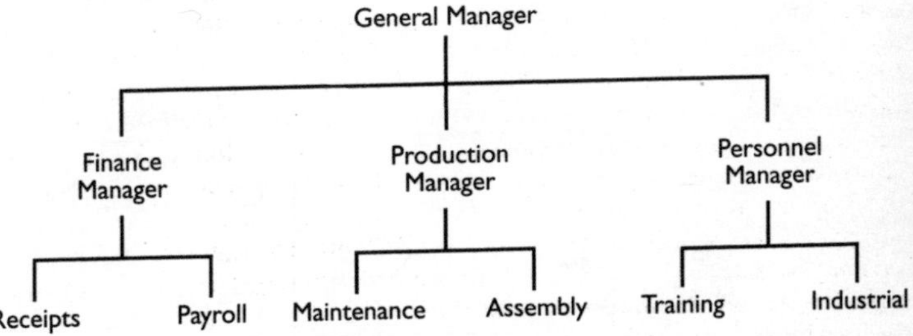

Fig. 43 **Functional structure.** A typical example.

g

G7 see GROUP OF 7.

GAAP (Generally Accepted Accounting Principles) see ACCOUNTING CONCEPTS.

gainsharing a PAY system where a proportion of employees' pay is linked to gains in productivity or reductions in costs. Its benefits are thought to include greater acceptance of changes in technology and work methods, more information sharing, more effective teamwork and greater personal effort. It can be used in organizations where profit-sharing schemes are inappropriate or impossible e.g. not-for-profit and public service organizations.

Two common forms of gainsharing are the Scanlon Plan where a portion of wages is based on movements in the ratio of the total wages bill to the total value of sales, and the Rucker Plan where wages are related to movements in the ratio of the total wages bill to total VALUE ADDED. The former provides an incentive to maximize saleable output whilst the latter encourages cost reduction.

game theory a conceptual framework used by business strategists to analyse the consequences of particular competitive actions. It is typically employed in oligopolistic markets (dominated by a few large suppliers) where the fortunes of the firm are *interdependent* and the actions of one firm will have a big impact on the position of its rivals, and vice versa. To illustrate: consider the 'pay-off' matrix shown in Fig 44. in which two tobacco companies, Philip Morris (PM) and BAT have the options of 'advertising' or 'not advertising' their, respective, cigarette brands 'Malboro' and 'Camel'. The 'best' course of action for BAT *if PM advertises* is to advertise itself, securing a profit of £2bn; *if PM doesn't advertise* BAT's 'best' strategy is still to advertise, securing £4bn in this case. By circular reasoning, PM's 'best' strategy is to advertise. Thus, both companies advertise and secure £2bn each. Note, however, if the two companies could 'agree' not to advertise then they would each secure £3bn. See COLLUSION.

Gantt chart a chart used for PRODUCTION SCHEDULING purposes which lists orders on the left of the chart and time along the right of the chart as in Fig. 45, depicting the

		Phillip Morris's Decision	
		Advertise	Don't Advertise
BAT's Decision	Advertise	• £2bn profit each	• Marlboro get £1bn profit • Camel gets £4bn profit
	Don't Advertise	• Marlboro gets £4bn profit • Camel gets £1bn profit	• £3bn profit each

Fig. 44 **Pay-off matrix.**

order no	customer	date					
		week 1	week 2	week 3	week 4	week 5	week 6
001	Pass						
002	Lowes						
003	Chadwick						
004	Pendleton						
005	Smith						

Fig. 45 **Gantt chart.** A typical example.

scheduling of orders on a day-by-day or week-by-week basis using bar lines to show the start and completion dates of each order. A similar chart can be used to show machine availability and utilization rates in producing orders.

gap analysis 1 the comparison between an organization's objective and its expected performance from its current and planned operations. Gap analysis helps to identify means by which the gap might be filled.
2 a technique used in the marketing of services to identify to what extent customers' *expectations* match up to the *perceived* level of services received. In some cases customers may get better service than they expected – a positive 'expected service-perceived service' gap – thus encouraging them to purchase the supplier's service again. By contrast, a negative 'expected service-perceived service' gap may apply such that customers will show their dissatisfaction with the supplier's service by ceasing to purchase it. Gap analysis identifies a number of potential problem areas which can emerge, including: (i) *management perception–consumer expectations gap:* the supplier fails to identify or understand consumers' expected service needs; (ii) *management perception–service quality specification gap:* the supplier knows what customers expect but fails to establish satisfactory service quality specifications resulting in the provision of an inferior service; (iii) *service quality specification–service delivery gap:* service quality specifications may be satisfactory but the firm's service delivery is unsatisfactory because, for example, contact persons are inefficient/unhelpful; (iv) *service delivery–external communications gap:* the supplier 'misleads' customers by promising (through advertisements etc.) more than the supplier can actually deliver.

Gap analysis thus helps managers identify and remove existing and potential negative service gaps which reflect the firm's *own* failings in meeting customers' demands for a quality service.

'garbage can' model of decision-making a pattern of decision-making in organizations, identified by the American Professor of Management, James March (1928–), in which organizational members generate a stream of problems and solutions, especially when choices need to be made. These are in effect 'dumped' into a 'garbage can'; only a small minority of solutions will be incorporated in the final decision (if one is made at all). The basis of this model is that organizational members frequently have favoured courses of action: wherever they can they seize the opportunity provided by a problem or the organization's needs to make a choice to advocate the implementation of their solution. In this sense organizations can be said to be a set of 'free floating' solutions waiting for problems to arise. Decisions can be seen as a more or less fortuitous by-product of problems, solutions and choices coming together at a particular junction. See ORGANIZATIONAL ANALYSIS, 'ORGANIZED ANARCHY'.

gardening leave a period of enforced leave from work.

gatekeeper a person who controls important information flows and access to other persons within an organization. The person concerned may have control over the information which goes up or down the organizational structure or in and out of the organization.

GATT see WORLD TRADE ORGANIZATION.

gazumping a situation in which a seller of an asset such as a house, having already agreed informally to sell the asset to one buyer at an agreed price, subsequently sells the asset to another buyer at a higher price.

GDP see GROSS DOMESTIC PRODUCT.

gearing see CAPITAL GEARING.

General Agreement on Tariffs and Trade (GATT) see WORLD TRADE ORGANIZATION.

general union see TRADE UNION.

generic a term that is used to identify a PRODUCT or product class as a whole (for example, 'cigarettes') rather than an individual supplier's BRAND of the product (for example, 'Marlboro' cigarettes).

geographical pricing the PRICING of products to customers based in different locations. In some cases differential PRICES may be charged to reflect the respective costs of physical DISTRIBUTION involved in moving goods from the factory to the buyer.

In other cases firms may simplify their pricing arrangements by means of a 'uniform delivered price system' which involves charging the same price to all customers irrespective of their location (for example post office letters). Alternatively, customers may be grouped into a number of delivery zones and a common price charged to all customers in each zone. Such 'basing point price systems' involve some cross-subsidization of delivery costs between customers in the interests of maximizing the firm's total sales. See PRICE DISCRIMINATION.

geographical segmentation a form of MARKET SEGMENTATION which divides a market into geographical areas on the basis of common customer characteristics. Geographical segmentation also provides a means of dividing a MARKET into sales regions and then subdividing them into sales territories to assist with the efficient deployment of sales representatives to service customers.

geographic mobility see LABOUR MOBILITY.

gilt-edged security a BOND issued by the government or a company as a means of borrowing money. Such bonds are called gilt-edged because they are a low-risk form of lending in so far as governments and well-established large companies rarely default on their debts.

glass ceiling the impenetrable yet invisible barrier which prevents most women from reaching senior management positions, despite attempts to tackle DISCRIMINATION in employment over the last twenty-five years. The glass ceiling exists because male senior managers tend to believe that the values and talents necessary for senior management positions are more likely to be found in men. In other words male managers recruit new managers in their own image.

global brand a BRAND which is sold in a very large number of national markets on the basis of a single unique BRAND NAME, for example Coca-Cola, rather than using different brand names for each separate national market. Such global brands offer considerable economies of scale in marketing and production, though care must be exercised in developing a brand name which is in keeping with the customs and sentiments of all the target nations. See MULTINATIONAL ENTERPRISE.

globalization the tendency for markets to become global, rather than national, as barriers to INTERNATIONAL TRADE (e.g. TARIFFS) are reduced and international transport and communications improve; and the tendency for large MULTINATIONAL ENTERPRISES to grow to service global markets. See INTERNATIONALIZATION.

Globex an international futures trading system which enables futures contracts to be traded outside the trading hours of their national FORWARD MARKETS. Globex is run by REUTERS and its members include the Chicago Mercantile Exchange, Matif (of

France) and DTB (of Germany). However, it has failed to attract the support of the London based LIFFE, the world's third largest futures market, while the world's largest futures exchange, the Chicago Board of Trade, withdrew from Globex in 1994.

GMB the UK's fourth largest TRADE UNION formed out of a merger between the GMB (a general union) and APEX (a white-collar union) in 1989. It currently has around 700,000 members.

GNP see GROSS NATIONAL PRODUCT.

GNVQ see NATIONAL VOCATIONAL QUALIFICATION.

goal displacement the process where by an organization's primary objectives (for example the provision of services to consumers) come to take second place to other subsidiary objectives (such as monitoring employee performance). Writers on ORGANIZATIONS have shown how there is the ever-present danger that the means adopted to achieve organizational goals will become ends in themselves and displace the original goals. This tension is inevitable because organizations generally need to develop procedures to guide their members' job activities. But time and effort have to be expended to ensure that the procedures are adhered to and that they are effective. In this way operation of the procedures can come to dominate the activities of managers to the exclusion of attaining the goals the procedures were initially intended to achieve. See BUREAUCRACY.

goals see BUSINESS OBJECTIVES.

going concern see ACCOUNTING CONCEPTS.

going-rate pricing see COMPETITION-BASED PRICING.

gold a mineral that is used both as an industrial base metal and for ornamental purposes, and is held by governments as part of their stock of INTERNATIONAL RESERVE assets in order to finance balance of payments deficits. Formerly, in the UK and many other countries, gold coins formed the basis of the domestic MONEY SUPPLY, but gold has now been replaced by banknotes and brass and nickel coins as the cash component of the money supply. See BULLION MARKET, WORLD GOLD COUNCIL.

goldbricking a hoarding of output by employees when PIECEWORK is in operation. Employees do not declare their full daily output, preferring to hide it and then declare it at a later date. Payment for it will thus be received in the future. This enables employees to regulate their earnings over time. On some days they can take it easy but by releasing previous output to management they can achieve their usual level of pay. See QUOTA RESTRICTION.

golden handcuff a form of BONUS PAYMENT (cash or share allocation) made to retain key staff. Bonuses are not paid out immediately but at some set future date provided the person is still working for the firm.

golden handshake a generous severance payment made to an employee as an inducement to leave an organization. The phrase is also sometimes used to describe payments made to retiring employees as a sign of gratitude for their services. See REDUNDANCY.

golden hello a large lump-sum payment made to a new employee of an organization as an inducement to join it.

golden parachute see TAKEOVER BID.

good *or* **commodity** an economic PRODUCT which is produced to meet some personal or business demand. Goods which are purchased by individuals are called *consumer goods* or *final goods*, while goods purchased by businesses are referred to variously as *producer goods, capital goods, industrial goods* or *intermediate goods*.

Some consumer goods (nondurables), such as bread and toothpaste, are used up immediately or within days of purchase, while others, referred to as *consumer durables*, such as cars, washing machines and televisions, are 'consumed' over a time scale often running into several years and are often considered to constitute part of an individual's personal assets or wealth.

Producer goods are items which are purchased by manufacturers, etc. to be used as factor inputs in producing other goods or services. They too may be used up in the short term (for example nuts and bolts, engines, etc.) as the production cycle repeats itself, or they may constitute the firm's stock of longer-lasting (durable) fixed capital assets such as plants, equipment and machinery.

The provision of goods (for example, a motor car, a perfume etc.) involve a number of characteristics which set them apart from the provision of a SERVICE (for example, window cleaning), in particular *tangibility* – the ability of a customer to see, touch, taste or smell the good, and *separability* – the fact that goods are typically produced and consumed at different points in time and thus can be stored. See MARKETING.

goods (inwards) received records documents used to inform the PURCHASING and production scheduling departments that goods have arrived from suppliers and are now in the materials store or warehouse.

goods on approval products which are supplied to a prospective buyer on the understanding that they will only be purchased if they prove to be suitable to the buyer.

goodwill the difference at a particular time between the STOCK MARKET valuation of a FIRM and the sum of its NET ASSETS recorded in a BALANCE SHEET. If another firm wishes to acquire this firm, goodwill represents the premium which the buyer must be prepared to pay for the firm over and above its asset value, because of the firm's trade contacts, reputation, established BRAND names, management expertise and general 'know-how'. Where a firm has a poor trading record its market value as a going concern to a potential buyer may be less than the balance sheet value of its assets, in which case goodwill is negative.

Goodwill is an intangible FIXED ASSET and may be shown in a company's balance sheet. However, many companies write off the goodwill premium which they pay to acquire a new subsidiary company immediately against their current year's profits with the result that goodwill does not appear in their balance sheets.

governance the arrangements for managing or controlling a firm or other organization. Particular interest has focused upon CORPORATE GOVERNANCE: who owns and controls JOINT STOCK COMPANIES.

government securities see BOND, TREASURY BILL.

Gozinto chart see MATERIALS FLOW MANAGEMENT.

GP Fundholder a UK doctors' practice which was given funds to purchase healthcare services, e.g. hospital treatment for its patients. See PURCHASER-PROVIDER SPLIT.

graduated measured day work see MEASURED DAY WORK.

graphology the study of handwriting and its associations with character types. There is some evidence that certain writing styles are associated with certain character traits. For this reason graphology is sometimes used as a quasi-PSYCHOLOGICAL TEST in RECRUITMENT AND SELECTION.

green *or* **environmental audit** an examination of an organization's production, distribution and marketing activities which concentrates upon the environmental impact of these activities. Green audits can assist an organization in identifying sources of environmental pollution or excessive resource usage so that it can then seek to improve its performance.

Greenbury Committee Report see CORPORATE GOVERNANCE.

'green' consumers buyers who are influenced by environmental considerations in purchasing products. For example, a typical green consumer of petrol would favour the purchase of a lead-free brand. Pressures from green consumer groups like Friends of the Earth or Greenpeace have on occasions forced companies to adopt production and waste disposal methods which reduce pollution levels. See CONSUMERISM.

greenfield investment the establishment of a new manufacturing plant, workshop, office, etc. by a firm. Greenfield investment is undertaken by a 'start-up' (i.e. new) business and by existing firms as a means of expanding their activities (see ORGANIC GROWTH). Establishing a new plant may be preferred to inheriting existing plants through takeovers and mergers (see EXTERNAL GROWTH), because it gives the firm greater flexibility in choosing an appropriate location (see INDUSTRIAL LOCATION). It enables it to build a scale of plant most appropriate to its operations and to install modern manufacturing processes, techniques and work practices, thus avoiding, for example, various problems associated with the rationalization and reorganization of existing plants and the removal of restrictive labour practices. See MARKET ENTRY, BARRIERS TO ENTRY.

greenfield location a geographical area usually consisting of unused or agricultural land (i.e. 'greenfield') which is developed to accommodate new industrial premises, often as part of a regional industrial regeneration programme. See REGIONAL DEVELOPMENT AGENCY. Contrast BROWNFIELD LOCATION. See INDUSTRIAL LOCATION.

greenmail see TAKEOVER BID.

grievance a complaint by an employee arising out of his or her employment. For instance, a typical grievance is that a mistake has been made in the calculation of wages and that a worker has been underpaid. If not sorted out satisfactorily grievances can lead to resentment or even INDUSTRIAL DISPUTES. See GRIEVANCE PROCEDURE, DISCRIMINATION.

grievance procedure a set of rules stipulating the procedures to be followed when an employee has a complaint arising out of his or her employment. Usually they require that the complaint be formally submitted in writing, that the employee and the immediate manager attempt to resolve the problem and that, failing that, the issue be dealt with by higher levels of management. In some cases the grievance procedure forms part of the PROCEDURAL AGREEMENT governing COLLECTIVE BARGAINING. Most, but not all, UK organizations operate a formal grievance procedure; it is a statutory requirement, however, that all employees other than those in small firms be notified, in the documentation setting out their CONTRACT OF EMPLOYMENT, as to what steps they can take if they have a grievance. Employees have a right to be accompanied by a fellow employee or trade union representative at a grievance hearing. See DISPUTES PROCEDURE.

gross domestic product (GDP) the total money value of all final goods and services produced in an economy over a one year period.

grossing up the process in the UK of converting *net* of tax payments of DIVIDENDS. INTEREST, etc., into *gross* figures by adding back the tax credits attached to those dividends or interest payments. This is done in order to allow an individual investor's INCOME TAX assessment to be based on his gross income. See CORPORATION TAX.

gross margin see PROFIT MARGIN, MARK UP.

gross national product (GNP) the total money value of all final goods and services produced in an economy over a one year period (gross domestic product) plus net property income from abroad (net profits, dividends, rent and interest).

gross profit the difference between SALES REVENUE and the COST OF SALES before the deduction of selling, distribution, administration and other costs in the PROFIT-AND-LOSS ACCOUNT.

group 1 a collection of people who interact with each other, are aware of each other and see themselves as a group. Very small groups, where each member knows the others well and can interact in a face-to-face manner, are often termed *primary groups*. Those with a larger membership where individuals are unable to interact directly with all the members are called *secondary groups*. Much of the work conducted in ORGANIZATIONS is done by groups. Work groups may take the form of either a number of people undertaking a particular task, directed by a manager (see MANAGEMENT) or SUPERVISOR, or a team in which coordination of a range of activities takes place and where status is more equal. The distinction is not a hard and fast one, but groups of production workers are generally referred to as 'work groups' whilst groups of managers tend to be referred to as teams. Both are *formal groups* in that they are consciously established to achieve certain work goals. By contrast, *informal groups* are those which emerge naturally, are based primarily on friendship, shared attributes or status, and whose membership does not necessarily coincide with that of formal groups. An early indication of the importance of social groups in organizations was provided by the HAWTHORNE STUDIES and exemplified in HUMAN RELATIONS philosophy. The Hawthorne researchers found that informal groups could emerge alongside formal groups, with work norms which contradicted those of management. An earlier investigation in the research programme, however, seemed to find that a style of management (see MANAGEMENT STYLE, LEADERSHIP) which displayed an interest in workers could help collections of workers to cohere into effective groups, committed to managerial goals.

Subsequently managers have adopted a variety of means to influence the activities of groups so as to harness them in support of managerial goals. One such measure is basing pay or bonuses on group output, so as to provide a stimulus to group members to work effectively together and to pressurize recalcitrant members into following group policy. Similarly, the creation of 'semiautonomous work groups' (see JOB DESIGN AND REDESIGN) with the power to allocate group members' tasks is designed to heighten both group cohesion and commitment to effective task performance. However, a question that still nevertheless vexes managers is why some groups are effective whilst others are not. For this reason substantial research has been conducted into group development and dynamics (i.e. the stages of growth that they go through and the patterns of interaction within them). One approach has suggested that groups go through four stages of development:

(a) *forming* (i.e. getting to know each other);

(b) *storming* (initial conflict as individuals compete for leadership positions and to influence the direction taken by the group);

(c) *norming* (the establishment of shared values);

(d) *performing* (where the group utilizes its strengths to perform desired activities).

Many groups find difficulty in moving beyond the second and third stages. Team-building exercises, to encourage group cohesion, are an attempt to solve such problems. Research has shown that individual contributions to groups differ, and that in some cases they are effective whilst in others they are not. Management writer Meredith Belbin (1926–) has argued that each individual has a preferred team role and a secondary role which he or she adopts if unable to occupy his or her preferred role. These roles are *chairman* (setting the agenda), *shaper* (defining the task), *plant* (generating ideas), *monitor/evaluator* (evaluating ideas), *company worker* (organizing the group), *resource investigator* (seeking out resources), *team worker* (maintaining group cohesion) and *finisher* (ensuring deadlines are kept). On the basis of research of this type managers have attempted to influence group performance by selecting appropriate team members.

Whilst team working is generally thought to be a useful approach to achieving organizational goals, it can have negative effects. The most damaging of these is *groupthink*, where pressures towards group conformity stifle creativity. See TEAM BREIFING.

2 a collection of interrelated JOINT-STOCK COMPANIES which usually consists of a HOLDING COMPANY and a number of SUBSIDIARY COMPANIES and ASSOCIATED COMPANIES which tends to operate as a single business unit.

group accounts see CONSOLIDATED ACCOUNTS.

group discussion see MOTIVATIONAL RESEARCH.

group incentive bonus scheme a form of PAYMENT BY RESULTS in which WAGES may be supplemented by additional payments based on the performance of the work group, the establishment or the enterprise as a whole rather than the performance of the individual worker (INCENTIVE BONUS SCHEME). For example, in addition to being paid a GUARANTEED BASIC WAGE, workers in a work group could be paid a 'bonus' for exceeding predetermined production targets. See PRIESTMAN PLAN, PERFORMANCE-RELATED PAY.

Group of 7 (G7) a group of seven major countries which in the late 1980s committed themselves to promote stable EXCHANGE RATES between their currencies in order to strengthen the world economy at a time when FLOATING EXCHANGE RATE SYSTEMS were threatening to undermine world economic recovery. The finance ministers and central bank governors of the US, Japan, Germany, France, UK, Italy and Canada meet regularly to discuss financial issues affecting their economies and occasionally they act in concert to intervene in the foreign exchange market to assist a particular currency.

On some issues they convene as the 'G8' (G7 plus Russia).

group replacement a PREVENTIVE MAINTENANCE system which replaces groups of items such as lightbulbs at predetermined intervals, even though they may not all have come to the end of their life. This is done because group replacement can be more cost-effective than the replacement of individual items as they fail, if the cost of replacement units is low and the labour and other costs of replacing them are high.

group survey see MARKETING INTELLIGENCE.

group technology (GT) see CELLULAR MANUFACTURING.

'groupthink' see GROUP.

growth see BUSINESS GROWTH, ECONOMIC GROWTH.

growth phase see PRODUCT LIFE CYCLE.

GT (Group Technology) see CELLULAR MANUFACTURING.

guarantee *or* **warranty** a legally binding promise by the seller of a product to the purchaser that in the event of the product failing to work properly the seller will either replace or repair it free of charge, or refund the purchase price. Guarantees and warranties usually operate for a limited time-period from the date of purchase, though some products like cars may relate guarantee conditions to both time and mileage. Guarantees and warranties are an important means of promoting a product, in so far as they assure the buyer about the product's expected QUALITY and reliability. See CUSTOMER SERVICE, MARKETING MIX.

guaranteed basic wage the amount which a worker will receive in remuneration irrespective of the level of company output. For example, in an INCENTIVE SCHEME, should a worker's output fall short of the target set, the guaranteed basic WAGE will still be paid.

h

'halo effect' the regarding of an individual by others, especially his or her superiors, as especially good at his or her job. The reality may be different but, because the belief is strongly held, any shortcomings may not be perceived. Those employees who have the halo effect often achieve rapid promotion, with the result that their occupancy of particular job roles may be brief. Any aspects of their performance which are not satisfactory may not come to light for some time, hence the halo effect remains undiminished. However, those with this attribute often attract resentment from their more discerning colleagues. The opposite of the halo effect is the *horns effect,* where an employee is viewed badly whatever his or her actual performance. See PETER PRINCIPLE.

Halsey Plan see ROWAN PLAN.

handling see MATERIALS HANDLING.

hard currency a FOREIGN CURRENCY that is in strong demand, but in short supply on the FOREIGN EXCHANGE MARKET. This usually arises when a country is in persistent balance of payments surplus. Compare SOFT CURRENCY.

hard disk a data storage device in which data is stored on a magnetic disk embodied in a COMPUTER. Most hard disks can store large amounts of data, such as 20 megabytes of numbers or letters.

'hard sell' a forceful and robust approach to marketing a BRAND or product. This style of ADVERTISING OF PERSONAL SELLING can sometimes be successful in convincing undecided buyers. See 'SOFT SELL'.

hardware the electrical circuits and electromechanical devices that make up a COMPUTER system, including the CPU (central processing unit), DISK DRIVES, keyboard, and VDU (visual display unit).

harmonization see STAFF STATUS.

harmonization of accounts the process of reducing differences in accounting practices between countries. Differences arise because of countries' different legal and commercial systems, differences in types of business organization and their ownership, varying taxation rules and variations in the strength of the accounting profession between countries. Harmonization of accounting on an international basis has been fostered by the International Accounting Standards Committee which prepares international accounting standards as a basis for national financial reporting standards. On a regional basis, the European Union (EU) has issued a number of Company Law Directives which have prescribed the form and content of ANNUAL REPORTS AND ACCOUNTS for all EU countries, set out common rules on ASSET valuation and offered common rules on CONSOLIDATED ACCOUNTS. See ACCOUNTING STANDARDS.

harmonized consumer price inflation rate a measure of INFLATION compiled by each of the fifteen countries of the EUROPEAN UNION (EU) alongside national indices such as in the UK the RETAIL PRICE INDEX. Harmonized indices of consumer prices (HICPs) are calculated in order to provide a *common* basis for measuring inflation in the EU for comparative purposes.

Hawthorne Studies a series of investigations into workers' attitudes and behaviour conducted in the late 1920s and early 1930s at Western Electric Company's plant at Hawthorne, Chicago, which provided the empirical underpinning for the management approach known as HUMAN RELATIONS. The research programme had four main stages. In the *first* (inconclusive) experiments the researchers tested the effect of environmental factors, such as the quality of lighting, on worker productivity. The suspicion that social factors may have been an important intervening variable led to the *second* stage. Here six women were placed in the Relay Assembly Test Room and a set of changes were made to their working conditions, such as alterations to the duration of work-breaks. Somewhat oddly, output rose throughout the experiments even when conditions were restored to their pre-experimental state. The only consistent variable seemed to be the presence of the researcher in the test room. From this was derived the so-called Hawthorne Effect – that people behave differently when they know they are under observation. Human relations writing further suggested that the observer had acted as a quasi-supervisor and had stimulated a growth in output by:

(a) showing interest in the workforce and thereby increasing JOB SATISFACTION; and

(b) helping the women to cohere as an effective team.

The *third* stage was a large scale programme of interviews (about 10,000) with workers, which found that employees were more complex social beings than had been assumed in management theory to date. Following on from this the *fourth* stage involved the observation of a work GROUP in the Bank Wiring Observation Room. Here it was found that an informal policy of restricting output was in operation. For the researchers this showed the importance of group influences on individual behaviour and how this could frustrate managerial objectives.

Overall human relations theory claimed that the Hawthorne studies showed that people were social beings, who both developed and were influenced by social networks out of a need to belong to a community. The task for management was to understand these processes and to intervene to mould them in the organization's favour. Whether this is the correct interpretation of the studies is open to question. The Hawthorne studies suffered from methodological weaknesses and, contrary to their conclusions, their data provides some evidence that financial incentives rather than social pressures are the main influence on worker behaviour. See SOCIOLOGY OF WORK.

Hay-MSL evaluation see JOB EVALUATION.

headline inflation rate see INFLATION.

health and safety the regulation of organizations' working methods so as to discourage dangerous practices. It is usually understood to focus on the avoidance of accidents rather than the active promotion of good health, although the latter can form part of a health and safety policy.

Concern for safety can be worthwhile for employers, as well as for employees. Absence from work due to accidents at work is costly. Nevertheless in many firms health and safety is not given the attention it deserves, in part because the benefits of safe working conditions may only become apparent once accidents have occurred, in part because the encouragement of safe working methods can slow down production speeds.

In the UK, legislation has regulated working conditions since the mid-nineteenth century. The main legislation today is the Health and Safety at Work Act 1974. This requires employers to formulate a written safety policy, places an obligation on employees to observe safety rules, and allows for the appointment of TRADE UNION safety representatives with time off from normal duties to attend to safety matters. The Act established the Health and Safety Commission to formulate safety regulations and codes of practice, and the Health and Safety Executive (HSE) to enforce the provisions of the Act. HSE inspectors are responsible for ensuring that employers obey safety regulations, and have the right to enter workplaces to carry out investigations.

hedge fund a pool of capital which fund managers (for example, international banks) used to speculate on the foreign exchange, stock and commodity markets. Fund managers aim to make windfall profits by 'correctly' guessing future price movements. Their activities, which have become increasingly global and largely unsupervised by national regulatory frameworks, have, on occasion, served to destabilize the financial markets. See HEDGING, OPTIONS, FORWARD MARKET, DERIVATIVE.

hedging the act of reducing uncertainty about future (unknown) price movements in a COMMODITY (rubber, tea, etc.), FINANCIAL SECURITY (share, stock etc.) and FOREIGN CURRENCY. This can be done by undertaking forward sales or purchases of the commodity, security or currency in the FORWARD MARKET; or by taking out an OPTION which limits the option holder's exposure to price fluctuations. See EXCHANGE RATE EXPOSURE. HEDGE FUND.

heterarchy an ORGANIZATION without a HIERARCHY or leader. All members of the organization have equal authority and involvement in decision-making. Such an organizational form is difficult to sustain beyond the smallest organizations because of the need to coordinate the organization's activities. See WORKERS' COOPERATIVE.

H-form a form of company structure in which constituent companies are completely or partially owned by a HOLDING COMPANY. Generally such structures arise out of merger or acquisition activity. The product range, production facilities and management structures are often left largely unchanged, and constituent companies can thus be said to be *undigested*. Little direct control is exercised by the holding company other than receipt of profits. The absence of central direction is often contrasted with that in the *M-form company* but in so far as the holding company confines itself to acquisitions, divestment and simple financial control it could be said to be a 'pure' form of the latter. H-form companies were at one time a common feature of UK industry but in the last thirty years the structure and activities of many have been rationalized (*digested*) to form multi-divisional companies. See PRODUCT-BASED STRUCTURE.

HICP see HARMONIZED CONSUMER PRICE INFLATION.

hidden *or* **disguised price rise** a decrease in the quantity or quality of a good or service sold at an unchanged price. Suppliers may reduce the quantity or quality of a good in order to improve unit profit margins or contain cost increases, but need to be mindful of consumers' reactions to these moves once they have become aware of the situation.

hidden reserve the undervaluation of the ASSETS, or overvaluation of the LIABILITIES, of a firm in its BALANCE SHEET. For example, the value of a firm's land and buildings may be shown in the balance sheet at HISTORIC COST or original cost, whereas the current market price of those assets may be considerably higher. Thus, if the assets were to be revalued to reflect current market values the difference would be formally recorded in the balance sheet as an addition to capital RESERVES. See INFLATION ACCOUNTING.

hierarchy 1 any pattern of social relationships where some individuals have AUTHORITY over others.

2 the vertical structure of an ORGANIZATION. Generally there will be a number of management levels in the hierarchy with each having authority over the one beneath it. In a very small organization there might be only two levels in the hierarchy – the manager and the managed. In larger organizations the number will be greater, though it is rarely above eight. Organizations with a high number of levels are said to be *tall* whilst those with only two or three are said to be *flat*. There is an inverse relationship with the SPAN OF CONTROL. Where the latter is high, i.e. each manager supervises a large number of subordinates, there will be a tendency towards a flat structure. For the same number of total staff, a low span of control will be associated with a tall structure. See ORGANIZATION CHART, DE-LAYERING.

hierarchy of needs see MOTIVATION.

Higgs Report see CORPORATE GOVERNANCE.

high geared see CAPITAL GEARING.

hire purchase see INSTALMENT CREDIT.

hiring see RECRUITMENT AND SELECTION.

historic cost the original cost of purchasing an ASSET (such as an item of machinery). For accountancy purposes, the asset is entered in a firm's BALANCE SHEET at historic cost. However, allowance has to be made for the REPLACEMENT COST of the asset which, because of INFLATION, may well be considerably greater than the original price paid. Thus, DEPRECIATION provisions which are generally based on the historic cost of assets may be inadequate in a period of rapidly rising prices. See INFLATION ACCOUNTING, MARKET VALUE.

historical costing COSTING systems where costs and revenues are calculated after the end of the accounting period in which they are incurred. Historical costing permits the accurate calculation of costs afterwards but is of little use for forward planning purposes. Contrast PREDETERMINED COSTING.

hoarding the nonproductive retention of resources, products or money. Rather than release particular workers when demand for its products falls, a firm may retain them so as to be in a position to expand production again quickly when demand picks up. Hoarding of money may be practised by people who are reluctant to use the banking system, etc. as a repository for their savings.

holding company a JOINT-STOCK COMPANY that controls another company or companies. Ownership may be *complete* (100%) or *partial* (ownership of 50%+ of the voting shares in the company). Such ownership confers powers to control the policies of SUBSIDIARY COMPANIES. The holding company will report the accounting results of these subsidiary companies as part of the accounting results for the group of companies.

In addition, the holding company may own between 20% and 50% of the voting shares of an ASSOCIATED COMPANY, which will continue to produce its own annual accounts and retain a degree of independence, though subject to the influence of the holding company.

Holding companies are most frequently used as a means of achieving diversified or conglomerate growth, with the firm operating separate companies in different lines of production activity, but with each company subject to varying degrees of centralized control by the *parent company.* See CONSOLIDATED ACCOUNTS, H-FORM. DIVERSIFICATION.

holding cost see STOCKHOLDING COST.

holding gains increases in value resulting from holding an asset, eg, a rise in the value of factory premises caused by inflation.

home shopping see DIRECT SELLING/ MARKETING.

homeworking work performed at home for an organization or individual. Such work is usually performed by those confined to the home for some reason (for example child-care commitments) and usually involves simple assembly or packaging and dispatch, though there are more sophisticated variants (see NETWORKING). It is commonly found in the clothing industry, either for simple manufacture at the bottom-end of the market, or for creation of one-off fashion design at the top end. Payment is usually based on output, and rates of pay are often very low. Since homeworkers are usually freelance, not employees, they receive little employment or earnings protection and do not contribute directly to the social INSURANCE system. For this reason homeworking can be advantageous to those business people who place a premium on minimizing labour costs as part of a policy of competing on prices. Labour costs may be kept at a level which makes it not financially worthwhile to automate the production process on the employer's premises. A recurrent problem, however, is a high drop-out rate amongst homeworkers (see LABOUR TURNOVER). Once they are no longer confined to the home conventional employment may be more financially and socially rewarding.

horizontal integration 1 the specialization of a firm at a particular level in the production or distribution of a product.
2 the increase in MARKET CONCENTRATION arising from the ORGANIC GROWTH of firms, or, more specifically, EXTERNAL GROWTH through MERGERS and TAKEOVERS, and the subsequent integration of firms supplying the same product.

Horizontal integration may be advantageous to firms if it permits them to lower unit costs by exploiting ECONOMIES OF SCALE, and to increase their market share, enabling them to exercise greater control over market conditions. On the other hand the firm may experience DISECONOMIES OF SCALE as it grows larger and be unable to adapt quickly and flexibly to change in customers demands because it is too bureaucratic (see DOWNSIZING). Moreover there are limits to horizontal expansion as a growth strategy for the firm. Overspecialization may increase the firms exposure (risk) to cyclical and secular downturns in demand. The former causes profits to vary and can lead to cash-flow problems while the latter threatens the very survival of the firm (see PRODUCT LIFE CYCLE). The internationalization of the firm's operations (see MULTINATIONAL EXTERPRISE) can help but in many cases DIVERSIFICATION may be necessary to sustain the expansion of the firm. In addition, firms' ability to increase market share by merger and takeover may be restricted by COMPETITION POLICY. In the UK, for example, mergers and takeovers which take a firm's market share of a product above 25% may be challenged by the OFFICE OF FAIR TRADING. See BUSINESS STRATEGY, COMPETITIVE ADVANTAGE, PRODUCT MARKET MATRIX.

horizontal segregation the division of a workforce by sex or some other criteria. It is common for certain jobs in an organization to be performed solely by women, whilst other jobs at the same level are performed by men. Most female employees in the UK work only with other women. This practice has a long history due to gender stereotyping but has been reinforced by legislation aimed at tackling DISCRIMINATION. To avoid claims by women for equal pay many employers removed all males from certain occupations so that there is no directly comparable male wage. The emergence of 'equal pay for work of equal value' undermines the rationale for this practice.

'horns effect' see 'HALO EFFECT'.

hoshin *or* **hoshin kanri** *or* **jishu kanri** a Japanese term referring to the setting of strategic direction for planning and communicating QUALITY and PRODUCTIVITY goals, the purpose being to communicate common objectives and to gain commitment for these throughout the organization. The term 'hoshin' is used to describe the breakthoughs of goals that are required to be achieved to meet an overall plan. See BUSINESS STRATEGY.

hot money short-term CAPITAL INFLOWS and CAPITAL OUTFLOWS between countries which occur in anticipation of likely EXCHANGE RATE changes (devaluations and revaluations), or in response to INTEREST RATE differentials between financial centres. See SPECULATION, ARBITRAGE.

hours of work the number of hours an employee is contracted to work each week for his or her employer. See CONTRACT OF EMPLOYMENT.

HP (hire purchase) see INSTALMENT CREDIT.

human asset accounting see PERSONNEL MANAGEMENT.

human capital the notion that human capabilities may be developed along the same lines as other forms of capital (e.g. PHYSICAL CAPITAL). Education and TRAINING are key elements of the human capital perpective. An economic perspective is typically applied to the analysis of human capital, and it is suggested that there are costs and returns to investments in human capital.

human engineering see ERGONOMICS.

human factor psychology see OCCUPATIONAL PSYCHOLOGY.

human relations a concept of the MANAGEMENT of human resources based on the belief that the character of social relationships at work has a profound effect on employee performance. The task of management is to understand and influence these so as to gain employee commitment to organizational goals and to improve individual and collective performance. The main way of doing this, according to human relations theory, is for management to be seen to be taking an active interest in employee aspirations and welfare, which in turn will stimulate the development of work GROUPS which cohere well and are committed to the formal objectives of the organization.

The main architect of human relations was Professor Elton Mayo (1880–1949) of Harvard University. He based his work on the investigations known as the HAWTHORNE STUDIES, though it is debatable how far Mayo was actually involved in these. The key findings of these studies were that informal work groups which operate against the organization's objectives could emerge and that friendly supervision was correlated with steady improvements in employee performance. Mayo placed these findings in a broader philosophy of modern industrial society. He claimed that people had a fundamental 'need to belong' (more powerful than economic needs) which had not been actualized in industrial society (see ANOMIE), and they therefore suffered a sense of loss which could be overcome by the creation of a *community* at work. The Hawthorne studies, according to Mayo, showed how managerial action could achieve this: the friendly supervisor had helped workers to cohere in an effective social group.

The upshot of this is that MANAGEMENT STYLE is a key consideration in the management of people. Managers should display concern for people as well as simply getting the job done. It can be argued that human relations put a welcome emphasis on the human dimension at work. However, the concept can be criticized for its manipulative character in that it advocates that managers should mould social relationships in a way that is conducive to organizational goals. It also requires that managers stifle the expression of interests which are contrary to those of the organization. Hence human relations practice can be hostile to trade unions. Human relations has also been criticized on the grounds that it understates the influence of other factors, such as financial incentives and job design (see JOB DESIGN AND REDESIGN), on worker behaviour and JOB SATISFACTION. Despite these criticisms human relations was an important stage in the development of the SOCIOLOGY OF WORK, in that it focused attention on the role of work groups and social factors in influencing individual attitudes and behaviour. Human relations was fashionable amongst managers in the UK in the 1940s and 1950s but lost favour subsequently. It has had something of a revival recently in the guise of such management methods as TEAM BRIEFING.

See SOCIOLOGY OF WORK.

hygiene factor see MOTIVATION.

hyperinflation a very high level of INFLATION.

hypermarket see SUPERMARKET.

human resource management (HRM)

The management of people in an organization. This term for people management is increasingly preferred to PERSONNEL MANAGEMENT. Operationally, human resource management (HRM) has a similar focus to personnel management: RECRUITMENT AND SELECTION, PAYMENTS SYSTEMS, TRAINING etc.

However, HRM is often seen to be qualitatively different to personnel management. The notion of people as a resource implies a sophisticated approach to getting the most out of this factor of production. This may include the nurturing of HUMAN CAPITAL, and may therefore involve a 'people-centred' approach to management. Some critics, however, see such an approach as manipulative and 'hard-edged'. A further claim is that HRM has a closer link to BUSINESS STRATEGY than traditional personnel management, and is also more focused on achieving key business outcomes, such as profits. In some countries (though not generally the UK), HRM is contrasted with INDUSTRIAL RELATIONS, and is seen as being anti-TRADE UNION. However, some critics argue that HRM is little more than personnel management with a trendy new name.

i

ICAEW see INSTITUTE OF CHARTERED ACCOUNTANTS IN ENGLAND AND WALES.

ICAS see INSTITUTE OF CHARTERED ACCOUNTANTS IN SCOTLAND.

idea generation a systematic search for new product ideas. Idea generation may involve BRAINSTORMING, visits to other countries to seek out new product opportunities, or simply monitoring the external environment in which the firm operates. See NEW PRODUCT DEVELOPMENT, DELPHI TECHNIQUE, NOMINAL GROUP TECHNIQUE.

ideal type see BUREAUCRACY.

idle time the time during which a machine or PRODUCTION operative is not producing components or products. Idle time can be caused by machine breakdowns, delays in obtaining raw materials or components. production delays at earlier phases of the production process, worker illness or injury, or industrial disputes. Idle time leads to lost output and reduces MACHINE UTILIZATION rates.

ILO see INTERNATIONAL LABOUR ORGANIZATION.

IM see INSTITUTE OF MANAGEMENT.

image building an aspect of SALES PROMOTION which seeks to influence buyers' perceptions of a BRAND in a favourable way, thus reinforcing BRAND LOYALTY. See also COMPANY IMAGE, PRODUCT IMAGE.

IMF see INTERNATIONAL MONETARY FUND.

immigration see POPULATION.

immunities see TRADE UNION IMMUNITIES.

implicit cost *or* **imputed cost** the OPPORTUNITY COST to a FIRM of using resources owned by the firm itself to produce its output. For example, if a firm occupies a building that it owns, it forgoes the opportunity of renting it out for some other use. Thus, implicit costs represent the sacrifice of income that could have been earned by renting out (or selling) the firm's resources to others.

To achieve an accurate measure of the total cost of producing goods or services, the firm must *impute* a rent to itself using a SHADOW PRICE based upon the current market rates for renting the property. See PROFIT, EXPLICIT COST.

implied terms those conditions of employment which are implicit rather than explicitly stated in the CONTRACT OF EMPLOYMENT between employer and employee. These normally derive from common law (e.g. that employees should normally obey reasonable instructions from the employer).

import 1 a good which is produced in a foreign country and which is then physically transported to and sold in the home market, leading to an outflow of foreign exchange from the home country (visible import).
2 a service which is provided for the home country by foreign interests, either in the home country (banking, insurance) or overseas (for example, travel abroad), again leading to an outflow of foreign exchange from the home country (*invisible* import).
3 capital which is invested in the home country in the form of portfolio investment, foreign direct investment in physical assets and banking deposits (*capital* imports).

Together these items comprise, along with

EXPORTS, a country's BALANCE OF PAYMENTS. See INTERNATIONAL TRADE, IMPORT DUTY, IMPORTING, IMPORT PENETRATION.

import deposit a sum of money paid to the government by importers of a specified good on arrival of the good in the country prior to its eventual sale. Import deposits are used primarily to discourage imports as a means of protecting a country's BALANCE OF PAYMENTS.

import duty a TAX levied by the government on imported products (see TARIFFS) as a means of protecting domestic industries from foreign competition, in order to assist the country's BALANCE OF PAYMENTS and to raise revenue for the government. See PROTECTIONISM.

importing the sale in the home market of a product which is produced in a foreign country. Domestic producers may IMPORT particular materials, components and final products either because they are unobtainable from domestic sources or because foreign producers can supply an input more cheaply or supply an alternative version of the final product. Similarly, importing may be undertaken (indirectly or directly) by foreign-based firms as an adjunct to their EXPORTING operations.

In some cases locally based agents may be contracted by overseas producers to develop sales outlets and importers/distributors may be appointed to handle physical distribution. In other cases, in order to build up a stronger position in the market, foreign producers may prefer instead to establish their own sales offices and subsidiary companies to handle local distribution and marketing. See INTERNATIONAL TRADE, MULTINATIONAL ENTERPRISE, PARALLEL IMPORTING, CUSTOMS AND EXCISE.

import penetration the proportion of domestic consumption accounted for by IMPORTS. In the case of particular products the displacement of domestic supply by imports may be beneficial, allowing consumers access to products at lower prices than can be obtained from local producers (see INTERNATIONAL TRADE). Widespread import penetration across the economy, however, when unmatched by an equivalent volume of EXPORTS, can result in BALANCE OF PAYMENT difficulties, falling domestic output and job losses (see UNEMPLOYMENT). In the case of the UK, import penetration in the competitive manufacturing sector has increased substantially, imports rising from 7% of domestic consumption of manufactures in 1955 to 51% in 2004. See also STRUCTURE OF INDUSTRY.

import surcharge an extra duty placed on an imported good by the government, over and above existing rates of import duty, customs duty or tariff. Import duties are used primarily to discourage imports as a means of protecting the country's BALANCE OF PAYMENTS.

imprest a system used to control the expenditure of petty cash. An opening balance of petty cash (called the imprest) is made available to cover the petty cash expenses for the next accounting period. At the end of the period, whatever cash has been spent is replenished to restore the petty cash balance. This system tends to limit any losses, for example, via fraud, because the maximum that can be misappropriated in any one period is the imprest or opening balance.

impulse buy see PRE-PURCHASE BEHAVIOUR.

imputation system see CORPORATION TAX.

IMRO see FINANCIAL SERVICES ACT, 1986.

incentive bonus scheme a form of PAYMENT BY RESULTS whereby an individual's WAGES may be supplemented by additional payments based on achievement of output or sales targets. See GROUP INCENTIVE SCHEME, PIECEWORK, PRIESTMAN PLAN, ROWAN OR HALSEY PLAN, PERFORMANCE-RELATED PAY.

incentive pay scheme any form of PAY system which rewards an employee or group of workers in such a way as to induce increased effort or production. Such reward systems include PIECEWORK PAYMENTS which are geared to an individual's or group's effort and output; BONUS SCHEMES which provide bonuses for reaching stipulated levels of production or sales;

PROFIT-RELATED PAY systems and PROFIT SHARING schemes which provide for employees to receive a proportion of the firm's profits. See INCENTIVE BONUS SCHEME, PERFORMANCE-RELATED PAY, EXECUTIVE SHARE OPTION SCHEME, LONG-TERM INCENTIVE PLAN, EMPLOYEE SHARE OWNERSHIP PLAN, PRINCIPAL-AGENT THEORY.

income money received by individuals, firms and other organizations in the form of WAGES, SALARIES, RENT, INTEREST, COMMISSIONS, FEES and PROFIT, together with grants, unemployment benefit, old age pensions, etc. See EARNED INCOME, DISTRIBUTION OF INCOME.

income-and-expenditure account see PROFIT-AND-LOSS ACCOUNT.

income-elasticity of demand see ELASTICITY OF DEMAND.

income measurement the calculation of the PROFIT or LOSS of a firm. See PROFIT AND LOSS ACCOUNT, ACCOUNTING.

income per head see PER CAPITA INCOME.

income segmentation a form of MARKET SEGMENTATION which divides consumers into groups according to their income levels. See SOCIOECONOMIC GROUP.

incomes policy see PRICES AND INCOMES POLICY.

income statement see PROFIT-AND-LOSS ACCOUNT.

income support see SOCIAL SECURITY BENEFIT.

income tax a DIRECT TAX imposed by the government on the INCOME (wages, rent, dividends) received by persons. The government uses income tax in order to raise revenue (see BUDGET), as a means of redistributing income (see DISTRIBUTION OF INCOME) and as an instrument of FISCAL POLICY. Income tax is usually paid on a progressive scale so that the greater the individual's earnings, the greater the rate of tax which is levied, up to some predetermined upper limit (currently 40% in the UK); low levels of income are usually tax exempt (by granting individuals an INCOME TAX ALLOWANCE), while the remainder is taxed according to various *bands* of income at rising tax rates up to the upper limit. In the UK, for example, there are currently *three* taxable income bands with taxable income up to £2,090 being taxed at 10%; £2,091 to £32,400 being taxed at 22%; and above £32,401 being taxed at 40% (as at 2005/06).

In the UK, the INLAND REVENUE assesses and collects taxes on behalf of the government for a fiscal year from 6 April to 5 April the following year.

Ideally, a progressive income tax structure should promote social equity by redistributing income but also encourage enterprise and initiative by avoiding penal rates of taxation at the upper end of the scale and, together with the SOCIAL SECURITY provisions, provide suitable incentives to work at the lower end of the scale. See DISTRIBUTION OF INCOME.

income-tax allowance *or* **personal allowance** the amount of income that a person is allowed to earn before beginning to pay INCOME TAX. In the UK, for example, the personal allowance is currently (2005/06) £4,895 for a single person. In addition, older persons, widows, single-parent families, married couples and blind persons receive an extra personal allowance so that they are able to earn more before paying tax.

income-tax schedules the classification by the INLAND REVENUE in the UK of various sources of INCOME to facilitate the assessment of TAXATION liability upon an individual. There are 6 schedules lettered A to F. Briefly, the income source of each schedule is as follows:

Schedule A: land and property

Schedule B: woodlands run as a business (not now used)

Schedule C: INTEREST and DIVIDENDS from public bodies (including government)

Schedule D: trades, businesses, professions and vocations, interest received gross

Schedule E: WAGES from employment (collected under the PAY-AS-YOU-EARN system – PAYE)

Schedule F: company distributions.

There are considerable rules and regulations concerning INCOME TAX and the expenses allowable against income.

incorporation see COMPANY FORMATION.

incremental cash flows see RELEVANT CASH FLOWS.

incremental pay scale a graduated PAY scale upon which an employee's position is determined usually by a combination of age, experience and length of service. After each year of service the employee will generally be given an increment, i.e. moved one position up the scale. However, organizations are increasingly determining movement on such pay scales according to job performance.

indemnity an arrangement whereby a financial institution such as an INSURANCE COMPANY agrees to compensate a client for any financial losses suffered as a result of damage, theft or loss of the client's property.

independent inventory an inventory item that is not reliant on other units for the quantities held. Thus a final product is an independent item; the components of the item are dependent. See STOCK, PRODUCT SPECIFICATION. Contrast DEPENDENT INVENTORY.

in-depth interviews see MOTIVATIONAL RESEARCH.

index-linked (of an income payment such as a wage, or the value of an asset such as a house), connected to a PRICE INDEX in some predetermined proportion, so that, for example, if the retail price index increases, a wage payment will be automatically adjusted by the same proportion. Indexation is a means of protecting the PURCHASING POWER of an income payment or the value of an asset against erosion by INFLATION.

indirect cost see OVERHEADS, COST.

indirect exporting see EXPORTING.

indirect investment any expenditure on FINANCIAL SECURITIES such as STOCKS and SHARES. This is sometimes referred to as *financial* or *portfolio investment*. See INVESTMENT.

indirect labour that part of the labour force in a firm which is not directly concerned with the manufacture of a good or the provision of a service. Indirect-labour cost depends on the amount of remuneration paid to all those factory employees who are not directly engaged in making products but who provide support services, for example supervision and clerical work. The wages of such indirect labour are usually counted as part of production OVERHEADS. See DIRECT LABOUR, FIXED COST, STANDARD COST.

indirect materials any raw materials which, while they are not incorporated in a product, are nonetheless consumed in the production process, for example lubricants and moulds for metal castings. The cost of such indirect materials is usually counted as part of production OVERHEADS. See DIRECT MATERIALS, FIXED COST, STANDARD COST.

indirect quotation see EXCHANGE RATE.

indirect tax a TAX imposed by the government on goods and services (which is incorporated into the product's final price) in order to raise revenues and as an instrument of FISCAL POLICY in managing the economy. The main forms of indirect tax in the UK are VALUE ADDED TAX, EXCISE DUTY and CUSTOMS DUTY. See BUDGET (GOVERNMENT), EXPENDITURE TAX.

individualism the philosophy that individuals have their own unique set of wants and interests, and that they should be given free rein to pursue them. Those promoting this philosophy therefore advocate the removal of laws and regulations governing how people should behave. In the economic and business spheres, they argue, regulation stifles entrepreneurial creativity and inhibits responsiveness to market forces; if people can be freed from regulation they will become more highly motivated to succeed, whilst markets will be able to function more effectively, leading to benefits to society at large. They tend to be critical of TRADE UNIONS since they believe that unions elevate group over individual interests, and place restrictions on both their members' and managers' freedom to behave as they wish. Critics of this philosophy argue, however, that interests are in fact often shared (for example between groups of employees), that power resources are unequal and hence that collective action is therefore often necessary, and that unbridled pursuit of individual goals can damage the interests of others. See COLLECTIVISM, DEREGULATION.

individual labour law see LABOUR LAW.

individual savings account (ISA) a SAVINGS scheme introduced by the UK government in 1999 to replace PERSONAL EQUITY PLANS which allows investors to secure tax-free interest and capital gains. ISAs provide for a maximum investment of £7000 per tax year. Initially, ISA investment was limited to stocks and shares growth and income funds. More recently, under 'mini ISA' rules up to £3000 can be invested in a mini stocks and shares ISA, up to £3000 in a mini cash ISA and up to £1000 in a mini insurance ISA. In the case of 'maxi ISAs' the above allowances still apply with the exception that it is possible to invest *all* £7000 in stocks and shares. See PORTFOLIO, TRACKER FUND.

indivisibilities the physical inability, or economic inappropriateness, of running a machine or some other piece of equipment at below its optimal operational capacity. For example, because of design and technical specifications a machine may optimally carry out 4,000 operations per day, it being physically impossible to build two 'half-machines' in its stead, each performing only 2,000 operations. Given this situation, a firm requiring, say, a machine which carried out 3,000 operations per day would be forced to invest in the minimum-sized machine of 4,000 operations per day capacity. As a result the machine would be under-utilized and the unit of AVERAGE COST would be greater than if the machine were optimally employed.

Indivisibilities may pose particular problems in the context of a PRODUCTION-LINE operation where a number of processes and machines, each having different optimal capacities, may be required. Suppose a firm needs to combine process A machines capable of carrying out 5,000 operations per day and process B machines capable of carrying out 2,000 operations per day. Only by producing 10,000 units a day, employing two process A machines and five process B machines, would the firm be able to use both types of machine in a cost-effective way. Any output level below this would result in either one or other machine, or both, being under-utilized. See MACHINE UTILIZATION, PRODUCTION-LINE BALANCING.

induction the initial TRAINING an employee may receive at the commencement of employment to familiarize him or her with the workings of the organization.

induction crisis a trauma suffered by new employees where the reality of their new employment differs sharply from their expectations. A widespread phenomenon, it generally results from a failure by management to portray accurately the job and organization at the RECRUITMENT AND SELECTION stage, and from neglect of the process of initial TRAINING and familiarization. Induction crises frequently result in decisions to quit. See LABOUR TURNOVER.

indulgency pattern a term coined by an American sociologist, Alvin Gouldner (1920–80), to refer to a relaxed approach to organizational rules by both management and workers, leading to generally harmonious relationships between them. See BUREAUCRACY, ORGANIZATION.

industrial action measures taken by one or more workers either to bring pressure to bear on employers during the course of an INDUSTRIAL DISPUTE or as a response to their conditions of work and employment. Industrial action can therefore be an element of a strategy to win concessions from employers, or an expression of discontent and CONFLICT (or both). Generally the most dramatic form of industrial action is where employees withdraw their labour by going on STRIKE. There are other methods, however, many of which are less costly to employees since they do not usually result in complete loss of wages for the duration of the action. These include:

(a) the *overtime ban*, where employees refuse to work any time in excess of the hours stipulated in their CONTRACT OF EMPLOYMENT;

(b) the *go-slow*, where employees work at a slower rate than usual;

(c) the *work-to-rule*, where employees observe strictly the terms of their job description and their contract of employment, thereby requiring a greater level of direct supervision by management than is usual and restricting FLEXIBILITY.

The success of these forms of action is based on the fact that the work process usually requires a degree of cooperation and flexibility from the workforce in excess of that which can be formally embodied in the contract. Withdrawal of this cooperation can thus be an effective sanction. These forms of action are especially useful to those occupational groups who are prohibited from withdrawing their labour or who find STRIKE action morally repugnant.

A rarer form of industrial action is the *work-in* or *occupation* ('sit-in') where workers take over the running of the workplace, usually in response to a threat of closure.

Workers may also take *individual* action either as an expression of discontent or as an element of a personal strategy to improve their working life. ABSENTEEISM, where workers stay away from work, and *quitting* altogether (see LABOUR TURNOVER) are good examples of this. *Sabotage* (i.e. deliberate interference with equipment and the work process) is often seen as an individual outburst of dissatisfaction but it can also be a collective action carefully designed to regulate the pace of work.

Although attention generally focuses on action taken by workers, *employers* also take industrial action on occasions. For instance they may *lock-out* the workforce (i.e. prevent their employees from entering the workplace) in an attempt to secure concessions or to counter employee action during a dispute. A more indirect form of action is where they deliberately foster a STRIKE or other form of employee action, possibly as a way of reducing labour costs when the order book is low. See ALIENATION, JOB SATISFACTION, SECONDARY ACTION.

industrial buyer a BUYER whose function it is to acquire raw materials, components, services and equipment on behalf of his or her company. See PURCHASING, INDUSTRIAL MARKETING, BUYER BEHAVIOUR.

industrial conflict see CONFLICT, INDUSTRIAL ACTION, INDUSTRIAL DISPUTE, STRIKE.

industrial democracy the participation of the workforce in the government of organizations. Various approaches to industrial democracy provide employees or their representatives with varying degrees of power to influence decision-making processes in their organization. All, however, involve the creation of institutions and mechanisms to permit transmission of employee interests and objectives into these processes.

Industrial democracy can take a number of forms:

(a) *workers' control*, where the workforce is the sole source of authority within the organization, even though the organization might be actually owned by another (i.e. the state), and managers are required to operate to policy determined by the collectivity. This can be said to be direct form of democracy in that potentially all workers are deeply involved in the formulation of policy;

(b) *workers' cooperative*, where the organization is actually owned by the employees, and where the management (selected by and possibly from the workforce) acts in accordance with policies formulated by or sanctioned by the workforce. See WORKERS' COOPERATIVE;

(c) *worker directors*, who are representatives of the workforce who sit on the BOARD OF DIRECTORS and are involved in determining broad company policy. In contrast to other forms of industrial democracy it is not anticipated that worker representatives will have a close involvement in operational decisions. However, in the CO-DETERMINATION system in Germany, worker directors operate in tandem with works councils, which have a more substantial involvement in these areas of management. See WORKER DIRECTOR;

(d) *collective bargaining* which is a form of industrial democracy in that it involves management formally relinquishing the right to take all decisions in the organization. See COLLECTIVE BARGAINING.

These various forms of industrial democracy can be contrasted with EMPLOYEE PARTICIPATION and EMPLOYEE

INVOLVEMENT, where employee involvement is often confined to immediate job issues and where employees or their representatives have few formal rights in decision-making. See BULLOCK REPORT, SOCIAL CHAPTER.

industrial dispute a dispute between an employer (or group of employers) and one or more workers usually arising over pay and conditions of employment, allocation of work, work discipline etc. The current official definition in the UK states that it is a dispute between workers and *their* employer (i.e. not another employer) and that it relates mainly or wholly to their conditions of employment (see CONTRACT OF EMPLOYMENT). The definition excludes disputes *between* workers (thereby excluding inter-TRADE UNION conflicts). Disputes that fall outside the official definition (for example INDUSTRIAL ACTION taken by workers or trade unions in furtherance of political objectives) are not covered by TRADE UNION IMMUNITIES and hence those involved are liable to legal action by employers in the civil courts.

A large number of UK employers are party (either directly or indirectly through EMPLOYERS' ASSOCIATIONS) to a DISPUTES PROCEDURE or GRIEVANCE PROCEDURE which governs how disputes of this kind should be dealt with and resolved. Where such procedures are absent or where it is not possible to resolve the dispute in this way, some form of INDUSTRIAL ACTION such as a STRIKE may occur. Industrial disputes may be settled in a number of ways, including voluntary agreement between the parties concerned or through some form of third party intervention. See ARBITRATION, COLLECTIVE BARGAINING, CONCILIATION, CONFLICT, MEDIATION.

industrial estate a purpose-built site designated for industrial and commercial use which is separate from residential accommodation, often located on the outskirts of major urban conurbations close to motorways and other transportation systems. In the main, industrial estates offer low-cost work space for light manufacturing industries and warehouse distribution facilities. A large proportion of the investment in infrastructure and buildings is provided by local authorities. See INDUSTRIAL LOCATION.

industrial goods raw materials, components, machinery, equipment, etc., which are used by firms as 'factor inputs' in the production of other goods. See GOOD, INDUSTRIAL MARKETING.

industrial location the geographical site or sites selected by a firm to perform its economic functions. The choice of an appropriate location is influenced by a range of considerations but two are particularly important:

(a) the nature and characteristics of the industrial activity that the firm performs (for example raw material extraction or crop cultivation, the manufacture of intermediate or final products, the provision of a service) and

(b) the relative costs of production at different locations balanced against the cost of physical distribution to target markets, and the importance of closeness to customers as a basis for establishing COMPETITIVE ADVANTAGES over rival suppliers.

Some activities are highly location-specific. For example, the extraction of iron ore can only occur where there are deposits of the metal. Likewise many service activities, for example retailing, have to be located in and around customer catchment areas, while some suppliers of components may find it advantageous to operate alongside their key customers in order to synchronize better the latter's input-production requirements. The manufacture of final products tends to be more 'footloose'. Certain locations may be preferred for their production advantages, because of, for example, lower labour costs, or the availability of investment subsidies (see REGIONAL POLICY) or the supply of skilled workers and access to related facilities. On the other hand, high distribution costs, especially in the case of bulky, low value added products, or, in the international context, the imposition of tariffs and quotas on imports, tend to favour a market-orientated location. See GREENFIELD

LOCATION, BROWNFIELD LOCATION, INDUSTRIAL ESTATE, MULTINATIONAL ENTERPRISE.

industrial marketing the MARKETING of goods and services to INDUSTRIAL BUYERS. The major characteristics of industrial marketing are that:

(a) industrial buyers tend to be fewer and possess greater bargaining power than final consumers;

(b) DISTRIBUTION CHANNELS tend to be more complex, with more intermediate steps in production, wholesaling and retailing than for consumer goods;

(c) the sales force in most cases needs to have a detailed technical knowledge of the products/services in which they are dealing because of the generally greater complexity of industrial products;

(d) PERSONAL SELLING plays a greater role in marketing industrial products and sales representatives have to make more pricing decisions on discounts and spend more time demonstrating products and dealing with technical queries;

(e) the PROMOTIONAL MIX for industrial goods tends to be different from that for consumer goods, with little use of MASS ADVERTISING MEDIA and greater emphasis on PERSONAL SELLING and on targeted advertising through trade/professional journals, industrial directories, direct mail, and samples and brochures. See BUYER BEHAVIOUR.

industrial policy a policy concerned with promoting industrial efficiency and competitiveness, industrial regeneration and expansion and the creation of employment opportunities. Industrial policy can be broadly based, encompassing, for example, measures to increase competition (see COMPETITION POLICY) and promote regional development (see REGIONAL POLICY), as well as specific across-the-board measures to stimulate efficiency and the adoption of new technology; or it can be more narrowly focused involving selective intervention in particular industries or support for particular projects and firms. Industrial policy in most countries is both *reactive* (responding, for example, to cases of market failure by acting to restructure and rationalize declining industries or support failing, 'lame duck' firms) and *proactive* (acting as a catalyst for change by encouraging, for example, the establishment of new businesses and the development of new technologies). Between 1962 and 1992 the National Economic Development Council (NEDC) and its satellites, the Economic Development Committees were responsible for the formulation of strategic programmes for improving efficiency and international competitiveness.

Currently in the UK, the thrust of industrial policy is directed towards strengthening the industrial base of the economy in a number of ways, including:

(a) the promotion of greater domestic competition by attacking in particular, CARTELS, anti-competitive practices and MERGERS and TAKEOVERS (see COMPETITION POLICY (UK)), together with the privatization and DEREGULATION of state-owned industries (see NATIONALIZATION VERSUS PRIVATIZATION);

(b) the stimulation of overseas trade by the provision of back-up export support services by the DEPARTMENT OF TRADE AND INDUSTRY (DTI) and its arms, the Export Market Information Centre, EXPORT CREDIT GUARANTEE DEPARTMENT, etc. (see EXPORTING);

(c) the regeneration of regions in industrial decline by the provision of financial support programmes for firms prepared to locate in the *assisted areas*. (see REGIONAL POLICY);

(d) the encouragement of innovation and the adoption of new technologies through DTI-sponsored 'collaborative research' between industry and government/university research departments and TECHNOLOGY TRANSFER programmes, the SMART scheme, Regional Technology Centres and the activities of the BRITISH TECHNOLOGY GROUP;

(e) the promotion of vocational training, again partly funded by the DTI, together with more general initiatives to create employment opportunities. See TRAINING.

Finally, in recent years particular emphasis

has been placed on the small- and medium-sized enterprise sectors (SMEs – see BUSINESS entry) of the economy. To encourage business start-ups and assist with initial development problems, the DTI offers a LOAN GUARANTEE SCHEME, which together with the ENTERPRISE INVESTMENT SCHEME, provides financial backing to small firms. Recently, financial support has been provided for various measures aimed at encouraging SMEs to adopt information technology and E-COMMERCE. These measures are dispensed through the SMALL BUSINESS SERVICE and the BUSINESS LINK network. Grants are available for small firms undertaking new investment in areas designated as 'assisted areas' under UK REGIONAL POLICY. (See ENTERPRISE GRANT SCHEME.) See MARKET STRUCTURE, MARKET PERFORMANCE, SCIENCE PARK, SUBSIDY, INVESTMENT INCENTIVE.

industrial product see SELLER.

industrial relations 1 the general state of relationships between management, TRADE UNIONS and workforce.

2 the process of determining rates of pay and conditions of employment by COLLECTIVE BARGAINING, the institutions and procedures in which this is done, and the relationships between the key people (for example SHOP STEWARDS and industrial relations managers) involved.

Industrial relations can therefore refer to both the day-to-day relationship between workers and their supervisor and the more specialized activity of formal NEGOTIATIONS and CONSULTATION. The main subjects of industrial relations include PAY and conditions and, from the employers' perspective, achieving desired levels of productivity, in part through the enforcement of work discipline. Industrial relations problems can arise where employees believe that too much effort is required from them for a given set of rewards or that work discipline is harsh or inequitable.

Industrial relations is often also referred to as 'labour relations' or (more commonly today) 'employee relations'. Many managers prefer the latter term since it is thought to avoid the connotations of conflict and trade unionism associated with both 'industrial relations' and 'labour relations'.

Within organizations, industrial relations management is often one of the duties of PERSONNEL MANAGEMENT, although in many cases negotiation over pay is done by managers whose primary responsibilities lie outside the field. Much of the day-to-day conduct of industrial relations is undertaken by LINE MANAGERS.

industrial relations audit a systematic examination and assessment of the quality and effectiveness of existing INDUSTRIAL RELATIONS procedures in an organization. The aim is not so much to quantify precisely their costs and benefits but to determine whether they are the most appropriate for the organization's needs. Issues that usually need to be considered are the incidence and resolution of grievances and conflicts, and the structure of and approach to COLLECTIVE BARGAINING over PAY and conditions of employment.

Industrial Society a UK organization (now called the Work Foundation) which aims to promote public awareness of industry and to encourage good practice amongst managers, especially in relation to EMPLOYEE INVOLVEMENT. It has strongly recommended the practice of TEAM BRIEFING.

industrial sociology see SOCIOLOGY OF WORK.

Industrial Tribunal see EMPLOYMENT TRIBUNAL.

industrial union see TRADE UNION.

industry a branch of commercial enterprise concerned with the output of related goods or services. For example, the beer/brewing industry might be defined as all those firms that produce bitter and mild ales, lagers, stouts and elders. However, beer production might be seen also as constituting part of a wider and bigger industry, the 'alcoholic beverages industry' which includes the production of spirits and wines as well as beer. Thus, there are specification problems with respect to how widely or narrowly a particular industry is defined. Moreover, STANDARD INDUSTRIAL CLASSIFICATIONS typically group together products on the basis of their *supply* characteristics, such as the use of common raw materials and manufacturing processes. This may or may not coincide with how goods and services are grouped together to define MARKETS, which requires account to be taken also of how products are seen from the point of view of buyers (that is, their *demand* characteristics). Thus although men's and women's' shoes are produced using the same materials and manufacturing processes, and often by the same firms, they are not considered by buyers as close *substitutes*, and hence, from a MARKETING point of view, they must be treated as constituting separate markets. See STRUCTURE OF INDUSTRY.

industry-wide bargaining see COLLECTIVE BARGAINING, MULTI-EMPLOYER AGREEMENT.

inertia selling the practice of attempting to sell goods by sending them to people who have not requested them in the hope that the recipients will keep and pay for these goods. See UNSOLICITED GOODS AND SERVICES ACT.

inflation

An increase in the general level of PRICES in an economy that is sustained over time. In the UK the rate of inflation has been measured since December 2003 by a CONSUMER PRICE INDEX (CPI) in order to bring it into line with European Union practice which uses a 'harmonised index of consumer prices' (HICP) to provide a common formula for calculating inflation rates for EU member countries. Formerly the UK measured inflation rates in two main ways: the RETAIL PRICE INDEX (RPI all items) the 'headline inflation rate', and the Retail Price Index (RPIX) which excludes mortgage interest payments – the 'underlying inflation rate'. The CPI is now used to monitor the inflation rate for purposes of applying the government's macroeconomic policy in general and MONETARY POLICY in particular (see RETAIL PRICE INDEX). Fig 46 shows movements in these three indices over the period October 1999 to October 2001. Because of the distorting effects of inflation on the functioning of the economy and the harm it does to certain sections of the community (particularly those people on fixed incomes), most governments accord a high priority to the control of inflation when formulating their ECONOMIC POLICIES.

There are two main causes of inflation:

(a) the presence of excess demand beyond the output capacity of the economy to supply goods and services, which 'pulls up' prices (*demand-pull* inflation);

(b) an increase in input costs – wages, raw materials and components – which 'push up' final prices (*cost-push* inflation).

According to the monetarist school (see MONETARISM), demand-pull inflation is caused by the excessive creation of money and they prescribe strict controls on the MONEY SUPPLY as a means of reducing excess spending (see MONETARY POLICY). Likewise the Keynesian school advocates cuts in spending as the way of tackling excess demand, but in their case mainly by increasing taxes and reducing government expenditure (see FISCAL POLICY). Cost-push inflation tends to be associated particularly with excessive increases in money wage rates (i.e. wage rates greater than can be paid for by increases in the underlying rate of productivity growth) and with occasional explosions in commodity prices

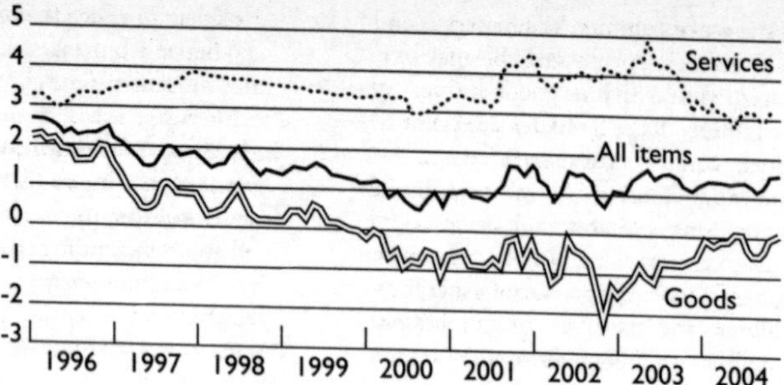

Fig. 46 **CPI annual percentage change.** Source: Office for National Statistics.

(the OPEC oil price increases of 1973 and 1979 being a case in point). Cost-push inflation caused by excessive wage demands can be modified or eliminated either directly by the use of controls on prices and incomes or more indirectly by 'moral suasion' and measures to reduce the monopoly power of trade unions.

In the past most UK governments have not formulated monetary policy with any specific inflation 'target' in mind. The present government, however, has committed itself to an annual inflation rate target of not more than 2%, and the remit of the MONETARY POLICY COMMITTEE at the Bank of England is to set official INTEREST RATES so as to achieve this target. The 'thinking' behind this strategy is that a low inflation economy is essential in order to create stable monetary conditions and thus lower unemployment. Likewise, in the European Union (EU) the EUROPEAN CENTRAL BANK (under Maastricht Treaty 'convergence' criteria for ECONOMIC AND MONETARY UNION) has set an average EU-wide inflation rate target of not more than 2%.

In general the business community dislikes inflation. It is administratively inconvenient and expensive constantly to change price lists and allow for the effects of inflation on firms' cash-flow positions and the valuation of assets (see INFLATION ACCOUNTING). A more important consideration is the effect of inflation on firms' competitive positions in the domestic and overseas markets against foreign rivals. Specifically, high rates of inflation, unless offset by compensatory EXCHANGE RATE movements, have the effect of making imports relatively cheaper and exporting more expensive, thus putting firms at a growing price disadvantage or squeezing their profit margins. See PURCHASING POWER, INDEX-LINKED.

inflation accounting adjustments to a firm's accounts to allow for the effects of INFLATION and arrive at a view of the real profitability of the firm. In a period of rising prices when the purchasing power of the money unit is declining, profit calculations based upon the HISTORIC COST of STOCKS and FIXED ASSETS are likely to overstate the real profit position. Various methods of allowing for the effects of inflation on the PROFIT-AND-LOSS ACCOUNT and the BALANCE SHEET have been tried.

One relatively simple method of inflation-adjusting a firm's accounting results is the *current purchasing-power method.* This uses a PRICE INDEX number to adjust the calculated profit figure from the profit-and-loss account, and to express it in real terms. A more detailed method is the *current cost-accounting method.* This produces a supplementary current-cost profit-and-loss account and balance sheet. In these current-cost accounts the deduction from revenue for COST OF SALES is based upon the REPLACEMENT COST of the goods sold (cost of sales adjustment); while DEPRECIATION is calculated on the replacement cost of fixed assets used and not on their historic cost (depreciation adjustment). See REVALUATION PROVISION, APPRECIATION, definition 1.

influencers individuals whose views, advice and recommendations are respected and acted upon during the making of a buying decision. Such individuals may often be OPINION LEADERS and they can provide useful market research data to a company in drawing up product specifications. See MARKETING RESEARCH.

informal organization see ORGANIZATION.

information knowledge possessed by persons and firms about products, customers, suppliers, prices, delivery terms, etc. Information has an economic value when it is scarce and is not available to all potential parties to a TRANSACTION OF CONTRACT.

Firms spend large amounts of money on product and process research and development and on market research and other forms of data-gathering in order to try to gain information to reduce UNCERTAINTY. However, firms need to balance the costs of gathering information against the value of additional information to them. See MARKETING RESEARCH, DATA PROCESSING, INFORMATION MANAGEMENT.

information agreement an agreement between rival suppliers which involves them in furnishing each other with details of their prices, discount terms, output and sales figures, profit margins etc. Although some of the information exchanged may be innocuous and could be obtained from normal trade sources (for example, rivals' prices), some data is of a highly confidential nature, and prompts one to ask why firms are prepared to disclose such information to competitors. In the UK, concern that information exchanges between competitors might well be used as a cloak for COLLUSION between firms has led to their prohibition. See COMPETITION ACT, 1998.

information highway a national or international ('super' highway) network which links up businesses and homes with information service providers (cable television, video telephones, interactive shopping etc.). Each user has a 'connection box' which links them via a cable to all kinds of services. In the case of cable television, for example, a customer connected to the highway could select a film from a large 'menu' and then receive it down the wire a few minutes later. See INTERNET.

information management the process of gathering, processing and interpreting data both from the firm's external environment and from inside the firm, generally using the information technology provided by COMPUTERS.

All business functions such as production, marketing and distribution involve both physical tasks and parallel information-processing activities. Computers, communications devices and other information technology hardware can be deployed to perform routine accounting, record keeping and order processing functions cheaply and efficiently. In addition to these basic data-processing tasks, information technology has enabled firms to collect more data than previously could be handled by the firm and subject it to more detailed analysis. This has the advantage of dovetailing production, marketing and distribution activities within the firm. In addition, greater communication with customers and suppliers through their computers facilitates closer relationships with these customers and suppliers, leading to, for example, just-in-time production and supply (see JUST-IN-TIME (JIT) SYSTEM). Such information technologies as COMPUTER-AIDED DESIGN and COMPUTER-AIDED MANUFACTURE facilitate the rapid development of new products or modification of existing products and the prompt production of such products through FLEXIBLE MANUFACTURING SYSTEMS, thereby allowing the firm to gain a COMPETITIVE ADVANTAGE by responding rapidly to changing customer requirements. See COMMUNICATION, BUSINESS PROCESS RE-ENGINEERING, INTERNET, E-COMMERCE, WORLD WIDE WEB, CUSTOMER RELATIONSHIP MANAGEMENT.

information technology see INFORMATION MANAGEMENT.

informative advertising see ADVERTISING.

infrastructure the investment by central government and local authorities in railways, roads, airports, shipping ports, schools, universities, hospitals, etc.

Infrastructure can play an important facilitating role in improving a country's industrial performance by providing, for example, a good communications network, and a stock of well-educated and trained workers, scientists and technologists.

inheritance tax a form of WEALTH TAX imposed by the UK government on a proportion of a person's private assets when these assets are transferred to the person's beneficiaries. Currently (as at 2005/06) 'chargeable assets' such as houses, stocks and shares, etc. up to a maximum of £275,000 are tax-exempt. Above £275,000 inheritance tax is levied at a flat rate of 40%. Assets transferred more than seven years before the donor's death are exempt from inheritance tax, while assets transferred between three and seven years before death are taxed at lower rates.

Inheritance tax superseded earlier UK arrangements for taxing wealth, including estate duty or death duty and capital transfer tax.

initial public offering (IPO) the first public sale of shares in a firm having newly obtained a STOCK MARKET listing.

injunction a court order issued to a person or company requiring them to desist from behaving in ways which are harmful to other people. See CONTRACT, TORT.

Inland Revenue the UK government department that is responsible for assessing individual and corporate TAXATION liabilities (HM Inspector of Taxes), and for the collection of taxation monies due (HM Collector of Taxes).

innovation see RESEARCH AND DEVELOPMENT.

innovator customer see DIFFUSION PROCESS, PRODUCT LIFE CYCLE.

input resources such as raw material, labour and capital which are used by a firm to produce goods and services (OUTPUT). See PRODUCTION

input-output control a means of managing the relationship between the amount of work or jobs arriving at a workstation (input) and the rate at which work is completed by that workstation (output). The output rate will depend upon the capacity of the workstation and the load or volume of work still to be processed by that workstation. See PRODUCTION-LINE BALANCING.

input tax see VALUE ADDED TAX.

inseparability a characteristic of most SERVICES (for example, window cleaning, legal advice etc.) that reflects the fact that they are produced and consumed at the same time and thus cannot be stored. Contrast GOODS.

insider dealing *or* **insider trading** transactions in FINANCIAL SECURITIES by persons having access to privileged (secret and confidential) information not yet available to the general investing public, and who in consequence stand to profit from exploiting this knowledge. For example, an employee of a merchant bank engaged in working out the financial details of a prospective TAKEOVER BID by a client firm for another company, might himself or through intermediaries buy shares in the target company prior to the public announcement of the bid.

In the UK, the provisions relating to the criminal offence of insider dealing are now contained in Part V of the Criminal Justice Act 1993 which replaced the Company Securities (Insider Dealings) Act 1985. In addition, the directors and the company will be bound by the Stock Exchange Model Code. See STOCK MARKET.

insolvency *or* **bankruptcy** a condition under which an individual or firm's LIABILITIES to CREDITORS exceed ASSETS. The individual or firm is therefore unable to discharge all accumulated liabilities from realizable assets. Insolvency occurs after a period in which an individual's expenditure has exceeded his income, or a firm's costs have exceeded its sales revenues (when LOSSES are made). In the UK the treatment of insolvent companies is governed by the terms of the Insolvency Act 1986. A number of possible steps are involved.

The first stage is often a *voluntary arrangement* under which the company and its creditors agree to a scheme of reduced or delayed debt payments. If it proves impossible to TURNROUND the company within a reasonable time the firm may ask the bankruptcy court to arrange for the company to be put into administration where an Administrator is appointed to try to reorganize the company and run it, and who will liquidate the company only if he is unable to rehabilitate it.

If the Administrator is successful in rehabilitating the company then it may be returned to its management. Otherwise the next stage is *receivership* where the Administrator may continue to run the company while selling assets to pay off secured creditors such as DEBENTURE holders whose loans are secured by a fixed charge on a particular asset.

Should the firm's fortunes continue to deteriorate the Administrator may have no alternative but to *wind up* the firm, i.e. LIQUIDATE its available assets, the proceeds being distributed amongst creditors. In this event the Administrator adopts the role of liquidator, whose function is to sell off the company's assets and pay back creditors.

When a joint-stock company's assets are liquidated then the proceeds of liquidation will be paid fully to firstly, 'preferential creditors' (the INLAND REVENUE for tax due, employees for wages owed etc.); secondly, other creditors (banks for loans and TRADE CREDITORS); thirdly, PREFERENCE SHAREHOLDERS; and finally, ORDINARY SHAREHOLDERS, if any funds still remain.

In the UK, under the terms of the Company Directors Disqualification Act 1986, if directors of a joint-stock company continue trading after they should have known that it was insolvent, then they can be charged with wrongful trading, lose the protection of limited liability and become personally responsible for the firm's debts. They may also be declared unfit to be directors and disqualified from acting as directors or managers of any company for up to 15 years.

Insolvency Act 1986 see INSOLVENCY.

inspection 1 the examination of raw materials, work in progress and finished goods to check that these items comply with predetermined QUALITY standards. The principal purpose of inspection is the identification of rejects, thereby ensuring that the standards set are maintained by weeding out unacceptable items (DEFECTIVE WORK). Inspection can involve examination of all items, or just a sample of items where the cost of examination is high.

2 the inspection of buildings, plant, machinery and equipment which is also necessary to identify MAINTENANCE problems which might cause machine failure and disruption to production, or inconsistent machine performance which would affect product quality. See QUALITY CONTROL, QUALITY COSTS.

instalment credit *or* **hire purchase** a contractual means of purchasing a product over an extended period of time using a

CREDIT facility provided either by a financial institution such as a FINANCE HOUSE, or by the firm selling the product concerned. An initial down payment is usually required followed by monthly fixed payments (including interest charges) for a specified period. See MONETARY POLICY, CONSUMER CREDIT ACT 1974.

Institute of Chartered Accountants in England and Wales (ICAEW) the largest of the UK bodies of professional accountants, whose members primarily undertake auditing and provide taxation advice.

Institute of Chartered Accountants in Scotland (ICAS) a body of professional accountants who practise primarily in Scotland.

Institute of Directors the UK organization representing the interests and views of company directors. Its membership is drawn especially from smaller businesses and hence its policies tend to reflect the interests of small employers. In particular it advocates reduction of those regulations governing how businesses operate, including those relating to employment protection, which are believed to stifle entrepreneurial initiative.

Institute of Management (IM) the main UK organization representing managers in general whose main aim is to improve standards of MANAGEMENT. The IM was formed in 1992 through the merger of the British Institute of Management and the Institution of Industrial Managers, and it currently has over 350,000 members. To be admitted to membership, managers must possess appropriate managerial experience and pass various examinations. See MANAGEMENT CHARTER, PROFESSIONAL.

Institute of Personnel Management (IPM) see CHARTERED INSTITUTE OF PERSONNEL AND DEVELOPMENT.

institutional investors the financial institutions that collect savings and other deposits and invest *long-term* in corporate STOCKS and SHARES, government fixed interest securities (BONDS), property and overseas securities. In the UK, PENSION FUNDS, INSURANCE COMPANIES, UNIT TRUSTS and INVESTMENT TRUST COMPANIES, together with the SAVINGS BANKS, INVESTMENT BANKS and specialized VENTURE CAPITAL agencies such as the 3i's (formerly Investors in Industry), constitute the main investing institutions. In many other countries the COMMERCIAL BANKS are major long-term investors. (In most of these countries the lack of any established STOCK MARKET and the availability of private capital from individuals was the main historical reason for their closer tie-in with industrial companies.)

Institutional investors have grown rapidly in the UK since the 1950s, encouraged in particular by tax concessions on contractual pension and life insurance schemes, and they now constitute the primary means of channelling personal savings into corporate investment. In 2004, pension funds, insurance companies, unit trusts and investment trust companies collectively owned around 64% of UK ordinary shares, compared with around 18% held by private individuals.

In the UK, the pensions funds, insurance companies, unit trusts and investment trust companies are represented collectively by the Institutional Investors Committee, which acts on their behalf in dealings with other institutional bodies such as the FINANCIAL SERVICES AUTHORITY. (See FINANCIAL SERVICES ACT 1986) and the government. See FINANCIAL SYSTEM.

Institutional Investors Committee the body which represents the collective interests of the PENSION FUNDS, INSURANCE COMPANIES, UNIT TRUSTS and INVESTMENT TRUST COMPANIES in the UK.

institutionalization of conflict see CONFLICT.

instrumentalism see ORIENTATION TO WORK.

insurance a method of protecting a person or firm against financial loss resulting from damage to, or theft of, personal and business assets (general insurance), and death and injury (life and accident insurance). Insurance may be obtained directly from an INSURANCE COMPANY or through an intermediary such as an INSURANCE BROKER/

AGENT. In return for an insurance premium the person or firm obtains insurance cover against financial risks. See ASSURANCE, COST, INSURANCE AND FREIGHT.

insurance broker *or* **insurance agent** a person or firm which acts as an intermediary in bringing together clients seeking INSURANCE cover and INSURANCE COMPANIES offering suitable policies. In some cases the agent may simply introduce the two parties to each other and receive a commission from the insurance company; or the agent may be employed by a particular insurance company to sell insurance policies on its behalf, partly on salary and partly on commission. Insurance brokers are usually independent intermediaries who are able to negotiate with a number of insurance companies on behalf of clients in order to secure for them the most advantageous cover and terms, as well as handling claims and offering general insurance advice. Most of the larger insurance brokers are members of LLOYDS, a corporation of brokers and insurance companies. Insurance brokers are regulated by the FINANCIAL SERVICES AUTHORITY in accordance with various standards of good practice laid down under the FINANCIAL SERVICES ACT 1986.

insurance company a financial institution which UNDERWRITES the risk of loss of, or damage to, personal and business assets (general INSURANCE) and life and limb (life and accident insurance). Some companies specialize in one or other of these areas, but others (referred to as 'composites') operate in both sectors. Insurance companies issue insurance policies to cover a variety of contingencies (fire, flooding, breakage, theft, death, etc.), involving potential financial loss to policy holders or their dependants in return for regular payments of a premium. An insurance company operates by pooling risk among a large number of policy holders; premiums are based on the probability of a particular event occurring and the average financial loss associated with each. This is done by the company's actuarial staff using statistical techniques to analyse past claims. For very large insurance risks an insurance company may resort to *reinsurance* sharing the insurance premium with other insurers in proportion to the share of potential claim which they are prepared to accept. In addition, many insurance companies offer contractual savings schemes (see ASSURANCE).

Insurance companies use the premiums they receive not only to settle day-to-day claims but also to generate additional income and profit by investing their funds in FINANCIAL SECURITIES, particularly UK and overseas government fixed-interest bonds and corporate stocks and shares (see INSTITUTIONAL INVESTORS). Their portfolios attempt to maintain a careful balance between immediate liquidity needs and longer-term investment returns. Life insurance business, in particular, because of its long-term contractual nature, is especially conducive to offering long-term investment returns to policy holders as well as the insurance company. *With profit* life insurance policies are now commonplace, as are *unit-linked* policies which are directly related to fund performance (see UNIT TRUST). Life insurance policies linked to the provision of MORTGAGE finance for house purchase are another innovation.

Most insurance companies are members of LLOYDS, a corporation of insurers and INSURANCE BROKERS. Insurance companies in the UK are represented by the Association of British Insurers which provides a forum for the discussion of matters of general concern to members and acts on behalf of members in dealings with other institutional bodies such as the Institutional Investors Committee and the government. The investment and management of funds by insurance companies is regulated by the FINANCIAL SERVICES AUTHORITY in accordance with various standards of good practice laid down under the FINANCIAL SERVICES ACT 1986.

Notably, also the Financial Services Act has enabled insurance companies to broaden the portfolio of services and financial products they are able to offer. Insurance companies such as the Prudential, for example, have set up estate agency chains and offer mortgages, as well as products such as personal pensions, unit trusts and INDIVIDUAL SAVINGS ACCOUNTS (ISAS). This development has introduced a powerful new competitive stimulus into the financial services industry breaking down traditional 'demarcation' boundaries in respect of 'who does what', allowing insurance companies to 'cross sell' these services and products in competition with traditional providers such as BUILDING SOCIETIES, UNIT TRUSTS etc.

intangibility a characteristic of most SERVICES (for example, window cleaning, legal advice etc.) that reflects the inability of a customer to see, touch, taste or smell the service. Contrast GOOD.

intangible fixed assets nonphysical FIXED ASSETS such as GOODWILL, PATENTS AND TRADEMARKS, which have a money value.

integrated marketing a business approach which stresses the need to coordinate all functions, departments and personnel in a firm and to harness their endeavours towards a common goal of attracting and retaining customers (see MARKETING CONCEPT).

Integrated marketing stresses how the activities of all functions and personnel in a firm have marketing implications. For example, the manner in which the firm operates its credit control procedures could win or lose customers, or customers could be put off by a poor delivery service.

Whether integrated marketing is effective depends to a large extent upon the position held by marketing in a business's ORGANIZATION STRUCTURE:

(a) if marketing is regarded as just one of a number of business functions alongside production, finance and personnel, insufficient integration will occur;

(b) if marketing includes all subfunctions from other departments which affect customers – credit control, customer service and distribution, then a fuller degree of integration will be attained;

(c) if a company fully accepts the marketing concept then marketing will be classed as the principal function, with all other functions (production, finance, personnel) being subordinate to it.

integration see HORIZONTAL INTEGRATION, VERTICAL INTEGRATION, DIVERSIFICATION, TRADE INTEGRATION, INTEGRATED MARKETING.

integrative bargaining see COLLECTIVE BARGAINING.

intellectual property right the legal ownership by a person or business of a COPYRIGHT, DESIGN, PATENT or TRADE MARK attached to a particular product or process which protects the owner against unauthorized imitation.

intensive distribution a physical DISTRIBUTION approach which seeks to maximize a firm's sales potential by attempting to ensure that its products are stocked by as many sales outlets as possible.

interaction see OCCUPATIONAL PSYCHOLOGY.

interbank clearing rate see INTEREST RATE.

interest the charge made for borrowing money in the form of a LOAN. Interest is payable on a number of short-term and long-term borrowing forms including LOANS, OVERDRAFTS, MORTGAGES, INSTALMENT CREDIT, LEASING, LOAN STOCK, DEBENTURES, BONDS, TREASURY BILLS and BILLS OF EXCHANGE.

Interest charges may be fixed or variable and payable weekly, monthly or annually depending on the size of the loan and the length of the loan period. When a loan is extended on a fixed-interest basis the rate remains unchanged throughout the life of the loan. However, in times of inflation the real or effective interest rate as opposed to the loan's agreed or nominal interest rate will fall as inflation reduces the PURCHASING POWER of money. In this case, where the lender is able to vary the interest charge, then the interest rate can be raised to offset the effects of inflation. For this reason, whereas most short-term loans are extended on fixed-interest terms, variable terms are usually applied to long-term loans.

Interest may be computed on a *simple* or *compound* basis. Simple interest is based only on the original amount of the loan, whereas compound interest is based on the original amount of the loan *plus* previous accumulated interest. For example, a £100 loan paying simple interest at 10% would accumulate to £110 at the end of the first year and £120 (i.e. £100 + £10 + £10) at the end of the second, whereas with compound interest the loan would accumulate to £121 at the end of the second year (i.e. £100 + £10 + £11 [10% of £110]).

See INTEREST RATE, APR.

interest cover *or* **times interest earned** a measure of the extent to which a firm's earnings (profit before tax) cover INTEREST payments due on LOANS. It expresses profit as a ratio of interest due.

interest rate

The particular amount of INTEREST which a borrower is required to pay to a lender for borrowing a particular sum of money to finance spending on consumption and the purchase of capital assets.

The rate of interest charged for any particular transaction will depend on such considerations as the purpose and duration of the loan, the amount of money borrowed, the COLLATERAL SECURITY offered (if any) and the creditworthiness of the borrower, all factors influencing the degree of perceived risk involved in making the loan as seen by the lender.

A number of key short-term interest rates may be identified in the UK including:

(a) *interbank clearing rate:* the rate of interest at which the COMMERCIAL BANKS lend short-term sterling funds to one another;

(b) *bill-discounting rate:* the rate of interest at which the central bank (BANK OF ENGLAND) is prepared to lend money to the DISCOUNT HOUSES in its capacity as 'lender of last resort' (i.e. if the discount houses are forced to borrow from the Bank because of their inability to obtain sufficient loans from the commercial banks to cover their TREASURY BILL positions);

(c) *base rate:* the 'floor' rate of interest which is used by the commercial banks as the basis for charging interest on loans and overdrafts to their customers. Typically, banks would charge an interest rate only slightly above base rate to large established business customers whose risks of default are small, and administrative charges low; whereas they would charge a rate much higher than base rate to, for example, a small new business.

These rates of interest (and others) are highly interrelated. The level of interest rates is determined by the forces of supply and demand for finance in the MONEY MARKET, subject to manipulation by the Bank of England as part of its application of MONETARY POLICY. Formerly, base rates etc. were linked directly to *bank rate*, and then its replacement the 'minimum lending rate', both of which were set by the government. In 1984 the minimum lending rate was abolished and from then until 1997 the government relied more on market forces to detemine interest rate levels although it did continue to 'massage' interest rates by OPEN MARKET OPERATIONS, buying or selling monetary instruments such as Treasury Bills (see REPO RATE OF INTEREST), and on occasions it intervened more aggressively to impose a particular level of

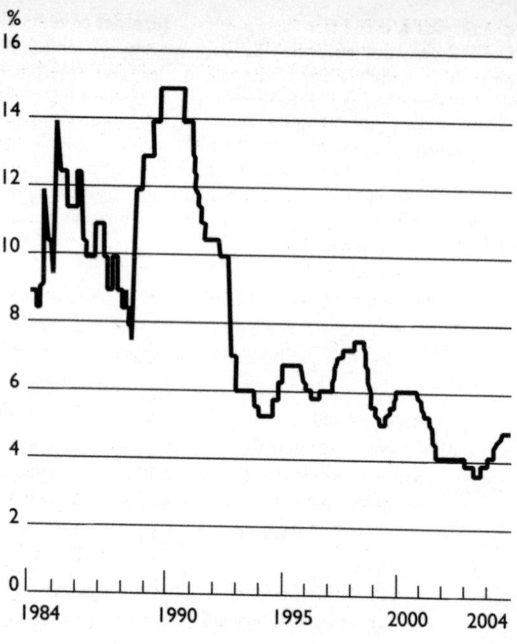

Fig. 47 **UK 'official' interest rate 1984–2004.**

interest rates on the economy. For example, the government set interest rates at 15% in late 1989 to head off an inflationary crisis and on 16 September 1992 interest rates were increased from 10% to 15% in a single day in a failed attempt to keep the pound in the 'exchange rate mechanism' of the EUROPEAN MONETARY SYSTEM. On May 6th 1997, in an unprecedented move, the government handed over the power to set interest rates to the Bank of England's MONETARY POLICY COMMITTEE whose main remit is to set interest rates so as to meet the government's 'target' rate of INFLATION (CPI) of no more than 2% per annum.

Fig. 47 shows UK 'official' short-term interest rates for the period since 1964 (currently, as at March 2005, 4.75%). See EUROPEAN CENTRAL BANK.

The rate of interest or COST OF CAPITAL is an important factor in relation to companies' investment decisions. See INVESTMENT APPRAISAL.

In a situation of INFLATION where prices are rising rapidly, it is important to distinguish between the 'nominal' interest rate stipulated in a LOAN contract and the 'real' rate of interest which allows for the effects of inflation in reducing the REAL VALUE OF PURCHASING POWER of the interest received. See APR, LIBOR, DISCOUNT RATE, SWAP.

interest-rate swap see SWAP.

interest yield the INTEREST paid on a BOND or LOAN STOCK etc., expressed as a percentage of the current market price of the bond or stock. For example, a bond offering an interest payment of £10 per year and having a current market price of £50 would have a yield of 20%.

interference allowance see ALLOWANCES.

interfirm comparison the comparison of one firm's accounting results with those of other firms in the same or similar industries. Such comparisons require the summarization of PROFIT-AND-LOSS ACCOUNT and BALANCE SHEET data in the form of ACCOUNTING RATIOS so that comparisons can be made between firms. Some industry trade associations and commercial organizations, such as the Centre for Interfirm Comparisons, operate industry-wide interfirm comparison schemes, whereby firms submit their accounting results on a confidential basis and receive in return information about their major competitors, these competitors being anonymously labelled company A, company B, etc. Alternatively a firm may use the published ANNUAL REPORT AND ACCOUNTS of competitors for comparison.

Interfirm comparisons allow a company's managers to gauge their *comparative* performance and are a useful adjunct to historical comparisons which merely look at the company's own performance over time. See BENCHMARKING.

interim dividend see DIVIDEND.

interim report an abbreviated form of the ANNUAL REPORT AND ACCOUNTS issued by the directors of a JOINT-STOCK COMPANY to SHAREHOLDERS during the accounting year. Interim reports are often prepared half-yearly to keep shareholders informed of a company's performance between the receipt of full end-year accounts. Such interim reports are not necessarily AUDITED.

intermediaries see DISTRIBUTION CHANNEL, MARKET INTERMEDIARY.

intermediate area see REGIONAL POLICY.

intermediate good see GOOD.

intermediation the role of financial institutions such as COMMERCIAL BANKS and BUILDING SOCIETIES as intermediaries in channelling funds from lenders to borrowers.

intermittent production see BATCH PRODUCTION.

internal audit see AUDIT.

internal appraisal see SWOT ANALYSIS.

internal customer a division or department of a vertically integrated firm (see VERTICAL INTEGRATION) which acts as a BUYER for raw materials, components or services supplied by other divisions or departments of the firm. The TRANSFER PRICE at which materials, components or services are 'bought' from *internal suppliers* by internal customers needs to be considered by managers; and the QUALITY standards of these items needsto be agreed. See TOTAL QUALITY MANAGEMENT.

internal financing the ability to finance a firm's growth from retained earnings. A company's NET PROFIT can be paid out in DIVIDENDS or retained for internal financing, or some mixture of these two. Generally, shareholders look for some immediate income in the form of dividends and some growth in the capital value of their shares (which depends on growth of the company). By paying out more dividends, growth is slowed. Achieving the optimum solution between two conflicting objectives is an important area of study in FINANCIAL MANAGEMENT. See COST OF CAPITAL, RETENTION RATIO, RESERVES.

internal growth see ORGANIC GROWTH.

internalization the combining in one firm of two or more related activities, as opposed to those activities being undertaken separately by different firms and then being synchronized through arms-length MARKET transactions. VERTICAL INTEGRATION where a series of vertically-related operations are combined together is the most frequent example of internalization. Internalization results from firms' desire to reduce their costs by achieving production economies in sequential operations, stock-holding economies and the avoidance of TRANSACTION COSTS in arranging contracts with outside suppliers or distributors. Security of input supplies and access to outlets may be additional considerations. (see also MAKE OR BUY, OUTSOURCING, SOURCING).

Diversified or conglomerate firms which operate in many different markets can internalize the funding of their capital investment programmes by recycling funds from some operating divisions to headquarters, which are then reallocated to other operating divisions. This avoids the need for these divisions to have to raise funds externally through a STOCK MARKET.

Internalization can also be a feature of the FOREIGN MARKET SERVICING STRATEGIES of MULTINATIONAL ENTERPRISES (MNEs); for example, MNEs may opt to replace the licensing of foreign producers and instead set up overseas manufacturing plants, the better to protect and exploit innovatory products. See DIVERSIFICATION, TRANSFER PRICE.

internal labour market a MARKET for LABOUR which operates within the organization. In other words, recruits for JOB positions in the organization are sought from within the stock of existing employees. In the 'pure' form, recruits from the labour market outside are sought for the lowest level jobs only ('points of entry'). These individuals then pass up through the organizational hierarchy, filling higher level posts as these become vacant. Economists and sociologists have discerned a long-term trend towards internalization of labour markets during which, as industrial societies and technology have developed, technology has become increasingly firm-specific. It has thus become increasingly difficult to find applicants already possessing suitable skills on the open market. The pay of employees in internal labour markets is set according to the firm's criteria and objectives. Some argue, therefore, that they are not really markets at all; the price of labour is not determined primarily by supply and demand.

The benefits of internalization stem from the individual becoming wedded to the organization by virtue of the fact that his or her skills and knowledge are not saleable elsewhere. The organization can invest heavily in training without fear of 'poaching' by other employers. A stock of skills and knowledge can therefore be built up. A potential disadvantage of internal labour markets is that the supply of 'new blood' is restricted and the organization may become insulated from new ideas.

Few organizations in the UK adopt the 'pure' form, though some have come close to it. Most modern large organizations use a mixture of external and internal labour markets. They have a number of points of entry (for example separate ones for production and managerial jobs) whilst jobs may be advertised both internally and externally, with the former often occurring first. See LABOUR MARKET.

internal market the creation of a network of divisions within an organization such as a public authority (the National Health Service for example) or a vertically integrated firm (see VERTICAL INTEGRATION), each division standing in a supplying or buying relationship with other divisions. To promote efficiency and cost-effectiveness each division may be required to operate as a PROFIT CENTRE thus imposing the same commercial 'discipline' on an organization as if it was dealing with external suppliers and buyers. See PURCHASER-PROVIDER SPLIT.

internal rate of return see DISCOUNTED CASH FLOW.

Internal Revenue Service (IRS) the United States equivalent of the British INLAND REVENUE which is responsible for assessing and collecting taxes.

internal supplier see INTERNAL CUSTOMER.

International Accounting Standards see ACCOUNTING STANDARDS.

International Bank for Reconstruction and Development see WORLD BANK.

international commodity agreement a form of CARTEL arrangement between producers in a number of countries (often organized by their governments) which operates to regulate the supply and prices of a particular COMMODITY such as tin, copper etc. on world markets.

international debt the outstanding LOANS owed by borrowing countries to the WORLD BANK, INTERNATIONAL MONETARY FUND, CENTRAL BANKS and private sector COMMERCIAL BANKS, and other lending institutions.

internationalization *or* **globalization** the expansion of a firm into foreign economies by EXPORTING, but more specifically by FOREIGN INVESTMENT in the establishment of components factories, manufacturing plants and sales subsidiaries. See MULTINATIONAL ENTERPRISE, FOREIGN MARKET SERVICING STRATEGY.

International growth provides additional sales opportunities for firms constrained by the small size of their national markets and serves to reduce their dependency on a single national market to generate profits. See STRATEGIC DIRECTION.

International Labour Organization (ILO) an organization run by the UNITED NATIONS whose basic remit is to assist in the improvement of social and working conditions throughout the world. The ILO provides technical assistance to countries with manpower training, advises governments on labour standards and work practices, and publishes regular series of international labour statistics.

International Labour Organization unemployment measure see UNEMPLOYMENT.

international liquidity see INTERNATIONAL RESERVES.

international marketing the MARKETING of a firm's products in a number of overseas markets as opposed to selling only in the firm's domestic market. In a limited number of cases a firm may be able to promote its product as a GLOBAL BRAND using the same broad MARKETING MIX format across all its export markets (for example Coca-Cola). More generally, however, differences in language, culture, laws and buyer characteristics (for example right-hand drive cars in the UK, left-hand drive cars in Europe) will require a firm to adopt a more customized approach to EXPORTING (see DIFFERENTIATED MARKETING STRATEGY). Products may have to be substantially adapted to meet foreign requirements or even new products developed to cater for those markets. The firm's marketing approach too may require significant modification to allow for differences in promotion (see PROMOTIONAL MIX) and DISTRIBUTION CHANNELS. In many cases lack of local knowledge and contacts may make it imperative for a firm to use overseas SALES AGENTS to market their products. See MARKET SEGMENTATION, ROLL-OUT MARKETING, MULTINATIONAL ENTERPRISE, FOREIGN MARKET SERVICING STRATEGY.

International Monetary Fund (IMF) an international organization established in 1947 to promote, alongside the General Agreement on Tariffs and Trade (now the WORLD TRADE ORGANIZATION), the expansion of INTERNATIONAL TRADE in a way consistent with the maintenance of BALANCE OF PAYMENTS equilibrium by individual member countries. This has involved the Fund in negotiating the removal of restrictions (such as FOREIGN EXCHANGE CONTROLS) on the convertibility of currencies, the establishment of 'orderly' EXCHANGE RATES between members' currencies and the provision of borrowing facilities and INTERNATIONAL RESERVES to members in balance of payments difficulties.

Up to the 1970s the IMF supervized a FIXED EXCHANGE RATE SYSTEM and established 'fixed' pivotal values for members' currencies for concluding trade and capital transactions. Countries could devalue or revalue their currency to a new fixed rate when their balance of payments situation warranted it, subject to Fund negotiation and approval. This procedure ensured that currency realignments were decided by multilateral agreement rather than initiated as a unilateral act. In the early 1970s, however, with a continued weakening of the US dollar, the pivotal currency in the Fund's operations, and the onset of a world recession, a large number of currencies were 'floated' to provide a greater degree of exchange rate flexibility (see FLOATING EXCHANGE RATE SYSTEM). As a result of these developments the Fund has lost formal control over exchange rate movements, but member countries are still obliged, in theory, to maintain orderly exchange rates, avoiding in particular the manipulation of their exchange rates to disadvantage trade partners.

The Fund's resources consist of a pool of foreign currencies (see FOREIGN EXCHANGE) and international reserve assets (excluding gold, however) subscribed by its members. Each country is allocated a 'subscription quota', weighted according to its economic status, and is required to pay 75% of its quota in its own currency and the remainder in international reserve assets. Included in the Fund's stock of reserve assets is the SPECIAL DRAWING RIGHT (SDR) unit, an asset which the Fund itself creates and holds in the form of a book-keeping entry (i.e. unlike currencies, SDRs have no tangible life of their own), and which is valued in terms of a weighted average of five major currencies. Countries needing extra resources over and above their own nationally-held reserves to finance a balance of payments deficit may borrow (i.e. exercise their 'drawing rights' on) the currencies they require from the Fund. A substantial proportion of these borrowings, however, are subject to the Fund's 'conditionality' rules, whereby the Fund stipulates the measures a member must implement to remove its payments deficit. Borrowings are normally required to be repaid within three to five years, but the INTERNATIONAL DEBT problem has not only forced the Fund to 'roll-over' credits but has led to the establishment of various new facilities to accommodate its poorer members. See GROUP OF 7.

international reserves *or* **international liquidity** monetary assets that are used to settle BALANCE OF PAYMENTS deficits between countries; specifically, GOLD, certain FOREIGN CURRENCIES (particularly the US dollar, the EURO, Swiss franc and Japanese yen), INTERNATIONAL MONETARY FUND 'Drawing Rights' and 'Special Drawing Rights'.

International Standard see ISO 9000.

International Standardization Organization (ISO) a body which produces international standards for products and processes. The ISO seeks to produce standards which harmonize national standards established by individual countries. In designing products and processes firms must generally meet the QUALITY, performance and safety standards laid down by the ISO if their products and processes are to be acceptable to consumers. See BRITISH STANDARDS INSTITUTION, ISO 9000.

international trade

Cross-frontier trade between countries in goods and services, with differences between countries in their COMPETITIVE ADVANTAGES (or 'comparative advantages') to supply particular products providing the basis of an international division of labour (location of production) and an associated flow of EXPORTS and IMPORTS between countries. International trade can bring both consumption and production gains to a country, serving to raise its living standards and improve its productive efficiency. International trade enables countries to consume some goods and services more cheaply by importing them, and also to obtain some resources and products from other countries which would otherwise be totally unavailable because domestic producers are unable to supply them (for example a scarce raw material or high-technology product). International trade promotes productive efficiency by encouraging a reallocation of resources away from areas of the economy best served by imports into industries where the country itself has a comparative advantage over trade partners.

Inter-country variations in comparative advantage are reflected both in terms of their differential cost structures (i.e. price competitiveness) and different skill levels (i.e. product differentiation competitiveness). These, in turn, are determined in large measure by the country's basic factor endowments (natural resources, labour and capital) and degree of economic maturity (level of per capita income, general cost and price levels, scientific and technical skills, etc.). Resource availability and skills indicate the product range which a country is technically capable of supplying, while *relative* cost, price and product differentiation factors dictate which of these products it is economically appropriate for the country to produce, i.e. those products in which it has a comparative advantage over other countries.

In its more simplified form, a two country – two product world economy, the theory of comparative advantage generates the following international production and trade relationship: assuming country A is well endowed with cheap labour and country B is well endowed with capital (capital is cheap relative to labour), and that product X is labour-intensive and product Y is capital-intensive, then country A will have a comparative advantage over B in the production of X, while country B will have a comparative advantage over A in the production of Y. It follows that both countries stand to gain from SPECIALIZATION and trade: country A produces X and exports some of it in exchange for imports of Y, while country B produces Y and trades some of it for imports of X.

A basic assumption of this presentation is that factor endowments, and hence comparative advantages, are 'fixed'. Dynamically, however, comparative advantage may well change. It may do so in response to a number of influences including:

(a) the initiation by a country's government of structural programmes leading to resource redeployment. For example, a country which seemingly has a comparative advantage in the supply of primary products such as cotton and wheat may nevertheless abandon or de-emphasize it in favour of a drive towards industrialization and the establishment of comparative advantage in higher value-added manufactured goods;

(b) international capital movements and technology transfer, and relocation of production by MULTINATIONAL ENTERPRISES. For example, Malaysia developed a comparative advantage in the production of natural rubber only after UK entrepreneurs established and invested in rubber tree plantations there.

Consideration of the benefits of international trade suggests that the optimization of such benefits is best achieved by conditions of FREE TRADE (i.e. the absence of restrictions on trade such as TARIFFS and QUOTAS), a view given operational validity by the international community by the establishment of the WORLD TRADE ORGANIZATION and the formation of various regional free trade blocs (see TRADE INTEGRATION). In practice, however, the benefits of international trade are often unequally divided between countries, and this inevitably tends to produce situations where national self-interest is put before international obligations.

In 2004 the USA was the world's leading exporter accounting for 10.7% of world goods exports, followed by Germany 9.5%, Japan 6.5%, France 5.1% and the UK 4.3%. The USA was also the world's leading importer accounting for 18.0% of the world's goods imports, followed by Germany 7.4%, Japan 5.2%, UK 5.0% and France 4.9%. See PROTECTIONISM, FOREIGN CURRENCY, FOREIGN EXCHANGE MARKET, BALANCE OF PAYMENTS, DUMPING, IMPORTING, PARALLEL IMPORTING, COUNTERTRADE, EMBARGO.

Internet a global 'web' of COMPUTER networks which use the same agreed 'protocols' (agreed methods of communication). The WORLD WIDE WEB (www or 'the web') is a vast collection of computers able to support multi-media formats and accessible via web-browsers' (search and navigation tools). Data stored in these computers ('servers') is organized into pages with hypertext links, each page having a unique address.

Connection to the web usually requires access to a personal computer, a modem and a telephone line, although it is now possible to receive television-based Internet services.

The Internet is increasingly used by businesses for the conduct of electronic commerce (E-COMMERCE, for short), and has thus provided a new powerful alternative means to conventional distribution channels of selling goods. See MARKET.

In 2004 around 9 million households in the UK owned personal computers with some 7 million of these using the Internet. The number of people worldwide using the Internet is estimated at 300 million and rising rapidly. See CUSTOMER RELATIONSHIP MANAGEMENT.

interstage store a work in progress STORE located between two production departments which serves to minimize production delays (IDLE TIME) by providing adequate levels of inter-process STOCKS.

intrapreneurial group a group of employees within an organization who are encouraged to act as ENTREPRENEURS by 'selling' their goods and services in competition with other groups, to other groups or departments within the organization. No real money necessarily changes hands. Instead notional payments may be made and received. However, they may seek contracts with other organizations. The allocation of work within the group can be determined by members of the group. The potential benefits of this form of organization are that by providing profit incentives and facilitating identification of individual and group output, employee motivation is increased, while inter-group competition can keep costs down. On the negative side, the encouragement of sectional interests could harm those of the organization as a whole.

Variants of this idea have been popular in the UK in recent years. Many organizations have pushed responsibility for profits down to as low a level as possible in the organization (see STRATEGIC BUSINESS UNIT), whilst many have developed the use of notional transfer payments between departments so as to identify and control the costs of activities. This can be particularly relevant to the work of those service departments (such as personnel) whose contribution to the 'bottom-line' is otherwise difficult to quantify.

introduction a method of raising new SHARE CAPITAL by issuing company shares at an agreed price to STOCKBROKERS and MARKET MAKERS rather than to the general public. Introductions are usually employed by established companies as a means of raising new capital with less administrative expense than other forms of SHARE ISSUE.

introduction phase see PRODUCT LIFE CYCLE.

invention see RESEARCH AND DEVELOPMENT.

inventory the STOCKS of finished goods, WORK IN PROGRESS and raw materials held by businesses. See INVENTORY INVESTMENT, STOCKHOLDING COSTS.

inventory control see STOCK CONTROL.

inventory investment the INVESTMENT in raw materials, WORK IN PROGRESS and finished STOCK. In contrast to FIXED INVESTMENT, inventories are constantly being 'turned over' as the production cycle repeats itself, with raw materials being purchased, converted first into work in progress, then into finished goods, then finally being sold.

The level of inventory investment made by a firm will depend upon its forecasts about future demand and its resulting output plans, and the amount of stock it needs to allow for delivery delays on raw materials and production delays in serving customers with appropriate buffer stocks to cover unforeseen contingencies. Frequently firms find that actual levels of demand differ from their forecasts, so that demand is less than expected and firms find that stocks of unsold goods build up (unintended inventory investment); or that demand exceeds expectations so that stocks run down (unintended inventory disinvestment). The cost of inventory investment includes order and delivery costs, deterioration and obsolescence of stock and interest charges on funds invested in stock. Firms seek to minimize these costs by establishing economic order quantities and optimum stockholding levels. See STOCKHOLDING COSTS.

Invest in Britain Bureau see INVEST UK.

investment 1 *physical* or real investment: capital expenditure on the purchase of assets such as plant, machinery and equipment (FIXED CAPITAL assets) and STOCKS or INVENTORY (WORKING CAPITAL assets). Fixed capital investment is undertaken by firms, both to replace worn-out and obsolete capital items (see DEPRECIATION) and to increase the firm's total assets (see CAPITAL EMPLOYED), so as to enable it to produce a greater volume of products, and, by investing in the latest technology, to remain competitive. In aggregate terms, net additions to the country's CAPITAL STOCK increase the economy's productive capacity, thus making an important contribution to the achievement of higher rates of ECONOMIC GROWTH and improved living standards.

2 *financial* investment: expenditure on the purchase of financial securities such as SHARES and BONDS. PORTFOLIO investment is undertaken by individuals, companies and financial institutions as a means of earning income in the form of dividend, interest and rent payments and through capital appreciation. See CAPITAL ALLOWANCES, ENTERPRISE INVESTMENT SCHEME, ENTERPRISE GRANT SCHEME, STOCK MARKET, FINANCIAL SYSTEM, FOREIGN INVESTMENT, SAVINGS, INVESTMENT INCENTIVE, INVESTMENT APPRAISAL, ACCOUNTING RETURN, PAYBACK METHOD, DISCOUNTED CASH FLOW.

investment bank a BANK which accepts deposits of money from savers and which specializes in investments in SHARE CAPITAL and the provision of LOAN finance for corporate borrowers (see VENTURE CAPITAL). Increasingly the leading investment banks are obtaining the greater part of their revenue from consultancy and advisory services to corporate clients; for example, in the recent £20bn takeover by Hewlett Packard of Compaq Computers (creating the world's largest PC maker), the former was advised by Goldman Sachs and the latter by Citigroup's Salomon Smith Barney arm (both in the USA). See BANKING SYSTEM, MECHANT BANK.

investment appraisal

The process of evaluating the desirability of INVESTMENT proposals covering such things as the replacement of worn-out plant and machinery, the establishment of a new factory, the takeover of another company, new product development or a sales promotion campaign.

Generally the desirability of an investment will be considered in terms of the PROFIT it will yield and managers will prefer those investments which promise the largest profit. Alternatively, they could measure the CASH FLOW associated with a project, and award priority to projects which promise the best contribution towards future cash flows. In making investment decisions managers will undertake investments which promise a rate of return greater than the cost of capital needed to finance it.

There are several techniques which can be used to assess investment opportunities, some based upon accounting profit measures, others upon cash flows. These methods include the ACCOUNTING RETURN, PAYBACK PERIOD and DISCOUNTED CASH FLOW.

investment centre an organizational subunit of a firm which is fully independent with full control over its costs and revenues (that is, a PROFIT CENTRE) but which also has responsibility for raising capital and for long-term investment.

investment grant see INVESTMENT INCENTIVE.

investment incentive a financial inducement given by the government to a firm as a means of encouraging new INVESTMENT. Such inducements can include cash grants to defray part of the costs of building a new factory and/or installing new machines and equipment; low interest rates; interest-free LOANS; or tax relief on the firm's profits. Investment incentives can be used to stimulate investment in general, or they can be targeted to encourage certain types of investment and to influence the geographical location of new investment. See CAPITAL ALLOWANCE, INDUSTRIAL POLICY, REGIONAL POLICY, SUBSIDY, ENTERPRISE INVESTMENT SCHEME, ENTERPRISE GRANT SCHEME.

investment income income which a company derives from TRADE INVESTMENTS rather than normal trading activities.

Investment Management Regulatory Organization (IMRO) see FINANCIAL SERVICES ACT 1986.

investment ratios ratios which are used to assess the performance of a company's shares, for example, PRICE EARNINGS RATIO, EARNINGS PER SHARE and EARNINGS YIELD. In addition to being of great interest to the ordinary shareholders, investment ratios are also of interest to potential investors, analysts and competitors.

investment trust company a financial institution which issues its own shares to the investing public and which specializes in investment in FINANCIAL SECURITIES, mainly UK and overseas corporate stocks and shares and government fixed-interest securities. They tend to be attractive to smaller investors who wish to secure a wider spread of risk than they could achieve for themselves by direct investment in a limited number of securities, or who require professional management of their investments.

Investment trust company shares are bought and sold on the STOCK MARKET so that, like other securities, their prices can go up or down reflecting general stock market price trends, but more particularly the company's own performance. Investment trust companies vary in the portfolios they put together and the expertise with which they are managed, so that the portfolio performance of different companies has varied from mediocre to excellent over the years.

In recent years most investment trust company shares have traded at a substantial DISCOUNT on their asset values (i.e. asset backing per share), partly reflecting small investors' preference for UNIT TRUSTS as an alternative investment medium.

Investment trust companies in the UK are represented by the Association of Investment Trust Companies (AITC), which provides a forum for the discussion of matters of general concern to members, and acts on behalf of members in dealings with other institutional bodies such as the Institutional Investors Committee and the government. The investment and management of funds by investment trust companies is regulated by the FINANCIAL SERVICES AUTHORITY in accordance with various standards of good practice laid down under the FINANCIAL SERVICES ACT 1986. See INSTITUTIONAL INVESTORS, FINANCIAL SYSTEM, PORTFOLIO.

investor a person, company or institution which uses either its own SAVINGS or LOAN finance to acquire financial and physical assets such as SHARES and BONDS, factories and offices, etc. See INVESTMENT, FINANCIAL SYSTEM.

Investors in People a recent UK government initiative to encourage ORGANIZATIONS to train their workforces. Those registering with the initiative are assisted to undertake a systematic analysis of BUSINESS STRATEGY and the training needs that result from this (see TRAINING). The organization is required to design and implement training programmes to meet these needs, and to agree personal training and development programmes with each employee, linked to the achievement of NATIONAL VOCATIONAL

QUALIFICATIONS where possible. The extent to which the organization meets the training targets set is assessed by external assessors, and those found to have met them are given an Investors in People award.

Invest UK a government body which seeks to promote FOREIGN DIRECT INVESTMENT in the UK by publicising the general attractiveness of the UK as a host country and by advising and assisting companies to find suitable locations.

invisible assets see INTANGIBLE FIXED ASSETS.

invisible export see EXPORT, BALANCE OF PAYMENTS.

invisible import see IMPORT, BALANCE OF PAYMENTS.

invoice a document sent by a supplier to a customer that itemizes the products supplied to the customer, their prices, and the total amount of money owed by the customer for these products. An invoice is usually sent after the products have been shipped with their associated DELIVERY NOTE, and serves to inform the customer that payment is required. See STATEMENT OF ACCOUNT.

invoice factoring see FACTORING.

inward investment see CAPITAL INFLOW, FOREIGN INVESTMENT, FOREIGN DIRECT INVESTMENT.

IPM see INSTITUTE OF PERSONAL MANAGEMENT.

irregular variations see SALES FORECASTING.

IRS see INTERNAL REVENUE SERVICE.

ISA see INDIVIDUAL SAVINGS ACCOUNT.

Ishikawa chart see FISHBONE CHART.

ISO see INTERNATIONAL STANDARDIZATION ORGANIZATION.

ISO 9000 a QUALITY standard drawn up by the INTERNATIONAL STANDARDIZATION ORGANIZATION. ISO 9000 is identical to the BRITISH STANDARDS INSTITUTION's quality standard BS 5750. To obtain certification a supplier is required to establish, document and maintain an effective and economical quality system.

isolating mechanisms see MOBILITY BARRIER.

issued share capital the amount of its AUTHORIZED SHARE CAPITAL that a JOINT-STOCK COMPANY has issued to SHAREHOLDERS in order to raise CAPITAL. This amount is disclosed in the company's BALANCE SHEET.

Issued share capital shows the initial investments made by shareholders in the company, though this investment is often increased to the extent that profits are retained in the firm and added to RESERVES rather than all being distributed as dividends. The market value of the issued share capital can differ considerably from its PAR VALUE, since market values depend upon the price at which issued shares are currently being sold on the STOCK MARKET.

issue price the price at which a SHARE or DEBENTURE is issued, which is not necessarily equal to its PAR VALUE (see SHARE PREMIUM).

issuing house a division of a MERCHANT BANK or similar organization that arranges and UNDERWRITES the issue of new STOCKS and SHARES on behalf of corporate clients, for an agreed fee. See SHARE ISSUE.

J

Japanization the adoption by organizations elsewhere of work organization and employment practices usually found in large Japanese companies. See QUALITY CIRCLE, JUST-IN-TIME (JIT) SYSTEM/TOYOTA PRODUCTION SYSTEM, KANBAN, KAIZAN, JIDOKA, KEIRETSU, HOSHIN, FIVE S, SEVEN WASTES, SINGLE MINUTE EXCHANGE OF DIES, SINGLE UNION DEALS, ENTERPRISE UNION (see TRADE UNION entry), NO-STRIKE AGREEMENT.

Jidoka a Japanese term used to describe the stopping of a process if an error is detected either in the process or in the product. Based in part on team working and empowerment, the application of the Jidoka allows an employee to stop a process, so that the error can be analysed and corrected so that it does not occur again. The process will then be restarted. See QUALITY, LEAN MANUFACTURING, JUST-IN-TIME (JIT) SYSTEM.

JIT see JUST-IN-TIME (JIT) SYSTEM.

job 1 a work task or series of work tasks to be performed. For factory operatives the work tasks are often clearly defined as a specific set of machining or assembly operations. By contrast, at senior management level, work tasks are less clearly defined and managers have more discretion as to the range of tasks to be performed and how they are performed.
2 a unit of good or service for which costs can be ascertained. The job or cost unit could consist of a single order. Alternatively, the job or cost unit could be a batch or group of identical products passing together through production.

job analysis a process of research to identify the tasks comprising a particular JOB and to determine whether they could be organized in a more productive or satisfying way. It is preferable not to analyse individual jobs in isolation but to examine the workflow in its entirety, since tasks could potentially be usefully shifted from one person or job to another. Job analysis can be carried out by simple observation of the workflow or by more scientific scrutiny (see WORK STUDY), and can make use of interviews with job holders. It can form the first step in compiling a list of job characteristics (job specification) for the RECRUITMENT AND SELECTION process or for investigating whether a different JOB DESIGN is feasible.

jobbing the function of buying and selling FINANCIAL SECURITIES such as STOCKS. SHARES and BONDS on the STOCK MARKET by a dealer who acts as a principal in 'making a market' in these securities. See MARKET MAKER.

jobbing production see PRODUCTION.

job card a document which records the materials and direct labour cost of a job. These ledger records collect data from MATERIALS REQUISITIONS and TIME SHEETS to ascertain the cost of a job.

job centre a government office, part of a national network of such offices operated by the Employment Service of the DEPARTMENT FOR WORK AND PENSIONS, where UNEMPLOYED persons can register as seeking work and where employers can notify job VACANCIES. Thus, job centres play a valuable role in facilitating the smooth functioning of the LABOUR MARKET. See JOBSEEKERS ALLOWANCE.

job costing see PRODUCT COSTING.

job description a statement of the work tasks which constitute a JOB and the responsibilities of the employee in performing that job. Job descriptions usually form part of an employee's CONTRACT OF EMPLOYMENT.

job design and redesign the process or outcome of grouping together work tasks to form individual JOBS. Jobs may comprise a single or small number of tasks (for example repetitive production work on an assembly line) or a considerable range (for example the job of a manager). Some jobs involve substantial decision-making whilst others require very little.

Job design is often said to have two main dimensions – SPECIALIZATION and discretion. The key questions facing the job designer are: how specialized a set of tasks should the individual perform? and how far should the individual decide which tasks are to be undertaken at a given moment and in what way? As regards the latter, it has been suggested that jobs could be categorized according to a TIME SPAN OF DISCRETION: the length of time that passes before a worker's task performance is checked and assessed by a superior.

Job design has an important effect on JOB SATISFACTION. Those jobs which are highly specialized and which involve little discretion often give rise to dissatisfaction, which may find expression in CONFLICT, INDUSTRIAL DISPUTES, ABSENTEEISM and LABOUR TURNOVER. Although specialization can be viewed as an efficient approach to job design these side-effects can lead to low levels of PRODUCTIVITY. To enhance job satisfaction and productivity some analysts have advocated job redesign. Most notable is the Quality of Working Life (QWL) movement, a loose-knit body of academics, managers and trade unionists, which from the 1970s onwards advocated sweeping changes to prevailing patterns of job design.

The changes recommended include:

(a) *job enlargement,* where additional tasks are given to the worker so as to provide more variety. In other words it is the horizontal expansion of the tasks;

(b) *job enrichment,* where workers are given greater scope in deciding how the tasks should be performed. Here the range of tasks is extended vertically, to enrich the quality of the job for the worker;

(c) *job rotation,* where workers rotate around the jobs in their department on a regular basis, on the grounds that greater variety will lead to greater job satisfaction.

As can be seen, these changes involve modification to the key dimensions of specialization and discretion. A more radical approach still is the creation of semi-autonomous work groups. Here workers are allowed to decide amongst themselves how to distribute and execute work tasks. This could involve replacing assembly-line working, where each individual performs an allotted task in a pre-planned series of tasks, by group working where who does what could be decided on a day-to-day basis. See FORDISM, SCIENTIFIC MANAGEMENT, WORK ORGANIZATION, AUTONOMOUS WORK TEAMS.

job enlargement see JOB DESIGN AND REDESIGN.

job enrichment see JOB DESIGN AND REDESIGN.

job evaluation a set of procedures to assess the relative worth of groups of jobs in an organization so as to place them in a rank order. This can then provide the basis of a grading and pay structure. Job evaluation is more widely used for assessing managerial and white-collar rather than blue-collar jobs but its use amongst the latter has been growing steadily in recent years. The primary advantage of job evaluation is that it puts differences in rates of pay between jobs on a systematic footing. By so doing the rationale for pay differences can be clearly shown. It is generally recommended that only broadly similar jobs (job family) be evaluated in a particular exercise, i.e. manual and managerial jobs are too different to be meaningfully evaluated together. It is also recommended that trade union representatives be fully involved (where TRADE UNIONS are present) in the evaluation to ensure that the eventual ranking is accepted as fair.

There are a number of different ways of conducting job evaluation:

(a) *Non-analytic:* these approaches do not break jobs into constituent factors but compare 'whole' jobs.

(i) *job ranking.* Here jobs are simply placed in an order on the basis of the content of job description that is felt to be fair by the evaluators.

(ii) *paired comparisons.* Here each job is compared with each other job and points are awarded for the comparative importance in each case. The total number of points for each job provides the basis for the rank order.

(iii) *job classification.* In this case the number and definition of grades are produced first, and then jobs are allocated to these grades according to the degree of 'fit' between job description and grade definition.

(b) *Analytic:* in approaches of this sort jobs are broken down into their core factors, such as degree of skill, responsibility, etc. and are then compared on the basis of these.

(i) *factor comparison.* Various facets of jobs, such as skill and responsibility, are considered and each is given a ranking. Jobs are then compared, factor by factor, to provide a grading structure.

(ii) *points rating.* The factors in each job are given a points score based on the importance of the factor relative to the others. The points for each factor are totalled for each job to produce a final rank order.

(iii) *Hay-MSL Evaluation.* This is a variant of the points rating system used for evaluating managerial jobs. The amount of knowledge, problem-solving and responsibility involved in each job is assessed, and each factor compared against the other to produce a final ranking.

The analytic approaches are plainly more rigorous than the non-analytic. Even these, however, cannot eliminate subjectivity. Job evaluators have to make decisions on the scores for each factor that can never be fully objective. Any score will inevitably involve an element of judgement. However, analytic job evaluation does enable jobs to be compared in a systematic and consistent way. Now that equal pay for men and women should be based on work of equal value, job evaluation free of sex bias is especially important. Those operating job evaluation schemes have to ensure that sexual discrimination does not enter into the ranking of jobs. The courts have decided that only analytic schemes may be used as a defence in an equal pay for equal value claim (see DISCRIMINATION). Where such a claim is made, the techniques of job evaluation are used to assess whether it is justified.

job grading see JOB EVALUATION.

job redesign see JOB DESIGN AND REDESIGN.

job rights the rights which employees may claim as theirs by virtue of performing a certain JOB. These may be an amalgam of their work conditions as laid down in a CONTRACT OF EMPLOYMENT: statutory rights, customary duties and benefits associated with a particular job. A good example of job rights is that of the (now abolished) Dock Labour Scheme: registered dockers were paid a wage even when there was no work available. Assertion of job rights is often a method of defence when managers seek to reorganize some aspect of work and employment.

job rotation see JOB DESIGN.

job satisfaction the satisfaction that an individual gains (or does not gain) from his or her job. It is generally believed that satisfied employees will be more highly motivated and will work more productively than dissatisfied employees. Job dissatisfaction may lead to ABSENTEEISM, LABOUR TURNOVER, INDUSTRIAL ACTION, etc.

The study of job satisfaction and its determinants has traditionally formed an important component of the SOCIOLOGY OF WORK. HUMAN RELATIONS writers argued that job satisfaction could be encouraged by managerial policies and practices that encouraged a sense of belonging. The rationale for this is that (in their view) people want to belong to a community: by experiencing a community at work workers will feel satisfaction in their work (see ANOMIE). More commonly, technology has been viewed as an important casual factor in job dissatisfaction. American sociologist Robert Blauner (1929–) argued that, in general, job satisfaction declined in the shift from craft through machine to assembly-line technology but then increased with the adoption of continuous process production, i.e. that found in modern petrochemical plants. In his view, the experience of dissatisfaction could have four dimensions: a sense of powerlessness, of meaninglessness, of isolation and of self-estrangement (see ALIENATION). Today most writers and practitioners take the view that, whilst technology can have certain effects on job satisfaction, there is no necessary form of WORK ORGANIZATION associated with any particular type of technology (see SOCIO-TECHNICAL SYSTEM). It is, therefore, possible to modify work organization to make work more satisfying (see JOB DESIGN AND REDESIGN).

Other writers, however, have followed Karl Marx (1818 – 83) in asserting that job dissatisfaction is an endemic feature arising from ALIENATION in capitalist society and hence can never be eliminated whilst capitalism remains in existence.

In recent years many analysts of job satisfaction have argued that in looking for the causes of dissatisfaction the focus of study should be widened from analysis of the job itself. Psychologists have argued that workers' experience of job satisfaction is influenced by their expectations of the job. If they have expected that a job would be tedious their dissatisfaction tends not to be as great as if they had expected it to be exciting. In a not dissimilar vein, sociologists have suggested that workers' experience of dissatisfaction is determined to some extent by their ORIENTATIONS TO WORK. If their primary reason for undertaking a certain job is to achieve a high income they do not experience strong dissatisfaction even if the job is tedious and repetitive (as long as it pays well). As one sociologist put it, 'they see the wound but feel no pain'.

job security the degree of certainty of continued employment with a particular organization. Job security is generally a function of statutory employment rights (i.e. protection against UNFAIR DISMISSAL), other elements of the CONTRACT OF EMPLOYMENT and the financial wellbeing of the organization. It can be said to be low where a company is suffering sustained losses or where the employment contract places a limit on the duration of employment (which may also debar the employee from certain statutory rights). Even where these conditions are not present, job security may be threatened by rationalizations which remove the need for certain jobs and hence lead to REDUNDANCY. See TEMPORARY WORK.

jobseekers allowance the weekly payment made to unemployed people to provide them with some minimum standard of living until they can secure new paid employment. The jobseekers allowance replaced 'unemployment benefit' in 1996, reflecting a more 'positive' approach to solving the problem of UNEMPLOYMENT. The current allowance rates payable (as at January 2005) are: £44.05p for age group 16 to 24 and £55.65p for persons over 25. See NEW DEAL, DEPARTMENT FOR WORK AND PENSIONS, JOB CENTRE.

job sharing the carrying out by two or more individuals between them of the duties of a particular JOB, each being paid pro rata according to the number of hours worked. For instance, two people might share a 40 hours per week job with each working 20 hours and each paid half the wage or salary attached to the post. The advantage to job sharers is that both may work part-time in jobs that are more highly paid than is usual for most PART-TIME jobs. It is more common for potential sharers to approach employers with a job-share package than for employers to initiate this form of working themselves. Employers are generally wary of job sharing because it can increase employment costs (for example INSURANCE payments), because the division of duties and responsibilities may be difficult to specify, and because the competencies of job sharers may be perceived as unbalanced.

job specialization see SPECIALIZATION, JOB DESIGN AND REDESIGN.

job specification see RECRUITMENT AND SELECTION.

joint account a BANK OR BUILDING SOCIETY account opened in the name of two or more people.

joint consultation see CONSULTATION.

joint costs the COSTS involved in producing several products from the same process, for example petrol, diesel, tar, etc. which derive from a common oil-refining process. Joint costs such as oil-refinery running costs are difficult to allocate precisely between the different products in determining the exact cost of each. See COSTING, BY-PRODUCT.

Joint Industrial Council see MULTI-EMPLOYER AGREEMENT.

joint products products which emerge from the same production process; for example, petrol, diesel and tar from a common oil refining process.

See JOINT COSTS, BY-PRODUCT.

joint-stock company a form of company in which a number of people contribute funds to finance a FIRM in return for SHARES in the company. Joint-stock companies are able to raise funds by issuing shares to large numbers of SHAREHOLDERS and thus are able to raise more capital to finance their operations than could a SOLE PROPRIETOR or even a PARTNERSHIP. Once a joint-stock company is formed then it becomes a separate legal entity apart from its shareholders, able to enter into contracts with suppliers and customers. Joint-stock companies are managed by the BOARD OF DIRECTORS appointed by shareholders. The directors must report on the progress of the company to the shareholders at an ANNUAL GENERAL MEETING where shareholders can in principle vote to remove existing directors if they are dissatisfied with their performance.

The development of joint-stock companies was given a considerable boost by the introduction of the principle of LIMITED LIABILITY which limited the maximum loss which a shareholder was liable for in the event of company failure. This protection for shareholders encouraged many more of them to invest in companies.

There are two main forms of joint-stock company:

(a) *private limited company.* Under UK Company Law the maximum number of shareholders in a private company is limited to 50 and the shares issued by the company cannot be bought and sold on the STOCK EXCHANGE. Such companies carry the term limited (Ltd) after their name;

(b) *public limited company.* Under UK Company Law there must be a minimum of seven shareholders in a public company, but otherwise a company can have an unlimited number of shareholders. Shares in a public company can be bought and sold on the stock exchange and so can be bought by the general public. Such companies carry the term public limited company (plc) after their name.

Most big firms are public companies since this is the only practical way of obtaining access to large amounts of capital. Although the shareholders are the owners of a public company, very often it is the company's management which in fact controls its affairs. See FLOTATION, SHARE ISSUE.

joint venture a business owned jointly by two (or more, in some cases) independent firms who continue to function separately in all other respects but pool together their resources in a particular line of activity. Firms set up joint ventures for a variety of reasons. The combining together of the resources of the two firms may facilitate the establishment of a larger-scale operation giving the joint venture access to economies of scale and increasing its penetration of the market. A joint venture is often a particularly effective way of exploiting complementary resources and skills, with one firm, for example, contributing new technology and products and the other providing marketing expertise and distribution channels. In the international context, joint ventures with local partners are often used by MULTINATIONAL ENTERPRISES as a means of entering unfamiliar foreign markets (see FOREIGN MARKET SERVICING STRATEGY).

Joint ventures are usually a less expensive way of expanding a firm's business interests than undertaking full mergers and takeovers (see EXTERNAL GROWTH); and they also allow firms to withdraw from a particular activity more easily (see DIVESTMENT). The main problem with joint ventures centres on the need to secure agreement between the two partners (especially if it is a 50–50 arrangement) as to how the business should be managed and developed. See BUSINESS STRATEGY, STRATEGIC ALLIANCE.

journal *or* **day book** a book of original entry in which information from documents and vouchers such as invoices and cheque stubs is entered, prior to entering or 'posting' this information to DOUBLE-ENTRY ACCOUNTS in the LEDGER. For example, the sales day book records invoices issued to customers in order of date and invoice number; these are then entered in the personal account of each customer in the sales ledger. Likewise the purchases day book records invoices received from suppliers in order of date; and these details are then posted or entered in the personal account of each supplier in the purchases ledger.

junk bond *or* **mezzanine debt** colloquial terms used to describe high-interest, high-risk LOAN STOCK which is issued by a company as a means of borrowing money to finance a TAKEOVER BID, MANAGEMENT BUY-OUT, or MANAGEMENT BUY-IN. A so-called 'leveraged' takeover bid or buy-out involves the company in increasing the proportion of its debt capital to equity capital, that is, increasing its CAPITAL GEARING.

Junk bond/mezzanine debt has come to the fore in recent years to plug the gap between the use of conventional loan finance such as DEBENTURES and the issue of SHARE CAPITAL, and the prices required to be paid for some takeover victims and DIVESTMENTS. Holders of mezzanine debt rank below conventional debt holders in terms of the repayment of loans, for which they receive a higher interest return or some shares in the company, or both. Mezzanine debt is often provided on a *bridging loan* basis; that is, it is used by a company to finance a takeover which, if successful, is then repaid out of the proceeds of disposing of some of the victim firm's businesses.

junk mail mail which is sent unsolicited and indiscriminately to a person or firm with a view to interesting them in a product.

juridification the process whereby the law has come to exert an increasing influence on the employment relationship and the conduct of industrial relations. See INDUSTRIAL RELATIONS.

just-in-time (JIT) system *or* **the Toyota production system (TPS)** a PRODUCTION MANAGEMENT system in which materials, components and products are produced for, or delivered to, the next stage of production (or customers) at the exact time they are needed. JIT seeks to minimize the amount of work-in-progress STOCKS held by a firm by synchronizing the flow of materials between production processes; and to economize on finished product stocks by matching the final assembly of products with the rate of customers' orders.

JIT is especially suited to high-volume production where uniform PRODUCTION-LINE OR ASSEMBLY-LINE schedules are operated on a continuous basis. Key elements in the successful application of JIT systems are:

(a) a high degree of cooperation and coordination with the (usually) single outside supplier of each particular material or component, who undertakes to supply on demand small consignments at frequent intervals and who carries sufficient stocks to permit immediate delivery;

(b) an internal control procedure which assists the smooth movement of materials and components from process to process at the required time. An illustration of this is provided by the Japanese car company Toyota's KANBAN (card) system which uses cards attached to component containers to monitor the flow of production through its factories.

The advantages of JIT include the reduction of stockholding costs; reduced space requirements; and faster manufacturing rates. On the other hand, JIT systems leave the firm more vulnerable to production losses occasioned by delivery hold ups or component defects. See PRODUCTION SCHEDULING, MATERIALS REQUIREMENTS PLANNING, MATERIALS PLANNING, LEAN MANUFACTURING, ANDON, OPTIMIZED PRODUCTION TECHNOLOGY. See also KAIZAN, JIDOKA, SUPPLIER DEVELOPMENT.

k

kabushiki kaisha the Japanese equivalent of a public limited company. See JOINT-STOCK COMPANY.

kaizan a Japanese term meaning 'continuous improvement'. Based on the 'philosophy' that QUALITY begins with the customer and that it is always possible to improve a product and a process. As customer requirements are always changing and because product standards are continually improving then the perception is that to stay in the market continual improvement is a necessary requirement for an organization. There are a number of guiding principals underpinning kaizan: these include, eliminating the task (in a similar way to BUSINESS PROCESS RE-ENGINEERING), reducing or changing activities and questioning the rules. Kaizan can be considered to be a part of LEAN MANUFACTURING.
See JAPANIZATION, QUALITY COUNCIL, QUALITY CIRCLE, JUST-IN-TIME (JIT) SYSTEM.

kanban a Japanese term meaning 'card'. It is used to describe part of the control mechanism for JUST-IN-TIME (JIT) and is at the centre of all JIT operations. A kanban is used to authorize the previous stage of production to make components. As such the system operates as a pull mechanism.
A kanban system, to work successfully, should operate within the following conditions.
1 A relatively stable demand pattern, with probably no more than 10% variation either side of the average.
2 QUALITY is imperative, defects for components in the system must be at a minimum. This is because kanbans normally work at pre-set component levels.
3 Good operator motivation. This is essential because a kanban is essentially a short-term, minute by minute inventory control mechanism. The simplest kanban is known as the kanban square. Here a square card (hence the name) is placed between two workstations. When the square is full (to a pre-set level) work at the previous station stops. When work is pulled from the square by the next operation (hence the alternative term 'pull-system') then work at the previous operation may start again. Kanbans exist in a number of variations, as stationary points attached to a work centre or as cards attached to an inventory bin, the principal remains the same however. See LEAN MANUFACTURING.

keiretsu a Japanese term relating to a network of customers and their suppliers working within a related industry, or with a single customer. Developed by the multinational organizations in Japan initially with the idea of exercising control over suppliers. Kereitsu has developed to mean closer links between customer and supplier and includes the sharing of technologies, of skilled employees and of product development. See SUPPLIER DEVELOPMENT, LEAN MANUFACTURING.

key account management an approach to SELLING which focuses resources on major customers and uses a team selling approach. See SALES FORCE.

keyboard a typewriter-style COMPUTER data input device.

key factor see LIMITING FACTOR.

key success factors see CRITICAL SUCCESS FACTORS.

kitting out the term used to describe the collection of sub-components into one area or one container for delivery to an assembly point.

know-how skill, expertise and trade contacts developed by a business over time, which serve to enhance its COMPETITIVE ADVANTAGE over rival suppliers.

knowledge worker a person who works in a professional or managerial capacity and whose tasks involve creating, processing and interpreting information.

l

label a paper or plastic attachment to a product, or part of the product's PACKAGING, which provides information about the product.

labour the human input to work activity. See JOB, CAPITAL.

labour cost variance the difference between the standard DIRECT LABOUR cost of a product (standard labour time x standard wage rate) and its actual direct labour cost (actual labour time X actual wage rate). This difference can be broken down into two parts:

(a) *labour efficiency variance*, which involves calculating the difference between the standard labour time specified and the actual labour time, converted into money terms by multiplying by the standard wage rate;

(b) *labour rate variance*, which involves calculating the difference between the predetermined standard wage rate and the actual wage rate, multiplied by the actual labour time.

With this distinction it is possible to trace whether an adverse direct labour cost variance is due to lower labour efficiency or higher wage rates. See STANDARD COST.

labour flexibility the ability of a firm to modify the employment and utilization of its labour force in the face of changing labour and product market conditions.

Several forms of labour flexibility can be identified:

(a) *numerical flexibility*, where the level and type of employment can be varied. For instance, PART-TIME WORK and TEMPORARY WORK can enable the employer to adjust the size of the labour force;

(b) *functional flexibility*, where the utilization of employees can be varied. Here the employer seeks to remove DEMARCATION LINES and RESTRICTIVE LABOUR PRACTICES so that, in theory at least, workers can perform a greater range of tasks. Further TRAINING may be necessary to achieve this;

(c) *temporal flexibility*, where the hours of work can be varied so as to match them to production or operations requirements. Use of part-time work, COMPRESSED HOURS and ANNUAL HOURS systems may assist this;

(d) *financial flexibility*, where levels of payment to employees can be varied in line with changes in profitability or individual performance. See PROFIT-RELATED PAY, MERIT PAY.

Firms require some degree of flexibility because of the inherent uncertainty of markets. However, it has arguably become more necessary in recent years because of intensifying competition in product markets. A firm which achieves flexibility in most or all of the dimensions above may be described as a 'flexible firm'. Such a firm would be composed of a *core workforce* of functionally flexible, well-paid employees and a *peripheral workforce* of numerically flexible PART-TIME WORKERS and temporal workers. Labour flexibility is usually viewed as a benefit to management; however, it can also benefit employees when it enables them to fit in paid employment with other (for example, domestic) commitments. See FLEXIBLE SPECIALIZATION, FLEXITIME, TEMPORARY WORK.

labour force *or* **workforce** 1 the total number of people employed by a firm or some other organization to produce goods and services.

2 the number of people currently in employment in an ECONOMY together with the number of people currently unemployed but actively seeking work. Fig. 48 shows labour statistics for the UK in Q1, 2004. This data is derived from the UK's monthly 'LABOUR FORCE SURVEY' using definitions recommended by the INTERNATIONAL LABOUR ORGANIZATION (ILO) and covering men in the population age group 16 years to 64 and women in the population age group 16 years to 59. People serving in the Armed Forces are not included in the Survey.

The labour force is made up of people in employment (employees, self-employment, unpaid family workers and people on government training and employment programmes) which together with 'ILO unemployed' equals 'total economically active'. In Q1, 2004 the labour force numbered 29,759,000 people of which 82% were employees, 12% were self-employed and 4% were unemployed. In addition 17,378,000 people were classified as 'economically inactive' (i.e. not in employment or seeking work) giving an employment rate of 75% (economically active as a % of the combined total of economically active and inactive). The labour force can be broken down in various other ways depending upon the purpose in hand. For example, men accounted for 51% of the labour force and women 49%. The proportion of women in the labour force has risen significantly in the last 20 years, reflecting in part the growing incidence of part-time work. In Q1, 2004 the number of part-time workers totalled 25% of the *employed labour force* and full-time workers 75%. In 1990, the respective figures were 21% and 79%. The distribution of *employees* in the employed labour force by industrial activity has changed over time with a growing proportion of people being employed in the service industries.

In 2004, 70% of employees were engaged in the service sector, 25% in the manufacturing and production sector (including gas, water and electricity), 4% in construction and 1% in the primary sector (agriculture and mining).

Categories		*Number of people, thousands*
1. In employment		
Employees		24,507
Self-employed		3,619
Unpaid family workers		107
Government training and employment programmes		113
= Total in Employment		28,346
2. ILO unemployment		1,413
3. Labour Force (1 + 2) = total economically active	men 16 years to 64	
	women 16 years to 59	29,759
4. Total economically inactive	men 16 years to 64	
	women 16 years to 59	17,378
5. Total Population in age groups – 16 years to 59 (women) 64 (men)		47,137[1]
6. Employment rate (3 as % of 5)		75%

[1]Note: Total population of UK (Category 5, plus under 16 and over 59 women, over 64 men) = 59 million

Fig. 48 **UK labour force Q1 (Jan-March) 2004.** Source: Monthly Digest of Statistics, Dec. 2004, ONS.

Labour Force Survey a UK survey which is undertaken to provide statistics relating to the size and composition of the LABOUR FORCE. A representative sample of some 120,000 people, men between the ages of 16 and 64 and women between the ages of 16 and 59, are interviewed over a three month period and asked to indicate details of their employment status: employee, self-employed, unpaid family worker, engaged on a government training and employment programme or unemployed. The Survey also provides other details of labour market conditions including average weekly earnings, paid holiday entitlements and average weekly number of hours worked. The Survey is organized by the Employment Service and is used to compile the International Labour Organization Unemployment Measure. See DEPARTMENT FOR WORK AND PENSIONS.

labour hour rate a COST RATE which is used in ABSORPTION COSTING to charge the OVERHEADS of a department or COST CENTRE in the cost of a product or job. It is usually used for those departments or cost centres which are less mechanized, and is computed by dividing the budgeted overheads which have been assigned to the department or cost centre by the estimated total number of labour hours for the period, to arrive at a rate per labour hour. The overhead charge for any product or job will depend upon the number of labour hours required for its production.

See also ABSORPTION.

labour intensiveness the extent to which labour is used in the PRODUCTION of goods and services. Where labour is relatively cheap and capital is comparatively expensive then firms will be inclined to use large amounts of labour in their production processes. See CAPITAL LABOUR RATIO. Compare CAPITAL INTENSIVENESS.

labour law the body of legislation and judicial decisions concerned with INDUSTRIAL RELATIONS, TRADE UNIONS and employment. Labour law has two main forms:

(a) *individual labour law,* relating to the rights and obligations of individual employees. From the 1960s onwards the volume of law in this area has grown considerably, partly as a response to European Union legislation. The Employment Act 1975 was particularly important as it established the right not to be unfairly dismissed (see UNFAIR DISMISSAL). Other important legislation in this era proscribed DISCRIMINATION on grounds of race or sex. In the 1980s individual rights were weakened somewhat. For example, the qualifying period for the right not to be unfairly dismissed was extended. However, legislation by the European Union counterbalanced this trend to some extent, and in the 1990s employees' rights in the areas of dismissal, MATERNITY RIGHTS, PARENTAL LEAVE and WORKING TIME were widened and strengthened;

(b) *collective labour laws,* relating to the activities of TRADE UNIONS and the conduct of INDUSTRIAL RELATIONS and COLLECTIVE BARGAINING. Traditionally, the law has not played an important role in industrial relations, and agreements made between unions and employers are not legally binding (see VOLUNTARISM). However, industrial relations has become increasingly subject to legal intervention in recent years (see JURIDIFICATION). In the 1970s a statutory union recognition procedure was established (subsequently repealed) by the Employment Act 1975. This law also required that employers consult over REDUNDANCIES and pass to unions information relevant to collective bargaining (see DISCLOSURE OF INFORMATION). In the 1980s and 1990s the conduct of STRIKES, TRADE UNION IMMUNITIES, SECONDARY ACTION, and the CLOSED SHOP were all the subjects of legislation, much of it aimed at eradicating what the government saw as trade union abuses. Recently a new STATUTORY UNION RECOGNITION PROCEDURE was introduced. Whilst union action continues to be highly regulated, labour law is now seen to be less hostile to unions than it was in the 1980s and 1990s. See MINIMUM WAGE.

labour management the activity or part of MANAGEMENT concerned with all aspects of managing the work of others. It involves both the managing of production itself and activities such as selection of labour, discipline etc. With the growing specialization of management in recent decades these activities have often been separated, with some becoming the responsibility of PERSONNEL MANAGEMENT. For this reason the term 'labour management' is not in widespread use today.

labour market a MARKET which brings together those persons seeking work (the supply of labour) and firms, government and other organizations seeking to fill JOB vacancies (the demand for labour). The labour market in practice is highly fragmented reflecting the diversity of work tasks, which range from unskilled or low-skill work (labourers, drivers, machine operators etc.) to tasks calling for specialist skills and expertise (research scientists, surgeons, managers, etc.). See LABOUR FORCE, INTERNAL LABOUR MARKET, PAY, COLLECTIVE BARGAINING, PAY DIFFERENTIAL, LABOUR MOBILITY.

labour mobility the movement of workers between firms, industries and regions in response to PAY DIFFERENTIALS and employment opportunities. Occupational mobility (the movement of workers between different types of JOB) depends upon, for example, the facilities for TRAINING and retraining workers provided by firms and the government, and upon the transferability of workers' occupational PENSIONS. Geographical mobility (the movement of workers between areas) depends upon, for example, the availability and cost of housing, relocation costs and social amenities (schools etc.).

labour process see SOCIOLOGY OF WORK.

labour relations see INDUSTRIAL RELATIONS.

labour turnover the proportion of an organization's labour force which leaves its employment over a given period. It can be composed of retirements, deaths, dismissals, redundancy or voluntary resignation. In general labour turnover is strongly influenced by the business cycle. In a period of growth when employment opportunities are expanding, turnover will increase. A certain amount of turnover is believed to be a good thing (as well as inevitable), since it enables the labour force to be revitalized. However, a high level of turnover in an organization can indicate that pay and conditions of employment are perceived as inadequate or that the organization is badly managed.

Two basic measures of leaving rate can be used:

(a) *wastage index*

$$\frac{\text{number of employees leaving in a period}}{\text{average number of employees in a period}} \times 100$$

(b) *stability index*

$$\frac{\text{number of employees with one year of service or more}}{\text{number employed one year ago}} \times 100$$

The wastage index is a fairly crude measure because it provides little indication of which employees are leaving. By contrast, the stability index can be used to pinpoint whether those quitting are new recruits or more established employees, and how long the duration of employment tends to be. This is important because turnover is often concentrated amongst new recruits (see INDUCTION CRISIS).

Turnover rates differ between industries. In general, those organizations with well-developed career structures have lower annual rates of turnover than those which rely heavily on the labour market to fill vacancies. See INTERNAL LABOUR MARKET, JOB SATISFACTION.

LAFTA see LATIN AMERICAN FREE TRADE ASSOCIATION.

LAN see LOCAL AREA NETWORK.

laptop a small battery-powered portable COMPUTER.

last-in, first-out see REDUNDANCY.

last-in, first-out (LIFO) see STOCK VALUATION.

last offer arbitration see ARBITRATION.

Latin American Free Trade Association (LAFTA) the former 'free trade area' established in 1960 comprising ten members: Argentina, Brazil, Paraguay, Mexico, Venezuela, Chile, Colombia, Ecuador, Peru and Bolivia. In 1995, a new trade bloc, MERCOSUR, was established, creating a customs union between Brazil, Uruguay, Argentina and Paraguay. Mexico is now a member of the NORTH AMERICAN FREE TRADE AGREEMENT. See TRADE INTEGRATION.

launch the introduction of a NEW PRODUCT onto the market. See PRODUCT LIFE CYCLE, TEST MARKETING, PROMOTIONAL MIX, ADVERTISING EFFECTIVENESS TESTS.

LAUTRO see FINANCIAL SERVICES ACT, 1986.

lay-off the termination of an employee's employment with an organization due to reduced demand for the goods or services produced by the organization. Lay-offs may be temporary, in which case employees will be re-employed when demand increases again, or permanent.

See REDUNDANCY.

lay official a TRADE UNION representative who is not actually employed by a union, and who performs union duties in his or her spare time or in time made available by their employer. See SHOP STEWARD.

lead body see NATIONAL VOCATIONAL QUALIFICATION.

leadership the process of influencing others to achieve certain goals. Effective leadership is often seen as the outcome of leadership qualities (traits) which some people have and some do not. In this conception, leadership is often seen as an autocratic activity, and leadership qualities are thought to include strength of personality, charisma, etc. Unfortunately, research into associated traits has been unable to prove conclusively a positive relationship between aspects of personality and effective management.

Academic work on leadership then shifted its attention away from what leaders are to what managers actually do in leadership roles. Two basic approaches to leadership were identified and have formed the core of theories of leadership and MANAGEMENT STYLE ever since. These are *concern for production*, as exemplified by SCIENTIFIC MANAGEMENT, and *concern for people*, as found in HUMAN RELATIONS philosophy. In the former, managers concentrate on getting the job done and their leadership style is essentially directive. In the latter, managers devote their efforts to ensuring that their subordinates are satisfied in their jobs, on the basis that a contented worker is an effective one. These twin dimensions are combined together in the Managerial Grid, devised by Americans Robert Blake (1918–)

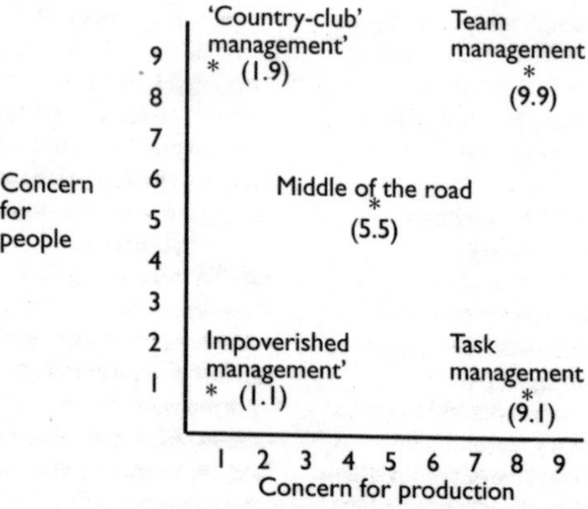

Fig. 49 **Leadership.** Blake and Mouton's managerial grid.

and Jane Mouton (1930–), as shown in Fig. 49. In their view the most effective form of management is Team Management, where leaders show a marked concern for people and for getting the job done.

However, research findings do not fully support this contention, leading some analysts to suggest that the *situation* in which leadership occurs needs to be considered too. American writer Fred Fiedler (1922–) has suggested that the extent to which tasks are structured and the nature of the leader–subordinate relationship (including the power resources of the leader) influence the effectiveness of leadership styles. A task-oriented approach is most effective where tasks are either highly structured or fairly unstructured and where the leader–subordinate relationship is very good or very poor. It is in the middling positions that a people-oriented style is most effective. Fiedler believed that managers find it difficult to change their styles and therefore advocated that managers should attempt to modify the situation to enhance effectiveness. Other writers, however, have argued, in what has come to be known as 'situational management', that leaders should adapt their style to the demands of the situation. It has been suggested that a critical factor is the job 'maturity' of subordinates, i.e. their capacity to direct their own job performance. At low levels of maturity a task-orientation is most appropriate to provide direction. As maturity increases leaders should adopt a people-orientation to provide support whilst reducing the amount of task direction. As individuals reach full maturity the manager can reduce both task- and people-orientation and allow individuals to perform the job as they see fit. In a sense, at this point successful leadership is the absence of overt leadership.

leading and lagging see EXCHANGE RATE EXPOSURE.

leading indicators the statistical time series that past experience has shown tends to reflect later changes, and which thus can be used to forecast these changes because they precede the changes in a consistent manner and by a relatively constant time interval. For example, current birth statistics would provide a firm basis for predicting primary school admissions five or six years ahead. Leading indicators like orders for new machine tools, overtime/short-time working in manufacturing and housebuilding starts are frequently used for SALES FORECASTING.

lead time the time between placing an order or reorder and the goods being received into stores. STOCK CONTROL systems take the lead time into account when deciding upon reorder levels, placing orders whilst there is sufficient safety stock or BUFFER STOCK to meet production requirements during the lead time. Lead time to manufacture is the time calculated to manufacture a component or final product.

lean manufacturing the use of a suitable combination of techniques enabling an organization to reduce costs and waste in any form, thus improving efficiency and effectiveness. The following techniques form the basis of lean manufacturing. Continuous improvement (KAIZAN); SUPPLIER DEVELOPMENT, (see KEIRETSU) CELLULAR MANUFACTURING (group technology); FIVE S (5S); VALUE ANALYSIS; PROCESS MAPPING; SEVEN (7) WASTES; single piece flow ('BATCH SIZE of one'); SINGLE MINUTE EXCHANGE OF DIES; STEP CHANGE; SUPPLY BASE REDUCTION (see SOURCING); KANBAN; TOTAL PRODUCTIVE MAINTENANCE. See PRODUCTION, COMPETITIVE ADVANTAGE, COMPETITIVE STRATEGY, PRODUCTIVITY.

Learning and Skills Council the UK body responsible for all post-16 education and TRAINING. It merges the activities of the Training and Education Councils and the Further Education Funding Council. The LSC oversees a network of 47 Local Learning and Skills Councils.

learning curve see EXPERIENCE CURVE.

learning for work see TRAINING.

learning organization an organization in which paramount importance is attached to the capacity for employees to learn from organizational events and developments in the external environment. Employees are encouraged to respond creatively to this learning. Systems for exchanging information are of great importance in such organizations.

lease a legal contract under which the owner (the lessor) of an ASSET such as a building or piece of machinery grants to a person or company (the lessee) the right to use that asset for a specified period of time in return for the payment of an agreed rental. See LEASING, LEASEBACK.

leaseback an arrangement which involves the selling of an ASSET by the owner to another person or company on condition that the asset is then LEASED (rented back) to the original owner for a specified period of time at an agreed rental. Leaseback is used primarily as a means of raising finance from the sale of surplus properties while allowing the firm to continue its existing business operations. See LEASING.

leasehold property property which is LEASED to a person or firm (the lessee) from its legal owners (the lessor) for an agreed period of time. Contrast FREEHOLD PROPERTY.

leasing the hiring out by one firm (the lessor) of an ASSET such as a factory building, piece of machinery or vehicle to another firm (the lessee) in return for the payment of an agreed rental. The lessor retains the ownership of the asset concerned and will repossess the asset on the expiry of the contract, or beforehand should the client require a replacement. A leasing arrangement can be useful to a client company in so far as it enables it to employ assets without having to tie up large amounts of capital for long periods of time. See LEASE, LEASEBACK, OFF-BALANCE SHEET FINANCING, FINANCE HOUSE.

least changeover cost a sequencing rule for the selection of the next item of work. The next job to be processed is the one that involves the least machine set-up cost. See PRODUCTION SCHEDULING.

least slack rule a sequencing rule for the selection of the next item of work. The next job to be processed is the one where the time difference between the due date and the operating time is the smallest for all jobs waiting. See PRODUCTION SCHEDULING.

ledger the ACCOUNTING records that keep a note of a firm's day-to-day financial transactions with outside parties. For example, the purchases or CREDITORS ledger would show the value of raw materials or services purchased from each supplier, payments made to suppliers for these, and any amounts still owing to suppliers. Similarly, the sales or DEBTORS ledger would show the value of goods or services sold to each customer, amounts they have paid for these, and any amounts still owed by customers. In former times such ledger accounts took the form of bound ledgers in which entries were recorded by hand; nowadays they are generally kept as computer records. Fig. 50 shows the main ledger accounts. See DOUBLE-ENTRY ACCOUNTS.

legal tender that part of a country's MONEY SUPPLY which, in the eyes of the law, is *totally* acceptable in discharge of a payment or debt. Coins and banknotes (CURRENCY) issued by the government fulfil this requirement. By contrast, a dealer or creditor is within his legal rights to refuse to accept as payment for a purchase or repayment of a debt a cheque drawn against a bank account.

lender a person, company or institution that provides a BORROWER with MONEY or some other asset (for example machinery, property) in the form of a LOAN, MORTGAGE or LEASING arrangement in order to finance consumption and investment. See DEBT, FINANCIAL SYSTEM, COLLATERAL SECURITY.

SALES LEDGER (Debtors' Ledger)
Account for each *customer*
PURCHASES LEDGER (Creditors' Ledger)
Account for each *supplier*
ASSET LEDGER (Plant Register)
Account for each *asset*
CASH ACCOUNT (Cash Book)
Record of all cash *incomings* and *outgoings*
NOMINAL LEDGER
Account for each *income* or *expense*
PAYROLL ACCOUNT
Record for each *employee*

Fig. 50 **Ledger**. The main ledger accounts.

'lender of last resort' the role of the BANK OF ENGLAND in making funds available to the DISCOUNT HOUSES when they are unable to cover their short-term liabilities from their own resources or from loans from the commercial banks. See DISCOUNT MARKET, INTEREST RATE, CENTRAL BANK.

letter of credit a document used to effect payment for internationally traded goods, usually as part of a contract for the sale of goods which ensures that the supplier receives prompt and guaranteed payment while the purchaser obtains a short-term CREDIT line. In brief, under this facility, a purchaser in country A of goods supplied by a firm in country B can arrange a letter of credit from his bank (the credit issuing bank) authorizing it to make payment to the supplier either through a branch of the bank in country B or, more usually, through a bank (the negotiating bank) holding the supplier's account. Under a contract of sale of goods this will be done on the presentation to the negotiating bank of documents stipulated in the letter of credit, such as the bill of lading, insurance policy, certificate of origin, etc. In the case of certain letters of credit relating to particular transactions and customers located in heavily indebted countries, a secondary market has developed to offset political as well as commercial risk. See EXPORTING.

level of activity see ACTIVITY LEVEL.

levels of hierarchy see HIERARCHY.

leverage see CAPITAL GEARING.

leveraged bid see TAKEOVER BID.

LGS see LOAN GUARANTEE SCHEME.

liability a claim on the resources of an individual or business in respect of monies borrowed. A liability is thus a form of DEBT, for example a bank overdraft or LOAN, a building society MORTGAGE. See ASSET, BALANCE SHEET.

LIBOR (London Interbank Offered Rate) the INTEREST RATE on dollar and other foreign currency deposits at which larger banks are prepared to borrow and lend these currencies in the EUROCURRENCY MARKET. The LIBOR rates reflect market conditions for international funds, and are widely used by the banks as a basis for determining the interest rates charged on dollar and foreign currency loans to business customers.

licence 1 the assignment by one firm to another (exclusive licence) or a number of firms (non-exclusive licence) of the right to use its technology or distribution network or to produce its product. Similarly, the grant by the government to an authority (for example an airport) or firm of the rights to supply a particular product. Licences are contractual arrangements which are entered into usually for a specified period of time, with the licensee paying a lump sum payment and/or a royalty or fee for the rights assigned. For an innovating firm with limited financial resources of its own, licensing offers a means of obtaining extensive national and international sales potential (see FOREIGN MARKET SERVICING STRATEGY) and a quick return on its risk capital. The danger is that the firm, by providing actual and potential (long run) competitors with its know-how etc., will lose control of core technology and products to rival producers. To safeguard this and also to provide greater technological collaboration between firms working both in complementary and diverse areas, a *cross licensing* arrangement may be established involving the reciprocal licensing of each other's products or technology.

2 a document issued by a licensing authority as a means of ensuring that persons or premises are 'fit and proper' for the activities in which they are engaged, for example, an investment adviser or premises for the consumption of alcoholic drink.

3 a document which shows proof of legal ownership (or entitlement) or compliance with a statutory or private requirement in which a fee is payable, for example a television licence issued by the government, or a private fishing licence. See EXPORT LICENCE.

Life Assurance and Unit Trust Regulatory Organization (LAUTRO) see FINANCIAL SERVICES ACT, 1986.

life cycle 1 the stage people have reached in their life, from single at home through young parents to solitary retired. See SOCIOECONOMIC GROUP, BUYER BEHAVIOUR.

2 see PRODUCT LIFE CYCLE.

life style an individual's living pattern as expressed by his or her interests, values, activities and opinions. Life styles influence people's buying behaviour and thus the types of products they are likely to purchase. See SOCIOECONOMIC GROUP, BUYER BEHAVIOUR.

LIFFE see LONDON INTERNATIONAL FINANCIAL FUTURES EXCHANGE.

LIFO 1 see REDUNDANCY.
2 STOCK VALUATION.

limited company (Ltd) see JOINT-STOCK COMPANY.

limited liability an arrangement that limits the maximum LOSS which a SHAREHOLDER is liable for in the event of company failure to the SHARE CAPITAL which he originally subscribed.

The principle of limited liability limits a shareholder's maximum loss in the event of his company failing to the original share capital which he invested, no further claims by creditors against the shareholder's other assets being permitted. Once shareholders were protected in this way many more people were encouraged to invest in companies and JOINT-STOCK COMPANIES grew rapidly. To warn potential creditors that any claims by creditors will be limited in total to the amount of the company's share capital, such companies carry the term: 'Limited' (Ltd) or 'Public Limited Company' (Plc) after their names.

When a business is subject to *unlimited liability*, as is the case with SOLE PROPRIETORS and unlimited PARTNERSHIPS, the owners of the business are liable in full for the debts of the business if it fails. This may involve their losing not only the capital that they have put into the business, but also most of their personal assets.

When the directors of a joint-stock company continue trading after they should have known the company was insolvent (see INSOLVENCY), they can lose the protection of limited liability and become personally responsible for the firm's debts.

limited-line strategy a product line strategy which involves offering only a small number of variations of a product. See PRODUCT RANGE. Contrast FULL-LINE STRATEGY.

limiting factor *or* **key factor** the critical constraint upon a firm's budgeted activity level. In most circumstances the limiting factor will be the amounts that the company can sell, but in certain cases the limiting factor might be shortage of production capacity, shortages of particular raw materials or the like. Here planning will be aimed at devising a sales programme which generates maximum profit from these limited resources. For example, Fig. 51 shows how a firm with limited production capacity might seek to maximize its CONTRIBUTION by concentrating upon production of the product which requires fewer direct labour hours to make. See BUDGET, BUDGETING, LINEAR PROGRAMMING.

	Chairs		*Sofas*
	£		£
Selling price	120		160
Unit variable cost	100		130
	20		30
Direct labour hours per unit	4 hours		8 hours
Contribution per direct labour hour	£5		£7.25
What 10,000 direct labour hours of capacity can make:			
	10,000 ÷ 4	or	10,000 ÷ 8
	2,500 units	or	1,250 units
Contributions	2,500 units x £20	or	1,250 units x £30
	£50,000	or	£37,500

Fig. 51 **Limiting factor.** Contributions and constraints.

line and staff an approach to structuring ORGANIZATIONS which distinguishes between those who are in the line or CHAIN OF COMMAND and are directly involved in the achievement of the organization's primary goals (line), and those who provide advice or a supporting service to them (staff). Typically, staff functions include those such as management services and personnel. However, the distinction is often less clear cut in practice because staff functions may exercise authority on behalf of line managers or acquire informal power and authority of their own. In addition, there is usually a line of command within staff departments. See MANAGEMENT.

linear programming a technique for utilizing limited resources to meet a desired objective, such as minimizing cost or maximizing profit, where the resource limits are expressed as constraints.

For example, consider a firm making only two products, bookcases and chairs, and trying to decide how many of each to make. The company's output will be limited by the productive resources which it has available, and these are depicted graphically in Fig. 52 where output of bookcases is represented on the horizontal axis and output of chairs on the vertical axis. If the company has only 40 hours of machine time available each week, while a bookcase needs 2 hours of machine time to make and a chair 2 hours of machine time, then the maximum output with the available machine would be represented by line XY. If there were only 42 hours of labour available, and each bookcase needs 3 hours' work while each chair needs 1.5 hours' work, then the maximum output with the available labour force would be represented by line RT.

The area OXZT represents all feasible combinations of bookcases and chairs which can be produced with the limited machine-hours and man-hours available (the *feasible region*).

If each bookcase (b) sold makes a profit of £5, and each chair (c) £4, then in order to maximize profit the firm would seek to maximize output:

$$5b + 4c.$$

For example, in order to earn a profit of £60 the company could produce 12 bookcases or 15 chairs or some combination of the two, as represented by the broken line MP in Fig. 52. Combinations of bookcases and chairs corresponding to larger total profits can be represented by other lines such as LN, which are parallel to MP but further out from the origin O. The line LN represents the largest profit which the firm can earn with its available man-hours and machine-hours, since it is the highest broken line which just touches the resource constraints represented by the feasible region OXZT. The firm will therefore settle at point Z producing OV chairs per week and OW bookcases each week in order to maximize its profits from available resources.

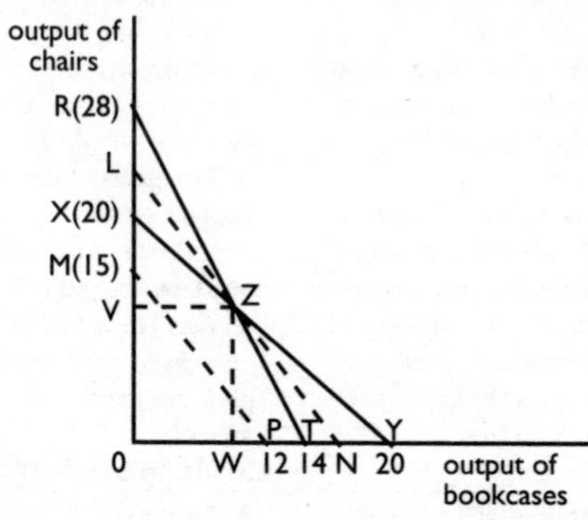

Fig. 52 **Linear programming.** Limitations on productive resources.

Linear programming also provides information about the value of additional resources to a company. For example, it shows how much extra profit could be earned by increasing the number of machine-hours or man-hours available, and thus indicates the maximum amount which the company should pay for additional units of these resources. These maximum amounts which the company could afford to pay for additional resources without prejudicing profitability are called SHADOW PRICES of the machine-hour and man-hour resources.

Where a company produces more than two outputs, two-dimensional graphical analysis is impossible. However, an optimum combination of outputs can still be calculated using a similar reasoning process called the *simplex method.*

line balancing see PRODUCTION-LINE BALANCING.

line manager a manager who has direct AUTHORITY over other employees in the ORGANIZATION. They exercise authority down the CHAIN OF COMMAND shown in the ORGANIZATION CHART. Often the term is used to denote those managers who have direct authority over production or clerical employees at the base of the organization. See LINE AND STAFF, MANAGEMENT.

line of balance (LOB) chart a chart which combines information on agreed product DELIVERY DATES with data on the availability of components required to make the products. LOB charts are used in PRODUCTION SCHEDULING to ensure that the correct number of components are available at the appropriate times, so that final assembly of the product can be completed by its scheduled date in time to meet promised delivery dates.

liquid assets those CURRENT ASSETS which are held in the form of cash, or assets which can be quickly converted into cash, notably DEBTORS but not STOCK. A company's liquid current assets show how much it could quickly raise in cash to meet the immediate demands of its CREDITORS if they were all to press for prompt payment.

liquidation the process by which a JOINT-STOCK COMPANY's existence as a legal entity ceases by the *winding-up* of the company. Such a process can be initiated at the behest of the CREDITORS where the company is insolvent (a compulsory winding-up), or by the company directors or SHAREHOLDERS, in which case it is known as a voluntary winding-up.

The person appointed as liquidator, either by the company directors/shareholders or by the creditors, sells off the company's ASSETS for as much as they will realize. The proceeds of the sale are used to discharge any outstanding liabilities to the creditors of the company. If there are insufficient funds to pay all creditors (INSOLVENCY), preferential creditors are paid first (for example the INLAND REVENUE for tax due), then ordinary creditors pro rata. If there is a surplus after payment of all creditors this is distributed pro rata amongst the ordinary shareholders of the company. See also LIMITED LIABILITY, SHAREHOLDERS, CAPITAL.

liquidator see LIQUIDATION, INSOLVENCY.

liquidity the possession by a person or business of a stock of monetary assets which can be used directly to finance the purchase of goods and services and capital assets. See MONEY, MONEY SUPPLY.

liquidity ratio see CURRENT RATIO.

listed company a public limited JOINT-STOCK COMPANY (Plc) whose shares are traded on the main STOCK MARKET. In the UK, to obtain a full listing on the main stock exchange a company is required to provide comprehensive information about its activities. Smaller companies unable or unwilling to provide the comprehensive information required for a full listing may seek to satisfy the less exacting information requirements of the UNLISTED SECURITIES MARKET and have their shares traded there. See QUOTED COMPANY.

list price the published PRICE of a good or service. The actual price paid by the buyer is often lower than this because suppliers are prepared to offer trade discounts for BULK BUYING.

Lloyds (of London) a corporation whose membership comprises a group of some 31,000 INSURANCE BROKERS and INSURANCE

COMPANIES engaged in the UNDERWRITING of INSURANCE risks. Lloyds itself does not perform any underwriting business; its member brokers and insurers either act individually in arranging insurance cover for clients, or, in the case of particular types of insurance risk, operate together on a consortium or syndicated basis. What Lloyds does is to provide a forum for organizing syndicated insurance groupings and to validate the integrity of its members in the eyes of the public (i.e. members of Lloyds are expected to conduct their business in a fair and honest way and to deposit funds with it as a surety).

load the work which is assigned to a workstation (machine or operative) during a specified period of time. See PRODUCTION-LINE BALANCING.

loading the balancing out of workloads over the available CAPACITY of a machine or item of equipment. Effective machine loading seeks to identify and avoid over- or under-loaded machines or equipment. See PRODUCTION-LINE BALANCING.

loan the advance of a specified sum of MONEY to a person or business (the BORROWER) by other persons or businesses, or more particularly by a specialist financial institution (the LENDER) which makes its profits from the INTEREST charged on loans. The provision of loans by COMMERCIAL BANKS, FINANCE HOUSES, BUILDING SOCIETIES etc. is an important source of CREDIT in the economy, serving to underpin a substantial amount of spending on current consumption and the acquisition of personal and business assets.

Loans may be advanced on an *unsecured* or *secured* basis; in the latter case the lender requires the borrower to offer some form of COLLATERAL SECURITY (for example property deeds) which the lender may retain in the event of the borrower defaulting on the repayment of the loan. See BANK LOAN, INSTALMENT CREDIT, MORTGAGE, LOAN STOCK, DEBENTURE, LOAN GUARANTEE SCHEME, INTEREST RATE, SOFT LOAN.

loan capital *or* **debt capital** the money employed in a company that has been borrowed from external sources for fixed periods of time by the issue of fixed-interest financial securities such as DEBENTURES. The providers of loan capital do not normally share in the profits of the company but are rewarded by means of regular INTEREST payments which must be paid under the terms of the loan contract. Interest payments are a business expense which must be charged against revenues in calculating profits. See SHARE CAPITAL, BALANCE SHEET, CAPITAL GEARING.

Loan Guarantee Scheme (LGS) a facility for encouraging the COMMERCIAL BANKS to provide LOAN finance to small firms who, because of the high risk involved or lack of collateral, are unable to obtain conventional loans. Under the scheme, the DEPARTMENT OF TRADE AND INDUSTRY guarantees repayment to the bank of (currently) 70% of the loan on default in return for an annual premium of 2.5% on the guaranteed portion of the loan.

LOB see LINE OF BALANCE.

local area network (LAN) a network of PERSONAL COMPUTERS used to undertake routine data processing functions in a business. Over the years these networks have become more complex and to this extent a 'system crash' or failure can be highly disruptive and expensive. Old-style PC networks were device-sharing facilities giving people access to a departmental printer or fax. If they went down, people could still carry on working. In modern networks, however, people use PCs to log on to the network for all their software, including word processing and databases, and to access information held on software in other departments. See INFORMATION MANAGEMENT.

local content rule *or* **rule of origin** the stipulation by a country that for a product to qualify as an authentic domestically manufactured product (that is, originating in that country) the product must be manufactured predominantly from locally supplied as opposed to imported components. Local content rules are used by governments mainly to prevent the operation of so called 'screwdriver' plants (plants producing final products from mainly imported components) established to circumvent TARIFFS, QUOTAS and anti-dumping duties imposed on imported final products. See DUMPING, CERTIFICATE OF ORIGIN.

local tax a TAX on property or persons by local authorities/councils which, together with central government grants, is used to finance the provision of various local services. Before 1990, in the UK, *rates* were levied on eligible properties; between April 1990 (April 1989 in Scotland) and April 1993 a *community charge* (*poll tax*) was levied on eligible persons; since April 1993 a *council* tax has been levied on eligible properties. The current means of raising local taxes, the council tax, is based on the rateable value of local properties, the amount payable in the case of residential dwellings being adjusted to take into account such things as the number of people living in the property, their incomes, and any disabilities they suffer. See UNIFORM BUSINESS RATE.

location see INDUSTRIAL LOCATION.

lock-out see INDUSTRIAL ACTION.

logistics the functions involved in moving raw materials and components into the firm, the movement of work-in-progress and stocks within the firm and the movement of finished products out of the firm. See MATERIALS MANAGEMENT, MATERIALS REQUIREMENT PLANNING, STOCK CONTROL, DISTRIBUTION, MARKETING LOGISTICS.

logo a company name or BRAND NAME written or illustrated in a distinctive way to heighten customers' recognition of the company or product concerned. See BRAND MARK.

log on the procedure for gaining access to a COMPUTER.

London Interbank Offered Rate see LIBOR.

London International Financial Futures Exchange (LIFFE) a FORWARD MARKET which is engaged in the buying and selling of FINANCIAL SECURITIES, COMMODITIES, FOREIGN CURRENCIES, DERIVATIVES and SWAPS. LIFFE was taken over in 2001 by the Euronext STOCK MARKET. See EUREX, FINANCIAL SERVICES ACT 1986.

London International Stock Exchange see STOCK MARKET.

London Metal Exchange see COMMODITY MARKET.

long position a situation in which a dealer or MARKET MAKER in a particular COMMODITY, FINANCIAL SECURITY or FOREIGN CURRENCY is selling less than he is buying, so that his working stock of the item increases (i.e. becomes 'long').

Longs BONDS, DEBENTURES and PREFERENCE SHARES which have a redemption date of 15 years or more.

long-term capital employed *or* **net worth** any long-term funds employed in a firm. For companies this takes the form of SHAREHOLDERS' CAPITAL EMPLOYED plus long-term loans such as DEBENTURES.

long-term debt see LOAN CAPITAL.

long-term incentive plan (LTIP) a scheme which involves the periodic grant of SHARES in a company to the company's executive directors as an incentive for them to improve the financial performance of the company and align their interests more closely with those of the company's SHAREHOLDERS. LTIPs are similar to EXECUTIVE SHARE OPTION SCHEMES insofar as they involve the periodic grant and exercise of share awards, again the exercise of share awards being conditional on the attainment of specified performance 'targets' usually over a three year period. However, there are some notable differences. Firstly whereas options are granted at an 'exercise price' LTIP shares are usually granted at zero price (ie. they are given 'free'). Secondly, 'benchmarking' is related specifically to the performance of other companies rather than the Retail Price Index, for example companies comprising a SHARE PRICE INDEX such as the FTSE-100, or more narrowly, a peer group of companies operating in the same industry. Thirdly, whereas options are exercised on an 'all or nothing' basis LTIPs are typically 'scaled' involving a minimum (partial exercise) point, rising to a maximum (full exercise) point. See PRINCIPAL-AGENT THEORY, BUSINESS OBJECTIVES, CORPORATE GOVERNANCE.

loss the shortfall between a firm's sales revenues received from the sale of its products and the total costs incurred in producing the firm's output (see BREAK-EVEN ANALYSIS). Losses may be of a temporary nature occasioned by, for example, a downturn in demand (see

BUSINESS CYCLE) or due to an exceptional level of expenditures (such as the launch of a series of new products). Short-term losses are usually financed by a firm running down its RESERVES or by an increase in borrowings. Losses which are sustained over time typically arise from a firm's poor competitive position in a market (see COMPETITIVE ADVANTAGE), and unless competitiveness can be restored market exit or DIVESTMENT may be the only practical way of remedying the situation. See MARKET SYSTEM.

loss leading the practice whereby a RETAILER sells a manufacturer's branded product at a PRICE below bought-in cost. Loss leading is used by retailers to attract customers into their stores in the hope that buyers will then purchase a selection of full-price products in addition to cut-price items, thus making a profit on the purchases taken as a whole. In the short run, manufacturers of products subjected to loss leading may well benefit from increased sales and profits (i.e. it is the retailer, not the manufacturer, who incurs the loss), but over the longer term the practice may undermine the product's price-quality reputation with consumers. In the UK, under the RESALE PRICE ACTS, manufacturers can take court action to stop retailers using their products as loss leaders.

lot for lot supplying the exact amount previously used or sold.

lot size see BATCH SIZE.

lot tolerance percentage defective (LTPD) as used in QUALITY CONTROL it is the amount of product that is considered unacceptable so that the complete batch or delivery is rejected.

low geared see CAPITAL GEARING.

low pay wages or salaries that are considered to be low relative to the average level of PAY or relative to needs. Official definitions tend to adopt the latter approach. Low pay is viewed as income that is insufficient to meet officially defined needs and hence can be supplemented by various state benefits (for example social security). Many argue, however, that poverty or impoverished lifestyle extends beyond the group able to claim such benefits, and therefore they prefer a relative definition. In the past the *lowest decile* of male earnings has been used as a yardstick, but increasingly in the UK the Council of Europe's 'decency threshold' of *two-thirds of median pay* has been adopted as a definition by those concerned to combat low pay.

Low pay, however defined, tends to be concentrated amongst certain social groups and industries. It is concentrated amongst the female workforce, and is especially prevalent in certain service industries, such as hotel and catering and hairdressing, and in such primary industries as agriculture. Some recent reports have indicated that nearly half the UK's employed adult workforce is receiving pay that falls below the decency threshold.

Low pay has been combated to some extent by the introduction of an official MINIMUM WAGE RATE in 2000. See DISCRIMINATION.

Low Pay Commission the UK body which advises the government on the MINIMUM WAGE RATE.

loyalty *or* **'points' card scheme** a facility which rewards customers of a retail business (for example, a supermarket or petrol station chain) for repeated purchases at the business's outlets. Customers accumulate 'points' based on their purchases which when aggregated entitles them to a cash discount, 'money-off' future purchases or gifts. The general purpose of such a scheme is to encourage customers to be 'loyal', purchasing all or the bulk of their requirements from the favoured retailer rather than 'shop around' splitting their purchases with rival traders.

The scheme is similar to AGGREGATED REBATES operated by suppliers of inputs to business customers. See BRAND LOYALTY.

Ltd (limited company) see JOINT-STOCK COMPANY.

LTIP see LONG-TERM INCENTIVE PLAN.

Mo, M3, M4 see MONEY SUPPLY.

Maastricht Treaty 1991 an agreement between member countries of the European Community (EC) which renamed the EC as the EUROPEAN UNION to reflect the move towards a deeper integration of the economies of member countries and the acceptance of broader political and social responsibilities.

The Treaty endorsed a formal commitment to the establishment of ECONOMIC AND MONETARY UNION (EMU) and the introduction of the EURO by 1999, intergovernmental cooperation covering justice and home affairs including policing, criminal actions, extradition and illegal immigration, and intergovernmental cooperation in external affairs, including the introduction of a Common Foreign and Security Policy (CFSP) covering defence, relationships with NATO etc. The Treaty also introduced the concept of EU citizenship as a supplement to national citizenship. See SUBSIDIARITY, SOCIAL CHAPTER, AMSTERDAM TREATY. See also BUDGET (GOVERNMENT), FISCAL POLICY.

machine bureaucracy an ORGANIZATION characterized by a high reliance on rules to govern how its members perform their jobs and interact with each other. Organizations of this type are usually found in stable environments. See MECHANISTIC AND ORGANISMIC.

machine code COMPUTER instructions written as a form of zero/one combinations which the computer can execute by activating off/on electrical pulses. All 'higher level' computer program languages like BASIC or COBOL have to be translated into machine code for use in a computer.

machine hour rate a COST RATE which is used in ABSORPTION COSTING to charge the OVERHEADS of a department or COST CENTRE in the cost of a product or job. It is usually used for those departments or cost centres which are highly mechanized, and is computed by dividing the budgeted overheads which have been assigned to the department or cost centre by the estimated total number of machine hours for the period, to arrive at the rate per machine hour. The overhead charge for any product or job will depend upon the number of machine hours required for its production. See also ABSORPTION.

machine register see PLANT REGISTER.

machinery 1 items of capital such as a lathe or ROBOT welder which are used in production. See PLANT, EQUIPMENT, CAPITAL STOCK, FIXED ASSET.

2 procedures for the conduct of negotiations between trade unions and management and the settlement of disputes. See PROCEDURAL AGREEMENT, GRIEVANCE PROCEDURE, DISPUTES PROCEDURE.

machine utilization the extent to which the productive capacity of a machine is used during a specified period of time. Machine utilization can be expressed as a percentage, for example:

$$\frac{\text{machine hours used}}{\text{total machine hours available}} \times 100$$

In order to maximize machine utilization, firms must examine IDLE TIME records to find out why machine time is being lost and take steps to remedy the situation.

macro-environment the broader, more general political, economic, social and technological forces which impinge on a firm's activities and viability in addition to those operating in the firm's immediate MARKETS. See PEST.

mail order a DIRECT MARKETING means of retailing products to consumers through the post. Mail order firms supply catalogues to prospective customers who either themselves or through agents make purchases for delivery to their homes. Mail order concerns typically combine wholesaling (stocking large quantities of products and breaking bulk) and retailing functions, supplying customers from a central warehouse. Such firms compete mainly by offering customers convenience (i.e. home shopping) and by the provision of INSTALMENT CREDIT facilities on purchases. Mail order methods may also be used to sell industrial products. See RETAILER, WHOLESALER, DISTRIBUTION CHANNEL.

mainframe a large-scale COMPUTER with big data-storage facilities which is often accessible simultaneously from many terminals. Mainframe computers are used by large data-processing departments in businesses for sales and purchase ledger record-keeping, etc.

As MICROCOMPUTERS and MINICOMPUTERS become more powerful in terms of data-processing, speed and data-storage capacity, the distinction between the three types of computer has become blurred.

mainstream corporation tax see CORPORATION TAX.

maintainability the ability of a product or component to be kept in a state in which it can perform its required function when maintained.

See MAINTENANCE.

maintenance the management process of repairing and maintaining buildings, plant, machinery and equipment to avoid breakdowns and disruption to production.

Effective maintenance requires the firm to draw up appropriate plans and timetables, taking into account the frequency of maintenance required, available personnel, ordering and stocking of spare parts etc.

The maintenance function provides an important service to production, marketing and administration departments. Routine maintenance within a firm is often undertaken by the firm's own maintenance department, while major refurbishment of machines may be contracted to specialist outside firms.

See TOTAL PRODUCTIVE MAINTENANCE, PREVENTIVE MAINTENANCE, INSPECTION, WORK-BASED MAINTENANCE, TIME-BASED MAINTENANCE, PRODUCTION MANAGEMENT, LEAN MANUFACTURING.

make for stock see PRODUCTION SCHEDULING.

make-or-buy decision the strategic choice confronting the firm as to whether it purchases its raw materials and components requirements from outside suppliers or produces them for itself as part of a vertically-integrated operation (see VERTICAL INTEGRATION). The main factors influencing this decision are the relative costs and risks involved. The main advantage of outside suppliers who specialize in the production of an input and produce for a large number of customers (not just one as in the case of self supply), is that they are able to benefit from the lower costs associated with economies of large-scale operations (see ECONOMIES OF SCALE). Thus, it may be cheaper to a user to buy in the input rather than to produce it internally; the more so if the firm has access to a number of supply sources (both domestic and international) and can take full advantage of price competition between them. Set against this are the risks in certain cases of over-dependency on particular suppliers, leading to possible problems of overcharging and disruptions to the firm's production schedules arising from supply shortages, failure to meet delivery times, and inputs lacking the desired degree of quality or precision. See SOURCING, OUTSOURCING, INTERNATIONALIZATION, PURCHASING.

make to order see PRODUCTION SCHEDULING.

management

The process of organizing and directing human and physical resources within an ORGANIZATION so as to meet defined objectives. The key management roles are:

(a) *planning* how to carry out the various activities which are required to achieve the objective. This involves establishing an action programme (see BUSINESS PLAN) and an appropriate organization structure within which tasks can be subdivided (for example into production, personnel, marketing and finance); RESPONSIBILITY for them delegated; and PAY and reward systems instituted (see JOB DESIGN AND REDESIGN, WORK ORGANIZATION);

(b) CONTROL, by comparing current performance with that planned in order to monitor progress of the work. Such comparisons reveal where additional resources may be needed to achieve desired performance or when plans may need to be modified in the light of experience;

(c) COORDINATION of the tasks being undertaken, which involves synchronizing and balancing work loads and ensuring effective collaboration between the various DEPARTMENTS and GROUPS within the organization;

(d) MOTIVATION of the members of the organization, encouraging them to work effectively in performing their assigned task.

CLASSICAL MANAGEMENT THEORY portrayed management as a rational activity largely concerned with establishing routines and procedures for administering the work. More recently this emphasis has been questioned in a number of respects. Research has shown that much of the manager's working day is spent on tasks other than those suggested in this approach, for example attending retirement presentations, responding to telephone enquiries etc. Much of the manager's job involves ad hoc reactions to events. Other research has shown that managers 'muddle through', aiming at achieving satisfactory rather than optimum outcomes (see SATISFICING).

Recent writing on management has emphasized the LEADERSHIP aspect of the managerial function. The key issue here concerns the means by which managers can achieve effective performance from their subordinates. Two basic approaches are identified in the literature (on MANAGEMENT STYLE):

(a) *task orientation*, where managers' relationship with their subordinates is essentially directive, being primarily focused on getting the job done;

(b) *people orientation*, where managers show a greater concern for their subordinates' well-being, on the grounds that a contented workforce performs effectively.

Some believe that good leaders are born with certain personal qualities whilst others believe that these can be instilled through MANAGEMENT DEVELOPMENT. Whatever perspective is taken it should be remembered that leadership involves more than a leader: it also involves subordinates and a context. Good leadership is that which produces appropriate behaviour from others in particular situations. See ORGANIZATIONAL ANALYSIS, BOARD OF DIRECTORS.

management accounting any accounting activities geared to the preparation of information for managers to help them plan and control a company's operations. Management accounts generally provide more detailed information than financial accounts; for example, breaking down revenues and costs between different products, factories or departments to provide comparative data and to help reveal profitable and unprofitable activities. Management accounts also tend to provide information about performance more frequently than financial accounts, with monthly or even weekly management accounts rather than annual financial accounts, to give managers prompt feedback and to enable them to act quickly to check inefficiencies. Management accounts are geared to estimates of future costs and revenues rather than simply reporting past revenues and costs as financial accounts do, thereby 'providing valuable management information for preparing accurate estimates and tenders and for use in negotiating price changes.

Fig. 53 shows how more detailed analysis of revenues and costs can provide more useful information than total information as reported in the PROFIT-AND-LOSS ACCOUNT. Compare FINANCIAL ACCOUNTING. See also BUDGETING.

management buy-in the TAKEOVER of a company, or of a division of a company, by a small group of shareholders (often ex-managers of the company) who then form the nucleus of a new management team to run the company or division. As with a MANAGEMENT BUY-OUT (the takeover of a company by its *existing* management) management buy-ins are often financed by the issue of loan capital subscribed by financial institutions such as merchant banks and VENTURE CAPITAL specialists. See JUNK BOND/MEZZANINE DEBT.

management buy-out (MBO) the TAKEOVER of a firm, or of a division of a firm, by its existing management team from, in the former case, the shareholders of the firm, or in the latter case, the firm's main board of directors subject to shareholder approval. The purchase of a division of a diversified firm (see DIVERSIFICATION) by its management is a form of DIVESTMENT which can be beneficial to both parties. The disposer's motive is usually to get out of a particular activity which is no longer considered to fit in with its strategic plans for developing the business, and to use the monies released to strengthen its activities or acquire new businesses. From the buyer's point of view, there is the challenge of running one's own business and the potential for making a greater success of an activity which perhaps, because of insufficient support from above in its divisional form, had previously been underperforming. The rekindling of entrepreneurship in the hands of owner-managers is seen to be a key advantage of a management buy-out.

A critical factor in the success of a management buy-out, apart from the obvious need for managerial competence (and a little luck!) is the price paid for the business and the related financial package for acquiring it. The members of the

Profit-&-Loss Account	Total	Beds	Divans	Suites
	£	£	£	£
Sales	300,000	190,000	70,000	40,000
less costs	274,000	178,000	52,000	44,000
Profit (loss)	26,000	12,000	18,000	(4,000)
Profit as % of sales	8.6%	6.3%	25.7%	Zero

Fig. 53 **Management accounting.** Trading results: Y Company Plc for year ending 20xx.

management team will provide a percentage of the purchase price from their own personal funds and own a large amount of the SHARE CAPITAL, with the balance of funds often being provided by LOANS from merchant banks and venture capital specialists. Alternatively, the balance can be obtained by selling shares to the workforce either directly, or indirectly to a trust, as part of an EMPLOYEE SHARE OWNERSHIP PLAN. One advantage of this solution is that it enables the management team to avoid an overdependency on outside interests and unrealistic CAPITAL GEARING levels. See JUNK BOND, MANAGEMENT BUY-IN, DEMERGER, BUSINESS STRATEGY, VENTURE CAPITAL.

management by exception a system whereby only the important variations from plan are brought to management attention. This avoids managers becoming too bogged down with paperwork containing unimportant detail. See VARIANCE ANALYSIS.

management by objectives (MBO) an approach to MANAGEMENT, popularized by American management writer Peter Drucker (1909 –), which emphasizes the need for clear organizational objectives which can be incorporated in the actions of individual managers. In Drucker's view organizations have a multiplicity of objectives; these should be clarified and prioritized so that all managers understand what the most important goals of the organization are. Then individual managers should set objectives for themselves, in conjunction with their superiors, which will assist in meeting organizational goals. This approach was popular in the 1960s and 1970s but subsequently fell from favour because all too often objectives were *imposed* on managers rather than generated by them, and because the extent to which objectives were met was often used simply to evaluate managers rather than as a basis to improve performance. Genuine commitment was difficult to engender in these circumstances. This approach to management has made a comeback recently with the emphasis attached to objective-setting in the PERFORMANCE APPRAISAL process.

management by walking around (MBWA) an approach to MANAGEMENT which emphasizes the value of observing what goes on in the ORGANIZATION and of displaying a high profile to subordinates. In this model, good managers are those who spend much of their time discussing work issues with colleagues and subordinates, rather than those who rely on issuing formal instructions from the seclusion of their offices. By wandering around in this way the manager will come to recognize and understand the informal relationships and activities that can both facilitate and obstruct the achievement of organizational goals. Compare MANAGEMENT BY OBJECTIVES.

Management Charter an initiative in the UK by the Council for Management Education and Development to create a national qualification of Chartered Manager. Managers thus qualified would become PROFESSIONALS like accountants or lawyers. Professionalization would require identification of the core skills or 'competencies' of management, and a system of training and examination in these areas. Critics of this proposal have argued that management is so diverse that it is difficult to identify a core of competencies that are relevant to all managers. Furthermore certain management skills, such as those relating to managing people, are not easily translatable into a simple set of skills that can be assessed by formal examination. See MANAGEMENT DEVELOPMENT.

management consultant a person or firm which specializes in advising companies and other organizations on matters relating to their business strategy, organizational structure and the management of operations in functional areas such as marketing and production. Management consultants are employed to examine a company's current business practices and management, with a view to making recommendations for change aimed at improving efficiency and profitability. Unlike 'insiders', often with a vested interest in maintaining the status quo, the use of an independent team of consultants can provide an objective and detached assessment of what a firm needs to do in order to strengthen its organization.

management development the preparation of managers for future work roles. It can have two components:

(a) The passing of *specific* skills to managers using programmes of TRAINING; and

(b) the *general* development of abilities thought to be useful to managers such as awareness, problem-solving, etc.

Whilst the former can be straightforward, the latter is usually more difficult because development of this kind is not very tangible, therefore it is difficult to evaluate the worth of development programmes.

The core of most management development programmes is short courses, run either in-house or by consultants, on such topics as managing difficult employees and interpreting customer needs. Usually selection of participants will be done by managers' superiors, possibly as a result of development needs identified during PERFORMANCE APPRAISAL. In some cases, however, courses are offered on a cafeteria basis, i.e. individuals choose what they think they need most. A more sustained programme of individual development can be had by enrolling for a Master in Business Administration course at a university or college.

One type of course, less popular now than in the 1970s, is that involving 'T groups' or 'sensitivity training'. Over a period of days participants meet in a group and explore the patterns of interaction between group members. Its rationale is that it can heighten awareness of others and understanding of oneself, thereby promoting a more perceptive approach to management. Many individuals, however, find this experience unpleasant as it can raise awkward truths which many would prefer left unstated.

Partly because of doubts about the effectiveness of the classroom approach to development, *action learning* has become popular in recent years. Here managers are presented with real problems, possibly arising in an organization other than their own. The theory is that concentration on dealing with these will enhance problem-solving abilities.

Another approach currently popular is that of mentoring. Here a junior manager is paired with an experienced and successful manager (mentor) who acts as a role model. The trainee is to learn good management by example, reviewing his or her progress in regular meetings with the mentor. The benefit claimed of mentoring is that it facilitates development of personal qualities and managerial skills which cannot easily be taught by formal training. For mentoring to be successful it is essential that a good personal relationship is established and that those responsible for management development fully appreciate which qualities are desirable and can discover which managers possess them.

Many UK organizations do not devote enough resources to development. The reasons for this include the difficulties of evaluating its benefits and the reluctance of organizations to release individuals from their normal duties to participate in development programmes. Those involved in the MANAGEMENT CHARTER initiative have proposed that this be rectified by developing a CODE OF PRACTICE establishing minimum standards of management development. All organizations subscribing to the Charter would abide by the proposed code.

management information system a procedure which is concerned with getting appropriate information to managers as and when they need it.

See INFORMATION MANAGEMENT.

management style 1 the general character of management's approach to INDUSTRIAL RELATIONS. The starting point for considering management style is usually the contrast between two frames of reference (i.e. perspectives) concerning industrial relations:

(a) *unitary frame of reference*, where employee and managerial interests are believed to be the same, and hence TRADE UNIONS are viewed as illegitimate. They are seen as troublemakers who provoke CONFLICT where no real conflict exists. Those subscribing to this philosophy often portray the organization as a team where each member is dependent on the others in the team. There is also usually a strong emphasis on management's prerogative of taking decisions, justified on the basis that they are working for the good of all in the organization;

(b) *pluralist frame of reference,* where it is accepted that employees' interests may differ from those of management or the organization on occasion, and that trade unions are a legitimate expression of this. It is necessary to create procedures for resolving these differences so that conflict, which is damaging to all, can be avoided.

Although the notion of industrial relations style can be criticized for a lack of clarity – it is an amalgam of philosophies, statements, policies and actions – it is useful as a shorthand term to designate clusters of attributes which can be found in reality.

2 (in ORGANIZATIONAL ANALYSIS) the character of LEADERSHIP and MANAGEMENT. In the literature, management style refers to two different, though closely related phenomena: the leadership styles of individual managers and the prevailing style or CULTURE of the organization. In the former a basic distinction is made between *concern for production* and *concern for people,* exemplified on the one hand by the autocratic, task-centred approach of SCIENTIFIC MANAGEMENT and on the other by the concern for employee welfare found in HUMAN RELATIONS. In recent writing on leadership these concepts have been considered in relation to the situation in which leadership is exercised, the characteristics of those to be led, and the relationship to managerial effectiveness. The underlying distinction is also found in analysis of collective management style. The best known example is Douglas McGregor's (1906–64) THEORY X AND Y. In Theory X approaches, emphasis is placed on coercion to get the task done, whilst in Theory Y organizations, employees are allowed greater freedom on the grounds that this will lead to better job performance. A more sophisticated variant was developed by Rensis Likert (1903–81). He discerned four styles or systems of management:

(a) *exploitative autocratic,* where decision-making is autocratic and where employee compliance is achieved through coercion;

(b) *benevolent authoritative,* where decision-making is still largely centralized but managers appear to take some note of employee views and interests;

(c) *consultative,* where managers seek EMPLOYEE INVOLVEMENT but nevertheless still take the lead in policy formulation and decision-making;

(d) *democratic,* where there is some genuine devolution of decision-making to subordinates, especially in relation to job performance (see JOB DESIGN AND REDESIGN).

Likert believed that in the long run the democratic style would be most effective because it would reduce job dissatisfaction and build up employee commitment. As in industrial relations analysis, notions of style such as Likert's seem to correspond with distinct organizational types. Similarly, there is the problem that they can be somewhat imprecise in analytical terms. See NEO-HUMAN RELATIONS.

managerial grid see LEADERSHIP.

manpower planning the process of determining the demand and supply of labour to ensure that the organization (or national economy) has the right people with the right skills at the right time. The starting point for manpower planning is consideration of the demand for labour required by the organization. Then a stocks and flows analysis should be undertaken:

(a) *stocks,* the number of existing staff and their profits in terms of age, skills etc.;

(b) *flows,* the movement of people through the organization, especially those out of the organization and those within the organization, for example promotions, transfers, etc.

By using wastage analysis (see LABOUR TURNOVER) it should be possible to forecast what the employment numbers and the profile of the workforce will be in the future. Any gap between this and the labour requirements of the business strategy will need to be filled by RECRUITMENT AND SELECTION of new staff, TRAINING etc.

Manpower planning fell into some degree of disrepute during the early 1980s because the future was viewed as so uncertain that reliable forecasts were difficult to make. However, some planning is better than none and generally speaking those organizations which undertake some measure of planning are better situated to respond to future developments than those which do not. The shortage of school leavers in the UK in the early 1990s and the need to find ways of covering potential shortfalls in employee numbers has given a renewed respectability to manpower planning. Sophisticated manpower planning does not concentrate exclusively on the future, however. It aims to identify weaknesses in and upgrade the quality of the current workforce. See HUMAN RESOURCE MANAGEMENT.

manual worker see WORKER.

manufacturer see PRODUCER.

manufacturer brands BRANDS which are created by producers and bear their chosen BRAND NAME. Contrast OWN-LABEL BRAND.

manufacturing account an accounting statement which summarizes the main items of manufacturing cost with a view to determining the cost of finished goods manufactured. The cost of finished goods manufactured can then be entered in the PROFIT-AND-LOSS ACCOUNT as the equivalent of purchases for a purely trading company, in order to determine the cost of goods sold and gross profit. Fig. 54 shows a typical manufacturing account.

manufacturing cycle see CYCLE TIME.

manufacturing resource planning (MRP II) a computer-based PRODUCTION planning system which integrates *all* the resource requirements of a firm, including not only the control of raw materials and components (the central concern of MATERIALS REQUIREMENTS PLANNING – MRP) but also labour, machines and other resource needs. See PRODUCTION MANAGEMENT.

Manufacturing, Science and Finance Union (MSF) see AMICUS.

margin the difference between selling price and cost price of a PRODUCT or FINANCIAL SECURITY. See PROFIT MARGIN, SPREAD.

marginal cost the extra cost that is incurred by a firm in increasing OUTPUT by one unit. Given that FIXED COSTS do not vary with output, marginal costs are entirely marginal VARIABLE COSTS. Marginal cost generally includes the DIRECT MATERIALS and DIRECT LABOUR COST of a product along with VARIABLE OVERHEADS. See MARGINAL REVENUE.

marginal costing a system of product COSTING which assigns variable materials and labour costs to units of product manufactured but which does not assign fixed OVERHEAD costs to products. Fig. 55 shows an illustration of marginal costing.

		£	£
Raw Materials used:	opening stock	100,000	
	add purchases	330,000	
	less closing stock	130,000	300,000
Direct labour			200,000
Direct cost			500,000
Factory overheads			100,000
Total manufacturing cost:			600,000
add opening work in progress		60,000	
less closing work in progress		110,000	(50,000)
Cost of finished goods manufactured			550,000

Fig. 54 **Manufacturing account.** Manufacturing account of Y Company for year ending 20xx.

	TOTAL £	Tables £	Chairs £	Stools £
Sales	500	200	200	100
Material cost	250	100	75	75
Wages	100	35	50	15
VARIABLE COST	350	135	125	90
CONTRIBUTION	150	65	75	10
FIXED COSTS	100			
PROFIT (LOSS)	50			
Contribution: Sales %	30%	32%	37%	10%
Contribution per £ wages	£1.50	£1.90	£1.50	£0.70
Contribution per £ mat	£0.60	£0.70	£1.00	£0.10

Fig. 55 **Marginal costing.** A typical example.

With marginal costing, work in progress and finished goods stocks are valued at direct materials and direct labour costs only, and fixed overhead costs are charged as a single block against revenues in the period when. they are incurred. By contrast, with ABSORPTION COSTING fixed overhead costs are included in the value of work in progress and finished goods stock.

See CONTRIBUTION, BREAK-EVEN.

marginal-cost pricing see COST-BASED PRICING.

marginal revenue the extra revenue that is obtained by a firm from the sale of additional units of product. If firms are profit maximizers they will seek to equate marginal revenue with MARGINAL COST to establish that price output/sales combination which yields an optimal return.

See BUSINESS OBJECTIVE.

market an exchange mechanism which brings together the sellers and buyers of a product. Markets, in practice, embrace a number of product, spatial and physical dimensions. In terms of product, a market can be defined as consisting of a group of goods or services which are viewed as *substitute* products by buyers. Thus, from a MARKETING point of view, women's' shoes and men's' shoes would be represented as constituting separate markets, that is, markets catering for the needs of different buyers (see MARKET SEGMENTATION).

Spatially, a market may be local, regional, national or international in scope, depending on such considerations as transport costs, product characteristics and the homogeneity of buyer tastes. For example, because of a high ratio of transport costs to value added, cement and plasterboard markets tend to be localized. Likewise, Bavarian beer caters for a specialized regional taste, while Coca-Cola, by contrast, is sold worldwide as a global brand.

Physically, seller and buyer exchanges may be transacted in a well-defined market place (for example a local fish market or wool exchange), or in a much more amorphous way (for example the buying and selling of stocks and shares by telephone through a nexus of international dealing offices). Finally, in some markets sellers deal directly with final buyers, while in others transactions are conducted through a chain of intermediaries such as wholesalers and retailers, brokers and banks.

Markets constitute the battlegrounds of business. Corporate success depends fundamentally on identifying and exploiting positions of COMPETITIVE ADVANTAGE which requires the effective application of appropriate strategies of PRODUCTION, MARKETING, etc. See COMMODITY MARKET, MONEY MARKET, STOCK MARKET, SPOT MARKET, FORWARD MARKET, INDUSTRY, MARKET STRUCTURE, MARKET-CONDUCT-PERFORMANCE SCHEME, MARKET SYSTEM, EQUILIBRIUM MARKET PRICE.

market based (approach to strategy) see BUSINESS STRATEGY.

market capitalization the total value of a company's ISSUED SHARE CAPITAL as determined by its current share price on the STOCK MARKET.

market challengers the sellers of a product who rank second, third etc. in terms of MARKET SHARE and are in a close position to challenge the current MARKET LEADER.

market channel see DISTRIBUTION CHANNEL.

market concentration the extent to which the production of a particular good or service is controlled by the leading suppliers (*seller concentration*), and the extent to which the purchase of a product is controlled by the leading buyers (*buyer concentration*). The degree of seller concentration in a MARKET is often measured by a concentration ratio which shows the proportion of market sales accounted for by the largest five, or ten, suppliers.

The significance of market concentration for BUSINESS STRATEGY and MARKETING lies in its effect on the nature and intensity of competition. Structurally, as the level of seller concentration in a market progressively increases, 'competition between the many' becomes 'competition between the few' until, at the extreme, the market is totally monopolized by a single supplier (see MARKET STRUCTURE). In terms of MARKET CONDUCT, as supply becomes concentrated in fewer and fewer hands (OLIGOPOLY), suppliers may seek to avoid mutually, ruinous price competition and channel their main marketing efforts into sales promotion and product innovation, activities which offer a more profitable and effective way of establishing COMPETITIVE ADVANTAGE over rivals.

Buyer concentration can also affect the competitive situation. In many markets (particularly end-consumer markets) buyers are too small to influence supply conditions, but in others (particularly in intermediary goods markets and in retailing), buying power is concentrated and purchasers are able to obtain bulk-buying discounts from suppliers. See ECONOMIES OF SCALE, HORIZONTAL INTEGRATION, COMPETITION POLICY, MONOPOLY.

market conduct the behavioural characteristics of suppliers and buyers operating in a MARKET/INDUSTRY. Key elements of market conduct include:

(a) the BUSINESS OBJECTIVES of suppliers (for example profit and sales growth targets), and the product requirements of buyers (for example low prices, product performance and sophistication);

(b) the MARKETING instruments and strategies available to firms which can be used to establish COMPETITIVE ADVANTAGE over rival suppliers. These include various pricing tactics (MARKET PENETRATION PRICING, MARKET SKIMMING, PRICING, etc.) and MARKETING-MIX combinations such as advertising and sales promotion, quality variations, packaging and design etc. The choice of appropriate marketing strategies will, of course, vary from market to market depending on product characteristics and, critically, on an understanding of those product attributes which command buyer satisfaction (see MARKET RESEARCH);

(c) the mutual interdependency of suppliers which serves to constrain individual freedom of action and often leads, particularly in markets characterized by high seller concentration, to coordinated behaviour patterns, for example PRICE LEADERSHIP and COLLUSION;

(d) the relationships between suppliers and buyers, in particular the impact of bulkbuying policies (see MARKET CONCENTRATION, MARKET STRUCTURE).

In sum, most markets exhibit both competitive and cooperative tendencies, and firms must be mindful of these forces in formulating appropriate business strategies.

COMPETITION POLICY interest in market conduct is centred on the potentially adverse effect of market power on MARKET PERFORMANCE, either exercised by a DOMINANT FIRM or deriving from collusion between firms. See MARKET STRUCTURE-CONDUCT-PERFORMANCE SCHEMA.

market development a BUSINESS STRATEGY pursued by a firm aimed at increasing sales of the firm's *existing* products by finding *new* markets for those products. This strategy could involve the firm in building up a network of export markets, or in finding new applications or uses for its product. See PRODUCT–MARKET MATRIX.

market dominance see DOMINANT FIRM.

market entry the entry into a MARKET of a new supplier in the form of either a GREENFIELD operation (i.e. an additional supply source) or the MERGER with, or TAKEOVER of, an existing supplier. Market entry constitutes a major BUSINESS STRATEGY decision, reflecting a strategic initiative on the part of a firm to develop, or reshape, its product/market positioning. Such entry occurs largely in response to the perceived long-run profit potential of the target market, which in turn is importantly influenced by the size of the market and its perceived growth potential, both with respect to the expansion of total primary demand and particular market segments. Successful new entry requires the firm not only to overcome any initial BARRIERS TO ENTRY, but also to develop a long-term strategy for establishing and sustaining COMPETITIVE ADVANTAGE over rival suppliers. See MARKET SYSTEM.

market exit the exit from a MARKET of an established supplier. Market exit constitutes a major BUSINESS STRATEGY decision, reflecting a strategic initiative on the part of a firm to reshape its product/market positioning. Such exit occurs largely in response to a sustained LOSS-making situation or poor PROFIT rate or low perceived growth potential. Successful exit requires the firm to overcome any BARRIERS TO EXIT. See DIVESTMENT.

market follower see MARKET CHALLENGER.

marketing the managerial process of identifying customer requirements and satisfying them by providing customers with appropriate products in order to achieve the organization's objectives. Marketing goes beyond merely selling what the firm produces, but starts by identifying underlying consumer needs through MARKETING RESEARCH; generating products which satisfy these needs through NEW PRODUCT DEVELOPMENT; promoting these products to consumers through various MARKETING MIX policies (pricing, advertising, sales promotion etc.); and physically distributing products to customers through DISTRIBUTION CHANNELS. See MARKETING CONCEPT, INTEGRATED MARKETING, CONSUMER ORIENTATION, PRODUCTION ORIENTATION, MARKETING STRATEGY, GAP ANALYSIS, CUSTOMER RELATIONSHIP MANAGEMENT.

marketing allocation the division of a company's SALES BUDGET between its PRODUCTS, MARKET SEGMENTS and SALES TERRITORIES.

marketing audit a systematic examination of a business's marketing environment, objectives, strategies, and activities with a view to identifying key strategic issues, problem areas and opportunities. See PEST, SWOT ANALYSIS.

marketing benchmarking see BENCHMARKING.

marketing communications see PROMOTION.

marketing concept a business philosophy which aims at the generation of profits by the recognition and satisfaction of customer needs.

The marketing concept emphasizes the need for a business to adopt a CONSUMER ORIENTATION, that is to start by identifying the needs of consumers and then develop products with the attributes and characteristics to meet these needs.

The marketing concept stresses the superiority of a customer-based marketing approach over a PRODUCTION ORIENTATION which is largely concerned with persuading customers to buy what the firm has chosen to produce. See INTEGRATED MARKETING, MARKETING MIX.

marketing effort the total amount of resources which a firm puts into the MARKETING MIX in order to stimulate demand for its goods and services (see SALES BUDGET). However, the firm's overall marketing success will depend not only on its marketing effort but also on the *effectiveness* of that expenditure in securing customers, and a firm would aim to generate greater sales than its competitors from an equivalent level of expenditure.

marketing information system a system in which marketing information is formally gathered, stored, analysed, and distributed to managers in accordance with their informational needs on a regular, planned basis. See MARKETING INTELLIGENCE.

marketing intelligence information about developments in a firm's market environment that can assist executives in formulating marketing plans. Such intelligence could include details of new products being introduced by competitors, and price changes, or more general economic and social statistics published by government and other bodies.

Various techniques may be employed to gather market intelligence. *Field studies* may be undertaken among samples of the population employing personally conducted or postal QUESTIONNAIRES, telephone and personal interviews, and group surveys; *focus groups*, which involve detailed discussions among small groups of invited respondents called together on one or two occasions; *desk research* can be employed using secondary published information and reports from government or other sources; finally, information about existing products or prototypes can be gained by recruiting *panels* of consumers who report regularly on their experience of using products, by setting up controlled experiments to test consumers' reactions to products and advertising messages, and by direct observation of customers who are buying or using a product or service.

Intelligence gathering is undertaken to seek out new market opportunities and identify possible threats to the sales of existing products. See MARKETING RESEARCH.

marketing logistics the analysis, planning, organization and control of all movement and storage operations connected with the PRODUCTION and DISTRIBUTION of goods.

Whereas distribution is concerned with simply moving products to customers, marketing logistics incorporates a broader responsibility for product distribution management which includes moving raw materials to factories, moving work in progress through the factory and moving finished goods from the factory to consumers. Such an integrated system involves siting of factories and warehouses and DISTRIBUTION CHANNELS used, in order to maximize the effectiveness of the system.See JUST-IN-TIME (JIT) SYSTEM.

marketing management the process of setting objectives, formulating policy, analysis, planning, implementation and control of activities aimed at the effective selling of the firm's goods or services. See MARKETING, MANAGEMENT.

marketing myopia the tendency for firms to take a narrow view of the MARKETS they currently serve based upon their present product offerings and thus to ignore broader market opportunities. For example, a producer who viewed his market solely as that for 'potato crisps' would be ignoring the potential for selling related products into the much broader 'snack products' market. See PRODUCT-MARKET MATRIX.

marketing objectives the general and specific aims which a firm sets for itself in selling its products. Marketing objectives together with similar objectives for the other functional areas of the firm (production, finance etc.) are closely related to the firm's overall BUSINESS OBJECTIVES. Operationally, marketing objectives may either be stated in general terms such as simply the increase of sales year by year, or set as quantitative targets: a minimum 10% increase in sales per annum, or an increase in the market share of a particular product from its current level of say 20% of the market to 30% over a five-year period. Such explicit objectives provide a focus for the deployment of the firm's resources and the application of appropriate MARKETING STRATEGIES to achieve them.

marketing mix

The range of measures used by firms to market their products to buyers. Important facets of the marketing mix are the 4 Ps: product, price, promotion and place.

(a) the product offering, in particular the QUALITY, styling and variety of the firm's established products (see PRODUCT RANGE), and its ability to provide buyers with new products over time (see NEW PRODUCT DEVELOPMENT), see PRODUCT POSITIONING;

(b) the prices charged for the firm's products (see PRICING, PRICING METHODS);

(c) the means used by the firm to promote its products, including ADVERTISING, SALES PROMOTION, MERCHANDIZING, PERSONAL SELLING, PACKAGING and PUBLIC RELATIONS;

(d) the place and means used to distribute the product into the hands of buyers (see DISTRIBUTION CHANNEL);

(e) also important is the provision of various on-going CUSTOMER SERVICES, particularly AFTER-SALES SERVICE facilities and GUARANTEES.

In the case of services three other elements (making the 7 Ps) to be taken into account are: process (meaning the operations involved in delivering the service), people (the frontline and back office staff involved in service delivery and management) and physical evidence (materials, décor, and settings used by organizations to make the service experience more concrete).

The relative importance of these elements will vary according to the *particular* buyer characteristics of the MARKET or MARKET SEGMENTS being served by a product. Thus, to take a broad example, in marketing *consumer* goods such factors as advertising, sales promotion and packaging might be emphasized, while in marketing *industrial* goods technical features of the product, price and personal selling might be stressed. See CONSUMER ORIENTATION.

marketing orientation see CONSUMER ORIENTATION.

marketing plan the specification of a firm's MARKETING OBJECTIVES, MARKETING STRATEGIES and policies and the various means of implementing these policies; e.g. MARKETING MIX SELECTION, MARKET SEGMENTATION and PRODUCT POSITIONING.

marketing research the systematic and objective classification, collection, analysis and reporting of information about a particular marketing problem. Marketing research can be ad hoc and specific or continuous and general.

Ad hoc (or one-off) marketing research sets out to obtain specific information which is needed for a particular purpose, for example a study of consumer attitudes and perceptions about an existing product. This information could then be used to modify the product or change the MARKETING MIX used to promote it. See CONJOINT ANALYSIS.

Continuous (or on-going) marketing research involves monitoring of the firm's market environment on a regular basis. Such research provides intelligence about competitors and their pricing and marketing policies, effects of proposed legislation on company brands, the potential impact of economic changes such as total consumer spending and social trends such as environmental awareness.

Marketing research uses a variety of techniques such as in-depth interviews and group surveys which can be used primarily for MOTIVATIONAL RESEARCH; in addition, field studies can be undertaken using QUESTIONNAIRES and interviews, and desk research of records and data, these being used primarily for MARKETING INTELLIGENCE. Finally, techniques such as consumer panels, market experiments and observation may be used to gain information about existing products.

Businesses carry out marketing research to enable them to identify market trends; to find out about market characteristics; to forecast market potential; to analyse MARKET SHARE; to find a MARKET SEGMENT; and to test consumer acceptance of new or existing products. See CONSUMER ORIENTATION, NEW-PRODUCT DEVELOPMENT.

marketing strategy the means of achieving a customer-related objective, specifically customer recruitment and customer retention. The key components of marketing strategy are MARKET SEGMENTATION, PRODUCT POSITIONING and the MARKETING MIX. See DIFFERENTIATED MARKETING OR TARGETING STRATEGY, UNDIFFERENTIATED MARKETING STRATEGY, CONCENTRATED MARKETING OR TARGETING STRATEGY.

market intermediary a business such as a WHOLESALER which acts as a 'middleman' in moving goods through a DISTRIBUTION CHANNEL, or an AGENT (for example, an INSURANCE BROKER) which brings together buyers and sellers of insurance. See TRADER/DEALER.

market leader the seller of a product who holds the largest MARKET SHARE. Generally firms become market leaders by establishing positions of COMPETITIVE ADVANTAGE over rival suppliers. See MARKET CHALLENGERS.

market maker a firm attached to the STOCK MARKET which is engaged in the buying and selling of FINANCIAL SECURITIES such as STOCKS, SHARES and BONDS and thereby acts to establish a market PRICE for these securities. Market making firms in the UK have (since the 1986 stock market reforms) combined the roles of jobber (acting as a *principal* in the buying and selling of securities) and stockbroker (acting as an *agent* on behalf of clients wishing to sell or buy securities); although the stockbroking function is still performed by firms specialized in that activity alone.

A market making firm usually specializes in a small group of securities, for example the shares of companies in a particular industry. The firm makes its profit out of the difference between the price at which it buys a security and the (higher) price at which it sells. The firm marks its buying and selling prices upwards or downwards according to whether its holding of a security is falling or increasing. For example, if there is a strong demand for a particular share, then as the firm sells some of its holdings it will mark the share price up to reflect its growing scarcity value. See BID PRICE, SHARE PURCHASE/SALE.

market niche see MARKET SEGMENT.

market penetration a BUSINESS STRATEGY pursued by a firm which is aimed at increasing the sales of the firm's *existing* products in its *present* markets thereby increasing its MARKET SHARE in those markets. This strategy involves the deployment of various MARKETING MIX elements (pricing, advertising etc.), together with appropriate MARKET SEGMENTATION policies aimed at competing more aggressively against rival suppliers. See PRODUCT MARKET MATRIX, MARKET PENETRATION PRICING, CONCENTRATED MARKETING STRATEGY.

market penetration pricing a pricing policy that involves charging a comparatively low PRICE for a product in order to secure growing sales and a high market share. This policy can be adopted by a firm where consumers are price sensitive. More specifically such a tactic may be used as a means of securing entry to a market, or where its product has moved into the growth phase of its PRODUCT LIFE CYCLE. Contrast MARKET SKIMMING PRICE. See PRICING OBJECTIVES, PRICING METHODS,

DUMPING, MARKET ENTRY, ELASTICITY OF DEMAND, MARKET PENETRATION.

market performance the effectiveness of suppliers in a MARKET/INDUSTRY in utilizing economic resource to their maximum efficiency and to the ultimate benefit of consumers. Key elements of market performance include:

(a) productive efficiency – the cost effectiveness of firms in producing their outputs. Ideally, outputs should be produced in plants of optimal scale, that is, plant sizes which fully exploit available ECONOMIES OF SCALE so that minimum cost levels are attained;

(b) distributive efficiency – the utilization of cost-effective channels of distribution and marketing techniques so as to minimize distribution costs;

(c) the setting of 'fair' prices to consumers, that is, prices which are consistent with the real economic costs of supplying the product, including a reasonable (i.e. non-monopolistic) profit return to suppliers;

(d) product performance – the satisfaction of consumer demands for product variety and sophistication, that is, the maximization of consumer choice and value-for-money attributes;

(e) technological progressiveness – the introduction of process and product innovations which enable supply costs and prices to be reduced in real terms and which provide consumers with technically superior products (see RESEARCH AND DEVELOPMENT).

Market performance is determined primarily by MARKET STRUCTURE and MARKET CONDUCT. For example, in markets where economies of scale are significant, a high level of MARKET CONCENTRATION may be required in order to minimize supply costs. In conduct terms, price COMPETITION between firms is likely to benefit consumers whereas COLLUSION is likely to have an adverse effect on consumer welfare. These and other elements of market structure and conduct are a major concern of a government's COMPETITION POLICY and INDUSTRIAL POLICY. See MARKET STRUCTURE-CONDUCT-PERFORMANCE SCHEMA.

market potential the total size of the MARKET for a product at a given time, measured in either volume or value terms. A single seller's share of the market potential will depend upon its MARKETING effort. However, the cumulative marketing efforts of all sellers can serve to expand market potential over time.

Changes in the broader economic environment can affect market potential. For example, a rise in interest rates will decrease the total DEMAND for certain electrical goods.

market power *or* **monopoly power** the ability of a firm (or group of firms) to dictate market prices and other terms and conditions of supply. Market power derives essentially from the possession of a dominant market share (see MONOPOLY) or from COLLUSION between the leading suppliers. Where firms possess market power there exists a danger that such power might be abused; for example, the charging of monopolistic prices to the detriment of consumers or selective price cuts to drive out smaller competitors. See COMPETITION POLICY, MARKET STRUCTURE, MARKET CONDUCT, MARKET PERFORMANCE, DOMINANT FIRM.

market research an aspect of MARKETING RESEARCH which is concerned with the collection and analysis of information about a particular market.

market research agency a firm which carries out MARKETING RESEARCH on behalf of clients.

market risk *or* **non-diversifiable risk** that part of total risk (within the CAPITAL-ASSET PRICING MODEL) attributable to the holding of a security, or portfolio of securities, which depends upon variations in general security prices on the STOCK MARKET. Market risk is associated with general market variations as measured by a market index, such as the Financial Times All-Share Index or the Dow-Jones Index. Unlike SPECIFIC RISK, it is not possible to diversify market risk away, because however large the portfolio of shares held, they are all influenced by the market generally to a greater or lesser extent. See BETA COEFFICIENT.

market segment a part of a MARKET which has its own distinct customer profile and buyer characteristics such that, for MARKETING purposes, it can be targeted separately from other segments of the market. See MARKET SEGMENTATION, DIFFERENTIATED MARKETING STRATEGY, CONCENTRATED MARKETING STRATEGY, FOCUS, COMPETITIVE STRATEGY.

market segmentation the division of a MARKET into identifiable submarkets or segments each having its own particular customer profile and BUYER characteristics. A market can often be divided up broadly into major customer segments as well as more narrowly into various submarkets within each of these segments. In MARKETING terms, markets can be segmented in a number of ways as Fig. 56 (overleaf) indicates, pyramiding down from the identification of major subgroups of customers, and their particular product-type requirements and preferences with reference to such things as range of quality gradations, colouring and packaging. Further elements in market segmentation include the distribution outlets used by buyers to make purchases and the geographical boundaries of the market.

Depending upon the complexity of a market as revealed by market segment analysis, a firm may choose to operate 'across the board' or decide to focus on a limited number of segments. Since most markets in practice possess segmentation characteristics to a greater or lesser degree, an UNDIFFERENTIATED MARKETING STRATEGY involving a uniform MARKETING MIX approach across all segments is likely to be of only limited effectiveness. A more attractive approach in these circumstances is a DIFFERENTIATED MARKETING OR TARGETING STRATEGY involving various 'customized' marketing mix formulations, each tailored to match the buyer characteristics of the segments targeted. A third approach, a CONCENTRATED MARKETING OR TARGETING STRATEGY, may be applied where the firm decides to target the whole of its marketing effort on one particular segment. See VALUE ADDED MODEL, CONSUMER SURPLUS, SOCIOECONOMIC GROUP, CONSUMER SEGMENTATION, DISTRIBUTION CHANNEL, PRODUCT RANGE, PRODUCT ATTRIBUTES, PACKAGING, INTERNATIONAL MARKETING, BRAND EXTENSION, PRODUCT POSITIONING, CUSTOMIZATION.

market share the proportion of total sales of a product accounted for by an individual BRAND of the product or all brands of the product offered by a firm in a particular MARKET.

A firm's market share relative to competitors' market share provides an indicator of its success in marketing its brand(s) over time. Some minimum market share may be necessary to achieve sufficient sales volume to enable the firm to produce efficiently (see ECONOMIES OF SCALE). Beyond this the firm may aspire to market leadership of the whole market or may seek to achieve high market share in one or more MARKET SEGMENTS.

Market shares can be only meaningfully related to a precise definition of the market serviced by the firm both in geographic terms (for example UK snack product sales or European snack product sales), and in product scope (for example, potato crisps and other snack products). See MARKET LEADER, MARKET CHALLENGERS, MARKET CONCENTRATION, COMPETITION POLICY.

market-skimming pricing a pricing policy that involves charging a comparatively high price for a product to secure large profit margins. This policy can be adopted by a firm where consumers are not price sensitive. More specifically, such a tactic may be used where a new product is still in the introductory phase of its PRODUCT LIFECYCLE and embodies novel features which enable it to command a premium price. Contrast with MARKET PENETRATION PRICING. See PRICING OBJECTIVES, PRICING METHODS, ELASTICITY OF DEMAND.

market structure the organizational characteristics of a MARKET/INDUSTRY. Key elements of market structure include:

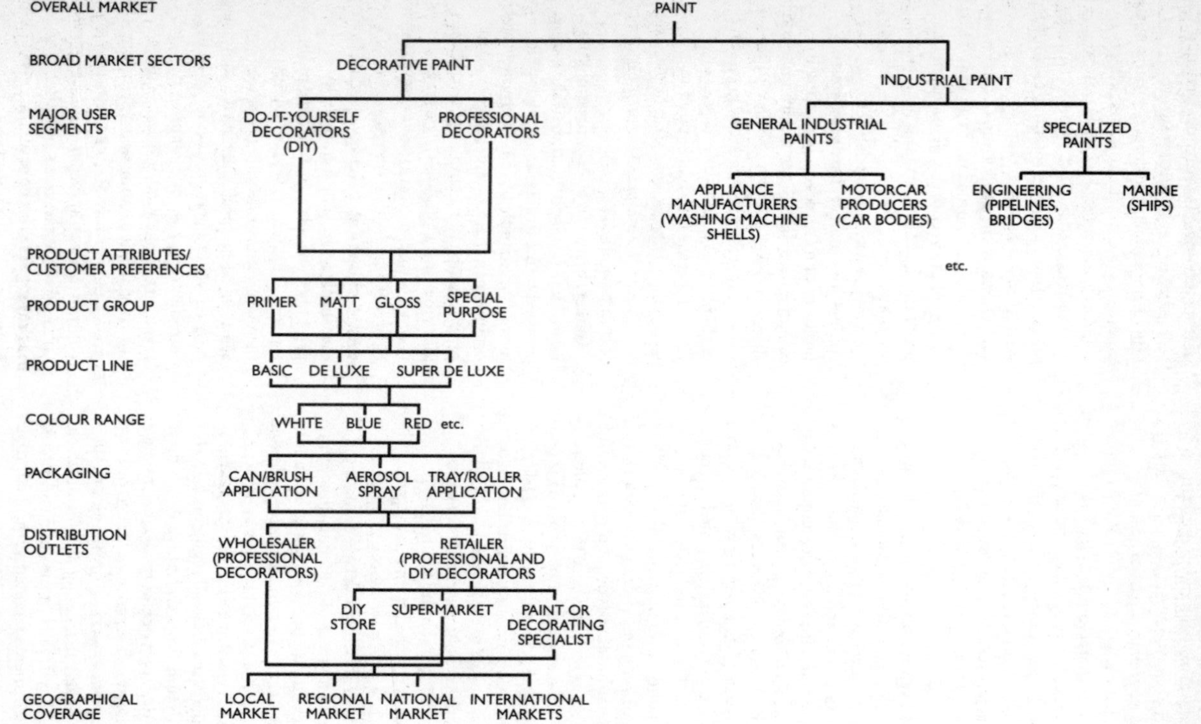

Fig. 56 **Market segmentation**. A matrix for paint.

(a) the number of suppliers and their relative size distribution, indicating the extent of seller concentration in the market (see MARKET CONCENTRATION, CONCENTRATION RATIO);

(b) the number of buyers and their relative size distribution, indicating the extent of buyer concentration in the market;

(c) the nature of the product, whether it is a standardized good or service, or differentiated in a variety of ways (see PRODUCT DIFFERENTIATION);

(d) the condition of entry to the market, that is, the extent and severity of BARRIERS TO ENTRY confronting potential newcomers;

(e) the degree of VERTICAL INTEGRATION, that is, the extent to which suppliers produce their own input requirements, or possess their own distribution outlets for their products.

These aspects of market structure, together with underlying cost and demand conditions, are significant in so far as they have a *strategic* influence on the nature and intensity of competitive behaviour in a market (see MARKET CONDUCT) and hence on MARKET PERFORMANCE. To illustrate: the greater the level of seller concentration, the more heightened is the degree of mutual interdependency such that the actions of one firm will have a discernible effect on the market position of other firms, causing them to respond with actions of their own. In this situation, for example, recognition that aggressive price competition is likely to prove mutually ruinous may well encourage suppliers to focus their competitive efforts on sales promotion and product innovation as these provide a more effective means of establishing COMPETITIVE ADVANTAGE. In turn, the greater the scope for the deployment of product differentiation strategies, the more prominent this area of competition is likely to become. Barriers to entry may arise naturally from the supply characteristics of the market (for example cost advantages to established firms arising from ECONOMIES OF SCALE), or they can be created predatorily by established firms to keep newcomers out (for example the use of EXCLUSIVE DEALING practices). In either case established firms are protected from new competition. Likewise, vertical integration by a DOMINANT FIRM may limit competition in a market by depriving rivals and potential entrants of inputs or distribution outlets. Additionally, a firm which is diversified into a number of markets (see DIVERSIFICATION) may be able to cross-subsidize its activities in a particular market in order to advance its position in that market.

In sum, market structure provides the backdrop to a firm's strategic actions as it seeks to establish competitive advantage over rivals, but, importantly, can itself be altered and controlled by firms' actions; for example, firms may seek to increase their market shares by TAKEOVERS and MERGERS, thereby raising the level of seller concentration.

COMPETITION POLICY interest in market structure centres on the association of market structure and conduct, and their impact on market performance. Mergers and takeovers, for example, which would reduce competition, may be prohibited on the grounds that they would unduly increase a firm's power to control market prices and profit levels. See MARKET STRUCTURE-CONDUCT PERFORMANCE SCHEMA, MONOPOLISTIC COMPETITION, MONOPOLY, OLIGOPOLY, PERFECT COMPETITION.

market structure-conduct-performance schema a conceptual framework which identifies key characteristics of MARKET STRUCTURE, MARKET CONDUCT and MARKET PERFORMANCE (see Fig. 57), and facilitates analysis of the interrelationships between these variables. The structure-conduct-performance schema is useful for the achievement of COMPETITIVE ADVANTAGE over rivals. Structure and conduct patterns enable an analysis to be made of the 'forces driving competition' in a market, which, together with observation of market performance results, enables an assessment to be made of the actual and potential strengths and weaknesses of established suppliers. Established firms may be relatively cost-inefficient because of their failure to exploit ECONOMIES OF SCALE, or, because of inertia or limited marketing

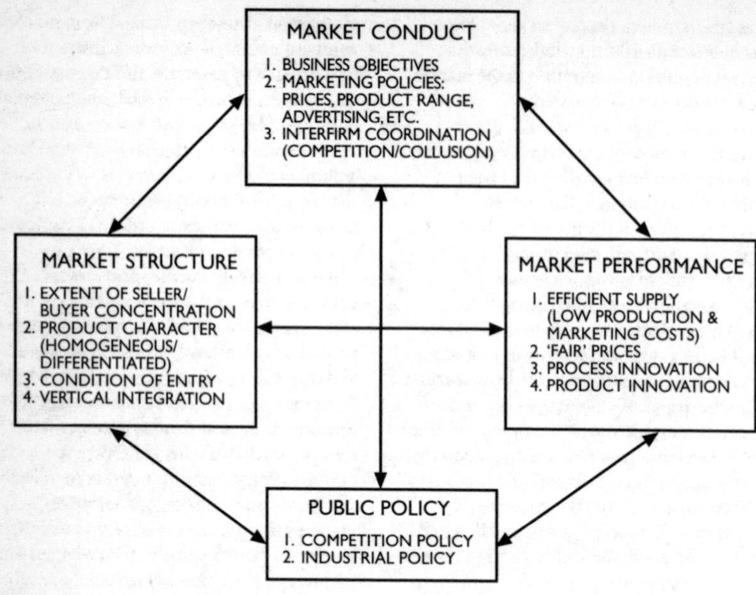

Fig. 57 **Market structure-conduct-performance schema.**

vision, neglect potentially lucrative market niches. Consideration of such factors may provide for successful MARKET ENTRY based on the establishment of optimal scale plant and MARKET SEGMENTATION strategies. The schema is particularly relevant to COMPETITION POLICY and INDUSTRIAL POLICY bodies in applying appropriate remedial measures to redress poor performance. For example, structural initiatives involving mergers and rationalization schemes may be the preferred means of reorganizing markets to eliminate excess capacity, or, alternatively, mergers between the leading firms in a market may be vetoed because they would lead to an undesirable degree of monopolization. Likewise, conduct measures may be used to improve cost efficiency and lower 'excessive' market prices and profit levels by, for example, the prohibition of price-fixing CARTELS, or the imposition of PRICE CONTROLS on dominant suppliers.

market system *or* **price system** an ECONOMY in which basic decisions about the allocation of resources, which goods and services are produced and in what quantities, are determined by the interaction of buyers and sellers in factor and product MARKETS. See EQUILIBRIUM MARKET PRICE, MARKET CONDUCT, MARKET PERFORMANCE, MARKET STRUCTURE, MARKET STRUCTURE-CONDUCT-PERFORMANCE SCHEMA.

market targeting see MARKET SEGMENT.

market testing the process of putting a good or service on to the market to gauge its viability. The term has been used in the UK in the context of the privatization and deregulation of public sector products.

market value the amount that a firm's FIXED ASSETS and CURRENT ASSETS such as STOCKS could be sold for on the open market. In a company's BALANCE SHEET such assets are usually recorded at their HISTORIC COST though market value may be substantially higher, reflecting current prices.

mark-up the PROFIT MARGIN on a good or service which can be expressed as a percentage of the cost of the product or a percentage of its selling price. See PRICING METHODS, COST-BASED PRICING.

mark-up pricing see COST-BASED PRICING.

mass customization the use of technology and sophisticated computing facilities to individualize mass produced (and therefore identical) products. For example, the manufacture of a pair of jeans specifically designed for an individual can be carried out using a mass production facility. The technique requires accurate measurements that are transmitted by Electronic Data Interchange to the manufacturing point. Cloth is cut by automatic cutting machinery, each piece is identifed by a bar code and the whole is then stitched together and forwarded to the customer. See MASS PRODUCTION.

mass marketing the process of promoting the sales of large numbers of a product in order to facilitate MASS PRODUCTION of the product. See PROMOTIONAL MIX.

mass media see MEDIA.

mass production a method of organizing PRODUCTION whereby a component or product such as a motor car passes through a sequence of predetermined operations or processes which constitute a PRODUCTION LINE OR ASSEMBLY LINE. Mass production systems are used to make components or products in comparatively large quantities using specialized machines on a continuous basis. See PRODUCT-FOCUSED LAYOUT, PRODUCTION SCHEDULING, MASS CUSTOMIZATION.

master budget a summary budgeted PROFIT-AND-LOSS ACCOUNT and budgeted BALANCE SHEET, incorporating the component functional budgets (sales, production, distribution etc.) as approved and employed by a firm's managers. See BUDGET, BUDGETING.

master production schedule a (usually) software-generated list that is divided into time periods (for example a day or a week) and which looks at all forecast and confirmed orders and compares this to the Bill of Materials for each item together with present inventory levels. The schedule produces a list of items that need to be made from final components, through sub-assemblies and orders material for inventory as required. See PRODUCT SPECIFICATION, PRODUCTION SCHEDULING.

matching the process of matching revenues and profits with the associated expenses incurred in earning these revenues. See ACCRUALS PRINCIPLE OF ACCOUNTING.

matching shares see SHARE INCENTIVE PLAN.

materials inputs into the PRODUCTION process most of which are embodied in the finished goods being manufactured. Materials include raw materials such as metal ores and cotton, and manufactured components. The materials which are embodied in the finished product are known as DIRECT MATERIALS whereas other materials such as lubricants and other consumables which are used up during the production process are known as INDIRECT MATERIALS. See VALUE ADDED.

materiality see ACCOUNTING PRINCIPLES.

materials cost variance the difference between the standard DIRECT MATERIALS cost of a product (standard materials usage x standard materials price) and its actual direct materials cost (actual materials usage x actual materials price). This difference can be broken down into two parts:

(a) *materials quantity variance,* which involves calculating the difference between the standard quantity of materials specified and the actual quantity used, converted into money terms by multiplying by the standard materials price;

(b) *materials price variance,* which involves calculating the difference between the standard price of materials specified and the actual price paid, multiplied by the actual quantity of materials used.

With this distinction it is possible to trace whether an adverse direct materials cost variance is due to excess usage of materials or to higher materials prices. See STANDARD COST.

materials flow management the organization of the flow of materials within a factory based upon the breaking down of manufacturing processes into detailed elements. The aim of materials flow management is to reduce manufacturing throughput time by seeking to reduce waste in the process.

Materials flow analysis generally involves three main types of documentation: *assembly drawings* which specify how the components in a manufactured product should be put together; *assembly* or *Gozinto charts* which are derived from the assembly drawings and which show each sequential step in the assembly process; *operations process sheets* or *routing sheets* which are derived from the assembly chart and which show in detail the operations and routing required for each individual component along with any tools and equipment needed.

In addition, where firms seek to analyse and improve materials flows they may employ ACTIVITY CHARTS which represent assembly activities in terms of standardized symbols. See MATERIALS MANAGEMENT, MATERIALS REQUIREMENT PLANNING, MANUFACTURING RESOURCE PLANNING, OPTIMIZED PRODUCTION TECHNOLOGY.

materials handling see MATERIALS MANAGEMENT.

materials management the administration and control of the materials used by a firm in the PRODUCTION process. This has two main aspects:

(a) the ordering and maintaining of STOCKS of materials so as to ensure that adequate amounts of materials are available at all times, thus enabling production to go ahead without interruption while at the same time attempting to minimize stockholding costs (see PURCHASING, MATERIALS REQUIREMENTS PLANNING, STOCK CONTROL, STOCKHOLDING MODEL);

(b) materials handling, the physical movement of materials from place to place, their packaging (in pallets and containers) and their storage (see INTERSTAGE STORE) as they proceed through various production processes. Materials handling seeks to minimize internal transport costs and damage to, and wastage of, materials. See MATERIALS FLOW MANAGEMENT.

materials price variance see MATERIALS COST VARIANCE.

materials quantity variance see MATERIALS COST VARIANCE.

materials requirement planning (MRP) a planning system for scheduling STOCK replenishment so as to ensure that adequate amounts of materials are available at all times thus enabling PRODUCTION to go ahead without interruption. Key features of MRP are the calculation of raw material and component requirements from the PRODUCTION SCHEDULES of the products in which the materials are to be embodied, and the time phasing of replenishment orders for materials so that they arrive in good time to avoid a *stockout* situation which would halt production. Thus, if production schedules indicate that stock of a particular material will need to be replenished in week 7 to avoid a stockout and the time it takes for the new stock to be delivered after the placement of the order is 2 weeks, then the order will need to be issued in week 5. See STOCK CONTROL, JUST-IN-TIME (JIT) SYSTEM, MANUFACTURING RESOURCE PLANNING, MATERIALS MANAGEMENT, MATERIALS FLOW MANAGEMENT, OPTIMIZED PRODUCTION TECHNOLOGY.

materials requisition a document which is used to authorize and record the issue of materials or components to production from stores. Information from the requisition is used to update the STORES RECORD CARD (bin card) and the STORES LEDGER, and to ascertain the DIRECT MATERIALS used on jobs or products as well as the INDIRECT MATERIALS used by various COST CENTRES.

materials usage variance see MATERIALS COST VARIANCE.

maternity rights the rights pregnant women and the mothers of very young children have in relation to their employment. Pregnant women in the UK have a right to a minimum of 18 weeks' maternity leave, and any dismissal of a female employee on the grounds of pregnancy constitutes UNFAIR DISMISSAL. Pregnant women also have the right to their usual employment benefits during these

18 weeks such as continuing use of their company car. These rights, based on a directive of the European Union, extend previous law on maternity rights which required minimum periods of employment. Those with one year's employment may take further maternity leave. See PATERNITY LEAVE, SICK PAY.

matrix an ORGANIZATION structure in which individuals report to managers in more than one DEPARTMENT or function. The simple CHAIN OF COMMAND found in the classic BUREAUCRACY is replaced by (potentially) a multiplicity of reporting relationships. This type of structure may characterize part of the organization – for project team management for instance, where a project manager assumes authority over team members drawn from a number of departments – or it may extend to the entire organization. See Fig. 58.

There is no standard form of matrix. Managers may have *equal* formal authority over subordinates or alternatively one of these may have *primary* authority with the others, assuming authority on particular issues, as in the dotted-line relationship (see ORGANIZATION CHART). The benefits of matrix organization are said to be that it facilitates interdepartmental coordination during innovation, and, by weakening departmental boundaries, encourages greater flexibility and creativity. However, many organizations that have assumed this form have found that the absence of clarity in lines of authority and responsibility can lead to inertia and conflict. See FUNCTIONAL STRUCTURE, PRODUCT-BASED STRUCTURE, CRITICAL FUNCTION STRUCTURE, CONCURRENT ENGINEERING.

maturity date see REDEMPTION DATE.

maturity phase see PRODUCT LIFE CYCLE.

maximum stock level the highest planned level of STOCK for a particular item in a STOCK CONTROL system.

MBO see MANAGEMENT BY OBJECTIVES, MANAGEMENT BUY-OUT.

MBWA see MANAGEMENT BY WALKING AROUND.

measured day work a system of PAY in which WAGES are output-based but do not fluctuate in response to short-term fluctuations in output. Typically, possible daily output will be established through WORK MEASUREMENT. Individuals' pay will then be based on the understanding that they will usually achieve this level of output. Pay relativities are established by JOB EVALUATION. The notable feature of measured day work is that daily output and WAGE RATES are usually set at higher levels than industry norms, and thus represent an attempt to achieve high output without the attendant INDUSTRIAL RELATIONS problems often associated with PIECEWORK. A variant is 'graduated measured day work' where an individual can choose from a range of output/wage options.

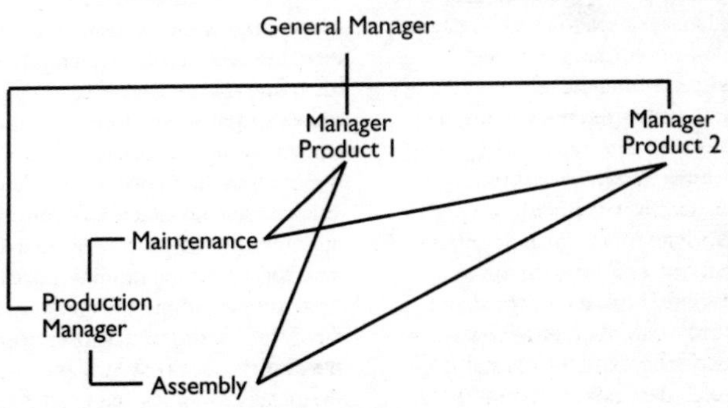

Fig. 58 **Matrix.** The matrix structure.

mechanistic and organismic organizations terms used by the British writers Tom Burns and G M Stalker to contrast two very different types of ORGANIZATION. *Mechanistic* organizations are characterized by high and rigid job specialization and centralized decision-making with vertical channels of communication. *Organismic* organizations, by contrast, display loose job definitions, greater horizontal communication and some devolution of decision-making to lower levels of the HIERARCHY. The nature of the environment is a critical determinant: stable conditions tend to encourage mechanistic organizations whilst fast-changing product markets tend to encourage the organismic form. See BUREAUCRACY, CONTINGENCY THEORY, CULTURE.

media the channels of communication available to a firm (or some other organization) through which the firm's products can be advertised to prospective buyers. The main media channels available in the UK and other major economies include commercial television and radio, newspapers and magazines, technical journals, poster sites, cinemas and theatres, display cards (on buses, in restaurants etc.) and direct mailing. A firm's selection of appropriate media for its ADVERTISEMENTS will depend critically on whether the whole MARKET or particular MARKET SEGMENTS are being targeted (for example, in the former case national newspapers may be used, in the latter case, appropriate specialist journals and magazines); the desired degree of ADVERTISING FREQUENCY required (daily, weekly, etc.); and the relative costs of placing advertisements in the various media combined with the firm's advertising budget limits. See ADVERTISING, INTERNET.

mediation a method of resolving INDUSTRIAL DISPUTES in which a neutral third party acts as a go-between to the parties in dispute. Typically, the mediator introduces proposals of his or her own as an aid to continued NEGOTIATIONS. It is a useful form of intervention where disputes have become especially acrimonious and the disputants are entrenched in their bargaining positions. Conceptually it is midway between CONCILIATION and ARBITRATION. See ADVISORY, CONCILIATION AND ARBITRATION SERVICES (ACAS), COLLECTIVE BARGAINING.

medium of exchange see MONEY.

Mediums BONDS, DEBENTURES and PREFERENCE SHARES which have a redemption date of between 5 and 15 years.

medium-sized firm see BUSINESS.

memorandum of association a legal document which must be filed with the REGISTRAR OF COMPANIES before a JOINT-STOCK COMPANY can be incorporated, and which governs the external relationship between the company and third parties. The memorandum must contain certain compulsory clauses stating:

(a) the name of the company;
(b) the objects of the company;
(c) the country in which the company is situated;
(d) whether it is limited by shares or other means;
(e) the amount and division of share capital;
(f) the signature of the subscribers forming the company, each of whom must take at least one share. See ARTICLES OF ASSOCIATION.

memory the part of a COMPUTER that stores information. The two main types of computer memory are RAM (Random Access Memory) and ROM (Read Only Memory). HARD DISKS and FLOPPY DISKS provide additional memory capacity for storing computer programs and data.

mentoring see MANAGEMENT DEVELOPMENT.

merchandise an alternative term for a GOOD or COMMODITY.

merchandising in-store promotional activity by manufacturers or retailers at the point of sale, designed to stimulate SALES. Such merchandising makes considerable use of POINT-OF-SALE DISPLAY materials and special buying incentives such as free trial samples, money-off packs and gifts. See SALES PROMOTION, PROMOTIONAL MIX.

merchant a business such as a RETAILER or WHOLESALER which acts as an intermediary in a DISTRIBUTION CHANNEL. Merchants 'take title' to goods (that is, purchase goods) which they then on-sell to customers.

merchantable quality a legal term used to describe products which are satisfactory insofar as they are fit for the purpose intended. See SALE OF GOODS ACT, 1979.

merchant bank a BANK which offers a range of financial facilities and services to clients. The merchant banks are still involved in what was their original business, namely the provision of merchandise finance, in the form of 'acceptance' notes on BILLS OF EXCHANGE to importers and exporters to cover products in transit. They have extended their interests variously into investment management, stockbroking, MARKET MAKING and corporate finance (see VENTURE CAPITAL). In the latter capacity, merchant banks arrange new stock and share issues on behalf of corporate clients (see SHARE ISSUES) and UNDERWRITE such issues. Merchant banks nowadays play a particularly prominent role in advising corporate clients on MERGERS and TAKEOVER BID tactics and in putting together the financial terms and details of such deals. See BANKING SYSTEM, INVESTMENT BANK.

Mercosur a regional 'customs union' established in 1995 to promote FREE TRADE between Brazil, Uruguay, Argentina and Paraguay. See TRADE INTEGRATION, LATIN AMERICAN FREE TRADE ASSOCIATION.

merger *or* **amalgamation** the combining together of two or more firms into a single business on a basis that is mutually agreed by the firms' managements and approved by their shareholders. Mergers are one form of EXTERNAL GROWTH involving firms in expanding in a horizontal, vertical or conglomerate direction:

(a) *Horizontal* mergers (mergers between firms in the same market) may enable the firms to lower their costs, by taking advantage of the economies of large-scale production and marketing and by increasing the market share of the combined group, thereby putting it on a stronger competitive footing (see HORIZONTAL INTEGRATION);

(b) *Vertical* mergers (mergers between firms operating at different levels in the same market) may enable the firms to lower their costs by combining together in one operation a number of sequentially linked processes and by cutting stockholding costs, while control of inputs and market outlets gives the firm greater security of supplies and access to distribution channels, often at a competitive advantage over non-integrated rivals (see VERTICAL INTEGRATION);

(c) *Conglomerate* mergers (mergers between firms engaged in unrelated markets) enable risk to be spread, and provide an opportunity to develop better the resources of each by cross-transference of management, production and marketing expertise and by the targeting of finance to areas of growth potential (see DIVERSIFICATION).

In terms of their wider impact on the functioning of market processes, mergers may, on the one hand, promote greater efficiency in resource use and lower market costs and prices, or, on the other hand, reduce competition and heighten the dangers of monopolistic control over markets. Thus they may simultaneously involve both benefits and detriments. For this reason, in the UK, under the FAIR TRADING ACT, 1973, mergers and TAKEOVERS which create or extend a firm's market share of a particular product in excess of 25%, or where the value of assets combined is over £70 million, can be referred by the OFFICE OF FAIR TRADING to the COMPETITION COMMISSION to determine whether or not they are in the public interest. See MARKET ENTRY, BARRIERS TO ENTRY, CITY CODE ON TAKEOVERS AND MERGERS, DEMERGER, BUSINESS STRATEGY, MERCHANT BANK.

merger accounting the preparation of financial statements according to the provisions of Financial Reporting Standard 6 'Acquisitions and Mergers' 1994. These provisions apply to business combinations which are not the acquisition of one entity by another, but substantially equal partnerships where no one party is dominant.

merit pay see PERFORMANCE-RATED PAY.

merit rating see PERFORMANCE-RELATED PAY.

method study an aspect of WORK STUDY which involves the systematic recording and analysis of the way in which a JOB is performed, with a view to developing and applying easier and more efficient methods of performing the task. More effective work methods can help increase PRODUCTIVITY and reduce labour costs.

Method study involves a number of steps:

(a) the selection of the work to be studied, giving priority to permanent jobs with a high labour content where potential cost savings are substantial;

(b) the recording of the existing work method. For DIRECT LABOUR involved in repetitive tasks this can be done by using an ACTIVITY CHART to record all the work tasks performed by a person and/or machine using standard symbols for the activities: operation, transportation, inspection etc. Alternatively, video tape records of the work being performed by direct operatives can be used. For managers, staff and INDIRECT LABOUR involved in a wide range of tasks ACTIVITY SAMPLING can provide information about the relative time spent on each main activity undertaken;

(c) the critical examination of these records to establish the purpose, place and sequence of activities, and the means by which they are performed, in order to facilitate

(d) the development of an improved work method by eliminating unnecessary activities, combining activities, changing their sequence or simplifying them;

(e) the installation of the new method and provision of appropriate training for

(f) the maintenance of the new work practice.

Method study is generally undertaken prior to WORK MEASUREMENT.

'me-too' product see MARKET POSITIONING.

mezzanine debt see JUNK BOND.

M-form see PARTS FAMILY CODING AND CLASSIFICATION SYSTEMS.

miclass see PARTS FAMILY CODING AND CLASSIFICATION SYSTEMS.

microcomputer a small-scale COMPUTER with modest data storage facilities, usually comprising a CPU (central processing unit), DISK DRIVES, KEYBOARD and monitor or VDU (visual display unit). Standalone, computers can be designed as desktop machines or as portable LAPTOP units.

As microcomputers have become more powerful in terms of data processing speed and data storage capacity the distinction between them and MINICOMPUTERS has become blurred.

middleman a person or firm which acts as an intermediary between a seller of a good or service and the buyer of that good or service. See WHOLESALER, AGENT, MARKET INTERMEDIARY.

middle manager any manager who occupies a middle position in the HIERARCHY of an ORGANIZATION, located between those senior managers who formulate business strategy and those with direct responsibility for overseeing the work of production or of clerical employees. In practice the term is used imprecisely; it can also refer to those managers who do not contribute directly to the organization's primary output and to those who do not have direct responsibility for budgets or overseeing the work of others (see LINE AND STAFF). In recent years many organizations have sought to reduce the number of their middle managers; information technology has rendered some of their information-processing roles unnecessary, whilst many have claimed that the absence of responsibility has led to poor job performance. See MANAGEMENT.

middle price the price of a FINANCIAL SECURITY, FOREIGN CURRENCY or COMMODITY which lies halfway between the bid (buy) and offer (sell) price quoted by market makers or dealers. Share prices, commodity prices and exchange rates published in newspapers are generally middle prices. See BID PRICE.

minicomputer a medium-scale COMPUTER with sizeable data storage facilities which is often accessible simultaneously from several terminals.

As MICROCOMPUTERS and minicomputers have become more powerful in terms of data-processing speed and data-storage capacity, the distinction between them and MAINFRAME computers has become blurred.

minimum agreement see MULTIEMPLOYER AGREEMENT.

minimum efficient scale see ECONOMIES OF SCALE.

minimum stock level the lowest planned level of STOCK for a particular item prior to replenishment in a STOCK CONTROL system.

minimum wage rate the minimum rate of PAY for work either decreed by the government or voluntarily agreed between trade unions and employers. Minimum wage rates are designed to ensure that workers are able to enjoy some basic standard of living.

In April 1999 the UK government introduced a statutory national minimum wage rate of £3.60p per hour for employees aged 22 and over and £3 per hour for employees aged 18-21; these rates have been increased progressively to £5.05p and £4.25p, respectively (as at October 2005). Many other countries have similar legislation. The minimum wage rate selected tends to reflect the outcome of a 'compromise' between various vested interests, the trade unions, employers and the government. Given the diversity of conditions in the LABOUR MARKET the introduction of a single economy-wide minimum wage is open to the objection that it will rarely correspond to 'market-clearing' rates in individual industries and trades. In particular, critics argue that pitching the wage rate too high (i.e. above the 'market clearing' rate) will tend, as noted above, to increase unemployment in many unskilled occupations. Moreover, there are practical complications relating to the imposition of the minimum wage rate where employees are traditionally paid on a 'piece-rate' basis rather than by the hour.

minority interest that part of a subsidiary company's listed SHARE CAPITAL which is not owned by the HOLDING COMPANY. Where the holding company owns more than 50% of the shares of a subsidiary company then it is able to control that company, but where it owns less than 100% of the shares then the minority interest of other shareholders in the subsidiary company must be recognized. In compiling CONSOLIDATED ACCOUNTS the claims of minority interests in certain group assets located in subsidiary companies must be recognized, and their entitlement to a share in the profits of subsidiary companies must be allowed for. See PREACQUISITION PROFITS.

minutes a summarized transcript or record of items discussed at a meeting and any proposals or resolutions made at the meeting.

mission statement an explicit written statement of an ORGANIZATION's long-term aims and objectives. Mission statements are designed to give substance to the perceived purposes of the organization and provide all employees with an indication of what they are attempting to achieve through their collective endeavours. See BUSINESS OBJECTIVES.

mixed economy see ECONOMY.

mixer company a subsidiary of a MULTINATIONAL ENTERPRISE (MNE) located in a low CORPORATION TAX country which 'collects' profits remitted from the MNEs other worldwide manufacturing and sales subsidiaries with the aim of minimizing its global tax bill. Usually under 'double taxation' treaties between countries once tax has been paid in one country no further liabilities are due when the profits are then remitted on to the MNEs parent company. However, under proposals introduced in its budget of 2000 the UK government indicated that it intends to tackle what it sees as tax evasion by imposing a tax 'surcharge' on profits sent back to the UK-based parent companies to bring the tax charge up to the UK's main corporation tax rate (currently 30%). See TRANSFER PRICE, TAX HAVEN.

MNC see MULTINATIONAL ENTERPRISE.

MNE see MULTINATIONAL ENTERPRISE.

mobility barriers *or* **isolating mechanisms** economic forces that limit the extent to which a firm's COMPETITIVE ADVANTAGE can be duplicated or neutralized through the activities of other firms.

There are two broad groups of mobility barriers. The first are *barriers to imitation*, which make it difficult for existing firms in a market or potential market entrants to duplicate the resources that form the basis of a firm's competitive advantage. These impediments include legal restrictions on imitation, such as PATENTS, copyrights, trademarks and licensing; superior access to factor inputs information, distribution channels and customers; ECONOMIES OF SCALE; and the specific know-how, collective wisdom and skills of the firm.

The second group of mobility barriers are *early-mover* advantages that allow a firm with competitive advantages to increase the magnitude of its advantages relative to competitors and potential market entrants over time. Early-mover advantages include EXPERIENCE-CURVE economies; reputation which reduces buyer uncertainty about product quality; and high buyer-switching costs.

Isolating mechanisms protect a single firm from immediate competitors in much the same way that BARRIERS TO ENTRY protect incumbent firms from potential market entrants. See RESOURCE-BASED THEORY OF THE FIRM, STATEGIC GROUP.

'mock bureaucracy' see BUREAUCRACY.

modem a device used to connect a COMPUTER to the public telephone network to enable the computer to transmit or receive information from other computers sited some distance away.

modern apprenticeship see APPRENTICESHIP.

modular design a product DESIGN which facilitates the production of a wide variety of styles of a product using a limited range of common interchangeable components.

Mondragon see WORKERS' COOPERATIVE.

monetarism a body of economic ideas concerning the role of MONEY, in particular the MONEY SUPPLY, in the functioning of the economy. The historical roots of modern monetarism lie in the *quantity theory of money:* MV = PT, where M = money supply, V = velocity of circulation of money, P = general price level, T = the number of goods and services produced by the economy. In simple terms, assuming V to be constant and T to be fixed in the short run, then an increase in M results in an increase in P. i.e. the quantity theory provides an explanation of INFLATION in the economy. The theory thus emphasizes the importance of the need for a *long-term* balanced relationship between the amount of money available to finance purchases of goods and services, on the one hand, and the ability of the economy to produce such goods and services, on the other. Thus, in order to avoid inflation the growth of the money supply must not exceed the supply capacity (i.e. growth rate) of the economy over time. See MONETARY POLICY, ECONOMIC POLICY.

monetary policy

The regulation of the MONEY SUPPLY, CREDIT and INTEREST RATES in order to control the level of spending in the economy (see ECONOMIC POLICY).

The monetary authorities (principally the BANK OF ENGLAND in the UK) can employ a number of measures to regulate the money supply, in particular that part of it which is used to underpin the provision of credit, including open market operations in government BONDS and TREASURY BILLS, special deposits and directives.

Open market operations are targeted at the liquidity base of the banking system and involve the sale or purchase of bonds and Treasury bills which alters the amount of bank deposits held by the COMMERCIAL BANKS and thus their capacity to advance LOANS and OVERDRAFTS to customers. For example, if the authorities wish to reduce the money supply they can sell long-dated bonds to the general public. Buyers pay for these bonds by running down their bank deposits – an important constituent of the money supply – which forces the banks in turn to reduce the volume of their lending.

A *special deposit* call by the authorities requires the banks to place a specified proportion of their liquid assets on deposit with the Bank of England which are then 'frozen', i.e. they cannot be used by the banks as the basis for advancing loans and overdrafts to customers, again reducing the money supply. A *directive* is a request by the Bank of England to the banks to keep their total lending below a specified global ceiling or to reduce their lending for particular purposes (for example car purchase).

The authorities can also operate INSTALMENT CREDIT controls on lending by FINANCE HOUSES to limit spending. They can, for example, discourage potential borrowers from using instalment facilities by increasing the down payment required and by reducing the time period of the loan; the former stipulation requires the borrower to find more ready cash, while the latter increases the effective interest charge payable.

The authorities may seek to influence interest rates more widely rather than just on particular categories of borrowing. In May 1997, responsibility or setting interest rates was handed over by the government to the Bank of England's MONETARY POLICY COMMITTEE, thereby making the determination of monetary policy 'independent' of political control.

In practice, the application of monetary policy is fraught with difficulties. The main problem is that there is no single reliable definition of the money supply (see MONEY SUPPLY for details), so that any attempt to target a particular specification of the money supply tends to be undermined by asset-switching from other categories. To illustrate briefly: if the authorities target M3 (mainly currency plus bank deposits) for control purposes and use the various instruments noted above to reduce the level of bank deposits, this may not be sufficient in itself to reduce spending. Spenders may simply switch to 'M4' type money, running down their building society deposits to finance current purchases. The central bank's ability to effectively control the money supply and interest rates has been increasingly questioned as a result of FINANCIAL INNOVATION outside the traditional banking system. For example, the proliferation of credit cards by non-bank operators such as retail stores has led to an increase in the availability of 'instant' credit without the traditional negotiation of a loan or overdraft with a bank manager; and even 'official' interest rates are being circumvented by durable goods retailers who have been increasingly prepared to offer customers "0%" interest deals on purchase of cars, furniture, televisions etc.

For most of the period since 1945, monetary policy has been used as a short-term stabilization technique but has largely taken second place to FISCAL POLICY. In the past authorities have occasionally set 'targets' for monetary policy; for example, in the 1980s the 'Medium Term Financial Strategy' set rolling annual targets for the money supply aimed at reducing the growth of the M3 money supply and INFLATION rate. In 1997 the incoming government singled out the control of inflation as its number one economic priority and set an inflation 'target' of an increase in the RETAIL PRICE INDEX (RPIX) of no more than 2½% per annum (now CPI – 2%). In an unprecedented move, as noted above, the government transferred the power to set 'official' interest rates from itself to the Monetary Policy Committee of the Bank of England. In doing this the government took the view that a low inflation economy was essential in order to achieve another of its priorities – low UNEMPLOYMENT. In the European Union, the EUROPEAN CENTRAL BANK (ECB) is responsible for monetary policy in general and for setting interest rates in particular for member countries of the ECONOMIC AND MONETARY UNION (EMU). The ECB has committed itself to a 'target' for INFLATION of no more than 2% per annum. See MONETARISM, BUSINESS CYCLE.

Monetary Policy Committee (MPC) a body, part of the BANK OF ENGLAND, which was established on May 6 1997 when, in an unprecedented move, the government transferred responsibility for setting UK 'official' INTEREST RATES from itself to the Bank of England. This was part of a move to give MONETARY POLICY a more independent stance, free from political 'interference'. The MPC currently has a membership of nine, five full-time Bank of England members including the Bank's Governor and Deputy Governor and four 'independent' members appointed from outside the Bank. The basic remit of the MPC is to set interest rates in order to secure the achievement of the government's INFLATION rate 'target' (RPIX) of, initially, a maximum of 2½% per annum (now CPI – 2%). To this end the MPC meets monthly and after reviewing prevailing and anticipated economic conditions decides whether any interest rate change is necessary. (See INTEREST RATE entry Fig. 47 and text for details of interest rate changes since 1997). The MPC monitors a varied set of economic data and indices including retail sales of goods and services, (see RETAIL PRICE INDEX) house sales, the growth in GDP, changes in the M0 and M4 money supply figures and the growth of earnings to 'gauge' the extent of inflationary pressure in the economy, and then take a *majority* vote on whether or not an interest rate change is called for, and, if so, by what magnitude.

monetary system the assets which make up a country's MONEY SUPPLY and the institutions involved in deposit-taking, money transmission and the provision of credit facilities, together constitute the monetary side of the ECONOMY.

The money supply consists of a number of assets (banknotes, coins etc.), denominated in terms of MONETARY UNITS (pounds and pence in the case of the UK). The institutions involved in handling money include various BANKS, FINANCE HOUSES, BUILDING SOCIETIES etc. The monetary system of a country is controlled by its CENTRAL BANK which uses a number of techniques to regulate the supply of money and interest rates (see MONETARY POLICY).

The monetary system also has an external dimension in that participation by countries in INTERNATIONAL TRADE and FOREIGN INVESTMENT requires the establishment of interactive mechanisms such as EXCHANGE RATES and INTERNATIONAL RESERVES. See INTERNATIONAL MONETARY FUND.

monetary unit one of the units of CURRENCY used in a country as the basis of payments and lending and borrowing transactions. The units of currency used in the UK, for example, are pounds and pence, while in the USA they are the dollar and cent. The monetary units of different countries are related to each other for INTERNATIONAL TRADE and INVESTMENT purposes through their EXCHANGE RATE values.

money an asset which is generally acceptable as a means of payment in the sale and purchase of products and other assets and for concluding borrowing and lending transactions. The use of money enables products and assets to be priced in terms of the monetary units of the country (pence and pounds in the UK, for example), and to be exchanged using money as a common *medium of exchange* rather than the bartering of one product against another. Money also acts as a *store of value* (money can be held over a period of time and used to finance future payments) and as a *unit of account* (money is used to measure and record the value of products and assets, as for example in compiling the country's NATIONAL INCOME accounts). See MONEY SUPPLY, MONETARY POLICY.

money-back guarantee a promise by a retailer or manufacturer that if a customer is not happy with the purchase he or she may return the product in good condition and get a full refund. See GUARANTEE.

money laundering the conversion of money (often obtained illegally through crime) into foreign currencies through multi-bank deposits to hide their source of origin, through bureaux de changes and through investments in 'legitimate' businesses.

In 2000 the OECD backed an initiative (made the more urgent by the terrorist attacks on the USA) for countries (in particular, TAX HAVENS) to require greater disclosure and scrutiny of 'suspect' bank accounts.

money market a MARKET engaged in the short-term lending and borrowing of MONEY, linking together the financial institutions (COMMERCIAL BANKS, DISCOUNT HOUSES etc.), companies and the government. To take one example: a company with surplus short-term funds might deposit these funds with its commercial bank, which in turn places them on 'call' (deposit) with a discount house. The discount house in turn uses the money to purchase TREASURY BILLS issued by the government. See DISCOUNT MARKET.

money measurement concept see ACCOUNTING CONCEPTS.

money purchase pension scheme see PENSION.

money supply the stock of MONEY in an economy. The money supply can be specified in a variety of ways: narrow definitions of the money supply include only a limited number of assets, while broader definitions extend the range of assets included; for example, the 'Mo' (narrow) money supply comprises currency (notes and coins), COMMERCIAL BANKS' till money and their operational balances at the Bank of England; 'M3' (broad) money supply is made up of Mo plus sight and time deposits with the commercial banks and UK public sector sterling deposits; and 'M4' is made up of M3 plus deposits with the building societies.

The size of the money supply is an important determinant of the level of spending in the economy and its control is a particular concern of MONETARY POLICY. However, the monetary authorities have a problem because given the number of possible definitions of the money supply, it is difficult for them to decide which is the most appropriate money supply category to target for control purposes. Moreover, having targeted a particular definition they face the added difficulty of actually controlling it because of the potential for asset switching from one category of money to another.

For most of the 1980s the authorities targeted M3 for control purposes, but in recent years have switched to Mo and M4 as 'indicators' of monetary conditions in setting 'official' INTEREST RATES (see MONETARY POLICY COMMITTEE). See LEGAL TENDER.

money values see REAL VALUES.

Monopolies and Mergers Commission (MMC) see COMPETITION COMMISSION.

monopoly a MARKET STRUCTURE characterized by a single supplier and high barriers to entry. In practice, the term 'monopoly' is usually given a wider interpretation, particularly within the context of COMPETITION POLICY, to cover DOMINANT FIRM situations and COLLUSION between rival suppliers. Monopoly is often depicted as an inefficient form of market organization since the lack of effective competition tends to remove the monopolist's incentive to reduce industry supply costs. Worse still, monopolists may abuse their market power both with respect to consumers (for example, by charging excessive prices), and actual and potential competitors (for example, by depriving them of market access through EXCLUSIVE DEALING practices). On the other hand, MARKET CONCENTRATION may lower industry supply costs by enabling firms to take advantage of ECONOMIES OF SCALE, and it is to be noted that governments go out of their way to encourage patent monopolies (see PATENT) as a means of encouraging innovation. See CONCENTRATION RATIO, MONOPOLY OF SCALE.

monopoly of scale see COMPETITION POLICY (UK).

monopoly policy a policy concerned with the regulation of MONOPOLIES, MERGERS and TAKEOVERS, ANTI-COMPETITIVE AGREEMENTS/RESTRICTIVE TRADE AGREEMENTS, RESALE PRICES and ANTI-COMPETITIVE PRACTICES. See COMPETITION POLICY for further discussion of these areas.

monopoly power see MARKET POWER.

moral hazard a situation in which one of the parties to a CONTRACT has an incentive, after the contract is agreed, to act in a manner that brings benefits to themselves at the expense of the other. For example, employees may work less conscientiously than expected by the terms of their CONTRACT OF EMPLOYMENT (i.e. they indulge in 'shirking' and time wasting). See PRINCIPAL-AGENT THEORY, AGENCY COST.

mortgage the advance of a LOAN to a person or business (the borrower/mortgagor) by other persons or businesses, in particular financial institutions such as BUILDING SOCIETIES and COMMERCIAL BANKS (the lender/mortgagee) which is used to acquire some asset, most notably a property such as a house, office or factory. A mortgage is a form of CREDIT which is extended for a specified period of time either on fixed INTEREST terms, or more usually, given the long duration of most mortgages, on variable interest terms. See SECOND MORTGAGE.

most favoured nation rule see WORLD TRADE ORGANIZATION.

mothballing see CAPACITY.

motion study see WORK STUDY.

motivation the force or process which impels people to behave in the way that they do. In a work setting, motivation can be viewed as that which determines whether workers expend the degree of effort necessary to achieve required task objectives. In OCCUPATIONAL PSYCHOLOGY two basic conceptions of motivation can be discerned: 'needs' theory and 'expectancy' theory. Possibly the best known of the former is the 'hierarchy of needs' identified by Abraham Maslow (1908–70). He argued that individuals have intrinsic needs which they are impelled to seek to satisfy. These needs, which are ordered in a hierarchy are *physical needs* (food, warmth, shelter), *security needs* (safety, home), *ego needs* (esteem, status) and *self-actualization needs* (the realization of individual potential). Initially, the lower order needs such as safety determine behaviour but once these are satisfied higher order needs come to dominate. Maslow's theory has been widely criticized, however, for assuming that such needs are universal and that they are always ordered in this particular hierarchy.

Other needs theories include Herzberg's 'Two Factor Theory of Motivation'. He argued that people are motivated by two kinds of need: *hygiene factors* (those basic needs such as shelter which, if not satisfied, lead to unhappiness but whose satisfaction does not in itself lead to happiness); and *motivators* (those higher order needs which when satisfied lead to contentment). The importance of this theory in a work setting is its insistence that managers have to ensure that both hygiene factors (i.e. pay, working conditions) and motivation (i.e. the need for personal fulfilment) are satisfied for a workforce to be content and highly motivated.

A further 'needs' theory is the ERG (Existence, Relatedness and Growth) theory of Clayton Alderfer (1940–). Like Maslow he suggests that there is a hierarchy of needs but that the less a high level need is satisfied the more important a lower level need becomes. Hence demands for more pay in fact really reflect a desire for work to be made more satisfying.

The main alternative approach to 'needs' theories is the 'expectancy' approach associated with Victor Vroom (1932–). This suggests that individuals are motivated to act in certain ways not by some basic inner need but by the strength of the expectation that the action will achieve a result seen by them as desirable. The desire for a particular outcome is known as the 'valence'. This theory is essentially a 'process' theory: it emphasizes the process of motivation rather than the nature or content of particular motivators. The strength of people's motivation will be determined by weighing up how much they want something and how far they believe a certain action will contribute to achieving it.

motivational research the measurement of attitudes and preferences likely to affect BUYER BEHAVIOUR. Motivational research is concerned with exploring the underlying reasons why consumers buy products, which can range from functional requirements to psychological needs like status and esteem. There are various techniques which may be employed to explore consumers' psychological needs, including in-depth interviews, psychoanalytical tests and group discussions. The results of motivational research can be used to generate ideas for new products, reposition existing products, and design ADVERTISING COPY to appeal specifically to the motives identified. See MARKETING RESEARCH.

mouse a device used to move a pointer around a COMPUTER screen.

moving average see SALES FORECASTING.

MRP see MATERIALS REQUIREMENT PLANNING.

MRPII see MANUFACTURING RESOURCE PLANNING.

MSDOS see DOS (DISK OPERATING SYSTEM).

MSF see MANUFACTURING, SCIENCE AND FINANCE UNION.

multi-channel marketing system see DISTRIBUTION CHANNEL.

multi-divisional company see PRODUCT-BASED STRUCTURE.

multi-employer agreement (in INDUSTRIAL RELATIONS) an agreement between a group of employers and TRADE UNIONS governing rates of pay and conditions of employment in all of these companies. In multi-employer COLLECTIVE BARGAINING in the UK the employers' interests are usually represented by an EMPLOYERS' ASSOCIATION, which aspires to represent all employers in that particular industry. Such agreements are thus often also called 'industry-wide agreements'. On the union side, the negotiations are usually conducted by paid regional or national officials rather than lay SHOP STEWARDS. The forum in which the agreement is made is known in some industries as a joint industrial council.

Multi-employer collective bargaining agreements developed in the UK from the 1920s onwards, but since the 1960s these agreements have declined in significance. Some firms have moved to company or plant-level bargaining whilst others do not subscribe to collective agreements with unions. However, multi-employer agreements are very important in some other European countries, such as Germany.

multi-employer bargaining see COLLECTIVE BARGAINING, MULTI-EMPLOYER AGREEMENT.

multilateral netting an arrangement whereby two or more associated companies offset their receipts and payments with each other, leaving a single net intra-company receipt or payment balance. Multilateral netting is used particularly by MULTINATIONAL ENTERPRISES which operate many overseas subsidiaries trading in different national currencies, in order to simplify the settlement of intra-group indebtedness. Multilateral netting also serves to reduce a company's EXCHANGE RATE EXPOSURE by minimizing the amount of external purchases and sales of foreign currencies.

multi-level marketing a system of selling a firm's product which involves a 'pyramid' of sales persons. Persons sell the product to friends, acquaintances etc. but are also offered a financial inducement to recruit other people as sales persons who, in turn, recruit yet more sales persons. In this way, person A recruits person B who recruits person C and so on thus creating an expanding chain of sales persons, each receiving a commission on their own sales and additionally further commissions based on the sales of people they have recruited directly or indirectly.

multinational company see MULTINATIONAL ENTERPRISE.

multiple activity chart see ACTIVITY CHART.

multiple channel – single phase in queuing where there is more than one point at which to QUEUE and where the customer has only one phase of activity. For example the till line at a supermarket. See SINGLE CHANNEL – MULTIPLE PHASE, SINGLE CHANNEL – SINGLE PHASE.

multiple sourcing obtaining raw materials, components, finished products, and services from many suppliers as opposed to single sourcing. See SOURCING.

multinational enterprise (MNE), multinational company (MNC) *or* transnational company

A firm that *owns* production, sales and other revenue-generating assets in a number of countries. Foreign direct investment by MNEs in the establishment or acquisition of overseas raw material and components operations, production plants and sales subsidiaries occurs because of the potentially greater cost-effectiveness and profitability in SOURCING inputs and servicing markets (see FOREIGN MARKET SERVICING STRATEGY) through a direct presence in a number of locations, rather than sole reliance on a single home base and IMPORTS and EXPORTS as the basis of the firms' international operations.

A firm may possess various COMPETITIVE ADVANTAGES over rival suppliers ('firm-specific advantages') in the form of patented process technology or a unique branded product which it can better exploit and protect by establishing overseas supply facilities. Direct investment may enable a firm to reduce its distribution costs and keep in touch more closely with local market conditions – changes in consumer tastes, competitors' actions etc. Moreover, direct investment enables a firm both to avoid governmental restrictions on market access such as TARIFFS and QUOTAS, and be able to benefit from other 'country-specific advantages' such as the availability of government cash grants and subsidies on inward investment. In the case of sourcing, direct investment allows the MNE to take advantage of some countries' lower labour costs or provides access to superior technological know-how.

See BUSINESS STRATEGY, CAPITAL INFLOW, HOST COUNTRY, FOREIGN DIRECT INVESTMENT, INDUSTRIAL LOCATION, INTERNALIZATION, TRANSFER PRICE, OFFSHORE PRODUCTION, INTERNATIONAL MARKETING, FOREIGN CURRENCY TRANSLATION, DOUBLE TAXATION, UNITARY TAXATION, WITHHOLDING TAX, EXCHANGE RATE EXPOSURE, SCREWDRIVER OPERATION, MIXER COMPANY, TAX HAVEN.

multi-unionism the presence of a number of potentially competing TRADE UNIONS in a workplace or organization, accompanied in some organizations by separate COLLECTIVE BARGAINING arrangements. It is believed to have a detrimental effect on INDUSTRIAL RELATIONS because it encourages disputes over DEMARCATION LINES, PAY DIFFERENTIALS etc. Once an integral element of UK industrial relations, the rationalization of bargaining procedures and the decline in the number of unions have reduced its extent and significance.

multi-unit pricing the sale of more than one unit of a product at a price lower than the total of individual units' prices. This technique is used as a form of SALES PROMOTION (for example, 'two-for-the price-of-one' offers).

mutuality the principle that managers should not change any aspect of WORK ORGANIZATION without first securing the agreement of SHOP STEWARDS or TRADE UNION officials. See COLLECTIVE BARGAINING.

n

NAFTA see NORTH AMERICAN FREE TRADE AGREEMENT.

NASDAQ the USA STOCK MARKET/EXCHANGE based in New York which specializes in the listing of high tech companies such as Microsoft, Dell and Amazon. The Nasdaq SHARE PRICE INDEX monitors and records the share price movements of the companies listed in the exchange. See DOW JONES INDEX.

In 1999 Nasdaq set up an exchange in London as a direct competitor to the London Stock Market's '*Techmark*' exchange.

national accounts large and important customers who may have centralized PURCHASING departments that buy or coordinate buying for decentralized, geographically dispersed business units.

National Association of Pension Funds (NAPF) the TRADE ASSOCIATION which represents the collective interests of PENSION FUNDS in the UK.

National Association of Schoolmasters and Union of Women Teachers (NAS/UWT) the second largest teaching TRADE UNION in the UK. Unlike the NATIONAL UNION OF TEACHERS, its membership is concentrated in secondary education. Currently its membership is around 210,000, and it is the UK's tenth largest union.

National Council for Vocational Qualifications the body overseeing the system of NATIONAL VOCATIONAL QUALIFICATIONS in England and Wales. See also TRAINING.

National Farmers' Union (NFU) the EMPLOYER'S ASSOCIATION representing employers in agriculture.

national insurance see SOCIAL SECURITY BENEFITS.

national insurance contributions the payments made by employers and their employees to the UK government up to a specified maximum limit. National insurance contributions, together with other government budgetary receipts, are used to finance state pensions, sick pay, jobseekers allowance, etc.

There are currently (2005) four classes of national insurance contributions; Class 1 (employees/employers), Class 2 and 4 (self-employed) and Class 3 (voluntary organizations). Under the most common class, Class 1, contributions are paid by employees at the rate of 11% on weekly earnings between £89 (minimum) and £585 (maximum); employers' contributions are paid at the rate of 12.2% on weekly earnings of employees greater than £84, with no upper limit. See BUDGET (GOVERNMENT), SOCIAL SECURITY BENEFITS.

nationalization versus privatization the taking into public ownership, in the case of nationalization, of an entire industry or an individual firm, and, in the case of privatization (denationalization), the removal of an industry or firm from the public sector and its sale back to the private sector.

In a fully centrally planned ECONOMY, most if not all of industry is owned by the State, while in a free enterprise economy, industry is in private hands. In a mixed economy such as the UK, some industries are State-owned, but most are in the private sector. In the 1980s in the UK the political tide placed a greater emphasis on free enterprise and this led the government to embark on a widespread privatization programme which has included the sale of the gas, telecommunications, water, electricity, bus and steel industries, together with various individual businesses including BP, BAA, TSB and Amersham.

national minimum wage see MINIMUM WAGE RATE.

national savings certificate a FINANCIAL SECURITY issued by the UK government as a means of raising money for the government and encouraging private SAVING. National Savings Certificates are issued in small denominations through post offices and banks; holders receive interest on them which is free of income tax, but the number held by any one person is limited to (currently) 20,000.

National Union of Teachers (NUT) the largest teaching TRADE UNION in the UK with members in both primary and secondary education. Currently it has over 300,000 members, and is the UK's seventh largest trade union.

National Vocational Qualification a qualification in England and Wales recognizing competence in a vocational or technical subject, usually awarded after a period of vocational TRAINING and formal assessment. Competence is primarily defined as the ability to perform a task successfully. The NVQ system has been developed to encourage firms to train more systematically and to encourage training in transferable SKILLS (i.e. skills of use to more than one organization). The UK government's intention is that there will be national standards of competence for all occupations, established by *lead bodies* for each occupation/industry. Many NVQ subjects are highly specific and are primarily concerned with task performance rather than more diffuse conceptual understanding (the ability to understand as well as perform a task is sometimes referred to as competency). Some NVQs, however, are broader and less immediately technical in scope, and are perceived as more practically focused alternatives to traditional academic qualifications such as A-Levels: these tend to be known as General NVQs or more usually GNVQs. NVQs are arranged in a set of 5 levels, ranging from basic to professional level.

The NVQ system is a major attempt to improve on the UK's poor record in vocational training. Critics of NVQs allege, however, that many NVQ courses pay insufficient attention to the development of the conceptual skills necessary to understand technical processes fully. It is also difficult to identify discrete competencies required for many tasks and occupations, particularly those that are highly complex in character. See ACCREDITATION OF EXPERIENTIAL LEARNING.

NCVQ see NATIONAL COUNCIL FOR VOCATIONAL QUALIFICATION.

needs *or* **wants** the physical, psychological and social requirements of human beings. The identification of consumer needs and the development and MARKETING of appropriate products to satisfy these needs lies at the heart of all business activity. See BUYER BEHAVIOUR, NEW PRODUCT DEVELOPMENT, OCCUPATIONAL PSYCHOLOGY, HUMAN RELATIONS, SOCIOLOGY OF WORK.

negotiation the process by which two or more parties attempt to achieve agreement on matters of mutual interest. It can occur at the interpersonal level, for example, to resolve who does the washing-up on a particular evening; or at the organizational and societal level, for example, negotiations between TRADE UNIONS and employers over the size of an annual pay award (see COLLECTIVE BARGAINING). It can be viewed as a way of resolving CONFLICTS of interest in a way that is at least acceptable, if not ideal, to all concerned. Negotiation between two parties can be relatively straightforward but becomes much more complex when more are involved.

Research into negotiation has established that the process works most smoothly when each party listens fully to the other so that the points of difference can be delineated precisely. In many cases this does not happen, with the result that each party's view of the other's position is in fact erroneous. Listening is also essential during hard bargaining to pick up any signals that the other party is prepared to change its bargaining position.

Inexperienced negotiators often believe that negotiation is a zero-sum activity: that one party's gain must be the other's loss. However, such an outcome is rarely effective in the long term. The defeated party may well harbour such resentment that when it is in a more favourable position it will strike back. More experienced negotiators tend to view bargaining as a positive-sum activity: all parties can gain something from the process. Negotiation is the activity through which the possibilities are explored. However in some cases, during INDUSTRIAL DISPUTES for example, negotiators find it impossible to reach agreement. At this point it can be useful to enlist the services of a neutral third party to conduct ARBITRATION, CONCILIATION or MEDIATION.

neo-human relations a body of theories, mainly developed in the 1950s and 1960s within the realm of OCCUPATIONAL PSYCHOLOGY, which suggested that prevailing patterns of WORK ORGANIZATION, leaving individuals with 'narrow' jobs and little responsibility, frustrate workers' needs for 'self-actualization' (i.e. development of their full potential) and hence lead to low levels of JOB SATISFACTION. The solution was seen to be the redesign of jobs (see JOB DESIGN and JOB REDESIGN), and especially job enrichment to make work more satisfying. As part of this process managers had to learn to trust their subordinates to act correctly without close or punitive supervision. In turn satisfied workers would become committed to organizational goals and their performance would improve. The emphasis of neo-human relations differs from that of human relations in that it assumes that worker behaviour is determined by material factors, such as work technology, as well as social relationships. Actual change in jobs is seen to be necessary as well as changes in MANAGEMENT STYLE. See ALIENATION, HUMAN RELATIONS, THEORY X AND Y.

net assets the combined amount of a company's FIXED ASSETS and WORKING CAPITAL (net current assets) as recorded in the company's BALANCE SHEET. The book value of a company's net assets provides a rough guide to the value of the company's resources being used to generate profit. Compare TOTAL ASSETS.

net asset value the asset value of a company to its ordinary shareholders. This consists of the BALANCE SHEET value of total assets (FIXED ASSETS plus CURRENT ASSETS) LESS CURRENT LIABILITIES, DEBENTURES, LOAN STOCKS and PREFERENCE SHARES. These net assets can be divided by the number of ordinary shares to indicate the net asset value per share.

net book value *or* **written down value** the accounting value of a FIXED ASSET in a firm's BALANCE SHEET that represents its original cost less cumulative DEPRECIATION charged to date.

net current assets see WORKING CAPITAL.

net income see NET PROFIT.

net investment method see FOREIGN CURRENCY TRANSLATION.

net margin see NET PROFIT.

net present value see INVESTMENT APPRAISAL, DISCOUNTED CASH FLOW.

net profit the difference between a firm's SALES REVENUE and all COSTS. In accounting terms net profit is the difference between GROSS PROFIT and the costs involved in running a firm (including DEPRECIATION costs and INTEREST charges). In the UK, net profit may be expressed before or after deduction of CORPORATION TAX. See PROFIT, PROFIT-AND-LOSS ACCOUNT.

net realizable value the amount for which a FIXED ASSET or CURRENT ASSET can be sold, less any selling expenses involved. Net realizable value of an asset may be below its Net Book Value in which case the ACCOUNTING PRINCIPLE of prudence would suggest that the value of the asset in the company's LEDGER accounts should be adjusted downward to avoid overstating asset values in the BALANCE SHEET.

netting see MULTILATERAL NETTING.

network analysis *or* **programme evaluation and review technique (PERT)** a method of planning, scheduling and controlling projects involving interrelated but distinct elements of work, or *activities*. Activities and their interrelationships are depicted in a *network* of arrowed links representing activities. For example, Fig. 59 shows a simple schematic network for the construction of a kitchen extension, with planned activities and their estimated duration in weeks. Certain activities (like preparing the ground) have to be performed before the next stage of production can be embarked upon (like constructing the shell of the building). The sequential path which takes the least time to complete the project is called the 'critical path' (here the route a-b-c-d-e-f, taking 20 weeks) and any delay to these critical activities will delay the project completion. Other activities (like preparing the ground) are non-critical and can be delayed (in this case by up to one week) without delaying the overall project. Such non-critical activities embody an amount of *slack* time (one week in the example). The total amount of slack time for all non-critical activities shows the extent to which these activities can be delayed before affecting the project completion date.

Network analysis is often applied to large-scale projects in civil engineering and shipbuilding or to major repair or maintenance projects or new product launches. It is used to identify problem areas where bottlenecks may occur and where additional resources may be needed.

networking 1 a form of WORK ORGANIZATION in which tasks are subcontracted to people who work away from the office (at home for instance) but who are connected to office information systems via COMPUTER-based ELECTRONIC MAIL and similar communications links. Usually networked staff are former employees who have become SELF-EMPLOYED and are now paid on a fee basis. Networking can be advantageous to all parties: employers benefit from lower employment costs whilst networked staff gain more control over their working time.
2 the establishment by a manager of contacts with other people whose knowledge and expertise might prove useful to the manager.
3 the linking of a number of firms or business units within a firm in order to develop a supply chain for a product. This could involve, for example, business unit (A) supplying components to business unit (B) which assembles these components into a final product which is then marketed by business unit (C). See MULTINATIONAL ENTERPRISE, JUST IN TIME (JIT) SYSTEM.
4 the process of linking together a number of PERSONAL COMPUTERS in order to facilitate communication between them.
See LOCAL AREA NETWORK.

net worth see LONG-TERM CAPITAL EMPLOYED.

New Deal a government programme introduced in 1998 aimed at reducing youth UNEMPLOYMENT and long-term unemployment amongst older workers. Persons qualifying for the youth scheme must be aged between 18-24 and have

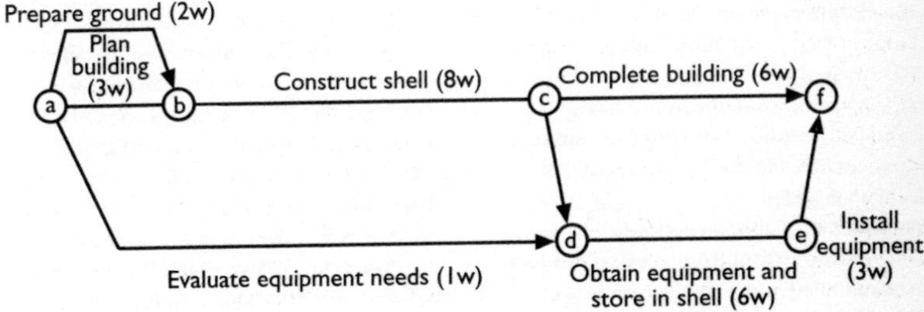

Fig. 59 **Network analysis.** Network for constructing kitchen extension. (w = weeks).

received the JOBSEEKERS ALLOWANCE for at least 6 months. Participants in the scheme are offered support and advice in seeking paid work for 4 months (the 'Gateway' period). After this if they are still unemployed they are placed on one of 4 options; (1) subsidized employment (2) work with a voluntary organization (3) work with an environmental task force (each of the options lasts 6 months) or (4) a one year training or education course.

Persons qualifying for the long-term unemployed scheme must be aged 25 or over and have received the jobseekers allowance for at least two years.

new economy/new economy company a term used to describe that part of the ECONOMY (and companies operating therein) which is based on new, innovative technologies and delivery systems, utilizing COMPUTERS and the INTERNET. The new economy embraces activities such as telecommunications (e.g. mobile phones, digital television, e-mail), computer software (e.g. Microsoft's 'Windows' system), biotechnology and genetic engineering to produce new drugs and 'genetically-modified' (GM) foodstuffs, and the 'dot.com' companies providing Internet access and facilities. By contrast, the 'old economy' consists of older established companies, producing, for example, beer, cigarettes and food. Of course, at the margin the distinction between the two is somewhat arbitrary since 'old economy' companies have embraced the new technologies to upgrade their manufacturing systems and widen their marketing reach. For example, car companies use robots on automated, computerized production lines to produce their models, while traditional service areas such as banking and insurance have developed telephone and internet banking and insurance facilities to augment their branch networks.

new product a good or service which is sufficiently different from existing products to be regarded as new by consumers. The degree of newness of a product depends upon the extent of its novelty and whether it embodies product attributes not previously available, and can range from relatively minor adaptations of existing products to entirely different product offerings like microwave ovens. Products which are radically different can rapidly establish COMPETITIVE ADVANTAGE as they open up an entirely new market and dominate the early stages of the PRODUCT LIFE CYCLE. See NEW-PRODUCT DEVELOPMENT, DIFFUSION PROCESS.

new product development the process of creating NEW PRODUCTS by a firm as part of its ongoing PRODUCT STRATEGY. New product development involves a number of steps as indicated in Fig. 60. New product ideas can arise from two broad sources:

(a) product concepts based on ideas for new products generated by the firm's own marketing or production staff, or ideas from customers or suppliers (see BRAINSTORMING, NOMINAL GROUP TECHNIQUE);

(b) product technology generated by the firm's RESEARCH AND DEVELOPMENT department or licensed from outside the firm.

Any product ideas arising from either of these sources are then subjected to an initial product screening which explores their viability in terms of possible consumer acceptance, technological feasibility and likely cost. Product ideas which seem viable in terms of this initial screening justify further development expenditures and proceed to the next phase. This phase involves:

(a) further testing of the product concept to gauge its consumer acceptability, perhaps using consumer discussion groups and questionnaire field research;

(b) product design to make product prototypes and test them in a laboratory situation.

The results of these two processes will then be subjected to further screening on marketing, technology and cost grounds, and a product design will be agreed upon for product ideas which survive the second screening. In order to test further both consumer acceptability and the operating efficiency of the product design, prototypes may be distributed to a consumer test panel for their use and results collected from them.

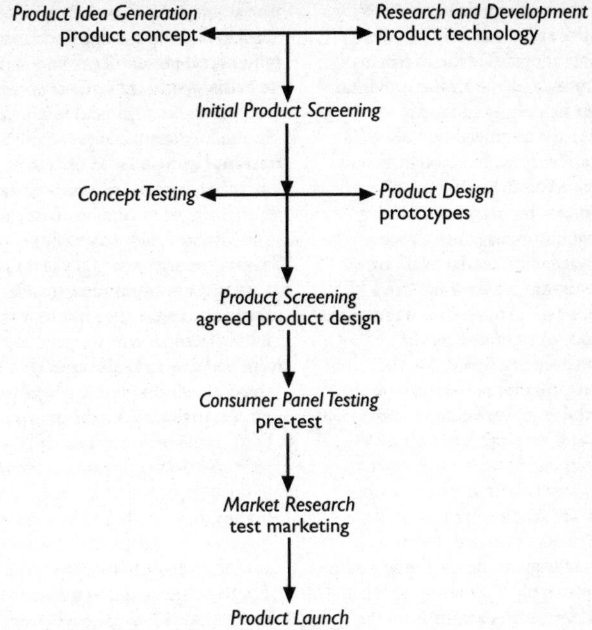

Fig. 60 **New product development.** Steps in the process of developing a new product.

Feedback from this pre-test can then be used to make final modifications to the product design if the basic design proves to be broadly acceptable.

Finally the firm may undertake extensive MARKETING RESEARCH into the potential market for the designed product, establish pilot production facilities for it and test market it in a limited geographical area in order to gauge consumer reaction. If TEST MARKETING proves successful then full-scale production facilities will be created and a full product launch undertaken, backed up by appropriate advertising and sales promotion.

A very high proportion of new product ideas are eliminated by the firm through its screening processes. Despite this only a small proportion of those surviving new products which are launched succeed in establishing themselves in the market. See CONCURRENT ENGINEERING.

new public management a new approach to the administration and delivery of public services which has found favour in the UK and elsewhere in the last fifteen years, and can be contrasted with 'old' public administration. Its hallmark is greater emphasis on private sector styles of management and efficiency. Large public bureaucracies with centralized decision-making have been broken up into smaller units with each unit operating at 'arms-length' from each other on the basis of explicit contracts, as in UK central government (see AGENCY STATUS) and the health service. These contracts typically include a range of output targets, and the organizations' achievement of these is measured by a set of PERFORMANCE INDICATORS. Competitive pressures have been increased in these organizations by the use of COMPETITIVE TENDERING which in some cases has resulted in private sector firms taking over the delivery of public services. The rationale for these changes is that the costs of public service provision will be easier to identify and hence to reduce. Furthermore, the fragmentation of public organizations will facilitate flexibility, and hence make service delivery more effective and efficient. An important component of the new public management has been a new approach to industrial relations: PERFORMANCE-RELATED PAY has been increasingly adopted in place of standardized pay systems. Critics of new public management argue, however, that the emphasis on entrepreneurial styles of management could weaken the commitment of public sector employees to disinterested public service, and at the extreme encourage corruption. See also CITIZENS' CHARTER.

Next Steps see AGENCY STATUS.

NFU see NATIONAL FARMERS' UNION.

NHS Trust an organization running health-care provision in the UK's National Health Service (NHS) at 'arms-length' from the other parts of the health service. NHS Trusts manage publicly-owned facilities such as hospitals and are accountable to central government in respect of their financial management but have operational autonomy in certain respects e.g. setting the pay and conditions of some employees. It is argued that hospital managers have greater freedom to manage than under the previous system of health service administration, and that this will lead to more effective and efficient use of resources. Controversy has surrounded the creation of NHS Trusts because local political influence on health-care delivery has been reduced, with critics arguing that the self-governing nature of some Trust functions is a form of privatization. Supporters argue that, besides the advantages listed above, consumer influences on health-care policy are more appropriately filtered through the health authorities and GP FUNDHOLDERS which purchase health services on their behalf from the Trusts (see PURCHASER-PROVIDER SPLIT). See NEW PUBLIC MANAGEMENT.

niche see MARKET SEGMENT, CONCENTRATED MARKETING OR TARGETING STRATEGY FOCUS.

Nikkei Index see SHARE PRICE INDEX.

no-frills products basic commodities such as bread, sugar and soft drinks sold in rudimentary packages at low prices.

nominal accounts records of items of income received by a business, such as rents from properties, or of expenses incurred, such as rates paid. This LEDGER information is summarized periodically in the PROFIT-AND-LOSS ACCOUNT. Contrast with REAL ACCOUNTS.

nominal capital see AUTHORIZED OR REGISTERED SHARE CAPITAL.

nominal group technique (NGT) a structured form of idea generation similar to BRAINSTORMING and the DELPHI technique. NGT draws on individual and group strengths using both as appropriate. One of its advantages is that it prevents domination of the group and has been widely used for QUALITY and PRODUCTIVITY improvement as well as organization strategy development. The technique requires a team of about 7 to 11 or 12 individuals who will form a multi-disciplined team and who are led by a facilitator. The technique has 8 steps, starting with a carefully prepared 'problem statement'. The second stage involves the facilitator encouraging the team to restate the problem in their own terms, this is followed by a silent generation period where individuals write down their responses, alternatives or suggestions to the statement. Ideas are then collected, recorded and clarified. The team then vote and rank each idea. The result is a ranked set of ideas towards a solution. NGT is frequently used instead of brainstorming as a means of idea generation. See NEW PRODUCT DEVELOPMENT.

nominal ledger the LEDGER which is used to record a firm's income and expenses.

nominal share capital see AUTHORIZED CAPITAL.

nominal share value see PAR VALUE.

nominal values the face value of an asset, wage, profit etc. expressed in current money prices without any adjustment for changes in the level of prices over time. Compare REAL VALUE.

nominee a company or trust which holds FINANCIAL SECURITIES on behalf of a person or other company. Nominees may be professional investment managers who hold portfolios of financial securities on behalf of investors (see UNIT TRUST). Alternatively, nominees may be used to buy and hold shares in a particular company on behalf of investors who wish to remain anonymous (often prior to making a TAKEOVER BID for the company). However, UK company law provisions on the DISCLOSURE OF SHAREHOLDINGS make it difficult for a BENEFICIAL OWNER to accumulate large blocks of shares in a company without being forced to reveal his identity. See SHARE REGISTER.

non-core business see CORE BUSINESS.

non-executive director see DIRECTOR, BOARD OF DIRECTORS.

non-diversifiable risk see CAPITAL-ASSET PRICING MODEL.

non-personal communication channels see COMMUNICATION CHANNELS.

non-productive time see IDLE TIME.

non-profit organization an organization which attempts to achieve an objective other than profit, for example, a charity.

non-voting shares *or* **'A'** shares ORDINARY SHARES which do not have any voting rights at a company's ANNUAL GENERAL MEETING. Non-voting shares often arose because company founders or directors sought to raise new share capital without diluting their control, by issuing large numbers of non-voting shares but retaining control of the original voting shares. Holders of voting shares have an advantage in company takeovers or disputes about company policy and so may have a higher market value than non-voting shares. Most STOCK MARKETS discourage companies from issuing new non-voting shares.

no par value share a company SHARE which has no face value. Such shares are used in North America. Contrast PAR VALUE SHARE.

normal curve a frequency distribution which has a bell-shaped symmetrical pattern where it is possible to calculate the height of the curve (the frequency) corresponding to any given numerical value.

Normal curves are used in statistical QUALITY CONTROL to establish the limits of variation in the size or other characteristic of a product which is to be regarded as acceptable in SAMPLES of a product being tested. For example, if a component is intended to measure an average of 100 mm across and the standard deviation is 2 mm, then the testers would expect 95% of a sample of components to measure between 96 mm and 104 mm across, and 99% of the sample to measure between 94 mm and 106 mm across. If the latter range of sizes was felt be acceptable in terms of the technical performance of the product, then this confidence interval would lead to the whole batch of components being rejected if more than 1% of sample components were larger or smaller than these broad limits. By contrast, if a tougher criterion was imposed and only components measuring 96 mm to 104 mm across were to be regarded as technically acceptable, then 95% of sample components would be acceptable. and if more than 5% of the sample were larger or smaller than these size limits then the whole batch of components would be rejected.

normal useful life see FAILURE RATE CURVE.

North America Free Trade Agreement (NAFTA) a regional 'free trade area' established in 1989 by the USA and Canada, which was extended to include Mexico in 1994. NAFTA aims to remove trade barriers for most manufactured goods, raw materials and agricultural produce over a 10-year period, as well as restrictions on cross border investment, banking and financial services. See TRADE INTEGRATION entry for further discussion.

no-strike agreement an agreement between an employer and a TRADE UNION in which the latter undertakes not to initiate or support STRIKE action by employees of the company. A number of Japanese companies which have recently established production facilities in the UK have reached agreements of this type. However, since collective agreements have no legal force in the UK there can be no absolute prohibition of strike action. Such agreements therefore can be viewed primarily as declarations of intent.

In fact most PROCEDURAL AGREEMENTS in INDUSTRIAL RELATIONS in the UK contain provisions which preclude strikes while issues are still under consideration within the COLLECTIVE BARGAINING procedures. Perhaps the main novelty of the new agreements is that most contain a provision for third party intervention, often in the form of pendulum ARBITRATION, should management and union be unable to resolve their differences. See SINGLE UNION AGREEMENT.

numerical control a system of controlling an automatic machine by means of a programme of instructions (often COMPUTER based) which relate to the particular operations being performed on a component. Machines which are operated by numerical control usually work with greater speed and accuracy than machines operated by hand and are particularly suited to MASS PRODUCTION OR PRODUCTION LINE manufacture.

numerical flexibility see LABOUR FLEXIBILITY.

NUPE see UNISON.

NUT see NATIONAL UNION OF TEACHERS.

NVQ see NATIONAL VOCATIONAL QUALIFICATION.

O

objectives see BUSINESS OBJECTIVES.

objectivity see ACCOUNTING PRINCIPLES.

observed time the time it takes an operator to perform a task when being observed for time study purposes. Observed times do not take into account contingencies like machine breakdowns or the operator's ability, and are simply the time taken by the particular operator being observed to complete the task. Thus, when setting a STANDARD TIME for a particular task several different operatives of differing levels of ability will be observed, and a contingency ALLOWANCE added. See WORK MEASUREMENT.

obsolescence 1 the tendency for products to become outmoded and to reach the end of their effective PRODUCT LIFE CYCLE. Obsolescence may be due to changes in style, fashion, materials used and the functions performed. With rapidly advancing technology and more fickle public tastes, product life cycles are tending to shorten as new, more sophisticated products supersede established products. Firms may respond by frequently updating their existing products in order to lengthen their life cycle. Alternatively, firms may deliberately follow a strategy of 'planned obsolescence' by bringing out a continuous stream of new products both to establish COMPETITIVE ADVANTAGE over rival suppliers, and to increase their total sales by inducing customers to replace products more frequently. See NEW-PRODUCT DEVELOPMENT, FASHION PRODUCT, PRODUCT STRATEGY.

2 the reduction in the value of a FIXED ASSET because of a significant change in demand or technology which renders the asset out of date, or comparatively inefficient.

Renting or LEASING plant, machinery and equipment avoids the risk of obsolescence, since at the end of the rental or lease period a firm may rent or lease a more modern fixed asset.

occupational mobility see LABOUR MOBILITY.

occupational pension see PENSION.

occupational psychology the branch of psychology concerned with the study of individual and group attributes and behaviour in work settings. Its potential benefit to managers is that understanding these can facilitate prediction and modification of future behaviour. Occupational psychology is therefore highly relevant to all aspects of organizational activities where individual performance and interaction are relevant to overall organizational performance, i.e. RECRUITMENT AND SELECTION, PERFORMANCE APPRAISAL.

Occupational psychology developed out of what came to be known as *human factor psychology*. This area of psychology is concerned with the relationship between the worker and the working environment. Specifically, it is concerned with the impact of environmental factors, such as the level of illumination on work performance, and how the environment can be changed to improve both job performance and JOB SATISFACTION. It is thus closely related to ERGONOMICS AND HUMAN ENGINEERING. Human factor psychology developed out of a concern to identify the causes of fatigue at work.

Initially fatigue was considered solely as a physiological phenomenon, i.e. adverse physical effects would be experienced as work pace reached a certain level. As time went on, however, it was realized that fatigue was at least in part a psychological occurrence and might arise from boredom which in turn could be traced to the character of JOB DESIGN AND REDESIGN.

Although human factor psychology continues to be an important element of occupational psychology, it is fair to say that the central concerns of the discipline relate to the central issues in psychology generally: *motivation, learning* and *personality.* Two basic approaches can be discerned in the study of MOTIVATION. One rests on the belief that people have certain basic needs which govern their behaviour (*content* or *needs theory*); the other, known as *expectancy theory,* suggests that individuals are motivated not by some inner need but the strength of their expectation that their actions will achieve a desired result, whatever that is.

The second main concern of occupational psychology is organizational learning. How do individuals learn (or how can they be taught) desirable modes of work behaviour? Once again there are two main approaches:

(a) *Behavioural psychology* suggests that there is a direct relationship between stimulus and response. A certain stimulus will cause a certain behavioural response. Psychologist B F Skinner (1904–90) is especially associated with this approach, which is notable for excluding mental processes themselves from analysis. He argued that behaviour could be conditioned or reinforced by using stimuli. In Skinner's view two forms of condition can be discerned:

(i) *respondent conditioning,* where there is a simple direct and temporal relationship between a certain stimulus and a certain response;

(ii) *operant conditioning,* where a range of environmental factors serves to shape behaviour over time, without there being a simple relationship between one stimulus and one response.

For example, a positive approach to performance appraisal by a boss can over time lead to good work performance by a subordinate. Recurrent praise by the boss will lead to better performance at some point in the future;

(b) The alternative approach to behavioural psychology is *cognitive psychology.* This emphasizes individual interpretation and understanding, and the active role of individuals in establishing their own objectives. A managerial strategy based on this approach would therefore attempt to influence individual goals and thought processes so as to make them complementary to the objectives of the organization.

The third main area of study and analysis is that of personality. Psychologists attempt to pinpoint the dimensions of personality (for example aggression, confidence etc.) and to determine which aspects are shaped by which experiences and whether some in fact are inherited ('nature-nurture debate'). The concern of occupational psychologists is to determine which aspects of personality are especially relevant to work performance, and whether certain traits are associated with effectiveness. It is widely believed, by managers if not by psychologists themselves, that certain traits, for example assertiveness, are LEADERSHIP qualities; hence an attempt to determine whether individuals possess these is often an important part of the recruitment and selection process. (See PSYCHOLOGICAL TESTS, BEHAVIOURALLY ANCHORED RATING SCALE, BEHAVIOURAL OBSERVATION SCALE, PERSONALITY INVENTORY.)

Besides these three core areas of occupational psychology, practitioners also deal with individual problems at work, such as stress. The method normally employed here is counselling. In face-to-face interviews the psychologist will encourage the individual to explore and understand the nature of the problem and to devise appropriate ways of dealing with it. The counsellor has a dual function: he or she listens (which can be highly important to the client) and also attempts to direct the way the client thinks about the problem.

OECD see ORGANIZATION FOR ECONOMIC COOPERATION AND DEVELOPMENT.

off-balance sheet financing the payment for use of an ASSET by hiring (LEASING) it rather than buying it. If a company wishes to install a new £50,000 photocopier it may enter into a lease agreement and agree to pay £12,000 per year over five years rather than buy the copier. Each year £12,000 is charged against profits in the company's PROFIT AND LOSS ACCOUNT. The copier does not appear in the BALANCE SHEET as a FIXED ASSET because the firm does not own it, but shows up as an annual operating cost which may be offset against PROFIT for TAXATION purposes. Off-balance sheet financing enables a company to make use of expensive assets without having to invest large sums of money in buying them. It also enables a company to keep its LONG-TERM CAPITAL EMPLOYED as small as possible, improving its measured RETURN ON CAPITAL EMPLOYED. See LEASEBACK.

offer see CONTRACT.

offer for sale a method of raising new SHARE CAPITAL by issuing company shares to the general public at a prearranged fixed price or by tender.

A company usually makes an offer for sale by placing its PROSPECTUS and application form for shares in a newspaper to invite the public to subscribe for shares. The application details will specify the deadline by which all application forms and accompanying cheques from prospective buyers must be received. At the deadline date, lists will be closed and shares allocated among successful subscribers (see ALLOTMENT); monies will be returned to unsuccessful applicants. See SHARE ISSUE, OVERSUBSCRIPTION.

offer price see BID PRICE.

office BUSINESS PREMISES used by a firm in the provision of services. See CAPITAL STOCK, FIXED ASSET.

Office for National Statistics (ONS) the UK government agency responsible for the collection, analysis and publication of economic, social and demographic statistics including the retail price index, national income accounts, balance-of-payments accounts, social trends, labour market data and periodic census of the population and health statistics.

ONS was formed in 1996 from the merger of the Central Statistical Office and the Office of Population Censuses and Surveys.

Office of Fair Trading an authority established by the FAIR TRADING ACT 1973, to administer all aspects of UK COMPETITION POLICY, specifically the control of MONOPOLIES. MERGERS and TAKEOVERS, ANTI-COMPETITIVE AGREEMENTS/ RESTRICTIVE TRADE AGREEMENTS, RESALE PRICES and ANTI-COMPETITIVE PRACTICES. The OFT, headed by the Director General of Fair Trading, collects data on industrial structure, monitors changes in market concentration and merger and takeover activity, and investigates and acts on information received from interested parties concerning allegedly 'abusive' behaviour in respect of trade practices, prices, discounts and other terms and conditions of sale. Where appropriate, the OFT may decide to refer particular cases for further investigation and report to the COMPETITION COMMISSION. The OFT also has other main responsibilities with regard to the protection of consumers' interests generally, including taking action against unscrupulous trade practices such as false description of goods and inaccurate weights and measures, and the regulation of consumer credit. See CONSUMER PROTECTION. TRADE DESCRIPTIONS ACTS 1968 AND 1972, WEIGHTS AND MEASURES ACT 1963, CONSUMER CREDIT ACT 1974, ESTATE AGENCY ACT 1979. CONTROL OF MISLEADING ADVERTISEMENTS REGULATIONS 1988.

Official List the prices of STOCKS and SHARES published daily by the UK STOCK MARKET. The prices quoted are the prices ruling at the close of the day's trading and are based on the average of the bid and offer prices. See BID PRICE.

off-line (of COMPUTER equipment) currently not under the control of the central processing unit (CPU).

offshore financial centre see TAX HAVEN.

offshore fund money and FINANCIAL

SECURITIES held by a FINANCIAL INSTITUTION which has its registered office in an overseas country (usually a TAX HAVEN such as Bermuda, the Cayman Islands or Jersey).

offshore production the devolvement, by a MULTINATIONAL ENTERPRISE engaged in the manufacture of a final product in a particular country, of part of its production operations to one or more of its overseas plants. In its strictest sense the term 'offshore production' refers specifically to the production overseas of *components* which are then exported and incorporated into the final product at the firm's main plant. With the increasing globalization of multinational firms' activities, the term is sometimes used also to describe the overseas production of some of the firm's *final products* which are then exported and sold alongside the firm's locally produced items as part of a comprehensive product range offering. Offshore production is undertaken primarily to enable a firm to maintain its international competitiveness by taking advantage of the lower labour costs of, and the financial subsidies offered by, HOST COUNTRIES wishing to attract FOREIGN INVESTMENT. See SOURCING.

old economy/old economy company see NEW ECONOMY/NEW ECONOMY COMPANY.

oligopoly a MARKET STRUCTURE characterized by concentrated supply conditions (i.e. a few large firms supply the bulk of industry output) and high barriers to entry. A key feature of oligopoly is the mutual interdependency of the leading suppliers, which has a major impact on the nature and intensity of their competitive relationships. For example, a price cut by one firm may seem advantageous as a unilateral act, but if rival suppliers are forced to follow suit rather than risk losing market share, such a move may escalate into a 'price war' leading to all firms suffering reduced profitability. For this reason, oligopolists tend to prefer to coordinate their price behaviour (see PRICE LEADERSHIP, CARTEL, COLLUSION) and to seek instead to establish COMPETITIVE ADVANTAGE over rival suppliers through PRODUCT DIFFERENTIATION initiatives. See COMPETITION POLICY.

ombudsman a UK body which is responsible for settling disputes between suppliers of goods and services and their customers, and public agencies and their clients. For example, the *Insurance Ombudsman* handles disputes between insurance companies and policyholders. The scheme is voluntary and not all insurers are members. By contrast, the *Building Societies Ombudsman* is a statutory scheme and all building societies are members. The *Revenue Adjudicator* considers complaints about delays, errors or discourtesy by INLAND REVENUE staff.

In most cases Ombudsmen have powers to award compensation to injured parties.

one worker – multiple machines production (OWMM) a method of PRODUCTION which involves one worker operating a number of *different* machines.

OWMM is usually employed in situations where production volumes are not high enough to justify a big production line involving a large number of operatives. OWMM economizes on the use of labour while enabling advantage to be taken of benefits of a production-line operation (for example less SET-UP time).

on-line (of COMPUTER equipment) currently under the control of the central processing unit (CPU).

ONS SEE OFFICE FOR NATIONAL STATISTICS.

OPEC SEE ORGANIZATION OF PETROLEUM EXPORTING COUNTRIES.

open market operation the sale or purchase by the monetary authorities of Government BONDS and TREASURY BILLS as a means of controlling the MONEY SUPPLY. See MONETARY POLICY for further discussion.

open union see TRADE UNION.

operant conditioning see OCCUPATIONAL PSYCHOLOGY.

operating characteristic curve a line which shows the relationship between the QUALITY of batches of raw materials or components and the probability of accepting any given batch. Fig 61 shows an operating

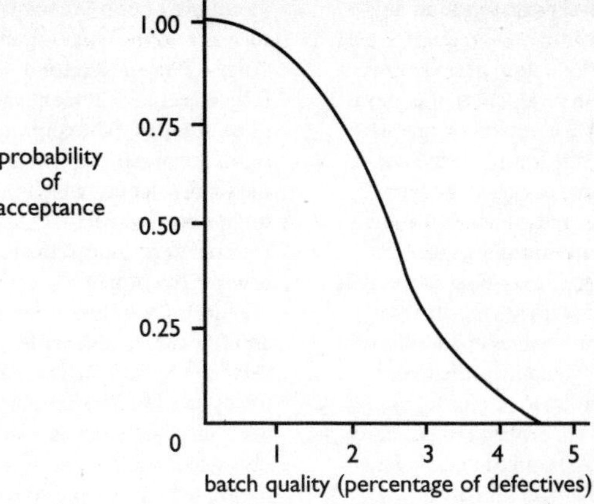

Fig. 61 **Operating characteristic curve.**

characteristic curve in which the vertical axis represents the probability of accepting a batch of raw materials or components (or the percentage of batches accepted from multiple batches) while the horizontal axis shows the percentage of defective units in a batch or batches of materials or components.

The operating characteristic curve is used as part of an ACCEPTANCE SAMPLING scheme and shows the performance of the sampling plan for any batch quality characteristic.

operating profit/loss the profit (or loss) arising from the manufacturing and trading operations of a business. Operating profit is not usually the same as NET PROFIT in the PROFIT-AND-LOSS ACCOUNT since it excludes non-operating income or expenditure such as dividends received on investments or loan interest paid.

operational research the application of mathematical and statistical techniques to industrial processes as a means of establishing optimal operating procedures and systems. Such techniques as LINEAR PROGRAMMING, NETWORK ANALYSIS, computer-based SIMULATION techniques, COMPUTER-AIDED DESIGN and STOCKHOLDING MODELS can be used in various areas of a firm's operations to establish cost-effective and efficient working practices.

operations management see PRODUCTION MANAGEMENT.

operations planning the planning of a firm's production operations including:

(a) the operations or work tasks to be performed;

(b) the order in which they will be carried out;

(c) the time which each operation should take;

(d) the layout of plant and machinery in the factory. Effective operations planning enables production to flow easily through out the factory, secures an efficient utilization of machines and labour, and facilitates good PRODUCTION SCHEDULING. See PRODUCTION-LINE BALANCING.

operating process sheets see MATERIALS FLOW MANAGEMENT.

opinion leaders individuals whose knowledge, skill or personality gives them an ability to influence other members of their REFERENCE GROUPS. In marketing goods and services, businesses try to identify opinion leaders and get them to try, use and endorse their product. See INFLUENCERS.

Opitz see PARTS FAMILY CODING AND CLASSIFICATIONS SYSTEMS.

opportunities and threats see SWOT ANALYSIS.

opportunity-based maintenance the performance of routine MAINTENANCE tasks outside normal production periods so as to avoid disruption to production operations.

opportunity cost a comparator against which to measure the return on the use of resources in some *particular* activity, as compared to the return which the *same* resources could earn in some other *alternative* activity. For example, a firm may employ its limited factory capacity in the production of dining tables or alternatively coffee tables, and would measure the opportunity cost of manufacturing dining tables in terms of the profits it might have earned from making coffee tables. For an illustration of the broader financial implications of this concept see the entry ECONOMIC VALUE ADDED. See LINEAR PROGRAMMING.

Opportunity 2000 an initiative by a group of employers (including the government) in the early 1990s to improve the position of female employees. Those subscribing to the initiative have introduced measures to overcome VERTICAL SEGREGATION and the GLASS CEILING, such as CAREER BREAKS. See DISCRIMINATION.

optimized production technology (OPT) a framework for identifying 'bottlenecks' in a PRODUCTION LINE which disrupts (i.e. holds-up) the smooth flow of work: OPT recognises that an hour lost at a bottleneck is an hour lost to the whole system and that bottlenecks govern both throughput and inventory (STOCK) in the system. Bottlenecks set the pace of the process (the 'beat' or 'drum'). Ideally, they must always have work (a 'buffer') placed in front of them, and material must be pulled (the 'rope') into the process from the bottleneck. Overcoming potential bottlenecks requires careful attention to PRODUCTION-LINE BALANCING needs and the availability of parts and components as and when required (see STOCK CONTROL). See MATERIALS REQUIREMENT MANAGEMENT, MATERIALS FLOW MANAGEMENT.

option a contractual right to buy (a 'call' option) or sell (a 'put' option) or buy/sell (a 'double' option) a FINANCIAL SECURITY such as a SHARE, FOREIGN CURRENCY, or a COMMODITY such as tea or tin, at an agreed (predetermined) price at any time within three months of the contract date. Option rights are purchased for a percentage of the share price etc. which varies according to the observed volatility of the share etc. (i.e. the magnitude of fluctuation in its price over the recent past).

Options are of two types: non-tradeable and tradeable. In the latter case the option itself can be bought and sold, which gives the option holder a greater degree of flexibility (see FORWARD MARKET); for example, if, in the case of a 'put' option, the share price should start to go down instead of up as anticipated, the option holder can cut his losses by selling his option. Options are frequently used to speculate (see SPECULATION) or hedge (see HEDGING) against future market prices.

The EUREX and the LONDON INTERNATIONAL FINANCIAL FUTURES EXCHANGE constitute the largest European Union centres for dealings in options and other forward contracts. See DERIVATIVE, SWAP. See also EXECUTIVE SHARE OPTION SCHEME.

optional extra a product which can be added to a basic product to enhance its performance or style, for example a sun roof or a radio cassette which may be added to a basic model of car. Optional extras are used by a seller to increase the market appeal of the basic product. See OPTIONAL EXTRAS PRICING, PRODUCT RANGE.

optional extras pricing the PRICING of OPTIONAL EXTRAS. Here, sellers must consider the cumulative price of the extras alongside the price of the basic model, vis-à-vis the price of the next most sophisticated model in the product line which incorporates these extras as standard features. See PRODUCT RANGE.

ordering cost the cost of placing an order for raw materials or components or machines, which includes management and clerical time, stationery, postage and other PURCHASING department costs. See STOCKHOLDING MODEL.

order interval the time interval between placings of orders for new STOCK. See STOCK CONTROL.

order level see STOCK CONTROL.

order quantity the quantity of an item to be ordered when STOCKS of the item fall to a predetermined minimum stock level. The reorder quantity should serve to replenish stock to the planned maximum stock level. The optimum order quantity may be ascertained by means of a STOCKHOLDING MODEL. See STOCK CONTROL.

order processing the procedure followed by a firm from receipt of a customer order to despatch or delivery and invoicing of the goods or services concerned. This procedure usually involves vetting the customer's credit limit and authorization of the customer's order; recording orders and sending copy orders to appropriate personnel, for example stores, despatch and accounts; and finally advising customers and sales personnel of delivery dates. See DELIVERY NOTE, INVOICE, WAREHOUSING, PICK LIST.

ordinary shares *or* **equity** a FINANCIAL SECURITY issued to those individuals and institutions who provide long-term finance for JOINT-STOCK COMPANIES. Ordinary SHAREHOLDERS are entitled to any net profits made by their company after all expenses (including interest charges and tax) have been paid and they generally receive some or all of these profits in the form of DIVIDENDS. In the event of the company being wound up they are entitled to any remaining ASSETS of the business after all debts and the claims of PREFERENCE SHAREHOLDERS have been discharged. Ordinary shareholders generally have voting rights at company ANNUAL GENERAL MEETINGS which depend upon the number of shares which they hold. However, some UK and overseas companies have both voting and NON-VOTING SHARES, where the company founders or directors have sought to raise new share capital without diluting their control by issuing non-voting shares. See also SHARE CAPITAL.

organic growth *or* **internal growth** a mode of business growth which is self generated (that is, expansion from within) rather then being achieved externally through MERGERS and TAKEOVERS. Organic growth typically involves a firm in improving its market share by developing new products and generally outperforming competitors (see HORIZONTAL INTEGRATION), and through market development (that is, finding new markets for existing products). Organic growth may also involve firms in expanding vertically into supply sources and market outlets (see VERTICAL INTEGRATION), as well as DIVERSIFICATION into new product areas.

The advantages of organic growth include the ability to capitalize on the firm's existing core skills and knowledge, to use up spare production capacity and to match available resources to the firm's expansion rate over time. Internal growth may be the only alternative where no suitable acquisition exists or where the product is in the early phase of the PRODUCT LIFE CYCLE. The disadvantages of organic growth are that in relying too extensively on internally generated resources, the firm may fail to develop acceptable products to sustain its position in existing markets, while existing skills and know-how may be too limited to support a more broadly based expansion programme.

For this reason, firms often rely on a combination of internal and external growth modes to internationalize their operations and undertake product/market diversifications.

See EXTERNAL GROWTH, BUSINESS STRATEGY, PRODUCT–MARKET MATRIX, NEW-PRODUCT DEVELOPMENT.

organismic organizations see MECHANISTIC AND ORGANISMIC ORGANIZATIONS.

organization a social grouping designed to achieve certain goals. In the modern world much of the provision of goods and services is undertaken by organizations, and they are the main providers of paid employment. The core features of the modern organization were outlined by Max Weber (1864–1920) in his analysis of BUREAUCRACY. In his view the bureaucratic organization was the dominant mode of organization in modern industrial societies. Organizations of this sort are often also called *formal organizations* since they exist independently of the individuals who belong to them at any given time, and the roles and activities of organization members are formally prescribed at least to some extent. *Informal organization*, by contrast, is where the differentiation of roles (for example leader, follower) is not formally specified and where roles emerge naturally. Small GROUPS are often referred to as informal organizations. They can be a source of difficulty within formal organizations because their respective roles and goals may conflict.

All formal organizations have a structure of roles and a set of arrangements to achieve the organization's objectives. This is known as the organization's *design*. It embraces the distribution of tasks that organization members perform and the mechanisms of coordination and control. Design is thus more than the simple lines of AUTHORITY and ACCOUNTABILITY shown in the ORGANIZATION CHART. In ORGANIZATIONAL ANALYSIS three dimensions of structure are usually seen as fundamental:

(a) *centralization:* the number of levels in the HIERARCHY and the extent to which decisions are taken at the top of the organization;

(b) *specialization:* the extent to which the total activities of the organization are broken down into specialized jobs for individuals. See JOB DESIGN AND REDESIGN;

(c) *standardization:* the extent to which the conduct of activities necessary to achieve the organization's goals are controlled and coordinated by standard, written rules.

Organizations differ along these dimensions. Small dynamic organizations in high growth sectors are often characterized by low centralization, specialization and standardization; by contrast, public administration often exhibits the opposite (see MECHANISTIC AND ORGANISMIC ORGANIZATIONS). See WORK ORGANIZATION, ORGANIZATIONAL STRUCTURE, PRODUCT-BASED STRUCTURE, FUNCTIONAL STRUCTURE, MATRIX STRUCTURE, H-FORM, TALL ORGANIZATION, FLAT ORGANIZATION.

organizational analysis the analysis and comparison of ORGANIZATIONS, especially their structure and the processes of decision-making within them. It is thus concerned with JOB DESIGN and the way work is organized (see WORK ORGANIZATION) in an organization. The body of knowledge on this subject is known as organization theory. Initially, theories in this area were concerned with developing universal principles of MANAGEMENT and organization structure, such as the optimum number of subordinates a manager should oversee (see CLASSICAL MANAGEMENT THEORY, SCIENTIFIC MANAGEMENT). Later analysts became aware of the differences between organizations. CONTINGENCY THEORY explores these differences, the reasons for them and the impact on performance (see also MECHANISTIC AND ORGANISMIC ORGANIZATIONS).

In recent years organizational analysis has been much concerned with decision-making processes in organizations. Researchers have investigated the types of decision that are taken by top managers and how the decisions are taken (for example by individuals or committee). There is considerable evidence that decisions are often not the outcome of a rational process of investigation and consideration but instead are substantially influenced by political processes within the organization. A further limit on rationality is the difficulty of obtaining sufficient information to make optimal decisions (see SATISFICE). As a result decision-making rarely occurs in the preplanned, rational way suggested in some of the literature on BUSINESS STRATEGY. Instead the parameters of the decision may change during the decision-making process. Much decision-making may be characterized as 'muddling through'.

organizational behaviour an umbrella term for theories and disciplines concerned with human behaviour in ORGANIZATIONS and the influences upon it. Approaches with this focus include INDUSTRIAL RELATIONS, OCCUPATIONAL PSYCHOLOGY, ORGANIZATIONAL ANALYSIS and the

SOCIOLOGY OF WORK. Though the boundaries between these are not distinct, they differ according to the emphasis they accord to individual or collective behaviour, and the relative importance they attach to structural (societal or organizational) or inter-personal determinants.

organizational buyer a member of an organization whose job is to negotiate terms of supply contracts. See PURCHASING.

organizational commitment the extent to which an employee is committed to an ORGANIZATION. It has both attitudinal components (i.e. the degree to which individuals identify with the goals of the firm) and behavioural aspects (i.e. the likelihood of an employee leaving the firm), and as such has been criticized for being a muddled concept. There are a number of standard scales for measuring commitment, and they are commonly applied using SURVEY methods.

organizational culture see CULTURE.

organizational slack the tendency for bureaucratic ORGANIZATIONS to use more resources than are strictly necessary to perform the functions of the organization, with the result that resources are used inefficiently and costs rise. See NATIONALIZATION VERSUS PRIVATIZATION.

organizational structure the particular way in which a firm or public authority is structured in order to perform its economic, social etc. activities.

A firm may be structured in two main ways: in a PRODUCT-BASED STRUCTURE activities are grouped together according to product, with each product being supported by its *own* functional teams of marketing, production, finance etc.; in a FUNCTIONAL STRUCTURE activities are grouped into departments by function – marketing, production, finance etc – which support *all* the firm's products.

Organizational structure can also be looked at in terms of the number of management layers involved, TALL ORGANIZATIONS having many management levels and FLAT ORGANIZATIONS only a few management levels.

The way in which a firm is organized around products and functions and the number of management layers can have a significant effect on the efficiency of the firm and its ability to respond quickly to changes in its market environment.

See CORPORATE RESTRUCTURING, BUSINESS PROCESS REENGINEERING.

organization chart a diagrammatic representation of the job tides and the formal patterns of AUTHORITY and RESPONSIBILITY in an ORGANIZATION. See Fig. 62.

Generally, such charts display the managerial HIERARCHY though they can be used to show all job positions within the organization. Though such charts are useful for presenting the overall structure, undue reliance should not be placed on such charts

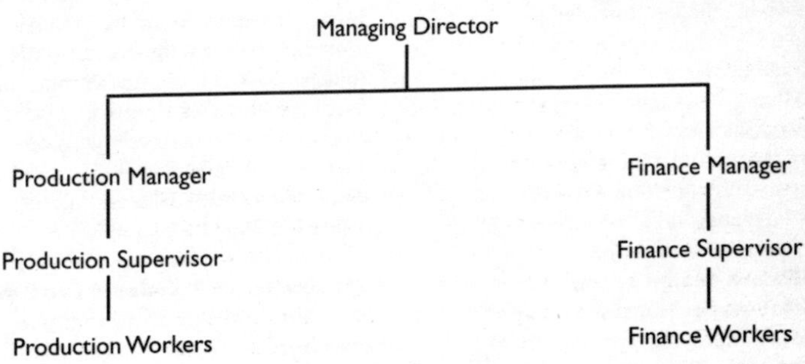

Fig. 62 **Organization chart.** A simple example.

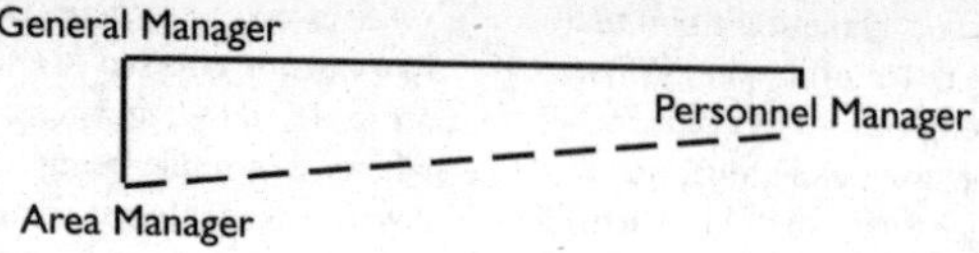

Fig. 63 **Organization chart.** A 'dotted line' relationship.

for the understanding of how organizations actually function. They rarely show the actual nature of job responsibilities.

They do not indicate what levels of cooperation may be necessary between departments, they do not show the actual communication flows nor the informal patterns of authority which may coexist with the formal channels. Organizations are usually much more complex and fluid than the organization chart suggests. In so far as the chart highlights the formal CHAIN OF COMMAND they can be said to embody a mechanistic conception of organization.,

More sophisticated organization charts may show 'dotted-line' relationships as well as the formal line of command. This is a representation of a relationship between two employees where one has no direct-line authority over the other but is empowered to give instruction on particular issues.

In Fig. 63 the Personnel Manager has a 'dotted line' relationship with the Area Manager, enabling him or her to give instructions on personnel issues. In theory the Personnel Manager's authority to do this flows from the powers of the General Manager. In practice those giving instructions through the 'dotted-line' may build up their own power base. See BUREAUCRACY, HIERARCHY, MECHANISTIC AND ORGANISMIC, SPAN OF CONTROL, LINE AND STAFF, PRODUCT-BASED STRUCTURE, FUNCTIONAL STRUCTURE, MATRIX STRUCTURE, DE-LAYERING, BUSINESS PROCESS RE-ENGINEERING.

organization design see ORGANIZATION.

organization development (OD) the process of improving organization performance by improving the pattern of interaction between members of the ORGANIZATION. The philosophy behind OD is that the core features of organization, such as task specialization, tend to obstruct the full use of individual talents and hence inhibit effectiveness. MECHANISTIC organizations can benefit from being loosened-up to enable faster response to environmental change. To do this individuals need to understand what others do and what motivates them, as well as themselves, and to identify the barriers to personal and group effectiveness. OD facilitates this through use of behavioural techniques such as T-Groups (see MANAGEMENT DEVELOPMENT). Many are wary of OD, partly because it seems to delve into the private domain and partly because its benefits are difficult to quantify. Also, if power relationships in the organization are left unchanged individuals may become resentful: they have been encouraged to modify their behaviour but their bosses, it seems, have not. See CULTURE. GROUP.

Organization for Economic Cooperation and Development (OECD) an international organization whose membership comprises mainly the economically advanced countries of the world. The OECD provides a regular forum for discussions among government finance and trade ministers on economic matters affecting their mutual interests, particularly the promotion of economic growth and international trade. The OECD is a main source of international economic data and regularly compiles and publishes standardized inter-country statistics.

Organization of Petroleum Exporting Countries (OPEC) an organization established in 1960 with a head office in Vienna to look after the oil interests of its 13 member countries: Saudi Arabia, Kuwait,

Iran, Iraq, Venezuela, Qatar, Indonesia, Libya, Abu Dhabi, Algeria, Nigeria, Ecuador and Gabon.

Ecuador withdrew in 1992 and Gabon in 1995. See CARTEL.

organization structure see ORGANIZATION.

organization theory see ORGANIZATIONAL ANALYSIS.

organized anarchy a behavioural model of how ORGANIZATIONS function which emphasizes the limits of rational action (compare with the rational model of BUREAUCRACY). As developed by the American management writers Richard Cyert (1921–) and James March (1928 –), this model suggests that organizations tend to formulate objectives *in response* to their activities rather than *in advance*, that organizational members do not fully comprehend the workings of the organization, and that their involvement in organizational activities is fluid and unpredictable. As a result, much of what organizations do can be said to be ad hoc and somewhat anarchic in character. However, the structure and procedures of the organization prevent unrestrained anarchy. See GARBAGE-CAN MODEL OF DECISION-MAKING, DISJOINTED INCREMENTALISM, ORGANIZATIONAL ANALYSIS.

orientation to work the objectives and expectations that employees have of their work, and which influences their interpretation of their work experience, thereby determining to some extent their JOB SATISFACTION. The notion of orientations to work first gained currency in the SOCIOLOGY OF WORK in the late 1960s after the publication of a major study of workers' attitudes (the Affluent Worker study) in a car assembly factory. The researchers found that these workers assessed the satisfaction obtained from their jobs not in absolute terms but in relation to what they wanted from their employment. Thus the technology, for instance, did not directly determine the level of job satisfaction; the orientations developed out of people's social experiences outside work. Three types of orientation were identified.

(a) *solidaristic*, where the value of work lies in its capacity to provide intrinsic satisfaction and social contact with other workers. Work is a central life interest and work friendships extend outside the factory gate.

(b) *bureaucratic*, where the worker sees work in terms of a lifelong career, and work satisfaction depends on the extent to which work meets career and status aspirations.

(c) *instrumental*, where no intrinsic satisfaction from work is sought and work has primarily an economic value to the worker. Those with this orientation attach little importance to friendship with workmates and tend to lead a 'privatized' existence separate from the rest of the community.

It was argued that the 'affluent workers' had the latter orientation. Although the work was undeniably tedious these employees did not express dissatisfaction with their jobs as long as high incomes could be gained. The Affluent Worker study was a landmark in the sociology of work because it emphasized the importance of the meanings people attach to their work.

original equipment a PART OR COMPONENT (e.g. a tyre) incorporated into a final product (e.g. a car) at the time of its initial manufacture or assembly. At a later date 'replacement parts' may be required to replace the original parts as a result of wear and tear, malfunction or damage.

OTC see OVER THE COUNTER MARKET.

output goods and services produced by a firm using resource INPUTS.

output tax see VALUE-ADDED TAX.

outsourcing the buying-in of components, finished products and services from outside the firm rather than self supply from within a firm. In some cases this is done because it is more cost-effective to use outside suppliers or because outside suppliers are more technically competent or can supply a greater range of items. For example, in 2000 the Bank of Scotland signed a 10 year outsourcing agreement with IBM which involves IBM taking over the Bank of Scotland's computer systems and operating them. The deal will enable the Bank of Scotland to 'save' up to £150 million on its information technology (IT) costs as well as being able to draw on IBM's expertise to create a more technically advanced IT infrastructure than it could have achieved on its own. On the debit side, however, reliance on outside suppliers may make the firm vulnerable to disruptions in supplies, particularly missed delivery dates, problems with the quality of bought-in components, and 'unreasonable' terms and conditions imposed by powerful suppliers. See SOURCING, INTERNALIZATION, MAKE OR BUY, VERTICAL INTEGRATION, VIRTUAL CORPORATION.

outward investment see CAPITAL OUTFLOW, FOREIGN INVESTMENT, FOREIGN DIRECT INVESTMENT.

overcapacity a situation in which a firm or industry has too much production CAPACITY on hand relative to current demand levels. This may be only temporary because of a downturn in the BUSINESS CYCLE. Alternatively, the decline in demand may be permanent (see PRODUCT LIFE CYCLE) or due to the industry having overinvested in new plant relative to long-run demand potential. In this case, overcapacity, leading to greater competition for limited sales is often removed by the disappearance of inefficient firms from the industry, or by RATIONALIZATION schemes involving the MERGER of firms and closure of redundant plant.

overdraft a financial facility for advancing MONEY to an individual or business (the borrower) by a COMMERCIAL BANK, SAVINGS BANK etc. (the lender). An overdraft is a form of CREDIT which allows the borrower to withdraw as much money as required up to a prearranged total limit, whereupon interest is charged at a rate related to the base rate of interest on outstanding balances (see INTEREST RATE). In the case of businesses, overdraft facilities are often provided on an indefinite basis, thus providing the borrower with a continuous line of credit used mainly to finance WORKING CAPITAL requirements. See BANK LOAN.

overhead *or* **indirect cost** any COST that is not directly associated with a product, that is, all costs other than DIRECT MATERIALS cost and DIRECT LABOUR cost. Production overheads (factory overheads) include the cost of INDIRECT MATERIALS and INDIRECT LABOUR along with other production expenses like factory heat, light and power, and depreciation of plant and machinery. The cost of factory departments such as maintenance, materials stores and the canteen which render services to producing departments are similarly part of production overheads. Most SELLING COSTS and DISTRIBUTION COSTS and all ADMINISTRATION COSTS are also counted as overheads since they cannot usually be directly related to units of product. See also FIXED COST, STANDARD COST.

overhead-cost variance the difference between the standard overhead cost of a product and its actual overhead cost. Use of COST RATES for charging OVERHEADS to products will recover the overheads actually incurred only if actual overhead costs correspond with BUDGET and if actual output is the same as budgeted output. If actual expenditure is larger than the budgeted amount, then the standard overhead cost per unit of product will be smaller than actual unit overheads incurred and overheads will be under-recovered in the price set (*expenditure variance*). Again, if actual output turns out to be smaller than planned output, then fixed overheads will remain as under-recovered overheads (*volume variance*). By contrast, over-recovery of overheads occurs when actual overhead costs are less than budget and/or more is produced than planned. See ABSORPTION, STANDARD COST.

overmanning the employment of more workers than is strictly required to perform efficiently a particular set of work tasks. This can occur because of an inefficient organization of work by management or through the operation of RESTRICTIVE LABOUR PRACTICES.

overriding discount see AGGREGATED REBATE.

Overseas Technical Information Centre see TECHNOLOGY TRANSFER.

oversubscription a situation in which the number of SHARES applied for in a new SHARE ISSUE exceeds the numbers to be issued. This requires the ISSUING HOUSE responsible for handling the share issue to devise some formula for allocating the shares. By contrast, *undersubscription* occurs when the number of shares applied for falls short of the number on offer, requiring the issuing house which has underwritten the shares to buy the surplus shares itself. See CALLED-UP CAPITAL, PAID-UP CAPITAL.

over-the-counter market (OTC) a MARKET for corporate SHARES which have not obtained a full listing on the main STOCK MARKET. The UK's OTC market was abolished in 1992. See ALTERNATIVE INVESTMENT MARKET.

overtime extra hours of work undertaken by an employee that are additional to the number of hours specified as constituting the 'basic' working week, and for which employees are paid a WAGE RATE higher than the 'basic' wage. Firms often resort to overtime working to meet sudden increases in orders, viewing overtime by the existing workforce as a more flexible and cheaper alternative to taking on extra workers. An *overtime ban* by employees can thus be a highly effective form of INDUSTRIAL ACTION.

overtime ban see INDUSTRIAL ACTION.

overtrading a situation in which a firm expands its production and sales without making sufficient provision for additional funds to finance the extra WORKING CAPITAL needed. Where this happens the firm will run into LIQUIDITY problems and can find itself unable to find the cash to pay suppliers or wages. See also WORKING-CAPITAL RATIO, CURRENT RATIO, CASH FLOW.

OWMM see ONE WORKER-MULTIPLE MACHINES PRODUCTION.

own-label brand a product which is sold by a RETAILER bearing the retailer's own BRAND NAME. In some cases own-label brands are manufactured by the retailer as part of a vertically integrated manufacturing-retailing operation (Boots the Chemist, for instance, both produces and retails a large number of its own pharmaceutical and cosmetic products). More usually, however, retailers' 'own labels' are produced by independent manufacturers on a contract basis. In many cases, these are the very same manufacturers who produce their own (manufacturers') branded products which sell in competition alongside the retailers' own-label version! The attraction to the manufacturer in producing 'own labels' is that they bring in a substantial volume of extra business on a regular basis. On the other hand, however, there is a danger that the own-label versions of the product will reduce the sales of the manufacturers' main branded products, especially as retailers tend to sell their own-label brands at lower prices than they sell the manufacturer's brand. For the retailer, own-label brands may increase unit profit margins and provide extra sales potential by building up store loyalty (for example, Heinz' baked beans can be bought in Tesco, Sainsbury's etc. but Tesco's baked beans can be bought only in Tesco).

p

P see CONTROL CHART.

packaging the means of physically protecting and selling a product. Functionally, packaging protects products whilst they are in transit and being stored, enables products to be sold in convenient retail packs in standard WEIGHTS AND MEASURES, and identifies the contents of the package by means of labelling.

In addition, packaging may play an important part in marketing a product, particularly when products are being sold on a SELF SERVICE basis. The attractiveness of the colour and design of the package is important in attracting the attention of the buyer. In addition, the use of BRAND NAMES on packaging reinforces the perceptions of the brand at the point of sale.

Packaging can take a variety of forms including metal and plastic containers, and paper and cardboard cartons, and a firm's choice of packaging material will depend upon the characteristics of the product (for example, liquid or solid), the comparative cost of the material and its appearance and customer appeal. See PROMOTIONAL MIX.

pac-man defence see TAKEOVER BID.

paid-up capital the amount of CALLED-UP CAPITAL which shareholders have paid to date, where a JOINT-STOCK COMPANY issues shares with phased payment terms. For example, a company may issue £1 shares with 50p payable immediately upon *application* by intending shareholders, a further 25p upon *allotment* of shares to shareholders and the final 25p three months later. Here the paid-up capital three months after allotment would be £1 per share times the number of shares allotted, equal to called-up capital, unless there is a shortfall from shareholders who have failed to pay their final 25p instalments (*calls in arrears*). See SHARE ISSUE.

pallet a portable platform or container used for transporting raw materials, work in progress and finished goods.

parallel importing the practice whereby independent importers buy a particular manufacturer's product from a low-priced market source and sell it in direct competition with the manufacturer's appointed distributors in the local market, usually at a lower price. Parallel importing has been prominent in the European Union where differences between member countries' price levels, along with manufacturers' practices of granting lucrative EXCLUSIVE DEALING rights to selected local distributors, have created profitable segments for independents to exploit.

Parallel importing is seen as beneficial by advocates of FREE TRADE and COMPETITION POLICY as it breaks down barriers to INTERNATIONAL TRADE and PRICE DISCRIMINATION between markets, leading to a greater harmonization of international price levels. See IMPORTING.

parallel loan see BACK-TO-BACK LOAN.

parallel system a means of improving the RELIABILITY of a product or machine by incorporating two or more components in the product or machine to operate in parallel, so that if one of the components fails, the product or machine will still continue to operate. Parallel systems are incorporated within products such as aircraft, where the importance of safety considerations warrants the extra cost of additional components.

parental leave the right of a parent to take time off work to care for a child. In the UK these rights have recently been enshrined in law following a European Directive on this issue. Such leave is unpaid and is restricted to employees who have at least one year's employment. See MATERNITY RIGHTS, PATERNITY RIGHTS.

parent company see HOLDING COMPANY.

parenting the manner in which the senior managers of a company manage their subordinate companies or business units. Good parenting in the form of dear goals for business unit managers, monitoring of their performance, appropriate rewards and tight financial controls can improve the performance of these business units. See DIVERSIFICATION.

Pareto analysis see ABC ANALYSIS.

Pareto distribution the tendency for a small proportion of the number of objects or items being considered to account for a large proportion of the feature under examination. More crudely, the Pareto 'law' suggests that 20% of items account for 80% of the total amount of stock or sales or whatever. In the case of stock, the Pareto law implies that a small proportion of the total number of items stocked accounts for a large proportion of the total value of stock held.

The business significance of the Pareto distribution is that if management devotes the greater part of its time to controlling the most important 20% of the stock items held, it is, in effect, controlling a large proportion of the total value of the firm's stocks. See ABC ANALYSIS.

Parkinson's law an observation by English management writer C Northcote Parkinson (1909–93) that 'work expands to fill the time available for its completion'. As a result employees generally feel overworked whatever their actual workload. A solution favoured by managers and officials alike is the appointment of more subordinates to relieve them of some of their workload. However, the greater the number of staff the more difficult the task of COORDINATION. Hence there is a tendency for certain coordinative mechanisms, such as committees, to proliferate. This in turn generates additional work which is reflected in pressure to increase employee numbers even further. Hence organizations have a tendency to grow in staff numbers even though the base workload may be unchanging. Parkinson's writings are generally viewed as humorous and perceptive asides on organizational life rather than propositions to be empirically tested.

part *or* **component** an item (e.g. a clutch) which is used in the assembly of a final product (e.g. a car). See PARTS FAMILY CODING AND CLASSIFICATION SYSTEM, ORIGINAL EQUIPMENT, REPLACEMENT PART, AFTER-SALES CARE.

partial agreement see MULTI-EMPLOYER AGREEMENT.

participating preference share see PREFERENCE SHARE.

participation see EMPLOYEE PARTICIPATION.

partly paid capital the difference between CALLED-UP CAPITAL and PAID-UP CAPITAL where shares are issued with phased payment terms.

partnership a BUSINESS owned and controlled by two or more persons who subscribe capital and share decision-taking as specified by a partnership agreement. Generally partners have *unlimited liability* for any debts incurred by the partnership and any of them may enter into contracts on behalf of the partnership. Partnerships are particularly prevalent in professional services, for example accounting, surveying and insurance. See SLEEPING PARTNER, SOLE PROPRIETORSHIP, JOINT-STOCK COMPANY, LIMITED LIABILITY.

partnership shares see SHARE INCENTIVE PLAN.

part period balancing a dynamic lot sizing technique that matches SET-UP COSTS with inventory holding costs. See BATCH SIZE, STOCKHOLDING MODEL.

parts family coding and classification system the identification and classification of parts and components which are used to make a final product, especially in CELLULAR MANUFACTURING operations. The coding structures in common use are typically multi-digit, faceted systems that identify, group and characterize components by finish, size, material, machining and other characteristics and process requirements. There are several systems available. The Brisch system is usually used within the UK. The Opitz system within Germany and the Miclass system in the Netherlands.

part-time work employment where the hours of work are substantially fewer than the usual working week. In the UK, part-time work is officially defined as that which is under 30 hours each week.

The advantage of part-time working to employers is that it *can* be relatively cheap as insurance contributions may not have to be made. It also enables them to adapt production or the provision of services to variations in demand, for example, a shop may stay open into the evening by employing part-time workers to cover the evening work. Part-time work can also be advantageous to employees themselves in so far as it allows them to fit work in with other commitments. Part-time employees are legally entitled to the same PENSION, MATERNITY RIGHTS, PARENTAL LEAVE, SICK PAY and TRAINING rights as full-time employees (though often on a pro-rata basis).

In the UK in recent years, growth in part-time work has formed a large part of the growth in employment. Approximately 25% of the employed labour force are now in part-time jobs. Most of these are women. It is often said that paid work is not as central a life interest to part-time workers as it is to full-timers and as a result pressure for high rates of pay is somewhat less. For these reasons also, TRADE UNIONS find it difficult to recruit and mobilize part-time workers. Thus, part-time work is generally not well paid, with the result that some employers find it attractive to replace full-time work-forces with part-time ones. See LABOUR FLEXIBILITY, LOW PAY, TEMPORARY WORK.

party plan see DIRECT SELLING.

par value 1 the face or nominal value of a SHARE in the UK. Par values may be of any amount, though 25p or £1 are the most common par values. The par value of a share bears little relationship to its market value, which is determined by demand and supply for the shares. A company can change the par value of its shares by a reorganization or SHARE SPLIT, for example issuing four 25p par value shares for every £1 share held. 2 the fixed price of a FOREIGN CURRENCY under a FIXED RATE EXCHANGE SYSTEM.

patent a grant of ownership rights by the government to a person or business in respect of the invention of an entirely new product or manufacturing process or a significant development of an existing product or process. In the UK, under the COPYRIGHT, DESIGNS AND PATENTS ACT 1988, the PATENT OFFICE can grant a patentee a monopoly to make, use or sell the invention for a maximum of twenty years from the date on which the patent was first filed. In order to obtain a patent approval, inventors are required to supply full details of the invention to the Patents Office and satisfy that body that the invention contains original features and that it has a demonstrable industrial application.

The monopoly protection given by a patent is not enforced by the Patent Office itself. It is the responsibility of patentees to look after their rights by detecting whether someone else is infringing them and then seeking redress for infringement through the courts.

Patents registered in one country may be valid in other countries if filed in a country which is party to a reciprocal treaty. The UK, for example, is a member of the 13-country European Patent Convention which allows inventors to obtain patent rights in the EPC countries by filing a single European patent application. Globally, patent applications are administered by the World Intellectual Property Organization (WIPO) under the Patent Cooperation Treaty which enables investors to apply for registration in member countries with a single registration. WIPO has no powers of enforcement. However, under a GATT (now the WORLD TRADE

ORGANIZATION) accord (negotiated at the 'Uruguay Round') it was agreed to give investors a minimum patent term of 20 years in all member countries with members being obliged to enforce patent protection on patents recognised by each others national authorities.

The patent system has the twin objectives of both encouraging inventors to undertake the risks and expenses of breaking new ground by offering them temporary monopoly rights to profit from their work, and providing for the eventual dissemination of advances in technology to the benefit of society as a whole. See RESEARCH AND DEVELOPMENT, BRAND.

Patent Office a UK body which is responsible for the administration of various aspects of 'intellectual property rights' legislation, in particular the COPYRIGHT, DESIGNS AND PATENTS ACTS 1988, the Registered Designs Act 1949 and the Trade Marks Act 1938. The Patent Office is the sole authority for the granting of PATENT rights on product and process inventions and for the registration of industrial designs (see DESIGN RIGHTS) and TRADEMARKS.

paternalism an approach to the management of employees or subordinates in which considerable importance is attached to looking after their interests as viewed and defined by the employer or superior. Paternalism is often associated with hostility to TRADE UNIONS since unions attempt to give independent expression to employee interests. See MANAGEMENT STYLE, WELFARE.

paternity leave time allowed off work to male employees on the birth of their children. In the UK male parents or carers are entitled to PARENTAL LEAVE.

pay the money paid to an employee for performing specified work tasks or JOBS. Payment to employees for the labour they provide takes two main forms:

(a) PAYMENT BY TIME, principally weekly WAGES and OVERTIME, together with monthly SALARIES;

(b) PAYMENT BY RESULTS, principally PIECEWORK, INCENTIVE BONUSES, GROUP INCENTIVE BONUSES.

The main distinction between the two is that 'payment by time' systems remunerate workers for the amount of labour supplied (i.e. the *input* of labour) per time period (hourly, weekly etc.) irrespective of the amount of output produced; whereas 'payment by results' systems remunerate workers specifically for the amount or value of the *output* produced in a given time period. 'Payment by results' is favoured by many firms because it is thought to provide a strong financial incentive for workers to strive to maximize their output rather than work at a more leisurely pace, but the firm may be required to install appropriate INSPECTION systems to ensure that extra output has not been achieved at the expense of product quality and reliability.

Pay rates are determined by a number of factors including the forces of supply and demand for particular types of job in the LABOUR MARKET, the bargaining power of TRADE UNIONS (see COLLECTIVE BARGAINING) and the general economic climate (see, for example, PRICES AND INCOMES POLICY). In addition to receipt of money employees may receive various other work-related benefits such as free or subsidized meals, travel allowances, a company car, etc. (see FRINGE BENEFITS). See ATTENDANCE BONUS, MERIT PAY, COMMISSION, FEE, PERFORMANCE-RELATED PAY, CAFETERIA BENEFITS, COMPARABILITY, INCREMENTAL PAY SCALE, WORK MEASUREMENT, PROFIT-RELATED PAY, EMPLOYEE SHARE OWNERSHIP PLAN, PAY DIFFERENTIALS, LOW PAY, GAINSHARING, EXECUTIVE SHARE OPTION SCHEME, LONG-TERM INCENTIVE PLAN, SHARE INCENTIVE PLAN, MINIMUM WAGE RATE, FINANCIAL PARTICIPATION.

pay-as-you-earn (PAYE), a scheme for collecting INCOME TAX due from the earnings of an individual by deducting the tax owing before an employer pays WAGES or SALARIES. PAYE is *not* a tax, merely a *scheme* for the collection of tax. See INCOME TAX SCHEDULES.

pay as you go a PENSION scheme where current payments to pensioners are financed by current savings contributions by employees in the scheme. This can be contrasted with 'FUNDED PENSIONS' where pension payments are funded by past contributions to a PENSION FUND.

payback method see PAYBACK PERIOD.

payback period a criterion used in INVESTMENT APPRAISAL to evaluate the desirability of an INVESTMENT project. Payback calculations involve measuring the CASH FLOWS associated with a project and indicate how long it takes for an investment to generate sufficient cash to recover in full its original capital outlay. For example, if a machine costs £5,000 to purchase at the start of year 1, then generates net cash inflows from the sale of products made by the machine of £5,000 in year 1 and £3,000 in year 2 then it would recoup the initial cash outlay in the first year. If a firm's target payback period for new investment projects was, say, two years or less, then this particular project would be undertaken.

Whether or not the machine pays back its initial outlay in one year depends upon how accurate the future estimates of sales volumes, selling prices, materials costs etc. turn out to be. Since all investments involve assessments of future re-venues and costs they are all subject to a degree of uncertainty. This problem, in part, can be handled by undertaking sensitivity analysis, by making not one but three estimates for each item of project cost or revenue ('optimistic', 'most likely', 'pessimistic') to indicate the range of possible outcomes.

pay bargaining see COLLECTIVE BARGAINING.

pay differential the difference between the WAGE RATES of different groups of workers. Pay differentials arise for a number of reasons:

(a) differences in skills, training and responsibilities between occupations (for example, doctors are paid more than nurses, managers more than factory operatives);

(b) differences in growth rates and PRODUCTIVITY levels between firms and industries, with high-growth, high-productivity firms and industries paying more;

(c) differences in regional employment levels reflecting differences in the supply and demand for labour in particular localities, with pay in prosperous areas generally being higher than pay in depressed areas.

Pay differentials serve to encourage LABOUR MOBILITY between occupations, industries and regions, facilitating the movement of workers into sectors of the economy where they can be more efficiently employed.

Maintenance of differentials is believed to foster poor INDUSTRIAL RELATIONS and encourage inflationary wage spirals; as one group wins a pay increase so another seeks a similar one to maintain the differential. See COLLECTIVE BARGAINING, COMPARABILITY, INFLATION.

pay dispersion the extent of PAY inequality within a firm or a country. Pay dispersion is usually measured as a ratio of average pay in the 9th decile to that in the 10th decile of the pay distribution. See PAY DIFFERENTIAL.

PAYE see PAY-AS-YOU-EARN.

payment by results a PAY system in which a worker's WAGES and other payments received are related to the amount (or value) of output produced. See PIECEWORK, INCENTIVE BONUS SCHEME, GROUP INCENTIVE SCHEME, MERIT PAY, WORK STUDY.

payment by time a PAY system in which a worker's WAGES are typically a function of the hourly 'basic' WAGE RATE for the job and the number of hours constituting the 'basic' working week, plus any OVERTIME payments. See SALARY, WORK STUDY.

payment in advance see PREPAYMENT.

payment system see PAY.

pay review body a committee whose function is to recommend levels of PAY for 'top people' (for example judges) and other groups of public sector PROFESSIONALS (for example hospital doctors and nurses) where it is believed by government that COLLECTIVE BARGAINING is an inappropriate method of pay determination. The acceptance of the pay review system by these occupational groups is premised on the assumption that the awards of these bodies will be honoured and financed by government (as the ultimate paymaster).

payroll accounts LEDGER accounts which show for each of a firm's employees the amount of gross salary or wage payment due, deductions of income tax and national insurance and the net amount of income to be paid out each week or month. Gross wages may be based on hours worked, for time-paid workers; or on units of output completed, for piece-rate paid workers.

pay round the series of negotiations between employers and TRADE UNIONS (COLLECTIVE BARGAINING) that takes place in some parts of UK industry each year to determine WAGE RATES, SALARIES and other forms of PAY.

PC see PERSONAL COMPUTER.

pendulum arbitration see ARBITRATION.

penetration see MARKET PENETRATION, MARKET PENETRATION PRICING.

pension a payment received by individuals who have retired from paid employment or have reached the government's pensionable age, in the form of a regular weekly or monthly income, or as a lump sum. There are three main types of pension scheme:

(a) *state retirement pensions* operated by he Government, whereby the employee pays NATIONAL INSURANCE CONTRIBUTIONS over his working life, giving entitlement to an old age pension on retirement of an amount considered to provide some minimum standard of living. State pensions may be based on earnings or may be a flat rate, or combination of the two. See DEPARTMENT FOR WORK AND PENSIONS;

(b) *occupational pensions* operated by private sector employers whereby the employee and the employer each make regular contributions to a PENSION FUND or INSURANCE COMPANY scheme, the pensioner then receiving a pension which is related to the amount of his contributions (annual contributions x number of years worked). Occupational pensions take two main forms: (1) defined benefit, where the pension is linked to final salary. Here the employer is liable to make up any shortfalls in the PENSION FUND. This type of scheme is also known as a 'final salary' scheme. (2) defined contribution, or money purchase scheme, where the size of contributions but not the final pensions benefits are fixed. The size of pension benefits are determined by the investment performance of the fund. The employee rather than the employer bears the risk.

In the UK there is a shift from defined benefit to defined contribution schemes, because of employer fears about their future liabilities;

(c) *personal pension plans* (*PPP*) operated by insurance companies, pension funds and other financial institutions which provide 'customized' pension arrangements for individuals depending on their personal circumstances. Since a PPP scheme is not tied to a particular employer the problem of transferring pension rights should the person move jobs is much reduced. A recent innovation in the UK is the 'stakeholder pension', aimed at low and medium income earners who work for employers who do not already have an occupational scheme. Employers with more than 5 employees are obliged to designate a 'stakeholder pension' provider for their workforce but they are under no obligation to make contributions to the scheme. Nor are employees obliged to subscribe. Approved providers of stakeholder pensions are required to levy low charges to participants. See CONTRACTING OUT.

pension fund a financial institution which specializes in the management and administration of personal and corporate PENSION schemes. Pension funds collect regular contributions from individuals, employees and employers in the case of occupational pension schemes, and make payments to retired beneficiaries.

Pension funds use the monies they receive not only to make day-to-day disbursements to pensioners but also to generate additional income and profit by investing their funds in FINANCIAL SECURITIES, mainly UK and overseas government fixed-interest bonds, corporate stocks and shares and property bonds (see INSTITUTIONAL INVESTORS). Their portfolios attempt to maintain a careful balance between immediate liquidity needs and longer term investment returns.

The pension fund movement in the UK is represented by the National Association of Pension Funds (NAPF), which provides a forum for the discussion of matters of general concern to members and acts on behalf of members in dealings with other institutional bodies such as the Institutional Investors Committee and the Government. The investment and management of monies by pension funds are regulated by the INVESTMENT MANAGEMENT REGULATORY ORGANIZATION (for in-company pension funds) and by the FINANCIAL SERVICES AUTHORITY (for retail pension funds) in accordance with various standards of good practice laid down under the FINANCIAL SERVICES ACT 1986.

pension holiday the suspension of contributions to a PENSION FUND by an employer. This typically occurs when the assets of the fund are judged to be sufficient to cover the future PENSION liabilities.

PEP see PERSONAL EQUITY PLAN.

per capita income *or* **income per head** the GROSS NATIONAL PRODUCT (national income) of a country divided by the size of its POPULATION. This gives the *average* income per head of population if it were all shared out equally. In 2003, the UK had a per capita level of $24,230, Japan $33,990, and the USA $34,870. Most developing countries, by contrast, had a per capita income level of under $1,000. See DISTRIBUTION OF INCOME

perceived benefit see CONSUMER SURPLUS, VALUE CREATED MODEL.

percent defective control chart (P) see CONTROL CHART.

percentage-of-sales method a rule of thumb used for determining a firm's SALES PROMOTION budget. The budgeted amount is calculated as a percentage of the product's past or projected sales revenue. See BUDGETING.

perceptual mapping see PRODUCT POSITIONING.

performance appraisal the process of considering and evaluating the performance of an employee with the objective of improving JOB performance. The information generated during appraisal can be used as a basis for measures to improve JOB SATISFACTION, career planning, MANPOWER PLANNING, TRAINING and as a basis for deciding levels of PAY.

Appraisal usually involves an employee and his immediate superior, although in some organizations employees appraise themselves (self-appraisal) or, much more rarely, are appraised by their immediate colleagues or subordinates. Whoever the appraiser, the focus of appraisal can take a number of forms:

(a) attitudes displayed at work. Experts believe this to be an undesirable form of appraisal since attitudes are not necessarily relevant to job performance whilst appraiser prejudice can bias the outcome;

(b) behaviour in work tasks, for example the proportion of incoming telephone calls answered in a period;

(c) meeting of objectives. These can be decided by the superior but in appraisal of managers it is usual for objectives to be agreed in advance (see MANAGEMENT BY OBJECTIVES).

For the last especially, interviews are the main vehicle for appraisal. Although the information generated can itself be of great use, there is a tendency for appraisal to involve an assessment of individual performance and competence. Often performance is condensed into an overall rating, ranging from 'excellent' to 'very poor'. Apart from the difficulties of producing such a rating – it often involves a judgemental leap from the data provided – this can introduce tension into the process. In so far as individuals feel they are on trial an element of distrust may enter the process and the validity of the information may become questionable.

These dangers become greater when pay is linked to the appraisal process (performance-related pay). Usually, the overall rating achieved will determine whether an employee receives a bonus (MERIT PAY) or is moved up the pay scale. This provides an incentive for individuals to exaggerate their achievement or to establish easily-met objectives, whilst the poor performer denied an increase is as likely to feel resentment as to be motivated to improve his or her performance. See CRITICAL INCIDENT TECHNIQUE, BEHAVIOURALLY-ANCHORED RATING SCALE, BEHAVIOURAL OBSERVATION SCALE.

performance indicator a proxy measure of organizational performance often used where profit or 'bottom-line' indicators are either inadequate or irrelevant guides to performance. Non-profit-making organizations or those with a multiplicity of objectives can find such indicators especially beneficial. Their use has been encouraged in the UK public sector in recent years, though private sector companies can also find them useful to measure and develop their quality of services. In the public sector their primary use has generally been to measure the relationship of inputs to outputs, thereby providing an indication of both efficiency and of the quality of output (effectiveness). Use of these indicators is thought to improve managerial decision-making and resource allocation. However, selection of appropriate indicators can be problematic whilst measurement and recording of output can be difficult. See MANAGEMENT BY OBJECTIVES, BALANCED SCORECARD.

performance-related pay a PAY system where part of an employee's pay is based on his or her performance. It is based on the principle, common to all PAYMENT BY RESULTS, that the opportunity to increase pay will act as an incentive to employees to work harder or more productively. At its simplest, performance-related pay may take the form of an annual cash bonus based on a simple subjective assessment of employee performance over the previous year. Most large organizations take a more systematic approach and attempt to base performance pay on more objective criteria. One approach, often used with clerical staff, is to observe employee behaviour, e.g. the number of telephone calls answered within a specified time period. A more common approach is based on systematic PERFORMANCE APPRAISAL. Typically a set of objectives will be agreed between the employee and the manager: the employee's achievement of these will be reviewed a year later, and an assessment made of his or her performance. Often this is expressed on a scale ranging from 'very good' to 'very unsatisfactory' (or similar) known as a merit rating. The performance pay is attached to the merit rating. The resulting payment may be an annual bonus, a percentage addition to monthly salary, or an extra increment. This payment may be made in addition to an annual cost of living pay increase or in place of it. Those deemed to be performing badly may be denied not just the performance supplement but also a cost of living increase.

The use of performance pay has been increasing in recent years, especially in the public sector (see CITIZENS' CHARTER) and particularly amongst white-collar and managerial employees. In most cases, however, it forms a relatively small portion of total pay. It has been associated with moves towards limiting the involvement of trade unions in pay determination, and is often introduced hand in hand with PERSONAL CONTRACTS. It is often criticized on the ground that good performers do not need financial incentives whilst financial penalties demotivate rather than incentivize poor performers. In any case poor performance may be due to factors other than lack of commitment or ability in individual employees. A further problem with performance pay systems is their tendency to encourage DISCRIMINATION against female employees and those from ethnic minorities.

performers' rights the legal protection given to persons and businesses from the making of unauthorized films, broadcasts, recordings or cable transmission of their performances.

In the UK, the Performers' Protection Acts 1958–72, as updated by the COPYRIGHT, DESIGNS AND PATENTS ACT 1988, give protection to original performances for 50 years. In cases of infringement, performers may seek an injunction through the Courts preventing further abuses, with offenders liable to pay unlimited damages/fines and to prison sentences in extreme cases.

period costs FIXED COSTS that are completely written off in the calculation of profit in the accounting period to which they relate and are not carried forward to subsequent accounting periods by being included in the valuation of unsold stock.

See MARGINAL COSTING, CONTRIBUTION and BREAK-EVEN ANALYSIS.

periodic review system of stock control see FIXED INTERVAL REORDER SYSTEM.

peripheral workforce see LABOUR FLEXIBILITY.

perishability 1 a characteristic of SERVICES, namely that the capacity of a service business, such as a hotel room, is perishable – if it is not occupied, that is lost income which cannot be recovered.
2 goods such as food which deteriorate over time and thus have a relatively short SHELF LIFE.

perk see FRINGE BENEFIT.

perpetual stock system see STOCK CONTROL, BIN CARD.

personal accounts the accounts which are recorded in the sales ledger and purchases ledger of debtors and creditors respectively. A business has to keep a record within its recording system of how much is owing from each individual customer and to each individual supplier. See LEDGER.

personal allowance see INCOME TAX ALLOWANCE.

personal computer (PC) a small COMPUTER used as a desktop data processing facility in business and for personal use. In the office, PCs and desk-top workstations are often linked together in LOCAL AREA NETWORKS enabling them to share data and peripherals such as printers, fax machines, scanners etc. For many tasks the PC has replaced the large mainframe computer (see DOWNSIZING). See INFORMATION MANAGEMENT.

personal contract a CONTRACT OF EMPLOYMENT which is determined solely by the employer and employee, and covers only that one employee. Many of the collective agreements underlying the terms of employment contracts, such as standardized conditions of employment reached by agreement by employer and trade unions, are explicitly excluded. The main purpose of most personal contracts is to take employees' pay out of the ambit of COLLECTIVE BARGAINING and to remove or limit employees' rights to representation by a trade union, thereby weakening trade unions. Instead an employee's pay is determined on a personal basis between employer and employee. For this reason personal contracts are often introduced alongside PERFORMANCE-RELATED PAY. Personal contracts often appear attractive to employees because it is common for substantial cash inducements to be given to encourage employees to sign them and because they appear to be more personalized than previous contracts. In practice most personal contracts are standardized with employees given little opportunity to negotiate over the contract's terms. Furthermore, most give greater discretion to employers than those they are replacing.

personal equity plan (PEP) a scheme introduced by the Government in 1987 to encourage small savers to invest tax-free in UK ORDINARY SHARES. PEPs were replaced in 1999 by INDIVIDUAL SAVINGS ACCOUNTS.

personal goals the individual goals or objectives of people working within a business or organization. In some cases these goals may run counter to and conflict with the goals/objectives of the business or organization. Possible goal conflict makes it important that the business or organization communicates its own goals clearly to all appropriate personnel and encourages them to adopt these goals as their own.

Personal Investment Authority (PIA) see FINANCIAL SERVICES ACT 1986.

personality inventory a profile of an individual's personality traits. Such profiles are usually constructed by asking subjects a series of questions about their behaviour in various situations and about their character. From these responses a profile or inventory of characteristics in key personality areas can be constructed. For example, a profile of an individual's degree of confidence, thoughtfulness, consideration for others etc. can be built up. In theory, there are no right or wrong answers to the questions asked but this is not always the case in practice. Inventories of this sort have been popular of late in RECRUITMENT AND SELECTION, especially of managerial employees. This reflects an emphasis on the importance of leadership qualities and an implicit belief that they are in part innate and not acquired. However, inventories of this sort can be flawed in a number of ways, hence their use as predictors of future performance is questionable:

(a) subjects can often discern the answers desired by the selectors;

(b) the presence of certain personality characteristics implied by certain answers may be dubious; for instance, 'lack of confidence' cannot be straightforwardly derived from a response such as 'I have not felt able to say anything at recent seminars'; it may have reflected an awareness that one's knowledge of the seminar topic was decidedly limited;

(c) the qualities seen as desirable by selectors (for example confidence) may not in fact be beneficial in actual work situations.

Despite these flaws the apparent insight the profile gives into the personality and characteristics of job applicants will ensure its continued popularity. See PSYCHOLOGICAL TEST.

personal pension plan see PENSION.

personal selling a means of increasing the sales of a firm's product which involves direct contact between the firm's SALES REPRESENTATIVES and prospective customers. Unlike passive means of communicating with buyers such as ADVERTISING, face-to-face meetings with customers facilitate a more proactive approach, with sales representatives being able to explain fully the details of a product, advise and answer customer queries about it, and, where appropriate, demonstrate the workings of the product. See PROMOTIONAL MIX.

personnel function see PERSONNEL MANAGEMENT.

personnel information system the collection of information on its employees stored by an organization. At its most basic such information will usually comprise employees' names and addresses, length of service and attendance, and will be maintained by the PERSONNEL MANAGEMENT department. It is common for this information to be kept separate from pay records (which are usually maintained by the finance department). Until the widespread adoption of computerized databases, many organizations found it difficult to analyse this information for MANPOWER PLANNING purposes; it was instead used mainly to deal with problems relating to individual employees. In addition such information was not readily available to other management departments. Nor did it generally include information on, for instance, skills and training which production departments, for instance, would find useful. A sophisticated personnel information system will comprise an extensive database capable of retrieval and analysis by all management functions.

personnel management

The branch of management concerned with administering the employment relationship and with achieving effective use of the human resources available to the organization. The rationale for employing personnel managers is that specialized knowledge of aspects of 'people management' – RECRUITMENT AND SELECTION, TRAINING, PERFORMANCE APPRAISAL, WELFARE, PAYMENT SYSTEMS, LABOUR LAW, INDUSTRIAL RELATIONS – will lead to better managerial and organizational performance. High standards of management in these areas will reduce certain potential costs such as those arising from ABSENTEEISM, LABOUR TURNOVER and INDUSTRIAL DISPUTES. Personnel management typically involves routine administration of employment matters, for example maintenance of personnel records (see PERSONNEL INFORMATION SYSTEM), provision of specialized advice on personnel issues to other managers, creation of procedures (for example DISCIPLINARY PROCEDURES) to guide and control the activities of these managers and, in some cases, conduct of COLLECTIVE BARGAINING with TRADE UNIONS. Often people management is largely undertaken by others, such as LINE MANAGERS; the objective of personnel managers is usually to ensure that these managers act consistently and equitably. The full range of personnel activities, be they undertaken by personnel managers or others, is known as the *personnel function.* In the UK personnel management developed out of the industrial welfare movement earlier in the twentieth century. These origins, coupled with the emphasis in personnel management on fairness (in part for good business reasons), lead some managers to view personnel managers with suspicion. They are sometimes seen as 'soft' on the workers and as not 'proper' managers. In part this may also be due to resentment at the interference of personnel managers in what they view as their area of decision-making. These attitudes are reflected in status insecurity amongst some personnel managers; they feel that they stand midway between workers and management, and are not properly part of either.

One development that has raised the status of personnel management in the UK in recent years is the emergence of *human resource management* (HRM). Some argue that HRM is nothing new; it is simply personnel management with a new title, adopted by personnel managers to advance their interests. Others argue that HRM does possess distinctive characteristics. These include greater sophistication in the use of personnel techniques (for example wider adoption of PSYCHOLOGICAL TESTS in employee selection); a concern with resource maximization (exemplified in an emphasis on training and MANAGEMENT DEVELOPMENT) rather than the traditional one of cost minimization; and a closer integration of personnel management activity with BUSINESS STRATEGY. In addition, many of the more routine aspects of personnel work are passed to line managers, leaving human resources managers with the task of devising strategies to guide and train them in these activities.

An advanced form of HRM, rarely practised, is *human asset accounting.* This approach attempts to assign an accounting value to the organization's human resources, and to determine whether these assets appreciate or depreciate in the same way as do capital resources. In this way HRM can be brought into the calculation of the 'bottom line'. The rationale of this approach is that the value of an organization's human resources has an important bearing on its long-term health. By generating data of this sort it provides managers with a higher quality of information upon which to base human resource decisions, and encourages them to adopt a more long-term perspective in the utilization of their workforces. See INSTITUTE OF PERSONNEL MANAGEMENT, MANPOWER PLANNING.

person-oriented culture see CULTURE.

person specification see RECRUITMENT AND SELECTION.

persuasive advertising see ADVERTISING.

PERT (programme evaluation and review technique) see NETWORK ANALYSIS.

PEST a framework used by business strategists to identify those factors operating in the 'outer' (macro) environment of a firm which impinge upon its activities and profitability, in addition to factors affecting its immediate product MARKETS. PEST has four elements: *political* (e.g. the UK government's policy on joining the EURO-zone); *economic* (e.g. recession/boom conditions. See BUSINESS CYCLE); *social* (e.g. DEMOGRAPHIC CHANGES) and *technological* (e.g. the impact of the INTERNET). See BUSINESS STRATEGY.

Peter Principle the principle, formulated by the American management writer Laurence Peter (1919–90), that in organizations people are promoted to the level of their incompetence. Individuals rise through ORGANIZATION hierarchies because job vacancies continually arise and need to be filled. The criteria for promotion is successful performance in current and previous posts. But at some point individuals are promoted to posts which are beyond the range of their abilities. From then on their job performance is characterized by incompetence, and promotion will cease. Individuals thus come to stay in jobs which they cannot adequately perform. Hence the principle that 'every employee tends to move to their level of incompetence'.

Every organization will contain a number of people in this situation. Indeed, in time 'every post tends to be occupied by an employee who is incompetent'. Thus organizational performance will virtually always be at suboptimum levels. The Peter Principle is generally viewed as a perceptive and humorous insight into organizational processes rather than as a proposition worthy of empirical investigation.

petty cash small sums of money held by a person or business to pay for small items of expenditure.

physical distribution see DISTRIBUTION.

picket a person involved in a STRIKE who seeks to prevent other persons from gaining access to a place of work during an INDUSTRIAL DISPUTE. In the UK, picketing one's own place of work is lawful; picketing other people's places of work (*secondary picketing*) is unlawful. See SECONDARY ACTION.

pick list an order list which has to be picked from various storage points in a WAREHOUSE so as to complete an order. The order may be for an external customer or may be composed of parts for assembly within a production unit. See ORDER PROCESSING, MATERIALS MANAGEMENT.

piecework a system of PAY in which an individual's WAGE is related to his or her output. In some cases payments are based entirely on the volume of output (for example fruit picking), in others employees receive a 'floor' wage supplemented by additional payments proportional to the value of the time saved where output is achieved in less than the time allotted. The latter relies on the calculation of standard times to perform given tasks and hence usually makes extensive use of WORK MEASUREMENT. In the past, piecework has often given rise to INDUSTRIAL RELATIONS difficulties, especially when workers are unable to achieve normal expected bonuses because of factors outside their control, for example non-availability of stock.

piggy backing a DISTRIBUTION term used to describe the movement of containers directly from shipboard to rail freight and from rail freight to heavy goods vehicle without unloading the containers' contents. See FREIGHT.

pioneering customer see DIFFUSION PROCESS, PRODUCT LIFE CYCLE.

PIMS (Profit Impact of Market Strategy) a database covering over 3000 businesses in Europe and North America which contains information on firms' sales, market shares, investment etc. and market characteristics (growth rates, concentration, customer power, etc.) and which seeks to establish associations between these variables and firms' profit performance. See BUSINESS STRATEGY, COMPETITIVE STRATEGY.

place an aspect of DISTRIBUTION concerned with ensuring that a firm's products are available for consumers to purchase at appropriate locations.

See DISTRIBUTION CHANNEL, MARKETING LOGISTICS, FOUR P'S OF MARKETING.

placing a means of raising new SHARE CAPITAL by issuing company shares to a selected group of investors rather than to the investing public at large. See SHARE ISSUE.

planned obsolescence see OBSOLESCENCE.

planning see BUSINESS STRATEGY, ECONOMIC PLANNING.

plant large items of capital such as a PRODUCTION LINE or furnace used in production. See MACHINERY, EQUIPMENT, CAPITAL STOCK, FIXED ASSET.

plant-and-machinery per employee an accounting measure of a firm's degree of mechanization, which expresses the firm's plant and machinery as a ratio of its number of employees. See CAPITAL LABOUR RATIO, PRODUCTIVITY.

plant bargaining see COLLECTIVE BARGAINING.

plant hire see LEASING.

plant layout see FACTORY LAYOUT.

plant register a record of information about each item of plant, machinery and equipment employed by a firm. Typically a plant register will include details of: description of the particular item and its expected life; its cost and DEPRECIATION details; its location; its MAINTENANCE requirements; any special operating considerations, such as safety features and breakdown implications; details of GUARANTEES and service contracts.

Plc (public limited company) see JOINT-STOCK COMPANY.

ploughed-back profit see RETAINED PROFIT OR UNDISTRIBUTED PROFIT.

pluralism a diffusion of power and interests in a society or ORGANIZATION, such that there is a plurality of interest groups. Those who subscribe to pluralism argue that there will inevitably be differences between individuals or groups in any complex social institution over, for instance, the distribution of rewards.

Pluralists claim that it is better to accept these differences than to suppress them, because once they are brought into the open it is possible to find mechanisms for resolving potential conflict to the benefit of all. In INDUSTRIAL RELATIONS the pluralist frame of reference is held by those who believe that the interests of management and workers will inevitably differ on occasions, for example over the size of an annual pay increase. They argue that it is better to accept that TRADE UNIONS are the legitimate expressions of *employee* interests rather than to refuse recognition on the grounds that employer-employee interests are identical. If the latter policy is adopted CONFLICT may break out without warning and with no acceptable means of resolving it. If, on the other hand, unions are recognized then management and unions can work together to devise procedures (for example GRIEVANCE PROCEDURES) that will prevent differences of interest from developing into open conflict and provide a means of resolving conflict if it should occur. See MANAGEMENT STYLE.

pluralist frame of reference see MANAGEMENT STYLE.

point of sale see RETAIL OUTLET.

point of sale display promotional material, such as banners and posters or demonstrations of a product inside a SHOP or store, which is used as a means of stimulating SALES. Such in-store displays and demonstrations are often used alongside an ADVERTISING campaign, and serve to reinforce and capitalize upon that advertising by attracting customers' attention whilst in the store. See SALES PROMOTION. MERCHANDISING.

poison pill see TAKEOVER BID.

poke yoke a Japanese term meaning 'to make fail-safe'. Any mechanism or process that prevents mistakes being made can be called a poke yoke. They are techniques and thinking designed to prevent errors in manufacture and service provision. The 3 pin plug is a simple poke yoke, it can only be inserted into the socket in one way, hence – fail-safe. Poke yokes have two broad functions, regulatory and setting. Regulatory devices are those that either control a process or give a warning about it. Control devices are used to shut a process down whenever it detects an abnormality. See PRODUCTION CONTROL.

political fund a fund maintained by a TRADE UNION or other body for the purpose of supporting a political party. In the UK such funds must be clearly distinct from other union budgets and union members have the right to be exempt from making payments into it. The TRADE UNION ACT 1984 requires that unions maintaining a political fund must ballot their members on its continuation at least every ten years.

poll tax a tax that is levied at a fixed rate per head of population. See LOCAL TAX.

polluter pays principle see POLLUTION.

pollution the contamination of the environment by the discharge of industrial substances, smoke emissions and the dumping of waste materials and products. In the past, little attention was paid to the social costs of polluting the atmosphere, rivers, the countryside etc., but increasingly governments have passed more onerous regulations covering the use and disposal of industrial materials and production methods. As a consequence industry itself is being forced to invest in appropriate pollution control and limitation systems, and take a more proactive approach to the production and marketing of products which are environment-friendly.

In the UK responsibility for matters relating to the environment resides with the Department for Environment, Food and Rural Affairs (DEFRA). The basic approach of government policy on the environment is that pollution should be prevented at source and that the polluter should pay for the necessary controls (the *polluter pays principle*). The main measure for achieving this is the Environmental Protection Act 1990. Under the Act the Inspectorate of Pollution is charged with the task of getting businesses to use the best available technology and techniques to prevent or minimize pollution in industrial processes.

Firms which do not comply with the new controls face fines of up to £20,000 in the magistrates' court, and unlimited fines in the Crown Court. Clean-up costs incurred by the enforcing authorities can also be recovered from the polluter. Many countries now have adopted 'practical' measures aimed at controlling pollution including the imposition of *environmental standards* and *emission permits* (limits set on permissible smoke emission, noise etc levels) and *environmental taxes* (on production processes and products which cause pollution). Member countries of the European Union (EU) are required to observe various environmental 'directives'. For example, all new cars produced in the EU are required to be fitted with a catalytic converter to reduce sulphur emissions (typically, adding around £400 to the price of a car); and in 2000, in a landmark case, Greece was fined heavily by the European Court for failing to halt the discharge of toxic waste into the River Kouroupitos in Crete.

Finally, governments have encouraged businesses and householders (through the provision of free 'wheeliebins' collected by the local authority) to RECYCLE waste products such as cans, glass bottles and paper.

International recognition and concern at the harmful impact on the ozone layer of toxic industrial emissions (so-called 'greenhouse gases' such as CFC and carbon dioxide gases) began to build up in the 1970s and 1980s leading to the Montreal Protocol in 1987. This set a target for the developed countries to ban CFC gases by 2020. In fact, this was achieved by 1995. Further attempts have proved to be more intractable. The 1997 Kyoto Protocol and the 2000 Bonn Accord committed countries to make substantial cuts in other greenhouse gases (particularly, carbon dioxide emissions for coal, gas and oil fuels). Although some 180 countries have signed the Bonn Accord, the biggest polluter nation, the USA, has not. See GREEN CONSUMER, EXTERNALITIES.

polyvalence the acquisition and application of a range of SKILLS. A polyvalent worker is one with a variety of job competencies and hence is able to perform a range of tasks which transcend traditional job boundaries. See LABOUR FLEXIBILITY.

population 1 the total number of people resident in a country at a particular point in time. The UK, for example, had a population of 59 million people in 2004. The size of the population is determined by past and present birth and death rates, together with net migration trends – the number of people leaving the country to live abroad (emigration) compared with the number entering the country to take up residence (immigration). The UK birth rate is currently 11 births per 1000 of the population per annum and the death rate 10 per 1000 of the population per annum. In most advanced countries, both birth and death rates have declined over the long run because of rising living standards and improved medical care; this has produced slow-growing, ageing populations.

The total size of the population and its composition in terms of proportion of males to females and age-group distributions, combined with various SOCIOECONOMIC factors influencing buying characteristics, are important to businesses in assessing the market potential for their products.

2 all possible observations of a certain phenomenon in statistical analysis, for example incomes of all people resident in a country. Where it is too time-consuming and expensive to record all possible observations it is necessary to take a SAMPLE, for example the incomes of 1000 citizens, and generalize about the incomes of all citizens from this sample. See STATISTICAL INFERENCE.

porcupine see TAKEOVER BID.

portable computer see COMPUTER.

portfolio 1 a collection of FINANCIAL SECURITIES held by an investor. Typically an investor would want to hold a number of different financial securities to spread his risk, and would seek a mixture of them, some offering high short-term DIVIDEND payments with others offering long-term capital appreciation as their market prices rise. Investors can assemble their own portfolio of shares, or they can opt to buy into funds offered by UNIT TRUSTS, INVESTMENT TRUSTS and other INSTITUTIONAL INVESTORS. The latter medium enables investors to invest in a much wider range of shares than their own limited resources would otherwise permit since unit trusts etc 'pool' the savings of many thousands of investors. Unit trusts etc. typically offer a number of different types of funds to appeal to different groups of investors, for example, 'growth funds' which aim to achieve *capital growth*, and 'income funds' which aim to secure high *income* returns to investors. Some funds are *passively* managed by fund operators who buy shares in companies comprising a selected share index, for example, the 'Financial Times Stock Exchange (FTSE) – 100 Share Index (see TRACKER FUND), while other funds are *actively* managed by fund managers who buy and sell shares regularly in a wider range of companies in order to maximize growth or income returns. See PORTFOLIO THEORY, INVESTMENT, INDIVIDUAL SAVINGS ACCOUNT.

2 a collection of products marketed by a firm. See PRODUCT RANGE, PRODUCT-MARKET MATRIX, BOSTON MATRIX.

portfolio theory the study of the way in which an individual investor may achieve the maximum expected return from a varied PORTFOLIO of FINANCIAL SECURITIES which has attached to it a given level of risk. Alternatively the portfolio may achieve for the investor a minimum amount of risk for a given level of expected return. Return on a security consists of INTEREST or DIVIDEND, plus or minus any CAPITAL GAIN or loss from holding the security over a given time period. The *expected* return on the collection of securities within the portfolio is the weighted average of the expected returns on the individual INVESTMENTS that comprise the portfolio. However, the important thing is that the risk attaching to a portfolio (its variability) is smaller than the variability of each individual investment. See CAPITAL ASSET PRICING MODEL, EFFICIENT MARKET HYPOTHESIS, UNCERTAINTY.

position audit see BUSINESS POLICY.

positioning see PRODUCT POSITIONING.

post an accounting term, meaning to enter the details of a transaction in a firm's LEDGER accounts from the details provided in the firm's JOURNAL.

post-acquisition profits the profits made by a company after the date of its acquisition or TAKEOVER by the HOLDING COMPANY. Such post-acquisition profits belong to the new shareholders of the company. See PRE-ACQUISITION PROFITS,

post-balance sheet events events occurring after the date of the annual BALANCE SHEET, that is, in the next ACCOUNTING PERIOD. Where events such as the outcome of a major legal trial or an important technological or market change have a significant effect upon the value of company ASSETS the BOARD OF DIRECTORS are required to spell out the financial implications of such events to shareholders in the Directors' Report in the ANNUAL REPORT AND ACCOUNTS.

post-entry closed shop see CLOSED SHOP.

post-purchase behaviour the stage in buyer decision-making where buyers take further action after making the purchase. Specifically sellers are interested as part of their MARKETING RESEARCH in whether buyers are satisfied or dissatisfied with their purchase since this will have a critical effect on BRAND LOYALTY and the likelihood of repeat purchases. Firms use buyer studies to elicit information about post-purchase behaviour. See BUYER BEHAVIOUR, PRE-PURCHASE BEHAVIOUR.

post-testing see ADVERTISING EFFECTIVENESS TEST.

pound (£) the standard monetary unit of the UK. See CURRENCY. STERLING.

power culture see CULTURE.

PR see PUBLIC RELATIONS.

pre-acquisition profits the profits made by a company up to the date of its acquisition or TAKEOVER by the HOLDING COMPANY. Such pre-acquisition profits belong to the original shareholders of that company and where the holding company acquires less than 100% of the subsidiary company's shares then a proportion of the pre-acquisition profits belong to the MINORITY INTERESTS. See POST-ACQUISITION PROFITS.

precedence diagram a chart which depicts the sequence of operations involved in an assembly operation by specifying which operations need to be completed prior to subsequent operations commencing. Precedence diagrams are a means of planning and controlling PRODUCTION operations.

predatory pricing a PRICING strategy which is aimed at the removal of troublesome competitors. It can take a number of specific forms including selective price cutting on particular brands or selective price cuts in particular sales territories, and the application of a PRICE SQUEEZE by a vertically-integrated supplier on non-integrated rivals. See PRICE WAR, LOSS LEADER, DUMPING, COMPETITION POLICY.

pre-determined costing COSTING systems such as BUDGETARY CONTROL and STANDARD COSTING, where costs and revenues are estimated in advance of the start of the accounting period in which they are to be incurred. Contrast HISTORICAL COSTING.

predetermined motion time system see WORK MEASUREMENT.

pre-entry closed shop see CLOSED SHOP.

preference share *or* **preferred stock** a FINANCIAL SECURITY issued to those individuals and institutions who provide long-term finance for JOINT-STOCK COMPANIES. Preference shares pay a fixed rate of DIVIDEND and are generally given priority over ORDINARY SHARES in receiving dividend. In the event of the company being wound up they also have first claim on any remaining ASSETS of the business after all debts have been discharged. Cumulative preference shares are entitled to be paid any arrears of their dividend before ordinary shares receive any dividends.

Certain preference shares, called Participating Preference Shares, entitle holders not only to a fixed dividend rate but also to anadditional distribution of profit in good trading years. Generally, preference SHAREHOLDERS have no voting fights at company ANNUAL GENERAL MEETINGS, though under the terms of a firm's ARTICLES OF ASSOCIATION they may be granted voting rights where their dividends are in arrears. See SHARE CAPITAL.

preferential creditor see INSOLVENCY.

preferred stock see PREFERENCE SHARE.

preliminary expenses the initial costs incurred in forming a JOINT-STOCK COMPANY, such as preparing a PROSPECTUS and issuing SHARES, prior to the company commencing trading.

premium 1 an addition to the published LIST PRICE of a product charged by a supplier to a customer. The premium could be charged for guaranteeing rapid delivery of the product, or could reflect the temporary scarcity of the product. A 'premium price' over similar products might be charged by a supplier who is able to convince buyers that his product is superior in some respect to competitors' offerings.

2 the purchase of a BOND for more than its nominal value. The price which people are prepared to pay for a bond can be more than its nominal value if the nominal rate of interest on that bond exceeds current market interest rates.

3 the sale of new STOCKS and SHARES at an enhanced price. In the UK this involves the issue of a new share at a price above its nominal value. Where shares have no nominal value it involves the sale of new shares above their current market price.

4 the rating of a particular company's shares at a price above the average market price of the shares of other companies operating in the same sector, the 'premium' reflecting investors' general optimism that this company is likely to perform much better than the others.

5 the amount by which a foreign currency's spot exchange rate stands above its 'official' par value under a FIXED EXCHANGE RATE system which allows some degree of short-term fluctuation either side of the par value.

6 the annual payment made to an INSURANCE COMPANY by persons or firms taking out an insurance policy.

premium bond a FINANCIAL SECURITY issued by the UK government as a means of raising money for the government and encouraging private SAVING. Premium bonds are issued in small denominations, but do not pay interest, nor can a capital gain be obtained on redemption, since they are issued and redeemed at their face value. Their appeal lies in the prospect of a 'gambler's chance' of winning a substantial lump sum of money in a monthly prize lottery (numbers being drawn electronically by 'ERNIE').

prepayment *or* **payment in advance** an expense which is paid in one trading period but which is properly chargeable against the revenues or profits of future trading periods. For example, if a company preparing accounts for the year to 31 December pays its annual rent on 1 April, then only three quarters of that rent relates to the current trading period, the remaining quarter being a prepayment for use of the building from 1 January to 31 March in the next trading period. Prepayments are counted as part of the company's assets at the end of the trading period and are usually included as part of DEBTORS in the firm's BALANCE SHEET. See ACCRUAL.

pre-purchase behaviour the stage in buyer decision-making where potential buyers get information about a product through advertisements, sales brochures and personal contacts. The degree of search behaviour undertaken by prospective buyers will vary according to the cost and technical complexity of the product and buyers' previous experience of the product. Purchasing decisions may be carefully pre-planned or may be a spontaneous impulse buy. As part of their MARKETING RESEARCH firms use MOTIVATIONAL RESEARCH to identify buyer needs in order to influence pre-purchase behaviour through ADVERTISING and SALES PROMOTION. See BUYER BEHAVIOUR, POST-PURCHASE BEHAVIOUR.

prescriptive (approach to strategy) see BUSINESS POLICY.

presenteeism a culture which encourages employees to spend excessive hours at work as a way of displaying ORGANIZATIONAL COMMITMENT. See WORK-LIFE BALANCE, ABSENTEEISM.

present value see DISCOUNTED CASH FLOW.

present value tables tables which are used in INVESTMENT APPRAISAL undertaken by means of DISCOUNTED CASH FLOW. The tables show how much we need to invest now, at a certain rate of interest and for a particular period of time, to produce £1. For example, the tables show that if we want to produce £1 in 5 years' time at 10%, we will need to invest £0.621 now. Alternatively, the tables show that £1 receivable in 5 years' time, taking into account a rate of interest 10%, will be worth only 62p (that is, £0.621).

president a North American term for the chief executive or MANAGING DIRECTOR of a corporation or JOINT-STOCK COMPANY.

pretest 1 a trial launch of a product to a sample group of consumers to test the product's operational efficiency and consumer acceptability. See NEW-PRODUCT DEVELOPMENT.

2 see ADVERTISING EFFECTIVENESS TEST.

3 see QUALITY CONTROL.

prevention costs see QUALITY COSTS.

preventive maintenance a planned MAINTENANCE programme aimed at minimizing or eliminating breakdowns to buildings, plant, machinery and equipment with their consequent disruption to production, or inconsistent machine operation which might affect product quality. A preventive maintenance programme would involve keeping an up-to-date PLANT REGISTER which notes the maintenance requirements of each machine; scheduling the frequency of inspections, lubrication and overhauls for each machine; GROUP REPLACEMENT of parts, where appropriate, or replacement of parts as they fail (see CONDITION-BASED MAINTENANCE); making modifications and improvements which increase reliability and at the same time bring the plant, machinery or equipment up to date.

price the money value of a unit of a GOOD, SERVICE, FINANCIAL SECURITY or ASSET which a buyer is required to pay a seller to purchase the item. Usually the price of a product is fixed by the seller in advance on the basis of the costs of producing and selling the product and the seller's desired profit margin. In other cases, however, prices are variable, being determined by prevailing demand and supply conditions as with the sale, for example, of a STOCK or SHARE, a house or items sold at an auction.

Because a purchase involves a money outlay on the part of buyers who operate within a budget constraint, the price of a product is an important factor in the buying decision. It may well be the paramount consideration in many cases, but for some purchases other elements in the MARKETING MIX (product quality and performance etc.) may be equally if not more important. Thus, although many products (especially COMMODITY-TYPE PRODUCTS) tend to be sold at low, competitive prices, many others can be sold at higher prices, providing customers with a variety of price-quality trade-offs and other product attributes. See MARKET STRUCTURE, MONOPOLY, BUYER'S MARKET, SELLER'S MARKET, PRICING, PRICING OBJECTIVES, PRICING METHODS, FOUR P'S OF MARKETING.

price competition see COMPETITION.

price discrimination the ability of a supplier to sell the *same* good or service in a number of *separate* MARKETS at *different* PRICES. Markets can be separated in various ways such as by different consumer requirements (for example bulk and low volume gas supplies to industrial and household consumers, respectively); by the nature of the product itself (for example original and replacement components for washing machines) and by geographical locations (for example domestic and foreign markets). In order for price discrimination to be viable, markets must differ in their demand profiles (that is, exhibit different demand elasticities, so that higher prices can be charged where demand is inelastic and lower prices charged when demand is elastic), and the supplier must be able to 'seal off' each market so that customers in lower-priced markets cannot resell to those in higher-priced markets.

Price discrimination can help a supplier to increase his sales and profits, improve market share and contribute to the full capacity utilization of manufacturing plant.

However, price discrimination may be exercised by a DOMINANT FIRM in a predatory manner aimed at removing troublesome competition or as a means of exploiting buyers. See OFFICE OF FAIR TRADING, ELASTICITY OF DEMAND, PRICE-SQUEEZE, DEMAND-BASED PRICING.

price-earnings ratio a ratio used to appraise a quoted public company's profit performance, which expresses the market PRICE of the company's SHARES as a multiple of its PROFIT. For example, if a company's profit amounted to £1 per share and the price of its shares was £10 each on the STOCK MARKET; then its price-earnings ratio would be 10:1. Where a company's prospects are considered by the stock market to be good, then it is likely that the company's share price will rise, producing a higher price-earnings ratio. Price-earnings ratio is the mirror image of EARNINGS YIELD. See EARNINGS PER SHARE.

price elasticity of demand see ELASTICITY OF DEMAND.

price index 1 a weighted average of the prices of a general 'basket' of goods and services produced in an economy over time, which is used in particular to indicate the rate of INFLATION. The RETAIL PRICE INDEX (RPI) is one commonly-used index, measuring the average level of the prices of final goods and services purchased by consumers. Each product in the index is weighted according to its relative importance in total consumer expenditure. A suitable base year is selected to commence the series (for example, index value 1990 = 100) and subsequent price changes are then reflected in changes in the index value over time (for example, 1999 = 200, indicating an annual rate of inflation of 10%). See INDEX-LINKED, PURCHASING POWER.

2 a weighted average of the prices of particular classes of financial securities or commodities, for example the Financial Times 100 share index or all-share index. See SHARE PRICE INDEX.

price leadership a situation where a particular supplier is generally accepted by other suppliers as the 'lead' firm in changing market PRICES. Price leadership systems are often seen by suppliers as a useful way of coordinating their price policies so as to limit price competition and avoid ruinous price wars (see OLIGOPOLY). They may, however, act as a cloak for COLLUSION, and as such operate in a way detrimental to the interests of consumers. See MARKET CONDUCT, COMPETITION POLICY.

Price Marking (Bargain Offers) Order 1979 a UK directive (made under the PRICES ACT 1974) which prohibits traders from making vague or misleading PRICE claims such as 'worth £10 our price £5' and 'reductions of up to 50%', and comparisons with prices of other unspecified traders. Genuine bargain-offer price claims must be related to the seller's previous prices (specifically a price the trader has charged for at least 28 consecutive days during the previous six months) or to the manufacturer's RECOMMENDED RETAIL PRICE. See TRADE DESCRIPTIONS ACT 1968, CONSUMER PROTECTION, DEPARTMENT OF TRADE AND INDUSTRY.

price promotion a form of SALES PROMOTION employed by manufacturers and retailers which involves 'introductory-price' offers, 'money-off' packs, 'two-for-the-price-of-one' packs and 'special-price' offers. In addition to increasing the sales potential of the products whose prices have been temporarily cut, price promotions also serve to attract customers into shops. See SALE, LOSS LEADING.

price–quality trade-offs a firm's MARKETING policy on what QUALITY of product or BRAND to sell and the PRICE at which it is sold. Such decisions can be made only in the context of the quality of rivals' brands and the prices they are charging. In this context, quality refers to both durability and performance and to technical sophistication.

A firm may choose to offer a high-quality brand and sell it at a high price to appeal to a particular quality-conscious MARKET SEGMENT; or to produce a lower-quality brand to sell at a lower price to a more price-conscious segment. In terms of PRODUCT

POSITIONING a firm, for example, may choose to upgrade slightly the quality of its brand and offer it at an unchanged price to make it more competitive; alternatively, the firm may modify a low-quality, low-price brand by significantly upgrading its quality and offering it at the same price to appeal to a new medium-quality price-conscious segment. Businesses often offer several different qualities or specifications of a product as a product line in order to appeal simultaneously to several market segments. See PRODUCT RANGE, PSYCHOLOGICAL PRICING.

Prices Act 1974 a UK Act which empowers the Secretary of State for Trade and Industry to issue 'orders', as appropriate, to protect consumers from vague, inaccurate and confusing PRICE claims made by traders. See PRICE MARKING (BARGAIN OFFERS) ORDER 1979, DEPARTMENT OF TRADE AND INDUSTRY, CONSUMER PROTECTION.

prices and incomes policy the application of controls on PRICES and INCOMES (particularly wages) in order to stop or slow down INFLATION in an economy. See ECONOMIC POLICY.

price squeeze the charging of discriminatory prices by a vertically integrated firm (see VERTICAL INTEGRATION) for the supply of inputs to non-integrated rivals, as a means of putting them at a competitive disadvantage. This occurs when the integrated firm produces both the input and the finished product, while the unintegrated firms produce only the finished product but have to rely on the integrated firm for their input supply. A 'squeeze' is applied if the integrated firm charges the non-integrated firms a *high* price for the input but sells its own finished product at a *low* price, thus allowing non-integrated firms only minimal profits or forcing losses on them. In market situations where there is a substantial number of alternative, independent supply sources, rival producers are unlikely to be harmed. However, the control by a DOMINANT FIRM of the input, combined with limitations on the establishment of new sources of supply, could have serious anti-competitive consequences. Under UK COMPETITION POLICY cases of vertical integration may be referred to the COMPETITION COMMISSION for investigation. See PRICE DISCRIMINATION, TRANSFER PRICE.

price system see MARKET SYSTEM.

price war a situation of aggressive price cutting by a group of rival suppliers as a means of gaining sales at each other's expense. Since price wars, however, tend to be mutually ruinous by destroying the profitability of the market, they are normally avoided, with suppliers preferring to compete instead through various PRODUCT DIFFERENTIATION strategies. See OLIGOPOLY, CARTEL, COLLUSION, PRICE LEADERSHIP.

pricing the decision-making process involved in setting a PRICE for a good or service. For most products, pricing decisions cannot be made in isolation but must consider all aspects of the MARKETING MIX, prices of the firm's related products, competitors' prices, product COSTS, DEMAND and the firm's PRICING OBJECTIVES. See PRICING POLICY, PRICING METHODS, PRICE-QUALITY TRADE-OFF, BY-PRODUCT PRICING, PRODUCT LINE PRICING, CAPTIVE PRODUCT PRICING, OPTIONAL EXTRAS PRICING, GEOGRAPHICAL PRICING, PSYCHOLOGICAL PRICING, BUNDLED PRICES, EVERYDAY LOW PRICES, PRODUCT POSITIONING, CONSUMER SURPLUS, VALUE CREATED MODEL.

pricing methods the approaches used by firms to PRICE goods or services. Three basic pricing methods may be distinguished:

(a) a COST-BASED PRICING method which relates the price of a product to the costs involved in producing and distributing it;

(b) a DEMAND-BASED PRICING method which relates the price of a product to the intensity of total demand for it and acknowledges differences in demand intensities between subgroups of buyers;

(c) a COMPETITION-BASED PRICING method which relates the price of a product to the prices charged by rivals. In practice, firms use a combination of these methods in setting their prices. Other pricing methods include: conversion cost pricing, target pricing, variable-cost pricing, marginal-cost pricing and return on investment pricing. See PRICING OBJECTIVES, PRICING POLICY.

pricing objectives the general and specific aims which a firm sets for itself in establishing the PRICE of its products. Pricing objectives are closely tied in with a firm's MARKETING OBJECTIVES which in turn are closely related to the achievement of the firm's overall BUSINESS OBJECTIVES.

Unit price x quantity sold is a key determinant of the firm's revenues which together with its underlying cost structures will determine the amount of PROFIT earned by the firm. Pricing objectives may be expressed generally in terms of achieving higher profit returns or related, for example, to some specified targeted RATE OF RETURN ON CAPITAL EMPLOYED. More specifically, in the case of particular products the pricing objective may be to increase MARKET SHARE in existing markets, or to enter a new market. In addition, a firm may seek to achieve price stability so as to avoid excessive fluctuations in its PROFIT MARGINS and the administrative costs associated with changing prices (for example, reprinting price lists). See PRICING, PRICING METHODS, PRICING POLICY, MARKET PENETRATION PRICING.

pricing policy the overall policy pursued by a multiproduct firm in PRICING its products. At the specific level pricing policy will include PRODUCT LINE PRICING, establishing price differentials between the brands making up a line, for example prices of the basic and de luxe versions of the Ford Mondeo car. At a general level, pricing policy would also embrace price relativities *between* product lines, for example prices of the Ford Mondeo, Focus and Ka cars.

Other areas involving a multidimensional pricing approach include BY-PRODUCT PRICING, CAPTIVE PRODUCT PRICING, OPTIONAL EXTRAS PRICING, PRICE-QUALITY TRADE-OFF, SELECTIVE PRICE CUTTING, BUNDLED PRICES.

Priestman plan a GROUP INCENTIVE SCHEME in which employees are paid a guaranteed basic wage plus a percentage based on the percentage by which output exceeded the target output. The principal problem for a business which wants to use this system is the setting of the target output figure: setting it too low will lead to large bonus payments, setting it too high will reduce the incentive for workers.

prime cost see DIRECT COST, COST.

principal 1 a sum of money or capital which can earn INTEREST.

2 the owner of a firm or other assets who assigns the management of the firm or assets to an AGENT who acts on behalf of the principal. See PRINCIPAL-AGENT THEORY, AGENCY COST.

principal-agent theory the relationship between the owner (principal) of an asset (for example, a company) and the persons (agents) CONTRACTED to manage that asset on the owner's behalf (for example, the appointed executive directors of the company).

Where contracts are *complete*, there is little scope for deviations from the objectives and requirements of the principal and the expected obligations and duties of an agent. However, most contracts are *incomplete* to a greater or lesser degree so that problems can arise (so-called 'agency costs'). For example, agents may pursue a 'hidden agenda', substituting their own objectives for those of the principal (see below), or ASYMMETRICAL INFORMATION favouring agents who (as 'insiders') are involved in day-to-day management may make it difficult for principals (as 'outsiders') to monitor the behaviour of executive directors. Further down the organization, problems of MORAL HAZARD may arise as employees indulgein 'shirking', working at less than optimal efficiency.

The principal-agent relationship is at the heart of the analysis of ownership and control issues in the modern JOINT-STOCK COMPANY, where it has been observed that although the SHAREHOLDERS of the company are its owners, effective control of the company is in the hands of the board of directors. Shareholders are usually too fragmented and too remote from the 'seat of power' to exercise strong control and are generally prepared to leave it to the executive directors to determine the affairs of the company. This can lead to conflicts of interests whereby directors may pursue courses of action which may be detrimental to shareholders (e.g. use current profits to diversify into risky new business ventures rather than pay higher dividends). See BUSINESS OBJECTIVES.

To get round these problems, principals may utilize various incentive payment schemes to align agents' interests more closely with their own and encourage dedicated attention to optimum performance. These include: EXECUTIVE SHARE OPTION SCHEMES, LONG-TERM INCENTIVE PLANS, EMPLOYEE SHARE OWNERSHIP PLANS and payment by PIECEWORK and COMMISSION.

printer a COMPUTER output device for producing hard copy of text or diagrammatic material on paper.

prior charges INTEREST payments on DEBENTURES and LOAN STOCK which must be paid by a company before any dividend payments can be made to shareholders. See ORDINARY SHARE, PREFERENCE SHARE.

priority-based budgeting a management accounting technique that seeks to improve profitability by requiring managers to reassess their activities and determine priorities. Priority-based BUDGETING aims to reduce costs and channel company resources into high-priority areas of the business.

prior year adjustments adjustments applicable to prior years arising from changes in ACCOUNTING PRINCIPLES, for example the use of a different DEPRECIATION rule for fixed assets. Prior year adjustments are made to ensure that previous years' accounting results (recalculated on the basis of the new accounting policy) are *consistent* with those of the current year (measured on the same new basis).

private enterprise economy see ECONOMY.

private label brand see OWN-LABEL BRAND.

private ledger a ledger that is used to keep the accounts relating to the directors and possibly other highly confidential accounts. Generally access to the private ledger is restricted to certain authorized personnel.

private limited company (Ltd) see JOINT-STOCK COMPANY.

privatization see NATIONALIZATION VERSUS PRIVATIZATION.

problem child see BOSTON MATRIX.

procedural agreement 1 any agreement between two parties which establishes procedures for future discussion and negotiations over issues of mutual interest. 2 (in INDUSTRIAL RELATIONS) an agreement between employers and trade union officials or representatives governing the conduct of negotiations and joint consultation over pay, conditions of employment etc. See COLLECTIVE BARGAINING.

process a flow of activities; a sequence of tasks.

process chart see ACTIVITY CHART.

process control see PRODUCTION CONTROL.

process costing a system for determining the cost of products made in a PROCESS PRODUCTION plant like an oil refinery. The continuous nature of such a process and the uniformity of the products emerging from it make it difficult to identify specific units of output. The cost of any particular unit must, therefore, be taken as the average cost of manufacture over a period. Process costing is further complicated by the tendency to experience process wastage from chemical reaction or evaporation and the production of waste products which have to be allowed for in costing products emerging from the process. Furthermore, in making the main product, BY-PRODUCTS may arise from the production process, making it difficult to determine the respective cost of main and by-products since they result from common expenditures on raw materials and processing of these materials. See BY-PRODUCT PRICING.

process-focused layout a FACTORY LAYOUT in which all PRODUCTION operations of a similar nature are grouped together in the same department or part of the factory. For example, separate areas may exist for drilling operations, milling, grinding, assembly and

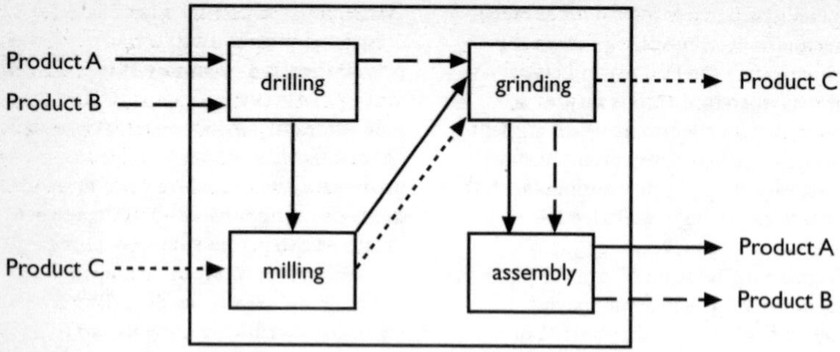

Fig. 64 **Process-focused layout.** A simple example.

so on (see Fig. 64). Process layout is appropriate where small quantities of a large range of products are to be manufactured, as for example in BATCH PRODUCTION or jobbing production. The nature of the layout permits flexibility in production, i.e. complex products, requiring processing in most of the functional departments, may be made alongside simple products requiring processing in only a few departments. This same flexibility, however, brings disadvantages, since batch production in process layouts necessitates frequent machine resetting; it normally operates with a comparatively high level of work in progress; and through-put time is high. Specialist supervision is possible, and the grouping of operatives of a similar type and skill within the same department promotes cohesiveness and enables individual incentive payment schemes to be used. The provision of services (for example water, power, removal of scrap) is simpler than in other forms of layout, but the cost of materials handling is high. See PRODUCT-FOCUSED LAYOUT, SET-UP COST, SET-UP TIME. See also CELLULAR MANUFACTURING.

process mapping a technique that uses graphic representation to map either in sequence or holistically a series of activities that together form a process. Process mapping is aimed at providing a better understanding of the process as visualized and to seek improvements (usually reductions) in the activities carried out, without altering the function of the process. See for example, PROCESS-FOCUSED LAYOUT. See LEAN MANUFACTURING.

processor an electronic device within a COMPUTER which is capable of interpreting and executing instructions.

process production a system of PRODUCTION in which a product passes through several processes or stages of production which are operated on a continuous basis; for example in oil refining and petrochemicals plants where the processes involve liquid or semisolid materials. In manufacturing a main product, say petrol, from such a production process, BY-PRODUCTS like tar or creosote may unavoidably arise. See PROCESS COSTING.

procurement see PURCHASING, BUYING PROCESS.

procurement lead time see STOCK CONTROL.

producer *or* **manufacturer** a business which is engaged in making consumer goods and capital goods using factor inputs such as raw materials, labour and capital. See VALUE ADDED.

producer good see GOOD.

producers' cooperative see WORKERS' COOPERATIVE.

product a generic term which covers both GOODS and SERVICES. *Final products* are goods and services which are purchased by consumers, while *intermediate products* are goods and services which are used by producers as factor inputs in producing other goods and services. See MARKETING MIX.

product attributes the various characteristics of a product which satisfy some particular consumer need. Product attributes such as quality, size, weight, price and reliability will affect the buyer's decision-making process. Buyers will tend to rank attributes according to their perceptions and needs. Companies generally focus on particular attributes when they advertise their brands or products. See MARKETING MIX.

product-based structure an ORGANIZATION structure where activities are grouped according to product or service, and formal COORDINATION of management functions occurs separately for each. See Fig. 65.

Although this structure duplicates management functions, potentially losing some economies of scale, it enables their activities to be tailored to the requirements of a particular product and its market. It is, therefore, said to be an appropriate structure for a diversified organization. The locus of AUTHORITY and coordination occurs at a relatively decentralized level (compared with FUNCTIONAL STRUCTURES), thereby facilitating swift adjustment to changing market conditions. The geographically based structure takes a similar form: each unit is based on a particular geographical area. Mixed geographical–product-based structures are quite common.

An extension of this form is the multi-divisional or M-form company. Here the units are organized as separate divisions or profit centres, with considerable autonomy in operational decision-making. Questions of strategy, i.e. which markets to be in and hence what divisions to have, are reserved to a head office. This also acts as a banker, setting profit targets for the divisions, receiving surpluses from them and providing capital. In practice this separation of responsibilities is not so clear cut: head offices often interfere in operational decisions which they perceive to be of great importance. This multi-divisional form is the predominant structure amongst large companies in the UK. See STRATEGIC BUSINESS UNIT, PROFIT CENTRE, FUNCTIONAL STRUCTURE, CRITICAL FUNCTION STRUCTURE, MATRIX STRUCTURE.

product champion an executive within a company who has specific responsibility for a *particular* product. Product champions may be needed in large multiproduct companies to provide a focus for integrating marketing, production and distribution of the product.

product churning the continuous introduction of NEW PRODUCTS by a firm in order to maintain its COMPETITIVE ADVANTAGE.

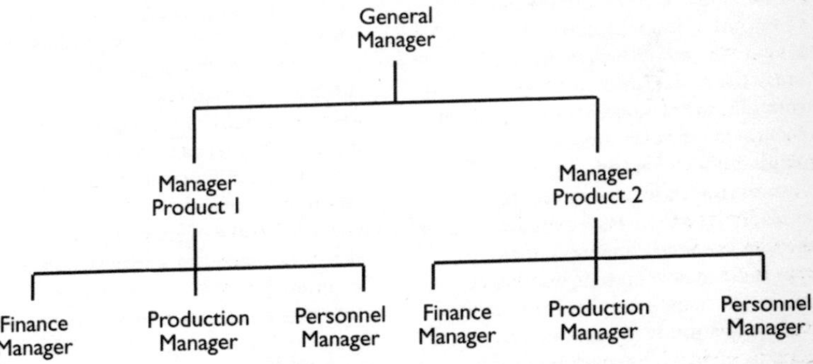

Fig. 65 **Product-based structure.** A typical example.

product class see PRODUCT RANGE.

product concept an idea for a product which is capable of fulfilling consumer needs. See NEW-PRODUCT DEVELOPMENT.

product cost the total cost of making a product which comprises its DIRECT MATERIALS cost and its DIRECT LABOUR cost plus its OVERHEAD cost. Product costs may be based upon the actual costs incurred in making products or the anticipated costs of making products in some future period. See STANDARD COST.

product costing *or* **job costing** a cost accounting method which applies to separate contracts, jobs or batches of products. Product costing seeks to determine PRODUCT COST which will include materials, labour and overheads.

product depth the number of variants of a product offered by a firm in each of its product lines. See PRODUCT RANGE.

product design see DESIGN.

product development a BUSINESS STRATEGY pursued by a firm aimed at increasing sales by developing *new* products which can be sold in its *existing* markets (see PRODUCT-MARKET MATRIX) or new products which take the firm into *new* markets. (See DIVERSIFICATION). In the former case, product development is especially important given both the life-cycle tendencies of products (see PRODUCT LIFE CYCLE) and in maintaining the firm's competitiveness. Most individual BRANDS follow a typical cycle of introduction, growth, maturity and eventual decline so that it is vital for the firm to develop and launch a constant stream of new brands to replace those in decline. Moreover, the ability of a firm to introduce innovatory new brands is often a key means of establishing a COMPETITIVE ADVANTAGE over rival suppliers. Developing new products involves the firm in undertaking MARKETING RESEARCH and committing resources to product RESEARCH AND DEVELOPMENT. See NEW-PRODUCT DEVELOPMENT, BOSTON MATRIX, PRODUCT-MARKET MATRIX.

product differentiation the means by which suppliers attempt to distinguish their own products from those offered by competitors. There are two basic ways in which products can be differentiated:

(a) by variations in the physical appearance and attributes of the product based on differences in design, styling, colouring and packaging, and differences in quality, composition, innovatory features and performance results;

(b) broadly similar products may be differentiated in the minds of buyers by the use of ADVERTISING and sales promotion techniques which emphasize imputed or subjective aspects of the product: for example 'better than', 'cleaner and whiter than'.

The purpose of product differentiation is to create and sustain a demand for the firm's products by nurturing consumer BRAND LOYALTY. Product differentiation is an important means of establishing COMPETITIVE ADVANTAGE over rival suppliers, and in some market structures, most notably OLIGOPOLY, it is regarded as constituting a more effective competitive strategy than price competition. The attraction of product-differentiation competition over price competition lies in the fact that whereas price cuts, for example, can be quickly and completely matched by competitors, a successful advertising campaign or the introduction of an innovatory product is less easily imitated. Moreover, whereas price competition lowers firms' profitability, product differentiation tends to preserve and even enhance profit returns. In particular, the establishment of product uniqueness may allow firms to command premium prices over competitors' offerings. Finally, product differentiation may serve to act as a BARRIER TO ENTRY, thereby protecting existing market shares against new competition.

See BRAND PROLIFERATION, MARKET CONDUCT, RESEARCH AND DEVELOPMENT, PRODUCT MIX, MARKETING MIX, DIFFERENTIATED MARKETING STRATEGY, PRODUCT POSITIONING.

product diversification a BUSINESS STRATEGY pursued by a firm aimed at increasing sales by developing (or acquiring) new products for new markets. See PRODUCT-MARKET MATRIX, DIVERSIFICATION.

product family see PRODUCT RANGE.

product-focused layout a FACTORY LAYOUT in which the equipment is arranged according to the needs of the product and in the same sequence as the operations (for example drilling, milling, grinding, assembly) necessary for production (see Fig. 66). Each production-line or assembly-line layout requires sufficient and stable demand to ensure a high utilization of equipment and a regular supply of raw materials and components. Failure in the supply of a piece of equipment results in the entire production line stopping, and quite remote failures can often result in disproportionately high losses.

The provision of machine services (power, maintenance, etc.) is difficult in product-type layouts, since where particularly elaborate machinery is used quite different pieces of equipment with different characteristics and requirements may be located adjacent to one another. A mixture of skills and operations frequently occurs, resulting in difficulties of payment and supervision; usually, however, little specialized supervision is required since the work performed is often highly rationalized. Minimum floor space is required, work in progress is minimized and through-put time is low. The requirements for handling materials are small and machine utilization is high.

A product layout is appropriate for the production of a small range of products in very large quantities and is a comparatively rigid production system. See PRODUCTION-LINE, PROCESS-FOCUSED LAYOUT. See also CELLULAR MANUFACTURING.

product group see PRODUCT RANGE.

product image the perceptions and attitudes of consumers towards an existing or proposed new product. Product image is affected both by the physical attributes of the product itself and by the psychological or imputed values of the buyer which can be cultivated and manipulated by ADVERTISING and other promotional forms. See BUYER BEHAVIOUR, PRODUCT POSITIONING, PSYCHOLOGICAL PRICING.

product imitation a MARKET POSITIONING strategy involving the introduction of a product which emulates or copies a product already on the market (in so far as it is legally possible under PATENT and TRADEMARK laws). Product imitation may be used to exploit high-volume market segments or to compete with new innovative products in a rapidly growing market (see PRODUCT LIFE CYCLE).

product innovation the improvement of existing products or the development of new products. Product innovation involves considerable expense in financing the generation of ideas, product design, development and testing, and since a high proportion of new products fail to secure customer acceptance it involves a high degree of risk. See RESEARCH AND DEVELOPMENT, NEW-PRODUCT DEVELOPMENT.

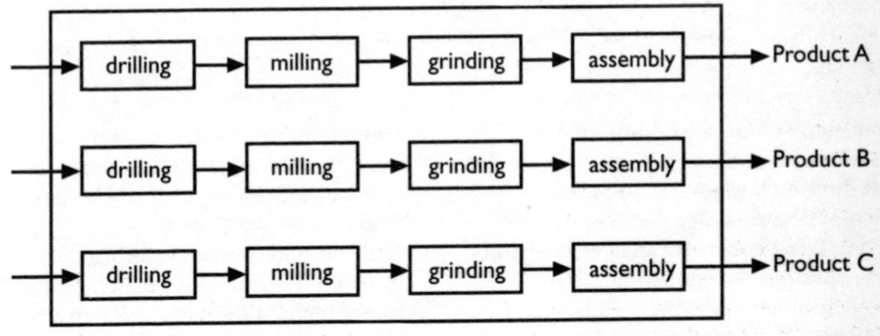

Fig. 66 **Product-focused layout.** A simple example.

production

The conversion process for transforming inputs such as materials, labour and capital into goods and services.

In the case of goods, production processes may be divided into three broad categories:

(a) *process* production involves the continuous production of a good in bulk often by chemical means, for example petrochemicals. Process production is used whenever raw materials in liquid or gaseous form need to be blended, heated or distilled, and the flow of these materials is facilitated by using pipelines which connect the various production stages;

(b) *mass* production involves the PRODUCTION-LINE OR ASSEMBLY-LINE production in very large numbers of goods such as motor cars or domestic appliances using PRODUCT-FOCUSED LAYOUTS. Mass production is used wherever demand for a product is sufficiently large and the product sufficiently standardized to justify laying out a specialized production line or assembly line for it in order to achieve the cost savings associated with ECONOMIES OF SCALE;

(c) *batch* production involves the manufacturing of similar goods together in batches and is used where demand is insufficient or the product cannot be standardized to enable mass production to be used. In batch production, batches of a product are subjected to a series of processes such as machining, drilling and grinding in work stations specializing in these processes, with machines generally being reset after each batch, ready to process the next batch (see PROCESS-FOCUSED LAYOUT).

In addition, a number of hybrid production systems such as CELLULAR MANUFACTURING and FLEXIBLE MANUFACTURING SYSTEMS combine various features of mass production and batch production methods, using AUTOMATION to facilitate the low-cost production of a variety of low-volume components or products. See LEAN MANUFACTURING, JUST-IN-TIME (JIT) SYSTEM.

Mass production and batch production are generally undertaken for STOCK and customer orders are met by drawing on this stock. Alternatively, the firm may manufacture to individual customer orders rather than for stock, that is, engage in jobbing production. See VALUE ADDED.

production benchmarking see BENCHMARKING.

production budget see BUDGET.

production capacity see CAPACITY.

production control *or* **process control** the coordination and monitoring of production programmes and targets. Production control involves a number of activities, in particular:

(a) minimizing operational variations from production schedules, PROGRESS CHASING and dealing with problems so as to avoid losing output;

(b) controlling manufacturing costs by monitoring the use of materials and labour inputs and taking action to avoid wastage where necessary (see COST CONTROL);

(c) controlling product quality by inspection to detect defective products and taking action to remedy deficiencies (see QUALITY CONTROL);

(d) controlling MACHINE UTILIZATION by monitoring machine usage and avoiding idle time or machine down-time. See also PRODUCTION MANAGEMENT, PRODUCTION SCHEDULING, OPTIMIZED PRODUCTION TECHNOLOGY, POKE YOKE.

production line *or* **assembly line** a means of organizing PRODUCTION whereby a product is manufactured by passing it through a series of operations, further materials or components being added as appropriate. This method of production is used in, for example, the production of motor cars and electrical products such as television sets.

In planning an assembly line careful attention must be paid to PRODUCTION-LINE BALANCING to ensure that all operations are synchronized so as to produce a preplanned volume of output.

Assembly-line methods usually involve breaking down production operations into many small tasks. This has the benefit of reducing the complexity of each task, reducing the skill demanded of production operatives and reducing training costs. Such lines also create opportunities to use specialized purpose-built machines to undertake particular production or assembly processes (see AUTOMATION, ROBOT). Assembly line methods also facilitate the use of special materials-handling devices like conveyor belts which reduce materials-handling costs. Finally, use of assembly lines serves to reduce stock holdings of raw materials and components between production processes by making it easier to estimate daily production and usage.

On the other hand, assembly lines are vulnerable to breakdowns and disruptions since a breakdown at any point on the assembly line stops the whole production process. In addition, the speed at which the line is operated can cause stress problems for operatives. Finally, the limited and repetitive nature of each operation can lead to worker demotivation. To counter such motivational problems some companies use job enrichment programmes whereby operatives undertake a wider range of activities, or interchange between activities (see JOB DESIGN AND REDESIGN). See PRODUCT-FOCUSED LAYOUT, JUST-IN-TIME (JIT) SYSTEM.

production-line balancing *or* **assembly-line balancing** the assignment of *equal* amounts of work to sequential work stations on the production line. This is necessary to avoid idle time or 'balancing loss' since the work stations at each production stage (for example drilling, milling, etc. in Fig. 67), although having different types of work to perform, are all required to work on the same number of items in any one time period (12 per hour in Fig. 67).

The task of production-line planning requires the total work to be divided among work stations where a worker or group of workers performs the same operation continuously on successive items. Alternatively, certain work stations may employ automatic machines (numerically-controlled machine tools or robots) to perform operations. The output of production lines is determined by the 'cycle time' at the work stations, i.e. the time it takes for the workers or machine to complete the work task required. The number of work-stations at each production stage must be balanced so that each production stage can deal with the same number of items (i.e. 12 in Fig. 67). If the average cycle time is, say, five minutes, then the output from the last work station, and consequently from the production line as a whole, is one item every five minutes or twelve items per hour.

A planned work pace of twelve items per hour could leave some machines underutilized; for example, the milling work station could be capable of producing 15 items per hour or one every four minutes but will be constrained to operate at less than capacity to maintain the same output rate as prior and succeeding work-stations. By contrast, if only one grinding work station rather than two were available this

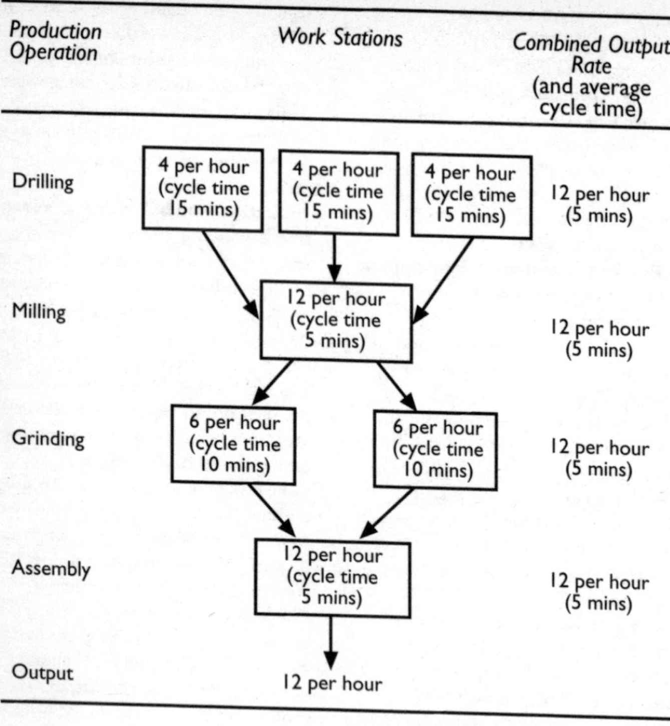

Fig. 67 **Production-line balancing.** A simple example.

would create a 'bottleneck' constraining the output of the whole production line to just six units per hour.

Whereas machine-based work stations have constant cycle times, work stations using human operatives are likely to experience a degree of variability in cycle time from the STANDARD TIMES established by work measurement techniques. To deal with this variability some flexibility can be built into the production line by introducing buffer stocks of materials or components between work stations. Buffer stocks also serve to prevent disruption to later 'down stream' production operations if machine breakdowns or labour problems have occurred at earlier production phases.

See INDIVISIBILITIES, INPUT-OUTPUT CONTROL.

production orientation the business philosophy of a company which emphasizes the *selling* of goods and services that it produces, through intensive use of advertising and sales promotion, but which pays only limited attention to the underlying needs of consumers. Such a philosophy is often found in companies dominated by production and engineering managers and stresses the pursuit of technical excellence of products. Since such products have not been designed with the needs of consumers sufficiently in mind they risk being rejected by them. Contrast with CONSUMER ORIENTATION.

production management *or* operations management

The administration of the conversion process which transforms labour, materials and capital inputs into final products. Production management involves:

(a) planning the design and construction of the production system. System design decisions include such things as the determination of manufacturing methods – batch production, mass production (see PRODUCTION), acquisition and arrangement of plant (see FACTORY LAYOUT), and the establishment of schedules for the production of each item (see PRODUCTION SCHEDULING);

(b) controlling the operation, performance and running of the physical facilities and predetermined production plans which constitute the production system. Decisions relating to the operation of the production system involve PRODUCTION CONTROL, PURCHASING, QUALITY CONTROL, STOCK CONTROL, WORK STUDY, and MAINTENANCE of equipment. See also MATERIALS MANAGEMENT, MATERIALS REQUIREMENTS PLANNING, JUST-IN-TIME (JIT) SYSTEM, MANUFACTURING RESOURCE PLANNING, DISTRIBUTION RESOURCE PLANNING, NETWORK ANALYSIS, WORLD CLASS MANUFACTURING, OPTIMIZED PRODUCTION TECHNOLOGY, POKE YOKE.

production scheduling the detailed planning of PRODUCTION so as to achieve production targets within specified timetables and avoid production bottlenecks, while making effective use of labour resources and ensuring a high rate of machine utilization. Production scheduling is generally undertaken by the production planning department and will be based upon orders received for products or forecasts of product demand. Where a firm schedules its production on the basis of *making to order* then it will plan its production in response to customers' specific orders and promised delivery dates. On the other hand, where a firm schedules its production on the basis of *making for stock* it will plan its production to maintain adequate STOCK levels of finished products from which it can, in turn, satisfy customer orders.

Production scheduling in BATCH PRODUCTION is concerned with fitting new orders into the spaces available in the manufacturing programmes. This requires knowledge of:

(a) the production operations required for the manufacture of each product, the order in which these operations must be undertaken and the machine or work stations at which operations will be performed;

(b) the available capacity of machines or work stations;

(c) the relative priorities of existing jobs;

(d) available labour and materials;

(e) the required delivery or completion date for the job.

Almost all production scheduling in batch production involves the successive subtraction of operation times from the required completion date. This is known as *due date* or *reverse scheduling*. The principal problem in due date scheduling is to decide what allowances shall be made for idle or waiting time. Operation times are known sufficiently accurately, but waiting times between operations are variable. Production schedules of this type are usually depicted upon bar charts (see GANTT CHART). The advantage of this type of presentation is that the load on any machine or on any department is clear at a glance, and available or spare capacity is easily identified. It will also indicate which resources are overloaded so that activities can be rescheduled or some of the work subcontracted.

Production scheduling in MASS PRODUCTION is more straightforward since usually a much more limited number of products is involved, sequences of production operations are predetermined and production is generally for stock rather than in response to direct customer orders.

Once production schedules have been established then PRODUCTION CONTROL will be concerned to ensure that products are manufactured according to the previously-determined production plan. See PRODUCT SPECIFICATION, MASTER PRODUCTION SCHEDULE, LINE OF BALANCE CHART, BACKLOG, ACTIVITY CHART, JUST-IN-TIME (JIT) SYSTEM, MATERIALS FLOW MANAGEMENT, DISPATCH, BACKWARD SCHEDULING.

productivity the relationship between the physical output of a product and the factor inputs which have gone into producing that output. Productivity is usually measured in terms of *output per man hour*, an improvement in productivity showing up as an increase in output per man hour.

Productivity is important to a firm because it enables the firm to establish a COMPETITIVE ADVANTAGE over rival suppliers: a *given output* can be produced at a lower resource cost, enabling a firm to supply this output at a lower price; or alternatively the firm can now produce more output from the *same amount* of inputs, enabling the firm to increase its total profit return. A high rate of growth of output per man hour also puts the firm in a better position to absorb inflationary cost pressures arising from wage increases and increases in raw material prices, should it be difficult (see PRICES AND INCOMES controls) or competitively inopportune to increase prices on a pro rata basis.

A firm can improve its productivity in a variety of ways, including the adoption of better working practices (particularly the removal of RESTRICTIVE LABOUR PRACTICES) and pay-incentive schemes (for example PROFIT-RELATED PAY and PROFIT-SHARING schemes); the adoption of methods for economizing on the STOCKHOLDING of raw materials (for example the JUST-IN-TIME stock ordering system). An especially important source of productivity improvement is the use of superior production methods (for example switching from labour-intensive BATCH PRODUCTION to continuous capital-intensive MASS-PRODUCTION processes), and investment in the latest 'state-of-the-art' technologies (for example COMPUTER-AIDED MANUFACTURING systems (CAM) and COMPUTER-AIDED DESIGN (CAD)). See LEAN MANUFACTURING, ECONOMIC GROWTH, EXPERIENCE CURVE, SPECIALIZATION, HOSHIN.

productivity bargaining see COLLECTIVE BARGAINING, PRODUCTIVITY.

product life cycle

The typical sales pattern of a PRODUCT over time from its introduction on to the market and its eventual decline as it is displaced by new, more innovative products or until demand for it falls, due to a change in consumer tastes.

The product life cycle for product A, as illustrated in Fig. 68, has four main phases: introduction/launch, growth, maturity/saturation and decline. Each phase can be characterized by the adoption of various MARKETING MIX formats (price, advertising, sales promotions etc.) to encourage both potential buyers to purchase the product and distributors to stock it:

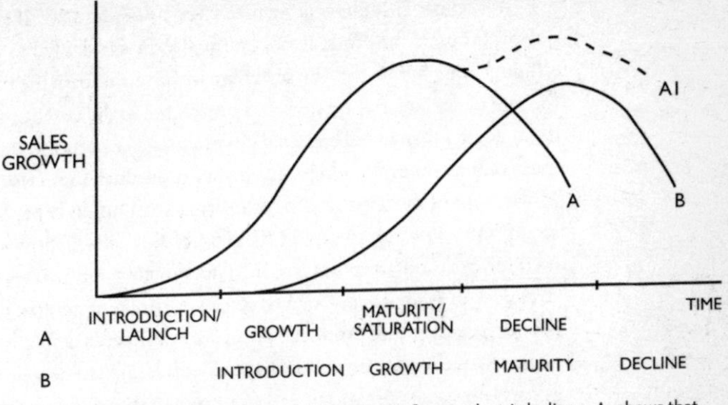

Fig. 68 **Product life cycle**. Product B is launched before product A declines. A1 shows that product life may be extended by product modification.

(a) *introduction/launch*. This occurs following the successful technical development of a NEW PRODUCT and indications, from MARKETING RESEARCH and TEST MARKETING trials, that the product is likely to be a commercial success. In the introductory phase, sales volume is relatively low and limited in the main to *pioneering* or *innovator customers*. Firms may adopt a high MARKET SKIMMING PRICING policy aimed at high-income, price-insensitive buyers, or, alternatively, they may wish to accelerate the move into the growth phase by a low MARKET PENETRATION PRICING policy backed by heavy advertising and other promotional spending to obtain the maximum physical distribution and consumer interest in the product;

(b) *growth* phase. In this stage, sales volume expands rapidly as the product increasingly commands acceptance by the mass market of consumers. The introduction of imitation brands by competitors tends to heighten competitive pressures, but at this stage the collective and cumulative marketing effort of suppliers expands the overall size of the market, resulting in sales gains for most producers;

(c) *maturity/saturation* phase. In this stage sales are largely repeat purchases to existing customers, since the majority of potential buyers have already made their first purchases. As the market becomes progressively saturated, firms *are* unable to benefit from further expansion of the market as a whole and must instead compete to increase or maintain their market share. It is at this point that BRAND LOYALTY becomes critical, leading to a heavy emphasis on advertising and sales promotion and back-up AFTER-SALES SERVICE etc. Fierce price competition is likely to be resisted, especially if the market is oligopolistic in structure (see OLIGOPOLY), in order to preserve the profitability of the market; firms may, however, have no choice but to compete on price if consumers see the product as increasingly a standardized item despite efforts by suppliers to differentiate their own particular brand of it;

(d) *decline*. This phase is characterized by falling sales. If left to follow this downward path, the product will eventually die as sales fall to very low levels, although long before this the firm may withdraw it from the market. However, the rate of decline may be slow and protracted in the absence of rapid technological change and bolstered by entrenched customer tastes, so that suppliers may continue to earn good profits from the product. (See ENDGAME STRATEGY).

In view of the product life cycle, firms must not only pay particular attention to how best to exploit their established products at various stages of their life cycle, but, importantly, must formulate appropriate PRODUCT RANGE strategies so as to provide for a balanced portfolio of new products, growth products and mature products. Thus, for example, as demand for product A begins to decline the firm must have *already* launched new products such as B as part of a regular programme of new product launches (see Fig. 68). In addition, it may be possible to modify an existing product such as A in order to extend its life cycle as depicted by Al in the figure (SEE PRODUCT MODIFICATION).

See NEW-PRODUCT DEVELOPMENT, OBSOLESCENCE, BOSTON MATRIX.

product line a number of closely-related versions of a product, for example variants of the Ford Focus car. See PRODUCT RANGE, PRODUCT LINE PRICING.

product line pricing the PRICING of all the different variants or models of a product which together constitute a product line, for example prices of the 'basic', 'de luxe' and 'super de luxe' versions of the Ford Focus car. Product line pricing seeks to establish appropriate price differentials between the brands making up a line, in relation to the relative quality, sophistication and cost of each brand, vis-à-vis equivalent competitors' offerings and the prices they are charging. In pricing a product line, price relativities *between* lines may also have to be considered, for example prices of the Ford Mondeo, Focus and Ka cars, since there can be overlaps between product lines, like that between the super de luxe model of the Ford Focus and the basic model of the Ford Mondeo. See PRODUCT RANGE, PRICING POLICY.

product manager *or* **brand manager** a manager who is responsible for planning and implementing the MARKETING of a particular product or brand.

product-market matrix

A framework for highlighting and analysing the various growth opportunities open to a firm which are used by corporate planners in formulating the firm's BUSINESS STRATEGY.

Fig. 69 shows the matrix which depicts products on one axis and markets on the other. By way of example let us consider a firm currently specializing in the production of rayon in the UK, a man-made fibre which is currently sold to UK textile fabricators to be made up into clothing. The matrix indicates that the firm has four main strategic possibilities open to it to develop its business (a fifth option, that of VERTICAL INTEGRATION, is closely linked with strategy (a):

		MARKET	
		Present	New
PRODUCT	Present	(a) market penetration	(b) market development
	New	(c) product development	(d) diversification

Fig. 69 **Product-market matrix.** A matrix showing four major strategies for growth.

(a) it can seek to achieve a greater penetration of its *existing* MARKET, increasing its share of the textile fabrication market by various competitive means – low costs and prices, product differentiation (see COMPETITIVE ADVANTAGE). However, if the firm is already a dominant supplier, or if the market itself is in the mature phase of the PRODUCT LIFE CYCLE, growth opportunities are strictly limited (see HORIZONTAL INTEGRATION);

(b) the firm can aim to develop *new markets* for its existing products, capitalizing on the firm's production expertise. In our example, the firm could adapt rayon for use as a packaging material for products such as crisps and cigarettes, or the firm could globalize its operations by selling rayon into international markets (see MULTINATIONAL ENTERPRISE);

(c) the. firm can seek to develop *new products* for its existing markets, exploiting the firm's marketing strengths. Our rayon firm could, for example, add other synthetic fibres to its product range, or blend together rayon with natural wool to create 'hybrid' fabrics of various strengths and textures for use by clothiers. This strategy, however, suffers from the same general limitations as strategy (a) above;

(d) the firm could aim to diversify (see DIVERSIFICATION) away from its existing activity by developing *new products* for *new markets*. The rayon firm might decide that the clothing industry overall had too little long-term growth potential, or that it had become too competitive to make decent profit returns. In this case, DIVESTMENT of its original business interests or a gradual move away from rayon production into, say, the electronics industry may be considered. This is generally the highest-risk strategy since it takes the firm furthest away from its core expertise in production and marketing. For this reason, merger and takeover (EXTERNAL GROWTH) rather than ORGANIC GROWTH is often the most viable way of developing entirely new business interests for the firm. See BOSTON MATRIX.

product mix see PRODUCT RANGE.

product modification the alteration by a firm of an existing product to update it and improve its competitiveness in serving existing MARKET SEGMENTS or to modify it to serve new market segments. Where technological change is rapid or where consumer tastes are changing rapidly, appropriate product modifications may be necessary to extend its life (see PRODUCT LIFE CYCLE). See PRODUCT STRATEGY.

product obsolescence see OBSOLESCENCE.

product portfolio see PRODUCT RANGE.

product positioning a process whereby a marketer identifies the set of products which compete with the product under analysis, identifies key product attributes in the set, collects information from customers/ prospects on perceptions of products and their attributes, determines the product's position on a perceptual map, determines customers' or prospects' ideal position(s), examines the fit between product position and market (customer) preference, and then selects a positioning strategy.

The technique of 'perceptual mapping' is often used to chart consumers' perceptions of brands currently on offer and to identify opportunities for launching new brands or to reposition an existing brand. This technique involves identifying perceived product characteristics which may be used to classify consumer opinions about brands of a product. Thus, in Fig. 70 the two axes of the 'map' show the perceived product attributes, 'strong'/ 'mild' and 'ordinary'/'classy' for cigarettes while B1 to B9 on the map indicate consumers' perceptions of existing brands of cigarettes on offer in terms of these characteristics. Brands show market segments which are currently being serviced by existing brands and 'clusters' of brands suggest larger volume segments.

A positioning strategy seeks to differentiate the firm's brand from competitors' brands in terms of product characteristics and 'image' so as to maximize sales potential. In positioning brands a firm may choose to offer a 'copy-cat' or 'me-too' brand in a well-served market segment which is very similar to competing brands, with minimal PRODUCT DIFFERENTIATION (Brands B1 to B5 in the figure). This stratagem may be viable where this segment represents a high proportion of total market sales so that even a small brand share would result in large sales. Alternatively, a firm's MARKETING RESEARCH may reveal untapped demand potential in different market segments, so that it may choose to distance its brand from competing brands

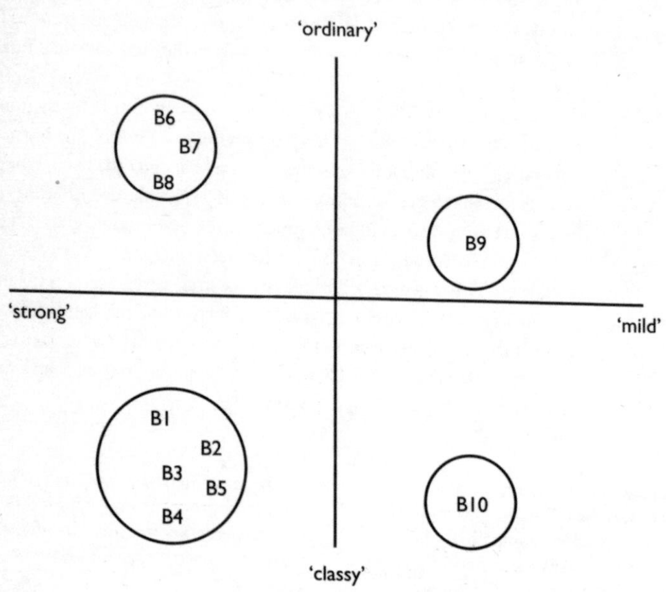

Fig. 70 **Product positioning**. Perceptual map.

with a high degree of product differentiation, introducing a new brand (B10). See MARKET SEGMENTATION, PRICE QUALITY TRADE-OFF, PRICING POLICY, PRODUCT IMAGE, PRODUCT VARIETY, BRAND EXTENSION.

product range the number of PRODUCTS and BRANDS sold by a firm. Depending upon the firm's degree of SPECIALIZATION or DIVERSIFICATION its product range may be classified as follows:

(a) *product line* or *product class:* a number of closely-related products. The products in a line may serve a particular consumer segment or price range, or may be used together by the consumer, or may employ common distribution outlets. For example, a motorcar supplier such as Ford offers a number of different versions of a particular model, say the Mondeo (differentiated by engine size, trim, accessories etc.), within a limited price band designated in Fig. 71 as 'basic', 'de luxe' and 'super de luxe'. Alternatively, a kitchenware supplier may market together as a product line such items as food mixers, toasters and kettles;

(b) *product group* or *product family:* a combination of individual PRODUCT LINES which together constitute a firm's product offering to a particular MARKET. A motorcar supplier like Ford, for instance, offers a number of different car models (Cougar, Mondeo, Focus and Ka) to serve different segments of the motorcar market (see Fig. 71);

(c) *product mix:* all the PRODUCT GROUPS and PRODUCT LINES which together constitute a firm's *total* product offering. The firm's product range might be closely related or very diverse depending upon the spread of the firm's business interests. Ford's product mix, for instance, consists primarily of motorcars, trucks and tractors, while a more diversified company will produce many different products. (see DIVERSIFICATION). See MARKET SEGMENTATION, PRODUCT LIFE CYCLE, PRODUCT-MARKET MATRIX, MARKETING MIX, PRODUCT LINE PRICING, PRODUCT VARIETY.

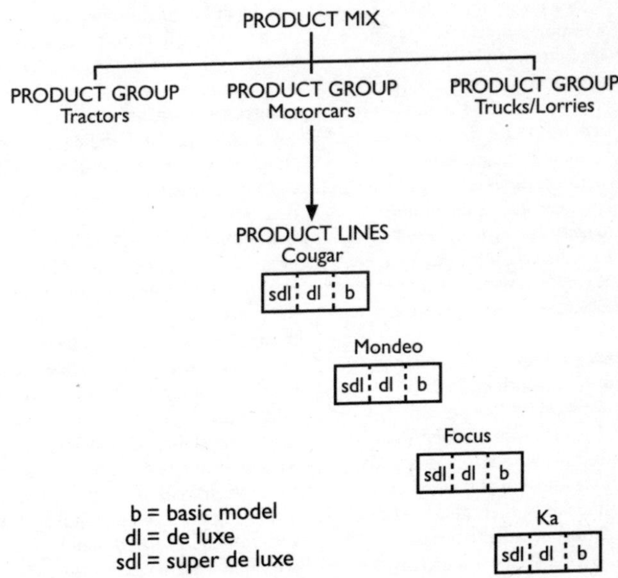

Fig. 71 **Product range.** An example from the car-manufacturing industry.

product rationalization the withdrawal by a firm of a product or products from the market. A firm may withdraw a product because demand for it has fallen to the extent that it is no longer profitable to sell (see PRODUCT LIFE CYCLE), or the firm may decide to withdraw a number of products from its PRODUCT RANGE in order to cut costs or focus its marketing efforts more narrowly. See PRODUCT STRATEGY, RATIONALIZATION. DIVESTMENT.

product repositioning see PRODUCT POSITIONING.

product sampling a form of SALES PROMOTION in which consumers are given a free trial sample of a brand so as to induce them to then purchase it.

product segmentation see PRODUCT POSITIONING.

product specification a detailed inventory of all the raw materials and components which comprise a product and their exact sizes and qualities (a 'bill of materials'). The product specification will also list all the manufacturing and assembly processes involved in making the product. Once a product specification is drawn up it can be used for organizational buying (see PURCHASING), PRODUCT COSTING purposes and as a basis for PRODUCTION SCHEDULING.

Product specifications for consumer products are strongly influenced by MARKETING considerations relating to the features and performance of the product considered to be appealing to buyers. For example, the product specification for a car could include comfort, speed, reliability, safety features etc. See MASTER PRODUCTION SCHEDULE.

product strategy a firm's policy on the range of PRODUCTS which it supplies. Product strategy involves the periodic updating and modification of the firm's existing products or brands (see PRODUCT RANGE); the introduction of NEW PRODUCTS; and the phasing out of old products whose sales are declining, in order to release production and marketing resources which can be devoted to newer, more active products.

Technological innovation results in new products, new cost-reducing production technologies and new materials. Some innovations can serve to improve existing products or reduce their production costs and so prolong their lives. However, many such technological changes serve to limit the lives of products, shortening the PRODUCT LIFE CYCLE and speeding the onset of decline as new products supersede existing products. Furthermore, rapid changes in consumer tastes may render a particular product obsolete after only a short time, as with, for example, fashion products. Consequently, a company's product development policy needs to maintain a constant stream of new products over time if it is to succeed in meeting its growth and profitability goals. Product range strategy should provide for launching new products and deleting old ones so as to avoid having a disproportionate number of products at any one stage of their lives. Indeed firms may deliberately follow a strategy of planned obsolescence, bringing out a continuous stream of new products as a means of increasing their total sales by inducing customers to replace products more frequently. See PRODUCT MODIFICATION, PRODUCT RATIONALIZATION, NEW-PRODUCT DEVELOPMENT.

product substitutes products which customers regard as fulfilling the same needs although they are technically dissimilar, e.g. butter and margarine. See ELASTICITY OF DEMAND.

product variety the number and range of BRANDS or PRODUCTS offered by a supplier. How many variants of a product a supplier markets will depend on the degree to which the market is segmented and the number of product variants offered by competitors. In making product variety decisions the firm must consider how to *position* its brands so as to serve its target market segments without excessive duplication of brands in any segment, and the additional costs of producing small volumes of many varieties with consequent loss of standardization economies. See MARKET SEGMENTATION, PRODUCT POSITIONING, BRAND PROLIFERATION, PRODUCT RANGE.

product warranty see GUARANTEE.

product width the number of different product lines offered by a firm. See PRODUCT RANGE.

professional a person with a recognized set of skills and knowledge which qualifies them to practise a certain occupation. Usually this knowledge is gained from lengthy TRAINING and is certified by examination, often by a professional association. This pattern of entry to an occupation is similar to that of apprenticeships; however, the professions are usually understood to be those occupations which are located at the top of the occupational structure in terms of status, for example doctors, architects, lawyers etc. In so far as professional associations (for example the Law Society) stipulate the form and content of training and examination, they define the nature of the job tasks and the work standards that should be achieved and they control entry into the profession. Once individuals have been admitted to the profession it is customary in most instances for them to join the association. Professional associations are similar to craft unions (see TRADE UNION) in that they seek to maintain high incomes for their members by restricting entry to these occupations. Some associations (especially those governing public-sector professionals) are registered as trade unions and have become more similar to other unions in recent years, in that they have felt forced to mount industrial action or publicity campaigns to influence government and management policy decisions.

The notion of professionalism, i.e. that professional workers are special by virtue of their knowledge, has been much criticized in recent years. Critics have claimed that it is used to advance sectional interests, for example high income levels, and to prevent regulation by government or employers of the way tasks are carried out. Attempts have been made to weaken the power of certain professions; for instance, the recent trend in the UK Health Service for the allocation of resources to be determined on grounds of efficiency and effectiveness by management teams rather than on medical grounds as defined by doctors and consultants.

MANAGEMENT *per se* has generally not been viewed as a profession in the UK because there has been little agreement on the skills and knowledge which are integral to management, and no professional body has been able to enforce mini-mum standards. However, numerous associations concerned with particular aspects of management, for example the INSTITUTE OF PERSONNEL MANAGEMENT, have identified training requirements and hold examinations in an attempt to achieve professional status. Recently the MANAGEMENT CHARTER initiative has attempted to identify core 'competencies' of management as a first step to creating a profession of management.

professional association see PROFESSIONAL.

professional bureaucracy an ORGANIZATION where much of the work is done by PROFESSIONALS. The organization depends on the extensive knowledge of these employees. This tends to encourage a certain degree of DECENTRALIZATION since it is difficult for superiors who do not possess the specialized knowledge to CONTROL what their subordinates do. There may well be conflict as managers attempt to enforce control.

profile segmentation a means of grouping people that allows them to be reached by the communications media (e.g. ADVERTISING, DIRECT MAIL). See MARKET SEGMENTATION.

profit the difference that arises when a firm's SALES REVENUE is greater than its total COSTS. GROSS PROFIT is the difference between SALES REVENUE and the COST OF SALES, while NET PROFIT is equal to gross profit less selling distribution, administration and financing costs. PROFIT AFTER TAX is the net profit attributable to shareholders after taxes have been paid.

Profit depends on two main factors:

(a) *average profit margins* or profit per £1 of sales. If costs increase the profit margins will be squeezed; if competition forces selling prices downward margins will be similarly squeezed, and vice versa;

(b) *sales turnover.* Any increase in sales value will tend to increase profits. See PROFIT AND LOSS ACCOUNT.

profitability the PROFIT earned by a firm in relation to the size of the firm, measured in terms of total ASSETS employed, long-term capital or number of employees. See RETURN ON CAPITAL EMPLOYED.

profit after tax the NET PROFIT attributable to SHAREHOLDERS of a company after all costs and taxes have been deducted. This is the amount left to be paid out as DIVIDENDS to shareholders as a return on their investment or to be ploughed back into the business as undistributed profits to add to the company's RESERVES.

profit-and-loss appropriation account an account that shows how any NET PROFIT recorded in the PROFIT AND LOSS ACCOUNT is divided between TAX payments, DIVIDEND payments and RESERVES.

profit centre an organizational subunit of a firm given responsibility for minimizing COSTS and maximizing REVENUE within its limited sphere of operations. Profit centres facilitate management control by helping to ascertain a unit's performance and profitability. Profit centres are, in effect, independent business units controlled by a local manager and financed by the parent company. See also COST CENTRE, INVESTMENT CENTRE.

Profit Impact of Market Strategy see PIMS.

profit margin the difference between the SELLING PRICE of a product and its PRODUCTION COST and SELLING COST. The size of the profit margin will depend upon the percentage profit mark-up which a firm adds to costs in determining its selling price. The size of the profit margin is measured by the PROFIT-MARGINS RATIO.

profit-and-loss account *or* income statement

An accounting statement that shows a firm's SALES REVENUE generated over a trading period and all the relevant costs experienced in earning that revenue. In the account, the COST OF SALES is deducted from sales revenue to calculate GROSS PROFIT; then the other costs involved are deducted from the gross profit to show any NET PROFIT earned.

In effect, the profit-and-loss account provides a summarized financial video-recording of the firm's trading activities. Fig. 72 shows the typical layout of a profit and loss account. See also VALUE ADDED, ECONOMIC VALUE ADDED.

		£	£
Sales revenue			980,000
less cost of sales:	opening stock of finished good	80,000	
	add purchases of finished good	550,000	
	deduct closing stock of finished good	100,000	530,000
Gross profit			450,000
Overhead costs:	manufacturing	60,000	
	selling and distribution	90,000	
	administration	40,000	
	financing	10,000	200,000
Net profit			250,000

Fig. 72 **Profit-and-loss account.** Profit-and-loss account of Y Co for year ending 31 December 20xx.

profit-margins ratio *or* **profit-to-sales ratio** a measure of a firm's PROFIT MARGINS, which expresses the firm's PROFITS as a percentage of its SALES REVENUE. Competitive pressure on selling prices or cost increases serve to squeeze profit margins and affect profits. The profit-margins ratio has a significant impact upon a firm's RETURN ON CAPITAL EMPLOYED.

profit per employee an accounting ratio which expresses a firm's PROFIT as a proportion of its size, measured in terms of numbers of employees. Where a company employs a high proportion of part-time workers, employee numbers may need to be adjusted to full-time equivalent numbers to assist comparability. Alternatively profit may be expressed as a proportion of total employee remuneration.

profit-related pay (PRP) a form of PROFIT SHARING in the UK. This was a very widespread scheme that gave employees significant INCOME TAX benefits if they took some of their WAGES as PROFIT-linked payments. In principal, their wages would vary according to company profitability. The objective was to combat the unemployment effects of 'wage stickiness' – i.e. that wages tend to remain unchanged when company profitability declines causing firms to adjust by reducing employment levels. However, a large proportion of these schemes were felt to be 'cosmetic' i.e. wages did not really respond to changes in profits. For this reason, the tax advantages have now been phased out. See FINANCIAL PARTICIPATION.

profit sharing the distribution of some portion of PROFITS to the employees of a company. It can take the form of an annual cash bonus based on the previous year's profits or it can form an element of weekly or monthly pay (see PROFIT-RELATED PAY). Less direct forms of profit sharing include allocation to employees of shares in the company, paid for out of company profits, and providing employees with the option to buy shares at some point in the future at current prices, thereby enabling them to benefit from both the share dividend and any growth in share value resulting from increases in profitability (see EMPLOYEE SHARE OWNERSHIP PLAN). Profit sharing is often advocated to improve employee commitment and thereby improve PRODUCTIVITY. See FINANCIAL PARTICIPATION.

profit-volume chart a conventional BREAK-EVEN chart which has been rearranged to show the effect on profits or losses of changes in output or sales. Fig. 73 shows a typical profit-volume chart. Sales or output is measured along the horizontal axis and profits (or losses) on the vertical axis. With

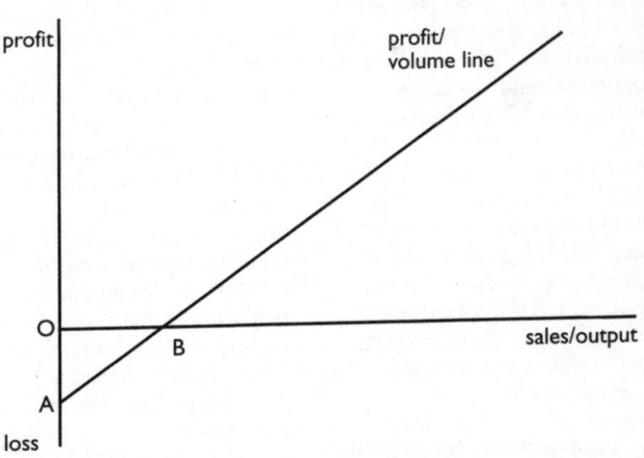

Fig. 73 **Profit-volume chart**

zero sales/output the firm experiences losses equal to the firm's fixed costs (OA). The break-even output (OB) is the output at which the firm makes neither a profit nor a loss. Losses or profits can be measured in terms of the distance of the profit/volume line from the horizontal axis. The slope of the profit/volume line reflects the CONTRIBUTION per unit of sales output, that is the price per unit less its unit variable costs.

profit-volume ratio a ratio used in MARGINAL COSTING and BREAK-EVEN analysis which shows the CONTRIBUTION as a percentage of sales. For example, if the profit–volume ratio is 42%, then for every £100 of sales a contribution towards fixed costs and profit of £42 will be generated, provided that selling prices and unit variable costs do not change.

pro forma prescribing a set form or procedure. For instance, a *pro forma* invoice may be sent to a customer in advance of a transaction to facilitate paperwork, or a *pro forma* projected SOURCES AND USES OF FUNDS STATEMENT may be constructed to show the bank manager the anticipated future financial situation as a basis for negotiating a short-term LOAN.

program see COMPUTER PROGRAM.

programme evaluation and review technique (PERT) see NETWORK ANALYSIS.

progress chasing the task of monitoring the progress of PRODUCTION orders through all stages of production from the time when the order is placed to the time when the work is completed, so as to detect variations of the order or production batch from schedule. This involves identifying jobs which have been started late or which are running behind schedule and the causes of deviations from schedule, for example because materials or components were not ordered in time. It also involves corrective action to overcome bottlenecks and ensure that jobs are completed by the scheduled date to help the business to keep to its delivery promises. See PRODUCTION MANAGEMENT, PRODUCTION CONTROL.

Projects and Exports Policy Division see EXPORTING.

promotion 1 the means of bringing products to the attention of consumers and persuading them to buy those products. See PROMOTIONAL MIX, ADVERTISING, SALES PROMOTION, MERCHANDIZING, PERSONAL SELLING, PACKAGING, PUBLIC RELATIONS, CAMPAIGN OBJECTIVES.

2 the elevation of a person to a position of greater authority and responsibility. See ORGANIZATION CHART.

promotional allowance a financial inducement which is offered by sellers of a product to wholesalers or retailers as a means of encouraging them to take part in a SALES PROMOTION campaign.

promotional mix the means which a firm can use to inform prospective customers of the nature and attributes of its products and to persuade them to buy and repeat-purchase those products. The promotional mix is made up of ADVERTISING, SALES PROMOTION, PERSONAL SELLING, DIRECT MARKETING and INTERNET MARKETING, PUBLIC RELATIONS.

Advertising involves the placement of ADVERTISEMENTS in the MEDIA (commercial television, newspapers, websites etc); *sales promotion* embraces such things as money-off-packs and free trial samples; *personal selling* involves visits by a firm's SALES REPRESENTATIVES to prospective customers; *direct marketing* involves the acquisition and retention of customers without the use of an intermediary; *internet marketing* refers to the use of the INTERNET to gain and keep customers; *public relations* is aimed at promoting the COMPANY'S IMAGE in general to establish a favourable public attitude towards the firm and its products.

In practice, most firms will use a combination of these methods to sell their products, varying the mix according to the product and buyer characteristics of a particular MARKET or MARKET SEGMENT. For example, low-price, frequently-bought consumer goods like tea are mostly promoted by mass media advertising and sales promotions, while high-price industrial or consumer goods such as cars are promoted largely by personal selling. See FOUR P'S OF MARKETING.

promotional price see PRICE PROMOTION.

promotional sample a free pack of a product given to prospective consumers to encourage them to try and subsequently to purchase the product. See SALES PROMOTION.

promotion-line union see TRADE UNION.

proof of purchase a receipt which is given by the seller of a product to a buyer at the time of purchase, which the buyer can then use to claim a refund, product exchange or repair under GUARANTEE conditions (see SALE OF GOODS ACT 1979). In the case of special offers and promotions, detachable vouchers or labels incorporated in the product packaging may be used as proof of purchase and entitlement to the offer or promotion (see SALES PROMOTION).

proprietor the owner of a business. See SOLE PROPRIETORSHIP, PARTNERSHIP, JOINT-STOCK COMPANY.

prospect an individual or organization who is a possible buyer of a product.

prospectus a document prepared by a JOINT-STOCK COMPANY as an invitation to the public to subscribe for shares in the company. The prospectus gives details of the company's past trading record, current capital structure and borrowings. Prospectuses are published as the first stage of an *offer for sale* of shares. See SHARE ISSUE.

protectionism the measures taken by a country to protect certain of its domestic industries from foreign competition and, on occasion, to assist the country's balance of payments. See TARIFF, QUOTA, DUMPING, LOCAL CONTENT RULES, SUBSIDIES, FREE TRADE, WORLD TRADE ORGANIZATION.

prototype an early, pre-market, model of a product which is being developed. Small numbers of prototypes of new products are often constructed to aid the process of testing the performance and consumer acceptability of the product prior to deciding whether or not to engage in full-scale commercial production and marketing of the product. See NEW PRODUCT DEVELOPMENT.

provision the sums charged in DOUBLE ENTRY ACCOUNTS against a firm's PROFITS in anticipation of costs which are likely to arise in the future. The most common general provision made by firms is the provision for DOUBTFUL DEBTS which is established in anticipation of some customers not paying what they owe. In addition, a firm may make a specific provision against, say, a damages claim which is presently not yet settled. Provisions are aimed at trying to ensure that profits are not overstated by making sure that all a firm's costs are charged, even those whose precise amount is not yet certain. See REVALUATION PROVISION, DEFERRED TAX.

proxy an authorization to a person or firm to act in place of another. During a JOINT-STOCK COMPANY'S ANNUAL GENERAL MEETING, for example, a SHAREHOLDER may be unable to attend and vote on items contained in the agenda. The shareholder may therefore give written authorization for someone else to attend and vote at the meeting in his stead. A shareholder's proxy is frequently given to the incumbent board of directors to vote with as they think fit, hence the term 'proxy vote'.

PRP see PROFIT-RELATED PAY.

prudence see ACCOUNTING PRINCIPLES.

PSBR see PUBLIC SECTOR BORROWING REQUIREMENT.

psychographic segmentation grouping people according to their lifestyle and personality characteristics. See MARKET SEGMENTATION.

psychological pricing an approach to PRICING which pays particular attention to the effect which a product's PRICE has upon consumers' perceptions of the product. This has a number of dimensions, including:

(a) the charging of very high prices for certain (generally high-quality) consumer products to convey an impression of product exclusiveness. High prices may appeal to particular high-income customers who wish to possess the product as a status symbol ('conspicuous consumption');

(b) the charging of high prices for technologically sophisticated consumer products in order to convey an impression of superior product quality and performance.

This may play an important part in the buying decision when consumers are ignorant about the comparative properties of *the* brands of the product facing them, and thus use price as an indicator of quality;

(c) the charging of a price for a product which is just below a 'round figure' threshold price (for example 99 pence rather than £1) so as to create an impression that the product's price is *considerably* below the threshold;

(d) the charging of relatively low prices for frequently purchased and familiar products so as to create or reinforce an impression of value for money.

psychological test a test of an individual's level of achievement or aptitude. There are two main types of test:

(a) *achievement test:* this tests an individual's acquired knowledge and skills, for example a driving test;

(b) *aptitude test:* this tests fundamental abilities or aptitudes, such as mental ability (for example, an intelligence test) or perceptual abilities.

Whereas (a) is used to determine what skills an individual already possesses, the purpose of (b) is to discover his or her capacity to acquire new skills in future. Tests of both types are often utilized in RECRUITMENT AND SELECTION. Achievement tests can be used to verify information that a candidate has submitted in his application, and aptitude tests can be used to gauge how individuals will respond to new challenges and hence to provide a degree of prediction of future work performance. See PERSONALITY INVENTORY.

psychometric testing see PERSONALITY INVENTORY, PSYCHOLOGICAL TEST.

public interest a yardstick used in the application of COMPETITION POLICY in the UK to judge whether or not a particular action or practice pursued by a supplier of a product, or a change in the structure of a market by, for example, MERGER or TAKEOVER, is 'good' or 'bad' in terms of its effects on efficiency and the interests of consumers.

public limited company (Plc) see JOINT-STOCK COMPANY.

public opinion see COMPANY IMAGE, PUBLIC RELATIONS.

public relations (PR) a general means of promoting a business's COMPANY IMAGE with a view to encouraging customers to buy its products and investors to buy its shares, as well, for example, as influencing government policies on issues relevant to the company. Companies often appoint a PR officer to liase with the MEDIA in providing them with information and news about the company's activities and its record on such matters as CONSUMER PROTECTION and environmental pollution. Sponsorship of sport and the arts, etc. represents an indirect way of building up customer goodwill towards the company's products. See PROMOTIONAL MIX.

public sector borrowing requirement (PSBR) the amount of money the government requires to borrow in order to finance a budget deficit (see BUDGET (GOVERNMENT)). The government can finance the PSBR in two basic ways:

(a) by the issue of short-dated TREASURY BILLS which are purchased in the main by DISCOUNT HOUSES and COMMERCIAL BANKS;

(b) by the issue of long-dated government BONDS which are purchased by INSTITUTIONAL INVESTORS (pension funds etc.) and by the general public.

How the government varies the borrowing between these two categories has an important effect on the level (and distribution) of spending in the economy. The issue of Treasury Bills increases the 'liquidity base' of the banking system, enabling it to make more credit available (i.e. it increases the MONEY SUPPLY and thus raises spending in the economy); by contrast, the issue of bonds reduces the liquidity base of the banking system as buyers of bonds run down their bank deposits to purchase them (i.e. it reduces the money supply and availability of credit, serving to decrease spending in the economy). See ECONOMIC POLICY, FISCAL POLICY, MONETARY POLICY.

public utility an undertaking which provides a certain basic good or service such as gas, electricity or telecommunications. In some countries public utilities are mainly owned by the State, while in others they are privately owned but subject to regulation by the government. See RATE OF RETURN REGULATION, NATIONALIZATION VERSUS PRIVATIZATION.

published accounts see ANNUAL REPORT AND ACCOUNTS.

'pull' strategy a manufacturing and marketing approach which emphasizes 'pulling' products through the DISTRIBUTION CHANNELS by spending on ADVERTISING and consumer promotions (free samples etc.) to increase the final demand for the products, so that consumers' demand encourages wholesalers and retailers to stock it.

In practice, SALES PROMOTIONS campaigns usually use trade promotions as well to encourage wholesalers and retailers to 'push' the product. See 'PUSH' STRATEGY.

punishment-centred bureaucracy see BUREAUCRACY.

purchaser-provider split an arrangement under which the unified management system of an organization is split into *purchasers* who buy goods or services and *providers* who supply goods or services. The purchaser-provider split serves to create an INTERNAL MARKET in which the true costs of making goods or services are easier to identify and incentives to reduce costs are provided. Purchase-provider splits were introduced in the UK health service in the 1980s. See NEW PUBLIC MANAGEMENT, COMPETITIVE TENDERING.

purchases day book see JOURNAL OR DAY BOOK, ACCOUNTING.

purchases journal see JOURNAL OR DAY BOOK, ACCOUNTING.

purchases ledger see LEDGER, ACCOUNTING.

purchasing the business function which is involved in procuring raw materials, components, finished goods and capital equipment, ordering and acquiring supplies of these items at competitive prices. Purchasing is charged with the task of maintaining adequate STOCKS of raw materials, components or finished goods, and placing orders to top up stocks as necessary. This involves seeking out and evaluating suppliers in terms of the quality of their offerings, reliability, delivery times and after-sales service, as well as prices. For standard commodities, industrial buyers will generally buy largely on price, seeking quotations or tenders from suppliers. The buyer can choose to place large orders with just one or two suppliers to secure BULK-BUYING price discounts or he or she may choose to spread orders among several suppliers to diversify supplies and avoid the risk of disruption to production if a single supplier defaults. Finally, industrial buyers need to keep up to date with materials and product prices and new materials becoming available in order to provide intelligence to production and marketing colleagues. See BUYING PROCESS, BUYING CENTRE, MATERIALS MANAGEMENT, JUST IN TIME (JIT) SYSTEM, APPROVED SUPPLIER, NATIONAL ACCOUNT, DECENTRALIZED PURCHASING, SOURCING. See also FOUR O'S OF PURCHASING.

purchasing power the amount of goods and services which can be purchased by a specified sum of money, *given* the prices of those goods and services. The greater the quantity of products which can be bought with, say, £20, the greater is the purchasing power of that sum of money. If prices go up (INFLATION), however, then purchasing power will fall. What is important for people and business is the long-run relationship of prices and the amount of money they have available to spend. If prices double, for example, but because people's wages are INDEX-LINKED, (i.e. related to a PRICE INDEX), wages also double, then purchasing power remains unchanged.

purchasing power parity the tendency for the EXCHANGE RATE between the currencies of two countries to reflect long-term differences in the INFLATION rates of these countries under a FLOATING EXCHANGE RATE SYSTEM. Thus, for example, if the inflation rate in country A were 10% per annum and that of country B 6% per annum, then in order to maintain parity between the PURCHASING POWER of the two currencies, country A's currency would have to depreciate by 4% against country B's currency.

'push' strategy a manufacturing and marketing approach which emphasizes 'pushing' a firm's products into wholesale and retail outlets using trade promotions (PROMOTIONAL ALLOWANCES etc.) to persuade WHOLESALERS and RETAILERS to stock and promote a product.

In practice, SALES PROMOTION campaigns usually use consumer promotions and ADVERTISING as well, in order to encourage consumers to demand the product and to 'pull' it through the distribution system. See 'PULL' STRATEGY.

put option see OPTION.

pyramid selling a form of MULTI-LEVEL MARKETING which involves a 'pyramid' of sales persons who recruit other people thus creating an expanding chain of sales persons.

reduce the payment or the time allowed per unit of output if output were to exceed initial expectations. By keeping output below the possible maximum, workers deter management from *decreasing* payment rates, or time allowed, and may even prompt them to *increase* them so as to stimulate greater effort on the workers' part. See GOLDBRICKING.

quotation 1 the price and terms on which a firm is prepared to supply a good or service. Quotations often include detailed technical specifications of the product to be supplied, delivery dates and credit terms. Several suppliers may quote for a contract put out to TENDER by the purchaser.

2 the price at which a MARKET MAKER is prepared to buy or sell a FINANCIAL SECURITY (STOCKS. SHARES etc.) or FOREIGN CURRENCY. Market makers often quote two prices, the price at which they are prepared to *buy* a financial security or currency and the price at which they are prepared to *sell* the security or currency.

3 permission from a STOCK MARKET's regulatory authority for a company's shares to be traded 'in that market. See LISTED COMPANY.

quoted company a public limited JOINT-STOCK COMPANY (Plc) whose shares are traded either on the main STOCK MARKET or related secondary markets such as the UNLISTED SECURITIES MARKET. See LISTED COMPANY.

quoted investments investments in FINANCIAL SECURITIES such as SHARES and DEBENTURES which are 'quoted' on a STOCK MARKET. Where a company holds such quoted investments they will be shown in its BALANCE SHEET at their purchase price with a supplementary note showing their current market value. See TRADE INVESTMENT.

r

Race Relations Act 1976 see DISCRIMINATION.

RAM (Random Access Memory) a COMPUTER memory device from which data can be read and on to which data can be written. The contents of such memory can be added to, or erased, by an operator. RAM is incorporated in microchips which allow the operative access to any part of the memory without having to move sequentially through the contents of the memory from start to finish.

R & D see RESEARCH AND DEVELOPMENT.

Random Access Memory see RAM.

rate fixer the person responsible for establishing the WAGE RATE per unit of output or the payment per time saved in PIECEWORK systems of wage payment.

rate of exchange see EXCHANGE RATE.

rate of interest see INTEREST RATE.

rate of pay see WAGE RATE.

rate of return the PROFITS earned by a business, measured as a percentage of the ASSETS employed in the business. See RETURN ON CAPITAL EMPLOYED.

rate of return regulation the control of a firm's or industry's level of profitability by the stipulation of maximum-permitted RATES OF RETURN ON CAPITAL EMPLOYED or investment. Such regulation is undertaken by government agencies to prevent the charging of 'excessive' prices by private sector monopolies and public utilities. See COMPETITION POLICY.

rates see UNIFORM BUSINESS RATE, COMMUNITY CHARGE.

ratio analysis the calculation and use of ACCOUNTING RATIOS to analyse the trading performance, liquidity and financial security of a company over time and by comparison with other firms. See INTERFIRM COMPARISON.

rational (approach to strategy) see BUSINESS POLICY.

rationalization the restructuring of a firm or industry to enable it to become more efficient or to reduce OVERCAPACITY. In some cases this may involve the firm in closing high-cost plant and concentrating production in larger, more modern plants; or it may involve the streamlining of a firm's organizational structure and reducing overhead costs. In the context of an industry, rationalization may require firms to merge, or inefficient firms to leave the industry, leading to higher levels of MARKET CONCENTRATION. See PRODUCT RATIONALIZATION. DIVESTMENT.

rational–legal authority see AUTHORITY.

raw materials basic materials such as iron ore, bauxite, wheat and coffee, which are converted into finished goods or components in the PRODUCTION process. See DIRECT MATERIALS, VALUE ADDED.

RDA see REGIONAL DEVELOPMENT AUTHORITY.

Read Only Memory see ROM.

real accounts ACCOUNTS OF LEDGER records that deal with assets and liabilities, for example the asset ledger. Assets and liabilities appearing in the real accounts are summarized periodically in the BALANCE SHEET. Contrast with NOMINAL ACCOUNT.

real values the value of an asset, wage, profit, etc. adjusted for changes in the level of prices (particularly INFLATION) over time; that is, expressing the value in terms of *constant* prices not current money prices. Thus, while workers' money wages may have increased due to inflation, giving the appearance that they are now better off, their real wage may well have remained the same; i.e. if wages go up at exactly the same rate as inflation, the PURCHASING POWER of that wage (the real wage) remains unchanged; if money wages go up by less than the rate of inflation then real wages will fall. See INFLATION ACCOUNTING. Compare with NOMINAL VALUES.

recall test see ADVERTISING EFFECTIVENESS TEST.

receipts and payments account a simplified form of PROFIT AND LOSS ACCOUNT which focuses upon cash received and cash paid over an accounting period, ignoring credit transactions, prepayments, accruals and depreciation.

receiver see INSOLVENCY, LIQUIDATION.

recession see BUSINESS CYCLE.

recognition test see ADVERTISING EFFECTIVENESS TESTS.

Recognized Investment Exchange (RIE) a body validated by the FINANCIAL SERVICES ACT 1986 as meeting the regulatory requirements of the Act in respect of dealings in financial securities and commodities.

Recognized Professional Body a professional body such as the Chartered Accountants of England and Wales, which is recognized as a self-regulating organization for maintaining standards of good business practice under the terms of the UK FINANCIAL SERVICES ACT 1986.

recommended resale price the stipulation by a manufacturer of a 'suggested' retail selling PRICE for his product. Suppliers have no powers legally to enforce such prices and the actual prices paid by consumers are usually much lower than those recommended, depending on the intensity of price competition between retailers. Retailers find the 'recommended price' tag a useful benchmark on which to base special offers and clearance sale prices. See RESALE PRICE MAINTENANCE, PRICE MARKING (BARGAIN OFFERS) ORDER 1979.

recovery see BUSINESS CYCLE.

recovery rate see ABSORPTION RATE.

recruitment agency see RECRUITMENT AND SELECTION, EMPLOYMENT AGENCY.

recruitment and selection

The process of filling JOB vacancies in an organization by hiring new employees. It is a recurring process for most organizations because new entrants will be needed to replace those leaving (see LABOUR TURNOVER). The challenge is to find and employ people with skills, knowledge and experience which match those required by the organization, and whose future performance will be conducive to the good of the organization. This latter is especially problematic since it is difficult to predict future performance on the basis of the past, and when much of the information flow during the recruitment and selection process is controlled by the job applicant. Many organizations now use quite sophisticated methods to deal with these issues, especially in the selection of managerial employees. Equally, in many cases recruitment and selection is handled in a haphazard way.

There are a number of stages to recruitment and selection, each of which should ideally be carefully managed by organizations.

(a) Creation of a *job specification*, i.e. the main characteristics of a job. Ideally this should be the result of careful JOB ANALYSIS;

(b) Creation of a *person specification*, i.e. the personal characteristics that match the requirements of the job specification. Two checklists are often used to guide recruiters here:

Fraser's Five-Fold Grading System

(i) impact upon others (appearance etc.)

(ii) qualifications

(iii) innate abilities

(iv) motivation

(v) adjustment (i.e. ability to respond positively in new situations).

Rodger's Seven-Point Plan

(i) physical makeup

(ii) attainments

(iii) general intelligence

(iv) special aptitudes

(v) interests

(vi) disposition

(vii) circumstances

(c) *recruitment*, i.e. the search for suitable applicants, using advertising, executive search agencies, etc. (see EMPLOYMENT AGENCY);

(d) *screening*, i.e. scrutiny of applications to determine which candidates appear to be capable of filling the post;

(e) *selection*, i.e. choosing the person to be employed. This can be the most difficult stage of the process for the reasons outlined above. The selection interview is the most favoured method but it is not without its problems, chiefly interviewer bias and (often) incompetence. PSYCHOLOGICAL TESTS and PERSONALITY INVENTORIES to determine abilities and to construct character profiles are being increasingly employed as a supplement to the interview, with the aim of uncovering the 'real' nature of the applicant in an apparently objective way. Some organizations also make use of the 'assessment centre'– a range of tests to determine suitability, including observation of candidates in complex decision-making and leadership situations.

The character of all stages of the selection and recruitment process can be influenced by the opinions of those operating it in such a way that DISCRIMINATION can occur. Legislation now prohibits explicit race or sex discrimination. However, members of disadvantaged groups may still be reluctant to apply for many types of job. To tackle this, many organizations now style themselves as 'equal opportunities employers' in their recruitment material. See HUMAN RESOURCE MANAGEMENT, GLASS CEILING.

rectification costs the cost of additional work which has to be performed in order to bring defective or damaged components or products up to standard. See QUALITY CONTROL.

recurrent cash flows transactions which are expected to recur in each accounting period, eg, taxation payments. See RELEVANT CASH FLOWS.

recycling the reprocessing of materials, containers and goods which would otherwise have been thrown away, to be used in the manufacture of some other product; for example the pulping of old newspapers to produce egg boxes and writing paper, and the melting down of used metal drinks cans to make new containers.

Recycling can help businesses keep their production costs down since materials which are recycled are generally less expensive than primary raw materials, and it helps the economy by conserving scarce natural resources and saving on energy costs: recycling paper preserves forests and is estimated to result in a 70% saving of energy compared to processing new timber. Recycling also helps control environmental POLLUTION by reducing the need for waste dumps.

redeemable financial security a financial security such as a DEBENTURE, PREFERENCE SHARE OF BOND issued for a fixed period of time and repayable on maturity.

Sometimes the borrowing company arranges debentures or loans which are repayable at the option of the company within certain time limits, the earliest and latest repayment dates being set out in the debenture or loan contract.

redemption date *or* **maturity date** the repayment date of a REDEEMABLE FINANCIAL SECURITY.

redemption yield see YIELD.

rediscounting the secondary purchase and sale of BILLS OF EXCHANGE, TREASURY BILLS and BONDS between their original issue and final redemption. When a bill of exchange is first issued it is usually purchased (i.e. 'discounted') by a DISCOUNT HOUSE. The discount house may hold on to the bill until maturity, or it may choose to on-sell it to another discount house, in which case the bill is then 'rediscounted'.

For example, if a bill with a face value of £1,000 redeemable in one year's time is sold initially for £900 (giving a £100 discount on its formal redemption value), then it might be resold or rediscounted for £950 after six months. See DISCOUNT, DISCOUNT MARKET.

red tape rules which stipulate in great detail how the members of an organization should carry out their duties, and which are seen to inhibit flexibility and detract from effectiveness. See BUREAUCRACY, GOAL DISPLACEMENT.

reducing balance depreciation see DEPRECIATION.

redundancy the termination of an individual's employment when the employer ceases trading or the job ceases to be required because of rationalization, change of product etc. When an employer decides to make part or all of a workforce redundant the European Collective Redundancies Directive requires that the workforce be consulted on the extent, distribution and rationale for redundancy. Advance notice must be given with the extent of this dictated by the number of planned redundancies. Consultation must take place with union representatives, specially elected employee representatives where a TRADE UNION is not present, or (exceptionally) directly with all employees.

Employees with more than two years' service are statutorily entitled to a redundancy or severance payment. For adult employees under 40 this is one week's pay for each year of service, for those of 40 plus it is one and a half week's pay for each year up to a maximum of twenty years. Many employers choose to make payments substantially above the statutory level (in some public sector organizations there are special schemes to support this) to sweeten the pill of redundancy.

Selection of employees for redundancy can be a traumatic process and, if the organization is to continue trading, needs to be conducted fairly if the morale of those remaining is not to be irretrievably dented. A favoured option is to seek voluntary recruits for redundancy among older employees, backed up by generous redundancy payments and possibly early access to pension benefits. An alternative method is 'last-in–first-out' (LIFO), i.e. those with shorter service are selected for redundancy. Whilst superficially fair the problem with this is that it potentially removes those young workers who have most to offer the organization in the long term.

Whatever the method chosen, redundancy is undoubtedly a distressing process for all those involved. Some more progressive organizations offer counselling services to aid adjustment and to rebuild confidence. Others, especially where very large numbers have been made redundant, have set up employment agencies in an attempt to find alternative work. Although trade unions sometimes declare their intention to fight redundancies, they and their members are generally unwilling to take any form of industrial action since this could imperil redundancy payments. Unions, therefore, usually come to devote their efforts to ensuring that individuals are treated fairly by those handling the redundancy process.

reference group a social group with which an individual identifies or to membership of which he or she aspires. The activities and values of the reference group provide a basis for the individual's beliefs and lifestyles. For example, young people often identify with rock stars.

The need to imitate the lifestyle of such idols can be exploited in MARKETING. Promotional material such as advertisements may feature these heroes, thereby suggesting that if consumers purchase a particular product they will be like their chosen reference group, and be viewed as such by others.

refusal to supply a business practice whereby a supplier acts to cut off supplies of his product to a distributor, either because the distributor has been found to be unsatisfactory in handling the product (i.e. failing to meet the terms of his CONTRACT), or as a means of coercing the distributor to accept such practices as EXCLUSIVE DEALING AND TIE-IN SALES. In the UK, a refusal to supply which is suspected of having detrimental effects on competition can be investigated by the OFFICE OF FAIR TRADING and the COMPETITION COMMISSION:

Regional Development Agency (RDA) a government body responsible for pursuing policies to achieve a combination of economic, social and environmental improvements in the regions of the UK (see REGIONAL POLICY). There are currently nine RDAs in England (North West, North East, Yorkshire and the Humber, West Midlands, East Midlands, East, South East, London and the South West) and one each covering Scotland, Wales and Northern Ireland. RDAs work closely with the local authorities and local businesses in their areas to foster industrial regeneration and expansion. See SMALL BUSINESS SCHEME, BUSINESS LINK, DEPARTMENT OF TRADE AND INDUSTRY.

regional policy

A policy concerned with promoting a balanced distribution of industrial activity, employment and wealth as between the various geographical areas of a country. The main thrust of regional policy in most countries is to ensure a fairly even spread of industry around the regions, so as to rectify or prevent economic decline, to rectify or prevent economic decline, UNEMPLOYMENT and low levels of PER CAPITA INCOME in some regions while avoiding congestion problems in more prosperous ones. A particular emphasis of regional policy is the regeneration of impoverished regions by encouraging new firms and industries to locate and invest in these areas (the so-called 'inward investment' approach to the regional problem). The rationale behind this approach is that the problems of the depressed areas stem largely from overspecialization in industries which have gone into decline (for example coalmining in South Wales, shipbuilding in North East England) rather than from any fundamental economic disadvantage. Accordingly, what is required is a diversification of the industrial base of such areas so as to provide new employment opportunities which, in turn, by increasing spending in the region, will help to create further jobs in, for example, local component suppliers, retailing and financial services.

The 'inward investment' approach to regional policy is implemented in three main ways: the provision of financial inducements (investment grants, tax and rent relief etc.) to firms prepared to locate in designated *assisted areas* to offset investment costs, together with other payments to cover, for example, retraining expenses; the use of physical controls on factory and office buildings to prevent firms from expanding in non-designated areas; investment by the government in improved road and rail communications and local amenities to increase the general attractiveness of these regions to potential investors. Critics of this approach to regional policy argue that directing firms to locate in areas which they might not otherwise have chosen to go to and subsidizing these activities might impair their efficiency. However, there is little evidence to suggest that this has been the case.

A possible alternative approach, that of encouraging labour migration out of depressed regions, has not found favour; not only does it tend to accentuate the problems of the depressed areas themselves (loss of skilled workers, reduced local spending etc.), but also it creates added difficulties for 'receiving areas', particularly if they are already overburdened with respect to housing, schools etc.

UK regional policy has as its main aim the reduction of disparities in unemployment between the regions and also the regeneration of smaller localities suffering particularly acute unemployment problems. To this end the government, through the DEPARTMENT OF TRADE AND INDUSTRY'S (DTI), SMALL BUSINESS SERVICE (SBS), the BUSINESS LINK network and the REGIONAL DEVELOPMENT AGENCIES (RDA) offers financial aid and other services to firms located in, or who are prepared to establish new plants and offices in, the areas designated as 'assisted areas'. Until recently the main areas qualifying for support were the *development areas* (large areas suffering from very high levels of unemployment, such as the North East of England); *intermediate areas* (smaller areas suffering from more moderate levels of unemployment, such as parts of South Yorkshire); *enterprise zones* (particular small areas suffering acute unemployment problems, such as Merseyside). These have now (2000) been replaced by the EUROPEAN UNION (EU) 'assisted areas' framework which is aimed at establishing a comparable regional aid system across all 15 EU member states. While unemployment remains an important consideration, under EU policy the main criteria for designating an assisted area is a (GDP) PER CAPITA INCOME level which is below 75% of the EU average.

In the UK the main assisted areas are 'Tier 1' areas (mainly former 'development areas') and 'Tier 2' areas (mainly former 'intermediate areas' and 'enterprise zones'). The government has proposed a number of areas for assistance (still under review by the European Commission). Proposed Tier 1 areas are Cornwall and the Scilly Isles, Merseyside, South Yorkshire, West Wales and the Valleys, together with the whole of Northern Ireland. Proposed Tier 2 areas totalling some 1550 *smaller localities* are 79 from the East of England region; 133 from the East Midland region; 44 from the London region; 228 from the North East region; 144 from the North West region; 440 from Scotland; 129 from the South East region; 20 from the South West region; 51 from Wales; 197 from the West Midlands region and 91 from the Yorkshire and Humber region. Regarding Tier 2 submissions, the European Commission's preferred policy is to support 'clusters' of adjacent localities providing sufficient 'critical mass' for industrial development rather than isolated localities.

In addition, a 'Tier 3' of assisted areas has been designated which covers areas of 'special need' (for example, coal fields and rural development areas).

The application of the new Tier structures is subject to an overall population requirement; specifically for any country the number of persons residing in the assisted areas should not exceed more than 28.7% of the total population of the country.

Financial aid in the assisted areas is mainly in the form of *Regional Selective Assistance* (cash grants.)

This is potentially available to *all* firms undertaking investments in the development and intermediate areas. Such aid, however, is discretionary – 'selectivity' requires that the investment project should have a good chance of paying its way, that assistance is vital for the project to go ahead (for example, without the grant the project could not go ahead at all, or only on a smaller scale), and that the project should contribute to both the regional and the national economy. A project grant is based on the fixed capital costs of a project and the number of jobs it is expected to create or safeguard. The amount of grant is negotiated for the minimum necessary for the project to go ahead on the basis proposed, up to a maximum ceiling of 30% of the project cost. This is obviously open to manipulation, but has been useful in enabling the development areas to attract foreign firms into the UK. It was the availability of a regional assistance grant that ensured the location of the Nissan car assembly plant in Washington, Tyne and Wear.

In addition, other grants and services are available to small firms including the ENTERPRISE GRANT SCHEME and training and consultancy through the SBS and Business Link.

Regional assistance is also available through the following:

a number of EU institutions including the European Social Fund, the

European Investment Bank, the European Coal and Steel Community, and, in particular, the European Regional Development Fund (ERDF). The ERDF has provided cash grants for a broad spectrum of projects in areas of industrial decline, ranging from tourism infrastructure in Wales to a regional airport in Lorraine. Support for such projects remains important, but increasingly the emphasis has shifted towards assisting the least developed areas of the Union, – Greece, Portugal and parts of Ireland, Spain and Italy. In these areas the ERDF supports infrastructure projects such as roads, railways, electricity and gas distribution, and provides funds to modernize traditional industries and establish new ones.

The European Investment Bank provides loans for schemes and investment projects of regional significance as well as projects considered to be beneficial in promoting the economic integration of the Union; while the European Coal and Steel Community provides loans to projects in areas specifically suffering job losses from the rundown of the coal and steel industries. Loans available from these two institutions are for up to half the fixed asset costs of the project.

regional selective assistance see REGIONAL POLICY.

Regional Technology Centres see TECHNOLOGY TRANSFER.

registered office the official address of a JOINT-STOCK COMPANY to which all official correspondence must be sent.

registered share capital see AUTHORIZED SHARE CAPITAL.

register of charges a record of the claims on a JOINT-STOCK COMPANY's assets (MORTGAGES. DEBENTURES etc.), which is kept at the company's head office with the COMPANY REGISTRAR for inspection by shareholders and creditors.

Registrar see COMPANY REGISTRAR, REGISTRAR OF COMPANIES.

Registrar of Companies the official (responsible to the DEPARTMENT OF TRADE AND INDUSTRY) who maintains a record of all JOINT-STOCK COMPANIES operating in the UK. All joint-stock companies must lodge a copy of their MEMORANDUM OF ASSOCIATION and ARTICLES OF ASSOCIATION with the Registrar at Companies House when they are first formed, and larger companies must continue to file their ANNUAL RETURN, ANNUAL REPORT AND ACCOUNTS and a REGISTER OF CHARGES on their assets with the Registrar each year. Any potential lender or investor can inspect the company records lodged with the Registrar in order to gain background information about a particular company.

Registrar of Friendly Societies the official (responsible to the DEPARTMENT OF TRADE AND INDUSTRY) who maintains a record of all FRIENDLY SOCIETIES in the UK and supervizes their activities.

registration fee a charge made by a JOINT-STOCK COMPANY for recording the transfer of ownership of STOCKS and SHARES.

regression analysis a statistical technique for estimating the equation which best fits sets of observations of dependent variables and independent variables, so generating the best estimate of the true underlying relationship between these variables. From this estimated equation it is then possible to forecast what the (unknown) dependent variable will be for a given value of the (known) independent variable.

Regression analysis is used in SALES FORECASTING to estimate trend lines in time series analysis and causal links with variables which affect sales; and in ECONOMETRICS to measure relationships between economic variables.

regulation the control of economic activities by the government or some other regulatory body, for example an industry trade association. Regulation can include PRICE CONTROLS to regulate inflation; FOREIGN EXCHANGE CONTROLS to regulate currency flows; and COMPETITION POLICY to regulate the operation of particular markets. More specific regulation may be imposed upon individual industries or activities, for example price control of denationalized industries (e.g. Oftel, which regulates telecommunication prices and Ofgas which regulates gas prices in the UK); and the regulation of financial services by the BANK OF ENGLAND and the FINANCIAL SERVICES AUTHORITY. See DEREGULATION, RATE OF RETURN REGULATION.

reinforcement advertising *or* **reminder advertising** ADVERTISEMENTS which seek to remind and 'reassure' established buyers of a product of the product's merits and values to them, thereby helping to reinforce BRAND LOYALTY.

reinsurance see INSURANCE COMPANY.

related company see ASSOCIATED COMPANY.

relationship chart (REL chart) a means of depicting the pattern and extent of inter-departmental movement of items within a factory. REL or cross charts are used to collect information about relationships between factory departments, identifying the numbers of items per day moved from each department and which department receives them. This information can be used to establish the best relative location for each department, thus assisting in planning FACTORY LAYOUT.

relativities any comparisons between the WAGES or SALARIES of workers in the same firm, the same industry, or between different industries. Such relativities reflect differences in training requirements, skill levels and responsibilities. See PAY DIFFERENTIAL.

relaxation allowance see ALLOWANCES.

REL chart see RELATIONSHIP CHART.

relevant cash flows the cash inflows or outflows which occur as a result of a project will be included as the relevant (also called incremental) cash flows. For example, specific fixed costs for a project are a relevant cost because they only have to be paid if the project goes ahead. Those costs which have to be paid out whether or not the project goes ahead are irrelevant. The relevant cash flows are the cash flows which should be used for capital investment appraisal purposes.

reliability the extent to which a product fulfils its function over a period of time.

The reliability of a product depends upon its design characteristics, the quality of materials and components embodied within it and the care with which it is made and assembled.

A product's reliability is an important part of its performance in use and thus affects the appeal of the product to customers and the likelihood of their buying it. See BRAND LOYALTY. See QUALITY CONTROL, FAILURE RATE CURVE, PARALLEL SYSTEM.

reminder advertising see REINFORCEMENT ADVERTISING.

remuneration the PAY or reward to workers and managers for their labour services, in the form of WAGES, SALARIES and bonuses.

remuneration per employee an accounting ratio which is used to assess the average remuneration of the labour force. It is computed by dividing the total wages and salaries paid to employees for the accounting period by the average number of employees on the payroll during the period.

rent the periodic payments made to the owners of ASSETS (for example, household and industrial premises, car hire) for the use of these assets. See LEASE, LEASING, LEASEBACK, INCOME.

renunciation form a form attached to the ALLOTMENT letter in respect of a new SHARE ISSUE or a RIGHTS ISSUE to existing shareholders, enabling a shareholder to sell his or her shares, or giving the right to additional shares in the period before receiving the SHARE CERTIFICATE.

reorder level a predetermined level for a particular item to which STOCKS must fall before an order for more of the item is placed. In fixing the reorder level, account has to be taken of the anticipated usage of the item during the reorder period. See STOCK CONTROL.

reorder point the time at which an order is placed for new STOCK. See STOCK CONTROL.

reorder point system see FIXED INTERVAL REORDER SYSTEM, STOCK CONTROL.

repeat purchases further purchases of a product by a BUYER who, after having tried the product, is sufficiently satisfied with it to make additional purchases. See BRAND LOYALTY.

replacement cost the cost of replacing a FIXED ASSET (such as an item of machinery) or STOCK. Unlike HISTORIC COST – the original cost of acquiring an asset – replacement cost makes due allowance for the effects of INFLATION in increasing asset prices over time. Prudence requires that stocks are valued in a company's accounts at historic or replacement cost, whichever is the lower. See also REVALUATION PROVISION, INFLATION ACCOUNTING, APPRECIATION, definition 1.

replacement investment the INVESTMENT that is undertaken to replace a firm's plant and equipment which has become worn out or obsolete.

replacement parts product PARTS and COMPONENTS which are stocked by suppliers of capital goods and consumer durables in anticipation of component failures. The comprehensiveness of a supplier's component stocks is an important part of his AFTER-SALES SERVICE, ORIGINAL EQUIPMENT.

Repo rate of interest the INTEREST RATE charged by the BANK OF ENGLAND on TREASURY BILLS to buyers (mainly the DISCOUNT MARKET houses) when they repurchase new bills to replace maturing bills. See MONETARY POLICY COMMITTEE.

repositioning changing a BRAND's design, physical properties or the identity it projects to alter the 'position' of the brand in a market. See MARKET POSITIONING.

representative bureaucracy see BUREAUCRACY.

resale price maintenance (rpm) a business practice whereby a supplier stipulates the PRICE at which his product is to be sold by retailers. By establishing a *uniform* retail price (that is, by preventing price cutting) the supplier may aim to ensure that his product is available through most retail outlets, as well as preserving the price-quality image of the product. On the other hand, in the absence of rpm, price competition between retailers may well increase the sales of the product. Rpm is virtually prohibited by UK COMPETITION POLICY on the grounds that it deprives consumers of the benefit of lower prices and gives too much protection to inefficient retailers. See OFFICE OF FAIR TRADING, RECOMMENDED RESALE PRICE, RESALE PRICES ACTS (1964, 1976).

Resale Prices Acts (1964, 1976) a body of UK legislation providing for the control of RESALE PRICE MAINTENANCE by suppliers of a product. The Acts make the practice of rpm illegal unless it is specifically exempted by the OFFICE OF FAIR TRADING, usually after investigation by the Restrictive Practices Court (now the COMPETITION COMMISSION). Under the Acts, suppliers must satisfy the Court that not only does rpm benefit buyers in one or more specified ways (for example through greater convenience, or the provision of after-sales services) but that, *on balance*, these benefits are greater than any detriments (for example higher prices resulting from the elimination of retail price competition). The Acts make one concession to manufacturers, allowing them legally to prevent a retailer from pricing products as a LOSS LEADER (i.e. selling the product at below bought-in cost). See COMPETITION POLICY (UK), RECOMMENDED RESALE PRICE.

research and development (R&D) the commitment of resources by a firm to scientific research (both 'pure' and 'applied') and the refinement and modification of research ideas and prototypes aimed at the ultimate development of commercially viable processes and products. Thus, R&D is concerned both with *invention* (the act of discovering new methods and techniques of manufacture and new products) and *innovation* (the task of bringing these inventions to the marketplace).

Invention is often an inspirational act, and studies have shown that the large firm with its well-equipped laboratories and research teams has been no more successful than the individual inventor working alone with minimal facilities. Innovation, however, is usually very resource-intensive and the substantial capital outlays required to pursue development work, coupled with a high risk of failing to come up with a marketable product, tend to favour the larger business which is able to cross-subsidize R&D out of profits from existing products and also pool risks. Nonetheless, in many industries small innovative firms continue to coexist alongside large firms as in, for example, computer software and electronics.

From an organizational point of view, R&D activities may be performed within a separate department but with links with the main operating divisions of the firm. Alternatively, a more customized approach may be preferred, involving the decentralization of R&D and a close integration of R&D work with the firm's ongoing production and marketing operations.

In technologically dynamic industries the ability to develop new processes which lower supply costs and introduce innovative NEW PRODUCTS is often a critical factor in establishing COMPETITIVE ADVANTAGE over rival suppliers. Although it may be possible to buy in the latest technology and products from other firms through LICENSING deals, this may represent a poor substitute in competitive terms for the establishment of the firm's own internal pool of skills and experience; i.e. it is the difference between the firm being able to assume the position of technological leader in the industry and it becoming a 'me too' follower. See PATENT, DIVERSIFICATION, PRODUCT DIFFERENTIATION, SCIENCE PARK, SMART SCHEME, INDUSTRIAL POLICY, DEPARTMENT OF TRADE AND INDUSTRY, NEW-PRODUCT DEVELOPMENT, TECHNOLOGICAL FORECASTING.

reserves 1 any additional claims of company shareholders which reflect increases in the value of company ASSETS in the BALANCE

Balance Sheet at Dec XX	£	*Balance Sheet at Dec XY*	£	*Balance Sheet at Dec XZ*	£
Fixed Assets	10,000	Fixed Assets	13,000	Fixed Assets	13,000
Net Current Assets	3,000	Net Current Assets	4,000	Net Current Assets	2,000
Net Assets	13,000	Net Assets	17,000	Net Assets	15,000
Share Capital	10,000	Share Capital	10,000	Share Capital	10,000
Reserves	3,000	Reserves	7,000	Reserves	5,000
	13,000		17,000		15,000

Profit and Loss A/c yr end XY	£	*Profit and Loss A/c yr end XZ*	£
Sales	20,000	Sales	15,000
Costs	16,000	Costs	17,000
Profit	4,000		(2,000)

Fig. 75 **Reserves.** Reserves and profit.

SHEET. Revenue reserves arise when some after-tax profit is retained in the business to finance the acquisition of extra assets, rather than being paid out as DIVIDENDS (see Fig. 75). Capital reserves arise when company assets such as buildings are revalued to reflect their increased market value due to inflation. Reserves serve to increase SHAREHOLDERS' CAPITAL EMPLOYED in a company. See also RETAINED PROFITS, CAPITALIZATION ISSUE, RETENTIONS RATIO, APPRECIATION, definition 1, REVALUATION PROVISION, INFLATION ACCOUNTING.

2 the proportion of a bank's total assets which it keeps in the form of liquid assets.

3 monetary assets held by countries to finance balance of payments deficits. See INTERNATIONAL RESERVES.

residual value *or* **scrap value** the amount for which a FIXED ASSET can be sold at the end of its useful working life. The anticipated residual value is taken into account in calculating the amount of DEPRECIATION to be charged against PROFITS each year for the use of the asset during its life. In many cases residual values are assumed to be nil, given the small residual values of many fixed assets and the difficulties of forecasting what such values may be many years ahead.

resource an input (e.g. raw material, people, machinery) which is combined with other inputs to supply a good or service.

resource allocation see MARKET SYSTEM, ALLOCATION.

resource based (approach to strategy) see BUSINESS STRATEGY.

resource based theory of the firm a conceptual framework developed by business strategists which focuses on the key resources and capabilities possessed by a business which forms the basis of establishing a *sustainable* COMPETITIVE ADVANTAGE over rival suppliers. The resource-based theory postulates that all firms are different to a greater or lesser degree – in essence, a firm consists of a 'unique bundle of resources and capabilities'. If a firm is to develop a sustainable competitive advantage, it must be underpinned by resources and capabilities that are scarce and imperfectly mobile otherwise its advantages could be quickly replicated by other firms. Thus, firm-specific assets such as patents, brand names, human assets and systems that arise from a firm's experience become the basis of long-term competitive advantage. See MOBILITY BARRIERS, CRITICAL OR KEY SUCCESS FACTORS.

The theory is useful in a wider context since it can provide an explanation of why some firms decline and fail while others thrive and increase their market shares. The resource-based theory suggests that, looking at market processes dynamically, some firms may be more efficient than others because they possess better resources and capabilities than rivals; for example, their internal organizations may be 'leaner and fitter' and better able to adapt to changes in customer demands, they may possess superior product methods and techniques, and their ability to create and market new products may be greater than that of rivals. See BUSINESS GROWTH, VALUE CREATED MODEL, VALUE CHAIN ANALYSIS, COSTS DRIVERS, BENEFIT DRIVERS, DISTINCTIVE CAPABILITIES, CORE SKILLS OR COMPETENCY.

respondent conditioning see OCCUPATIONAL PSYCHOLOGY.

responsibility the obligation to carry out specified duties and tasks. For instance, someone who has responsibility for cash transactions in an ORGANIZATION is obliged either to carry them out himself or herself or to ensure that others do so. Failure to do so can result in action being taken against the person with responsibility for them. A common problem in organizations is that responsibilities are weakly defined: it is not fully clear who is responsible for what, with the result that certain functions are not carried out effectively. Similarly, some office holders are unwilling to take full responsibility for their actions and decisions. See ACCOUNTABILITY, AUTHORITY.

responsibility centre see COST CENTRE, REVENUE CENTRE, PROFIT CENTRE.

restrictive labour practice a practice, usually operated by a TRADE UNION or group of employees, which inhibits PRODUCTIVITY.

A union may insist that certain work tasks are undertaken by several employees when arguably a smaller number of workers would be sufficient to perform the tasks (*overmanning*); efficiency may be impaired by DEMARCATION LINES, laid down by different unions operating in the same plant, which serve to limit job interchangeability. See COLLECTIVE BARGAINING.

Restrictive Practices Court (RPC) the former regulatory body responsible, in part, for the implementation of UK COMPETITION POLICY covering RESTRICTIVE TRADE AGREEMENTS and RESALE PRICES.
The responsibilities of the RPC were taken over by the COMPETITION COMMISSION under the COMPETITION ACT, 1998.

restrictive trade agreement an agreement entered into by two or more suppliers of a product which contains restrictions relating to such matters as prices, terms and conditions of supply, restrictions on the type of persons or businesses supplied etc. Such agreements, while conferring advantages to those firms party to them (for example enabling them to charge higher prices), may serve to limit or suppress competition in a market to the detriment of other suppliers and to the buying public. Restrictive trade agreements are prohibited by the COMPETITION ACT, 1998. See COLLUSION, CARTEL, CONCERTED PRACTICE.

The term restrictive trade agreement can be used also for an agreement entered into between a supplier and his distributors if it contains restrictions (for example EXCLUSIVE DEALING provisions) which deprive other suppliers of access to distribution outlets. See COLLUSION, CARTEL, RESTRICTIVE TRADE PRACTICES ACTS (1956, 1968, 1976).

restrictive trade practice a commercial practice operated by a firm which has the effect of restricting, distorting or eliminating competition (especially if operated by a dominant firm) to the detriment of other suppliers and consumers. Examples of restrictive practices include EXCLUSIVE DEALING, REFUSAL TO SUPPLY, FULL LINE FORCING, TIE-IN SALES, AGGREGATED REBATES, RESALE PRICE MAINTENANCE and LOSS LEADING.

Under the COMPETITION ACT, 1998, exclusive dealing, full line forcing, tie-in sales and aggregated rebates can be investigated by the OFFICE OF FAIR TRADING and (if necessary) the COMPETITION COMMISSION, and prohibited if found to unduly restrict competition. The RESALE PRICE ACTS 1964, 1976 make the practice of resale price maintenance illegal unless it is, very exceptionally, exempted by the Office of Fair Trading.

Restrictive Trade Practices Acts (1956, 1968, 1976) a body of UK legislation providing for the control of RESTRICTIVE TRADE AGREEMENTS between rival suppliers. See COMPETITION LAW, COMPETITION ACT, 1998.

restructuring see CORPORATE RE-ENGINEERING.

retail audit the continuous monitoring of sales by a retailer as part of its stocking policy. See EPOS.

retail cooperative an organization that is owned by its consumers. This form of organization provides an alternative mechanism for a firm to identify consumer wants: meetings with consumers replace market forces. In many cases not all consumers hold share capital. Nevertheless, they will receive a small annual dividend based on profits on sales. In this instance ownership is notional rather than real. See WORKERS' CO-OPERATIVE.

retailer a business which stocks a particular type of product (such as a shoe shop) or an extensive range of products (such as a DEPARTMENT STORE) for sale to consumers. Retailers operate at the final end of a DISTRIBUTION CHANNEL for a product or products, which also involves MANUFACTURERS and WHOLESALERS.

Although some retailers (for example, butchers) are involved in the preparation and packaging of products before their final sale and provide personal service, most retailers are engaged in selling prepacked, complete items on a self-service basis. Formerly, in the UK and elsewhere, retailers played a relatively passive role in the distribution channel, merely providing a convenient point of sale for manufacturers' products (in many trades at prices controlled by the manufacturers through RESALE PRICE MAINTENANCE). However, with the emergence of large CHAIN STORE retailers (SUPERMARKETS, DO-IT-YOURSELF groups) the 'balance of power' in the channel has switched towards retailers. Retailers have been able to use their BULK-BUYING power to obtain substantial price discounts from manufacturers and this, together with the demise of rpm, has given retailers greater discretion in the use of price as a competitive weapon (see DISCOUNT STORE). Moreover, the larger retailer groups have established an extensive OWN-LABEL BRAND business in direct competition to manufacturers' brands, which has also increased their MARKETING MIX opportunities to compete against other retailers. See SPECIALIST SHOP, CATEGORY DISCOUNTER, WAREHOUSE CLUB, MAIL ORDER, FACTORY OUTLET.

retailing the function of selling products to the ultimate buyers of those products. See RETAILER, DISTRIBUTION CHANNEL.

retail outlet business premises or facilities for selling products to CONSUMERS. A retail outlet may take the form of a SHOP or STORE which buyers visit to make purchases, or it could be an AUTOMATIC VENDING MACHINE or kiosk located in a hotel or restaurant. Apart from 'points of sale' geographically located within easy reach of prospective customers, retail sales can be made by direct delivery or through the post to a buyer's home as, for example, in MAIL ORDER selling. See RETAILER, DISTRIBUTION CHANNEL, EPOS.

retail price index/consumer price index a weighted average of the PRICES of a general 'basket' of goods and services bought by final consumers. Each item in the index is weighted according to its relative importance in total consumers' expenditure (See Fig. 76). Starting from a selected base year (index value = 100), price changes are then reflected in changes in the index value over time. Thus, in the case of the UK's CPI the current base year is 1996 = 100; in February 2005 the index value stood at 111.9 indicating that consumer prices, on average, had risen 12% between the two dates.

Composition of the CPI	weights in 2003
1 Food and non-alcoholic beverages	108
2 Alcoholic beverages and tobacco	47
3 Clothing and footwear	62
4 Housing, water, electricity, gas and other fuels	104
5 Furniture and household equipment	68
6 Health	23
7 Transport	144
8 Communication	25
9 Recreation	163
10 Education	20
11 Restaurants and hotels	135
12 Miscellaneous goods and services	101

Fig. 76 **Composition of the CPI, 2003.** Source: Office for National Statistics.

Since December 2003 the CPI has been used by the UK government as a measure of the rate of INFLATION in the economy for the purposes of applying macroeconomic policy in general and monetary policy in particular (see MONETARY POLICY COMMITTEE). Previously the RETAIL PRICE INDEX (RPI) was used for this purpose, but the CPI measure was adopted to harmonise the way the UK measured its inflation rate with that of other countries in the EUROPEAN UNION. See Fig. 46 in the main INFLATION entry.

retail services mix the range of services offered by a RETAILER to its customers to encourage loyalty to the store. Some of the main elements of the retail services mix include special displays, convenient opening hours, easy exchanges and returns, restaurants and parking facilities.

retained profit *or* **undistributed profit** any after-tax PROFIT that is reinvested (*ploughed back*) in the firm rather than being paid out to the owners of the company in DIVIDENDS. Such retained earnings form a valuable source of capital to be invested in additional FIXED ASSETS and CURRENT ASSETS. They serve to swell the value of the company to the shareholders and increase

SHAREHOLDERS' CAPITAL EMPLOYED by adding to revenue RESERVES, See also RETENTIONS RATIO.

retentions ratio a measure of the proportion of NET PROFIT which a company ploughs back into the business rather than distributing it to shareholders. Specifically the retentions ratio expresses net profit after tax and interest less DIVIDENDS declared/paid as a percentage of net profit. Thus, for example, if a company retains three-quarters of its profits and pays out only one-quarter as dividends, then its retentions ratio is 75%. The retentions ratio is the opposite of the DISTRIBUTION RATIO, See also RESERVES, RETAINED PROFITS.

retirement the termination of an individual's working career at a certain age with the expectation that he or she will no longer undertake paid employment. In the UK the normal retirement age for men has been 65 and for women 60. European law has a big effect on retirement benefits in the UK. For some time it has been required that men and women have the same pension rights in occupational schemes despite differing retirement ages, thereby meaning that women's benefits are more favourable than men's. The European Court of Justice has now ruled that benefits should be the same. This could mean that the retirement age for women will become 65. Another recent innovation, stemming from the Court, is that part-time workers can no longer be excluded from occupational pension schemes. Until recently many occupational pension schemes excluded part-time workers but the Court has ruled that since many part-time employees are female, exclusion could be a form of DISCRIMINATION.

retrenchment see DIVESTMENT.

return on assets see RETURN ON CAPITAL EMPLOYED.

return on capital employed (ROCE) an accounting measure of a firm's PROFITABILITY, which expresses the firm's PROFITS for an accounting period as a percentage of its period-end capital employed. Generally, profit is taken before deduction of tax and is related to LONG-TERM CAPITAL EMPLOYED, though broader comparisons are possible, which relate profit before tax and interest payments to all ASSETS employed, and narrower comparisons which relate after-tax profit to shareholders' capital. A firm's return on capital depends upon its PROFIT MARGINS RATIO and its ASSET TURNOVER RATIO, the first being a multiple of the last two, thus

$$\frac{\text{profit}}{\text{long-term capital}} = \frac{\text{profit}}{\text{sales}} \times \frac{\text{sales}}{\text{long-term capital}}$$

Return on capital employed provides a key measure of management performance in earning profits from the assets which they control. To improve return on capital employed managers need to:

(a) improve profit margins either by reducing unit production and selling costs, or by increasing selling prices of products;

(b) improve asset turnover either by increasing sales volumes using present assets, or by reducing the FIXED ASSETS and CURRENT ASSETS employed to achieve present sales volumes.

return on equity see RETURN ON SHAREHOLDERS' FUNDS.

return on investment see RETURN ON CAPITAL EMPLOYED, RETURN ON SHAREHOLDERS' FUNDS.

return on shareholders' funds an accounting measure of the rate of return that shareholders have obtained on the capital which they have invested in the business. It is calculated by dividing PROFIT after interest and tax by SHAREHOLDERS' CAPITAL EMPLOYED (issued share capital plus RESERVES).

Reuters a company which collects and disseminates worldwide general news items for press publication and which provides support facilities for the financial markets. See GLOBEX.

revaluation 1 the increase in the valuation of a FIXED ASSET to its current market value. Revaluation of fixed assets such as land and buildings may be necessary to reflect their APPRECIATION as property prices rise. Where revaluation takes place, the increase in the value of the fixed asset over its NET BOOK VALUE is added to the company's RESERVES.

2 an administered increase in the EXCHANGE RATE of a currency against other currencies under a FIXED EXCHANGE RATE SYSTEM; for example, an increase in the value of the UK pound (£) against the US dollar ($) from one fixed or 'pegged' level to a higher level, say, from £1 = $2 to £1 = $3. Governments resort to revaluations as a means of eliminating a BALANCE OF PAYMENTS surplus. The effect of a revaluation is to make imports (in the local currency) cheaper, thereby inducing an increase in import demand, and exports (in the local currency) more expensive, thereby reducing export demand. Contrast DEVALUATION.

revaluation provision an accounting PROVISION made for the increased cost of replacing a FIXED ASSET, over and above its HISTORIC COST. DEPRECIATION charges spread the original cost of a fixed asset over its estimated life, preventing the cost of the asset from being ignored in calculating net profit and so preventing the firm's LONG-TERM CAPITAL EMPLOYED from being distributed as DIVIDENDS. However, where the REPLACEMENT COST of a fixed asset is expected to exceed its original cost, a prudent firm may withhold additional profits instead of distributing them, in anticipation of having to pay this additional sum. See INFLATION ACCOUNTING.

revenue 1 the money received by a firm from the sale of its output of GOODS or SERVICES (SALES REVENUE).
2 money received by the government from TAXATION.

revenue account see PROFIT-AND-LOSS ACCOUNT.

revenue centre an organizational subunit of a firm under the control of a manager, who is able to affect output levels and revenues but has no direct control over costs. See COST CENTRE, PROFIT CENTRE.

revenue expenditure expenditure that is written off completely in the PROFIT-AND-LOSS ACCOUNT in the ACCOUNTING PERIOD to which it relates. Contrast CAPITAL EXPENDITURE.

reverse engineering a situation where a firm obtains a competitor's product so as to disassemble it and from the resultant component analysis decide how to build a similar product.

reverse takeover the TAKEOVER of one company by another company which has a lower stock market valuation (i.e. the value of the bidder's ISSUED SHARE CAPITAL traded on the stock market is less than that of the victim firm). A reverse takeover bid usually involves the bidding firm issuing shares or raising LOAN CAPITAL to finance the deal.

reverse yield gap see YIELD GAP.

rework costs see FAILURE COSTS.

RIE see RECOGNIZED INVESTMENT EXCHANGE.

right first time see ZERO DEFECTS.

rights issue the issue by a JOINT-STOCK COMPANY of additional SHARES to existing SHAREHOLDERS at a price which is generally a little below the current market price. Rights are issued to existing shareholders in proportion to their existing shareholdings, and shareholders can sell their rights if they do not wish to subscribe for extra shares. Compare CAPITALIZATION ISSUE.

rightsizing a colloquial term for an ORGANIZATION's restructuring efforts to improve its efficiency and cost-effectiveness which involve reducing the size of its workforce.

risk see UNCERTAINTY AND RISK.

risk analysis the systematic analysis of the degree of risk attaching to capital projects. Risk reflects the variability of expected future return from a capital INVESTMENT, and as such the statistical technique of probability may be applied to assist a decision. See also CAPITAL BUDGETING, UNCERTAINTY AND RISK, DECISION TREE.

risk aversion the tendency for managers, consumers and other decision-makers to avoid undertaking risks and to choose less risky alternatives. See RISK PREMIUM.

risk capital any business capital subscribed by an individual ENTREPRENEUR or group of ORDINARY SHAREHOLDERS which entails some risk of loss in the event of the enterprise failing.

risk premium the additional return on an INVESTMENT which an investor requires to compensate for the possibility of losing all or part of that investment if future events prove adverse. The size of the risk premium will depend to an extent upon the personality of the investor. Some cautious investors are 'risk averse' and require a substantial risk premium to induce them to undertake risky investments. Other less cautious investors are 'gamblers' and demand little risk premium. Attitudes to risk also depend upon the size of the potential gains or losses involved. Where a project risks making a loss which is so large as to endanger the future solvency of the investor then investors would tend to adopt a cautious view about the downside risk involved, even when such losses are highly unlikely, and would demand a substantial risk premium. See DECISION TREE, UNCERTAINTY AND RISK, CAPITAL ASSET PRICING MODEL.

Road Haulage Association Limited the EMPLOYERS' ASSOCIATION representing employers in the road haulage industry. As well as representing their interests in the political sphere, this association negotiates WAGE RATES with the industry's TRADE UNIONS. See MULTI-EMPLOYER AGREEMENT.

robot a form of programmable automatic machine that performs repetitive PRODUCTION tasks in place of human operatives on a PRODUCTION LINE. Robots can be used for tasks such as welding or spray painting, which can be unhealthy for human operatives to perform, and assembly tasks, which can be performed more rapidly and consistently than by human workers. The use of robots can therefore improve the PRODUCTIVITY of production operations and the QUALITY of products.

ROCE see RETURN ON CAPITAL EMPLOYED.

Rodger's seven-point plan see RECRUITMENT AND SELECTION.

role culture see CULTURE.

rolling settlement see ACCOUNT PERIOD, TALISMAN.

rollout marketing the planned introduction of a firm's products to its target markets one area at a time. The firm will seek to rank sales areas according to their market potential and competition so as to determine the order in which each area will be targeted. See MARKETING SEGMENTATION, INTERNATIONAL MARKETING.

ROM (Read Only Memory) a COMPUTER memory device from which data can be read but which cannot be written on to. The contents of such memory are fixed when the computer is manufactured, being incorporated in ROM micro chips.

routing sheets see MATERIALS FLOW MANAGEMENT.

Rowan *or* **Halsey Plan** a form of PAYMENT BY RESULTS where a component of WAGES is based on the achievement by a factory worker of output in excess of a predetermined output target.

Royal College of Nursing the main professional body for nursing staff in the UK. Faced with far-reaching changes in the health service recently, the RCN has increasingly acted as a TRADE UNION, taking some limited forms of INDUSTRIAL ACTION. Nevertheless, it has maintained its policy against STRIKE action despite challenges to it from some sections of the membership. With over 325,000 members it is the UK's fifth largest union.

Royal Mint see CENTRAL BANK.

royalties payments made for the use of an INTELLECTUAL PROPERTY RIGHT (copyrights, patents etc.) or physical property rights (mineral extraction rights etc.).

RPC see RESTRICTIVE PRACTICES COURT.

RPI see RETAIL PRICE INDEX.

RPIX see RETAIL PRICE INDEX.

rpm see RESALE PRICE MAINTENANCE.

Rucker Plan see GAINSHARING.

rule of origin see LOCAL CONTENT RULE.

rule of thumb an aid to decision-making involving the use of conventions or mechanistic formulas to determine prices, production schedules, advertising budgets etc. Rules of thumb are used as rough guides or approximations when, because of uncertainty, it is impossible to determine optimal solutions. Many firms, for example, use cost-based formulas to set prices, adding a conventional unit profit mark-up to costs, in the absence of totally reliable information about demand. Similarly, firms often set the value of their advertising budget as a fixed percentage of their sales revenue. See COST-BASED PRICING, UNCERTAINTY AND RISK.

run to start executing a specific PROGRAM on a COMPUTER.

S

sabotage see INDUSTRIAL ACTION.

safety see HEALTH AND SAFETY.

safety stock see STOCK CONTROL.

salary a payment made to employees for the use of their labour. Unlike WAGES, salaries are not strictly related to the actual number of hours worked (though the CONTRACT OF EMPLOYMENT will usually stipulate the required working hours each week). Instead salaries are expressed in an annual sum, a portion of which is paid to the employee each month. An employee's salary is generally a function of the individual's age and experience, and the level of the job in the organization. Increasingly, an element of the employee's salary is based on some measure of individual performance. See INCREMENTAL PAY SCALE, PERFORMANCE APPRAISAL, MERIT PAY.

sale 1 the purchase of a good or service by a buyer from a seller at a stated PRICE or, in some instances, through a BARTER or COUNTERTRADE arrangement.

2 price reductions applied to individual items or across the board for a limited period of time by a seller, to increase sales of existing products (a sales period), to clear old stocks prior to selling new lines (an end of season sale), or to sell off the stock of a bankrupt business (a closing down sale).

3 a specially convened gathering of sellers and buyers organized as a one-off event such as a jumble sale or on a regular basis such as a monthly AUCTION of second-hand cars.

sale and leaseback see LEASEBACK.

Sale of Goods Act 1979 a UK Act which provides protection to the purchaser of a GOOD by laying down certain legal obligations which a supplier must fulfil as part of the CONTRACT OF SALE. These obligations include that the goods supplied correspond with the description of the goods and that goods are of merchantable quality, that is, 'fit for the purpose' for which they are intended. See CONSUMER PROTECTION.

Sale of Goods and Services Act 1982 a UK Act which provides protection to the purchaser of a SERVICE (which may also involve the provision of a GOOD, for example, the supply of new parts in servicing a car) by laying down certain legal obligations which a supplier must fulfil as part of the CONTRACT OF SALE. These obligations include compliance with description and 'fitness for purpose' (see SALE OF GOODS ACT 1979) and that the supplier will use 'reasonable' care and skill in providing the service. See CONSUMER PROTECTION.

sales agency a business which specializes in promoting the SALES of a client firm. Typically agents do not take title to goods but are employed on a commission basis by, for example, a producer to obtain new wholesale customers or new retail accounts. A company may employ a sales agency to handle its entire selling activities or to augment its own sales force. Agents are often used by smaller companies and are particularly useful in the context of INTERNATIONAL MARKETING where foreign agents familiar with overseas markets and distribution networks can be used to establish an EXPORT market for a firm's products. See SALES COMMISSION.

sales analysis the recording, analysis and evaluation of a firm's SALES data. Sales analysis is usually designed to give a breakdown of sales by product, by sales person, by sales area, and by customer (age group, sex etc.). See SALES FORECASTING.

sales commission incentive payments made to the firm's own SALES REPRESENTATIVES for reaching/exceeding specified SALES targets. Where a firm employs AGENTS to sell its products, commissions are used as the primary form of remuneration. See SALES AGENCY.

sales concept a business philosophy which aims at the generation of profits through the selling and promotion of products. The sales concept is an extension of a firm's PRODUCTION ORIENTATION where emphasis is placed on the effective selling of what the firm has chosen to produce. Contrast MARKETING CONCEPT.

sales conviction test see ADVERTISING EFFECTIVENESS TESTS.

sales force the salespeople employed by a firm to sell its goods or services. Their functions range from relatively passive tasks such as taking repeat orders from established customers and making deliveries, to more active PERSONAL SELLING aimed at securing additional business from established and new customers. See KEY ACCOUNT MANAGEMENT.

The sales force can consist of:

(a) SALES REPRESENTATIVES who visit wholesalers, retailers or final customers, making face-to-face contact with those prospective buyers as a means of selling;

(b) telephone sales staff who contact prospective customers by telephone to establish an initial contact which can then be followed up by a visit from a sales representative;

(c) product demonstrators who operate in wholesale or retail stores or visit customers to provide an opportunity for prospective buyers to see a product in action or to sample it;

(d) sales managers who are responsible for organizing and controlling the activities of the field sales force, and the recruitment, selection and training of sales-force personnel.

In organizing the field sales force, sales persons may be required to represent *all* the firm's products in small SALES TERRITORIES, or may specialize in selling limited product lines in larger territories. See TEAM SELLING.

sales forecasting

The process of predicting future product demand to help in making decisions about marketing expenditure, investment in production capacity and the scheduling of factory output. Various sales forecasting methods can be used to make predictions about both future levels of industry demand and the company's own particular sales (which depend on its market share). These methods vary greatly in terms of their subjectivity, sophistication, data requirements and cost, and a manager's choice of method will depend on the level of accuracy he requires, on the distance into the future to be forecast, and on expense. The main forecasting methods are:

(a) *survey* methods, the most subjective of the demand-estimating techniques available. Surveys generally involve the use of interviews or mailed QUESTIONNAIRES asking individual consumers about their future buying intentions; alternatively, opinions of the sales force may be obtained. Such data can often be useful for making short-term projections about future spending, and, in the case of new products, surveys may provide one of the few methods available in the absence of historical data. However, their subjectivity can detract from their accuracy. Buyers may be unwilling to give correct answers for reasons of commercial secrecy, or be uncertain about their future buying intentions; or interviewer bias may occur in the way in which questions are asked. Sales-force opinions represent 'second-hand' data and can be distorted by optimism or pessimism of sales representatives. For these reasons surveys are frequently used to supplement rather than replace other forecasting methods.

(b) *Extrapolation* methods employ time-series data, using past sales to predict future sales. These techniques assume that the historical relationship between past and future sales will continue to hold. Time-series data usually comprise:

(i) *secular trend,* which shows the relatively smooth, regular movement of the time series over the long term.

(ii) *cyclical variation,* which consists of medium-term, regular repeating patterns, generally associated with BUSINESS CYCLES. The recurring upswings and downswings in economic activity are superimposed upon the secular trend.

(iii) *seasonal variation,* which consists of short-term regular repeating patterns, generally associated with different seasons of the year. These seasonal variations are superimposed upon the secular trend and cyclical variations.

(iv) *irregular variations,* which are erratic fluctuations in the time series caused by unpredictable, chance events. These irregular variations are superimposed upon the secular trend, cyclical variation and seasonal variation (see Fig. 77).

Time-series analysis is concerned with isolating the effect of each of these influences upon a time series with a view to using them to project this past experience into the future. In order to identify the underlying secular trend in a time series, the forecaster may 'fit' a line by eye to time-series observations depicted on a graph. Alternatively, the forecaster may use a moving average to smooth the time series and help identify the underlying trend. For example, he could use a five-period *moving average,* replacing each consecutive observation by the average of that observation and the two preceding and two succeeding observations. *Exponential smoothing* provides yet another technique which can be used to smooth time-series data. It is similar to the moving-average method but gives greater weight to more recent observations in calculating the average.

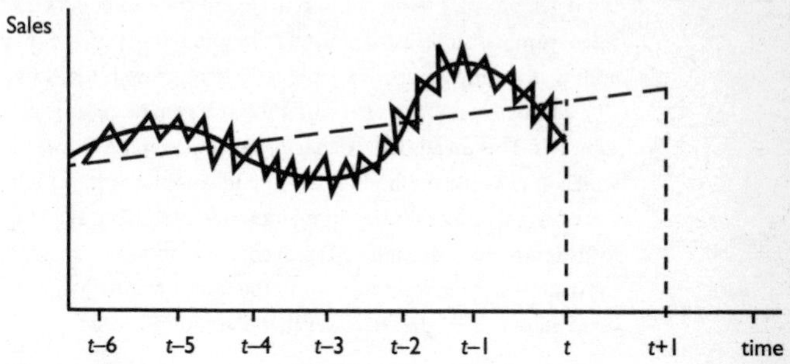

Fig. 77 **Sales forecasting.** Time-series analysis.

In order to identify the effect of seasonal variations, the forecaster can construct a measure of seasonal variation (called the *seasonal index*) and use this to 'deseasonalize' the time-series data and show how the time series would look if there were no seasonal fluctuations. Once the trend has been identified it is possible to extrapolate that trend, and estimate trend values for time periods beyond the present time period. In Fig. 77, for example, the trend for time periods up to and including time t can be extrapolated to time $t + 1$. Such trend-projection techniques are generally more useful for longer-term forecasting than short-term estimation. Their big drawback is that they make no attempt to represent the factors which causally affect demand, simply assuming that historical relationships involved in the time series will continue into the future. This renders them unable to predict sharp upturns or downturns in sales associated with dramatic changes in demand-influencing variables.

(c) *Barometric* methods seek to predict the future value of sales from the present values of particular statistical indicators which have a consistent relationship with sales. Such leading indicators as business capital investment plans and new house building starts can be used as a barometer for forecasting product demand, and they can be useful for predicting sharp changes in demand.

(d) *Econometric* methods predict future sales by examining other variables which are causally related to it. Econometric models link variables in the form of equations which can be estimated statistically and then used as a basis for forecasting. Judgement has to be exercised in identifying the independent variables which causally affect demand. For example, in order to predict future quantity of a product demanded (Qd) we would formulate an equation linking it to product price (P) and disposable income (Y):

$$Qd = a + bP = cY$$

then use past data to estimate the numerical value of the coefficients a, b and c. This method can be expensive in terms of data collection and processing costs, but it can produce reasonably accurate forecasts and offers the opportunity to learn from past forecasting mistakes by amending the forecasting equations, adding new independent variables etc., to improve future forecasts.

Ultimately no forecasting method will generate consistently accurate forecasts. This means that managers need to exercise judgement in choosing which forecasting methods to use and in combining information compiled from several different forecasting methods in arriving at a judgement about future demand conditions. Moreover, in making any forecast the forecaster must allow for a margin of error in the forecast, anticipating that future demand may be higher or lower than the forecast value.

sales journal see JOURNAL, ACCOUNTING.

sales ledger see LEDGER, ACCOUNTING.

salesmanship the art of SELLING.

sales-per-employee ratio a measure of a firm's sales/size relation, that expresses the firm's SALES REVENUE as a ratio of its size measured in terms of number of employees.

Where a company employs a high proportion of part-time workers, employee numbers may need to be adjusted to full-time equivalent numbers to assist comparability. Alternatively sales may be expressed as a proportion of total employee remuneration.

It is useful to compare sales per employee in a firm with the company's average employee remuneration.

sales per square foot/metre a common measure of efficiency in RETAILING which relates sales revenue generated to the OVERHEAD costs (rent, rates, heating, lighting, etc.) of providing selling space.

sales potential a particular seller's share of MARKET POTENTIAL.

sales promotion the measures used by firms alongside other elements of the PROMOTIONAL MIX (advertising, personal selling etc.) to increase the SALES of their products.

In the case of CONSUMER GOODS, while ADVERTISING seeks to develop and sustain sales by creating BRAND LOYALTY over the long run, sales promotions are largely used in short, sharp bursts to support, for example, the introduction of a new brand, to renew interest in a product whose sales have fallen and, periodically, to stimulate extra demand for a well-established brand. A variety of techniques are used for these purposes, including: free-trial samples, money-off packs, 'two-for-the-price-of-one' offers, extra quantities for the same price, product competitions offering prizes, coupons offering gifts, trading stamps, in-store demonstrations, point-of-sale displays, etc.

These methods can succeed only if the product being promoted is widely available for consumers to buy, so that it is important also to encourage retailers to stock it. This is done using various trade promotions including special cash offers on purchases, free extra quantities, gifts and prizes.

In the case of industrial products, trade fairs, exhibitions and demonstrations are used to back up the most commonly used mode, PERSONAL SELLING. See MERCHANDISING, PACKAGING.

sales representative (rep) *or* **sales executive** a salesperson employed to represent his or her company's products to prospective buyers. Sales representatives usually visit potential buyers at the buyers' premises and are generally responsible for visiting numbers of customers within their designated sales territory.

Sales representatives are responsible for securing repeat orders from established customers, gaining orders from new customers, informing customers about their firm's new products and collecting market intelligence from customers. In many cases the selling task also involves representatives in demonstrating products, offering technical advice and arranging credit terms. Sales representatives are often remunerated partly by means of SALES COMMISSION in order to provide them with incentives to secure sales.

See PERSONAL SELLING, CALLS.

sales response the rate at which SALES of a product or brand change as a result of changes in marketing expenditure or price. In order to make rational decisions about marketing expenditures on products or brands, firms need to estimate the likely sales response of each product or brand. See ELASTICITY OF DEMAND.

sales revenue the income generated from the sale of GOODS and SERVICES. Sales revenue depends upon the volume of a product sold and the price of the product.

In a company's PROFIT-AND-LOSS ACCOUNT, sales revenue is generally recorded net of VAT and any trade discounts given, for subsequent comparison with costs.

sales–revenue variance the difference between the budgeted value of SALES and the actual value of sales achieved. This variance can be broken down into two parts:

(a) *sales–price variance*, which shows the difference between the predetermined price of a product and the actual price;

(b) *sales–volume variance,* which indicates the extent to which sales revenue has been lost because smaller volumes of products were sold than were budgeted for.

Both of these are affected by sales mix, and the *sales–mix variance* shows the effect on revenue of achieving an actual mix of sales different from the product mix anticipated in the sales budget.

sales territory a geographical area containing potential customers who can be approached through DIRECT SELLING and to which salespersons can be assigned. The number and sizes of territories scheduled by a firm will depend upon such considerations as numbers and size of potential customers to be covered, how densely they are grouped (since this affects travelling time between customers) and the complexity of the selling operation (which will determine the number and length of sales calls required). Where a sales territory contains insufficient potential customers to warrant the cost of deploying its own sales personnel (see SALES REPRESENTATIVE) a firm may instead choose to sell its products through a SALES AGENCY.

sales to fixed assets ratio an efficiency ratio which looks at the sales generated by a firm in relation to its fixed assets. It is computed by dividing sales by fixed assets and provides a measure of fixed asset utilization. See ACCOUNTING RATIO.

sales volume the quantity of a firm's product or brand sold within a given time period. Sales volumes are important because of their implications for sales revenues (volumes multiplied by prices) and for PRODUCTION SCHEDULING and production costs, especially where a high rate of capacity utilization is necessary to BREAK EVEN.

salvage value see SCRAP.

sample 1 part of a total population that can be analysed to make inferences about the whole population (see SAMPLING).
2 a small amount of raw material or finished product whose quality or performance can be tested as a guide to the quality or performance of a whole batch of material or product (see QUALITY CONTROL, ACCEPTANCE SAMPLING).
3 a small trial pack of a product or brand which is used to encourage buyers to try it out (see SALES PROMOTION).

sampling the selection of part of a total population of consumers or products whose behaviour or performance can be analysed, in order to make inferences about the behaviour or performance of the total population, without the difficulty and expense of undertaking a complete census of the whole population.

Samples may be chosen *randomly,* with every consumer or product in the population having an equal chance of being included. Random samples are most commonly used by firms in QUALITY CONTROL where they are used as a basis for selecting products, components or materials for quality testing.

Alternatively, samples may be chosen by dividing up the total population into a number of distinct *sub-groups* or strata, then selecting a *proportionate number* of consumers or products from each sub-group since this is quicker and cheaper than random sampling. In MARKETING RESEARCH and opinion polling, *quota* sampling is usually employed where interviewers select the particular consumers to be interviewed, choosing the numbers of these consumers in proportion to their occurrence in the total population.

Samples may be:

(a) *cross-sectional,* where sample observations are collected at a particular point in time, for example data on company sales and the incomes of consumers in the current year, embracing a wide range of different income groups, as a basis for investigating the relationship between sales and income;

(b) *longitudinal,* where sample observations are collected over a number of time periods, for example data on changes in company sales over a number of years and changes in consumer incomes over the same time periods, as a basis for investigating the relationship between sales and income. See STATISTICAL INFERENCES, QUESTIONNAIRE.

Sarbanes-Oxley Act see CORPORATE GOVERNANCE.

satisfice an approach to decision-making which aspires to achieve satisfactory but not optimum results. It can be a rational approach because it accepts that the perfect knowledge necessary to make the best decision is usually unattainable. Instead decision-makers will act in accordance with RULES OF THUMB which they know will at least achieve acceptable results. See ORGANIZATIONAL ANALYSIS, BUSINESS OBJECTIVES.

saturation phase see PRODUCT LIFE CYCLE.

save as you earn (SAYE) scheme see SAVE AS YOU EARN (SAYE) SHARE OPTIONS.

save as you earn (SAYE) share options a UK SHARE OPTIONS scheme introduced in 1980. Where schemes are in operation employees can subscribe to options to buy shares in their employing company in three, five, or seven years time but at up to a 20% discount on the current market price. In the meantime they make regular savings of between £5 and £250 a month using a 'save as you earn' savings scheme. When the savings contract expires employees may purchase their options or may choose to take the money instead. This scheme attracts favourable tax concessions: employees receive a tax free bonus at the expiry of the savings schemes, whilst the award of shares on favourable terms is not subject to income tax. See EMPLOYEE SHARE OWNERSHIP PLAN.

saver a person, company or institution who sets aside a proportion of current income by forgoing immediate spending on consumption. See SAVINGS.

savings the proportion of income of a person (personal saving), company or institution (retained profits) that is not spent on current consumption. Savings are typically placed on deposit with a BANK, BUILDING SOCIETY, etc., or used to acquire financial and physical assets such as SHARES or plant. By forgoing immediate spending on consumption, savers seek to augment their future income through dividends, interest and rent receipts and through capital appreciation.

In real terms, savings are important in that they finance physical INVESTMENT in the economy, enabling a country to increase its CAPITAL STOCK and hence its overall capacity to produce a greater volume of products. See FINANCIAL SYSTEM, NATIONAL SAVINGS CERTIFICATE.

savings bank a BANK which offers clients a variety of savings accounts to attract deposits, mainly from the general public, and which specializes in investments in financial securities such as STOCKS and SHARES and government BONDS. In recent times, however, some savings banks, such as the Trustee Savings Bank, have become JOINT-STOCK COMPANIES and operate more like the COMMERCIAL BANKS, offering their clients money transmission services (cheque books and credit cards), bank loans and mortgages, and other financial services.

SAYE see SAVE AS YOU EARN (SAYE) SHARE OPTIONS.

SBS see SMALL BUSINESS SERVICE.

SBU see STRATEGIC BUSINESS UNIT.

'scab' see BLACKLEG.

scalar concept a principle of ORGANIZATION design whereby job posts are arranged hierarchically with clear lines of AUTHORITY passing down the HIERARCHY. This view is a central component of CLASSICAL MANAGEMENT THEORY.

Scanlon Plan see GAINSHARING.

scenario writing see TECHNOLOGICAL FORECASTING.

scheduling see PRODUCTION SCHEDULING.

'science of muddling through' see DISJOINTED INCREMENTALISM.

science park *or* **business park** a cluster of firms, mainly high-technology businesses, which are located together on a purpose-built site adjacent to a university, polytechnic or some other centre of research, which facilitates the transfer of basic technology and know-how from research laboratories to commercial applications. The term is also applied more generally to embrace *technology parks* or *technopoles* (commonly found in Continental Europe), where emphasis is on attracting established research-based companies and *innovation centres* which cater for smaller high-technology companies.

In most countries a large proportion of the investment in science-park infrastructure and buildings is provided by the public sector as part of a wider programme to stimulate regional enterprise and promote technological advance. See RESEARCH AND DEVELOPMENT, REGIONAL POLICY, INDUSTRIAL POLICY.

scientific management an approach to JOB DESIGN advocated by F. W. Taylor (1856–1915), an American WORK STUDY engineer. Taylor sought to increase output by improving management competence and by careful attention to job design. Specifically, he advocated close analysis of job tasks through the methods of work study as a basis for achieving an extreme degree of job specialization. All decision-making about task performance was to pass to management, who were to create 'thinking departments' to analyse and plan work tasks. Supervision of performance was to be undertaken by 'functional foremen', responsible for particular aspects of the production process (for example maintenance). Workers would be motivated by pay incentives to work to the full extent of their abilities, and the best workers should be selected for each particular job. Taylor believed that adoption of his system would lead to high levels of efficiency. In reality his theory ignored the importance of JOB SATISFACTION. Adoption of his methods led to STRIKES and CONFLICT. See FORDISM, METHOD STUDY.

Scotvec the Scottish Council for Vocational Training. The Scottish equivalent of the NATIONAL COUNCIL FOR VOCATIONAL QUALIFICATIONS in England and Wales, it oversees vocational training in Scotland and the SVQ, the Scottish version of the NATIONAL VOCATIONAL QUALIFICATION. See TRAINING.

scrap seriously defective or damaged components or products that are rejected by a firm's QUALITY CONTROL system as incapable of being rectified and which have to be disposed of for the salvage value of their materials.

scrap value see RESIDUAL VALUE.

screening the process of evaluating product ideas in terms of consumer acceptance, technical feasibility and cost. See NEW PRODUCT DEVELOPMENT.

screwdriver operation an overseas subsidiary of a MULTINATIONAL ENTERPRISE which simply assembles parts delivered to it by the parent company from abroad. Such screwdriver subsidiaries have only limited opportunities for creating jobs in the host country where the subsidiary is located and offer few opportunities for TECHNOLOGY TRANSFER. LOCAL CONTENT RULES are often established by governments which specify the minimum proportion of a product to be manufactured from locally supplied parts if the product is to be regarded as domestically produced.

scrip issue see CAPITALIZATION ISSUE.

SDR see INTERNATIONAL MONETARY FUND.

sealed-bid pricing see COMPETITION-BASED PRICING.

sealed minimum stock a STOCK CONTROL system for STOCK items where re-orders are placed when the sealed minimum stock level is reached. Sealed stock systems tend to be used for inexpensive items such as rivets, which are available to operatives on free issue. The reorder stock level is sealed in a bag and this bag is opened only when all the other stock has been used up. A tag or card attached to the bag is used to initiate a replenishment order.

SEAQ see STOCK MARKET.

seasonal index see SALES FORECASTING.

seasonal unemployment see UNEMPLOYMENT.

seasonal variation see SALES FORECASTING.

secondary action a form of INDUSTRIAL ACTION in which a group of employees STRIKE or take some other action against their employer, as a means of putting pressure on another employer currently engaged in an industrial dispute with his or her workforce. By taking industrial action, the provision of goods and services from the one employer to the employer in dispute can be disrupted. The Employment Act 1980 made secondary action lawful only when the firms involved had contracts with each other.

The Employment Act 1990 made all secondary action unlawful.

second mortgage a second LOAN raised by a property owner against the COLLATERAL SECURITY of his or her property. See MORTGAGE.

secular trend see SALES FORECASTING.

secured creditor see CREDITORS.

Securities and Exchange Commission the US government body that regulates the operations of the New York STOCK MARKET.

Securities and Futures Authority (SFA) see FINANCIAL SERVICES ACT, 1986.

Securities and Investment Board (SIB) see FINANCIAL SERVICES ACT 1986.

securitization an arrangement which involves putting together a claim on particular assets of a business which is then sold as a negotiable security in the financial markets. Securitization is mainly undertaken by financial institutions; assets involved typically include commercial paper, mortgages, car loans, export credits and credit card receivables.

Securitization enables the issuing institution to raise ready cash, thus improving its liquidity. Purchasers of such securities seek to profit by obtaining claims on assets at less than their redemption value, but they may choose to on-sell their claims in the market.

security 1 a FINANCIAL SECURITY such as a STOCK, SHARE or BOND.

2 the provision of a 'collateral' to obtain a LOAN. See COLLATERAL SECURITY.

segmental reporting the practice of reporting separately on the SALES REVENUES, COSTS and PROFITS of different segments of a company's business. Company law in the UK requires the DIRECTOR'S REPORT to offer information to shareholders about the performance of different market segments or sectors of the company. Segmental reporting is often necessary in large groups which are highly diversified, operating in many different markets at home and abroad.

selection see RECRUITMENT AND SELECTION.

selective distribution a DISTRIBUTION strategy used by manufacturers which makes a product available only to certain RETAILERS rather than to retailers in general. 'Approved' retailers are required to meet standards set by the manufacturer with regard, for example, to presentation of the product, and to employ trained staff who can advise customers about the product.

selective price cutting a PRICING strategy which involves price cuts on particular brands or in particular sales territories in order to boost demand. More predatorily, price cuts may be deployed in order to remove competitors.

self-appraisal see PERFORMANCE APPRAISAL.

self-management see WORKERS' COOPERATIVE.

Self-Regulatory Organization (SRO) see FINANCIAL SERVICES ACT 1986.

self service a form of retailing whereby customers of RETAIL OUTLETS (shop, filling station etc.) select for themselves the goods they wish to purchase and pay for them at a checkout. Self service can be applied to both large and small-scale retailing operations and by cutting down on operating costs (i.e. eliminating the wages of sales assistants) it can assist a retailer or some other business (restaurant, cafeteria, etc.) to become more price competitive. See RETAILER.

sell see SELLING.

sell by date see SHELF LIFE.

seller a supplier of a GOOD, SERVICE or FINANCIAL SECURITY. In the first two cases, a broad distinction can be made between suppliers of goods and services such as raw materials, components, plant and equipment which are used to produce other products (that is, suppliers of *industrial products*) and sellers of products for personal consumption (that is, suppliers of *consumer products*).

The distinction between these two groups is important in terms of the application of appropriate MARKETING STRATEGIES.

seller concentration see MARKET CONCENTRATION.

seller's market a MARKET situation in which the demand for a product or financial security is greater than the supply of it at existing PRICES, which leads to the bidding-up of prices to the advantage of sellers. Compare BUYER'S MARKET.

selling the process of persuading potential BUYERS to purchase products. This process is undertaken by a firm's SALES REPRESENTATIVES who visit buyers, or by sales assistants in retail shops or by wholesalers. See PERSONAL SELLING, SALES FORCE, KEY ACCOUNT MANAGEMENT.

selling costs the expenditures incurred by suppliers in creating and sustaining a demand for their products. Selling costs include ADVERTISING expenditures; packaging and styling; salaries, commissions and travelling expenses of sales personnel; and the cost of shops and showrooms. See also PROMOTIONAL MIX, PRODUCT DIFFERENTIATION, OVERHEADS.

semiautonomous work groups see JOB DESIGN AND REDESIGN.

semivariable overheads any OVERHEADS that are partly FIXED OVERHEADS and partly VARIABLE OVERHEADS with respect to output, so that they vary roughly with output but not in exact proportion to it. They include such items as electricity and telephone costs which combine a fixed quarterly payment with a charge per unit consumed. In arithmetic terms, semivariable costs (*S*) can be represented as:

$$S = F + V.Q$$

where *F* is the fixed cost element, *V* is variable cost per unit and Q is output.

To facilitate cost analysis, semi-variable overhead costs are often broken down into their fixed and variable parts, leaving only two categories of cost:

Variable Costs = direct materials + direct labour + variable overheads + variable component of semivariable overheads.

Fixed Costs = fixed overhead + fixed element of semivariable overheads.

This allows accountants to represent the behaviour of costs graphically by straight lines using BREAK-EVEN ANALYSIS.

senior manager a manager who has a substantial role in formulating the objectives and policy of the ORGANIZATION. Usually managers at the top of the HIERARCHY are described in this way but where there is substantial DECENTRALIZATION of decision-making, managers at lower reaches of the organization may have this status. See MANAGEMENT.

sensitivity analysis a means of testing the extent to which the results of an analysis of an INVESTMENT project or company budget would change if one or more of the assumptions on which the analysis is based were to change. For example, in estimating the rate of return on an investment, such as a new machine, a firm will need to input various assumptions about the cost of the machine, the anticipated life of the machine, its running costs, annual output, residual value etc. Sensitivity analysis shows how much the expected rate of return on the machine would change if any one of these factors were to be higher or lower than originally expected. Sensitivity analysis thus allows managers to anticipate a range of possible outcomes where uncertainty about the factors involved make it impossible to predict the exact outcome. See UNCERTAINTY AND RISK, DISCOUNTED CASH FLOW.

sensitivity training see MANAGEMENT DEVELOPMENT.

SEPON (Stock Exchange Pool Nominees) the official UK STOCK MARKET company which receives details of all STOCKS and SHARES transfers, and facilitates prompt settlement of accounts and transfer of SHARE CERTIFICATES, making use of the TALISMAN computerized transfer system.

sequestration the confiscation of an organization's assets by a court following contempt of court by the organization. Its assets come under the control of a sequestrator, usually an accountant, until the organization can show that it has purged its contempt. Sequestration can be used to ensure that funds are available to pay any fines resulting from the contempt of court. In the late 1980s a number of TRADE UNIONS were subject to sequestration orders, in most cases as a result of violating the law on SECONDARY ACTION and strike ballots.

service an economic activity which is performed to meet a personal or business demand. Some services are either specifically personal (for example hairdressing, dentistry), or business (for example factory maintenance, freight forwarding), but a large number are multifaceted, catering for both sectors, for example, household and industrial painting, telephone services.

The provision of most services (for example, window cleaning) involves a number of characteristics which set them apart from the provision of a GOOD (for example, a motorcar), in particular *intangibility* – the inability of a customer to see, touch, taste or smell the service, and *inseparability* – the fact that services are produced and consumed at the same time and thus cannot be stored. See also MARKETING MIX, GAP ANALYSIS. See PRODUCT, PERISHABILITY, VARIABILITY.

service contract a CONTRACT OF EMPLOYMENT covering the terms and conditions applied to directors and senior managers of a joint-stock company.

service costing a special application of PROCESS COSTING used where services are supplied, eg, computer services, management consulting.

service level see STOCK CONTROL.

settlement day see ACCOUNT PERIOD.

set-up cost the cost involved in preparing and setting up a machine for the next work task, including cleaning, replacement of cutting tools or jigs etc. Set-up costs include the labour costs of preparing machines, the cost of new tools and frequently higher scrap rates immediately after machine resetting.

set-up time the time involved in setting up a machine ready for the next work task. Set-up times represent IDLE TIME when machines are not producing output, and production managers will seek to set up machines as quickly as possible and return them to production mode. In BATCH PRODUCTION, in particular, set-up times are an important constraint upon factory output, and firms may prefer long production runs making particular components in order to minimize the number of machine resettings needed. See MACHINE UTILIZATION, ALLOWANCES, SINGLE MINUTE EXCHANGE OF DIES.

seven P's of marketing see MARKETING MIX.

seven (7) wastes part of the Toyota production system. The 7 Wastes are: waste from producing defects, waste in transportation, waste from inventory, waste from overproduction, waste from waiting time, waste in processing and waste of motion. See JUST-IN-TIME (JIT) SYSTEM, LEAN MANUFACTURING.

severance pay see REDUNDANCY.

sex discrimination see DISCRIMINATION.

Sex Discrimination Act 1975 see DISCRIMINATION.

shadow price the imputed PRICE or value of a good or service where such a price or value cannot be determined accurately owing to the absence of a market for the good or service, or to gross distortions in any markets which exist. To impute a price or value is to make the best estimate possible of what that price or value would be if a normal market existed.

One use of shadow pricing is when intra-firm trading occurs. The inputs of company division B may be the outputs of company division A. The products in which the two company divisions trade may not have an equivalent market price because no open market for them exists (for example intermediate components or managerial services). The transactions are given shadow prices, usually based on estimated costs plus a return on the capital involved.

A particular application of shadow pricing can be found in LINEAR PROGRAMMING where the solution to a problem yields hypothetical prices for scarce factor inputs, showing how much additional profit would result from an extra unit of each fully used resource. See TRANSFER PRICE.

share a FINANCIAL SECURITY issued by a JOINT-STOCK COMPANY as a means of raising long-term capital. Purchasers of shares pay money into the company's bank account and in return receive a SHARE CERTIFICATE signifying their ownership of the shares and have their ownership recorded in the company's SHARE REGISTER. The

SHAREHOLDERS of a company are its legal owners and are entitled to a share in its profits. Shares are traded on the STOCK MARKET. There are two broad kinds of shares: PREFERENCE SHARES and ORDINARY SHARES. See also SHARE CAPITAL, SHARE ISSUE, CAPITAL GEARING.

share buyback the purchase by a company of its *own* shares thereby reducing the amount of its ISSUED CAPITAL. Share buybacks are undertaken to return 'surplus' cash reserves to shareholders; more particularly they are undertaken to increase EARNINGS PER SHARE and DIVIDEND per share and thus (hopefully) lead to a rise in the company's share price. See SHARE ISSUE.

share capital the money employed in a JOINT-STOCK COMPANY that has been subscribed by the SHAREHOLDERS of the company in the form of ORDINARY SHARES (equity) and PREFERENCE SHARES, and which will remain as a permanent source of finance as long as the company remains in existence. See also LOAN CAPITAL, CAPITAL GEARING, STOCK.

share certificate a document which is issued to a SHAREHOLDER in a company, which serves as proof of ownership of SHARES in the company. See TRANSFER DEED.

shareholders the individuals and INSTITUTIONAL INVESTORS who contribute funds to finance a JOINT-STOCK COMPANY in return for SHARES in that company. There are two main types of shareholder:

(a) holders of PREFERENCE SHARES who are entitled to a fixed DIVIDEND from a company's PROFITS (before ordinary shareholders receive anything), and who have first claim on any remaining assets of the business after all debts have been discharged;

(b) holders of ORDINARY SHARES who are entitled to a dividend from a company's profits after all other outlays have been met and who are entitled to any remaining ASSETS of the business in the event of the company being wound up (LIQUIDATED).

Generally only ordinary shareholders are entitled to vote at ANNUAL GENERAL MEETINGS and elect DIRECTORS, since they bear most of the risk.

shareholders' capital employed SHARE CAPITAL originally invested by SHAREHOLDERS plus any RESERVES which arise, for example, as retained profits are ploughed back into the company.

Share Incentive Plan a UK scheme introduced in 2000 (originally as the *All Employee Share Ownership Plan*) which enables employees to acquire SHARES in their company. The Plan is aimed at motivating employees to work more productively and in aligning their interests more closely with those of outside shareholders.

Under the Plan shares can be offered to employees in three ways: *partnership shares* where employees can buy shares out of their gross pay up to a maximum of £1500 per year (or 10% of gross pay, whichever is lesser). Because shares are bought out of gross pay the employee pays less income tax and national insurance; *matching shares* given by the employer on the basis of two matching shares for every partnership share bought; *free shares* given without charge by the employer up to a maximum of £3000 per year.

Shares obtained in this way receive dividends and employees are accorded the normal rights of a shareholder. If the shares are held for a minimum of five years they are free of capital gains tax. See EMPLOYEE SHARE OWNERSHIP PLAN. See also EXECUTIVE SHARE OPTION SCHEME.

share issue the process of issuing shares in a JOINT-STOCK COMPANY.

New share capital is most frequently raised through issuing houses or merchant banks which arrange for the sale of shares on behalf of client companies. Shares can be issued in a variety of ways, such as direct to the general public by way of an 'offer for sale' (or an 'introduction') at a prearranged fixed price; an 'offer for sale by TENDER' where the issue price is determined by averaging out the bid prices offered by prospective purchasers of the share subject to a minimum price bid; a RIGHTS ISSUE of shares to existing shareholders at a fixed price; or a *placing* of the shares at an arranged price with selected investors, often INSTITUTIONAL INVESTORS. See INITIAL PUBLIC OFFERING.

Where shares are issued by means of an offer for sale the company issues a PROSPECTUS inviting members of the public to subscribe for shares, such *applications* for shares being accompanied either by a proportion of the purchase price of the shares or by the full purchase price. Then the company arranges for the ALLOTMENT of shares to intending shareholders. If the share issue is oversubscribed with more applications for shares than the number of shares being issued, then the firm must use some formula to allocate shares among applicants. To cover for the possibility that the share issue will be undersubscribed companies usually contract with a merchant bank to have the issue underwritten, the bank purchasing any unsold shares. Successful applicants then pay any balance of the share price or a second instalment towards the final price in response to a 'call' by the company. At this stage the names of successful applicants are entered on the company's SHARE REGISTER and they become entitled to full shareholders' rights, including the right to receive ANNUAL REPORTS AND ACCOUNTS and to vote at the company's ANNUAL GENERAL MEETING. See STOCK MARKET, CALLED-UP CAPITAL, PAID-UP CAPITAL, ALLOTMENT, SHARE CERTIFICATE.

share option a contractual right to buy a SHARE in a company at a predetermined price within a predetermined period. A company seeking to raise new capital can grant existing shareholders options to buy new shares in proportion to their existing shareholdings. Shareholders can either exercise their options and buy the shares or can sell their option rights on the STOCK MARKET. Share options can also be granted by a company to its executives and other employees as a means of improving their motivation and loyalty to the company. See RIGHTS ISSUE, EMPLOYEE SHARE OWNERSHIP, EXECUTIVE SHARE OPTION SCHEME, LONG-TERM INCENTIVE PLAN, ENTERPRISE MANAGEMENT INCENTIVE SCHEME, SHARE INCENTIVE PLAN.

share ownership plan see EMPLOYEE SHARE OWNERSHIP PLAN.

share portfolio see PORTFOLIO.

share premium the proceeds from issuing SHARES at a price higher than their PAR VALUE or present market value. Such proceeds are added to a JOINT-STOCK COMPANY'S revenue RESERVES.

share price index a measure of the change in the average prices of company shares over time. In the UK the *Financial Times All-Share Index* records day-to-day movements in the average price of all company shares listed on the London STOCK MARKET. The Financial Times 100 share index (FTSE-100), the FTSE-250 share index and the FTSE-350 share index show movements in the share prices of, respectively, the top 100, 250 and 350 companies by market capitalization. A similar role is performed in the US by the *Dow-Jones Index* and the *Nasdaq Index*, and in Japan by the *Nikkei Index*.

In technical terms, a share price index is compiled by noting the prices of the shares included in the index at some 'base' point in time (for example, 2 January 2001) and assigning an index number (say 1000) to begin the series. If share prices generally start to increase then this is translated into an upward movement in the value of the index (for example, the value of the index at 2 January 2002 may be, say, 1500, indicating that share prices on average have increased by 50% over a one-year period). Likewise, general falls in share prices are recorded as a decline in the value of the index.

Share price indices reflect the corporate sector's underlying profit and growth record and also act like a barometer of investor confidence or lack of it, about the state of industry and the economy generally. See PRICE INDEX.

share purchase/sale the process of buying and selling STOCKS and SHARES on the STOCK MARKET. This involves a number of procedures where small purchases or sales are involved:

(a) the buyer/seller can approach a STOCKBROKER or COMMERCIAL BANK and instruct them to buy or sell a specific number of shares in a particular company. The stockbroker or bank will then undertake this task for a commission (a minimum fixed amount or a percentage of the value of the transaction);

(b) the stockbroker or bank approaches a MARKET MAKER (formerly called a 'jobber') to buy or sell the shares as instructed. The market maker holds a stock of shares and other financial securities in a limited range of companies determined by the market maker's speciality. The market maker will quote two prices to the stockbroker or bank, a lower 'bid' price at which the market maker is prepared to buy shares, and a higher 'offer' price at which he is prepared to sell the shares. The difference or 'spread' between these prices provides the market maker's profit margin. In quoting two prices the market maker does not know whether the stock-broker intends to buy or sell shares and the stockbroker will only disclose whether he wishes to buy or sell and conclude the transaction if he finds the market maker's prices competitive with those being quoted by other market makers. At this stage a 'bargain' is struck and legal title to the shares passes to the buyer. In contrast to the above '*quote-driven*' exchanges, '*order-driven*' exchanges (such as used by *Tradepoint* (see STOCK MARKET) involve clients posting their own buy/sell instructions.

(c) Trading in the stock market takes place within a 'rolling settlement' system (see ACCOUNT PERIOD) in which settlement for purchases and sales takes place five working days after a deal has been struck.

(d) In order to record the transfer of ownership of the shares to the buyer, the market maker will notify the COMPANY REGISTRAR of the company whose shares have been bought, who will amend his share register and issue a new share certificate to the buyer and cancel share certificates held by the seller. See TALISMAN, CREST.

INSTITUTIONAL INVESTORS such as pension funds follow a broadly similar procedure in transacting shares, though they often bypass stockbrokers and sometimes market makers, buying and selling large volumes of securities direct between themselves. See SPECULATION.

share register a record of a company's SHAREHOLDERS which lists the names and addresses of shareholders and the number of shares and other company securities held by them. The COMPANY SECRETARY is legally obliged to maintain an up-to-date record of all share owners, which necessitates noting all transfers of ownership of shares shortly after they are bought and sold on the STOCK MARKET. TRANSFER DEEDS are used to record share purchases and these in turn are used to update the share register and issue new SHARE CERTIFICATES.

Where shares are held by NOMINEES it is impossible to identify the ultimate beneficial holders of these shares. However in the UK, where an individual shareholder acquires more than 3% of a company's issued shares through one or more nominees, the company's directors are legally entitled to insist on knowing the identity of the shareholder.

share split *or* **stock split** an increase in the number of SHARES in a JOINT-STOCK COMPANY matched by an offsetting reduction in the PAR VALUE of each share so that it does not affect the capitalization of the company. For example, Company X has 10,000 authorized, issued and fully paid up shares each with a par value of £1; and total SHAREHOLDERS' CAPITAL is shown in the BALANCE SHEET at £10,000. The STOCK MARKET values the company at around £100,000, making each share worth £10. The company wishes to attract a wider shareholder base by reducing the market PRICE of each share, and so undertakes a two-for-one stock split, giving existing shareholders two new 50p shares for each £1 share held. The company now has 20,000 authorized, issued and fully paid-up shares of 50p nominal value, and capitalization of the company remains unchanged at £10,000. However, now the stock-market price of the shares will be around £5, which hopefully will improve the marketability of the shares. See also SHARE CAPITAL.

shark repellents see TAKEOVER BID.

shelf life the specified expiry date of a perishable product, usually denoted by a 'sell by date' or 'best before' date instruction.

shelf space the amount of space allocated to a particular product or brand by a wholesaler or retailer. Shelf space is particularly important in the case of consumer goods sold through self-service retail outlets such as SUPERMARKETS, where the amount and location of shelf space devoted to a brand can have a significant impact upon sales volume. See SHELF LIFE.

shell company a company whose shares are currently listed on the STOCK MARKET but which is not actively trading. The share prices of such companies are generally very low and they may offer an attractive means for a business without a stock-market listing to acquire one by TAKEOVER.

shift pay see SHIFT WORK.

shift work a method of organizing work which enables production or services to be operated beyond normal working hours. Employees' working days are known as shifts and may be timed to commence at varying times of the day or night. Where shifts are of equal lengths it is common for employees to rotate around them, working, say 'earlies' one week, 'lates' the next.

There are several forms of shift work:

(a) *double-day shifts,* where there are two shifts of equal length each working day, usually 6 a.m. to 2 p.m. and 2 p.m. to 10 p.m.;

(b) *three-shift working,* where there are three shifts of equal length so that operations can be maintained round the clock either throughout the week including weekends (*continuous*) or from Monday to Friday (*discontinuous*). Where there are peaks of activity, a four-shift system can be used to provide some overlap at certain times of the day;

(c) *continental shift,* where there is a three-shift system but workers change from shift to shift every two or three days rather than each week;

(d) *split-shift working,* where an employee's working day is cut in two, with a middle period off duty. This may be found in industries such as public transport, where demand peaks in the early morning and late afternoon;

(e) *permanent night shifts,* where a separate group of employees work solely at night, thereby achieving the benefit of an extended working day but without disturbing the working patterns of day employees;

(f) *'twilight' shift working,* where a separate group of part-time workers (see PART-TIME WORK) take over from the day shift in the late afternoon and work through until mid or late evening. By this method the productive day is extended but some of the costs of shift work are avoided, such as the need to pay a shift *premium* (see below).

Most shift systems involve a regular pattern of signing-on times but in some cases, for example the railway industry, signing-on times vary from day to day (though they usually broadly correspond to a three-shift working system).

The benefits of shift work to employers include more intensive use of production facilities and, especially in service industries, the capacity to adapt operations to the pattern of demand. Also, some forms of technology, for example in the chemical industry, need to be operated continuously and require some form of shift working. Maintaining productivity in shift work can be problematic, however. People are generally less productive in the small hours of the night, whilst control of performance may be ineffective (witness the occasional media horror stories about night-shift workers getting a good night's sleep alongside their machines). It is recognized that shift work imposes costs on employees, chiefly in the disruption to their social and domestic life. For this reason it is common for some form of shift premium to be paid on top of the hourly pay rate, especially when night work is involved. There is also some evidence that frequent changes to waking hours damage body rhythms and can be harmful to health in the long term.

shop a business premise which is engaged in the retailing of products to customers who visit the shop or store to make purchases. The range of merchandise they stock and sell varies considerably from, at one extreme, total specialization on the one product (as in a shoe shop, for example) to retail operations involving thousands of different lines (as in a large DEPARTMENT STORE). Shop sizes too vary considerably, ranging upwards from small 'corner shop' premises to massive 'hypermarket' complexes (see SUPERMARKET). See RETAIL OUTLET, RETAILER, DISTRIBUTION CHANNEL.

Shop Act 1950 an Act applying to England and Wales which contains provisions relating to SHOP opening times and shop workers' hours. The Act requires every shop to be closed on Sundays except for the sale of a restricted list of products but this has now been amended by the Sunday Trading Act. Daily opening hours are also governed in so far as all shops (with a limited number of exceptions such as shops having an off-licence to sell liquor) must be closed by 8 p.m. except for one 'late day' per week which is until 9 p.m. There are no statutory provisions covering the time shops may open in the morning.

Local courts have the power to fine a trader for infringements of the Act.

In 1994 the Sunday Trading Act made it legal for retailers to open their stores on Sundays. Small shops are permitted to open as normal but larger shops (for example, supermarkets) are restricted to a maximum of six hours.

shop floor the basic level within an organization at which goods (or services) are produced. In a typical manufacturing business the shop floor would consist of operatives working in a factory to produce components or finished goods under the supervision of first line managers.

See SUPERVISOR, SHOP STEWARD.

shopping goods products such as motorcars which represent a major purchasing decision and thus justify the buyer in 'shopping around' to compare suitability, price, quality and style. Contrast with CONVENIENCE GOODS.

shop steward a shop-floor employee who represents his/her colleagues' interests in workplace negotiations with management. Their functions include rectifying with management GRIEVANCES arising at work and the maintenance or creation of patterns of WORK ORGANIZATION desired by their constituents. Although shop stewards are usually TRADE UNION members and are viewed as union representatives, they often function independently of the rest of the union. However, until CHECKOFF AGREEMENTS became widespread, it was common for shop stewards to collect union membership subscriptions.

shortest processing time a scheduling rule that looks at the jobs waiting to be processed and chooses the one with the shortest time for the task. See PRODUCTION SCHEDULING.

short position a situation where a dealer or MARKET MAKER in a particular COMMODITY, FINANCIAL SECURITY or FOREIGN CURRENCY is selling more than he is buying so that his working stock of the item becomes depleted (i.e. runs short).

Shorts BONDS and DEBENTURES which have a redemption date of less than five years.

SIC see STANDARD INDUSTRIAL CLASSIFICATION.

sick pay the payments made to an employee who is unable to work normally due to illness. In principle these payments could be made in place of a wage, from a national insurance fund, or by the employers themselves. The current system of 'statutory sick pay' in the UK (in operation since 1986) combines elements of both. The employer makes payments to the sick employee at a level determined by social security regulations, which are financed out of the National Insurance contributions held by the employer. No payments can be made until the fourth day of absence (unless there has been a previous period of absence due to illness shortly before). After seven days of absence a doctor's certificate is necessary; prior to that the employee provides self-certification. After a prolonged period of sickness absence (currently 28 weeks) responsibility for payment transfers to the DEPARTMENT OF WORK AND PENSIONS.

Many UK employers choose to operate their own sick-pay scheme alongside statutory sick pay, and provide more favourable benefits than the state scheme. Although, traditionally, occupational sick-pay schemes have been applied to managerial and white-collar rather than to blue-collar workers, most UK employees are now covered, by such a scheme. Often they will provide for the employee to receive full pay for up to 28 weeks. Provision of favourable sick pay is often thought to encourage ABSENTEEISM but the evidence suggests that this a short-run phenomenon largely confined to the period immediately after the scheme is introduced.

sight deposit see COMMERCIAL BANK.

SIMO chart see SIMULTANEOUS MOTION CHART.

simple interest see INTEREST.

simple structure an ORGANIZATION where the formal structure is in a rudimentary state, with few rules and regulations to govern how work is done or AUTHORITY exercised. Small organizations in their early stages of development often take this form.

simplex method see LINEAR PROGRAMMING.

simulation a technique for dealing with complex resource allocation problems which cannot be solved exactly by LINEAR PROGRAMMING or similar analytical methods. The technique involves creating a typical life history of a system to represent the actual problem and its rules of operation. Repeated runs of the simulation, slightly altering the operating rules each time, provides experimentation aimed at discovering methods of improving the performance of the system. Such simulation techniques are frequently employed in examining STOCKHOLDING and QUEUE problems. For example, in simulating a queue problem, such as cars queuing at a petrol-station forecourt, it is possible to note how well existing service facilities are coping with customers and the extent to which existing service capacity is utilized. It is also possible to investigate the effects of such changes as increasing the number of service channels or changing the arrangement of channels to discover ways of improving the performance of the garage.

simultaneous motion chart (SIMO chart) a chart used in METHOD STUDY to record a worker's rapid hand movements in performing work tasks. The work elements involved are often identified using slowed down video recordings or films and presented in chart form using THERBLIG symbols. SIMO charts can be used to identify non-productive pauses or awkward hand motions caused by poor workplace layout or badly designed tools. See WORK MEASUREMENT.

single-bin system see STOCK CONTROL.

single channel – multiple phase in queuing where there is a single channel but the customer has to go through several phases. For example renewing or applying for a passport. See QUEUE, SINGLE CHANNEL – SINGLE PHASE, MULTIPLE CHANNEL – SINGLE PHASE.

single channel – single phase in queuing where there is a single channel with the customer going through only one phase. For example queuing to pay in a store where there is only one till. See QUEUE, SINGLE CHANNEL – MULTIPLE PHASE, MULTIPLE CHANNEL – SINGLE PHASE.

single currency see EURO.

single employer bargaining see COLLECTIVE BARGAINING.

Single European Act 1986 (referred to popularly as the '1992' initiative) an Act which extended the principles enshrined in the founding legislation of the EUROPEAN UNION with the objective of creating a 'single market' (by 1992) by the removal of various internal obstacles to the free movement of goods, services, capital and persons between the member states of the Union. Under the Act, the European Commission has submitted some 400 Directives for eliminating disparities between members in respect of physical, technical and fiscal rules and regulations, so as to create a unified Union-wide set of practices: for example, individuals and freight transport will be able to move across national frontiers without undergoing passport and customs checks; common technical specifications are to be introduced relating to product descriptions and design, health and safety standards, etc.; while VAT and other sales taxes are to be applied on a uniform basis. See EUROPEAN ECONOMIC AREA.

single minute exchange of dies (SMED) the concept of exchanging the forming die in a metal press or injection or blow molding machine in less than 10 minutes (hence single minute). Developed as part of the Toyota production system, the technique is part of the JUST-IN-TIME philosophy, allowing very quick SET-UP TIMES for complex and accurate equipment. In some instances the technique has shortened set-up times from greater than four hours to less than 6 minutes. See LEAN MANUFACTURING.

single sourcing obtaining raw materials, components, finished products, and services from one supplier as opposed to multiple sourcing. See SOURCING, LEAN MANUFACTURING, APPROVED SUPPLIER, SUPPLY BASE REDUCTION.

single table bargaining a form of COLLECTIVE BARGAINING where all the trade unions in an organization sit together in negotiations over pay and conditions of employment. The alternative is separate negotiations between each union and management. The benefit of single table bargaining is that it inhibits leapfrog bargaining where each bargaining group tries to outdo the others. The trend in the UK is towards greater use of single table bargaining in those organizations that negotiate with trade unions.

single union deal an agreement between an employer and a TRADE UNION in which the former agrees to recognize the one union in respect of employee representation and COLLECTIVE BARGAINING. In return the union may agree to prohibit strike action by its members (see NO-STRIKE AGREEMENT). Such agreements are not new but they have been the subject of contention recently (especially in relation to Japanese and other foreign companies establishing factories in the UK), because signing such agreements has sometimes resulted in certain trade unions moving outside their traditional sphere of influence to represent occupational groups normally represented by another union.

sinking fund a fund into which periodic payments are made which, with compound INTEREST, will ultimately be sufficient to meet a known future capital commitment or discharge a LIABILITY. Such a fund may be used to finance the replacement of FIXED ASSETS at the end of their useful life or to purchase back company loan stock or DEBENTURES upon maturity. See also DEPRECIATION, definition 1.

sit-in see INDUSTRIAL ACTION.

situational leadership see LEADERSHIP.

skill any competence possessed by someone; in an employment context it often refers to a combination of knowledge and manual dexterity amongst manual workers. JOBS are often categorized as *skilled, semiskilled* or *unskilled* according to the level of skills apparently required to perform them. However, many argue that there is a mismatch between skills that are actually necessary to perform certain jobs and the nomenclature of the job. Jobs classed as skilled may in reality require little skill (perhaps because of the introduction of new technology) whilst unskilled jobs may require more knowledge than is often recognized (tacit skills). It is therefore argued by some that skills are socially constructed. By defining certain jobs as skilled, entry to them can be restricted to those who possess certain recognized competencies or characteristics. If acquisition of these can be controlled then entry to the job can be restricted. In this way the rewards stemming from the job can be maintained at a high level. This has traditionally been the strategy of craft TRADE UNIONS and of PROFESSIONALS. See SOCIOLOGY OF WORK, TRAINING.

skills gap see TRAINING.

skimming pricing see MARKET SKIMMING PRICING.

slack see NETWORK ANALYSIS, ORGANIZATIONAL SLACK.

sleeping partner a partner in a PARTNERSHIP who contributes capital to finance the business but takes no active part in managing the company. Sleeping partners still retain unlimited liability for the debts of the partnership alongside active partners.

slump see BUSINESS CYCLE.

Small Business Council (SBC) an independent body which represents small BUSINESSES in advising the government on policy issues affecting their interests. It does this mainly by liaising with the SMALL BUSINESS SERVICES division of the DEPARTMENT OF TRADE & INDUSTRY (DTI). The SBC has been particularly active in the area of employment policies and regulations.

Small Business Service (SBS) an agency of the DEPARTMENT OF TRADE AND INDUSTRY, established in 2000 to promote the interests of small BUSINESSES (see entry). The SBS's specific tasks are to provide a forum for small firms within government; assist in the formulation of government support mechanisms for small firms, and help small firms in dealing with regulatory provisions. The SBS is responsible also for the development of the BUSINESS LINK network which provides business information, advice and support in England.

Similar business support agencies have been established in Scotland *(the Small Business Gateway* and the *Business Information Source* (operating, respectively, in the *Scottish Enterprise* area (the lowlands) and the *Highland and Islands Enterprise* area); in Wales *(Business Connect)* and in Northern Ireland *(Local Enterprise Development Units).*

The SBS also coordinates various financial support schemes to small and medium sized businesses (SMEs) under the *Enterprise Fund* which has three components: the LOAN GUARANTEE SCHEME which underwrites bank loans etc against default; the *High Technology Fund* (which provides finance for existing funds that support investment in the high technology sector; and *Regional Venture Capital Funds* (which provides equity finance to small local businesses). See SMALL BUSINESS COUNCIL.

small-sized firm see BUSINESS.

SMART scheme (Small Firms Merit Award for Research and Technology) a programme sponsored by the DEPARTMENT OF TRADE AND INDUSTRY, designed to stimulate innovation effort by individuals and small firms to cover feasibility/ consultancy services and the development of prototypes of new processes and products, by providing initial finance. See BUSINESS LINK, INDUSTRIAL POLICY, RESEARCH AND DEVELOPMENT.

SME (small- and medium-sized enterprise) see BUSINESS.

social audit an examination of an organization's employment and equal opportunities performance, its responsiveness to customers; its environmental impact (pollution); and its impact upon the community. Social audits can assist an organization in identifying deficiencies in its performance in the above respects, so that the organization can develop policies to improve its performance. See AUDIT, GREEN AUDIT.

social chapter the EUROPEAN UNION (EU) protocol which established (under the MAASTRICHT TREATY 1991) a set of basic rights at work throughout the EU. These include the right to join a TRADE UNION, the right to take INDUSTRIAL ACTION, the right to equal treatment for men and women (including equal pay) and various provisions relating to collective REDUNDANCIES.

Initially, the UK refused to sign up to the social chapter regarding these as matters for SUBSIDIARITY. However, this stance was reversed in 1997 when the UK signed the AMSTERDAM TREATY, including also the adoption of the WORKING TIME DIRECTIVE and other Directives relating to the employment of young workers and part-time workers, parental leave and worker consultation

social class stratification the division, into groups, of people who tend to possess similar characteristics in terms of values, interests, aspirations and behaviour. See SOCIOECONOMIC GROUP.

social dialogue the involvement of the main European SOCIAL PARTNERS in the development of European Union level policy-making in the areas of enterprise, employment, and INDUSTRIAL RELATIONS.

social group see CORPORATE SOCIAL RESPONSIBILITY.

social partners a European term for representatives of employers and labour i.e. EMPLOYERS ASSOCIATIONS and TRADE UNIONS. See SOCIAL DIALOGUE.

social partnership a relationship between TRADE UNIONS and employers where both SOCIAL PARTNERS work together for the good of the company, and hence of the employees. Typically, social partnership in the UK involves unions agreeing to flexible working practices in return for promises of job security and employer commitment to TRAINING. It also involves the development of institutions to promote dialogue (SOCIAL DIALOGUE) between firms and unions. See COLLECTIVE BARGAINING.

social security benefits benefits provided by the government as a means of assisting low-income members of society such as the unemployed (the JOBSEEKERS ALLOWANCE), the retired (basic old age PENSIONS), the sick (sick pay and free medical treatment), the disabled, single-parent families etc. See DEPARTMENT OF WORK AND PENSIONS.

societal marketing the satisfaction of the needs and wants of consumers in an effective and efficient manner which avoids environmental pollution or waste of the Earth's resources. See SOCIAL RESPONSIBILITY.

socioeconomic group the potential BUYERS of a product grouped together in terms of certain common personal and economic characteristics. Such groups are likely to differ in the level and pattern of their spending and thus can be used as the basis for identifying strategic MARKET SEGMENTS which can then be exploited by targeting 'customized' products to meet the particular customer requirements of those segments.

A commonly used *general* method of classifying potential customers is the 'A to E' social-class grading system:

GRADE A – 'upper middle class': higher managerial, administrative or professional occupations;

GRADE B – 'middle class': middle to senior managers and administrators;

GRADE Cl–'lower middle class': junior managers, supervisory and clerical grades;

GRADE C2 – 'skilled working class': qualified tradespersons;

GRADE D – 'working class': semiskilled and unskilled workers such as labourers;

GRADE E – pensioners.

For most consumer product marketing, a much finer, more detailed customer profile is required based on such data as sex (male, female), age (1–4, 5–10, 11–18, 19–34, 35–49, etc.), income level (£50,000+, under £5,000), housing status (owner-occupier, council-house tenant), etc.

Using such information it is possible, for example, to establish the approximate number of professional, high-income earning women, in the age bracket 35–49, who might provide a potential market for a new premium price exotic perfume. See MARKET SEGMENTATION.

sociology of work a branch of sociology concerned with the attitudes, behaviour and relationships of those engaged in productive activity. As such, it has a number of levels of concern: the individual WORKER, the work GROUP, the ORGANIZATION and society. Traditionally the subject was known as industrial sociology and tended to focus on the attitudes and behaviour of production workers in industry. In recent years its subject matter has widened to take account of the shifts in occupational structure and the importance of work activities conducted outside formal employment (for example DOMESTIC LABOUR).

Industrial sociology emerged in the 1930s with the HAWTHORNE STUDIES. These studies were concerned with the social determinants of job behaviour, especially worker productivity. A notable feature of the Hawthorne studies was the (at the time) novel finding that JOB SATISFACTION was strongly influenced by the social experience of work and that satisfaction was itself an important determinant of worker output. These studies also highlighted the importance of GROUP influences on individual behaviour. Subsequent research in the new discipline was concerned with deepening the analysis of group dynamics and development, and with pinpointing more precisely the determinants of job satisfaction. For a while technological determinism – the notion that technology is the dominant influence on attitudes and behaviour – held sway (see ALIENATION). However, in the 1950s and 1960s, a growing body of thought suggested that there was no necessary relationship between technology and the social organization of work (see SOCIOTECHNICAL SYSTEM, JOB DESIGN AND REDESIGN) and hence a given type of technology could be used in various ways with varying effects on worker satisfaction. In addition sociologists came to appreciate the importance of individuals' expectations and requirements from work in determining their assessment of the quality of work experience (see ORIENTATIONS TO WORK).

In recent years the subject matter of the sociology of work has changed somewhat. Radical commentators have shifted the discipline to some extent to focus more explicitly on the structure of the relationship between employees and employers, and the inequities that flow from this. Arguing that the relationship is essentially one of exploitation, 'labour process' writers have argued that we need to examine the whole process by which employers achieve the 'subordination' of labour. In other words, how do employers control their workforces? It has been argued that there is a long-run tendency for employers to use the principle of SCIENTIFIC MANAGEMENT to reduce their reliance on workers' skills and independent thought. Control of labour is to be achieved by reducing workers to simple 'cogs in the machine'. Critics have argued that many managements lack this degree of planning, and that workers resist such objectives anyway. Both radical sociologists and their critics share, however, a concern with CONFLICT at work and its sources.

In response to the growing participation of women in paid employment in recent years, sociologists have come to examine the characteristics of gender relationships at work, focusing especially on the inequalities of work and its rewards between the sexes, as well as the interrelationship between work and broader societal experiences. In addition, changes in the labour market – the decline of manufacturing employment, for instance – have generally caused sociologists to widen their focus from (male) production workers in paid employment to all kinds of work activity. See also ANOMIE, LABOUR FLEXIBILITY, FLEXIBLE SPECIALIZATION, HOMEWORKING, PART-TIME WORK.

socio-technical system an approach within ORGANIZATION THEORY, associated with the Tavistock Institute in London, which stresses that WORK ORGANIZATION has both a technical and a social dimension. In a study of coalmining, researchers found that the replacement of group working by MASS PRODUCTION methods had disrupted the prevailing social systems with adverse effects on JOB SATISFACTION. With the specialization of work tasks, miners had fewer opportunities for job rotation, and the cohesive work groups were fragmented. The researchers concluded that, to be effective, work organization should not be determined by technology alone but should take account of the prevailing social system. They found that several forms of work organization, each with its own social and psychological effects, were compatible with a given level of technology. It was thus possible to choose a method of work organization that was efficient and also provided benefits to the participants. See JOB DESIGN AND REDESIGN.

soft currency a FOREIGN CURRENCY that is in weak demand, but in abundant supply on the FOREIGN EXCHANGE MARKET. This situation usually arises when a country is in persistent balance-of-payments deficit. Compare HARD CURRENCY.

soft loan a LOAN that bears an INTEREST RATE charge which is much lower than the market rate of interest for such loans. Soft loans are made available by the government to encourage investment in particular types of industrial activity or in particular regions, and by international organizations such as the INTERNATIONAL MONETARY FUND and

WORLD BANK to help countries with balance-of-payments difficulties, provide economic aid and to assist industrial development. See INDUSTRIAL POLICY, REGIONAL POLICY.

soft sell a gentle and indirect approach to marketing a BRAND or product. This style of ADVERTISING or PERSONAL SELLING can appeal to more discerning prospective buyers who require more objective information about a product. See HARD SELL.

software the PROGRAMS or instructions that make a COMPUTER system perform particular data-processing tasks. Some software makes the computer system operate while other software packages like SPREADSHEETS or WORD PROCESSING provide solutions to particular business problems.

sole proprietorship a BUSINESS or firm which is owned and controlled by a single person. See PARTNERSHIP, JOINT-STOCK COMPANY, LIMITED LIABILITY.

solidaristic (orientation to work) see ORIENTATION TO WORK.

SORP see ACCOUNTING STANDARDS.

sources and uses of funds statement *or* **funds-flow statement** an accounting statement that shows the sources from which a firm derives its cash and the use to which this cash is put during a trading period. The major source of funds is usually the net cash generated from sales, though this can be added to by cash raised from selling FIXED ASSETS and by raising further LOANS or new SHARE ISSUES. The major applications of funds are the purchase of new FIXED ASSETS, repayment of LOANS and payments of TAXES and DIVIDENDS. When further allowance is made for the cash-flow effect of changes in STOCKS, DEBTORS and CREDITORS, the sources and uses of funds statement shows the net inflow or outflow of cash to the firm. See CASH FLOW STATEMENTS.

sources of finance the provision of finance to a company to cover its short-term WORKING CAPITAL requirements and longer-term FIXED ASSETS and investments.

In financing their business operations, companies typically resort to a mix of internally generated funds and external capital. The company's own RETAINED PROFIT is the primary source of internal funds. Short-term external finance is obtained largely in the form of TRADE CREDITS extended by suppliers, and BANK LOANS and OVERDRAFTS from the commercial banks. Long-term external finance takes the form principally of SHARE CAPITAL (ordinary and preference shares) subscribed by private investors, the institutional investors, merchant banks and venture capital specialists; LOAN CAPITAL (loan stock and debentures) SUBSCRIBED by the above plus the commercial banks; and miscellaneous grants and loans made available by governments (see, for example, INDUSTRIAL POLICY, REGIONAL POLICY). See also FACTORING, LEASING, LETTER OF CREDIT, FORFAITING, LOAN GUARANTEE SCHEMES, BUSINESS ENTERPRISE INVESTMENT SCHEME, ENTERPRISE GRANT SCHEME.

sourcing the selection by a firm of its sources of supply – raw materials and components in the case of a manufacturer, final products in the case of a retailer. Strategically, a firm may chose to buy in a particular input (or product) from an outside supplier (OUTSOURCING), or produce it for itself as part of a vertically integrated operation (see VERTICAL INTEGRATION, MAKE-OR-BUY DECISION). In the former case, a firm may choose to favour one or a number of suppliers, both domestic and overseas-based, depending on various cost and risk considerations. For example, relying on a single supplier may allow the firm to benefit from discounts given on bulk purchases, but on the other hand may expose the firm to great risk of supply disruptions. For this reason multiple-supplier locations may be preferred, especially in the case of MULTINATIONAL ENTERPRISES which may deploy global sourcing strategies to take advantage of differences in supply costs between countries and obtain access to new component technologies and products. See LOCAL CONTENT RULE, JUST-IN-TIME (JIT) SYSTEM, INTERNATIONALIZATION, PURCHASING SUPPLIER DEVELOPMENT.

span of control the number of people a manager has formal AUTHORITY over and is responsible for. Most ORGANIZATIONS are structured on the premise that there are practical limitations to the number of people one manager can effectively supervise without becoming overloaded or losing sight of what the subordinates are doing. CLASSICAL MANAGEMENT THEORY held that the optimum span of control was around six people. It is now generally believed that the effective width of the span is to some extent determined by the distribution of decision-making. Where this is decentralized a wider span is feasible. The span of control is often inversely related to the number of levels in the HIERARCHY of an ORGANIZATION. The more levels, the smaller the span of control, and vice versa.

spare parts see REPLACEMENT PARTS.

special deposit see MONETARY POLICY.

Special Drawing Right see INTERNATIONAL MONETARY FUND.

specialist shop a RETAIL OUTLET which concentrates exclusively on selling either a particular type of product or a narrow range of related products: a shoe shop, a butcher's shop, an electrical goods shop, a chemist's shop etc. Specialist shops may be under a single shop ownership or run as a multiple CHAIN-STORE business. Traditionally, specialist shops have competed mainly by offering personal service and good quality products. Increasingly, however, with the appearance of SUPERMARKETS and DISCOUNT STORES, specialist shops have been forced to compete on price. In this regard, the large specialist shop chains have been able to obtain significant price discounts by BULK BUYING from manufacturers, while single shops have found it advantageous to participate in VOLUNTARY GROUP organizations to obtain similar concessions. See RETAILER, DISTRIBUTION CHANNEL.

speciality goods products such as designer clothes or photographic equipment which have unique characteristics and brand identification, and which particular buyers seek to purchase through specialist sales outlets.

specialization a form of division of labour whereby each individual or firm concentrates its productive efforts on a single or limited number of activities. By specializing on a single work task or JOB, an individual is usually more productive since familiarity and repetition improve work skills and time is not lost moving from one job to another. Labour specialization is a feature of PRODUCTION LINE or ASSEMBLY LINE operations used in mass production.

Likewise firms may choose to specialize in the production of a limited range of products (see HORIZONTAL INTEGRATION) to focus their business interests and to take advantage of economies of large-scale production. See ECONOMIES OF SCALE.

See also JOB DESIGN AND REDESIGN, PRODUCTIVITY, INTERNATIONAL TRADE.

specific risk *or* **diversifiable risk** that part of total risk (within the CAPITAL-ASSET-PRICING MODEL) uniquely attributable to the holding of a specific financial security. Unlike MARKET RISK, specific risk is independent of general market variations. Events unique to a particular security may comprise such corporate decisions as dividend policy, changes in capital structure, recruitment of top personnel and so forth. Changes in a firm's share price may be positive or negative depending upon the opinion of investors. The argument is that such specific variations occur randomly, and therefore if a sufficiently large and well-diversified PORTFOLIO of shares is held, such variations will cancel each other out. This means that investors can eliminate specific risk by diversifying their portfolio.

specific tax a TAX which is levied at a fixed rate per physical unit of output. Compare AD VALOREM TAX.

specifier an individual in an organization who is responsible for determining the specification of a product which is to be bought. See PURCHASING.

speculation the buying and selling of COMMODITIES (tea, tin etc.), FINANCIAL SECURITIES (shares etc.) and FOREIGN CURRENCIES whose market prices are characterized by substantial fluctuations over time, by individuals and firms (speculators) in the hope of making windfall profits. For example, in the STOCK MARKET and FOREIGN EXCHANGE MARKET, a speculator may take a 'bullish' view that a share price or the exchange rate of a currency will rise and may gamble on this possibility by buying that share or currency, using either his or her own money or short-term credits, and hoping to resell it at a higher price after a few days or weeks, in order to make a capital gain on the difference between the two prices. On the other hand, the speculator may take a 'bearish' view that a share price or currency value will fall and may gamble on this possibility by selling the share or currency (even though he or she does not currently own any), using the proceeds from this sale to buy at a lower price the shares or currency he or she has promised to deliver a week or two later.

Speculative activity may have a destabilizing effect on share prices or exchange rates if speculators take a collective view that prices will rise or fall, accelerating and magnifying upward or downward price movements. Because of the disruptive effects of speculation on international trade, countries' central banks often intervene in the foreign exchange markets to maintain 'orderly' exchange rates. See ARBITRAGE, FORWARD MARKET, FLOATING EXCHANGE RATE SYSTEM, STAG, ACCOUNT PERIOD.

speculator see SPECULATION.

split-shift working see SHIFT WORK.

sponsorship a business relationship between a provider of funds, resources or services and an individual, event, or organization which offers in return some rights and association that may be used for commercial advantage.

spot market a market which provides for the buying and selling of FINANCIAL SECURITIES (shares, stocks), FOREIGN CURRENCIES, and COMMODITIES (rubber, tin etc.) for immediate delivery, as opposed to a FORWARD MARKET which provides for delivery at some future point in time. Spot prices reflect current demand and supply conditions for the financial security, currency or commodity being traded (see EQUILIBRIUM MARKET PRICE). Spot prices for commodities and financial assets transacted at different locations are harmonized by ARBITRAGE dealings. See FOREIGN EXCHANGE MARKET, COMMODITY MARKET, STOCK MARKET.

spread the difference between the bid (buy) and offer (sell) price of a FINANCIAL SECURITY, FOREIGN CURRENCY OR COMMODITY quoted by a MARKET MAKER or dealer. See BID PRICE.

spreadsheet a COMPUTER software program package which enables data to be analysed in columns and rows. Spreadsheets are widely used for financial analysis.

SRO see FINANCIAL SERVICES ACT 1986.

SSAP see ACCOUNTING STANDARDS.

stability index see LABOUR TURNOVER.

staff see LINE AND STAFF.

staff association an association of employees of an organization formed (often by management) to pursue issues of common interest, such as the provision of recreational facilities at work. Such associations are rarely given the right to negotiate over WAGE RATES and conditions of employment. See COMPANY UNION, TRADE UNION.

staff status the status held by those individuals (usually 'white-collar' WORKERS) whose conditions of employment, including hours of work, holiday and pension entitlements are generally more favourable than those possessed by manual workers in an organization. It is also common for those enjoying staff status to have separate canteen arrangements. Many believe that these differences foster a 'them and us' attitude at work, and some organizations have attempted to overcome this by a process of harmonization – bringing the conditions of employment of all or most employees into line (usually towards the more favourable ones of those with staff status). See JAPANIZATION.

stag a person who subscribes for a new SHARE ISSUE by applying for a large number of shares in the hope that the demand for new shares exceeds the number being issued and that this will lead to an increase in the share price when they are first transacted on the STOCK MARKET. Stags are speculators who buy shares to make a quick profit rather than as long-term investors.

stakeholder someone having an interest or stake in the operations and performance of a firm. *Shareholders* in a company have an interest in so far as they have invested money in the company and look for a return on that investment in the form of dividends and share appreciation. *Employees* have a stake since they work in the firm and are dependent on the firm for their jobs and incomes. *Customers* have a stake since they buy products from the firm and require a stable supply of products that are safe, effective and affordable. *Suppliers* have a stake as providers of raw materials and services. Finally the broader *community* has a stake in the firm and looks to the firm to behave as a 'good citizen' who will avoid polluting the environment and will help in solving community problems such as inner city decay etc.

Until recent years managers were expected to run companies largely in the interests of shareholders; however in recent years firms have been urged to adopt broader responsibilities to *all* stakeholders.

See CORPORATE SOCIAL RESPONSIBILITY, CORPORATE GOVERNANCE.

stakeholder mapping a technique for assessing the potential effect of STAKEHOLDERS upon an organization. Stakeholder mapping seeks to assess, first, the power of different stakeholders' groups to effect the organization and, second, the level of interest which stakeholders have in the organization's activities. By plotting power and interest levels of different stakeholders in a matrix it is possible to track the changes in the potential influences of different stakeholders' groups; and to assess the impact of a particular strategic development in stakeholders.

stakeholder pension see PENSION.

stamp duty a UK TAX on the value of SHARES purchased on the STOCK MARKET.

standard cost an estimated product cost, prepared in advance of production, that

		£	£
Standard direct materials cost			
Frame Wood	5m at £4 per m	20.00	
Spring Unit	one at £10 each	10.00	
Upholstery	$3m^2$ at £10 per m^2	30.00	60.00
Standard direct labour cost			
Assembling	2hrs at £5 per hr	10.00	
Upholstering	1hr at £10 per hr	10.00	20.00
Standard prime cost			80.00
Production overheads (£10 per unit)*		10.00	
Standard factory cost			90.00
Selling, distribution, administration overheads (30%)**			27.00
Standard total cost			117.00

* Production overhead cost rate:

$$\frac{\text{budgeted production overheads}}{\text{budgeted output}} = \frac{£20{,}000}{2{,}000 \text{ units}} = £10 \text{ per unit}$$

** Selling etc. overheads cost rate:

$$\frac{\text{budgeted selling, distributed and administration overheads}}{\text{standard factory cost of total output}} = \frac{£30{,}000}{£100{,}000} = \text{30\% on factory cost}$$

Fig. 78 **Standard cost.** Table showing the standard cost of an upholstered chair.

shows what a product ought to cost given reasonably efficient working. Standard cost includes the direct materials cost of the product, direct labour cost and production overheads, as well as distribution, selling and administration overheads. Overheads are charged to products using an appropriate COST RATE derived by dividing budgeted overheads by budgeted output. Fig. 78 shows a simplified standard cost for a product. Such predetermined standard costs are used to provide a basis for price fixing and for cost control through VARIANCE ANALYSIS. See also DIRECT-LABOUR COST VARIANCE, DIRECT-MATERIALS COST VARIANCE, OVERHEAD-COST VARIANCE.

Standard Industrial Classification (SIC) a system which codifies and measures groups of economic activity at various levels of aggregation and disaggregation. In the UK, the Standard Industrial Classification comprises 10 major divisions, 60 classes, 222 groups and 334 activities. Activities, or their equivalent 'industries' (see INDUSTRY), are derived on the basis of their *supply* characteristics, in particular the use of common raw materials and processes of manufacture. Such a classification provides a useful source of information on industry structure and statistical details of employment, output and investment by the industrial sector. However, for purposes of MARKETING strategy, SIC data usually needs to be reinterpreted in order to provide more meaningful specifications of MARKETS, defined in terms of groups of products which are regarded by *buyers* as close substitute products. To illustrate, glass jars and metal cans are assigned to different industries by the SIC (Division 2, Activity 'glass containers', Division 3 'packaging products of metal', respectively), but would be regarded by a user of packaging materials such as a coffee manufacturer as substitute products. See STRUCTURE OF INDUSTRY.

standardization 1 the limitation of a firm's product and component range as a means of controlling production and marketing costs. By limiting the PRODUCT RANGE a firm can mass-produce each product and achieve ECONOMIES OF SCALE through long production runs, but forgoes potential sales by serving only a limited number of market segments. However it may be possible to cut production costs while maintaining product VARIETY through standardization and interchangeability of components. Standardization serves to reduce the variety of finished product stocks or materials and component stocks held, simplifying purchasing and STOCK CONTROL. Compare CUSTOMIZATION.

2 see ORGANIZATION.

standard of living the general level of economic prosperity in an economy as measured by, for example, the level of per capita income (GROSS NATIONAL PRODUCT divided by the size of the POPULATION). A country's standard of living will depend on such things as its level of economic maturity, investment and productivity and the provision by the government of various social welfare programmes. Advanced industrial countries like Japan (income per head $33,990 in 2003) and the UK (income per head $24,230 in 2003) are much more prosperous than developing countries such as the Upper Volta, Chad etc. (whose levels of income per head are less than $500).

standard rate the average work rate at which an operative possessing the appropriate skill level and motivation performs a work task. For example, if the 'observed time' for an operative performing a task was 5 minutes and the operative was judged to be working at a faster work pace than the standard rate, say twice as fast, then the observed time would need to be lengthened to 10 minutes in calculating the 'basic time' which an operative working at standard rate would take to perform the task. See WORK MEASUREMENT.

standard time the time that it should take a motivated operative with the appropriate level of skill to complete a work task, including an ALLOWANCE for relaxation, machine break-down and interruptions. See WORK MEASUREMENT.

standing order see COMMERCIAL BANK.

star see BOSTON MATRIX.

statement of account a periodic statement sent to a customer by a supplier that sets out both the money value of products supplied to the customer over a monthly or other period, and any amounts still owed by the customer for these products. A statement of account is sent by a supplier some time after an INVOICE has been sent. Compare DELIVERY NOTE.

statements of recommended practice (SORP) see ACCOUNTING STANDARDS.

statements of standard accounting practice (SSAPs) see ACCOUNTING STANDARDS.

statistical inference a process by which we infer conclusions about a statistical POPULATION from which only a SAMPLE has been drawn. For example, if one million Britons buy bicycles each year, and 200 are asked why they do so, 50% may say because it helps to keep them fit. From this sample one may infer that 50% of the total population of one million Britons buying bicycles do so for this reason. However, it is not possible to say with 100% accuracy that this is the case unless the views of all one million were obtained. Nevertheless, it is possible to say with reasonable confidence that the estimation of 50% is correct for the whole population.

statistical quality control an aspect of QUALITY CONTROL which involves inspecting and testing a sample of a raw material, component or product in order to make inferences about the quality of all the output of that material, component or product. Where inspection and testing involves destruction of the product, statistical quality control based on sampling is the only means of monitoring quality.

statistics 1 methods of collecting and analysing numerical data.

2 a group of data.

Businesspeople make considerable use of statistical methods such as collecting SAMPLES in order to make STATISTICAL INFERENCES in such areas as MARKETING RESEARCH and QUALITY CONTROL. They also use government economic data in monitoring changes in the business environment.

status see BUYER BEHAVIOUR, PSYCHOLOGICAL PRICING.

statute law the law laid down by government legislation (in the UK, an Act of Parliament). Examples include the FAIR TRADING ACT 1973 and the Companies Act 1989. Once such legislation is on the statute books, it is then up to the courts to interpret and enforce the provisions of this legislation. Compare COMMON LAW. See COMPANY LAW, LABOUR LAW, COMPETITION LAW.

statutory ESOP see EMPLOYEE SHARE OWNERSHIP PLAN.

statutory formats the formats in which the final accounts of companies (PROFIT AND LOSS ACCOUNT and BALANCE SHEET) have to be reported, which in the UK is governed by company law.

statutory sick pay see SICK PAY.

statutory union recognition procedure a legal entitlement for TRADE UNIONS to be recognized by an employer for COLLECTIVE BARGAINING purposes where it is the clear wish of the workers involved. Where a union is unable to obtain the employer's agreement, it may submit a claim for recognition to the CENTRAL ARBITRATION COMMITTEE (CAC). The CAC can award recognition where more than half of the relevant workforce are members of the union making the claim. Alternatively, it can organize a ballot of the workers. Recognition will be granted if a majority of those voting and 40% of the eligible workers vote for recognition.

stealth tax a 'buzzword' for a relatively obscure TAX increase (e.g. stamp duty) announced with little publicity and explanation, usually to be implemented some months later by which time people generally have 'forgotten' about it. See FISCAL POLICY.

sterling the name given to the UK POUND when used in international dealings, primarily to distinguish it from other countries also using the pound as a domestic currency. Formerly, large amounts of sterling were held by members of the British Commonwealth (the so-called 'sterling area bloc') and others, as part of their INTERNATIONAL RESERVES.

step change a method for creating a change in an organization's ways of working that is neither gradual nor incremental. The described methodology seeks a jump in PRODUCTIVITY, usually using enabling technology and knowledge. The introduction of FLOW LINE production by Ford could be considered a step change from the previous batch method of working, as could the introduction of CAD, CAM into what was previously a craft machine shop. See LEAN MANUFACTURING.

stewardship accounting records kept by business entities of all their transactions, outstanding debts, and the way in which their capital employed has been invested. For example, in a public limited company, the directors have a stewardship role, and manage the company on behalf of the shareholders. Hence the need to keep proper books of account.

stimuli the various components, verbal, written or visual, of an ADVERTISEMENT for a product which are designed to encourage consumers to buy the product. See ADVERTISING COPY.

stock 1 the part of a firm's ASSETS that are held in the form of raw materials, work in progress and finished goods. These are also known as INVENTORIES. Finished goods are held in stock to ensure that goods are available when required by customers. Raw materials and components are held in stock to prevent disruptions to production caused by lack of materials or components and to secure economies from BULK BUYING. Decisions as to what *level* of stock to hold may not be entirely in the businessman's hands. Involuntary investment may occur when demand turns out to be less than a producer's expectations. Fig. 79 shows the main components of stock. See STOCK VALUATION, STOCK CONTROL, CONSIGNMENT INVENTORY, DEPENDENT INVENTORY, INDEPENDENT INVENTORY.

2 a FINANCIAL SECURITY issued by a JOINT-STOCK COMPANY or by the government as a means of raising long-term capital. In some countries (for example the US) stockholders are the equivalent of shareholders and are the owners of the company. In other countries (for example the UK) stock is a form of repayable, fixed-interest DEBT and stockholders are creditors of the company not shareholders. Stocks are traded on the STOCK MARKET. See SHARE CAPITAL.

stock appreciation the increase in the market value of STOCK held during a specific time period, generally because of INFLATION. Accountants value stock at the lower of either cost or net realizable value in the BALANCE SHEET, not at replacement cost, and when stock is sold, tax is paid on the profits arising. This gives rise to 'phantom profits' and is one reason why British firms were given stock relief in taxation calculations during the inflationary period of the 1970s. Where prices are falling, *stock depreciation* results. See also HISTORIC COST, INFLATION ACCOUNTING, STOCK VALUATION.

stockbroker a business which acts as a market intermediary in bringing together buyers and sellers of financial securities s uch as STOCK, SHARES and BONDS. See STOCK MARKET, AGENT, TRADER/DEALER, STOCKBROKING.

stockbroking the function of buying and selling FINANCIAL SECURITIES such as STOCKS SHARES and BONDS through the STOCK MARKET by a dealer (*stockbroker*) who acts as an agent on behalf of clients wishing to buy or sell securities. In the UK, some dealers act solely as stockbrokers, but others combine stockbroking with JOBBING and act also as principals in 'making a market' in securities. See MARKET MAKER, SHARE PURCHASE/SALE, DUAL CAPACITY.

stock depreciation see STOCK APPRECIATION.

stock dividend a DIVIDEND payment whereby a SHAREHOLDER is paid a dividend in the form of additional SHARES or STOCKS in the company rather than in the form of cash. See also STOCK SPLITS.

stock exchange a MARKET which deals in the buying and selling of company stocks and shares and government bonds. See STOCK MARKET entry for fuller discussion.

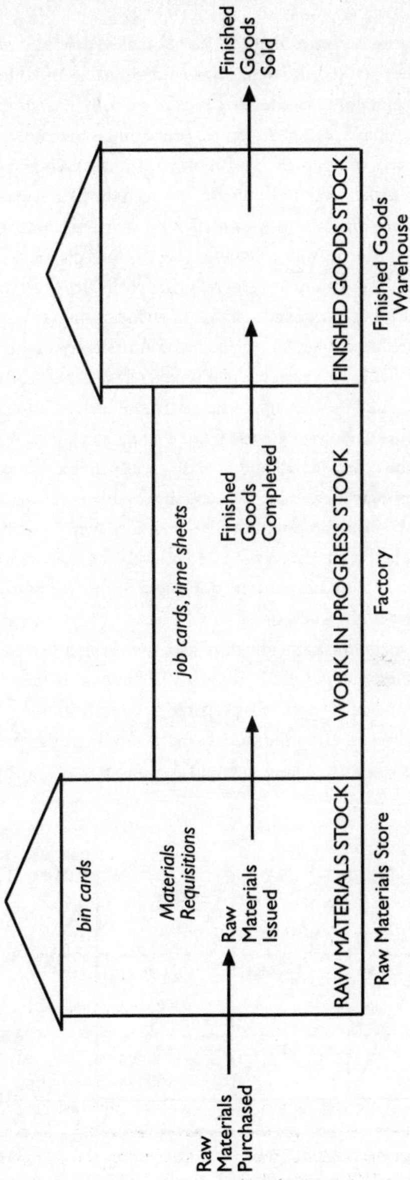

Fig. 79 **Stock.** Diagram showing the main components.

stock control

The process of controlling STOCKS of finished products, work in progress and raw materials, in order to minimize warehousing and other stockholding costs, while maintaining an adequate level of stock to meet usage requirements.

The object of a stock-control procedure is to maintain records of existing stock levels, compare these with planned stock levels and place orders for new stock to make good the difference between the two. Replenishment of stock is achieved by placing outside orders for purchased raw materials or components, or by initiating further production for finished goods or components.

Fig. 80 illustrates the general principle by depicting a simple stockholding problem where usage of stock is known in advance, rate of usage is constant and where stocks can be replenished completely once they run out. Once the firm is out of stock then it will immediately order and bring into stock fresh items to build its stock up to the maximum level M. After this the stock level will again fall as items are used. The average stock level A will depend upon the size of the orders placed and how frequently they are placed, with large orders placed at infrequent intervals necessitating high average stocks. In placing orders the firm may establish a stock *reorder level* R, placing orders for new stocks when stocks fall to the reorder level. The stock reorder level will be set to take into account usage of the stock item during the reorder period or *lead time* between placing a new order and delivery of the replacement items into stock. Operating on this principle the firm would replenish stock at order intervals between reorder points T_1, T_2 and T_3. The *minimum stock level,* S. is the smallest stock level which the firm is prepared to tolerate immediately prior to replenishment. This minimum stock level is usually greater than zero because the firm will wish to hold a certain amount of *safety stock* or *buffer stock* to

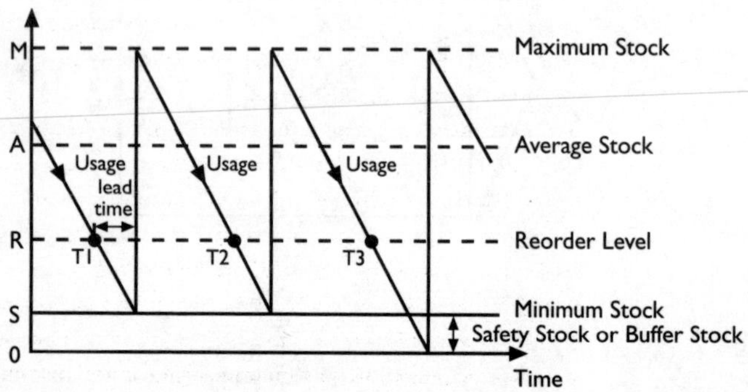

Fig. 80 **Stock control.** A simple stock-holding system.

meet unexpectedly rapid usage or delays in delivery which extend the lead time. Without a safety stock, usage and lead time variability could lead to costly 'stockouts' with disruptions to production or delivery delays to customers. The size of safety stock carried will seek to balance the extra stockholding costs such as warehousing costs and interest charges associated with safety stocks on the one hand, and the cost of stockouts on the other hand. Since the precise cost of stockouts is difficult to determine the firm may start by deciding the 'service level' or number of stockouts per period considered acceptable, then estimate the safety stock necessary to ensure this level of service.

The stock-control system depicted here is known as the reorder level system. One specific version of the reorder level system is the *two-bin* system which is frequently used where large quantities of inexpensive items are concerned, the stock being held in two bins or containers. Stock is drawn from one bin only until it is empty, at which stage a further full bin of items is ordered. Whilst this is being obtained, stock is drawn from the second bin. This is a simple and effective system which requires the minimum of clerical work and administration, since the physical division of stock into two areas (bins) makes the order decision almost automatic. The same result can be achieved by marking the reorder level on a single bin.

Sealed minimum stock systems operate along similar lines, where the reorder stock level is sealed in a bag and orders are placed when 'open' stock is exhausted and the bag must be opened.

Finally, *base stock* systems make provision to place a replenishment order every time a withdrawal is made from stock, ordering an amount which exactly replaces the amount withdrawn so as always to maintain a given level of base stock. Operation of reorder level systems requires the firm to maintain *perpetual stock* records, that is, up-to-date daily records of the stock situation of all items.

As an alternative to reorder level systems, firms may operate *reorder point* systems, placing orders for variable amounts of an item at fixed time intervals. With such reorder point or periodic review systems the stock of each item is checked at preplanned intervals and orders of varying size placed to replenish stocks. Such replenishment at fixed time intervals is administratively cheaper, allows orders for several items from a common supplier to be combined, and requires stocks to be checked only at the order point avoiding the expense of daily stock checks. One specific version of the reorder point system is the *single-bin* system where the desired maximum stock is marked on the side of a single bin and orders are placed for an amount to replenish the contents of the bin up to that mark at regular intervals. See STOCKHOLDING MODEL, MATERIALS MANAGEMENT, MATERIALS REQUIREMENTS PLANNING, JUST-IN-TIME (JIT) SYSTEM, STOCK-TURNOVER RATIO, OPTIMIZED PRODUCTION TECHNOLOGY.

Stock Exchange Automated Quotation System (SEAQ) see STOCK MARKET.

Stock Exchange Pool Nominees see SEPON.

stockholding model *or* **economic order quantity model** a method used in STOCK CONTROL of raw materials, components or finished goods which seeks to balance stockholding costs and delivery costs for a STOCK item in order to determine the optimum order quantity for that item.

The principal objective of stock-control procedures is to maintain stocks at the lowest total cost consistent with satisfying demand. This involves balancing two sets of cost:

(a) *stockholding costs:* the cost to firms of holding stocks of finished products and raw materials in order to provide immediate customer service or to prevent disruptions to production caused by lack of materials. Stockholding costs include costs of warehouse space, insurance, deterioration and obsolescence of stored items and interest on capital tied up in stocks. Such costs are roughly proportional to the value of the stock held, and to contain such costs, stock levels need to be kept low;

(b) *order costs:* costs for ordering and delivering goods for stock such as communicating with suppliers or the firm's own production department, accounting transactions, transport and unloading and inspecting goods. Many of these ordering and delivery costs will remain the same irrespective of the size of the order. Since many order and delivery costs are fixed costs, in order to reduce these costs the firm should place large orders at infrequent intervals, and such a policy would have the additional benefit of allowing the firm to earn price discounts for BULK BUYING. However if orders are placed at in frequent intervals then stocks, and thus stockholding costs, will be high. It is desirable to strike a balance between these two groups of costs so as to achieve the minimum stock cost, as in Fig. 81 which shows the *optimum order quantity* or *economic order quantity* which serves to minimize total stock cost. Order and delivery costs decrease as larger and less frequent deliveries are made; however, larger deliveries at less frequent intervals involve holding a larger average stock and thus entail higher carrying costs. The optimum order quantity OB corresponds to the minimum point on the total stock-cost curve. See BATCH SIZE.

stockist a WHOLESALER or RETAILER who holds STOCKS of products, components and replacement parts for a particular manufacturer.

stockout see STOCK CONTROL.

stockpiling the holding of levels of STOCK which are greater than would be normally required by a person, firm or government agency. Stockpiling usually occurs at times of an actual or expected shortage of a product or in anticipation of a price rise.

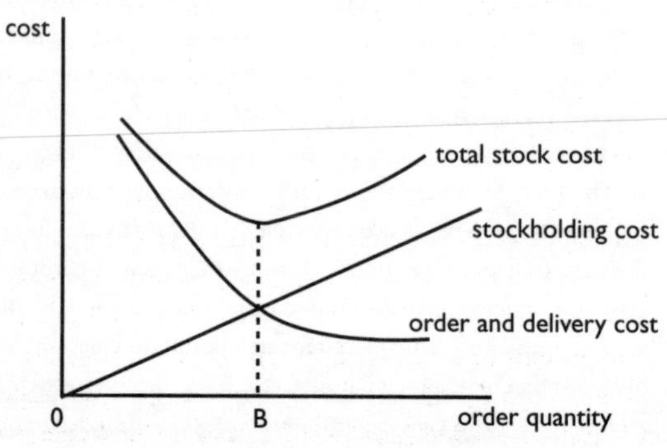

Fig. 81 **Stockholding model**. Stockholding cost.

stock market/exchange *or* capital market

A MARKET which deals in the buying and selling of company STOCKS and SHARES and government BONDS. The stock market, together with the MONEY MARKET (which deals in short-term company and government securities), are the main sources of external capital to industry and the government.

Institutions that are involved in the UK Stock Market include MARKET MAKERS (who perform JOBBING and STOCKBROKING functions), specialist stockbrokers, ISSUING HOUSES, MERCHANT BANKS, and, as general buyers and sellers of securities, the CENTRAL BANK, COMMERCIAL BANKS, PENSION FUNDS, INSURANCE COMPANIES, UNIT TRUSTS and INVESTMENT TRUST COMPANIES, together with private individuals, industrial companies and overseas investors and institutions.

The stock market performs two principal functions. It provides:

(a) a *primary* or 'new issue' market where capital for investment and other purposes can be raised by the issue of new stocks, shares and bonds (see SHARE ISSUE);

(b) a *secondary* market for dealings in existing securities (see SPOT MARKET), including forward dealings (see FORWARD MARKET), which facilitates the easy transferability of securities from sellers to buyers (see SHARE PURCHASE/SALE). Day-to-day movements in the prices of shares (and other securities) are recorded by various SHARE PRICE INDICES, for example, the FTSE-100. See EQUILIBRIUM MARKET PRICE.

In the UK, the London Stock Exchange is the country's main centre for dealings in securities, supported by five provincial exchanges (Glasgow, Liverpool, Birmingham, York and Belfast).

In order to obtain a full listing or quotation on the London stock exchange for their shares, companies must satisfy various, requirements, including proof of their financial standing and previous business history, and be prepared to issue at least 25% of their shares to the investing public. Additionally, smaller companies can raise capital without obtaining a full listing through the ALTERNATIVE INVESTMENT MARKET.

In recent years, stock markets worldwide, such as those based in London, New York, Tokyo, Zurich and Paris, have become increasingly interdependent with the growth of MULTINATIONAL ENTERPRISES whose securities are traded on a number of exchanges while financial institutions and securities firms themselves have become more internationally based. This has led to an increase in competitive pressures, which has brought about a number of important changes, particularly in the case of the UK stock market, including:

(a) the so-called *big bang* – the termination (under the prodding of the OFFICE OF FAIR TRADING) of the CARTEL arrangements for fixing minimum commissions on securities transactions and the ending of the traditional division between the stockbroking and jobbing functions;

(b) various *mergers* and joint ventures between UK securities firms and international securities and banking groups, so as to provide clients with a more diversified range of financial services and geographical spread

(c) the *computerization* of dealing systems, using the *Stock Exchange Automated Quotation System* (SEAQ) which provides a mechanism for linking buying and selling transactions on a global basis. This has largely transferred day-to-day business from a physical presence on the stock exchange floor to telephone exchanges and the use of VDU computer terminals in dealing rooms.

In recognition of the growth in international dealings, the London Stock Exchange merged in the 1990s with the International Securities Regulatory Organization (ISRO) which represented the big international securities firms. In November 1999, a new competitive stimulus emerged when the London Stock Exchange set up a new sub-exchange (*Techmark*) for the listing of shares in high tech companies, only to be followed days later by NASDAQ (the US high tech stock exchange) setting up a rival exchange in London as part of its plan to build a pan-European operation. In addition, the London Stock Exchange has faced competition from *Tradepoint*, an electronic stock exchange based in London and owned by a consortium headed by Reuters and a number of American investment banks and fund management groups. Like NASDAQ, Tradepoint aims to build a pan-European trading system.

In 2000 the Paris, Amsterdam and Brussels stock exchanges merged to form the 'Euronext' exchange, and SWX, the Swiss stock exchange, joined up with Tradepoint to form the *Virt-X* exchange. Also in 2000 hostile bids for the London Stock Exchange by the German exchange, Deutsche Bourse, and the Swedish exchange failed. However, in 2005, the Deutsche Bourse and Euronext both put in hostile takeover bids for the London Stock Exchange. (Watch this space!)

In 2001 Euronext took over the LONDON INTERNATIONAL FINANCIAL FUTURES EXCHANGE (LIFFE) to form a combined 'spot' and forward exchange facility. See FORWARD MARKET.

On the UK stock market, transactions (transfers and settlements) are processed by the TALISMAN and CREST systems using a *rolling settlement* procedure which has replaced the traditional ACCOUNT PERIOD arrangement. The UK stock market is a *Recognized Investment Exchange,* and operates under the regulatory framework laid down by the FINANCIAL SERVICES ACT 1986. See FINANCIAL SYSTEM, CITY CODE ON TAKEOVERS AND MERGERS, INSIDER DEALING, SPECULATION, DUAL CAPACITY, SINGLE CAPACITY, PORTFOLIO, INDIVIDUAL SAVINGS ACCOUNT, LONDON INTERNATIONAL FINANCIAL FUTURES EXCHANGE (LIFFE), EUREX.

stock split see SHARE SPLIT.

stocktaking the process of checking physical STOCKS of raw materials, components or finished goods against STORES records of materials quantities on BIN CARDS.

stockturn see STOCK TURNOVER RATIO.

stock-turnover ratio a measure of a firm's stockholdings that expresses the firm's SALES REVENUE as a ratio of its period-end STOCK, to show how many times stocks are turned over in sales during a period's trading. See also STOCK CONTROL, STOCKHOLDING MODEL.

stock valuation the placing of an appropriate money value upon a firm's STOCKS of raw materials, WORK IN PROGRESS and finished GOODS. Where INFLATION causes the price of several different batches of finished-goods stock bought during a trading period to differ, the firm has the problems of deciding:

(a) what money value to place upon the period-end physical stock in the BALANCE SHEET;

(b) what cost to attach to the units sold in the PROFIT-AND-LOSS ACCOUNT.

The second decision has a direct bearing upon the COST-OF-GOODS SOLD and so upon GROSS PROFIT.

Different formulas used to value stock can lead to variations in the balance-sheet value of stock and in the cost of goods sold. For example, the *first-in, first-out* (*FIFO*) method assumes that goods are withdrawn from stock in the order in which they are received so that the cost of goods sold is based on the cost of the oldest goods in stock, while the value of closing stock is based on the prices of the most recent purchases (see Fig. 82). By contrast, the *last-in, first-out* (*LIFO*) method assumes that the most recently purchased goods are (theoretically) withdrawn from stock first so that the cost of goods sold is based on the costs of the most recent purchases, while the value of closing stock is based on the oldest goods available (see Fig. 82). The last-in, first-out method gives a higher figure for cost-of-goods sold, i.e. one which more closely approximates to the replacement cost of goods sold, but it tends to understate the value of period-end stocks.

In the interests of prudence the firm would tend to value stocks at cost or market value, whichever was the lower, to avoid overstating profits. Generally stocks of work in progress and finished goods will include the raw materials, direct labour and OVERHEAD costs involved in manufacturing them. See also STOCK APPRECIATION, INFLATION ACCOUNTING.

storage cost see HOLDING COST.

store 1 a secure area for the storage of raw materials or components not required immediately for production, or of finished goods not required immediately for despatch to customers.

Storekeeping procedures involve checking deliveries of materials or components against orders and receiving them into stores for safekeeping against damage or theft. Thereafter materials or components are issued to production departments in

FIFO		LIFO	
sales (100 x £15)	£1,500	sales (100 x £15)	£1,500
cost of goods sold:		cost of goods sold:	
20 x £10 = £200		100 x £12	£1,200
80 x £12 = £960	£1,160		
100			
profit	£340		£300
closing stock (20 x £12)	£240	closing stock (20 x £10)	£200

Fig. 82 **Stock valuation.** Two methods. The opening stock is 20 units, costing £10 each; the purchases are 100 units at £12 each; the sales are 100 units at £15 each; the closing stock is 20 units.

quantities authorized by MATERIALS REQUISITIONS, and appropriate entries made on BIN CARDS to maintain up-to-date records of stock in hand. Period STOCK CONTROL checks serve to ensure that stocks recorded agree with physical stocks held. When stocks fall to reorder levels new orders are placed for materials, to avoid production holdups. Accurate and systematic storekeeping procedures are needed if the raw materials and component cost of products is to be accurately ascertained.

Similar stores-control procedures operate in the finished goods store to ensure that stocks are available to fulfil sales orders. See WAREHOUSE, MATERIALS MANAGEMENT, INTERSTAGE STORE, AUTOMATED GUIDED VEHICLE, AUTOMATED STORAGE AND RETRIEVAL SYSTEM.

2 an alternative term for a SHOP.

store of value see MONEY.

stores issue note see MATERIALS REQUISITION.

stores record card *or* **bin card** a paper or computer record which is kept for each STOCK item held by a firm showing the balance in hand, details of stock received and issued, stock reserved to meet current production orders and the residual balance which is free for future use.

The information contained in stores record cards, when supplemented by data on the prices of stock items, forms the basis for stores ledger records.

straight line depreciation see DEPRECIATION.

strategic alliance the combining together of the resources and competencies of two or more firms in a particular activity (but who continue to function separately in all other respects). Strategic alliances can be contractually based or ownership based (with each partner putting equity into the business) and can take a number of formats, for example, co-marketing (with one firm undertaking to market the product supplied by the other firm); co-production (with one firm undertaking to manufacture a product using components supplied by the other firm); and joint research and development (cross fertilization of ideas).

Strategic alliances can enable firms to obtain access to technologies, know-how, capital and markets to augment their own resources and capabilities. Pooling resources and capabilities in this way enables firms to achieve synergistic effects otherwise unobtainable on an individual basis. International alliances in particular can assist MULTINATIONAL ENTERPRISES to ensure that products reach the market place more quickly and more effectively, especially where products need to be modified to meet local regulations covering product standards and packaging, and the preferences of local customers.

While strategic alliances can yield positive benefits to partners there are some potential drawbacks. Arm's length cooperation agreements need careful planning and nurturing and involve 'agency' costs in negotiating, securing and monitoring CONTRACTS; they also require the establishment of mutual trust and commitment. Joint ventures go some way to implementing a stronger link between partners, but problems of joint control of operations may again limit the effectiveness of alliance. See JOINT VENTURE, FOREIGN MARKET SERVICING STRATEGY, EXTERNAL GROWTH, LICENCE.

strategic analysis see BUSINESS STRATEGY.

strategic business unit (SBU) a division of a multi-product firm which represents a discrete area of business. Each SBU is responsible for a group of interrelated products serving a core MARKET; for example, within Unilever margarines and fats re-present one SBU while soap powders and detergents represent another. SBUs generally operate autonomously within the firm with their own chief executive, production and marketing staff etc., but are usually subject to overall control by the firm's main board of directors in such matters as capital investment.

SBUs are an attempt to decentralize responsibility for profit generation. It is believed that this will increase motivation and improve individual performance, thereby improving overall organizational performance and the achievement of strategic goals. See PRODUCT-BASED STRUCTURE.

strategic choice see CONTINGENCY THEORY.

strategic direction deciding, as part of a firm's overall BUSINESS STRATEGY, which business activities the firm should operate in, and where. For example, the firm may decide to specialize in one particular activity (see HORIZONTAL EXPANSION) or it may decide to deepen its involvement in an industry by undertaking VERTICAL INTEGRATION; or it may wish to broaden the scope of its activities by DIVERSIFICATION into new product areas. The geographical markets in which the firm operates also require consideration. Some firms, for example, may choose to operate on a purely local/regional basis, some may establish themselves as national suppliers or as MULTINATIONAL ENTERPRISES supplying markets on a global basis. See PRODUCT MARKET MATRIX, DIRECTIONAL MATRIX.

strategic fit the extent to which a new business activity undertaken by a conglomerate firm is compatible with its existing activities. In some cases, the new activity may be closely related to the firm's existing activities, thus providing scope for achieving SYNERGY gains across these activities. See DIVERSIFICATION.

strategic group a group of firms within a MARKET OR INDUSTRY which each pursue broadly similar policies in respect of product and market coverage, pricing, vertical integration etc. Thus, an industry may comprise a number of distinct groups of firms depending upon differences in their business strategies: for example, one strategic group in an industry might consist of suppliers who offer a full product range from basic to luxury items and sell nationally; other suppliers in the same industry might concentrate solely on luxury items and sell in a limited number of local markets. See MOBILITY BARRIER.

Strategic-group analysis is used by corporate planners as a means of positioning and repositioning a firm in a market, so as to establish COMPETITIVE ADVANTAGES over rival suppliers as well as to identify possible gaps in the market which might be exploited. See BUSINESS STRATEGY, COMPETITIVE STRATEGY.

strategic management see BUSINESS STRATEGY.

strategic withdrawal a repositioning of a firm's marketing effort involving its withdrawal from particular MARKET SEGMENTS in order to concentrate its efforts in market segments where its competitive position is stronger.

strategy a unified set of plans and actions designed to secure the achievement of the basic objectives of a business or of some other organization: BUSINESS OBJECTIVES represent the goals of the organization, i.e. the economic (and social) *purposes* for which the business exists; strategy is the *means* used to attain these goals. See BUSINESS STRATEGY, MARKETING STRATEGY, FOREIGN MARKET SERVICING STRATEGY.

strategy development see BUSINESS POLICY.

strategy implementation see BUSINESS POLICY.

strengths and weaknesses see SWOT ANALYSIS.

strike a stoppage of work by a group of workers as part of an INDUSTRIAL DISPUTE with the aim of bringing pressure to bear on the employer. In the UK most strikes arise out of disputes over pay and conditions of employment. In the UK strike activity is normally measured in three ways: the number of stoppages, the number of workers involved, and the number of working days lost per 1000 employees. Of these the best indicator of 'strike proneness' (i.e. how likely workers are to take industrial action) is the number of working days lost per 1000 employees, because it captures more of the intensity and extent of stoppages than the other indices.

Strikes are generally both a protest and an attempt to secure concessions from employers. Their effectiveness is premised on the costs of a loss of output and the damage of relationships with suppliers, customers and employees that a stoppage of work can result in. However, strikes are costly to employees too since they usually suffer a loss of earnings for the duration of the stoppage. Employees therefore often take alternative forms of INDUSTRIAL ACTION, such as overtime bans, which are considerably cheaper. The conduct of strikes by unions is regulated by LABOUR LAW in the UK. A postal ballot of employees must be held, and employers must be given advance notice of the strike, for the strike to be lawful (and hence TRADE UNION IMMUNITIES to be retained). SECONDARY ACTION is unlawful.

strike ballots see STRIKE.

structural unemployment see UNEMPLOYMENT, STRUCTURE OF INDUSTRY.

structure the pattern of roles and relationships in a GROUP OF ORGANIZATION. See also BUREAUCRACY and ORGANIZATION CHART.

structure of industry the productive activities of an ECONOMY classified according to broad groupings of activities by sector, or on an individual INDUSTRY basis (see STANDARD INDUSTRIAL CLASSIFICATION).

The three basic sectors of the economy are the *primary* sector (agriculture, minerals etc.), the *industrial* sector (manufacturing, construction, electricity etc.) and the *service* sector (banking, retailing etc.). The relative importance of these sectors tends to change as an economy matures: less developed countries are characterized by large primary sectors, whereas developed countries are characterized by large industrial and service sectors.

In the advanced countries, as Fig. 83 shows, there has been a relative decline in the industrial sector and a corresponding increase in the importance of the service sector. In the main this reflects a change in the pattern of final *demand* for goods and services over time, favouring services, and as such may be considered a natural development associated with a maturing economy. Despite this general tendency, *deindustrialization,* however, has aroused particular concern in the UK because it has been accompanied by slow growth in total output in the economy, high unemployment and balance of payments difficulties (i.e. the service sector has not been able to absorb all the slack created by industrial decline). The fact that deindustrialization has been more severe in the UK than elsewhere has been put down to mainly *supply-side* deficiencies: a low level of investment, higher supply costs and prices and lack of product sophistication and innovation has put the UK at a competitive disadvantage in INTERNATIONAL TRADE, resulting in imports taking up a rising share of the UK domestic market See IMPORT PENETRATION.

subcontractor see CONTRACTOR.

subcultures see CULTURAL VALUES.

subsidiarity a principle enshrined in the MAASTRICHT TREATY which affirms that, wherever possible, decision-making in the EUROPEAN UNION (EU) should be 'taken as close as possible to the citizens' affected. This implies that matters affecting *all* member countries need to be resolved at

	Primary Sector		*Industrial Sector*		*Service Sector*	
	1960 %	2003 %	1960 %	2003 %	1960 %	2003 %
UK	3	1	43	29	54	70
USA	4	2	38	27	58	71
Japan	13	1	45	32	42	67
Germany	6	1	53	31	41	68

Fig. 83 **Structure of Industry.** Distribution of gross domestic product, 1960 and 2003. (Source: World Development Report, World Bank, 2004).

an EU-wide level whereas matters affecting only an individual member country are best left to the member concerned. See SOCIAL CHAPTER, COMPETITION POLICY (EU).

subsidiary company a JOINT-STOCK COMPANY that is owned by another company (the HOLDING COMPANY). Specifically, a subsidiary company is one in which the holding company owns between 50% and 100% of the voting shares. The accounting results of subsidiary companies are consolidated (see CONSOLIDATED ACCOUNTS) in the annual accounts of the holding company. A subsidiary company is regarded as different from an ASSOCIATED COMPANY (where the holding company owns between 20% and 50% of its shares) which is less subject to the influence of the holding company and continues to produce its own annual accounts. A subsidiary company may continue to trade under its own name, but it is subject to control by the parent company.

subsidy the provision of finance and other resources by the government or a firm to support a business activity or person. Subsidies can be direct (cash grants, interest free LOANS etc.) or indirect (DEPRECIATION write-offs, RENT rebates) and can be used for a variety of purposes. They include:

(a) PRODUCTION subsidies: the subsidization of suppliers by government to encourage them to increase the output of particular products by partially offsetting their production costs or even financing losses. The objective may be to expand production at a low price of some product which is deemed to be 'essential' (for example a particular foodstuff thereby also subsidizing consumers); or, for example, to assist in the start-up of a new firm (see ENTERPRISE INVESTMENT SCHEME) or industry (see INDUSTRIAL POLICY), and encourage firms to locate in particular areas (see REGIONAL POLICY). Also such subsidies are used to support failing firms and declining industries to facilitate orderly restructuring. See PROTECTIONISM;

(b) EXPORT subsidies: the subsidization by the government of exports in general or of a particular product which is exported, as a means of assisting the country's balance of payments;

(c) EMPLOYMENT subsidies: the subsidization of wages by the government as an incentive to businesses to provide more job opportunities, thereby reducing the level of unemployment in the economy;

(d) INCOME subsidies: the subsidization of persons through government transfer payment systems (for example, social security benefits) in order to allow them to enjoy some minimum standard of living;

(e) *cross-subsidization:* businesses themselves regularly practise internal or cross-subsidization as a means of expanding their activities, for example, using the profits generated by established products to finance NEW-PRODUCT DEVELOPMENT and DIVERSIFICATION into new-product markets.

substitutes see PRODUCT SUBSTITUTES.

suggestion scheme a facility for employees to submit suggestions for revision of production equipment and working methods which will lead to improvements in efficiency or product quality. Rewards are generally given for those proposals adopted by management, usually in relation to the improvement in performance which is likely to be achieved. Suggestion schemes have been in vogue recently since they are widely seen as a simple, effective and cheap way of promoting employee identification with the company. However, they require careful management to ensure that the pattern of rewards is seen as fair and worthwhile. See EMPLOYEE INVOLVEMENT.

Sunday Trading Act 1994 see SHOP ACT.

sunk cost the cost of durable and specific assets such as plant and machinery which cannot be used for other purposes or easily be resold. Where sunk costs represent a high proportion of a firm's total costs the firm may be 'locked in' to its existing products and markets, the sunk costs forming a BARRIER TO EXIT from the market. Since such specific assets have little alternative use they have no OPPORTUNITY COST and so naturally should not enter into management decision-making. Consequently in MAKE-OR-BUY DECISIONS the firm need not consider the sunk costs involved in making products but only the additional production costs as opposed to buying from outside suppliers.

supermarket a RETAILER which typically sells a wide range of products on a self-service basis. Supermarkets may be under single-shop ownership or run as multiple CHAIN-STORE businesses. The bigger supermarket chains are able to achieve significant economies in distribution both on a group basis by being able to obtain favourable price discounts from manufacturers by BULK BUYING, and at the individual store level by the use of capital-intensive methods of retailing (see EPOS). Initially, supermarkets appeared mainly in the grocery trade, but groups there have moved into a variety of non-food lines (hardware, television and radio, paint, etc.). Similar supermarket-type operations have been established for most mass-retailed products.

Hypermarkets or *superstores* are an extended form of supermarket, usually located on the outskirts of towns and cities where space is plentiful.

Supermarkets compete mainly by offering consumers highly competitive prices on manufacturers' prepacked branded products. However, as part of their MARKETING-MIX policies, emphasis is also placed on product range (including the provision of fresh foods – bread, cheeses, meat, etc.) and various ancillary facilities – cafeteria or restaurant, petrol station etc. The most significant development, however, has been the introduction of OWN-LABEL BRANDS selling under the retailer's own name in direct competition to manufacturers' brands. See DISTRIBUTION CHANNEL.

superstore a very large RETAILER which is often located on the edge of a large town with extensive parking facilities, selling such products as groceries, furniture and do-it-yourself items.

supervisor an employee with RESPONSIBILITY for monitoring the work of others to ensure that they fulfil work targets generally established by middle managers. As such supervisors usually have little AUTHORITY in their own right, they often experience role uncertainty as they are neither 'proper' managers nor fully part of the group they supervise, and can thus be described as 'men (*sic*) in the middle'. With the recent trend towards devolving managerial authority, many organizations have attempted to enlarge the decision-making powers of supervisors. See MANAGEMENT.

supplier a producer or distributor of a GOOD or SERVICE. See also INTERNAL SUPPLIER.

supplier certification see CERTIFICATION.

supplier development the practice of buying firms seeking closer relationships with their suppliers in order to provide mutual benefits: a better coordination of input requirements, a reduction in supply costs and the creation of opportunities for refining/developing compatible parts and product technologies. See KEIRETSU, LEAN MANUFACTURING, JUST-IN-TIME (JIT) SYSTEM, SUPPLY CHAIN MANAGEMENT, SOURCING.

Supplier Trade Procedures Board see EXPORTING.

supply based reduction the reduction in the number of suppliers used to provide a firm with its input requirements. Some firms use a single supply source to provide all their requirements of a particular input. Relying on a single supplier may allow a firm to reduce its costs (through the discounts given on bulk-buying) and facilitate the operation of a JUST-IN-TIME (JIT) production system. On the other hand, relying on a single source of supply may expose the firm to a greater risk of supply disruptions. See SOURCING, LEAN PRODUCTION.

supply chain the network of vertically-related raw material and component suppliers, manufacturers, distributors and customers for a product which collectively make up the VALUE-ADDED CHAIN. See SUPPLY CHAIN MANAGEMENT.

supply chain management a term used to describe the management of inventory (STOCK), not only within a firm but also along the network of suppliers and customers which constitute the SUPPLY CHAIN or VALUE-ADDED CHAIN. Supply chain management employs a variety of methods such as STOCK CONTROL, MATERIALS REQUIREMENT PLANNING and DISTRIBUTED REQUIREMENT PLANNING to both minimize stock-holding costs while maintaining effective distributed levels of servicing customer orders. See SUPPLIER DEVELOPMENT.

supply curve see EQUILIBRIUM MARKET PRICE.

survey a research tool which is used to elicit information about respondents' attitudes, opinions and preferences. In MARKETING RESEARCH, surveys are employed to discover more about potential consumers' views and perceptions of existing and proposed new products, and more specifically about the buying intentions of customers.

Surveys may also be used to discover employees' views on aspects of company policy and to assess employees' MOTIVATION, ORGANIZATIONAL COMMITMENT etc.

See MARKETING INTELLIGENCE.

survey method see SALES FORECASTING.

SVQ the Scottish equivalent of the NATIONAL VOCATIONAL QUALIFICATION (NVQ) found in England and Wales. See TRAINING.

swap the bilateral (and multilateral) exchange of a product, business asset, interest rate on a financial debt, or currency for another product, business asset, interest rate on a financial debt, or currency, respectively;

(a) *product* swaps: individual A offers potatoes to individual B in exchange for a bicycle. See BARTER;

(b) *business asset* swaps: chemical company A offers its ethylene division to chemical company B in exchange for B's paint division. This enables both companies to divest (see DIVESTMENT) parts of their business they no longer wish to retain while simultaneously entering, or strengthening their position in, another product area;

(c) INTEREST-RATE swaps on financial debts: a company that has a *variable-rate* debt, for example, may anticipate that interest rates will rise; another company with *fixed-rate* debt may anticipate that interest rates will fall. It therefore contracts to make variable interest-rate payments to the first company and in exchange is paid interest at a fixed rate. Interest-rate swaps may be undertaken simultaneously on a variety of debt instruments thereby enabling corporate treasurers to lower the company's total interest payments;

(d) *currency* swap: the simultaneous buying and selling of foreign currencies. This can take two main forms: a spot/forward swap (the simultaneous purchase or sale of a currency in the SPOT MARKET coupled with an offsetting sale or purchase of the same currency in the FORWARD MARKET); or a forward/forward swap (a pair of forward currency contracts involving a forward purchase and sale of a particular currency which mature at different future dates).

Currency swaps are used by firms which trade internationally to minimize the risk of losses arising from exchange rate changes (see EXCHANGE RATE EXPOSURE).

'sweating' assets the process of increasing the profits generated from a company's ASSETS where the RETURN ON CAPITAL EMPLOYED is inadequate. This could involve increasing selling prices of products; reducing unit production and selling costs; increasing sales volumes using present assets; or reducing the FIXED ASSETS and CURRENT ASSETS employed to achieve the present sales volume. Sweating assets is often a strategy employed after a company has been taken over.

sweetheart union see COMPANY UNION.

SWOT analysis a framework for identifying the *internal* strengths (S) and weaknesses (W) of a firm, and the *external* opportunities (O) open to it and the threats (T) it faces, which can be used by corporate planners in formulating the firm's COMPETITIVE STRATEGY and MARKETING STRATEGY in individual product markets and its overall BUSINESS STRATEGY.

The internal appraisal of a firm's strengths and weaknesses involves looking at the firm's current resources: the amount and quality of these resources, how well they are being managed in terms of achieving operating economies and developing core skills, and how the firm's resources match up to the requirements of the MARKET place as identified by the external appraisal of threats and opportunities. This kind of audit typically reveals a checklist of strengths and weaknesses of the firm as seen by its incumbent management (but their perception could be endorsed or changed by employing the services of an outside team of MANAGEMENT CONSULTANTS). For example, the analysis may reveal that the firm is especially strong in PRODUCTION but that the firm's products have failed to sell well because of poor MARKETING. This can then be remedied by upgrading the marketing function with a more careful focus on understanding customer needs.

The appraisal of the firm's external environment involves looking both at the immediate threats and opportunities encountered in the firm's present markets and also at the long-term strategic possibilities open to the firm for developing its business interests in other directions (see PRODUCT-MARKET MATRIX, BOSTON MATRIX). A typical threat facing a firm in its existing market is loss of business to competitors and to new entrants (due possibly, as in our example above, to the firm's poor marketing), but for firms possessing COMPETITIVE ADVANTAGE (lower costs, superior products) over rivals, opportunities abound, particularly in expanding markets. The ultimate threat facing firms in an existing market is, of course, the danger of market obsolescence, i.e. the market itself goes into decline as new substitute products emerge. In consequence, careful attention needs to be paid to the identification of opportunities for successful DIVERSIFICATION, where, for example, the firm's core internal skills can be carried over and transferred to new markets.

Having drawn up a checklist of possible SWOT factors, caution needs to be exercised in interpreting them. For example, many feature film makers who made movie films for screening through cinemas (often their own vertical chains), initially saw the advent of television as a threat to their traditional business and refused TV companies permission to screen their films. The reality was and still is, of course, that television is simply another form of viewing, representing an opportunity for market development and concentric diversification, i.e. the basic materials and skills involved in film-making (actors, film crews *etc.*) are the same irrespective of whether a film is being produced for the cinema or television; the key thing, strategically, is the perception of the true dimensions of the market which is being supplied. See also PEST.

syndicated loan a LOAN which is provided by a number of financial institutions on a collective basis, each subscribing a specified amount of money. Syndicated loans are usually put together by a 'lead' organization, for example, a commercial bank.

synergy the phenomenon whereby the *overall* return on a firm's resources is greater than the sum of its parts (the so-called '2 + 2 = 5 or more effect'). Synergy often results from the exploitation of complementary activities or from the carry over of management capabilities, synchronizing individual, group or organizational activities in a way which achieves a better result than any of the activities by themselves: for example, in the case of a MERGER, one firm may have a strong production organization, while the other excels in marketing; joining the two can make the combined firm more effective overall. See DIVERSIFICATION.

synthetic time see WORK MEASUREMENT.

systems analysis the process of analysing management problems into their constituent operations and then specifying these operations in a form suitable for COMPUTER programming.

t

tactical marketing decisions decisions which have as their objective the achievement of an appropriate balance between the various elements of the MARKETING MIX.

tacit skill *or* **knowledge** see SKILL.

takeover *or* **acquisition** the acquisition by one firm of another firm. For companies listed on the STOCK MARKET this involves the *acquiring* firm either buying in the open market, or bidding for the voting SHARES in the *target* firm (See BID, TAKEOVER BID). Unlike a MERGER, which is usually arranged by mutual agreement between the two firms' management, a takeover is often resisted by the target firm's management, so that the bidder must convince shareholders that selling out to the acquirer, or taking shares in it in the case of a share exchange, is of benefit to them. Although a 51% stake in the target company would be sufficient to allow the acquiring company to exercise effective control, generally it would wish to take full control so as to be free from the interference of minority interests.

Takeovers are a form of EXTERNAL GROWTH by which firms expand in a horizontal, vertical and conglomerate direction. *Conglomerate* takeovers (the acquisition of a firm in an unrelated market) are undertaken primarily as a means of spreading business risks and to enable the firm to reorientate itself away from static or declining markets into areas offering good long-term growth and profit potential (see DIVERSIFICATION). *Vertical* takeovers (the acquisition of a firm which supplies inputs to the acquirer or which distributes its products) may enable the firm to cut its costs by, for example, linking together a series of sequentially related input assembly operations or reducing stockholding costs; vertical takeovers give the firm greater security of input supplies and access to distribution channels and the potential to put non-integrated competitors at a disadvantage (see VERTICAL INTEGRATION). *Horizontal* takeovers (the acquisition of a competitor operating in the same market) may allow the firm to reduce its costs by realizing economies of scale in production and marketing, and by taking over the rival supplier the firm can increase its market share and perhaps exercise some degree of monopolistic control over the market (see HORIZONTAL INTEGRATION).

From society's point of view takeovers may be beneficial in so far as they improve efficiency and cut costs and prices, but also (potentially) harmful if they eliminate competition and create monopolies. For this reason, in the UK, under the FAIR TRADING ACT, 1973, takeovers and mergers which lead to, or extend, a firm's market share of a particular product beyond 25%, or where the value of assets taken over is greater than £70 million, can be referred by the OFFICE OF FAIR TRADING to the COMPETITION COMMISSION to decide whether or not they are in the public interest. See MARKET ENTRY, BARRIERS TO ENTRY, CITY CODE ON TAKEOVERS AND MERGERS, BUSINESS POLICY, MANAGEMENT BUY-IN, MANAGEMENT BUY-OUT, COMPETITION POLICY (UK), COMPETITION POLICY (EU).

takeover bid an attempt by one or a number of companies to achieve the TAKEOVER of another company by bidding for (see BID) all or the majority of voting SHARES in the target company. A number of terms are used to describe the various tactics available to the bidding and defending firms, including:

(a) *black knight;* a firm that launches an unwelcome (contested) takeover bid for some other firm;

(b) *concert party;* a number of investors who each buy shares in a company with a view to pooling their shareholdings and acting in concert to take over the company;

(c) *dawn raid;* an attempt to buy up as many shares in a company as possible on the STOCK MARKET over a short period of time, as a prelude to making a full takeover bid for the company;

(d) *golden parachute;* any generous severance terms written into the employment contracts of the directors of a firm that makes it expensive to sack the directors if the firm is taken over;

(e) *greenmail;* a situation in which a firm's shares are being bought up by a (potential) takeover bidder, who is then headed off from making an actual bid, by that firm's directors buying these shares from him at a premium price;

(f) *leveraged* bid; a takeover that is financed primarily by the issue of LOAN CAPITAL rather than share capital, which increases the CAPITAL GEARING of the enlarged firm. (see JUNK BOND);

(g) *pac-man defence;* a situation in which the firm being bid for itself now makes a bid for the acquiring firm (see REVERSE TAKEOVER);

(h) *poison pill;* a tactic employed in a takeover bid whereby the intended victim itself takes over or merges with some other firm, in order to make itself financially or structurally less attractive to the potential acquirer;

(i) *porcupine*; any complex agreements between a firm and its suppliers, customers or creditors that make it difficult for an acquiring company to integrate this firm with its own business;

(j) *reverse takeover;* an attempt by a smaller firm to take over a larger firm. Since the smaller aggressor company has a smaller capital than the victim, it must usually issue additional shares or raise loans to finance the takeover (see pac-man defence);

(k) *shark repellent;* any measures specifically designed to discourage takeover bidders; for example, altering the company's ARTICLES OF ASSOCIATION to increase the proportion of shareholders' votes needed to approve the bid above the usual 50% mark;

(l) *white knight;* the intervention in a takeover bid of a third firm which itself takes over or merges with the intended victim firm to rescue it from its unwelcome suitor.

See also ARBITRAGEUR, MERCHANT BANK.

Talisman (Transfer Accounting Lodgement for Investors) the UK STOCK MARKET computerized transfer system which handles the administrative work involved in transferring STOCKS and SHARES and settling accounts through the official stock market company, SEPON. In 1994 a *rolling settlement* system was introduced in which settlement takes place ten working days after the completion of a deal. This replaces the traditional ACCOUNT PERIOD system. Settlement was cut to five working days in 1995 thus speeding up the whole process of concluding deals. See CREST, SHARE PURCHASE/SALE.

tall organization an ORGANIZATION which has many managerial layers. Such an organizational structure tends to be characteristic of large firms or public utilities and government departments.

Tall organizations tend to have a number of drawbacks – excessive bureaucracy, remoteness of decision-making from ultimate customer needs and an inability to respond quickly to changes in the organization's external environment.

In recent years many larger firms have attempted to make themselves 'leaner and fitter' by reducing the size of their managerial hierarchies and by establishing more focused business divisions. See FLAT ORGANIZATION, STRATEGIC BUSINESS UNIT, RIGHTSIZING, HIERARCHY, DE-LAYERING.

tangible fixed assets physical FIXED ASSETS such as land, buildings and machinery which have a money value.

tap 1 a FINANCIAL SECURITY such as a government STOCK which can always be obtained on demand because there is continuous supply.

2 the issue of TREASURY BILLS and government BONDS which are sold directly to government departments as opposed to being sold on the open market.

target audience the group of people at which an ADVERTISEMENT or message is aimed.

targeting 1 MARKETING STRATEGY. See CONCENTRATED MARKETING OR TARGETING STRATEGY, DIFFERENTIATED MARKETING OR TARGETING STRATEGY.

2 BUSINESS STRATEGY. See COMPETITIVE STRATEGY.

target market the MARKET or MARKET SEGMENTS which form the focus of a firm's MARKETING efforts.

target-profit pricing see COST-BASED PRICING.

tariff 1 a TAX (import duty) levied by a country on IMPORTS of products from foreign countries which *may* increase their prices in the domestic market. There are two main types of tariff;

(a) an *ad valorem* duty which is levied as a fixed percentage of the value of the product;

(b) a specific duty which is levied as a fixed sum of money per physical unit of the product.

Governments impose tariffs primarily to protect domestic industries from overseas competition, in order to maintain a local production base and to prevent job losses. Additionally, governments use tariffs to assist the BALANCE OF PAYMENTS, and also as a means of raising revenue.

Since 1950, the tariffs which were once applied at substantial rates on an extensive range of internationally traded products have been either reduced or eliminated, as a result of the work of the WORLD TRADE ORGANIZATION and the formation of various free trade blocs. (See TRADE INTEGRATION).

Firms facing tariff obstacles to overseas markets may choose to absorb the duties payable by lowering profit margins, or they may be able to remain price-competitive by increasing productivity and reducing their supply costs. A further option open to MULTINATIONAL ENTERPRISES is for them to replace exporting by setting up manufacturing plants in the markets concerned. See PROTECTIONISM, DEINDUSTRIALIZATION, FOREIGN MARKET SERVICING STRATEGY, LOCAL CONTENT RULE.

2 a charge for the consumption of a product or service, for example a meals tariff at a restaurant, or a tariff for gas and electricity supplies. Two-part tariffs are often used in connection with the supply of gas, electricity, telephone services etc., involving a charge per unit of the good or service consumed, plus a fixed annual or quarterly charge to cover overhead costs. Two-part tariffs can be used by PUBLIC UTILITIES or firms to achieve the benefits of marginal cost pricing whilst raising sufficient revenues to cover total outlays (so avoiding a deficit). Additionally, multi-part tariffs can be utilized to reflect the different marginal costs involved in offering products such as electricity, and rail and bus services at peak and off-peak periods. See COST-BASED PRICING.

task culture see CULTURE.

tax a levy imposed by the government on GOODS and SERVICES (INDIRECT TAX) and the INCOME and WEALTH of persons and businesses (DIRECT TAX). The government uses taxes for a number of purposes such as:

(a) to raise revenue to finance government spending (see BUDGET);

(b) to promote social equity by redistributing income and wealth (see DISTRIBUTION OF INCOME);

(c) to regulate the level of total spending in the economy (see FISCAL POLICY);

(d) to protect domestic producers from imports (see TARIFF). See INCOME TAX, CORPORATION TAX, CAPITAL GAINS TAX, WEALTH TAX, INHERITANCE TAX, VALUE-ADDED TAX, CUSTOMS DUTY, EXCISE DUTY.

taxable income the amount of an individual's income that is subject to TAXATION once any tax allowances to which the taxpayer is entitled have been deducted.

taxation the government receipts from TAXES on personal and business income, expenditure and wealth. Taxes on income include personal INCOME TAX and CORPORATION TAX; taxes on expenditure include VALUE-ADDED TAX and EXCISE DUTIES. Taxes are used to finance government spending and as instruments of FISCAL POLICY in regulating the level of total spending in the economy. See INLAND REVENUE, BUDGET (GOVERNMENT).

tax avoidance any efforts by taxpayers to arrange their financial affairs so as to avoid paying TAX by taking maximum advantage of taxation allowances and reliefs. In this way taxpayers can legally minimize their tax burden. Compare TAX EVASION.

tax burden the total amount of TAXATION paid by the citizens of a country in the form of INCOME TAX, CORPORATION TAX, VALUE-ADDED TAX, etc.

tax credit see CORPORATION TAX, DIVIDEND.

tax evasion any efforts by taxpayers to evade TAX by various illegal means, such as not declaring all of their income to the tax authorities or falsely claiming reliefs to which they are not entitled. Compare TAX AVOIDANCE.

tax haven a country which imposes low rates of personal and corporate TAXES, and which as a consequence tends to attract wealthy individuals, MULTINATIONAL ENTERPRISES and FINANCIAL INSTITUTIONS seeking to minimize their taxation liabilities. At the present time, countries operating low-taxation systems include Bermuda, Jersey and the Cayman Islands. An OECD report published in 2000 listed 35 'offshore financial centres' which it classed as 'tax havens that harm trade and investment'. The OECD defined harmful jurisdictions as those that offered zero or low tax rates but fell short in legal and administrative transparency. The latter factor makes it difficult for other countries 'tax authorities' to detect and observe the complex financial transactions undertaken by criminals and MNEs (MULTINATIONAL ENTERPRISES) to 'hide' their tax liabilities.

There are two main types of tax haven arrangements: (a) *tax exempt companies* beneficially owned by non-residents of a country which pay a small annual administration fee (under £2000) in return for being exempt from income and withholding taxes; there are no capital gains or inheritance taxes. Tax haven countries themselves 'gain' from the creation of local employment and the extra income this creates, often in an impoverished country or a country lacking other resources (e.g. the Channel Islands and the Isle of Man); (b) *international business companies* that are 'accommodated' by 'designer' taxation, whereby tax havens 'tailor' rates of tax to help individual MNEs to minimize their 'onshore' tax liability. MNEs negotiate low tax rates which in turn allows them to meet thresholds for tax exemptions in onshore jurisdictions. See also TRANSFER PRICE, MIXER COMPANY, MONEY LAUNDERING.

tax point see VALUE-ADDED TAX.

tax return a form which must be completed by all taxpayers and potential taxpayers for the INLAND REVENUE, giving details of their INCOME and CAPITAL GAINS and any allowances and reliefs to be set against this income.

team see GROUP.

team briefing a form of COMMUNICATION in which supervisors or managers pass information about company affairs to their subordinates (who in turn brief *their* subordinates) via the medium of a regular meeting. In this way information can be cascaded down the organization. Advocates of team briefing maintain that, as well as providing information useful to job performance, communication of this sort results in employees feeling more involved. As a result they become more committed to their organizations, with the benefit that performance may improve further. Team briefing can therefore be said to embody a HUMAN RELATIONS philosophy. The efficacy of team briefing, however, can be questioned. Mechanisms for transmitting employee recommendations *up* the organization hierarchy are generally absent, with the result that employees may soon question whether team briefing permits genuine involvement. Some also maintain that team briefing is an attempt to weaken TRADE UNIONS in the organization, by providing alternative channels of communication to those provided by SHOP STEWARDS. See EMPLOYEE INVOLVEMENT.

team production the organization of PRODUCTION based on a specific group of workers in order to improve efficiency and product quality. See CELL, CELLULAR MANUFACTURING. Appropriate reward structures may be required to encourage commitment to group targets and discourage 'shirking'. See GROUP INCENTIVE BONUS SCHEME.

team selling the use of the combined efforts of salespeople, product specialists, engineers, sales managers and even directors to sell products. See SALES FORCE.

TEC see LEARNING AND SKILLS COUNCIL.

Techmark see STOCK MARKET/EXCHANGE.

Technical Help to Exporters see EXPORTING.

technological determinism the belief that technology is the dominant influence on employee behaviour. See SOCIOLOGY OF WORK.

technological forecasting the process of predicting the direction and scope of future technological advances. With rapid advances in science and technology, shortening PRODUCT LIFE CYCLES and improving production techniques, firms need to forecast technological developments. Technological forecasting helps the firm to formulate its BUSINESS STRATEGY by identifying opportunities and threats presented by technical change, and assists in the planning of RESEARCH and DEVELOPMENT programmes by identifying new areas to explore. Technological forecasting can be done in several ways, by means of:

(a) methods which identify and extrapolate trends derived from historical data; for example, in plotting trends in data storage capacity and information processing speed over time, it is possible to identify the development of, first, valve-based computer technology, then transistor-based technology, present semiconductor (silicon chip)-based technology, and future fibre optics-based technology;

(b) methods based upon the subjective impressions of practising technologists. A single expert may write in some detail about the possible future of his own field of technology ('scenario' writing), or a consensus of expert opinion may be sought, using the DELPHI approach where the experts first independently give opinions concerning the development of a scientific field, then distil these opinions to produce an overall view of likely advances. See BRAINSTORMING, NOMINAL GROUP TECHNIQUE.

technology the application of scientific principles and know-how in the development and operation of industrial processes, systems and products. See AUTOMATION, NUMERICAL CONTROL, ROBOT, COMPUTER, PRODUCTION LINE, INFORMATION TECHNOLOGY, TECHNOLOGICAL FORECASTING, NEW-PRODUCT DEVELOPMENT.

technology transfer the diffusion of technological know-how and expertise concerning processes, methods of manufacture and innovative products across industries, within an industry or, in the international context, from country to country. Intra-industry technology transfer occurs when, for example, an exclusive PATENT accruing to one firm expires and other firms are then free to adopt the technology concerned, or alternatively, the rate and scale of diffusion may be speeded up if the patentor firm is prepared to LICENSE the technology to other firms. Technology transfer between countries often occurs as a result of the FOREIGN MARKET SERVICING STRATEGIES adopted by MULTINATIONAL ENTERPRISES (MNES). For example, an MNE may choose to establish a manufacturing plant, incorporating innovative production techniques, in an overseas market, or grant licensing rights to local producers to use its technology.

Technology transfer effects can be important in upgrading the technical competence of an industry, giving it an advantage over international competitors. Similarly, from a host country perspective, technology transfer enables the country to acquire technological expertise otherwise unavailable domestically, as a means of establishing new industries.

More generally, new technologies may be developed which are applicable, in modified forms, to a wide range of industries. For example, information technology and computer-aided manufacturing systems. In the UK, the DEPARTMENT OF TRADE AND INDUSTRY has established Regional Technology Centres to disseminate information on new technology and assist in its application at local industry level, while the DTI's Overseas Technical Information Service provides details of developments elsewhere which may have reference and application in the UK. See INDUSTRIAL POLICY.

telecommunication see COMMUNICATION.

telephone selling a form of DIRECT MARKETING in which a seller of a product contacts customers by telephone in order to establish an initial contact with them. Interested customers may then be visited by a SALES REPRESENTATIVE of the firm with a view to completing a sale.

temporal flexibility see LABOUR FLEXIBILITY.

temporal method see FOREIGN CURRENCY TRANSLATION.

temporary work employment which is of a less than permanent duration, i.e. where the employees are on fixed-term contracts or where they take jobs for a limited time. The reasons for employing temporary workers are that the job duties may themselves be temporary, or that the employer is uncertain about the future prospects of the organization and wishes to retain the flexibility to adjust employment levels downwards. Temporary work can be unsettling for those seeking long-term employment since it is difficult to plan for the future. However, some groups, for example students wanting holiday jobs, actively seek such employment. The amount of temporary work has increased substantially in recent years. In universities, for instance, a high proportion of staff are now on fixed-term contracts. See LABOUR FLEXIBILITY, PART-TIME WORK.

tender 1 an invitation from a buyer who requires particular goods or services to prospective suppliers of those products to put in competing price bids. The buyer will usually detail the precise specifications of the product, and will make a final decision about which supplier's bid to accept on the basis of comparative price and how well bids match up to the stated requirements. See QUOTATION, definition 1.

2 a means of making a SHARE ISSUE by offering shares to the general public, who are invited to make a bid for shares, subject to a minimum bid price. The issue price of the shares is determined by averaging out the bid prices offered by prospective purchasers. Anyone making a bid which is below the final issue price will not be offered any shares, whilst those making a bid at or above the price will be allotted shares in full at the final price.

Tenders may be similarly used to sell other financial securities such as TREASURY BILLS.

terminal a COMPUTER input/output device linked to the computer, usually comprising a KEYBOARD and VDU (visual display unit). MAINFRAME and MINICOMPUTERS are usually capable of serving several terminals simultaneously.

terotechnology "the combination of management, financial, engineering, building and other practices applied to physical assets in pursuit of economic life cycle costs. Its practice is concerned with the specification and design for reliability and maintainability of plant, machinery, equipment, buildings and structures, with their installation, commissioning, operation, maintenance, modification and replacement with feedback of information on design, performance and costs". (BRITISH STANDARD BS 3811 definition) See TOTAL PRODUCTIVE MAINTENANCE.

testing the checking of raw materials, components and finished products to ensure that they meet specified performance standards. In principle all materials, components and products could be tested but in practice firms will usually only test a sample of such items. See QUALITY CONTROL. See also ADVERTISING EFFECTIVENESS TEST, NEW PRODUCT DEVELOPMENT, TEST MARKETING.

test marketing a prelaunch trial run of a NEW PRODUCT involving a representative sample of prospective buyers who are given the product to try. Consumers' opinions and views about the performance of the product, its quality and the satisfaction they derive from it are compiled, often alongside consumer reaction to a range of possible prices that could be charged for the product. This data is then used by the firm to decide whether or not to go ahead and launch the product on to the market. Test-market reactions are useful not only in establishing whether actually to launch the product, but also in indicating whether changes in its attributes (quality, shape and form, styling etc.) would strengthen its appeal and which consumer perceptions about the product might usefully form the basis of advertising the product to maximize its impact on prospective buyers. See ADVERTISING COPY, ADVERTISING EFFECTIVENESS TESTS, NEW-PRODUCT DEVELOPMENT.

T-group see MANAGEMENT DEVELOPMENT.

theory of constraints see OPTIMIZED PRODUCTION TECHNOLOGY.

Theory X and Theory Y two opposed philosophies of MANAGEMENT and ORGANIZATION, so named by the American social psychologist Douglas McGregor (1906–64). Theory X assumes that people dislike work and prefer to avoid responsibility. It therefore emphasizes that coercion is necessary to achieve satisfactory performance. By contrast, Theory Y believes that people can enjoy the activity of working and exercising responsibility and that if they are given the opportunity they can become committed to organizational goals. McGregor concluded from this that Theory Y could lead to superior organizational performance. See MANAGEMENT STYLE.

Theory Z the application to Western ORGANIZATIONS of the Japanese approach to management. Theory Z-type companies typically prioritize generating and sustaining employee commitment by EMPLOYEE PARTICIPATION and CONSULTATION. They also tend to invest heavily in training. See JAPANIZATION.

therbligs a coding system which breaks down the elements of a JOB into a number of discrete tasks. For example, therbligs could include 'search' (attempting to find an item manually or visually), 'grasp' (gaining control of an item by touch or grasping), 'position' (aligning an item for purposes of assembly) etc. By analysing a work task in this way, it may be possible to find ways of improving the methods used to do the job. See METHOD STUDY.

The Securities Association (TSA) see FINANCIAL SERVICES ACT, 1986.

threats and opportunities see SWOT ANALYSIS.

Three i's (**3i's,** formerly **Investors in Industry**) a company which provides LOAN and SHARE CAPITAL for VENTURE CAPITAL projects, MANAGEMENT BUY-OUTS and other activities requiring specialized financing, particularly small project 'start up' funding.

three-shift working see SHIFT WORK.

tie-in sale a business practice whereby a supplier encourages a dealer/purchaser not only to buy the GOOD or SERVICE of primary interest to him but to buy also, as part of the same transaction, some other related good or service. For example, a supplier of colour film might attempt to tie the processing of that film to himself by including an inclusive processing charge in the price paid for the colour film. The practice of tie-in sales may help the supplier to increase his total sales and also to protect BRAND LOYALTY (for example, in the case of colour film, inefficient processing by an independent processor might lead the purchaser to believe, erroneously, that poor picture reproduction is due to the poor quality of the film itself). However, if undertaken by a DOMINANT FIRM, the practice may serve to limit competition in a market by discouraging purchasers from placing their custom with rival businesses. See OFFICE OF FAIR TRADING, COMPETITION POLICY (UK).

tier 1 and tier 2 assisted areas see REGIONAL POLICY.

time and motion study see WORK STUDY.

time-based maintenance an approach to MAINTENANCE which provides for the overhaul of machinery, plant and equipment at planned regular intervals, for example, once every three months.

time card see CLOCK CARD.

time deposit see COMMERCIAL BANK.

time management 1 the organization of a manager's working practices so as to make the optimum use of the manager's scarce time.
2 the process of reducing the amount of time taken in developing new product ideas into products, and getting them on to the market. Firms which are able to shorten new product lead times can often gain a significant COMPETITIVE ADVANCE over rival suppliers. See NEW PRODUCT DEVELOPMENT, CONCURRENT ENGINEERING.

time rate system see PAY.

time saved the difference between the time allowed for completing a work task, the 'standard time' (see WORK MEASUREMENT) and the actual time taken. INCENTIVE BONUS SCHEMES often use a percentage of the time saved in their bonus calculations.

times covered see DIVIDEND COVER.

time-series see SALES FORECASTING.

time sharing 1 the joint use of a COMPUTER facility by two or more users in return for a rental payment.
2 the joint use of a holiday home by several users, each of whom contributes a share of the capital cost of the property and upkeep expenses in return for the right to use the property for specified weeks each year.

time sheet document completed by a worker in which he or she itemizes the work tasks undertaken and the time spent on each task. This information can be used for COSTING purposes in computing the direct labour cost of JOBS and as a basis for calculating PAY.

times interest earned see INTEREST COVER.

time span of discretion the length of time that elapses before an employee's work is checked by a supervisor. The concept was developed by the social psychologist Elliott Jacques (1917–) who believed it was a viable way of quantifying the level of judgement and discretion involved in a job. Jobs that involve little decision-making, such as assembly-line work, have a very short time span of discretion whereas managerial jobs, which have a much greater judgemental element, have a much longer span.

The time-span theory can be said to be an attempt objectively to incorporate the notions of responsibility and judgement into systems of WORK MEASUREMENT and JOB EVALUATION. Jacques has argued that it could form the basis of an equitable pay system, with rewards being based on the amount of discretion involved in each job. See JOB DESIGN AND REDESIGN.

time standards see WORK MEASUREMENT.

time study see WORK STUDY.

time value of money see DISCOUNTED CASH FLOW.

tolerance limit the limits of permitted variation in the size, colour or other attribute of a component or product. See QUALITY CONTROL.

tort a civil wrong. The laws of tort are general laws which protect the personal rights of an individual to non-violation of his or her property, reputation and person:

(a) offences against property rights include *trespass; negligence* (where there is a breach of a legal duty to take care which results in unintended damage to the plaintiff); and *nuisance* (where there is an unlawful and unreasonable interference with a person's use or enjoyment of his or her property);

(b) offences against reputation include *libel*, and *slander* (making a false and malicious statement which damages another person's reputation);

(c) offences against one's person include *assault, battery; negligence;* and *intimidation* (a threat to perform an unlawful act interfering with the victim's freedom of action).

It may be noted in this context that an employer may be made liable for the torts of his employees which are committed during the course of their employment, having vicarious liability for their actions. In a tort action the plaintiff will usually be seeking either financial compensation (damages) for harm done to him or her by the defendant, or an injunction from the court ordering the defendant to discontinue harming the plaintiff.

total absorption costing see ABSORPTION COSTING.

total assets the combined amount of a company's FIXED ASSETS and CURRENT ASSETS as recorded in the company's BALANCE SHEET. This shows *all* the assets used by a company regardless of how they are financed. Compare NET ASSETS.

total productive maintenance (TPM) a PRODUCTION control system which monitors the availability, efficiency and effectiveness of a firm's MACHINERY and EQUIPMENT. The potential of an item of machinery and equipment usually depends on its function and on the environment it operates in. In particular how well the machine meets the requirements of availability, meaning that the machine is operational when needed; efficiency, meaning that it always performs at its rated throughput; and quality, meaning that it produces no defects or non-conforming products. TPM moves beyond preventing breakdowns and includes machinery and equipment restoration and design, a goal being to upgrade equipment so that it performs better and provides less maintenance than when it was new. See MAINTENANCE, LEAN MANUFACTURING.

total quality management (TQM) a business philosophy which seeks to instil in *all* employees of a firm an *individual* as well as a *collective* responsibility for maintaining high QUALITY standards, in respect of both the products supplied by the firm and the attention paid to customer services and requirements. TQM has both an internal and an external dimension. Fundamentally, the success or failure of the firm will depend on its ability to satisfy the demands of its external customers. Product quality may well be the most important source of a firm's COMPETITIVE ADVANTAGE over rival suppliers. TQM emphasizes that the firm's ability to generate and sustain quality advantages stems from the totality of its internal operations. The firm is made up of a network of interrelated departments, each one standing in a customer or supplier relationship with others in terms of the internal flow of raw materials and components, processing and assembly operations, through to final product, stockholding and dispatch. TQM seeks to establish a unity of interests and commitment to the maintenance of the highest possible quality standards at each of these interfaces.

TQM in particular attempts to minimize the amount of time and money spent on QUALITY CONTROL by the PREVENTION of quality problems (e.g. component and product defects and waste) arising in the first instance, thus shifting the focus of quality control away from merely detecting and rectifying cases of failure and waste. Individual commitment to quality can be reinforced by the operation of QUALITY CIRCLES and various EMPLOYEE PARTICIPATION schemes. See QUALITY ASSURANCE, EUROPEAN FOUNDATION FOR QUALITY MANAGEMENT, ACCEPTANCE SAMPLING, ACTIVITY CHART, FISHBONE CHART.

total shareholder return (TSR) the nominal capital growth (share price increase plus dividends) that would have been achieved by a shareholder over a specified time period assuming all dividends were reinvested. The TSR of a company is used as a comparative measure of that company's financial performance against other companies. See EXECUTIVE SHARE OPTION SCHEME, LONG-TERM INCENTIVE PLAN, SHARE PRICE INDEX.

Toyota production system see JUST-IN-TIME (JIT).

TQM see TOTAL QUALITY MANAGEMENT.

tracker fund a PORTFOLIO of company SHARES which is designed to exactly mirror in composition and relative 'weighting' the shares making up a selected share index uch as the 'Financial Times Stock Exchange (FTSE) – 100 Share Index'. Tracker funds are operated by UNIT TRUSTS, INVESTMENT TRUSTS and other INSTITUTIONAL INVESTORS. Unlike many funds which are *actively* managed by fund managers who buy and sell shares at their discretion in a wide range of companies, tracker funds are *passively* managed and, as their name implies, simply 'track', in a robotic way, the shares comprising the target index. See INDIVIDUAL SAVINGS ACCOUNT (ISA).

trade the exchange of goods, services and financial securities between BUYERS and SELLERS. In most cases trade takes place using MONEY as a means of exchange in buying and selling transactions, though occasionally trade can involve direct BARTER. See MARKET SYSTEM, INTERNATIONAL TRADE.

trade association an organization which represents the interests of firms operating in the same INDUSTRY. Trade associations collect data on industrial production, sales and exports for circulation to member firms, provide a forum for the discussion of trade affairs, and represent the interests of members in dealings with other trade organizations or government departments. See INTERFIRM COMPARISON.

trade credit a deferred-payment arrangement whereby a supplier allows a customer a certain period of time (typically one to two months) after receiving the products in which to pay for them. See CREDITORS, CREDITORS RATIO, WORKING CAPITAL.

trade creditors see CREDITORS.

trade cycle see BUSINESS CYCLE.

trade debt a deferred-payment arrangement whereby a customer is allowed a certain period of time in which to pay for products after receiving them. See DEBTORS, DEBTORS RATIO, WORKING CAPITAL, CREDIT CONTROL, AGE ANALYSIS PROFILE FOR DEBTORS.

Trade Descriptions Acts 1968 *and* **1972** a UK Act (1968) which makes it an offence to apply a false or misleading description to a GOOD OR SERVICE and a false or misleading indication as to the PRICE of a good or service. The term 'trade description' is defined broadly to include, for example, quantity, size of gauge, composition, fitness for purpose, performance, strength, accuracy, method of manufacture, place and date of manufacture, etc. Offenders can be punished by a fine or imprisonment. The Act is administered by local authority WEIGHTS AND MEASURES officials, in conjunction with the DEPARTMENT OF TRADE AND INDUSTRY and the OFFICE OF FAIR TRADING, which keeps a central register of convictions.

The 1972 Act requires that certain imported products should have their country of origin clearly displayed. See CONSUMER PROTECTION, PRICE MARKING (BARGAIN OFFERS) ORDER 1979, CONSUMER PROTECTION ACT 1987.

trade discount see QUANTITY DISCOUNT.

trade dispute see INDUSTRIAL DISPUTE, TRADE UNION IMMUNITIES.

traded options market a market where investors trade in the right to buy or sell shares or commodities at a predetermined price and time. OPTION prices reflect in more accentuated form movements in the prices of shares or commodities, so that prices in traded options markets are more volatile. See FORWARD MARKET.

trade fair an organized gathering of firms from different industries for the display and promotion of their goods and services to prospective customers. See TRADE SHOW, PROMOTIONAL MIX.

trade-in an allowance made by a supplier to a customer against the price of a good when the customer simultaneously trades in an older version of the good. As such, trade-ins are a form of price DISCOUNT offered to customers to induce them to buy.

trade integration the establishment of FREE TRADE between a number of countries with the aim of securing the benefits of international SPECIALIZATION and INTERNATIONAL TRADE. There are four main forms of trade integration, ranging from a loose association of trade partners to a fully integrated group of nation states:

(a) a FREE TRADE AREA, where members eliminate trade barriers between themselves but each continues to operate its own particular barriers against nonmembers.

(b) a CUSTOMS UNION, where members eliminate trade barriers between themselves and establish uniform barriers against nonmembers, in particular a common external tariff.

(c) a COMMON MARKET, that is, a customs union that also provides for the free movement of labour and capital across national boundaries.

(d) an ECONOMIC UNION, that is, a common market that also provides for the unification of members' general objectives in respect of economic growth, etc, and the harmonization of monetary, fiscal and other policies.

Examples of 'free trade areas' are the EUROPEAN FREE TRADE ASSOCIATION (EFTA), the NORTH AMERICAN FREE TRADE AGREEMENT (NAFTA), the ASSOCIATION OF SOUTHEAST ASIAN NATIONS (ASEAN), ASIA PACIFIC ECONOMIC COOPERATION (APEC), and the former LATIN AMERICAN FREE TRADE ASSOCIATION (LAFTA). A splinter-group from LAFTA, MERCOSUR, is an example of a 'customs union'; the ANDEAN PACT, another LAFTA splinter-group, is an example of a 'common market'; while the EUROPEAN UNION is rapidly transforming itself from a common market into a full-blown 'economic union' (see ECONOMIC AND MONETARY UNION).

Partial trade integration as exemplified by the above arrangements are beneficial insofar as they create additional trade between members, but they also involve discrimination against nonmembers, which may reduce trade with these countries. Thus, many economists view the promotion of free trade on a *multilateral* basis through the auspices of the WORLD TRADE ORGANIZATION as generally preferable to limited regional alliances.

trade investment the acquisition of STOCKS and SHARES in one FIRM by another firm. Trade investments may be undertaken for a variety of reasons including the profitable investment of surplus cash; the protection or advancement of an existing contractual trade relationship by a more direct involvement (for example, a supplier might buy a stake in a customer firm); the provision of a launching pad for a possible future TAKEOVER or merger. Where the trade investment involves the acquisition of a large but not controlling proportion of a company's shares then that company becomes an ASSOCIATED COMPANY.

See QUOTED INVESTMENTS, UNQUOTED INVESTMENTS.

trade mark a symbol (a word or pictorial representation) which is used by a business as a means of identifying a particular good or service so that it may be readily distinguished by purchasers from similar goods and services supplied by other businesses. See BRAND NAME.

In the UK, under the Trade Marks Act 1938 and the Trade Marks (Amendments) Act 1984, trade marks can be registered with the PATENT OFFICE. Registration of a trade mark confers a statutory monopoly in the use of that mark in relation to the products for which it is registered, and the registered owner has the right to sue in the courts for infringement of the mark. In order to qualify for registration, a trade mark must be judged by the Patent Office to be uniquely distinctive (i.e. non-identical or confusable with symbols used by other traders).

Trade marks protect the registered owner from unfair competition through piracy and they provide consumers with a means of unambiguously identifying the products of their choice.

trade partners see EXPORTING.

Tradepoint see STOCK MARKET.

trade price the PRICE paid by a RETAILER to a WHOLESALER or PRODUCER for products which will be resold at a higher price. See MARK-UP, DISCOUNT.

trade promotions the incentives given by a seller of a product to encourage WHOLESALERS and RETAILERS to stock and promote the product. Such inducements include TRADE DISCOUNTS, free merchandise and gifts etc. See PROMOTIONAL MIX.

trader/dealer generic terms which cover both businesses which *take title* to goods (that is, purchase goods) which they then on-sell to customers – food RETAILERS, car dealers; and businesses which act purely in an agency or brokerage capacity, bringing together buyers and sellers of a good or service – ESTATE AGENTS, INSURANCE BROKERS. Traders and dealers thus act as 'middlemen' or 'market intermediaries' in the economic system.

trades council an association of TRADE UNION branches, drawn from a variety of unions, with the objective of advancing their mutual interests and promoting trade unionism in a locality.

trade show an organized gathering of firms, usually from a particular industry, for the display and promotion of their goods and services to prospective customers. See TRADE FAIR, PROMOTIONAL MIX.

Trades Union Congress (TUC) the TRADE UNION federation to which most UK unions are affiliated. The TUC represents the trade union movement in dealings with government and formulates policy for the movement as a whole. Unlike some continental federations it has no direct role in COLLECTIVE BARGAINING, though on occasions TUC officials intervene in major INDUSTRIAL DISPUTES. The TUC can intervene in disputes (for example over membership between unions (see BRIDLINGTON RULES)). The TUC is governed by a General Council elected by constituent members in proportion to their membership.

trade union an organization of employees whose primary objective is to protect and advance the economic interests of its members by negotiating WAGE RATES and conditions of employment with employers or managers. There are a number of different types of union:

(a) *craft union*, a union that represents a particular group of skilled workers (for example electricians) who may work in many industries. A sub-species is the 'promotion-line union' which also represents those who, after a period of training, will join the skilled group;

(b) *enterprise union*, a union that represents all those employed in a particular organization;

(c) *general union*, a union composed of employees drawn from a variety of occupations and industries;

(d) *industrial union*, a union that aspires to represent all or most of those employed in a particular industry.

Traditionally, UK unionism has been a complex amalgam of (a), (c) and (d), with the result that managers in a given organization may have to negotiate with a number of unions (see MULTI-UNIONISM). It has been argued, however, that this classification is not helpful in the analysis of union behaviour: a better distinction is between *open* and *closed* unions. Open unions are those which respond to industrial change by broadening their membership base, whilst closed unions are those which maintain their exclusivity. Whilst a useful distinction, it perhaps does not do justice to the variety of union organizations in the UK. Those mergers between unions in which small craft-based unions are incorporated into larger, more general unions can result in a union having both open and closed sections.

Enterprise unions are an important feature of the large-firm sector in Japan, whilst most union members in Germany are to be found in industrial unions. Trade unions may also be organized on political or religious lines, as in France.

A distinction can also be drawn between differing philosophies of trade unionism. In *business unionism* the union's sole objective is the improvement of the pay and conditions of its members. Such unions do not concern themselves with wider social and political issues. In this model the job of the union leader is simply to sell the labour of the membership at the highest price. By contrast, in *welfare unionism* unions seek improvements in social benefits (for example child benefit payments) through political action as well as improvements in pay and conditions. In so far as many British trade unions have concerned themselves with social and political issues, welfare unionism could be said to be the main approach in Britain. Nevertheless, improvements in pay and conditions remain their primary objective.

The basic unit of organization of trade unions is generally the union branch, composed of all members in a particular workplace or locality. In many industries, representation of members' interests in particular workplaces is undertaken not by officers of the branch but by lay officials elected separately (see SHOP STEWARDS). Union policy is determined by a periodic conference attended by delegates from the branches, whilst the running of the union is overseen by an executive committee elected by the members (Trade Union Act 1984). Day-to-day management of the union is in the hands of paid officials. Critics of trade unions have argued that the officials and activists do not adequately represent the views and interests of the ordinary member. However, the conduct of most unions is based on democratic procedures, and the union member does have the opportunity to influence union policy-making and behaviour.

Union membership and union density (i.e. the proportion of labour force in union membership) declined in most advanced industrialized countries during the 1980s. In the UK, membership fluctuated at around 45% of the labour force for much of the post war period but rose to over 50% in the 1970s as a result of governmental and managerial encouragement of union membership and the CLOSED SHOP. Currently (2005) union membership is about 30% of the total workforce. See COLLECTIVE BARGAINING, INDUSTRIAL RELATIONS, WHITE-COLLAR UNION, STATUTORY UNION RECOGNITION PROCEDURE.

trade union immunities legal protection from civil action for TRADE UNIONS taking lawful STRIKE action in furtherance of an INDUSTRIAL DISPUTE. Without these, employers could take legal action against unions every time they caused employees to breach their CONTRACT OF EMPLOYMENT in this way. The immunities in effect confer a negative right not to be sued for such action. For immunity to be held, it is essential that a strike be officially sanctioned by the union and that the union follows the procedures for taking strike action stipulated in recent labour laws. Immunity is restricted to trade disputes between employees and their employer concerning the terms and conditions of employment, allocation of work, discipline, union membership and facilities and INDUSTRIAL RELATIONS procedures. All forms of SECONDARY ACTION are now excluded from immunity.

trade war the use by a number of countries of beggar-my-neighbour trade restrictions such as Tariffs and QUOTAS to restrict imports, and subsidies and tax rebates to increase exports. These actions are usually self-defeating, leading to lower trade and income levels for all. See WORLD TRADE ORGANIZATION.

trading account the section of a PROFIT-AND-LOSS ACCOUNT where the COST OF SALES is deducted from SALES REVENUE to show the amount of GROSS PROFIT made.

trading period the period of trading between two successive sets of financial accounts. To comply with the requirements of company law and taxation authorities, companies generally adopt a one-year trading period, producing an ANNUAL REPORT AND ACCOUNTS at the end of each trading period. However, because for internal management control purposes, much more frequent results are generally required, a company may produce PROFIT AND LOSS ACCOUNTS and BALANCE SHEETS at monthly or even weekly intervals.

trading profit see OPERATING PROFIT.

trading stamp a coupon attached to a product, which purchasers can collect with a view to redeeming them for cash or gifts. See SALES PROMOTION.

traditional authority see AUTHORITY.

training the process of extending and improving the SKILLS and knowledge of people so as to improve JOB performance. A distinction can be made between *vocational* training, i.e. the acquisition of specific occupational skills, and *pre-vocational* training, i.e. the development of awareness of the world of work and employment. Education develops those basic skills such as writing and numeracy which form the bedrock for more specialized occupational skills.

To determine what training is required in an organization or economy, it is beneficial to undertake a *training needs analysis.* As a first step the main goals or priorities have to be established; then it is necessary to consider what skills are necessary to achieve these objectives. These are compared with the existing stock of skills amongst workers. Any deficiency is referred to as *a skills gap* and represents the skills that should be provided by training. A comprehensive approach to training will involve a needs analysis, a programme to close this gap and a monitoring and evaluation process to determine whether it has been successful.

Although it is generally accepted that training improves job performance, UK employers are often reluctant to provide training. The UK in fact has a poor record compared with its main competitors such as Germany. Training in the UK is widely viewed as a cost rather than an investment, and one whose potential benefits are difficult to quantify on the balance sheet. Employers fear that employees, once trained, will leave or be poached for higher paid employment.

Traditionally, the training system in the UK was *voluntarist* (see VOLUNTARISM) in that the state had little role in directing the structures and content of training programmes and institutions. However, state intervention has grown in recent years. Currently, the system of vocational training is overseen by the recently-created national and local LEARNING AND SKILLS COUNCILS and the government has established a framework of vocational qualifications (see NATIONAL VOCATIONAL QUALIFICATION). There is also an emphasis on skill development and training amongst the unemployed in the Welfare-to-Work programme. Participants in this programme receive training as part of work placements. See MANAGEMENT DEVELOPMENT, ACCREDITATION OF EXPERIENTIAL LEARNING, ACCREDITATION OF PRIOR LEARNING, APPRENTICESHIP, NEW DEAL.

Training and Enterprise Council see LEARNING AND SKILLS COUNCIL.

training needs analysis see TRAINING.

transaction the exchange of an INPUT, GOOD, SERVICE or ASSET between two or more individuals or firms. Transactions can take place on an 'arm's length' basis, with individuals and firms buying and selling through a MARKET, or transactions may be 'internalized' and conducted through an internal ORGANIZATION, involving exchanges between the various departments/divisions of a VERTICALLY INTEGRATED firm (or DIVERSIFIED FIRM or MULTINATIONAL ENTERPRISE).

Transactions have a number of characteristics, which have an economic significance, including their 'size' (e.g. the transfer of a single item or large number of items), their 'frequency' (e.g. transfers may occur on a 'one-off' basis or may occur continuously, daily or weekly), and their 'complexity' (e.g. transfers may be relatively simple or highly technical and sophisticated).

The specification of transactions and the terms of exchange (e.g. prices to be paid) are usually incorporated into a legally binding CONTRACT between the parties involved when transfers take place through the market.

Transactions are conducted within the firm through established procedures and protocols governing input procurement, production, distribution and marketing. Typically, a system of internal TRANSFER PRICES is used to value interdepartmental exchanges of inputs, goods and services.

A key focus of modern theories of the firm and markets are the determinants of the relative efficiencies of conducting transactions through the market or within the firm. A number of considerations are relevant to this issue:

(a) the relative costs of transactions through the market compared to within the firm *per se* (see TRANSACTION COSTS);

(b) the importance of transaction costs vis-a-vis the firm's *total* supply costs (production and selling); and

(c) strategic considerations such as controllability of inputs. For example, the transaction costs of using the market may be substantially higher than transactions within the firm arising from the need to find suitable external input suppliers and distributors and draw up and monitor contracts with them. Superficially, this would indicate that an internal organization is preferable to using the market. However, the 'savings' on transaction costs may be offset by higher internal administrative costs and AGENCY COSTS.

transaction costs the costs associated with the activities of buying and selling in a MARKET system (see TRANSACTION). For example, firms incur costs in finding satisfactory input suppliers and distributors for their products and in negotiating, concluding and monitoring CONTRACTS with other firms. In some market situations, transaction costs may be inflated by the application of monopoly surcharges by powerful suppliers. Although a firm may avoid some transaction costs by VERTICAL INTEGRATION (i.e. performing some functions internally), these may well be offset by the higher administrative, stockholding and other costs involved in running a vertically integrated business. See AGENCY COSTS.

transaction exposure see EXCHANGE RATE EXPOSURE.

Transfer Accounting Lodgement for Investors see TALISMAN.

Transfer and Automated Registration of Uncertificated Stock see CREST.

transfer deed a document used to record the transfer of ownership of SHARES from a seller to a buyer. Transfer deeds are used to update a company's SHARE REGISTER and become the basis for cancelling old SHARE CERTIFICATES and issuing new ones.

Transfer of Undertakings (Protection of Employment) Regulations 1981 (TUPE) a set of UK regulations which stipulate employee rights when the ownership of a business changes. Derived from the European Union's Acquired Rights Directive of 1977, the Regulations stipulate that an employee's CONTRACT OF EMPLOYMENT is automatically transferred to the new employer when a business changes hands, with the result that the employee's rights and duties are unchanged. These Regulations only applied to commercial ventures and hence it was supposed that large parts of the public services were not covered by them. However, a succession of recent judgements by the European Court of Justice has implied that this interpretation, upon which the government's COMPETITIVE TENDERING programme was based, infringed European law. The Regulations were therefore amended to include public service activities.

TUPE has been widely considered in relation to the CONTRACTING-OUT of public services as well as competitive tendering. Whilst TUPE provides protection for employees at the point of transfer there is some debate as to the duration of the protection against changes to employment conditions and wages.

Employers are obliged by law to consult with employee representatives over transfers of undertakings, in the same manner as is required with REDUNDANCY.

transfer price the internal PRICE at which raw materials, components and final products are transacted between the divisions or subsidiaries of a vertically integrated or conglomerate firm.

The transfer price charged may be set by reference to the prices ruling in outside markets for inputs and products (arms-length pricing). Alternatively, the transfer price may be set at a lower or higher level than the going market price, according to some internal accounting convention (for example, cost of production plus standard profit mark-up) and the desired 'profit split' between the firm's activities. Such administered transfer prices would generally be designed to achieve the firm's overall profit goals, but in transfer pricing decisions there may often be an inherent conflict between the overall goals of the firm and the goals of its subunits. For example, if one COST CENTRE is allowed to transfer components at cost of production plus a specific mark-up, then it has little incentive to minimize its production costs. Again, where a PROFIT CENTRE does not have discretion over its buying or selling prices but must buy or sell some or all of its inputs or outputs to other subunits at transfer prices established by headquarters, then the profit performance of the subunit will not depend solely upon the efforts of local managers, making it difficult to evaluate the performance of subgroup managers and motivate them to improve efficiency.

Transfer pricing gives a firm added flexibility in pricing its products. It may deploy transfer pricing to gain a competitive advantage over rival suppliers (to PRICE SQUEEZE a non-integrated rival), in the case of a MULTINATIONAL ENTERPRISE, transfer pricing provides an opportunity to increase its profits by setting transfer prices across national frontiers in such a way that most of the firm's profits accrue in countries where company taxation rates are the lowest. In addition, inflated transfer prices for components or services may be used to remit surpluses back to the parent company from subsidiaries located in countries which limit the repatriation of profits through dividend controls or EXCHANGE CONTROLS. See INTERNALIZATION, TAX HAVEN, VERTICAL INTEGRATION, DIVERSIFICATION, SHADOW PRICE, MIXER COMPANY.

translation exposure see EXCHANGE RATE EXPOSURE.

transnational company see MULTINATIONAL ENTERPRISE.

Transport and General Workers' Union the UK's third largest TRADE UNION with some 870,000 members in a large number of industries. For many years it was the UK's largest trade union and at its peak had nearly two million members.

transportation model a means of selecting the best way to distribute a product from a number of factories or warehouses to a number of destinations so as to minimize transportation costs while meeting customers' requirements. The transportation model uses LINEAR PROGRAMMING to analyse such physical DISTRIBUTION management problems.

treasury 1 the department within a firm which is responsible for managing the firm's finances, making arrangements to collect cash speedily from debtors; profitably invest any short-term cash surpluses; and arrange with lenders to cover any short-term cash shortages. In large multidivisional companies the treasury department may also arrange to transfer cash from company divisions earning surpluses to divisions experiencing liquidity problems so as to minimize external borrowings. In MULTINATIONAL ENTERPRISES the treasury department may also transfer funds between countries and convert currencies in order either to minimize the risk of losses or to take advantage of possible windfall gains from EXCHANGE RATE changes.

2 the Treasury, the UK government department responsible for managing the government's finances, authorizing the expenditure plans of government DEPARTMENTS, and overseeing the tax-gathering work of the INLAND REVENUE and CUSTOMS AND EXCISE. In addition the Treasury advises the Chancellor of the Exchequer on the government's annual Budget. See BUDGET (GOVERNMENT).

Treasury bill a redeemable FINANCIAL SECURITY bearing a three-month redemption date which is issued by the Bank of England. Some Treasury bills are purchased *on tap* at undisclosed sums by government departments with temporary cash surpluses, but the vast majority are sold at periodic *tender* auctions to DISCOUNT HOUSES and overseas banks. Treasury bills bear a nominal face value which is repaid in full on redemption, but the price paid for them on issue depends on the outcome of a competitive tender, with discount houses and overseas banks bidding against each other for an allocation. The Treasury bills which are bought by the discount houses are usually then sold (rediscounted) in the DISCOUNT MARKET to other buyers, principally to COMMERCIAL BANKS which hold them as part of their 'liquidity base' to support their lending operations. Treasury bills are issued alongside BONDS both to raise finance for the government to cover BUDGET deficits and also as a means of controlling the MONEY SUPPLY and level of INTEREST RATES. See MONETARY POLICY.

Treaty of Nice, 2000 see EUROPEAN UNION.

Treaty of Rome, 1958 see EUROPEAN UNION.

trend 1 the direction of movement of a variable such as sales over time. See SALES FORECASTING.

2 a broad change in attitude and behaviour in society over time. These can serve to influence the acceptability of products by consumers with some products going out of *fashion* whilst others become more popular.

trendsetter see OPINION LEADERS.

trial balance a listing of the balances on a firm's LEDGER accounts that is prepared prior to the PROFIT-AND-LOSS ACCOUNT and BALANCE SHEET, as an initial check on the arithmetic accuracy of the ledger accounts.

If the total of all DEBIT balances in ledger accounts equals the total of all CREDIT balances in ledger accounts then this suggests (but does not guarantee) that the DOUBLE-ENTRY ACCOUNTS have been accurately recorded and that the data from them might be used to prepare the profit-and-loss account and balance sheet.

tripartism a system of cooperation between both sides of industry and the state. Tripartite institutions typically include representatives of TRADE UNIONS, managers and owners, and government on the grounds that each has an interest in and worthwhile contribution to make to economic and industrial policy. Insofar as these organizations become *de facto* extensions of the state (i.e. they make and implement government policy) the more advanced forms of tripartism are sometimes referred to as *corporatism*. Tripartism developed in the UK from the 1960s. Examples of tripartite organizations include the now defunct National Economic Development Council and the Manpower Services Commission (see TRAINING). UK governments since 1979 have been hostile to tripartism on the grounds that trade unions have no legitimate role in the formulation and implementation of policy, and the trend since then has been to abolish tripartite bodies or to terminate union involvement. This contrasts with other European countries, such as Germany, Austria and the Scandinavian nations where tripartism continues to be viewed as a valued approach to formulating industrial policy.

true and fair view the opinion formed by an AUDITOR about a JOINT-STOCK COMPANY'S accounts, based upon evidence obtained from auditing the company's LEDGER accounts. The auditor is required to report to a company's shareholders about the accuracy and presentation of a firm's annual report and accounts. After undertaking the appropriate tests, usually on a sample basis, the auditor must be convinced that no material errors or omissions have occurred either in the firm's system of recording accounting transactions or in their summary and presentation. If the auditor is satisfied that no material irregularities have occurred, he or she will conclude that the financial statements present a 'true and fair view' for the period (year) under review. If irregularities are noted, the accounts may be prefaced with the qualification that 'subject to the following ... the financial statements audited ... present a true and fair view'. See also FINANCIAL ACCOUNTING.

trust 1 a collection of ASSETS held and managed by appointed *trustees* on behalf of an individual or group of people. Trusts are often established to minimize the amount of INCOME TAX and WEALTH TAX an individual or group is required to pay. See TRUSTEE INVESTMENTS.

2 see UNIT TRUST.

3 an alternative term for a CARTEL (most commonly used in the USA).

trustee see TRUST.

trustee investments investments made by a trustee on behalf of an individual or group through a TRUST. In the UK such investments are governed by the Trustee Investment Act of 1961, which lays down rules obliging trustees to maintain part of their portfolio in the form of Government BONDS, and restricting shareholdings to SHARES in larger quoted companies.

TUC see TRADES UNION CONGRESS.

TUPE see TRANSFER OF UNDERTAKINGS (PROTECTION OF EMPLOYMENT) REGULATIONS.

turnkey project a one-off major construction project such as the building of a dam, power station etc. in another country where usually a contracted foreign firm (operating either alone or as the leader of a consortium of firms) is responsible for the design and construction of the facility. See BUILD, OPERATE, TRANSFER PROJECT.

turnover see SALES REVENUE, LABOUR TURNOVER.

turnover tax see VALUE-ADDED TAX.

turnround a situation where a firm or a division of a firm that has been experiencing a protracted decline in profits is able to institute measures which not only halt the decline but form the basis of a *sustained* recovery in its profitability. A turnround situation reflects something more than a downturn in profits associated with the BUSINESS CYCLE which affects to a greater or lesser degree most companies operating in a particular activity. In essence it is a crisis situation which is firm-specific, reflecting various internal problems: ineffectual management (an autocratic chief executive, an unbalanced management team, lack of attention to the formulation of BUSINESS STRATEGY), poor financial structure (an inappropriate capital GEARING level), poor financial control (unsystematic allocation of overhead costs, lack of information on which products are generating cash and which ones are making losses) etc. All these factors can contribute to a lack of efficiency, higher costs, loss of competitive vigour and a failure to respond adequately to the changing needs of the market.

Recovery can only be achieved if there is a willingness and ability to identify the major sources of the firm's problems, followed by the initiation of action programmes involving managerial, administrative and financial reorganization, cost reduction and better directed marketing efforts aimed at re-establishing COMPETITIVE ADVANTAGE over rival suppliers. A tardiness or failure to implement appropriate turnround measures may well end in insolvency. However, before this point is reached the firm may well be TAKEN OVER, or in the case of a division, divested. See DIVESTMENT, ENDGAME STRATEGY.

twilight shift see SHIFT WORK.

two-bin system see STOCK CONTROL.

two factor theory of motivation see MOTIVATION.

two-part tariff see TARIFF.

U

UBR see UNIFORM BUSINESS RATE.

U-form see FUNCTIONAL STRUCTURE.

ultra vires (of an action by a JOINT-STOCK COMPANY) exceeding its powers as defined in its MEMORANDUM OF ASSOCIATION. For example, if a company's memorandum authorizes it to trade in the motorcar business, and its directors then set up an ice-cream business, then they may be regarded as trading *ultra vires* and the company's CONTRACTS with ice-cream suppliers and customers may be regarded as void. To avoid falling foul of the *ultra vires* doctrine, companies now tend to draw up very wide-ranging business powers in the MEMORANDUM OF ASSOCIATION.

UMA see UNION MEMBERSHIP AGREEMENT.

umbrella branding a MARKETING tactic which involves a firm selling completely different products or different versions of the same general product under the same BRAND NAME. The attractions of umbrella branding are that it enables the firm to capitalize on the 'goodwill' accruing to an existing brand to facilitate the introduction of a new product and also 'spread' the cost of promoting a related group of brands. Buyers who have found the existing brand to be satisfactory will be 'reassured' the new product will also be satisfactory. Umbrella branding thus increases marketing effectiveness and can reduce both the initial launch cost and the subsequent advertising and promotional unit cost of supporting the brand.

Hoover, for example, used its original 'Hoover' vacuum cleaner brand name to effect entry into the washing machine and other electrical products markets. Likewise, 'Nestlé' has employed the 'Nescafé' brand name to extend its coverage of the instant coffee market through new brand launches: Nescafé Gold Blend, Nescafé Blend 37, Nescafé Cap Colombia, Nescafé Alta Rica, Nescafé Decaffeinated etc. See ECONOMIES OF SCOPE.

unaided recall test see ADVERTISING EFFECTIVENESS TESTS.

unapproved employee share ownership plan an EMPLOYEE SHARE OWNERSHIP PLAN that does not comply with the requirements of UK legislation on share schemes and hence is not approved by the INLAND REVENUE. These schemes do not attract the tax concessions available to approved schemes.

unbundling a colloquial term used to describe a DE-MERGER (the break-up of a company originally formed through a MERGER into two or more separate companies) or more generally the sale of a number of its business divisions by a conglomerate company (see DIVERSIFICATION).

uncertainty and risk the comparative unpredictability of a firm's future business environment, bringing with it the possibility that the firm might incur losses if future economic and market conditions turn out to be radically different from those anticipated by the firm in, for example, pricing its products, moving into new activities etc.

Since managers cannot foretell the future, they are forced to guess the most likely outcome of any decision. All such estimates must, by their very nature, be subjective, though some estimates will be better than others depending upon the amount and availability of information.

Uncertainty arises because it is difficult to predict changes and to estimate accurately the likelihood of events, including possible losses. Unfortunately, many management decisions are based on this uncertainty, since circumstances rarely repeat themselves and there is little past data available to act as a guide. Such market uncertainty can only be gauged by managers, when launching a new product, through combining the limited data available with their own judgement and experience. Managers can improve upon their subjective estimates by collecting information from forecasts, market research, feasibility studies, etc., but they need to balance the cost of collecting such information against its value in improving decisions.

The term 'risk' rather than uncertainty is used to describe business situations where large amounts of information are available about the extent of possible losses and the likelihood of such losses occurring. For example, an insurance company dealing with fire INSURANCE policies and claims from large numbers of manufacturers will be able to compile detailed statistics about numbers of fires and the amount of damage done by each, and can use this information to predict the likelihood of a business experiencing a fire. This detailed statistical information allows the insurance company to charge manufacturers premiums for indemnifying them against fire losses, and thereby to make a profit. By contrast, a single manufacturer would find it very difficult to predict the likelihood of his premises being damaged by fire and the amount of damage, since such an event would probably be a unique experience for him. Faced with a possibility of fire, the manufacturer can either choose to bear the risk of losses resulting from a serious fire or can avoid the risk of fire damage by paying an insurance company a premium to bear the risk. Again, the manufacturer can take the risk that the prices of its main raw materials will be much higher next year, or it can contract now through a commodity FORWARD MARKET to buy raw materials supplies for future delivery at a fixed price. See DECISION TREE, SALES FORECASTING, DISCOUNTED CASH FLOW, BUSINESS CYCLE, SENSITIVITY ANALYSIS.

UNCTAD see UNITED NATIONS CONFERENCE ON TRADE AND DEVELOPMENT.

under-capacity scheduling the allocation of extra time in a schedule for non-production tasks. For example, maintenance and problem-solving. See PRODUCTION SCHEDULING.

underlying inflation rate see INFLATION.

underwriting the acceptance by a financial institution of the financial risks involved in a particular transaction, for an agreed fee. For example, INSURANCE COMPANIES underwrite INSURANCE risks such as damage to property, paying out monies to policy holders wholly or in part to cover *bona fide* claims for compensation; MERCHANT BANKS underwrite new SHARE ISSUES, guaranteeing to buy up any shares that are not sold in the open market, and BILLS OF EXCHANGE. See LLOYDS, EXPORT CREDIT GUARANTEE DEPARTMENT.

undifferentiated marketing strategy a MARKETING STRATEGY for a product based on the use of the *same* MARKETING MIX format right across the market (uniform pricing, advertising messages, retail outlets, etc.). Contrasted with a DIFFERENTIATED MARKETING OR TARGETING STRATEGY OR CONCENTRATED MARKETING OR TARGETING STRATEGY which seeks to exploit particular MARKET SEGMENTS, the undifferentiated approach attempts to reach all classes of buyer. This approach is best suited to a market where the product being sold is relatively standardized and buyers require little in the way of product variety. Mass marketing the product on a uniform basis is simpler to organize and manage than a fragmented approach, and may yield lower unit selling and production costs by enabling the firm to take advantage of economies of scale in advertising and production. On the debit side, undifferentiated marketing may fail to realize fully a product's sales potential because of its inability to appeal to key customer segments.

undistributed profits see RETAINED PROFIT.

unearned income see EARNED INCOME.

unemployment the non-utilization of part of the economy's available labour (and capital) resources. Because idle resources lead to a loss of potential output to the economy and the divisive social effects of unemployment, most governments accord a high priority to the achievement of a high level of employment in formulating their ECONOMIC POLICIES.

In the UK two measures are commonly used by the government to calculate the UNEMPLOYMENT RATE:

(a) the 'claimant count unemployment measure' which is based on the number of people who register as unemployed at JOB CENTRE offices and qualify for the JOBSEEKERS ALLOWANCE;

(b) the 'International Labour Organization (ILO) unemployment measure' which is based on a LABOUR MARKET SURVEY which identifies people who 'are currently out of work but are actively seeking a job'. In recent years there has been a steady fall in the numbers unemployed. In 2000 the number unemployed fell to below 1 million (a figure last achieved 25 years before), with the unemployment rate (2004) standing at 2.9% of the LABOUR FORCE (claimant count measure).

There are a number of different types of unemployment, including *cyclical* unemployment (short-term unemployment associated with a fall in the level of business activity, see BUSINESS CYCLE); *seasonal* unemployment (short-term unemployment associated with changes in the demand for particular products at different seasons of the year); *frictional* unemployment (short-term unemployment associated with people changing jobs); *structural* unemployment (long-term unemployment associated with the decline of particular industries and automation of production processes); '*voluntary*' unemployment (when people who are available for work nonetheless choose not to offer themselves for employment at 'going' wage rates because they are 'cushioned' by social security benefits).

There are two basic causes of long-term unemployment:

(a) a level of total demand in the economy which is too low in relation to the supply capacity of the economy to produce goods and services. The traditional prescription for dealing with this situation is for the government to boost spending in the economy by decreasing taxes and by increasing its own expenditure (see FISCAL POLICY), and by expanding the money supply and lowering interest rates (see MONETARY POLICY);

(b) supply-side deficiencies, particularly a lack of investment in plant and new products, low productivity and LABOUR MARKET distortions.

Remedies for supply-side problems include improving industrial efficiency and stimulating innovation, enterprise and business start-ups. (See INDUSTRIAL POLICY, COMPETITION POLICY, ENTERPRISE INVESTMENT SCHEME, ENTERPRISE INVESTMENT GRANT, REGIONAL POLICY); encouraging people to seek paid work (see JOBSEEKER ALLOWANCE, WORKING FAMILIES TAX CREDIT); and promoting more flexible labour markets by a variety of trade union legislation aimed at curbing disruptive INDUSTRIAL DISPUTES (see STRIKE, INDUSTRIAL ACTION).

In the past most UK governments have not formulated fiscal and monetary policy with any specific unemployment 'target' in mind. The present government, however, is committed to reducing unemployment as much as possible and see the best way of achieving this is to sustain stable monetary conditions. Specifically, the government has committed itself to an annual inflation rate 'target' of not more than 2% and the remit of the MONETARY POLICY COMMITTEE of the Bank of England is to set official INTEREST RATES so as to achieve this target. See VACANCY RATE, DE-INDUSTRIALIZATION, STRUCTURE OF INDUSTRY.

unemployment benefit see JOBSEEKERS ALLOWANCE.

unemployment rate the number of unemployed persons expressed as a percentage of the total LABOUR FORCE. See UNEMPLOYMENT.

unfair dismissal the unfair termination of a person's employment by the employer. Dismissal can be held to be unfair if the employer cannot show a 'fair' reason and acted 'unreasonably' in taking the decision to dismiss. A fair reason is one where for some reason the employee is not able to carry out satisfactorily the duties associated with the employment or where the job is no longer needed because of REDUNDANCY. For instance, it would probably be considered fair to dismiss a chauffeur who had been disqualified from driving but unfair to dismiss someone on the grounds of personal dislike. To have acted reasonably the employer should have clearly informed the employee of the grounds for dismissal and given the employee the opportunity to put a personal point of view.

Constructive dismissal is where an employee feels forced to leave because the employer acts unlawfully, unfairly or otherwise breaches the CONTRACT OF EMPLOYMENT. A female employee who is subject to sexual harassment by her manager and who feels forced to leave her job as a result could possibly claim that she had been constructively dismissed.

An individual who believes the dismissal to be unfair may pursue a claim for reinstatement or compensation at an EMPLOYMENT TRIBUNAL. In determining whether dismissal is fair, tribunals draw on case law and an ADVISORY, CONCILIATION AND ARBITRATION SERVICE code of practice on DISCIPLINARY PROCEDURES. A very small minority of those who take unfair dismissal claims to tribunal actually achieve reinstatement. The number of claims taken to tribunal has increased in recent years and policy makers have sought ways of limiting this growth. For instance, claimants have to pay a deposit, and CONCILIATION prior to a formal hearing is strongly encouraged. See EMPLOYMENT APPEALS TRIBUNAL.

unfranked investment income see FRANKED INVESTMENT INCOME.

UNICE Union of Industrial and Employers Confederations of Europe. The main private sector employer body at European level, and one of the main SOCIAL PARTNERS. It represents the combined interests of national business organizations, such as the CBI, in the European SOCIAL DIALOGUE.

uniform business rate (UBR) the annual charge made by local authorities in England and Wales on business premises, factories, warehouses, offices and shops. The UBR is fixed at a set rate throughout the country (for 2005/06 the rate has been fixed at 42.2p in the £). Thus, for any given premises anywhere in England and Wales the rate payable is calculated simply by multiplying the above rates by the assessed rateable value of the premises. The UBR came into effect in April 1990, replacing the previous system of rating which gave individual local authorities discretion in setting the base rates payable in their particular areas. Inevitably, this created anomalies with large variations from area to area, as some authorities increased their local services and put the burden of paying a higher proportion of the bill on to businesses rather than householders. The introduction of the UBR required all business premises to be revalued at 1990 prices with further revaluations scheduled every five years.

uniform delivered price system see GEOGRAPHICAL PRICING.

union branch see TRADE UNION.

union democracy see TRADE UNION.

union density see TRADE UNION.

union dues TRADE UNION membership fees. See CHECK-OFF AGREEMENT.

union mark-up the WAGE premium that derives from membership of a TRADE UNION.

union membership agreement (UMA) see CLOSED SHOP.

Union of Shop, Distributive and Allied Workers a UK TRADE UNION for retail employees with over 300,000 members. The UK's sixth largest union.

UNISON the UK's largest TRADE UNION formed from a merger of the Confederation of Health Service Employees, National Association of Local Government Officers and the National Union of Public Employees in 1993. It currently has around 1,270,000 members in the health service, local government, schools and universities. It includes amongst its membership both manual workers, such as cleaners, and white collar workers such as managers and secretaries. It is notable for having a high proportion of female members.

unitary frame of reference see MANAGEMENT STYLE.

unitary taxation a system of TAXATION operated by a country that taxes a foreign-owned MULTINATIONAL ENTERPRISE on a predetermined proportion of its total worldwide income, rather than on the income which the multinational actually earned within that country. This involves the use of some rule of thumb to apportion tax liability: for example, if 10% of the total world ASSETS of a multinational are located in that country, then the country may seek to tax 10% of the multinational's world income, making no allowance for any foreign taxes paid. Countries might adopt unitary taxation to increase their taxation revenues and to counter manipulative TRANSFER PRICING by multinationals, but must bear in mind that such a taxation system is likely to discourage inward INVESTMENT. Compare DOUBLE TAXATION.

unit cost see AVERAGE COST.

United Nations an international organization consisting of most of the world's countries whose primary objective is the maintenance of world peace and security and the promotion of social harmony and economic development. The UN operates a number of satellite agencies, including the Food and Agriculture Organization, the INTERNATIONAL LABOUR ORGANIZATION and the UNITED NATIONS CONFERENCE ON TRADE AND DEVELOPMENT, and works closely with other international bodies such as the WORLD BANK and the WORLD TRADE ORGANIZATION.

United Nations Conference on Trade and Development (UNCTAD) an international institution which promotes the economic interests of DEVELOPING COUNTRIES by sponsoring INTERNATIONAL COMMODITY AGREEMENTS to improve export earnings on primary foodstuffs and minerals; by negotiating QUOTA and TARIFF reductions on developing countries' exports of manufacturers to the developed world; and by securing economic aid packages for its members.

unit of account see MONEY.

unit pricing the practice of marking on product packs not only the PRICE per pack but the price per common unit of weight or volume, for example price per 500 grammes or price per litre. Unit pricing is generally undertaken for products like groceries which can be offered in a number of pack sizes for a particular brand, or where different brands are offered in a variety of sizes, in order to give consumers more accurate comparative price information. See WEIGHTS AND MEASURES ACT 1964.

unit trust a financial institution which specializes in investment in FINANCIAL SECURITIES on behalf of its 'unit' holders. Some unit trusts offer a single fund, but more usually they operate a number of funds catering for different investment requirements. Unit trusts pool together the monies of a large number of investors which they use to purchase a varied portfolio of investments, mainly UK and overseas corporate stocks and shares and government fixed-interest securities. They are ideal for smaller investors who wish to secure a wider spread of risk than they could achieve for themselves by direct investment in a limited number of securities, or who require professional management of their investments.

Unit trusts issue 'units' in their funds to buyers, and repurchase units from sellers on the basis of a bid price (lower, for buying) and an offer price (higher, for selling). An initial management charge is required of buyers, followed by a smaller annual charge. The value of the individual units in a fund is obtained by dividing the total value of the fund investments plus cash held, by the number of units in existence every day. A fund which is growing will need to create new units, while one in decline will liquidate units on redemption. The value of the total investments of a fund is determined by the value of the securities it holds and the fund's valuation, and hence unit prices can go up or down with the ebb and flow of STOCK MARKET prices in general. Unit trusts usually offer investors a variety of funds to choose from, ranging from general funds which aim at a balance between current income and capital growth, to those specialized in achieving either capital growth or high current income.

The unit trust movement in the UK is represented by the UNIT TRUST ASSOCIATION (UTA) which provides a forum for the discussion of matters of general concern to members, and acts on behalf of members in dealings with other institutional bodies such as the Institutional Investors Committee and the government. The investment and management of funds by unit trusts are regulated by the FINANCIAL SERVICES AUTHORITY in accordance with various standards of good practice laid down under the FINANCIAL SERVICES ACT 1906. See INSTITUTIONAL INVESTORS, FINANCIAL SYSTEM, INSURANCE COMPANY.

Unit Trust Association the TRADE ASSOCIATION which represents the collective interests of UNIT TRUSTS in the UK.

unity of command the principle that an employee should receive instructions from only one superior. See CLASSICAL MANAGEMENT THEORY.

universal management theory see CLASSICAL MANAGEMENT THEORY.

unlimited liability see LIMITED LIABILITY.

unlisted securities market (USM) a market for corporate STOCKS and SHARES that have not obtained a full STOCK MARKET listing. See ALTERNATIVE INVESTMENT MARKET.

unofficial strike see STRIKE.

unquoted investment investments in UNQUOTED SECURITIES such as SHARES and DEBENTURES which are not quoted or traded on a STOCK MARKET. Where a company holds such unquoted investments, they will be shown in its BALANCE SHEET at their purchase price. See TRADE INVESTMENT.

unquoted securities SHARES or DEBENTURES in JOINT-STOCK COMPANIES which are not traded in the STOCK MARKET or for which no price is regularly quoted. It is difficult to determine the value of an unquoted security since no regular market exists for such a security.

unsecured creditor see CREDITORS.

unsecured loan money BORROWED by a company or individual without offering any COLLATERAL SECURITY to the lender.

Unsolicited Goods and Services Acts 1971 and **1975** UK Acts which make it an offence for a person or business to make a demand for payment from persons or businesses to whom unrequested goods have been sent or delivered. See CONSUMER PROTECTION, INERTIA SELLING.

upgrade to replace an existing COMPUTER system (HARDWARE and/or SOFTWARE) by a more powerful model capable of processing data faster or storing larger amounts of data. When upgrading, computer users can experience problems of compatibility with existing programs and machines.

up-selling persuading an existing customer to buy a more valuable product from the firm's portfolio.

upstream integration see VERTICAL INTEGRATION.

Urgent Issues Task Force see ACCOUNTING STANDARDS.

USM see UNLISTED SECURITIES MARKET.

V

vacancy rate the number of available jobs ('officially' notified to local JOB CENTRES) which remain unfilled as a percentage of the total LABOUR FORCE.

valence see MOTIVATION.

value the money worth of a PRODUCT OR ASSET. Value is measured in terms of the PRICE which buyers are prepared to pay for the product or asset. The amount which they are prepared to pay depends upon the benefits which they expect to derive from consuming or owning the item. See PRICE–QUALITY TRADE-OFF, PSYCHOLOGICAL PRICING, VALUE CREATED MODEL, CONSUMER SURPLUS.

value added the difference between the value of a firm's (or industry's) *output* (i.e. the total revenues received from selling that output) and the cost of the *input* materials, components or services bought in to produce that output. Value added focuses attention on the value that a company adds to its bought-in materials and services through its own production and marketing efforts within the company.

A firm will measure its value added as the difference between its SALES REVENUE and the COST of its bought-in materials and services. Where a firm operates at only one level of production or distribution in a VALUE-ADDED CHAIN, it will generally add less value than a vertically integrated firm which embraces several production and distribution stages. See VALUE CREATED MODEL, CONSUMER SURPLUS, VERTICAL INTEGRATION, VALUE-ADDED TAX, VALUE-ADDED STATEMENT, VALUE ADDED PER EMPLOYEE, PROFIT AND LOSS ACCOUNT, ECONOMIC VALUE ADDED.

value-added chain a chain of vertically linked activities which each add value (see VALUE ADDED) in producing and distributing a product. Depending on the nature of the product the value-added chain may involve a large number of vertically linked activities or only a few. Fig 84 overleaf, for example, shows one particular value-added chain in the petrochemical industry. Here the value-added chain involves converting a raw material (oil) into intermediate materials (ethylene and PVC), then into a finished product (plastic kitchenware), then packaging and physically distributing this kitchenware to consumers.

Strategically, where a firm 'positions' itself in the value-added chain for an industry can have an important bearing on its profitability since different activities within the chain may (because of technical and competitive considerations) generate different levels of profitability. For example, supplying unprocessed basic raw materials may yield low levels of profit compared to more skill-intensive later stage processing activities or the supply of high-technology 'speciality' inputs.

In many cases, firms will choose to embrace a number of 'stages' in the value-added chain as part of a vertically integrated operation in order to reduce costs or secure 'tied' input supplies or market outlets. See VALUE CREATED MODEL, VALUE CHAIN ANALYSIS, VERTICAL INTEGRATION.

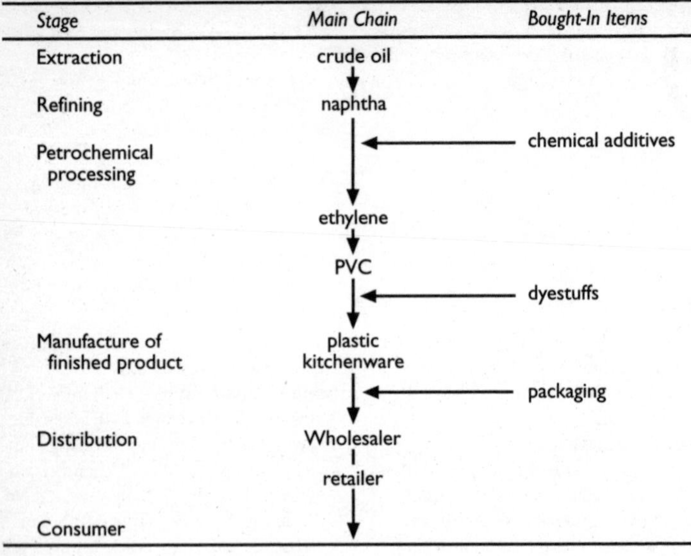

Fig. 84 **Value-added chain.**

value added per employee a measure of a firm's value added/size relation, that expresses the firm's VALUE ADDED as a ratio of its size, measured in terms of number of employees, It is useful to compare value added per employee in a firm with the company's average employee remuneration.

value-added statement an ACCOUNTING statement showing the value added by a company during an accounting period and how this created wealth has been shared among employees, providers of capital and others contributing towards its creation. Fig. 85 shows the typical layout of a value-added statement.

			£
Sales			980,000
Less materials and services purchased			560,000
VALUE ADDED			420,000
Applied to meet:			
Remuneration	(to employees)	150,000	
Interest	(to lenders)	30,000	
Tax	(to government)	80,000	
Dividends	(to shareholders)	40,000	300,000
Retained for use in business			120,000

Fig. 85 **Value-added statement.** Value-added statement of Y Co for year ending 31 December 20xx.

value-added tax (VAT) an INDIRECT TAX imposed by the government on the VALUE ADDED to a good or service. Governments use value-added taxes both as a means of raising revenue (see BUDGET) and as an instrument of FISCAL POLICY.

A value-added tax is based on the difference between the value of the OUTPUT over the value of the INPUTS used to produce that output. The final amount of tax is added on to the selling PRICE of the product and is paid by the buyer.

The 'mechanics' of a value-added tax may be illustrated as follows: producer Y sells his output for £10 per unit having spent £8 on inputs. Thus, value added is £2 per unit. If VAT is set at 10%, the selling price of the product is £11 with £1 being the amount of tax paid by the final buyer. Producer Y would then set off against the £1 VAT-output tax collected from the final buyer the 80p VAT-input tax which he has already paid on his £8 of inputs bought, and remit the difference of 20p to the CUSTOMS AND EXCISE. In the same way. supplier X (who has supplied producer Y with his input for £8 per unit) will have collected 80p VAT-output tax from producer Y, against which he will offset any VAT-input tax which he paid on his inputs, and remit the difference to the Customs and Excise. The total of all these sums remitted by firms X, Y etc. to the Customs and Excise will equal the £1 charged on the final sale to the customer.

VAT rates may be applied uniformly at a single rate across the board, or, as in the UK, applied on a discretionary basis. In the UK (as at 2005) there are two VAT rates (a) zero (for example, many food and drink products, books and newspapers, children's shoes); (b) a standard rate of 17.5% on all non zero-rated products and services.

VAT is a cumbersome tax system to operate, involving as it does thousands of 'tax points' and related paperwork. It does, however, require all the firms contributing to a taxed product to be involved in the tax collection operation, not just final sellers.

value analysis *or* **value engineering** the evaluation and review of a product's DESIGN, with the aim of reducing its material or manufacturing cost without impairing its function or performance. By examining all a product's components and their manufacture it may be possible to identify cheaper raw materials to replace expensive ones, or opportunities to reduce the degree of precision with which components are made. See CONCURRENT ENGINEERING, LEAN MANUFACTURING.

value chain see VALUE ADDED CHAIN, VALUE CHAIN ANALYSIS, VALUE CREATED MODEL.

value chain analysis

A conceptual framework which examines how the particular activities undertaken in a firm creates VALUE either through their impact on *cost* or through the *benefits* they provide customers (see VALUE CREATED MODEL for details).

Fig. 86 presents Michael Porter's schematic model of the value chain. Value activities can be divided into two broad types, 'primary activities' and 'support activities'. Primary activities are those activities which involve the production of a good or service and its sale and movement to the buyer as well as after-sales facilities, whilst support activities provide purchased inputs, technology, human resources and various firm-wide information functions which support the primary activities.

There are five broad categories of primary activities:

Inbound logistics activities which involve receiving, storing and disseminating inputs to the product manufacturing process (e.g. materials handling, warehousing, stock control etc).

Operations activities involving the transformation of inputs into products (e.g. machining, assembly, packaging etc).

Outbound logistics activities associated with storing and distributing the product (e.g. finished goods warehousing, order processing, delivery etc).

Marketing and sales activities associated with generating customer demand for the firm's products such as advertising and sales promotion etc.

Service activities such as installation, repairs and parts supply etc. which help maintain the value of the product.

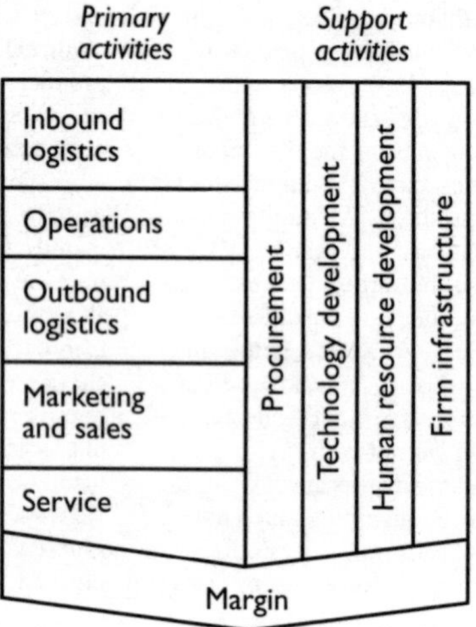

Fig. 86 **The Porter value chain.**

Due attention to primary activities is important in the context of establishing and maintaining COMPETITIVE ADVANTAGE (lower costs, superior products etc) over rival suppliers. Differences in the value chains of major competitors reflect the emphasis each firm places upon particular activities as its major competitive strength, so that, for example, one firm in a market may rely primarily upon the efficiency of its production operations, whilst another may emphasize marketing expertise.

In addition, the scope of an *individual firm's* value chain has to be considered in the context of the *industry* VALUE-ADDED CHAIN. Some firm's value chains may encompass only one stage of the industry chain, whilst other firms value chains may embrace several industry stages (see VERTICAL INTEGRATION). See RESOURCE BASED THEORY OF THE FIRM, VALUE ADDED ANALYSIS, CRITICAL OR KEY SUCCESS FACTORS.

value created model an analytical framework which builds on the concepts of VALUE ADDED and the CONSUMERS SURPLUS which assists business strategists to identify opportunities for establishing COMPETITIVE ADVANTAGES over rival suppliers and to increase the firm's profits.

'Value created' is the difference between the value that resides in a product and the cost of producing it. In Fig. 87 'C' is the cost of producing the product which includes 'bought-in costs (materials etc) and the 'additional costs incurred by the firm itself in making-up the product in its final form. 'P' is the price charged for the product and 'B' represents the value *(perceived benefits)* of the product to the consumer. 'Value created' consists of two elements (a) the *firm's profit* which is the difference between the price (P) charged for the product and the cost (C) of producing it (i.e. P-C); (b) the value of *perceived benefit* of the product to the consumer (B), part of which is the value of the product embodied in the *actual* price the customer is required to pay (P) and part of which is the *extra value* received by the consumer in the form of the consumer surplus (B-P). The consumer surplus (see entry for further discussions) is the difference between the price the consumer *actually pays* compared to the price the consumer *would be prepared* to pay, ie. if the product's actual price is £50 and the consumer would have been prepared to pay £75 the 'consumer surplus' is £25. The total 'value created' thus consists of the firm's profit and the consumer surplus.

The model is useful to strategists in that it enables them to explore various ways of establishing competitive advantage over rival firms and increase profit potential. To illustrate it the firm can *reduce its costs* (while keeping 'perceived benefits' unchanged) then either it can continue to keep its price unchanged and obtain higher unit profit margins, or it could lower its price, undercutting the prices of its competitors thus gaining market share. See COST DRIVERS. Conversely, if it can *increase the 'perceived benefits'* to the consumer (while keeping costs unchanged) it will encourage customers to switch away from competitors, thus gaining market share. Increasing 'perceived benefits' can be done through ADVERTISING extolling the attractions of the product and increasing the quality of the product. See BENEFIT DRIVERS.

The firm can also explore ways of 'capturing' – more of the consumer surplus through differential pricing (see CONSUMER SURPLUS entry for details) and various MARKET SEGMENTATION strategies. See RESOURCE BASED THEORY OF THE FIRM, VALUE CHAIN ANALYSIS, CRITICAL OR KEY SUCCESS FACTORS.

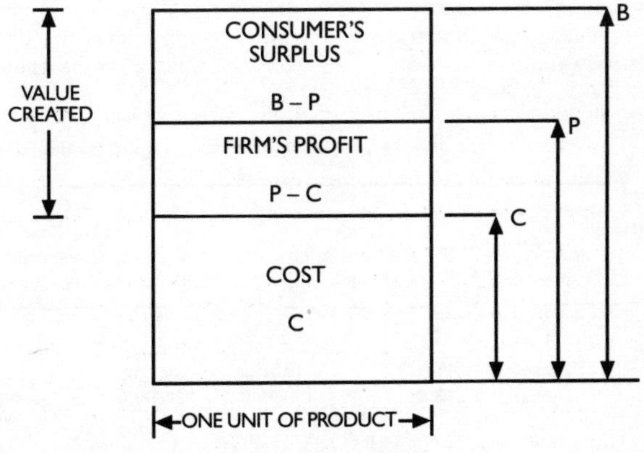

Fig. 87 **Value created model.**

value engineering see VALUE ANALYSIS.

value for money the extent to which a government, business person or consumer gets a good deal from the money which they spend on goods or services.

value-for-money audit an audit of a private sector organization which looks at the extent to which the organization achieves *economy* (reducing waste and cutting costs); *efficiency* (ensuring that scarce resources are fully utilized); and *effectiveness* (achieving targets and fulfilling the objectives laid down by management).

variability a characteristic of SERVICES, namely that being delivered by people, the standard of their performance is open to variation.

variable costs any COSTS that tend to vary directly with the level of output. They represent payments made for the use of variable factor-inputs, notably raw materials and direct labour.

A firm will leave a market if in the short run it cannot earn sufficient SALES REVENUE to cover its total variable cost. If it can generate enough total revenue to cover total variable cost and make some CONTRIBUTION towards total FIXED COST then it will continue to produce in the short run even though it is still making a loss.

variable overheads any OVERHEADS that vary proportionately with the level of output of a product, so that variable-overhead cost per unit of output is constant. They include such items as fuel and lubricants, and salespersons' commissions. See also FIXED OVERHEADS, SEMIVARIABLE OVERHEADS.

variance 1 the difference between budgeted and actual results (see BUDGETING), or between STANDARD COSTS/revenues and actual costs/revenues. Variances can be:

(a) adverse or negative when actual revenues fall short of budget or standard, or when actual costs exceed budget or standard;

(b) favourable or positive when actual revenues exceed budget or standard, or when actual costs are less than budget or standard.

2 a measure of variation within a group of numerical observations, specifically the average of the squared deviations of the observations from the group AVERAGE.

See STANDARD DEVIATION.

variance analysis the breakdown of differences between the STANDARD COST (revenue) of a product and its comparable actual cost (revenue) into their constituent parts. Variance analysis highlights matters which are not proceeding to plan, enabling managers to take corrective action to deal with losses or inefficiencies. The main variances are MATERIALS-COST VARIANCE, the LABOUR-COST VARIANCE, the OVERHEAD-COST VARIANCE and the SALES-REVENUE VARIANCE. Fig. 88 shows the main cost variances and how they are linked.

variance reports tabulations which compare actual results with the BUDGET or STANDARD COST and show the VARIANCES. It is especially important that such reports highlight variances which are adverse and of a significant value. It is also important from a control point of view that all variances which are being reported and

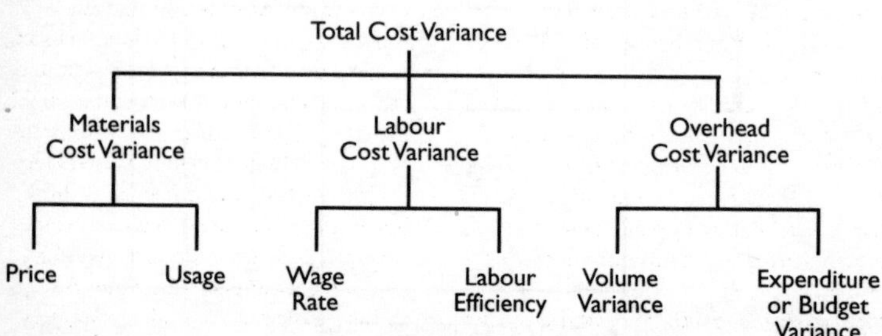

Fig. 88 **Variance analysis.** The relationship of the main cost variances.

which require management action are supported by sufficient narrative to explain the reasons why the variances have occurred. See VARIANCE ANALYSIS.

variety the number of products sold by a firm as part of its PRODUCT RANGE. A firm may make many different products and many variants of each product in order to appeal to most market segments and maximize its potential sales. However, the providing of variety can be expensive if this is associated with short production runs, high stockholding costs, complex production scheduling and high marketing costs. Consequently, firms may aim to eliminate unnecessary variety in products or components by means of variety-reduction programmes and STANDARDIZATION of components.

VAT see VALUE-ADDED TAX.

VCT see COMPETITIVE TENDERING.

VDU see VISUAL DISPLAY UNIT.

vendor the seller of a good or service. The vendor can be a person (see PERSONAL SELLING) or a machine (see AUTOMATIC VENDING).

venture capital money subscribed in the form of SHARE CAPITAL and LOAN CAPITAL to finance new firms and activities which are considered to be of an especially risky nature and hence unable to attract finance from more conventional sources. There are a number of specialist institutions covering this sector of the capital market (see STOCK MARKET), including THREE I'S (formerly Investors in Industry) and the venture capital arms of the COMMERCIAL BANKS, INVESTMENT BANKS and MERCHANT BANKS.

Venture capital investors originally concentrated most of their funding on small start-up businesses offering innovative products, but recently a substantial proportion of their funds has been directed towards the less risky business of financing MANAGEMENT BUY-OUTS of established companies.

The British Venture Capital Association represents firms and institutions operating in this area.

vertical disintegration the withdrawal of a firm from a particular stage in a vertically linked production and distribution chain. A firm which is currently vertically integrated into a number of stages may decide to exit from a particular stage for cost or strategic reasons. For example, as a result of technical advances or a change in competitive conditions, it may be cheaper for the firm to buy in materials from outside suppliers than continue to self-supply (see MAKE OR BUY); or the emergence of new distribution channels for the firm's products may remove the imperative for it to own distribution outlets. In some cases the volatility of profits in the face of cyclical downturns in demand or a long-term secular decline in demand may force a firm to reduce the size and depth of its investment in a multi-stage operation. See VERTICAL INTEGRATION, SOURCING, OUTSOURCING, DIVESTMENT, VIRTUAL CORPORATION.

vertical integration the combining in one firm of two or more vertically related activities, as opposed to these activities being performed separately in different firms and then being synchronized through arms-length market transactions. For example, a firm engaged in assembly operations may integrate backwards ('upstream') to produce its own components, or forwards ('downstream') to distribute its products. Vertical integration may involve ORGANIC GROWTH on the part of the firm, or firms may choose to expand by MERGER with, or TAKEOVER of, established suppliers and distributors.

Vertical integration may be advantageous to firms if it permits them to lower their operating costs by production savings arising from the linking of technically related processes (for example the linking together of casting and rolling operations in steel mills, and continuous motorcar assembly operations), and reduce STOCKHOLDING COSTS by a closer matching of inventory and production requirements. Vertical integration also enables firms to avoid various TRANSACTION COSTS in dealing with outside suppliers/distributors, including the costs of finding suppliers/ dealers, agreeing contract terms and conditions, and ensuring that there is strict adherence to these undertakings. Additionally, vertical integration gives firms greater security of supplies and access to customers, as well as the potential for applying competitive pressure on non-integrated rivals by depriving them of supplies/outlets (FORECLOSURE) or PRIZE SQUEEZING.

On the other hand the firm may experience increasing costs because 'captive' transfers of inputs within the firm puts little pressure on divisions to hold costs in check while such transfers may make the firm myopic to 'outside' buying and selling opportunities (see VERTICAL DISINTEGRATION). Moreover, there are limits to vertical integration as a growth strategy for the firm. Vertical integration 'converts' a variable cost (buying in the market) into a fixed investment cost (self-supply) thus increasing the firms exposure (risk) to cyclical and secular downturns in demands. The former causes profits to vary and leads to 'ripple-on' effects down the vertical chain thus exacerbating cash-flow problems while the latter threatens the very survival of the firm (see PRODUCT LIFE CYCLE). Vertical disintegration can help but in many cases DIVERSIFICATION may be necessary to sustain the expansion of the firm. In addition, firms' ability to expand vertically, particularly by merger and takeover, may be restricted by the OFFICE OF FAIR TRADING, because of anti-competitive effects. See MAKE OR BUY DECISION, COMPETITIVE ADVANTAGE, BUSINESS STRATEGY, TRANSFER PRICE, VALUE ADDED, VALUE ADDED CHAIN, VALUE ADDED ANALYSIS, DISTRIBUTION CHANNEL, VERTICAL MARKETING SYSTEM, INTERNALIZATION, OUTSOURCING, INTERNAL CUSTOMER, INTERNAL MARKET, COMPETITION POLICY (UK), AGENCY COSTS.

vertical marketing system (VMS) a distribution system in which a firm in a DISTRIBUTION CHANNEL undertakes as a vertically integrated operation a number of channel functions (wholesaling, retailing), or is able to control independent firms in the channel by, for example, contractual arrangements such as EXCLUSIVE DEALING and FRANCHISING.

vertical segregation the division of the HIERARCHY of an ORGANIZATION by sex or some other criterion. It is common for all or most jobs at high levels of the hierarchy to be performed by men and all or most jobs at lower levels to be performed by women. Women find it hard to obtain jobs at higher levels because of DISCRIMINATION. See GLASS CEILING.

vicarious liability see TORT.

video conferencing a form of interactive COMMUNICATION which involves the use of PERSONAL COMPUTERS. Desktop or personal video systems provide one-to-one video communications, usually by adding a video camera and a plug-in video card to a personal computer attached to a digital telephone line or office network.

Video conferencing can be a time-saving and cost-effective means of communication since it reduces or eliminates the need for business travel. See INFORMATION MANAGEMENT.

virtual corporation a firm which minimizes its *internal* hierarcy and *maximizes* its dealing with *outside* (i.e. market) suppliers and customers. Given today's rapidly changing technological and competitive conditions a firm needs to be more flexible in responding to changing business circumstances. To this end the firm should avoid VERTICAL INTEGRATION (and its associated AGENCY COSTS) and OUTSOURCE inputs as much as possible and deal only with independent distributors and dealers, using such new technologies as E-COMMERCE to reduce external TRANSACTION COSTS. See VERTICAL DISINTEGRATION.

virt-x see STOCK MARKET/EXCHANGE.

visible export see EXPORT, BALANCE OF PAYMENTS.

visible import see IMPORT, BALANCE OF PAYMENTS.

visual display unit (VDU) a means of displaying COMPUTER output, usually on a television-style screen or liquid crystal display unit.

VMS see VERTICAL MARKETING SYSTEM.

voice messaging a form of COMMUNICATION which involves the use of answering machines attached to fixed-wire and cordless telephones to store messages until such a time as recipients are present, or it is convenient for them to receive them. Around one-half of all business calls are for one-way communication only but they often interrupt work which is more important than the call itself.

See INFORMATION MANAGEMENT.

voluntarism the philosophy that the activities of organizations should be governed by their own codes of conduct rather than by the law. In INDUSTRIAL RELATIONS it refers to the widespread belief amongst both TRADE UNIONS and employers that the form and outcome of COLLECTIVE BARGAINING should be determined by themselves and not be subject to legal regulation. See LABOUR LAW.

voluntary competitive tendering see COMPETITIVE TENDERING.

voluntary group a business which operates as a WHOLESALER to a group of small RETAILERS who undertake to place a certain volume of orders with the voluntary group, in return for price concessions on the purchases they make and various backup services (promotions etc.). Voluntary groups such as SPAR in groceries and Unichem in chemists' goods are able to use their BULK-BUYING power to obtain price discounts from manufacturers, some of which are passed on to their members. See DISTRIBUTION CHANNEL.

voluntary organization an organization in which most of the members are not paid but give their time voluntarily because they identify with its objectives.

voluntary redundancy see REDUNDANCY.

voluntary winding-up see INSOLVENCY, LIQUIDATION.

voting shares the ORDINARY SHARES that allow the SHAREHOLDERS to cast a vote for each share held at a company's ANNUAL GENERAL MEETING. See also SHARE CAPITAL.

Vredeling Directive a draft directive of the European Union (EU) concerning DISCLOSURE OF INFORMATION and CONSULTATION with employees. Named after the former European Union Commissioner Henk Vredeling, it proposes that employee representatives have rights to information concerning the organization's structure, its financial situation, investment plans and employment prospects. It also proposes that management plans which are likely to have serious consequences for the workforce should be the subject of meaningful consultation. This directive, originally formulated in the early 1980s, has not been adopted by the EU, in part because of resistance by the UK Government.

W

wage the money payment made to a worker, usually on a weekly basis, for the use of his or her labour. A worker's basic wage will depend on the hourly WAGE RATE and the number of hours worked. The latter is usually related to the number of hours specified as constituting the 'basic' working week, but in some cases workers may be given a GUARANTEED BASIC WAGE to protect them against loss of earnings due to *short-time working*, and in other cases workers may be able to add to their basic wage by OVERTIME earnings. In addition to PAYMENT BY TIME, workers may be paid in proportion to their output under a PAYMENT BY RESULTS scheme. See PAY, MEASURED DAY WORK.

wage differential see PAY DIFFERENTIAL.

wage drift the propensity for employees' actual earnings to rise faster than increases in their WAGE RATE. This tends to occur when there is full employment or when there are labour shortages in particular labour markets, and often results from informal bargaining between workers, their representatives (SHOP STEWARDS) and managers supplementing formal COLLECTIVE BARGAINING. It was considered to be a widespread problem in the UK in the 1960s and contributed to the decision to create a Royal Commission to investigate the state of UK INDUSTRIAL RELATIONS (See DONOVAN COMMISSION). See PRICES AND INCOMES POLICY, PAY, PAYMENT BY RESULTS.

wage rate the money payment made to a worker for each 'unit' of his or her labour input, usually measured either on hourly time basis (see WAGES), or for each unit of output produced (see PIECEWORK). See PAY, PAYMENT BY TIME, PAYMENT BY RESULTS, WORK STUDY.

wage round see PAY ROUND.

Wages Council a UK body which stipulated minimum levels of WAGES and CONDITIONS OF EMPLOYMENT in certain industries. Wages Councils were abolished in 1993. See MINIMUM WAGE RATE.

wage system see PAY.

waiting time see IDLE TIME.

wants see NEEDS.

warehouse business premises used by a manufacturer to STORE both raw materials, components etc. (materials store) and final products (finished goods store), and by WHOLESALERS and RETAILERS to store finished products in the course of distribution to buyers. See DISTRIBUTION CHANNEL, MATERIALS MANAGEMENT, AUTOMATED STORAGE AND RETRIEVAL SYSTEM, ORDER PROCESSING, PICK LIST.

warehouse club a RETAILER which sells an extensive range of products to club members only, at heavily discounted prices on a SELF SERVICE basis. See DISCOUNT STORE, DISTRIBUTION CHANNEL.

warrant a FINANCIAL SECURITY issued by a company to raise capital, which gives the holder the right to purchase SHARES in the company at some specified future date at a set price. Warrants are quoted on the STOCK MARKET and thus can be bought and sold in the same way as the issuing company's shares, usually at a much lower price. In essence a warrant is similar to convertible LOAN STOCK (but without interest payments) which can be converted into equity at the appointed time. The holder of a warrant forgoes current income in the hope of making a sizable capital gain on conversion.

warranty see GUARANTEE.

wastage see LABOUR TURNOVER.

wastage index see LABOUR TURNOVER.

wasting asset FIXED ASSETS such as mines, quarries and oil wells, which are used up during their working lives. It is especially important to make adequate provision for DEPRECIATION of such assets.

weaknesses and strengths see SWOT ANALYSIS.

wealth the total stock of ASSETS owned by the population of a country. Wealth represents past income flows which have been used to buy such assets as houses, land, stocks and shares etc. One commonly used measure of wealth in the UK is that of 'marketable wealth', consisting of those assets which are readily saleable. Wealth in the UK, like income, (see DISTRIBUTION OF INCOME), is unevenly distributed (see Fig. 89). See WEALTH TAX.

wealth tax a DIRECT TAX imposed by the government on a person's private assets when those assets are transferred to the person's beneficiaries. Wealth taxes are used by governments principally as a means of promoting social equity by reducing disparities in WEALTH holdings. In the UK INHERITANCE TAX is the current means of taxing wealth.

wear out period see FAILURE RATE CURVE.

web see WORLD WIDE WEB.

Weibull analysis see FAILURE RATE CURVE.

weight note a document that lists the gross weight of packages, crates, etc. containing GOODS OR COMMODITIES issued by the supplier to the buyer. See EXPORTING.

Weights and Measures Act 1963 a UK Act which empowers the DEPARTMENT OF TRADE AND INDUSTRY to prescribe permitted weights and measures for the sale of certain products such as food and beverages. The act established a network of local authority officials to inspect goods sold in shops, public houses and other establishments to see if specified weights and measures are applied correctly and, on finding shortages, instigate proceedings against offenders through the courts. The OFFICE OF FAIR TRADING now acts as a coordinating body, keeping a central register of convictions under the Act. See CONSUMER PROTECTION, UNIT PRICING.

Weights and Measures Act 1985 a UK Act which lays down the legal weights and measures to be used for trading and other purposes. For example, the UK 'primary standards' are the yard or metre as the unit of measurement of length, and the pound or kilogram as the unit of measurement of mass or weight.

welfare that aspect of management concerned with the wellbeing, both physical and emotional, of employees. It is an umbrella term for a range of services and activities. HEALTH AND SAFETY (the regulation of working conditions) is probably the most important but is often managed separately from other welfare functions. Other welfare activities include

Total marketable wealth		*£3,364 billion* *%*
Most wealthy	1%	23
" "	5%	43
" "	10%	56
" "	25%	75
" "	50%	95

Fig. 89 **Wealth.** The distribution of marketable wealth in the UK, 2002. The total includes land and dwellings (net of mortgage debt), stocks and shares, bank and building society deposits and other financial assets, but excludes life assurance and pensions. (Source: Social Trends, 2004).

the provision of canteens and social clubs, sports facilities, medical officers etc. Some organizations also provide counselling services to help individuals cope with, for instance, work-related stress.

The reasoning behind employer concern with welfare suggests that a contented workforce is likely to be more productive. Some employers also feel that it is a social obligation to their employees. Welfare activities usually come under the remit of the PERSONNEL MANAGEMENT function. In fact, in the UK the origins of personnel management lie in the concern to improve employee welfare felt by certain employers in the early years of the 20th century. See FRINGE BENEFIT, HUMAN RELATIONS. See also SOCIAL SECURITY.

welfare unionism see TRADE UNION.

whistle-blower someone who publicizes or reports to the relevant authorities what they perceive to be unlawful or unethical practices by their employer or fellow employees. Whistle-blowing has become more prominent in recent years, in part because of the trend towards commercialization of public services (e.g. in the health service). Many CONTRACTS OF EMPLOYMENT now preclude employees from publicizing any aspect of the employing organization without prior authorization, and this has made whistle-blowing a more secretive and more dramatic activity. Those blowing the whistle, rather than those committing the unlawful or unethical act, are often those penalized by the employer. However, in some circumstances (e.g. health and safety violations) whistle-blowers now have legal protection.

white-collar union a TRADE UNION which largely or exclusively represents clerical, administrative and technical employees. In the past, such unions have generally been concerned to maintain for their members conditions of employment, rates of PAY, and status superior to those of manual WORKERS. With the growth of public sector employment and the gradual shift in the UK from manufacturing to services, such unions have generally achieved big increases in their membership since the 1960s.

white-collar worker see WORKER.

white knight see TAKEOVER BID.

Whitley Councils the COLLECTIVE BARGAINING institutions found in each department of the UK civil service and in the National Health Service.

wholesaler a business which buys products in relatively large quantities from manufacturers which it stocks and 'breaks bulk', on-selling in smaller quantities to RETAILERS. Thus, wholesalers act as *middlemen* between the PRODUCERS and retailers of a product in the DISTRIBUTION obviating the need for the producers themselves to stock and distribute their goods to retailers, and likewise retailers to undertake their own warehousing.

Wholesalers typically sell to retailers by adding a MARK-UP on their buying-in prices from suppliers or by obtaining a commission from the retailer.

Traditionally, wholesalers have provided their retail customers with credit facilities and a delivery service, but in recent years CASH AND CARRY wholesaling has become a prominent feature of distribution systems both in the UK and elsewhere. Moreover, with the emergence of large CHAIN STORE retailers (for example supermarkets, and DIY groups) the wholesaling function of stocking and breaking-bulk has itself become increasingly integrated with the retailing operation, with retailers taking particular advantage of the price discounts associated with BULK BUYING directly from manufacturers.

Independent wholesalers may operate a single warehouse or a chain of warehouses giving wider regional coverage and in many cases national distribution. See VOLUNTARY GROUP, CATEGORY DISCOUNTER.

wholesaling the function of buying products in relatively large quantities from manufacturers and 'breaking bulk', on-selling these products in smaller quantities to RETAILERS. See WHOLESALER. DISTRIBUTION CHANNEL.

wildcat strike see STRIKE.

windfall profit an exceptional gain or PROFIT arising from a sudden and unexpected change in market conditions which serves to raise the price of a FINANCIAL SECURITY, FIXED ASSET or STOCK.

winding-up see LIQUIDATION, INSOLVENCY.

window dressing the use of discretion in the application of ACCOUNTING PRINCIPLES so as to report PROFIT and ASSET figures which are flattering to the company. Window dressing is a form of CREATIVE ACCOUNTING which is concerned with making modest adjustment to sales, debtors and stock items when preparing year-end ANNUAL REPORTS AND ACCOUNTS.

withholding tax TAX deducted at source from INTEREST or DIVIDEND payments. Withholding taxes are often levied by a country upon interest and dividends paid by a domestic company to non-residents. It is a means of taxing cash flows from the company before such monies move out of their jurisdiction. Such taxes are levied in order to encourage investment at home and raise money for the government. Looked at more broadly from an international community perspective witholding taxes are harmful because they reduce the free flow of international investment and distort the geographical location of such investment. See DOUBLE TAXATION.

'word of mouth' recommendation the personal endorsement of a product by a satisfied customer who creates additional sales potential by extolling the merits of the product to friends, neighbours etc.

word processor a COMPUTER software program package designed for the manipulation of text. Word processors have dramatically improved the speed with which business documents can be produced by making the correction of errors or rearrangement of blocks of text easier.

work see JOB, LABOUR, WORK ORGANIZATION, SOCIOLOGY OF WORK, HOMEWORKING, DOMESTIC LABOUR.

work-based maintenance an approach to MAINTENANCE which provides for the overhaul of machinery, plant and equipment at intervals, based on the usage or output of each machine.

work centre a generic term used to describe a manufacturing 'cell' composed of a number of machines or a single machine (often computer numerically controlled) capable of multiple operations. See CELLULAR MANUFACTURING, WORK STATION. Can also be used to describe a location where one or more individuals carry out multiple tasks (e.g. a customer service centre or typing pool).

worker a person employed by an organization to perform a JOB or work tasks either on a paid basis (as an employee) or on an unpaid basis (as, for example, a charity worker).

Traditionally, paid employees have been categorized into two groups of workers:

(a) *manual workers*, i.e. those working mainly with their hands. Although manual workers may be engaged in service occupations such as pavement sweeping, the dominant image of the manual worker is that of an employee engaged in production in a factory. Often these workers are referred to as *blue-collar workers* because their physical working environment is such that (blue) overalls are necessary;

(b) *non-manual workers*, i.e. those who can be said to work with their heads rather than their hands, providing administrative services rather than directly creating material goods. As with manual workers, the term is somewhat artificial: some non-manual employees, typists for example, require considerable manual dexterity. *White-collar worker* is an alternative term in common use, though it tends to be applied mainly to clerical rather than managerial or PROFESSIONAL employees. White-collar workers are so called because their apparently favourable working environment makes a light-coloured shirt or blouse practical work wear, and because smart clothing is often viewed as appropriate dress for work of this type and status. In sociology 'black-coated worker' has also been used to refer to clerical workers because a sober, dark jacket similarly has been seen as essential work wear.

Although these categorizations are somewhat imprecise in terms of the type of work performed, there is often a clear difference in the conditions of employment (see CONTRACT OF EMPLOYMENT) associated with each. Those workers classed as non-manual tend to have more favourable conditions (for example, better holiday entitlements) than manual workers (see STAFF STATUS).

The difference in working conditions between the two groups has been thought in the past to give rise to two distinct sets of attitudes. Manual workers were thought to subscribe to COLLECTIVISM and to a confrontational view of their relationship with their employer, whilst non-manual workers were thought to be more individualist (see INDIVIDUALISM) in their attitudes and to adopt a deferential approach to their managers. Though always an oversimplification, the picture has become more complex in recent years with the apparent spread of individualism amongst manual workers and the growth of highly repetitive, routinized clerical work, leading, some say, to the 'proletarianization' of white-collar work.

Probably the most widespread popular image of the worker is that of a male employee employed in factory work. However, this image is now a long way out of step with reality. Only 25% of the UK labour force are now employed in manufacturing, with a corresponding growth in services in recent years. In addition, there has been a large increase in the number of women workers, with the result that nearly half of the employed force is female. In the UK, the employment of males in full-time manufacturing jobs has been steadily replaced by the employment of females in PART-TIME, service sector jobs. See DISCRIMINATION, ORIENTATION TO WORK, TEMPORARY WORK, WHITE-COLLAR UNION.

worker director a representative of the workforce on the BOARD OF DIRECTORS. These directors may be selected by management or elected by the workforce (all those employed in an organization or all those in a TRADE UNION). Where worker directors are elected the scheme is a form of INDUSTRIAL DEMOCRACY. The rationales for worker directors include the practical consideration that it can promote commitment to and understanding of organizational goals; and the moral consideration that employees should be able to influence the direction of the organization of which they are a part.

See CO-DETERMINATION, EMPLOYEE SHARE-OWNERSHIP PLAN.

workers' collective see WORKERS' COOPERATIVE.

workers' control an advanced form of INDUSTRIAL DEMOCRACY in which employees have tight control over both policy and operational activities of managers.

workers' cooperative an organization that is owned and controlled by those who work in it (though some in the UK have a few external shareholders). To be fully accepted as a workers' cooperative, such an organization must adhere to the general principles of the International Cooperative Alliance, including the requirement that each member has an equal vote at general meetings. Voting should not be proportional to share capital.

A critical issue that faces all cooperatives is how to organize the MANAGEMENT function: should all cooperative members be actively involved in management (as in a workers' collective), or should managerial functions be delegated to specialist managers? There is the obvious danger with the former that decision-making could be slowed down, that RESPONSIBILITY will be unclear and that many of those involved in management will not be sufficiently competent. But if specialists are employed, some of the democratic character of the cooperative will be lost. The question arising from this dilemma is whether the need to compete in markets will force cooperatives to 'degenerate' into conventional hierarchically organized firms.

Many believe that cooperatives are not a sustainable alternative to conventional business organizations. Proof that they could be comes from the Mondragon area of northern Spain. Here some 20,000 workers are employed in a large number of cooperatives in all sectors of the local economy. Critical to their success have been cooperation between cooperatives, facilitating the sharing of skills and resources, and the existence of a strong support structure, including a bank, providing finance and business skills. Such support is not as well advanced in the UK.
See INDUSTRIAL DEMOCRACY.

workflow analysis see JOB ANALYSIS.

workforce see LABOUR FORCE.

work group see GROUP.

work-in see INDUSTRIAL ACTION.

working-capital ratio a measure of a firm's ability to pay its short-term liabilities out of CURRENT ASSETS, which expresses the firm's current assets as a ratio of CURRENT LIABILITIES. See also CURRENT RATIO, WORKING CAPITAL, CASH FLOW.

working families tax credit (WFTC) a fiscal measure introduced in the UK in 1999 which provides financial assistance to low income parents who work. The basic rate is payable for an adult with one child who works a minimum of 16 hours per week, with higher rates being payable the more children and the more hours worked.

The WFTC replaces Family Credit – a benefit paid by the Department for Work and Pensions – and is paid by the Inland Revenue through the tax system. Like the NEW DEAL initiative, the WFTC is part of the government's attempt to 'reward' people for working as a means of reducing the level of UNEMPLOYMENT.

working capital *or* net current assets

An accounting term denoting a firm's short-term CURRENT ASSETS which are turned over fairly quickly in the course of business. They include raw materials, work in progress and finished goods STOCKS, DEBTORS and cash, less short-term CURRENT LIABILITIES. Fig. 90 shows the major components of the working capital cycle.

Increases in the volume of company trading generally lead to increases in stocks and amounts owed by debtors, and so to an increase in working capital required (see OVERTRADING). Reductions in delays between paying for materials, converting them to products, selling them and getting cash in from customers, will tend to reduce the working capital needed. Decisions to hold larger than normal stocks to take advantage of bulk-order discounts or special prices, or in anticipation of materials scarcity, would tie up working capital. Increases in prices of materials or wage rates would also mean that extra working capital would be needed to cover INFLATION.

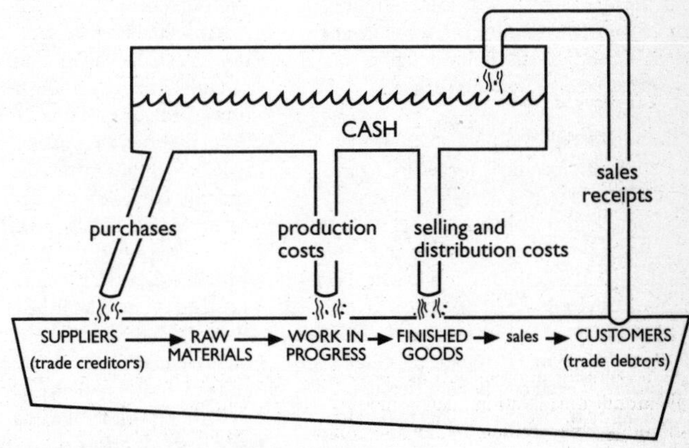

Fig. 90 **Working capital.**

working time the amount of time spent working for an employer. In the European Union this is regulated by the Working Time Directive and the Young Worker's Directive. In general this legislation restricts weekly hours of work to 48 but this may be averaged out over a period of time. Workers can also choose to work longer hours, and some groups of workers are excluded in both the Directive and national legislation implementing the Directive. The legislation also provides rights to rest periods and to a minimum of four weeks paid holiday each year.

working time directive see WORKING TIME.

work in progress any goods that are still in the process of being made up into their final form. Work in progress together with raw materials and STOCKS of finished goods constitute INVENTORY INVESTMENT.

work-life balance the idea that the demands of work and domestic life be balanced so as to optimize the well being of employees and their families. Specifically, initiatives in this area are targeted at reducing excessive working hours. See PRESENTEEISM, WORKING TIME.

work measurement an aspect of WORK STUDY which involves the application of measurement techniques to establish the time it takes for a trained worker to carry out a particular JOB. The purpose of measuring the time required to complete a job is to provide management with information for PRODUCTION SCHEDULES, for PRODUCT COSTING, and to assist in the design of incentive payment systems such as PIECEWORK.

Timestudy is the most often used work measurement technique for recording the time it should take to complete a specified job. Time study involves a number of steps:

(a) Recording details of the job and checking that no obvious improvements in method can be made (see METHOD STUDY);

(b) Dividing up the job being done into discrete operational elements to facilitate the timing of each component element;

(c) Timing the work elements to obtain the *observed time*;

(d) Rating the performance of the worker by comparing his or her actual rate of working against the defined STANDARD RATE (the average rate of working of a skilled, motivated operative) and using this to adjust the observed time and arrive at the *basic time*;

(e) Determining the percentage *allowances* to be added to the basic time to compensate for fatigue, contingencies like machine breakdowns and interruptions, in order to establish the *standard time* for the job.

Time study is appropriate for short-cycle repetitive work. If, however, it is necessary to establish work standards in situations where irregular long-cycle work is conducted or where many different jobs are performed, these techniques may well be quite inappropriate. In such circumstances it may well be advisable to use some form of *activity sampling*, which in its simplest form consists of visual sampling and recording of activities in order to establish the proportion of time in which employees or machines are working or idle (see ACTIVITY CHART).

Time study is a *direct* work measurement technique. Alternatively, various *indirect* measures may be employed to generate standard times. One method uses data collected from previous time studies to provide a *synthetic standard time* for a job which differs only marginally from a job which has already been subject to direct time study or a new job which has not yet begun. A second method, the *predetermined motion time* system lists all motions that workers can utilize in performing tasks, together with times for these motions. From this general list of motions it is possible to select the specific motions involved in a particular job and thus compile a standard time for this particular job. Finally, *analytical estimating* can be used where there is insufficient synthetic data available to allow time standards to be established for all job elements and where the time required for these elements has to be based on knowledge and practical experience. See SIMULTANEOUS MOTION CHART, THERBLIGS.

work organization the distribution and coordination of work tasks, skills and authority in an ORGANIZATION. Work organization is the way that tasks are distributed amongst the individuals in an organization and the ways in which these are then coordinated to achieve the final product or service. For instance, in a school the work organization comprises those workers providing tuition, secretarial staff giving administrative support and ancillary workers, such as the caretaker, who ensure that the facilities are ready for teaching to take place. These activities are coordinated in part by staff meetings, in part by the headteachers and their assistants. An alternative form of work organization would be where teachers also undertake some secretarial and ancillary tasks.

Some modes of work organization may be more efficient in terms of labour utilization than others. The quality of work organization may thus have an important impact on the performance of the organization. Work organization may be determined by a number of factors:

(a) the nature of the technology used (in turn influenced by the nature of the product or service). Assembly-line technology, for instance, tends to discourage group working and to encourage a pattern of work organization where each worker does a single repetitive task;

(b) managerial choice. Technology may potentially be used in a number of ways (see SOCIOTECHNICAL SYSTEM) according to managerial objectives. Managerial competence is also important. Poor knowledge of production management may lead to inefficient work organization;

(c) workforce aspirations. Groups of workers are often able to modify informally the way that work is done and the way that tasks are distributed among them. In addition TRADE UNIONS or SHOP STEWARDS may regulate the way work is organized, either unilaterally (see DEMARCATION LINE, RESTRICTIVE LABOUR PRACTICE), or jointly with management (see COLLECTIVE BARGAINING).

Many commentators believe that much of the UK's economic difficulties in recent decades are due to inefficient patterns of work organization. These are variously attributed to a failure to invest sufficiently in new technology, 'over-mighty' unions, poor management etc. There is a growing recognition that the managerial approach to work organization should be more rigorous and strategic than in the past (see JAPANIZATION). Many also believe that greater task scope should be given to MANUAL WORKERS, supported by improved TRAINING. Operators of sophisticated equipment should be given the opportunity to program or maintain it. As well as improving JOB SATISFACTION this would lead to better standards of work. See JOB DESIGN AND RE-DESIGN, SOCIOLOGY OF WORK.

workplace bargaining see COLLECTIVE BARGAINING.

work sampling see ACTIVITY SAMPLING.

works committee see CONSULTATION.

works council see CONSULTATION, CO-DETERMINATION.

works manager the manager with overall RESPONSIBILITY for the operation of a factory or plant. See MANAGEMENT.

work station a specific productive activity (e.g. drilling a piece of metal) which typically forms one link in a PRODUCTION-LINE sequence of activities involving the processing of materials through to final assembly of the product (see PRODUCTION LINE BALANCING entry for further details).

work study *or* **time and motion study** an area of PRODUCTION MANAGEMENT concerned with ensuring the best possible use of human and material resources in carrying out a specified activity. Work study embraces the techniques of METHOD STUDY, which analyses the ways JOBS are done with a view to improving these methods, and WORK MEASUREMENT, which seeks to measure the time required to perform jobs.

work-to-rule see INDUSTRIAL ACTION.

World Bank (International Bank for Reconstruction and Development) an international institution established in 1947 whose purpose is to assist countries to develop their economies by the provision of economic aid in the form of loans and technical assistance. The World Bank supports a wide range of projects in the less developed countries including the establishment of infrastructure (roads, gas and water supplies, schools and hospitals), the modernization of traditional industries (farm mechanization and cultivation techniques) and the setting up of new industries (iron and steel, textiles etc.).

The Bank's resources are provided largely by subscriptions from the advanced countries, although it also issues its own securities to raise additional funds. Generally, the Bank lends on a commercial basis – loans are repayable and bear market-related interest charges – but it also provides low-interest ('soft') loans through its affiliate the *Industrial Development Association*, while a further affiliate, the *International Finance Corporation* invests in share capital in selected companies.

world-class manufacturing the ability of a firm to compete successfully against the best anywhere in the world. This requires the firm to have the right manufacturing capability to supply products at competitive prices and high levels of product quality and sophistication, depending on customers' demands. Achieving world-class status involves the firm embracing sound PRODUCTION AND OPERATIONS MANAGEMENT practices (for example, METHOD STUDY), concepts and techniques (for example, TOTAL QUALITY MANAGEMENT), systems (for example, MANUFACTURING RESOURCE PLANNING) and technologies (for example, COMPUTER-INTEGRATED MANUFACTURING).

World Gold Council an organization based in Geneva whose main objective is to promote the sale of GOLD bullion (bars and coins) to investors, and to widen the appeal of gold as an ornamental (jewellery) material and as an industrial base metal.

World Trade Organization (WTO) an international organization which was established in 1995 to administer the international trading system. The WTO took over the activities and responsibilities of its predecessor the '*General Agreement on Tariffs and Trade*' (GATT) which was set up in 1947 to promote FREE TRADE. The change of name partly reflects the wider responsibilities the WTO has assumed for managing INTERNATIONAL TRADE and the new name more accurately reflects what the organization stands for as opposed to the 'cumbersome' title of its predecessor.

The essential functions of the WTO are (1) administering and implementing the multilateral trade agreements which collectively make up the WTO; (2) acting as a forum for multilateral trade negotiations; (3) seeking to resolve trade disputes; (4) reviewing national trade policies and (5) cooperating with other international institutions involved in global economic policy-making. The highest authority of the WTO is the Ministerial Conference, which is composed of representatives of all WTO member countries and meets every two years to determine the general policies of the WTO, while the day-to-day work of the WTO is undertaken by a number of subsidiary bodies, in particular the General Council and Dispute Settlement Body. In 2005, 148 countries were members of the WTO which is headquartered in Geneva.

The WTO embraces the two main operational principles of the original GATT: (1) reciprocity – arranging for countries to receive foreign tariff reductions in return for TARIFF cuts of their own and (2) the 'most favoured nation' rule – requiring that a country should apply its lowest tariff for any particular product to all of its suppliers.

The GATT supervized 11 major multilateral 'rounds' of tariff negotiations, including the 'Kennedy Round' of 1962-67 which secured an average cut in tariffs of around 35% and the 'Tokyo Round' of 1973-79 which provided further significant cuts in tariffs. In the main these tariff cuts applied only to manufactured goods. The last 'round' supervized by GATT – the 'Uruguay Round' of 1988-93 also led to tariff cuts on manufacturers but concessions were also agreed on agricultural products, the liberalization of trade in commercial services, and protection of INTELLECTUAL PROPERTY RIGHTS. See PROTECTIONISM.

Currently, a new round (the 'Doha Round') has been set in motion.

While the WTO has sought to liberalize international trade on a global, multilateral basis, trade liberalization has also taken place on a more limited basis through the formation of various 'free trade areas' and 'common markets' (see TRADE INTEGRATION entry).

World Wide Web (www) a multimedia presentational tool that uses computers and other media to communicate, often through the INTERNET. The World Wide Web permits two-way interactive communications with large numbers of people simultaneously. The World Wide Web is an important tool of E-COMMERCE insofar as Internet marketing can be undertaken by developing colourful and attractive web pages to gain visitors' attention. As the number of people 'surfing' the web grows the potential to market goods through web browsers has become a significant element of firms' promotional mix.

write off (*accounting*) to charge a cost item as an expense in computing a firm's profit or loss. Certain cost items which are fixed assets but which are of insignificant value may still be written off and charged as an expense in their year of purchase.

writing down allowance see CORPORATION TAX.

written down value see NET BOOK VALUE.

y

yield the return on a FINANCIAL SECURITY, expressed in money terms, related to the current market price of that security, to show the percentage return on the investment. Yield can refer to the INTEREST RATE payable on the market price of a BOND (INTEREST YIELD); or DIVIDEND rate payable on the market price of a SHARE (DIVIDEND YIELD); or company profit per share (after tax) related to the price of the share (EARNINGS YIELD). For example, a bond with a face value of £100 and a rate of interest of 10% generates a nominal return of £10 per year. If, however, the bond can be purchased for £50 on the open market, then the yield is 20%, representing 20% return on the £50 invested. The lower the purchase price of a bond or share with a given coupon rate of interest or dividend or profit, the higher its yield will be, and vice versa. There is thus an inverse relationship between the price paid for a bond or share and its yield.

The term *flat yield* or *current yield* is sometimes used to describe a yield calculation which does not take account of the redemption value of a bond. Yields which take into account not only the annual interest receivable but also any capital profit/loss on redemption of the bond are termed *redemption yields.* Where the current market price of a bond is below its specified redemption price, the potential profit on redemption must be divided by the number of years to the redemption date of the bond, and this annual profit equivalent added to the flat yield on the bond to arrive at its redemption yield. Where the current market price of the bond is above its specified redemption price the annualized potential loss on redemption must be deducted from the flat yield in calculating redemption yield. For example, a bond offering an interest payment of £10 per year and with a current market price of £50 would have a flat yield of 20%. If, in addition, the specified redemption price of the bond is £100 in five years' time, then the bond promises a potential profit of £100 – £50 = £50 which is equivalent to an annualized profit of £50 ÷ 5 = £10 per year or an additional return of £10 ÷ £50 or 10%. This would be added to the flat yield of 20% to give a redemption yield of 30%.

yield gap the difference between the YIELD on established undated or long dated gilt-edged BONDS and the average yield on SHARES. Before 1960, the yield on gifts was less than the yield on shares, and it was argued that such a gap was justified by the greater riskiness or variability in the return on shares. However, since about 1960, some countries like the UK have experienced a reverse yield gap with the yield on gifts exceeding the yield on shares as a result of high inflation and high interest rates.

Z

zero-based budgeting a management accounting technique that seeks to re-examine and challenge the assumptions underlying a firm's costs. Zero-based BUDGETING involves preparing from scratch a budget for each company department, starting from the basic premise that each department's budget is zero, then justifying every activity and its associated expenditure before including it in the budget. This contrasts with conventional budgeting, where departmental budgets are often based on last year's budget suitably updated. The purpose of this process is to identify and remove inefficient or obsolete activities within the firm.

zero defects a business philosophy which emphasizes the need to make all products 'right first time' in order to minimize QUALITY COSTS.

zero-rated products see VALUE-ADDED TAX.

Z-score a composite score, summarizing the weighted results of a number of ACCOUNTING RATIOS, that claims to predict a company's likelihood of failure. Z-scores were developed by distinguishing the values of various performance-and-liquidity ratios for companies which had gone bankrupt and for those which had prospered. Those accounting ratios which proved t o discriminate effectively between failed companies and successful ones were incorporated in a standard formula to calculate an aggregate Z-score. Analysts can calculate Z-scores for particular companies, and use the results to try to predict whether companies are likely to fail.

Internet Links

Finding business resources on the internet

The internet has a vast amount of information on business available to academics, students and people in business. Finding reliable data should not be difficult although a few points need to be borne in mind. The material should be up to date. Small organizations and departments within academic institutions sometimes encounter funding difficulties and are unable to continue with their researches. Make sure to look at the 'Last updated' section of the main website page before using any data. Try clicking on the links to make sure that they have been maintained properly and do not result in error messages. Ideally information should be obtained from websites run by universities, research institutes, and other reputable organizations. Websites maintained by individuals may not be up to date and comprehensive. It is also possible that the prejudices of those maintaining the websites will be reflected in the content and list of links.

General business sites

www.bized.ac.uk
A service for students and educators in business and economics. It has a catalogue of over 4,000 internet links which is regularly updated. It also contains a glossary of terms and a selection of downloadable diagrams along with a wealth of other material relevant to the study of business.

http://gethelp.library.upenn.edu/guides/business
University of Pennsylvania Lippincott Library Research Guides to over 40 areas of business activities from accounting to US economic statistics, detailing websites and other reference sources.

www.libraries.rutgers.edu/rul/rr_gateway/research_guides/busi/business.shtml
This Rutgers University Research Guide provides assistance in doing research in a variety of business and management topics, with descriptions of databases, and links to more than 3,000 selected business and management-related internet resources are included.

www.sosig.ac.uk/business
This gateway provides free access to high-quality resources on the internet. Each resource has been evaluated and categorized by subject specialists based at UK universities, with the aim of matching resources to the business curriculum.

http://vlib.org/BusinessEconomics
Maintained by the Virtual Library, this portal has hundreds of links to individual websites and gateway directories.

Business magazine and resources

BBC
http://news.bbc.co.uk/1/hi/business/

Business Week
www.businessweek.com

Bloomberg.com
www.bloomberg.com

Business 2.0
www.business2.com/b2

Business Ethics
www.business-ethics.com

Canadian Business
www.canadianbusiness.com

CIA World Factbook
www.cia.gov/cia/publications/factbook

CNN Money
http://money.cnn.com

The Economist
www.economist.com

The Financial Times online
http://news.ft.com

Forbes
www.forbes.com

Fortune magazine
www.fortune.com/

Key Note Publications
produce a range of information on market performance in the UK
www.keynote.co.uk/

Reuters news agency
www.reuters.com and www. reuters.co.uk

Time magazine
www.time.com

Wall Street Journal
www.wsj.com

Institutions and organizations

Accounting Standards Board
www.asb.org.uk/asb

Advertising Standards Authority (ASA)
www.asa.org.uk/asa

Advisory, Conciliation and Arbitration Service (ACAS)
www.acas.org.uk

Alternative Investment Market (AIM)
www.londonstockexchange.com/en-gb/products/companyservices/ourmarkets/aim

Asia Pacific Economic Cooperation (APEC)
www.apecsec.org.sg/apec.html

Association of British Chambers of Commerce
www.chamberonline.co.uk

Association of British Insurers
www.abi.org.uk

Association of Friendly Societies
www.afs.org.uk

Association of Investment Trust Companies (AITC)
www.aitc.co.uk

Association of Southeast Asian Nations (ASEAN)
www.aseansec.org

Auditing Practices Board
www.asb.org.uk/apb

Baltic Mercantile and Shipping Exchange
www.balticexchange.com

Bank of England
www.bankofengland.co.uk

Banque de France
www.banque-france.fr/home.htm

British Standards Institution (BSI)
www.bsi-global.com/British_Standards/index.xalter

British Venture Capital Association
www.bvca.co.uk

Business Link
www.businesslink.gov.uk/bdotg/action/home

Central Arbitration Committee
www.cac.gov.uk

Chartered Association of Certified Accountants (ACCA)
www.acca.co.uk

Chartered Institute of Management Accountants (CIMA)
www.cimaglobal.com

Chartered Institute of Marketing (CIM)
www.cim.co.uk

Chartered Institute of Personnel Development (CIPD)
www.cipd.co.uk

Chartered Management Institute
www.managers.org.uk/institute/home_3.asp

Common Agricultural Policy
europa.eu.int/pol/agr/index_en.htm

Companies House
www.companieshouse.gov.uk

Competition Commission (CC)
www.competition-commission.org.uk

Confederation of British Industry (CBI)
www.cbi.org.uk

Consumers' Association
www.which.net

Council of the European Union
ue.eu.int/showPage.ASP?lang=en

Customs and Excise
www.hmrc.gov.uk

Department for Education and Skills (DfES)
www.dfes.gov.uk

Department for Environment, Food and Local Affairs (DEFRA)
www.defra.gov.uk

Department for Transport
www.dft.gov.uk

Department for Work and Pensions (DWP)
www.dwp.gov.uk

Department of Trade and Industry (DTI)
www.dti.gov.uk

Deutsche Bundesbank
www.bundesbank.de/index.en.php?print=no&

Disability Rights Commission
www.drc-gb.org

Dow-Jones Index
www.dowjones.com

Economic and Monetary Union (EMU)
europa.eu.int/pol/emu/index_en.htm

Engineering Employers Federation (EEF)
www.eef.org.uk/UK

Equal Opportunities Commission
www.eoc.org.uk

ETUC (European Trade Union Confederation)
www.etuc.org

Eurex
www.eurexchange.com/index.html

'Euronext' exchange
www.euronext.com

European Central Bank (ECB)
www.ecb.int/home/html/index.en.html

European Commission
europa.eu.int/comm/index_en.htm

European Community (EC)
europa.eu.int/index_en.htm

European Court of Justice
europa.eu.int/institutions/court/index_en.htm

European Economic Area (EEA)
europa.eu.int/comm/external_relations/eea

European Foundation for Quality Management (EFQM)
www.efqm.org

European Free Trade Association (EFTA)
www.efta.int

European Investment Bank
www.eib.org

European Parliament
www.europarl.org.uk/index.htm

European Regional Development Fund
europa.eu.int/grants/topics/erdf/erdf_en.htm

European Union (EU)
europa.eu.int/index_en.htm
www.eurunion.org/infores/BestBusSites.HTM
A site that guides you to the essential website about the European Union.

Export Credit Guarantee Department (ECGD)
www.ecgd.gov.uk

Federal Reserve
www.federalreserve.gov

Financial Services Authority (FSA)
www.fsa.gov.uk

General Agreement on Tariffs and Trade (GATT)
www.wto.org/english/tratop_e/gatt_e/gatt_e.htm

Inland Revenue
www.hmrc.gov.uk

Institute of Chartered Accountants in England and Wales (ICAEW)
www.icaew.co.uk

Institute of Chartered Accountants in Scotland (ICAS)
www.icas.org.uk

Institute of Directors
www.iod.com

Internal Revenue Service (IRS)
www.irs.gov

International Labour Organization (ILO)
www.ilo.org

International Monetary Fund (IMF)
www.imf.org

International Standardization Organization (ISO)
www.iso.org/iso/en/ISOOnline.frontpage

Invest UK
www.invest.uk.com

Investment Management Association (Association of Unit Trusts and Investment Funds)
www.investmentfunds.org.uk

Investors in People
www.investorsinpeople.co.uk

Latin American Integration Association
www.aladi.org/nsfweb/redisenioSitioi/index.htm

Learning and Skills Council
www.lsc.gov.uk

Lloyds (of London)
www.lloyds.com

London Clearing House
www.lchclearnet.com

London International Financial Futures Exchange (LIFFE)
www.euronext.com

London Metal Exchange
www.lme.co.uk

London Stock Exchange
www.londonstockexchange.com/en-gb

Low Pay Commission
www.lowpay.gov.uk

Monetary Policy Committee (MPC)
www.bankofengland.co.uk/monetarypolicy/overview.htm

Monopolies and Mergers Commission (MMC)
See Competition Commission

NASDAQ
www.nasdaq.com

National Association of Pension Funds (NAPF)
www.napf.co.uk

The National Institute of Economic and Social Research
www.niesr.ac.uk

Nikkei Net Interactive
www.nni.nikkei.co.jp

North American Free Trade Area (NAFTA)
www.nafta-sec-alena.org

Office for National Statistics
www.statistics.gov.uk

Office for National Statistics (ONS)
www.statistics.gov.uk

Office of Fair Trading
www.oft.gov.uk

Organization for Economic Cooperation and Development (OECD)
www.oecd.org/home

Organization of Petroleum Exporting Countries (OPEC)
www.opec.org/home

Patent Office
www.patent.gov.uk

Queen's Award for Enterprise
www.queensawards.org.uk

Regional Development Agency (RDA)
www.englandsrdas.com/home.aspx

Registrar of Companies
www.companieshouse.gov.uk

Registrar of Friendly Societies
See Association of Friendly Societies

Securities and Exchange Commission
www.sec.gov

Small Business Council (SBC)
www.sbs.gov.uk

Small Business Service (SBS)
www.sbs.gov.uk

Trades Union Congress
www.tuc.org.uk

UNICE Union of Industrial and Employers Conference of Europe
www.unice.org/Content/Default.asp?

United Nations Conference on Trade and Development (UNCTAD)
www.unctad.org

Work Foundation
www.theworkfoundation.com

World Bank (International Bank for Reconstruction and Development)
www.worldbank.org

World Trade Organization (WTO)
www.wto.org